EU Competition Law: General Principles

EU Competition Law: General Principles

David Vaughan CBE QC
Barrister, Brick Court Chambers, London

Sarah Lee
Barrister, Brick Court Chambers, London

Brian Kennelly
Barrister, Blackstone Chambers, London

Philip Riches
Barrister, Stone Chambers, London

Published by:
Richmond Law & Tax Ltd.
12-14 Hill Rise
Richmond TW10 6UA
United Kingdom
Tel. +44 (0) 20 8614 7650
Fax +44 (0) 20 8614 7651
info@richmondlawtax.com
www.richmondlawtax.com

ISBN 1-904501-63-X

British Library Cataloguing in Publication Data
A catalogue record for this book is available from the British Library

Cover design by Bill Anderson Associates.
Printed and bound by Antony Rowe Ltd.

Table of Contents

All references are to paragraph numbers

TABLE OF CASES ix
TABLE OF LEGISLATION xxi

1. INTRODUCTION

A. General 1
1. The rules of competition 1
2. The rules of competition in the context of the EC Treaty 2
3. Objectives of the rules of competition: earlier statements (1) 3
4. Objectives of the rules of competition: earlier statements (2) 5
5. Objectives of competition policy: more recent statements 17
B. Implementation of the rules of competition 26
1. Role of the Council 29
2. General Treaty powers of the Commission 32
3. Legislative powers of the Commission 33
4. Quasi-legislative powers of the Commission 34
5. Administrative and executive powers and duties of the Commission 36

2. SCOPE OF THE RULES OF COMPETITION

A. Territorial application 37
1. The territory of the common market 37
2. Treaties with third countries 38
3. Application to trade with third countries 39
4. Extra-territorial jurisdiction 41
5. Extra-territorial application 47
B. Personal application 52
1. Meaning of 'undertaking' 52
2. Public undertakings 60
3. Member States 61
C. Temporal application 70
1. Time limits generally 70
2. Limitation periods 72
D. Sectoral application 74
1. Coal and steel 75
2. Nuclear energy 76
3. Agriculture 77
4. Transport 82
5. Telecommunications and broadcasting 83
6. Security and defence products 84
7. Banking and insurance 86
8. Utilities 88

9. Electronic communications and e-commerce 89
10. Other sectors 90

3. AGREEMENTS, DECISIONS OF ASSOCIATIONS OF UNDERTAKINGS AND CONCERTED PRACTICES

A. Introduction 91
1. The prohibition of anti-competitive agreements and practices 91
2. Exemption 96
B. Agreements, decisions and concerted practices 98
1. Agreements 98
2. Decisions by associations of undertakings 105
3. Concerted practices 108
4. Exchange of information 119
5. Application of Article 81 to 'unilateral' conduct 122
6. Concerted behaviour between companies in the same group and agreements between principals and agents 129
C. The object or effect of preventing, restricting or distorting competition 133
1. Introduction 133
2. Object or effect 135
3. Prevention, restriction or distortion of competition 138
4. Horizontal agreements 141
5. Vertical agreements 143
6. Restrictions necessary for the promotion of competition 148
D. Effect on trade between Member States 155
1. Introduction 155
2. Agreements which 'may' affect inter-State trade 160
3. Agreements which limit, or affect the terms of, cross-border transactions 163
4. Partitioning of national markets 166
5. Network effect 169
6. Altering the pattern of inter-State trade 174
E. The requirement of 'appreciable' effect on competition and on trade between Member States 178
1. An appreciable effect on competition 178
2. An appreciable effect on trade between Member States 188
F. Exemption 197
1. Introduction 197
2. Exemption under Article 81(3) 199
3. The conditions for exemption 201

4. ABUSE OF DOMINANT POSITION

A. The prohibition 219
1. Prohibition of abuse of dominant position 219
2. The prohibition 220
3. Structure of Article 82 221

4. Interpretation of Article 82 223
5. Interrelationship with Article 81 225
B. Dominant position 229
1. Meaning of 'dominant position' 229
2. Determination of dominant position 230
3. Relevant product market 234
4. Relevant geographic market 245
5. Substantial part of the common market 247
6. The temporal market 248
7. Assessment of market power 249
8. Undertakings 265
C. Abuse 270
1. Meaning of 'abuse' 270
2. Fault 273
3. Causation 274
4. Objective justification 275
5. The list of abuses in Article 82 EC 278
6. Pricing 279
7. Conditions with tying effects 289
8. Requiring supplementary obligations 291
9. Refusal to deal 292
10. Refusals to supply competitors and essential facilities 295
11. Abuse and intellectual property rights 298
12. Limiting production, markets or technical development 304
13. Restricting parallel trade between Member States 306
14. Other unfair trading conditions 307
15. Other abuses 308
16. Duration of abuse 309
17. Abuse and mergers 310
D. Affecting trade between Member States 311
1. Inter-State trade 311
2. Trade and other activities 313

5. STATE INVOLVEMENT AND THE APPLICATION OF THE RULES ON COMPETITION

A. Article 86 314
1. The provisions of Article 86 314
2. The purpose of Article 86 and the relevance of Articles 3(g) and 10 of the Treaty 316
3. Balancing competing interests 320
4. Requirement to apply Article 86(1) in conjunction with another Treaty provision 322
5. Article 86 and direct effect 324
B. Article 86(1) 325
1. Article 86(1) only applies to certain types of undertaking 325
2. The prohibited conduct under Article 86(1) 342

3. Particular examples of the grant of special or exclusive rights infringing Article 86(1) in conjunction with Article 82 350
C. Article 86(2) 361
1. Purpose 361
2. Undertakings having the character of a revenue producing monopoly 362
3. Undertakings entrusted with the operation of services of general economic interest 363
4. Obstruction of the performance of the tasks entrusted 368
5. No adverse effect on trade contrary to the interests of the Community 372
6. Direct effect 373
D. Article 86(3) 375
1. Powers of the Commission under Article 86(3) 375
E. Article 81 in conjunction with Article 10 380
1. Requiring or favouring the adoption of anti-competitive agreements or reinforcing their effects 383
2. Delegating to private traders responsibility for taking decisions affecting the economic sphere 387

Table of Cases

References are to paragraph number

Aberdeen Journals v Director General of Fair Trading (No 1) [2002] UKCLR 167 237, 243, 279, 280, 281
Acciaierie Laminatoi Magliano Alpi SpA v High Authority Case 8/56 [1957-58] ECR 95 49
ACF Chemiefarma NV v Commission Case 41/69 [1970] ECR 61 99
AEG-Telefunken AG v Commission Case 107/82 [1983] ECR 3151, [1984] 3 CMLR 325 125, 126, 127, 186
Aéroports de Paris v Commission Case T-128/98 [2000] ECR II-3929 229, 267, 328, 331, 332
Ahlström Osakeyhtio v Commission Cases 89, 104, 114, 116, 117, 125-129/85 [1988] ECR 5193, [1988] 4 CMLR 901 44, 45, 69, 92, 105, 107, 108, 113, 115, 117, 140, 147, 176, 188
Ahmed Saeed Flugreisen v Zentrale zur Bekampfung unlauteren Wettewerb eV Case 66/86 [1989] ECR 803, [1990] 4 CMLR 102 64, 129, 226, 227, 234, 236, 248, 265, 270, 286, 366, 369, 385
Air Inter v Commission Case T-260/94 [1997] ECR II-997 366, 370, 372
AKZO Chemie v Commission Case 62/86 [1991] ECR I-3359, [1993] 5 CMLR 215 237, 252, 273, 280, 285, 291, 308
Alaska Airlines v United Airlines, 948 F.2d 536 (9th Cir 1991) 296
Albany International BV v Stichting Bedrijfspensioenfonds Textielindustrie Case C-67/96 [1999] ECR I-5751, [2000] 4 CMLR 446 52, 53, 54, 100, 267, 324, 326, 330, 331, 347, 351, 353, 354, 363, 366, 369, 385, 387
Almelo Case C-393/92 [1994] ECR I-1517 340, 366, 369
Altmark Trans GmbH v Nahverkehrsgesellschaft Altmark GmbH Case C-280/00 [2003] ECR I-7747 367
Ambulanz Glöckner v Landkreis Süswestplaz Case C-475/99 [2001] ECR 8089, [2002] 4 CMLR 726 52, 57, 267, 268, 326, 328, 329, 331, 337, 341, 343, 347, 351, 358, 359, 366, 369, 370
Amministrazione Autonoma dei Monopoli dello Stato v Commission Case T-139/98 [2001] ECR II-3413 306
AOK Bundesverband v Ichthyol-Gesellschaft Cordes, Hermani & Co Cases 264/01, 06/01, 354/01 and 355/01 [2004] ECR I-2493 54, 326, 328, 329, 331
ARD v Commission Case T-158/00 [2003] ECR II-3825 222
Arduino Case C-35/99 [2002] ECR I-1529 383, 385
Argos and Littlewoods v OFT [2004] CAT 24 92
Arkin v Borchard Lines Ltd [2003] EWHC 687 94
Associated Press v US, 326 US 1 308
Association des Centres distributeurs Edouard Leclerc v Au BléVert Sàrl Case 229/83 [1981] ECR 1, [1981] 2 CMLR 282 269
Atlantic Container Line AB v Commission Cases T-191/98, T-212/98 and T-214/98 [2003] ECR II-3275 38, 197
Atlantic Container Line v Commission Case T-191/99 [2001] ECR II-3677 82
Attheraces Ltd v BHB Ltd and BHB Enterprises Ltd [2005] EWHC 1553 286
Banchero Case 387/93 [1995] ECR I-4663 330, 337
BAT Cigaretten-Fabriken GmbH v Commission Case 35/83 [1985] ECR 363, [1985] 2 CMLR 470 99, 194

Bayer AG and Maschinenfabrik Hennecke GmbH v Heinz Süllhofer Case 65/86 [1988] ECR 5249, [1990] 4 CMLR 182 145
Bayer AG v Commission Case T-41/96 [2000] ECR II-3383, [2001] 4 CMLR 126 98, 104, 122, 127
Bayer AG v Commission Cases C-2 and 3/01 [2004] 4 CMLR 653 98, 104
Bayer AG v Süllhofer Case 65/86 [1988] ECR 5249, [1990] 4 CMLR 182 99, 174
Becu Case C-22/98 [1999] ECR I-5665, [2001] 4 CMLR 968 324, 326
Béguelin Import Co v GL Import Export SA Case 22/71 [1971] ECR 949, [1972] CMLR 81 39, 41, 43, 129, 196
Belgische Radio en Televisie (BRT) v SV SABAM Case 127/73 [1974] ECR 51, [1974] 2 CMLR 238 53, 93, 94, 267, 303, 307
Benzine en Petroleum Handelsmaatschappij BV v Commission Case 77/77 [1978] ECR 1513, [1978] 3 CMLR 174 236, 248, 275, 292
BEUC v Commission Case T-37/92 [1994] ECR II-285, [1995] 4 CMLR 167 140, 175
BHB Enterprises Ltd v Victor Chandler (International) Ltd [2005] EWHC 1047 286, 289
BMW Belgium SA v Commission Cases 32, 36-82/78 [1979] ECR 2435, [1980] 1 CMLR 370 99
BMW v Commission Case 32/78 [1979] ECR 2435, [1980] 1 CMLR 370 101, 123
BNIC v Aubert Case 136/86 [1987] ECR 4789 384, 386
Bodson v Pompes Funèbres des Regions Liberées Srl Case 30/87 [1988] ECR 2479, [1989] 4 CMLR 984 53, 54, 61, 129, 130, 223, 229, 234, 254, 265, 269, 279, 286, 311, 312, 313, 336, 340, 343
Boehringer Mannheim GmbH v Commission Case 45/69 [1970] ECR 769 72
BPB Industries and British Gypsum v Commission Case T-65/89 [1993] ECR II-389 272
BPB Industries Plc and British Gypsum Ltd v Commission Case C-310/93 [1995] ECR I-825 228, 254, 291
Brasserie de Haecht SA v Wilkin Case 23/67 [1967] ECR 407, [1968] CMLR 26 137, 152, 171
Brentjens Cases C-115/97 to C-117/97 [1999] ECR I-6025 330, 337, 348, 352
British Airways v Commission Case T-219/99 [2004] 4 CMLR 19 237, 249, 252, 272, 273, 275, 282, 283
British American Tobacco Co Ltd and RJ Reynolds Industries Inc v Commission Cases 142, 156/84 [1987] ECR 4487, [1988] 4 CMLR 24 137, 311
British Broadcasting Corpn and BBC Enterprises Ltd v Commission Case T-70/89 [1991] ECR II-535, [1991] 4 CMLR 669 235, 247, 265, 267, 311, 312
British Gypsum v Commission Case C-310/93 [1995] ECR I-865 273
British Leyland Motor Corpn Ltd v Armstrong Patents Co Ltd [1984] FSR 591, [1984] 3 CMLR 102 261, 262, 263, 269
British Leyland plc v Commission Case 226/84 [1986] ECR 3263, [1987] 1 CMLR 85 229, 236, 249, 262, 275, 279, 286, 289, 292, 307, 310, 312, 313
British Telecommunications v Commission Case C-302/94 [1996] ECR I-6417 341
BRT v SV SABAM Case 127/73 [1974] ECR 313 364, 365, 367, 373
Budesrepublik Deutschland v ISIS Cases C-327/03 and C-328/03, judgment of 20 October 2005 343, 359
Bulk Oil (Zug) AG v Sun International Ltd (No 2) Case 174/84 [1986] ECR 559, [1986] 2 CMLR 732 37, 69
Bunderverband der Arzneimittel-Importeure EV and Commission v Bayer AG Cases C-2 and 3/01 [2004] 4 CMLR 653 122, 127, 379
Bundeskartellamt v Volkswagen AG and VAG Leasing GmbH Case C-266/93 [1995] ECR I-3477 132
Bureau National Interprofessionel du Cognac (BNIC) v Aubert Case 136/86 [1987] ECR 4789, [1988] 4 CMLR 331 78, 107, 156

Bureau National Interprofessionnel du Cognac (BNIC) v Clair Case 123/83 [1985] ECR 391, [1985] 2 CMLR 430 63, 64, 78, 98, 99, 105, 107, 135, 156
Cableuropa v Commission Case T-346/02 [2003] ECR II-4251 234
Cadillon SA v Höss, Maschinenbau KG Case 1/71 [1971] ECR 351, [1971] CMLR 420 158, 178, 179
Cali e Figli Case C-343/95 [1997] ECR I-1547, [1997] 5 CMLR 484 54
Camera Care Ltd v Commission Case 792/79 [1980] ECR 119, [1980] 1 CMLR 334 95
Campus Oil v Minister for Industry and Energy Case 72/83 [1984] ECR 2727 372
Carlo Bagnasco v BPN Case C-215/96 [1999] ECR I-135, [1999] 4 CMLR 624 195
CBEM Case 311/84 [1985] ECR 3261 238, 346, 358
Centrafarm BV v Sterling Drug Inc and Winthrop Cases 15 and 16/74 [1974] ECR 1147, [1974] 2 CMLR 480 55, 129, 131
Centre belge d'etudes de marché-Telémarketing (CBEM) SA v Compagnie Luxembourgeoise de telédiffusion SA Case 311/84 [1985] ECR 3261, [1986] 2 CMLR 558 229, 249, 261, 267, 269, 275, 283, 293, 294, 296
Centro Servizi Spediporto Srl v Spedizione Marittima del Golfo Srl Case C-96/94 [1995] ECR I-2883, [1996] 4 CMLR 613 64, 386
Charmasson v Minister of Economic Affairs and Finance (Paris) Case 48/74 [1974] ECR 1383, [1975] 2 CMLR 208 80
Cheil Jedang Corpn v Commission Case T-220/00, 9 July 2003 42
Chelmkalm Motors Ltd v Esso Petroleum Co Ltd [1979] 1 CMLR 73 279
Chemidus Wavin Ltd v Societe pour la Transformation et l'Exploitation des Résines Industrielles SA [1977] FSR 181, [1978] 3 CMLR 514 CA 94
Chemische Afvalstoffen Dusseldorp BV v Minister van Volkshuisvesting, Ruimtelijke Ordening en Milieubeheer Case C-203/96 [1998] ECR I-4075, [1998] 3 CMLR 873 268, 318, 331, 338, 343, 346, 349, 351, 356, 363, 365, 366, 369, 370
Chiron Corpn v Murex Diagnostics Ltd [1993] FSR 324, [1994] FSR 187, [1994] 1 CMLR 410 261, 262
CICCE v Commission Case 298/83 [1985] ECR 1105, [1986] 1 CMLR 486 229
CICRA v Renault Case 53/87 [1988] ECR 6039, [1990] 4 CMLR 265 261
CIF v Autorita Garante della Concorrenza e del Mercato Case C-198/01 [2003] ECR I-8055 381, 383
CILFIT Srl v Ministero della Sanità Case 77/83 [1984] ECR 1257 78
Cisal di Batatistello Venanzio & Co v Instituto Nazionale per L'Assicurazione Contro Gli fortune Sul Lavoro (INAIL) Case C-218/00 [2002] ECR I-691, [2002] 4 CMLR 833 52, 54, 329
Claritas (UK) Ltd v (1) Post Office (2) Postal Preference Services Ltd [2001] UKCLR 2 238
Claymore Dairies Ltd and Arla Foods UK plc v OFT [2005] CAT 30 272, 280, 281
CMA CGM v Commission Case T-213/00 [2003] ECR II-913 70
CNSD Case C-35/96 [1998] ECR I-3851 384, 387
Coca-Cola v Commission Cases T-125/97 and T-127/97 [2000] ECR II-1733 222
Comet BV v Produktschap voor Siergewassen Case 45/76 [1976] ECR 2043, [1977] 1 CMLR 533 70
Comité des Industries Cinématographiques des Communautes Européennes v Commission Case 298/83 [1985] ECR 1105, [1986] 1 CMLR 486 279
Commission v Belgium Case 156/77 [1978] ECR 1881 82
Commission v France Case 232/78 [1979] ECR 2729, [1980] 1 CMLR 418 80
Commission v France Case C-159/94 [1997] ECR I-5815 373
Commission v France Case C-359/95 346, 381
Commission v Greece Case 226/87 [1988] ECR 3611 376
Commission v Ireland Case 249/81 [1982] ECR 4005 344

Commission v Italy Case 118/85 [1987] ECR 2599 61, 327, 328, 332, 333
Commission v Italy Case C-35/96 [1998] ECR I-3851 332
Commission v Italy Case C-158/94 [1997] ECR I-5789 373
Commission v Netherlands Case 157/94 [1997] ECR I-5699, [1997] 5 CMLR 601 364, 367, 369, 370, 371, 373
Commission v Solvay Case C-287/95 [2000] ECR I-2391 252
Commission v Spain Case C-463/00 [2003] ECR I-4581 333
Commission v T-Mobil Austria Case C-141/02, 22 February 2005 317, 379
Commission v Tetra-Laval BV Case C-12/03, judgment of 15 February 2005 222, 311
Commission v United Kingdom Case 231/78 [1979] ECR 1447, [1979] 2 CMLR 427 80
Compagnie Commerciale de l'Ouest Cases C-78/90 to C-83/90 [1992] ECR I-1847 319
Compagnie Maritime Belge Transport v Commission Case T-24/93 [1996] ECR II-1201 267, 272
Compagnie Maritime Belge Transports SA v Commission Case C-395/96 [2000] ECR I-1365, [2000] CMLR 1076 219, 228, 270
Compagnie Royale Asturienne des Mines SA and Rheinzink GmbH v Commission Case 29, 30/83 [1984] ECR 1679, [1985] 1 CMLR 688 101, 117, 124, 135, 136, 163, 194
Connect Austria Gesellschaft fur Telekommunikation GmbH v Telekom Control-Kommission and Mobilkom Austria Case C-462/89 [2003] ECR I-5197 343
Consiglio Nazionale degli Spedizionieri Dognali v Commission Case T-513/93 [2000] ECR II-1807 332
Consorzio Industrie Fiammiferi v Autorita Garante della Concorrenza e del Mercato Case C-198/01, 9 September 2003 197, 286, 303
Consten and Grundig v EEC Commission Cases 56, 58/64 [1966] ECR 299, [1966] CMLR 418 135, 154, 207
Coöperatieve Stremsel-en Kleurselfabriek v Commission Case 61/80 [1981] ECR 851, [1982] 1 CMLR 240 53, 78, 79, 81, 106, 158, 161, 164
Coöperatieve vereniging Suiker Unie UA v Commission Cases 40-48, 50, 54-56, 111, 113, 114/73 [1975] ECR 1663, [1976] 1 CMLR 295 39, 55, 58, 69, 79, 80, 109, 114, 117, 118, 119, 132, 139, 229, 245, 247, 248, 252, 261, 265, 274, 275, 283, 291, 292, 304, 308
Corbeau Case C-320/91 [1993] ECR I-2533, [1995] 4 CMLR 621 88, 261, 269, 319, 338, 343, 344, 359, 366, 369
Corsica Ferries Case C-18/93 [1994] ECR I-1783 236, 247, 261, 283, 315, 338, 346, 355, 366, 369, 383, 387
Costa v ENEL Case 6/64 [1964] ECR 585, [1964] CMLR 425 66
Courage Ltd v Crehan Case C-453/99 [2001] ECR I-6297, [2001] 5 CMLR 28 94, 123, 221
Cullet v Centre Leclerc Toulouse Case 231/83 [1985] ECR 305, [1985] 2 CMLR 524 64, 269, 385
Cutsforth v Mansfield Inns [1986] 1 WLR 558 QB 247
Daimler Chrysler v Commission Case T-325/01 132
Dansk Pelsdyrovlerforening v Commission Case T-61/89 [1992] ECR II-1931 78, 81
Dansk Rorindustri Cases C-189/02, C-205/02, C-208/02 and C-213/02 [2005] ECR I-0000 326
De Norre v NV Brouwerij Concordia Case 47/76 [1977] ECR 65, [1977] 1 CMLR 378 171
Deesen v Professional Golfers' Association, 358 F.2d 165 (9th Cir 1966) 90
Delimitis v Henninger Bräu AG Case C-234/89 [1991] ECR I-935, [1992] 5 CMLR 210 97, 136, 137, 144, 151, 152, 154, 171
Demo-Studio Schmidt v Commission Case 210/81 [1983] ECR 3045, [1984] 1 CMLR 63 253
Deutsche Bahn v Commission Case T-229/94 [1997] ECR II-1689, [1998] 4 CMLR 220 259, 282

Deutsche Grammophon Gesellschaft GmbH v Metro-SB-Grossmarkte GmbH & Co KG Case 78/70 [1971] ECR 487, [1971] CMLR 631 2, 229, 234, 260, 261, 262, 269, 279, 288, 302
Deutsche Post AG v Gesellschaft fur Zahlungssysteme mbH (GZS) and Citicorp Kartenservice GmbH Case C-147-8/97 [2000] ECR I-825 361, 366, 369, 370
Diego Cali & Figli Srl v Servizi ecologici porto di Genova SpA (SEPG) Case C-343/95 [1997] ECR I-1547 53, 54, 61, 267, 326, 328
Dijkstra v Friesland Coöperatie Case C-319/93 [1995] ECR I-4471, [1996] 5 CMLR 178 79, 81
DIP SpA v Commune di Bassano del Grappa Cases C-140, 141, 142/94 [1995] ECR I-3257, [1996] 4 CMLR 157 64, 265, 367, 386
Distillers Co Ltd v Commission Case 30/78 [1980] ECR 2229, [1980] 3 CMLR 121 186
Dona v Montera Case 13/76 [1976] ECR 1333 324
Dow Chemical Iberia SA v Commission Cases 97-99/87 [1989] ECR 3165, [1991] 4 CMLR 410 48
Dresdner Bank ea v Commission Cases T-44, 54, 56 and 60-61/02, 14 October 2004 111
Dunlop Slazenger v Commission Case T-43/92 [1994] ECR II-441, [1994] 5 CMLR 201 118, 120, 126, 127, 135
Eco Swiss China Time Ltd v Bennetton Case C-126/97 [1999] ECR I-3055, [2000] 5 CMLR 816 94
Elliniki Radiofonia Tileorasi v Kouvelas Case C-260/89 [1991] ECR I-2925, [1994] 4 CMLR 540 229, 247, 269, 275, 282, 319, 324, 348, 353, 369, 375
EMI Records Ltd v CBS Graamofon A/S Case 86/75 [1976] ECR 871, [1976] 2 CMLR 235 259, 301
EMI Records Ltd v CBS Schalipiatten GmbH Case 96/75 [1976] ECR 913, [1976] 2 CMLR 235 259, 301
EMI Records Ltd v CBS United Kingdom Ltd Case 51/75 [1976] ECR 811, [1976] 2 CMLR 235 39, 43, 259, 262, 301
Enichem Anic SpA v Commission of the European Communities Case T-6/89 [1991] ECR II-1623 58, 186
Enirisorse SpA v Ministero delle Finanze Cases C-34/2001 to C-38/2001 [2003] ECR I-14243 336, 367
Enterprenorforeningens Affals Miljosektion (FFAD) acting for Sydhavnens Sten & Grus ApS v Kobenhavns Kommune Case C-209/98 [2000] ECR I-3743, [2001] 2 CMLR 936 268, 331, 336, 338, 343, 347, 356, 366, 369, 370
Erauw-Jacquéry SPRL v La Hesbignonne Case 27/87 [1988] ECR 1919, [1988] 4 CMLR 576 152, 155, 158
ERT v DEP Case C-260/89 [1991] ECR I-2925, [1994] 4 CMLR 540 261
Esso Espanola v Communidad Autonoma de Canarias Case C-134/94 [1995] ECR I-4223, [1996] 5 CMLR 154 66
ETA Fabriques d'Ebauches SA v DK Investment SA Case 31/85 [1985] ECR 3933, [1986] 2 CMLR 674 129, 135, 139, 146
Etablissements Consten SARL and Grundig-Verkaufs-GmbH v EEC Commission Cases 56, 58/64 [1966] ECR 299, [1966] CMLR 418 137, 139, 144, 148, 149, 155, 158, 159, 160, 165, 205, 225
European Night Services v Commission Cases T-374, 375, 384 and 388/94 [1998] ECR II-3141, [1998] 5 CMLR 718 135, 187, 215, 225, 297
Europemballage Corpn and Continental Can Co Inc v Commission Case 6/72 [1973] ECR 215, [1973] CMLR 199 2, 42, 49, 56, 219, 223, 225, 234, 235, 236, 241, 254, 259, 261, 263, 273, 275, 279, 311
Farbenfabriken Bayer AG v Commission Case 51/69 [1972] ECR 745 70

Fédération Française des Sociétés d'Assurances v Caisse Nationale d'Assurance Vieillesse Mutuelle Agricole Case C-244/94 [1995] ECR I-4013, [1996] 4 CMLR 536 52, 53
Felixestowe Dock and Rly Co and European Ferries Ltd v British Transport Docks Board [1976] 2 Lloyd's Rep 656, [1976] 2 CMLR 655 230
FENIN v Commission Case T-319/99 [2003] ECR II-357, [2003] 5 CMLR 34 54, 329, 331
Ferriere Nord SpA v Commission Case T-143/89 [1995] ECR II-917 186
Fiatagri v Commission Case T-34/92 [1994] ECR II-905 119
Florimex v Commission Cases T-70/92 and T-71/92 [1997] ECR II-697, [1997] 5 CMLR 796 78
Ford of Europe Inc and Ford Werke AG v Commission Cases 228, 229/82 [1984] ECR 1129, [1984] 1 CMLR 649 105, 112, 126, 131
Ford-Werke AG and Ford of Europe Inc v Commission Cases 25, 26/84 [1985] ECR 2725, [1985] 3 CMLR 528 125, 126, 127, 131, 205
France, Italy and United Kingdom v Commission Cases 188-190/80 [1982] ECR 2545, [1982] 3 CMLR 144 33, 332, 333
France v Commission Case 188/80 [1982] ECR 2545 381
France v Commission Case C-202/88 [1991] ECR I-1223 340, 353, 358, 371, 376, 379, 381
France v Commission Case C-327/91 [1994] ECR I-3641, [1994] 5 CMLR 517 38
France v Commission Cases C-68/94 and C-30/95 [1998] ECR I-1375 245
France v Ladbroke Racing Case C-379/95 346, 381
Gamco Inc v Providence Fruit and Produce Building Ltd, 194 F.2d 484 (1st Cir 1952) 296
Garden Cottage Foods Ltd v Milk Mareketing Board [1984] AC 130, [1983] 2 All ER 770, [1983] 3 CMLR 43 79, 94
GB-INNO-BM v Verenigning van Kleihandelaars in Tabak Case 13/77 [1977] ECR 2115, [1978] ECR 283 62, 64, 223, 229, 267, 268, 275
Geitling Ruhrkohlen-Verkaufsgesellschaft GmbH v High Authority Case 13/60 [1962] ECR 83, [1962] CMLR 113 225
GEMO Case C-16/2001 [2003] ECR I-13769 367
Gencor Ltd v Commission Case T-102/96 [1999] ECR II-753 46
General Motors Continental NV v Commission Case 26/75 [1975] ECR 1367, [1976] 1 CMLR 95 229, 236, 247, 261, 262, 267, 269, 279, 286, 289, 306, 309, 313
Genzyme Ltd v OFT [2004] CompAR 358 229, 272, 277, 282, 290
Germany v Delta Schiffarts-und Speditionsgesellschaft GmbH Case C-153/93 [1994] ECR I-2517, [1996] 4 CMLR 21 64
Gibbs Mew plc v Gemmell [1998] Eu LR 588 Ca 94
Giovanni Carra Case C-258/98 [2000] ECR I-4217 324, 351
Gottrup-Klim Grovvareforening v Dansk Landbrugs Grovvareselskab AmbA Case C-250/92 [1994] ECR I-5641, [1996] 4 CMLR 191 53, 78, 105, 152, 222, 223, 225, 250, 252
Greenwich Film Production v SACEM Case 22/79 [1979] ECR 3275, [1980] 1 CMLR 629 2, 40, 50, 303, 311, 312, 313
Groupement des Cartes Bancaires 'CB' v Commission Cases T-39, 40/92 [1994] ECR II-49 86, 135, 166
GT-Link A/S v Danske Staatsbaner Case C-242/95 [1997] ECR I-4449, [1997] 5 CMLR 601 324, 355, 364
GVL v Commission Case 7/82 [1983] ECR 483, [1983] 3 CMLR 645 2, 52, 236, 247, 267, 272, 282, 292, 303, 311, 312, 313, 366, 367
Hanner Case C-483/02, judgment of 31 May 2005 363, 372, 373
Hans Just I/S v Danish Ministry for Fiscal Affairs Case 68/79 [1980] ECR 501, [1981] 2 CMLR 714 70
Hasselblad (GB) Ltd v Commission Case 86/82 [1984] ECR 883, [1984] 1 CMLR 559 111, 118, 120, 166

Heintz van Landewyck Sàrl v Commission Cases 209-215, 218/78 [1980] ECR 3125, [1981] 3 CMLR 134 52, 92, 105, 139, 158, 218
Herlitz v Commission Case T-66/92 [1994] ECR II-531, [1995] 5 CMLR 458 137, 147, 156, 162
HG Oude Luttikhuis v Verenigde Coöperatieve Melkindustrie Coberco BA Case C-399/93 [1995] ECR I-4663, [1996] 5 CMLR 178 81
Hilti AG v Commission Case C-53/92 [1994] ECR I-667 229, 236, 240, 242, 262, 278, 286, 292, 307
Hilti AG v Commission Case T-30/89 [1991] ECR II-1439, [1990] 4 CMLR 602 229, 236, 240, 241, 242, 249, 252, 255, 261, 262, 278, 286, 292, 303, 307, 312
Hoffmann-La Roche & Co AG v Commission Case 85/76 [1979] ECR 461, [1979] 3 CMLR 211 2, 3, 42, 223, 226, 228, 229, 236, 249, 252, 254, 255, 258, 259, 260, 270, 283, 286, 291, 299, 306, 311, 312
Höfner and Elser v Macroton GmbH Case C-41/90 [1991] ECR I-1979, [1993] 4 CMLR 306 52, 53, 61, 247, 261, 267, 268, 269, 275, 306, 311, 313, 324, 326, 328, 330, 347, 348, 354, 366, 371
Hugin Kassaregister AB v Commission Case 22/78 [1979] ECR 1869, [1979] 3 CMLR 345 39, 129, 158, 162, 229, 234, 236, 245, 262, 311, 313
Hüls AG v Commission Case C-199/92 [1999] ECR I-4287, [1999] 5 CMLR 1016 110
Hydrotherm Gerätebau GmbH v Compact de Dott Ing Mario Andreoli & CSAS Case 170/83 [1984] ECR 2999, [1985] 3 CMLR 224 52, 129
IAZ International Belgium NV v Commission Cases 96-102, 104, 105, 108, 110/82 [1983] ECR 3369, [1984] 3 CMLR 276 92, 99, 105, 365, 366, 370, 371
ICI v Commission Case 48/69 [1972] ECR 619, [1972] CMLR 557 72, 129
ICI v Commission Case T-36/91 [1995] ECR II-1847 117
ICI v Commission Case T-37/91 [1995] ECR II-1901 252, 286, 291
ICI v Commission (PVC II) Case T-328/94 72
Imperial Chemical Industries Ltd v Commission ('Dyestuffs')Case 48/69 [1972] ECR 619, [1972] CMLR 557 3, 42, 43, 49, 50, 51, 92, 109, 111, 114, 117, 130
IMS Health GmbH & Co OHG v NDC Health GmbH & Co KG Case C-418/01 [2004] 4 CMLR 1543 229, 234, 261, 262, 298, 300
Independent Television Publications and Radio Telefis Eireann (RTE) v Commission Cases C-241, 242/91 [1995] ECR I-743, [1995] 4 CMLR 718 228, 229, 235, 247, 261, 262, 265, 267, 299, 300, 304
Independent Television Publications Ltd v Commission Case T-76/89 [1991] ECR II-575, [1991] 4 CMLR 745 228, 235, 265, 267, 298, 311, 312
Industria Gomma Articoli Var v Ente Nazionale per la Cellulosa e per la Carta Case 94/74 [1975] ECR 699, [1976] 2 CMLR 37 269
Industrie des Poudres Sphériques v Commission Case T-5/97 [2000] ECR II-3755 282
Instituto Chemioterapico Italiano SpA and Commercial Solvents Corpn v Commission Cases 6, 7/73 [1974] ECR 223, [1974] 1 CMLR 309 2, 42, 50, 51, 52, 129, 130, 156, 223, 234, 236, 238, 263, 265, 273, 279, 292, 295, 296, 311, 312, 313
Intergraph v Solid Systems [1993] FSR 617 262
Irish Continental Group v CCI Morlaix Case IV/35.388 [1995] 5 CMLR 17 236, 296, 315
Irish Sugar v Commission Case C-497/99 [2001] ECR I-5333 251, 267, 309
Irish Sugar v Commission Case T-228/97 [1999] ECR II-2969 271, 309
Italy v Commission Case 41/83 [1985] ECR 873, [1985] 2 CMLR 368 36, 53, 60, 156, 229, 267, 275, 282, 291, 313, 329, 369, 370, 376
Italy v Commission Case C-35/96 [1998] ECR I-3851, [1998] 5 CMLR 889 53

Italy v EEC Council and EEC Commission Case 32/65 [1966] ECR 389, [1969] CMLR 39 52, 144
Italy v Saachi Case 155/73 [1974] ECR 409, [1974] 2 CMLR 177 53
ITT Promedia NV v Commission Case T-111/96 [1998] ECR II-2937 272, 308
Javico International and Javico AG v Yves Saint Laurent Parfums SA Case C-306/96 [1998] ECR I-1983 39
JCB Service v Commission Case T-67/01 [2004] 4 CMLR 1346 128
Jean Claude Becu Case C-22/98 [1999] ECR I-56656, [2001] 4 CMLR 968 55
Jersey Produce Marketing Organisation v States of Jersey Case C-293/02 37
JJB Sports and Allsports v OFT [2004] CAT 17 92, 229
Job Centre Case C-55/96 [1997] ECR I-7119, [1998] 4 CMLR 708 53, 330, 331, 338, 346, 348, 351
John Deere Ltd v Commission Case C-7/95 [1998] ECR I-3111, [1998] 5 CMLR 311 119
John Deere Ltd v Commission Case T-35/92 [1994] ECR II-957 119
JR Geigy AG v Commission Case 52/69 [1972] ECR 787, [1972] 1 CMLR 557 42, 49
Kali and Salz AG v Commission Cases 19, 20/74 [1975] ECR 499, [1975] 2 CMLR 154 235
Kiedinguerkoopbedrijf de Geus en Uitdenbogerd v Robert Bosch GmbH Case 13/61 [1962] ECR 45, [1962] CMLR 1 93
Kish Glass v Commission Case C-241/00 [2001] ECR I-7759 234
Kish Glass v Commission Case T-65/96 [2000] ECR II-1885 234
Lancôme SA v Etos BV Case 99/79 [1980] ECR 2511, [1981] 2 CMLR 164 135
Langnese-Iglo GmbH v Commission Case T-7/93 [1995] ECR II-1533, [1995] 5 CMLR 602 157, 173
LC Nungesser KG v Commission Case 258/78 [1982] ECR 2015, [1983] 1 CMLR 278 60, 99, 137, 150, 151, 154, 276, 371
Leclerc v Au Blé Vert Case 229/83 [1985] ECR 1, [1985] 2 CMLR 286 64, 385
L'Oreal NV v De Nieuwe AMCK PVBA Case 31/80 [1980] ECR 377, [1981] 2 CMLR 235 135, 171, 229, 234, 270
Lucazeau v Société des Auteurs, Compositeurs et Editeurs de Musique (Sacem) Case 110, 241, 242/88 [1989] ECR 2811, [1991] 4 CMLR 248 53, 117, 228, 286, 292
Mannesmann Anlagenbau Austria AG v Strohal Rotationsdruck GmbH Case C-44/96 [1998] ECR I-73 333
Marks and Spencers Ltd v Commissioners for Customs and Excise [1999] EuLR 450 229
Marlines v Commission Case T-56/99 [2003] ECR II-0000 82
Matra Hachette v Commission Case T-17/93 [1994] ECR II-595 204, 205, 208, 214, 216, 223
Maxmobil v Commission Case T-54/99 [2002] ECR II-313 317
Meca-Medina and Majcen v Commission Case T-313/02 (30 September 2004), [2004] 3 CMLR 60 90
Meng Case C-2/91 [1993] ECR I-5751 385
Merci Convenzionali Porto di Genova SpA v Siderurgica Gabrielli SpA Case C-179/90 [1991] ECR I-5009, [1994] 4 CMLR 422 61, 236, 247, 261, 262, 269, 315, 323, 324, 336, 338, 346, 348, 354, 366
Metro SB-Grofimankte GmbH and Co KG v Cartier SA Case C-376/92 [1994] ECR I-15, [1994] 5 CMLR 331 129, 205
Metro SB-Grossmarkte GmbH & Co KG v Commission Case 26/76 [1977] ECR 1875, [1978] 2 CMLR 1 3, 152, 205, 211, 228, 252, 254
Metro SB-Grossmarkte GmbH & Co KG v Commission Case 75/84 [1986] ECR 3021, [1987] 1 CMLR 118 228, 265
Métropole Télévision SA (M6) v Commission Case T-185/00 [2002] ECR II-3805, [2003] 4 CMLR 707 205
Métropole Télévision SA v Commission Cases T-528, 542, 543 and 546/93 [1996] ECR II-649, [1996] 5 CMLR 386 205

Métropole Télévision v Commission Case T-112/99 [2001] ECR II-2459, [2001] 5 CMLR 1236 152, 154, 155, 205
Michelin v Commission Case 322/81 [1983] ECR 3461 222, 234, 245, 271
Michelin v Commission Case T-203/01 [2004] 4 CMLR 18 222, 249, 283
Microsoft v Commission Case T-201/04 [2005] 4 CMLR 406 249, 261, 262, 290, 304
Miller v Commission Case 19/77 [1978] ECR 131, [1978] 2 CMLR 334 147, 161, 163, 186
Minister Public de Luxembourg v Muller Case 10/71 [1971] ECR 723 366, 369
Ministère Public v Asjes (Nouvelles Frontières) Cases 209-213/84 [1986] ECR 1425, [1986] 3 CMLR 173 64, 385
Ministère Public v Tournier Case 395/87 [1989] ECR 2521, [1991] 4 CMLR 248 117
Ministerio dell'Economia e delle Finanze v Cassa di Risparmio di Firenze SpA Case C-222/04, 27 October 2005 331
Mobistar SA v Commune de Fleron, Belgacom Mobile SA v Commune de Schaerbeek Cases C-544/03 and C-545/03, judgment of 8 September 2005 343, 359
Molinas v National Basketball Association, 190 F.Supp 21 (DCNY 1961) 90
Morris Communications Corp v PGA Tour, 235 F.Supp.2d 1269 (M.D.Fla. 2002) 90
Municipality of Almelo v Energiebedrijfl Ijsselmij Case C-393/92 [1994] ECR I-1477 226, 265, 286, 304
Musique Diffusion Française SA v Commission Cases 100-103/80 [1983] ECR 1825, [1983] 3 CMLR 221 111, 118, 166, 186
Napp Pharmaceuticals Holdings Ltd v DG of Fair Trading [2002] CAT 5 229, 280, 283, 287
National Carbonising Co Ltd v Commission Cases 109, 114/75 [1977] ECR 381 70, 275
National Collegiate Athletic Association v Board of Regents of University of Oklahoma, 104 S.Ct. 2948 (1984) 90
Nederlandse Banden-Industrie Michelin NV v Commission Case 322/81 [1983] ECR 3461, [1985] 1 CMLR 282 223, 229, 234, 236, 239, 241, 246, 247, 249, 251, 254, 257, 259, 270, 283, 284, 311, 312
Nederlandse Sigarenwinkeliers Organisatie v Commission Case 260/82 [1985] ECR 3801, [1988] 4 CMLR 753 69
Nederlandse Vereniging voor Fruit en Groentenimporthandel 'Frubo' v Commission Case 71/74 [1975] ECR 563, [1975] 2 CMLR 123 39, 78, 79, 80, 99, 105, 107
Netherlands and Koninklijke PTT Nederland v Commission Cases C-48/90 and C-66/90 [1992] ECR I-565 377, 378
Nungesser v Commission Case 258/78 [1982] ECR 2105, [1983] 1 CMLR 278 53
NV GB-INNO-BM v ATAB Case 13/77 [1977] ECR 2115, [1978] 1 CMLR 283 317, 319, 337, 381
Ohra Case C-245/91 [1993] ECR I-5851 385
OPEL Austria v Council Case T-115/94, 22 January 1997 38
Oscar Bronner GmbH & Co KG v Mediaprint Case C-7/97 [1998] ECR I-7791, [1999] 4 CMLR 112 25, 286, 295, 297, 298
Otter Tail Power Co v US, 410 US 366 308
Ottung v Klee and Weilbach A/S and Thomas Schmidt A/S Case 320/87 [1989] ECR 1177, [1990] 4 CMLR 915 145, 146
Parke, Davis & Co v Probel Case 24/67 [1968] ECR 55, [1968] CMLR 47 222, 261, 275, 279, 286, 288, 302
Parker Pen v Commission Case T-77/92 [1994] ECR II-549, [1995] 5 CMLR 435 137, 147, 162, 178
Passmore v Morland Plc [1999] 3 All ER 1005 93
Pavlov v Stichting Pensionenfonds Medische Specialisten Cases C-180-184/98 [2000] ECR I-6451, [2001] 4 CMLR 30 52, 53, 100, 326, 330, 332, 385, 387

Pigs and Bacon Commission v McCarren & Co Ltd Case 177/78 [1979] ECR 2161, [1979] 3 CMLR 389 79
Portugal v Commission Case C-163/99 [2001] ECR I-2613 247, 343, 355, 377
Portugese Republic v Commission Case C-163/1999 [2001] ECR I-2613 37, 376
Poucet and Pistre v Assurances Generales de France Cases C-159, 160/91 [1993] ECR I-637 52, 53, 54, 61, 326, 329
Procureur do la République v Giry and Guerlain SA Cases 253/78 and 3/79 [1980] ECR 2327, [1981] 2 CMLR 99 311
Procureur du Roi v Dassonville Case 8/74 [1974] ECR 837, [1974] 2 CMLR 436 137
Procureur General v Buys Case 5/79 [1979] ECR 3203, [1980] 2 CMLR 493 270
Pronuptia de Paris GmbH, Frankfurt am Main v Pronuptia de Paris Irmgard Schillgalis Case 161/84 [1986] ECR 353, [1986] 1 CMLR 414 150, 154
Provimi Ltd v Aventi Animal Nutrition SA [2003] EWHC 961 42
Publishers Association v Commission Case C-360/92 [1995] ECR I-23, [1995] 5 CMLR 33 105, 178, 218
Publishers Association v Commission Case T-66/89 [1992] 5 CMLR 120 105, 205, 206, 217
R v Competition Commission, Director General of Telecommunications, ex p T-Mobile [2003] EWHC 1555 282
Radio Telefis Eireann v Commission Case T-69/89 [1991] ECR II-485, [1991] 4 CMLR 586 235, 247, 265, 267, 311, 312
RCA/BHB v OFT [2005] CAT 29 153, 229, 235, 242
Regie des Télégraphes et des Téléphones v SA-GB-INNO-BN Case C-18/88 [1991] ECR I-5941 247, 269, 275
Reiff Case C-185/91 [1993] ECR I-5801, [1995] 5 CMLR 145 64, 383, 385, 386, 387
Remia BV v Commission Case 42/84 [1985] ECR 2545, [1987] 1 CMLR 1 135, 154, 166, 205, 206, 211
Rewe-Zentralfinanz v Landwirtschaftskammer Case 33/76 [1976] ECR 1989, [1977] 1 CMLR 533 70
Reyners v Belgium Case 2/74 [1974] ECR 631 324
Rhône-Poulenc SA v Commission Case 179/86 45
Rhône-Poulenc SA v Commission Cases T-1, 4, 6-15/89 [1990] ECR II-637, [1991] ECR II-867 45, 58, 92, 119, 119231
Riseria Luigi Geddo v Ente nazionale Risi Case 2/73 [1973] ECR 825, [1974] 1 CMLR 13 269
RTT v GB-INNO-BM Case C-18/88 [1991] ECR I-5941 323, 324, 344, 346, 350, 353, 358, 367, 369, 371
SA Hercules NV v Commission Case C-51/92 [1999] ECR I-4235, [1999] 5 CMLR 976 110
Sacchi Case 155/73 [1974] ECR 409, [1974] 2 CMLR 177 52, 229, 267, 282, 307, 313, 324, 366, 371, 373, 375
Salonia v Poidomani Case 126/80 [1981] ECR 1563, [1982] 1 CMLR 64 158, 166, 179, 292, 304, 312, 313
Sandoz AG v Commission Case 53/69 [1972] ECR 845, [1972] CMLR 557 42
Sandoz prodotti Farmaceutici SpA v Commission Case C-277/87 [1990] ECR I-44 98, 99, 124, 135, 136
SAT Fluggesellschaft v Eurocontrol Case 364/92 [1994] ECR I-43, [1994] 5 CMLR 208 52, 53, 54, 61, 316, 329
Shearson Lehman Hutton Inc v Maclame Watson & Co Ltd [1989] 3 CMLR 429 3
Shell v Commission Case T-11/89 [1992] ECR II-757 129
Silvano Raso Case 163/96 [1998] ECR I-533, [1998] 4 CMLR 737 338, 346, 348, 350, 352
Sirena Srlv Eda Srl Case 40/70 [1971] ECR 69, [1971] CMLR 260 222, 229, 234, 261, 262, 275, 279, 286, 288, 302

SIV v Commission (Italian Flat Glass) Case T-68/89 [1992] ECR II-1403, [1992] 5 CMLR 302 250
Società Italiano Vetro SpA v Commission Case T-68, 77, 78/89 [1992] ECR II-1403, [1992] 5 CMLR 302 117, 226, 234, 235, 267
Société Agricole du Centre d'Insémination de la Crespelle v Cooperative d'Elevage et d'Insemination Artificielle du Départment de la Mayenne Case C-323/93 [1994] ECR I-5077 268, 319, 336, 346, 348, 350, 357
Société alsacienne et lorraine de telecommunications et d'electronique (Alsatel) v Novasam SA Case 247/86 [1988] ECR 5987, [1990] 4 CMLR 434 222, 223, 226, 229, 236, 245, 252, 261, 265, 312
Société Cooperative des Asphalteurs Belges (Belasco) v Commission Case 246/86 [1989] ECR 2117, [1991] 4 CMLR 96 168
Société de Vente de Ciments et Betons de l'Est SA v Kerpen and Kerpen GmbH & Co KG Case 319/82 [1983] ECR 4173, [1985] 1 CMLR 511 93
Société Rhinane d'Exploitation et de Manutention v High Authority Case 67/63 [1964] ECR 151, [1964] CMLR 350 99, 107
Societe Vente de Ciments et Betons de l'Est SA v Kerpen and Kerpen GmbH & Co KG Case 319/82 [1983] ECR 4173, [1985] 1 CMLR 511 144
Sociéti Technique Minière v Maschinenbau Ulm GmbH Case 56/65 [1966] ECR 235, [1966] CMLR 357 93, 135, 136, 149, 151, 155, 158, 190, 196
Solvay v Commission Case T-32/91 [1995] ECR II-1825, [1996] 5 CMLR 91 252, 286, 291
Solway v Commission Case T-30/91 [1995] ECR II-1775, [1995] All ER 600, [1996] 5 CMLR 57 111, 113
Spain, Belgium and Italy v Commission Cases C-271, 281, 289/90 [1992] ECR I-5833 358, 371, 381
Spanish Courier Services [1990] OJ L233/19=[1991] 4 CMLR 560 53
SPO v Commission Case T-29/92 [1995] ECR II-289 119
Srl Ufficio van Ameyde v Srl Ufficio Centrale Italiano di Assistenza Auotmobilisti in Circolazione Internazionale Case 90/76 [1977] ECR 1091, [1978] 3 CMLR 478 86
SSI v Commission Cases 240-2, 261 and 262/82 [1985] ECR 3831, [1987] 3 CMLR 661 98
Stichting Sigarettenindustrie v Commission Cases 240-242, 261-262, 268-269/82 [1985] ECR 3831, [1987] 3 CMLR 661 69, 157
Stik Strip BV v Polaroid Nederland and Polaroid UK [1984] 1 CMLR 132 291, 292
Syfait Case C-53/03, 28 October 2004 229
Tepea BV v Commission Case 28/77 [1978] ECR 1391, [1978] 3 CMLR 392 99, 118, 165
Tetra Laval v Commission Case T-5/02 [2002] ECR II-4381 311
Tetra Pak International SA v Commission Case C-333/94 [1996] ECR I-5951 226, 237, 245, 252, 261, 280, 308
Tetra Pak International SA v Commission Case T-83/91 [1994] ECR II-755 226, 237, 245, 247, 252, 261, 272, 273, 283, 291, 308
Tetra-Pak v Commission Case T-51/89 [1990] ECR II-309 222, 225, 228, 240, 276, 302, 308, 311
Tiercé Ladbroke v Commission Case T-504/93 [1997] ECR II-923 235, 245, 297
TNT Traco SpA v Poste Italiane SpA Case C-340/99 [2001] ECR I-4109 364
Toscano v PGA Tour, 201 F.Supp.2d 1106 (E.D.Cal. 2002) 90
Trefileurope Sales Sarl v Commission Case T-141/89 [1995] ECR II-791 98, 135, 136
UEFA's Broadcasting Regulations [2001] OJ L171/12, [2001] 5 CMLR 654 53
Union Royale belge des sociétés de football association v Bosman Case C-415/93 [1995] ECR I-4921, [1996] All ER 97, [1996] 1 CMLR 645 90
United Brands Co v Commission Case 2/76 [1978] ECR 207, [1978] 1 CMLR 429

2, 3, 39, 42, 48, 223, 229, 230, 235, 236, 241, 246, 247, 249, 251, 252, 254, 255, 256, 260, 261, 262, 263, 275, 283, 286, 287, 292, 304, 312
United States v El du Pont de Nemour and Co, 351 US 377 (1956) 242
United States v Terminal Railroad Association of St Louis, 224 US 383 (1912) 296, 308
VAG France SA v Etablissements Magne Sa Case 10/86 [1986] ECR 4071, [1988] 4 CMLR 98 93
Van Ameyde v Srl Ufficio Centrale Italiano di Assistenza Assicurativa Automobilisti Case 90/76 [1977] ECR 1091, [1977] 2 CMLR 478 267, 305, 313
Van Binsbergen v Bestuur van de Bedrijfsvereniging voor de Metaalnijverheid Case 33/74 [1974] ECR 1299 323
Van den Bergh Foods v Commission Case T-65/98 [2003] ECR II-4653 249, 272
Van der Woude v Stichting Beatrixoord Case C-222/98 [2000] ECR I-7111, [2001] 4 CMLR 93 100
Van Eycke v ASPA Case 267/86 [1988] ECR 4769, [1990] 4 CMLR 330 64, 86, 156, 382, 383, 384, 387
Van Landewyck v Commission Cases 209-215, 218/78 [1980] ECR 3125, [1981] 3 CMLR 134 98, 99, 105
VBA and Florimex v Commission Case C-265/97 [2000] ECR I-2061, [2001] 5 CMLR 1343 78
VBA and Florimex v Commission Case C-266/97 [2000] ECR I-2135 78
VBVB and VBBB v Commission Cases 43, 63/82 [1984] ECR 19, [1985] 1 CMLR 27 53, 90, 99, 105, 159, 160, 163, 205, 206
Verband der Sachversicherer BV v Commission Case 45/85 [1987] ECR 405, [1988] 4 CMLR 264 86, 105, 106, 135, 156, 165
Vereeniging van Cementhandelaren v Commission Case 8/72 [1972] ECR 977, [1973] CMLR 7 98, 105, 166, 167
Vereniging van Vlaamse Reisbureaus v Sociale Dienst van de Plaatselijke en Gewestelijke Overheidsdiensten Case 311/85 [1987] ECR 3801, [1989] 4 CMLR 213 64, 171, 177
Vereniging voor Energie, Milieu en Water v Directeur van de Dienst uitvoering en toezicht energie Case C-17/03, judgment of 7 June 2005 343
Viho v Commission Case C-73/95 [1996] ECR I-5457, [1997] 4 CMLR 419, [1997] All ER 163 122, 129, 132
Viho v Commission Case T-102/92 [1995] ECR II-17 122, 131, 132
Vlaamse Televisie Maatschappij NV v Commission Case T-266/97 [1999] ECR II-2329 377, 381, 386
Völk v Vervaecke Case 5/69 [1969] ECR 295, [1969] CMLR 273 158, 178
Volkswagen v Commission Case C-338/00 [2003] ECR I-9189, [2004] 4 CMLR 351 101, 123
Volkswagen v Commission Case T-208/01 [2004] 4 CMLR 727 128
Volvo AB v Erik Veng (UK) Ltd Case 238/87 [1988] ECR 6211, [1989] 4 CMLR 122 261, 262, 298, 303
VTM v Commission Case T-266/1997 [1999] ECR II-2329 366
VZW Vereniging van Vlaamse Reisbureaus v VZW Sociale Dienst van de Plaatselijke en Gewestlijke Overheidsdiensten Case 311/85 [1987] ECR 3801, [1989] 4 CMLR 213 132
Walrave and Koch Case 36/74 [1974] ECR 1405 90
Windsurfing International Inc v Commission Case 193/83 [1986] ECR 611, [1986] 3 CMLR 489 134, 155
Wireless Group v RJAR, 16 December 2004 229
Wouters v Alegemene Raad van de Nederlandse Order van Advocaten Case C-309/99 [2002] ECR I-1577, [2002] 4 CMLR 913 52, 53, 90, 98, 100, 105, 152, 190
Züchner v Bayerische Vereinsbank AG Case 172/80 [1981] ECR 2021, [1982] 1 CMLR 313 86, 109, 116, 156, 228, 266, 313, 366

Table of Legislation

References are to paragraph number

Act of Accession 1972 37
Art 26(1) 37
Art 26(3) 37
Art 28 37
Act of Accession 1979 37
Art 20 37
Act of Accession 1985 37
Art 24 37
Art 25 37
Act of Accession 1994 37
Art 18 37
Art 28 37
Protocol 2 37
Act of Accession 2003 37
Art 2 37
Art 5(1) 37
Art 19 37
Art 53 37
Competition Act 1998 44, 220
Chap. II 276
s 47A 220
s 60 44
Criminal Law Act 1977 94
s 5(1) 94
Decision 64/233 [1964] CMLR 237 43
Decision 68/317 [1968] OJ L201/1 154
Decision 68/318 [1968] OJ L201/4 180
Decision 68/376 [1968] CMLR D78 39
Decision 69/152 [1969] OJ L122/8 139
Decision 69/195 [1969] OJ L165/12 129, 130
Decision 69/202 [1970] CMLR D1 39
Decision 69/243 [1969] CMLR D23 42, 111
Decision 69/243 [1969] OJ L195/11 92
Decision 70/332 [1970] CMLR D19 39, 130
Decision 70/333 [1970] OJ L148/9 105, 106
Decision 70/488 [1970] CMLR D49 39
Decision 71/224 [1971] CMLR D35 53, 262
Decision 71/337 [1971] OJ L227/26 105, 106
Decision 72/21 [1972] CMLR D11 42, 50, 261
Decision 72/22 [1972] OJ L13/34 167
Decision 72/23 [1972] OJ L13/14 180
Decision 72/238 [1972] CMLR D45 39
Decision 72/390 [1972] OJ L26 105, 107
Decision 72/403 [1973] CMLR D2 42, 55
Decision 72/457 [1973] CMLR D50 42, 50

Decision 72/480 [1973] CMLR D43 42, 135
Decision 73/323 [1973] CMLR D250 53
Decision 74/292 [1974] OJ L160/1 99
Decision 74/433 [1974] OJ L237/16 81, 99, 105, 106, 107
Decision 74/634 [1975] 1 CMLR D8 39, 43, 98, 135
Decision 75/74 [1975] OJ L29/11 174, 306
Decision 75/77 [1975] OJ L29/26 43, 80, 135
Decision 75/94 [1975] 1 CMLR D31 39
Decision 75/95 [1975] 1 CMLR D68 139
Decision 75/358 [1975] OJ L159/22 167
Decision 75/482 [1975] OJ L212/23 180
Decision 75/494 [1975] 2 CMLR D40 39
Decision 75/497 [1975] OJ L228/3 99, 135
Decision 76/29 [1976] 1 CMLR D14 55
Decision 76/159 [1976] OJ L28/19 39, 170
Decision 76/185 [1976] OJ L35/2 275, 282
Decision 76/248 [1976] 2 CMLR D1 76
Decision 76/249 [1976] 2 CMLR D15 76
Decision 76/353 [1976] 1 CMLR D28 42, 49
Decision 76/593 [1992] OJ L192/27 48
Decision 76/642 [1976] 2 CMLR D25 42, 49
Decision 76/684 [1976] OJ L231/24 69, 105, 376
Decision 76/743 [1976] 2 CMLR D44 39, 55, 194
Decision 76/915 [1977] 1 CMLR D61 42
Decision 77/66 [1977] OJ L16/8 99
Decision 77/100 [1977] 1 CMLR D82 39
Decision 77/129 [1977] 1 CMLR D44 43, 73, 99
Decision 77/160 [1977] OJ L48/32 159, 178
Decision 77/327 [1977] OJ L117/1 236, 259
Decision 77/543 [1977] 2 CMLR D69 39, 174
Decision 77/592 [1977] OJ L242 119
Decision 77/722 [1977] OJ L299/18 105
Decision 78/24 [1978] 1 CMLR D63 48
Decision 78/59 [1978] 2 CMLR 194 99, 105, 106
Decision 78/66 [1978] OJ L111/23 80, 81
Decision 78/68 [1978] OJ L22/23 51, 129, 247, 259
Decision 78/155 [1978] OJ L46/33 99
Decision 78/193 [1978] OJ L60/19 99
Decision 78/251 [1978] OJ L70/47 139
Decision 78/252 [1978] OJ L70/54 43, 51, 119
Decision 78/253 [1978] 2 CMLR 397 39
Decision 78/516 [1978] 3 CMLR 306 55
Decision 78/571 [1978] 2 CMLR 758 84
Decision 78/670 [1978] OJ L224/29 92, 105
Decision 78/823 [1978] 3 CMLR 434 60, 376
Decision 78/921 [1978] OJ L322/26 84, 226
Decision 78/922 [1978] OJ L322/26 99, 124, 128, 146
Decision 79/68 [1979] 1 CMLR 448 42, 99, 118
Decision 79/86 [1979] 1 CMLR 511 55
Decision 79/90 [1979] OJ L21/16 43, 111, 118, 119
Decision 79/253 [1979] 1 CMLR 650 53

Decision 79/934 [1979] OJ L286/32 99, 118, 119, 129
Decision 80/182 [1980] 2 CMLR 285 111, 161, 187, 210
Decision 80/183 [1980] OJ L39/64 80
Decision 80/234 [1980] 2 CMLR 402 53, 106
Decision 80/256 [1980] OJ L60/21 42, 118
Decision 80/257 [1980] OJ L62/28 105, 106
Decision 80/917 [1980] OJ L260/24 105
Decision 80/1071 [1980] OJ L318/1 106
Decision 80/1283 [1981] 2 CMLR 287 42, 51, 99
Decision 80/1334 [1980] OJ L383/19 99, 175
Decision 81/1030 [1981] OJ L370/49 52, 156
Decision 82/86 [1982] OJ L360/36 267
Decision 82/123 [1982] OJ L54/36 99, 105
Decision 82/174 [1982] OJ L80/36 53, 86, 92
Decision 82/204 [1982] 2 CMLR482 262
Decision 82/367 [1982] OJ L161/18 111, 118, 120
Decision 82/371 [1982] OJ L167/39 92, 99, 105, 106, 107
Decision 82/506 [1982] OJ L232/1 99
Decision 82/742 [1983] 1 CMLR 619 60, 76
Decision 82/821 [1982] OJ L360/36 247
Decision 82/853 [1982] OJ L354/28 99
Decision 82/861 [1982] OJ L360/36 53, 60, 156, 282, 291, 313, 376
Decision 82/866 [1982] OJ L362/40 135, 136
Decision 82/896 [1982] OJ L379/1 69, 105
Decision 82/897 [1983] 1 CMLR 412 73, 194
Decision 83/390 [1983] OJ L224/45 213
Decision 83/462 [1983] OJ L252/13 279
Decision 83/546 [1983] OJ L317/1 52, 73, 163
Decision 84/191 [1984] 2 CMLR 484 86, 210
Decision 84/379 [1984] OJ L207/11 236, 247, 263, 275, 289, 292, 311
Decision 84/405 [1985] 2 CMLR 108 73
Decision 85/74 [1985] OJ L35/1 55, 58, 111, 118
Decision 85/75 [1985] OJ L35/20 86, 105, 106, 156
Decision 85/76 [1985] OJ L35/35 78, 79, 80, 81, 105
Decision 85/77 [1985] 3 CMLR 434 86, 202, 208
Decision 85/202 [1985] OJ L85/1 38, 43, 45, 69, 92, 105, 176
Decision 85/206 [1985] OJ L92/1, [1987] 3 CMLR 813 42, 43, 52, 60, 69
Decision 85/563 [1985] OJ L369/28 105
Decision 85/564 [1985] OJ L369/28 105
Decision 85/565 [1985] OJ L369/31 105
Decision 85/566 [1985] OJ L369/34 105
Decision 85/609 [1985] OJ L347/1 228, 237, 270
Decision 85/615 [1985] OJ L376/15 86
Decision 86/398 [1986] OJ L230/1 45, 52, 58, 73
Decision 86/499 [1985] OJ L291/46 105
Decision 86/507 [1987] 2 CMLR 601 86
Decision 86/596 [1986] OJ L348/50 80, 81
Decision 87/3 [1987] OJ L5/13 69
Decision 87/13 [1987] OJ L7/27 86, 105
Decision 87/103 [1989] 4 CMLR 238 86
Decision 87/500 [1987] OJ L286/36 228, 259, 294

Decision 87/602 [1987] OJ L374/19 31
Decision 88/84 [1988] 4 CMLR 513 58
Decision 88/87 [1988] OJ L50/18 209
Decision 88/109 [1988] OJ L59/25 80
Decision 88/138 [1988] OJ L65/19 228, 242
Decision 88/330 [1988] OJ L150/35 208, 209, 210, 213, 214, 219
Decision 88/491 [1988] OJ L262/27 79, 81
Decision 88/501 [1988] OJ L272/27 228, 240, 254, 311
Decision 88/518 [1988] OJ L284/41 228, 275, 283, 290, 294
Decision 88/541 [1988] OJ L301/68 39
Decision 88/587 [1988] OJ L316/43 78, 81
Decision 88/589 [1988] OJ L317/47 228, 237, 270, 275, 283, 294, 296
Decision 88/604 [1988] OJ L332/38 156, 202
Decision 89/22 [1989] OJ L10/50 228, 255, 275, 291, 294
Decision 89/44 [1989] OJ L26/12 105, 217
Decision 89/93 [1989] OJ L33/44 117, 226
Decision 89/95 [1989] OJ L36/16 207, 210
Decision 89/113 [1989] OJ L43/27 226, 237, 249, 275, 294
Decision 89/190 [1989] OJ L74/1 58
Decision 89/191 [1989] OJ L74/21 58
Decision 89/205 [1989] OJ L78/43 228
Decision 89/512 [1989] OJ L253/1 86, 163
Decision 89/515 [1989] OJ L260/1 73, 98, 155
Decision 89/536 [1989] OJ L284/36 52
Decision 90/16 [1990] OJ L10/47 306
Decision 90/22 [1990] OJ L13/34 86
Decision 90/25 [1990] OJ L15/25 86
Decision 91/38 [1992] OJ L19/25 208, 210
Decision 91/128 [1991] OJ L60/19 105, 210
Decision 91/130 [1991] OJ L63/32 214
Decision 91/299 [1991] OJ L152/21 252, 291
Decision 91/300 [1991] OJ L152/40 252, 291
Decision 91/301 [1991] OJ L152/54 140
Decision 91/335 [1991] OJ L185/23 130
Decision 91/408 [1991] OJ L258/18 202, 207
Decision 91/562 [1991] OJ L306/22 202, 207
Decision 92/96 [1992] OJ L37/16 86, 202, 207
Decision 92/163 [1992] OJ L72/1 226, 252, 261, 308
Decision 92/212 [1992] OJ L95/50 86
Decision 92/213 [1992] OJ L96/34 227, 236, 296, 297
Decision 92/261 [1992] OJ L131/32 118, 120, 124
Decision 92/262 [1992] OJ L134/1 267
Decision 92/521 [1992] OJ L326/31 177
Decision 92/568 [1992] OJ L366/47 105
Decision 93/3 [1993] OJ L4/26 86, 105
Decision 93/50 [1993] OJ L20/23 207
Decision 93/82 [1993] OJ L34/21 39, 255, 267, 279
Decision 93/252 [1993] OJ L116/21 311
Decision 93/403 [1995] 4 CMLR 56 262
Decision 93/438 [1993] OJ L203/27 55
Decision 94/19 [1994] OJ L15/5 236, 261, 296, 315

Decision 94/119 [1994] OJ L55/2 236, 247, 261, 265, 267, 296, 315
Decision 94/296 [1994] OJ L131/15 211
Decision 94/601 [1994] OJ L243/1 52, 55
Decision 95/1 37
Art 19 37
Protocol 2 37
Decision 95/145 [1995] OJ L95/51 30
Decision 95/188 [1995] OJ L122/37 55
Decision 95/364 [1995] OJ L216/8 236, 247, 297
Decision 95/695 [1999] OJ L275/17 204
Decision 96/454 [1996] OJ L188/37 86
Decision 97/606 [1997] OJ L244/18 366
Decision 99/421 [1999] OJ L161/61 215
Decision 2000/475 [2000] OJ L187/47 212
Decision 2001/124 311
Decision 2001/418 [2001] OJ L152 119
Decision 2002/914 [2002] OJ L318/17 204
Decision, Adaptation Decision
Art 15(1) 37
Art 15(2) 37
Decision of 29 May 1998, [1998] OJ L173/26 38
Directive 80/723 [1980] OJ L195/35 333, 367, 379, 381
Art 2(1)(b) 333
Directive 87/601 [1987] OJ L374/12 31
Directive 88/301 [1988] OJ L131/73 33, 340, 358, 379, 381
Directive 90/337 [1990] OJ L185/16 88
Directive 90/377 [1990] OJ L185/16 88
Directive 90/388 [1990] OJ L192/10 33, 340, 358, 379
Art 2(1)(b) 340
Art 2(1)(c) 340
Art 3c 343
Directive 90/547 [1990] OJ L 313/30 88
Directive 91/296 [1991] OJ L147/37 88
Directive 94/46 [1994] OJ L268/15 340
Directive 95/49 [1995] OJ L 233/86 88
Directive 96/2 343
Directive 96/19 340
Directive 96/92 [1997] OJ L27/20 88
Directive 97/13 359
Directive 98/30 [1998] OJ L204/1 88
Directive 2000/52 [2000] OJ L193/75 333, 379
Directive 2002/19 [2002] OJ L108/7 381
Directive 2002/20 [2002] OJ L108/21 381
Directive 2002/21 [2002] OJ L108/33 381
Directive 2002/22 [2002] OJ L108/51 381
EC Treaty 1, 2, 3, 15, 33, 37, 51, 70, 109, 275, 310
Annex II 78
Art 1-16 2
Art 2 90, 223
Art 3(1)(g) 223, 311, 377
Art 3(3) 130

Art 3(f) 64
Art 3(g) 316, 317, 380, 381, 385, 387
Art 4(1) 2
Art 5(2) 64
Art 10 62, 64, 65, 316, 318, 319, 380, 381, 382, 383, 384, 385, 386, 387
Art 10(2) 377
Art 12 314, 322
Art 23-31 2
Art 28 343, 371
Art 31 363
Art 32-38 2
Art 33 77, 78
Art 36 77
Art 37(2) 77
Art 37(3) 77
Art 39 323
Art 39-60 2
Art 43 323
Art 70-80 2, 82
Art 81 26, 27, 28, 29, 30, 32, 38, 42, 45, 46, 52, 55, 60, 61, 62, 63, 64, 65, 69, 70, 91, 93, 94, 95, 97, 98, 99, 101, 102, 105, 107, 111, 121, 122, 124, 125, 126, 128, 129, 130, 131, 132, 133, 134, 135, 136, 139, 143, 146, 148, 152, 154, 155, 156, 159, 162, 169, 170, 174, 177, 179, 189, 191, 192, 193, 194, 195, 198, 199, 211, 219, 220, 225, 226, 228, 235, 262, 265, 267, 311, 317, 319, 326, 339, 340, 373, 376, 377, 380, 381, 382, 383, 384, 385, 386, 387
Art 81-82 322
Art 81-86 1, 78
Art 81-89 1, 314
Art 81(1) 37, 52, 55, 64, 78, 79, 81, 87, 91, 93, 94, 96, 97, 100, 101, 103, 122, 124, 126, 127, 132, 133, 135, 137, 138, 139, 140, 145, 148, 149, 150, 152, 153, 154, 155, 160, 178, 179, 181, 188, 197, 199, 200, 201, 203, 212, 227, 228
Art 81(1)(a) 91, 219, 279, 307
Art 81(1)(b) 91, 219, 304
Art 81(1)(c) 91
Art 81(1)(d) 91, 282
Art 81(1)(e) 91, 291
Art 81(2) 93, 94, 197, 220
Art 81(3) 26, 28, 30, 33, 38, 82, 93, 96, 97, 150, 197, 198, 199, 201, 202, 203, 204, 206, 207, 211, 212, 215, 218, 227, 228, 275
Art 82 3, 25, 26, 27, 28, 29, 30, 32, 38, 42, 45, 46, 52, 60, 61, 62, 63, 69, 70, 78, 94, 97, 122, 133, 156, 177, 179, 189, 191, 192, 193, 194, 198, 211, 219, 220, 221, 222, 223, 224, 225, 226, 228, 229, 230, 237, 238, 246, 248, 265, 266, 267, 268, 269, 275, 276, 278, 279, 280, 283, 284, 286, 290, 292, 295, 298, 303, 311, 313, 317, 319, 344, 350, 351, 352, 354, 355, 358, 360, 373, 376, 381
Art 82(2)(b) 350, 351
Art 82(a) 219, 279, 307
Art 82(a)-(d) 278
Art 82(b) 219, 304, 358
Art 82(c) 219, 282, 283, 289
Art 82(d) 220, 291
Art 83 381

Art 83(1) 29
Art 83(2) 29
Art 84 64, 97
Art 85 63, 64, 138, 387
Art 85-94 1
Art 85(1) 32, 98
Art 85(2) 32
Art 85(3) 86
Art 86 60, 61, 62, 267, 268, 292, 314, 315, 316, 317, 320, 321, 322, 323, 324, 325, 327, 328, 333, 339, 340, 343, 345, 346, 347, 348, 350, 351, 352, 355, 356, 358, 360, 375, 378, 379, 380, 387
Art 86(1) 64, 268, 315, 316, 317, 318, 319, 322, 324, 325, 326, 331, 334, 335, 340, 341, 343, 344, 350, 351, 352, 354, 359, 375, 376, 381
Art 86(2) 69, 315, 317, 326, 331, 341, 343, 351, 353, 354, 359, 361, 363, 364, 365, 367, 368, 369, 370, 371, 372, 373, 374, 376
Art 86(3) 33, 315, 316, 321, 375, 376, 377, 378, 379, 381
Art 87 29, 331
Art 87-89 1, 322
Art 88 29, 62
Art 88(1) 78
Art 88(3) 78
Art 89 62
Art 90 323, 343, 359
Art 91 1
Art 95 68, 379, 381
Art 96 62, 65, 66, 68
Art 97 62, 65, 66, 68
Art 97(1) 66
Art 97(2) 66
Art 157 12
Art 157(1) 2
Art 211 32, 375
Art 230 378
Art 234 64
Art 256 51
Art 296(1) 84
Art 296(1)(b) 84
Art 296(2) 84
Art 296(3) 84
Art 298 85
Art 299(1) 37
Art 299(2) 37
Art 299(4) 37
Art 299(6) 37
Art 305(1) 75
Art 305(2) 76
Part I 2
Part III 1, 2
Preamble 2
Euratom Treaty 52, 76
Art 196(b) 52

European Coal and Steel Community Treaty 49, 275
Art 35 70
Art 65 105, 107
Art 65-67 75
Art 80 52
Patents Act 1977 291
s 44(1) 291
Regulation 17/62 [1962] OJ Spec Ed 87 2, 26, 30, 64, 72
Art 3 95, 304
Art 9(1) 97, 198
Art 11(1) 48
Art 13(1) 48
Art 14(1) 48
Art 15 95
Art 15(1)(b) 48
Art 16 95
Art 19(2) 53
Art 20 48
Regulation 26/62 [1962] OJ 030/993 30, 78
Art 1 78, 79
Art 2 78, 81
Art 2(1) 78, 79, 80, 81
Art 2(2) 79
Art 4 78
Regulation 141/62 [1962] OJ L124/2751 30
Regulation 19/65 [1965] OJ P036/533 30
Art 1 33
Regulation 67/67 33, 129
Regulation 1017/68 [1968] OJ L175/1 30, 82, 200
Art 29 33
Regulation 2821/71 [1971] OJ L285/46 30
Art 1 33
Regulation 2779/72 33
Regulation 2988/74 [1974] OJ L319/1 30, 70, 72
Art 1(2) 73
Regulation 3604/82 33
Regulation 1983/83 33
Regulation 1984/83 33
Regulation 2349/84 33, 228
Regulation 123/85 33
Regulation 417/85 [1985] OJ L53/1 33, 142
Regulation 418/85 33, 210
Regulation 4056/86 [1986] OJ L378/4 30, 33, 82
Regulation 4057/86 [1986] OJ L378/14 200
Regulation 3975/87 [1987] OJ L374/1 30, 82
Regulation 3976/87 [1987] OJ L374/9 30, 33
Regulation 2671/88 33
Regulation 2672/88 33
Regulation 2673/88 33
Regulation 4087/88 33
Recital 7 202

Regulation 4260/88 33
Regulation 4261/88 33
Regulation 556/89 33
Regulation 2299/89 [1989] OJ L220/1 31
Regulation 4064/89 [1989] OJ L395/1 26, 30, 33
Regulation 2342/90 [1990] OJ L217/1 30, 31
Regulation 2343/90 [1990] OJ L217/8 30, 31
Regulation 2344/90 [1990] OJ L217/15 30, 82
Regulation 2367/90 33
Regulation 82/91 33
Regulation 83/91 33
Regulation 84/91 33
Regulation 294/91 [1991] OJ L36/1 30
Regulation 295/91 [1991] OJ L36/5 30
Regulation 1534/91 [1991] OJ L143/1 30, 33, 87
Regulation 479/92 [1992] OJ L55/3 30, 33
Regulation 2408/92 [1992] OJ L240/8 30
Regulation 2409/92 [1992] OJ L240/15 30
Regulation 3932/92 [1992] OJ L398/7 87
Regulation 151/93 33
Regulation 1617/93 33, 200
Regulation 3652/93 33, 200
Regulation 3666/93 33
Regulation 3384/94 33
Regulation 70/95 33
Regulation 304/95 [1995] OJ L332/1 30
Regulation 870/95 33, 82
Regulation 1475/95 209
Regulation 240/96 33, 228
Regulation 1523/96 [1996] OJ L190/11 200
Regulation 2842/98 49
Regulation 2790/99 [1999] OJ L336/21 26, 200, 202, 209
  Art 11 129
Regulation 823/2000 [2000] OJ L100/24 200
Regulation 2658/2000 [2000] OJ L304/3 26, 142
Regulation 2659/2000 [2000] OJ L304/7 26, 142, 200, 208
Regulation 2790/2000 147
Regulation 1400/2002 33, 123, 200, 209
Regulation 1/2003 [2003] OJ L1/1 26, 28, 30, 31, 70, 71, 72, 79, 82, 180, 198, 211
  Art 1(1) 199
  Art 1(2) 199
  Art 2 229
  Art 3 194
  Art 5 199
  Art 6 199
  Art 7 71, 95
  Art 7(1) 73
  Art 8(3) 26
  Art 9 200
  Art 10 200
  Art 18(1) 48

Art 20 48
Art 23 48, 73, 95
Art 24 73, 95
Art 25 70
Art 25(1) 73
Art 25(3) 73
Art 25(5) 73
Art 25(6) 73
Art 26 70
Art 26(1) 73
Art 26(2) 73
Art 26(3) 73
Art 26(4) 73
Art 26(5) 73
Art 33 33
Art 36 82
Art 36-43 82
Art 37 72, 73
Art 38 33, 82
Art 39 82
Art 40 33
Art 41 33
Art 42 33
Art 43 26
Regulation 358/2003 [2003] OJ L53/8 87, 200
Regulation 139/2004 [2004] OJ L24/1 (EC Merger Regulation) 3, 26, 30, 154
Art 2(3) 3
Regulation 261/2004 [2004] OJ L046/1 30
Regulation 411/2004 [2004] OJ L68/1 200
Regulation 772/2004 [2004] OJ L123/11 26, 33, 200, 217
Regulation 773/2004 [2004] OJ L123/18 49
Art 2(2) 49
Art 10 49
Single European Act 14
Treaty Establishing a Constitution for Europe 1, 2
Art 1-3(2) 2
Art I-3(3) 2
Art III-52-III-58 1
Treaty of Amsterdam 1
Treaty of European Union 2, 12
Art 2 18

1

INTRODUCTION

A. GENERAL

1. The rules of competition

[1]

The competition rules of the EC Treaty are contained in Articles 81 to 89.[1] They form the first chapter of the sixth[2] title of Part Three, which contains common rules on competition, taxation and the approximation of laws. Section 1 of that chapter (Articles 81 to 86) contains the rules applying to undertakings, Section 2 (Articles 87 to 89) relates to aids granted by States.[3] This section deals with Articles 81 to 86. The Treaty Establishing a Constitution for Europe, signed on 16 December 2004, incorporates these provisions.[4]

1 All article numbering in Vaughan, *Law of the European Union,* Section 21 ('Competition') reflects the renumbering brought about by the Treaty of Amsterdam. Formerly, the competition rules were found in Articles 85 to 94 of the EC Treaty. In addition, the former Article 91 (relating to intra-Community dumping in the transitional period) has been removed from this chapter of the EC Treaty.

2 Formerly the fifth title before the Treaty of Amsterdam renumbering.

3 For discussion of the rules concerning State aids, see Vaughan, *Law of the European Union,* Section 29 ('State Aid', forthcoming).

4 [2004] OJ C310/1, yet to be ratified by all the Member States. See in particular, Articles III-52 to III-58.

2. The rules of competition in the context of the EC Treaty

[2]

The rules of competition are not necessarily ends in themselves.[1] They are to be considered in the context of the fundamental principles[2] of the EC Treaty.[3] The rules of competition are designed to ensure that the objectives of the treaty[4] are effective and are not distorted.[5] Thus, in an appropriate case, the rules of competition are to be considered in the light of the treaty provisions designed to establish a single market,[6] to ensure the protection of the freedom to provide services,[7] or to avoid discrimination on the grounds of nationality.[8] Without the rules of competition, numerous other provisions of the treaty would be pointless.[9] It should be noted that though the Treaty of Rome came into force in 1958, it was not until 1962 that the competition rules began to be enforced.[10]

1 Commission XXXIII Report on Competition Policy (2003), p 3

2 For the fundamental principles of the EC Treaty, see Articles 1 to 16. In addition, reference should be made in the context of competition to Articles 4(1) and 157(1). See also the Treaty Establishing a Constitution for Europe [2004] OJ C310/1, Articles I-3(2) and I-3(3).
3 See, for example, Case 78/70 *Deutsche Grammophon GmbH v Metro-SB-Grossmarkte GmbH & Co KG* [1971] ECR 487, [1971] CMLR 631, ECJ; Case 6/72 *Europemballage Corpn and Continental Can Co Inc v Commission* [1973] ECR 215, [1973] CMLR 199, ECJ; Joined Cases 6, 7/73 *Istituto Chemioterapico Italiano SpA and Commercial Solvents Corpn v Commission* [1974] ECR 223, [1974] 1 CMLR 309, ECJ; Case 27/76 *United Brands Co v Commission* [1978] ECR 207, [1978] 1 CMLR 429, ECJ; and Case 85/76 *Hoffmann-La Roche & Co AG v Commission* [1979] ECR 461, [1979] 3 CMLR 211, ECJ. See also the reference to 'fair competition' in the EC Treaty preamble.
4 For these objectives, see EC Treaty, Parts One and Three, as amended by the TEU and the Treaty of Amsterdam. They comprise the principles (Articles 1–16), the free movement of goods (Articles 23–31), agriculture (Articles 32–38), the free movement of persons, services and capital (Articles 39–60), and transport (Articles 70–80).
5 Case 85/76 *Hoffmann-La Roche & Co AG v Commission* [1979] ECR 461 at 554, [1979] 3 CMLR 211 at 301, ECJ.
6 Case 85/76 *Hoffmann-La Roche & Co AG v Commission* [1979] ECR 461, [1979] 3 CMLR 211, ECJ.
7 Case 22/79 *Greenwich Film Production v SACEM* [1979] ECR 3275, [1980] 1 CMLR 629, ECJ.
8 Case 7/82 *GVL v Commission* [1983] ECR 483, [1983] 3 CMLR 645, ECJ.
9 See Case 6/72 *Europemballage Corpn and Continental Can Co Inc v Commission* [1973] ECR 215 at 244,245, [1973] CMLR 199 at 224, ECJ.
10 With the passing of Regulation 17 ([1962] OJ Spec Ed 87).

3. Objectives of the rules of competition: earlier statements (1)

[3]
The objectives of the rules of competition, as derived from decisions of the Court of Justice, concentrate in the main upon the promotion of fair competition in a basically free market economy and upon the creation of a single market.[1] Thus, the court sees the objectives of such rules as including:

(a) keeping prices down to the lowest possible level and encouraging the movement of goods between Member States, thereby permitting the most effective possible distribution of activities in relation to productivity and the capacity of undertakings to adapt themselves to change;[2]

(b) interpenetration of national markets and, as a result, direct access by consumers to the sources of production of the whole Community;[3]

(c) the establishment of workable competition, that is to say the degree of competition necessary to ensure the observance and the attainment of the basic objectives of the EC Treaty, in particular the creation of a single market achieving conditions similar to those of a domestic market.[4] The Commission has also often used language referring to the aim of 'effective' competition;[5]

(d) ensuring that structural rigidity is not reinforced.[6]

1 See *Shearson Lehman Hutton Inc v Maclame Watson & Co Ltd* [1989] 3 CMLR 429, QB, where Webster J cited with approval a statement to this effect in Vaughan, *The Law of the European Communities* (Butterworths, 1985).
2 Case 48/69 *Imperial Chemical Industries Ltd v Commission* [1972] ECR 619 at 660, [1972] CMLR 557 at 627, ECJ.
3 Ibid. See also Case 85/76 *Hoffmann-La Roche & Co AG v Commission* [1979] ECR 461 at 554, [1979] 3 CMLR 211 at 301, ECJ.

4 Case 26/76 *Metro SB-Grossmarkte GmbH & Co KG v Commission* [1977] ECR 1875 at 1904, [1978] 2 CMLR 1 at 33, ECJ.

5 See, in relation to Article 82, the Commission's description of a dominant position as involving an undertaking's power to 'prevent effective competition being maintained on the relevant market' (Case 2/76 *United Brands v Commission* [1978] ECR 207, [1978] 1 CMLR 429, para 65; Case 85/76 *Hoffmann-La Roche & Co AG v Commission* [1979] ECR 461, [1979] 3 CMLR 211, para 38). See also the EC Merger Regulation (Council Regulation 139/2004 [2004] OJ L24/1), Article 2(3), which sets out the grounds of prohibition of a merger as being that it would 'significantly impede effective competition'.

6 Case 26/76 *Metro SB-Grossmarkte GmbH & Co KG v Commission* [1977] ECR 1875 at 1905, [1978] 2 CMLR 1 at 34, ECJ.

[4]

The annual Reports on Competition Policy of the Commission provide valuable help in defining in more detail the objectives of competition policy:

(a) stimulating economic activity by guaranteeing the widest possible freedom of action to all;[1]

(b) making it easier for supply and demand structures continually to adjust to technological development;[2]

(c) through the interplay of decentralised decision-making machinery, enabling enterprises continuously to improve their efficiency, which is the essential condition for a steady improvement in living standards and employment prospects within the countries of the Community, and thus satisfying to a great extent the individual and collective needs of society;[3]

(d) taking action against restrictive or improper practices which hamper the creation of a single market and the maintenance of effective competition within this uniform market;[4]

(e) strengthening the competitive position of undertakings by exempting desirable forms of co-operation;[5]

(f) maintaining and promoting competition so that competition can perform its task of guiding and stimulating the economy;[6]

(g) providing an essential part of the armoury to be deployed against inflation;[7]

(h) ensuring that competition performs its proper role in achieving a market economy in which fair, undistorted competition ensures that available resources are allocated to the most productive sectors, and stimulating firms to make use of their know-how and skills, and encouraging them to exploit efficiently new techniques and new products;[8]

(i) safeguarding the operation of fair and workable competition, which is the only way to ensure optimum allocation of resources, the development of innovation and a long-term improvement in the competitiveness of the European economy;[9]

(j) stimulating firms' potential and encouraging adoption of industrial structures to changing economic conditions;[10]

(k) contributing to improving the allocation of resources and raising the competitiveness of Community industry, and, thanks to this greater competitiveness, secured largely by encouragement of research and development, enabling the Community at length to overcome the economic problems facing it and in particular to combat structural unemployment and thus play its part in securing lasting economic recovery;[11]

(l) contributing to the encouragement of the better use of available factors of production, stimulating firms to better their performance relative to their competitors, and encouraging new products, new production processes and new distribution techniques.[12]

1 Commission I Report on Competition Policy, p 11.
2 Ibid.
3 Ibid
4 Commission II Report on Competition Policy, points 1, 2.
5 Ibid.
6 Commission V Report on Competition Policy, point 3.
7 Ibid.
8 Commission XI Report on Competition Policy, Introduction, where it was said that the competition policy is not based on a laissez-faire model, but is designed to maintain and protect the principle of workable competition.
9 Commission XII Report on Competition Policy, Introduction, which said that without such competition free trade would be at risk, and that active competition policy can play a useful part in solving the persistent economic difficulties.
10 Commission XII Report on Competition Policy, Introduction.
11 Commission XIII Report on Competition Policy, Introduction.
12 Commission XIV Report on Competition Policy, Introduction.

4. Objectives of the rules of competition: earlier statements (2)

[5]
The Commission's focus increasingly turned to the importance of competition policy in achieving the internal market:

[6]

(a) 'Vigorous competition policy has a key role to play in the Commission's overall strategy for dynamic economic development — and thus for prosperity and employment. Its task is to keep markets open and adaptable and in doing so to break down rigidities. It is part of a comprehensive policy designed to motivate entrepreneurs to undertake risk, to innovate, to stimulate technical progress and to develop active market strategies. Competition policy is at the same time an important instrument for creating a Community-wide market free of internal barriers. Without competition, technological policy within the Community would not be able to achieve its moderising effects throughout all levels of the economy. The price mechanism, based on competition by performance, is the most effective — and also the most democratic — co-ordinator of the countless buying and selling, investment and planning decisions taken daily in the marketplace.'[1]

1 See Commission XV Report on Competition Policy, Introduction.

[7]

(b) 'Competition policy has a key role to play in ensuring that the opening of the market yields all the benefits expected of it. It must ensure that these barriers are not replaced by divisions of markets resulting from restrictive business practices or protectionist measures taken by the Member States. The control of state aid is of particular importance in this context. Member States may use aid to give their industry an advantage over industry elsewhere in the Community. Public funds may also be used to prop up uncompetitive businesses and industries. This generally only renders ultimately more difficult the task of finding a genuine solution and in the meantime tends to cause difficulties for more competitive firms that are providing real jobs.'[1]

1 See Commission XVI Report on Competition Policy, Introduction.

[8]

(c) 'The future growth of the Community economy entails improving the allocation of production factors, increasing market profitability and boosting innovation, in order to increase the international competitiveness of Community undertakings. Dynamic growth of supply is precisely the contribution that competition policy can bring to the economy of the Twelve. Much remains to be done in this field, both at international level, where protectionism - whether hidden or deliberate, general or selective - has flourished since the Tokyo Round, and within the Community itself, particularly in those sectors where the anachronisms of market barriers and market partitioning remain prevalent. There is no doubt that more dynamic competition in the coming years will enable latent Community resources to be brought into play, and would facilitate the release of dormant growth potential as well as promoting stable employment and greater competitiveness of EC firms, both inside the EC and in third country markets. A clear illustration of the cost of 'non-Europe' is to be found in the tertiary sector whose capacity to create new jobs is hindered by the continued existence of barriers in the internal market. For example, the action instituted by the Commission to reinforce competition in the telecommunications sector reflects this need to introduce healthy intra-Community competition. The greatest opportunities for developing supply, stimulating demand and improving the job situation lie in the service sector. It is now increasingly accepted that subsidised jobs are unstable jobs and that successful firms find the incentives for growth within themselves and on the market place. A competition policy can thus be a growth policy inasmuch as it aims to eliminate the structural blockages still hampering the European economy, notably as regards the mobility of productive resources.'[1]

1 See Commission XVII Report on Competition Policy, Introduction.

[9]

(d) 'An effective competition policy is the sole means of making the most of the potential offered by the completion of the large market and thus, by increasing competitive pressure, of producing a more competitive Community economy. More competition will also strengthen the position of European industry in both world and domestic markets. Without such a policy, there is the risk that Community consumers would be unable to enjoy the promised benefits of a large integrated market.'[1]

1 See Commission XVIII Report on Competition Policy, Introduction.

[10]

(e) 'At the threshold of the new decade, the European economy faces major challenges. While the Community has re-established a sound economic base it must further underpin the internal factors underlying its growth and ensure that growth does not fade under the build-up of inflationary pressures and external or budgetary disequilibria that could undermine its cohesion. The Commission has on numerous occasions drawn attention to the essential contribution which competition policy can make to the completion of the single market and to strengthening the competitiveness of the Community's economy. Such contribution, which is more necessary than ever against the background of the recovery in the Community economy, is a long-term process. However, continuity does not rule out change and 1989 saw substantial developments in areas in which there had previously been gaps or deficiencies in competition policy.'[1]

1 See Commission XIX Report on Competition Policy, Introduction.

[11]

(f) 'Since the very beginning of the creation of the common market competition policy has been an important Community instrument used both to promote economic integration and to ensure an efficient allocation of resources. Effective competition is the main stimulus to innovation and higher productivity which underpins policies designed to increase economic growth and welfare. Not only does competition lead to higher output but it also enables consumers to obtain a fair share of this growth. Living standards therefore depend on the maintenance of effective competition.

This traditional role of competition policy has been given increased importance by the completion of the internal market by 1992. The full benefits of the internal market in terms of higher output, growth and employment can only be attained if competition intensifies as a result of the dismantling of the barriers to trade that still remain. The increase in competition expected as a result of this integration process can be thwarted in a number of ways, so the Commission must be vigilant to guard against any such attempts. Member States must not be allowed to replace forms of protectionism abolished in the market integration process by state aids or exclusive rights accorded to monopolies. Companies must not be allowed to thwart integration (e.g. to create cartels to split up markets, to block exports and imports, to abuse local dominant positions, to block new entrants or to create new dominant positions through anti-competitive mergers). In all these areas where anti-competitive measures threaten the market integration process, the Commission will reinforce its policy ...'[1]

1 See Commission XX Report on Competition Policy, Introduction.

[12]

(g) 'When in its 1990 communication on industrial policy the Commission opted clearly for a system of open and competitive markets, it reaffirmed the role to be played by competition policy in boosting the competitiveness of Community industry. Competition policy has been taking on growing importance as the Community advances towards economic and monetary union and nears the completion of the single market. It can only have the desired effect if great vigilance is exercised in applying the competition rules. The new Article 130 [the present Article 157] to be inserted into the EC Treaty pursuant to the Maastricht Treaty on European Union confirms this approach: it states that the objective of ensuring 'that the conditions necessary for the competitiveness of the Community's industry exist' must not lead to the introduction 'of any measure which could lead to a distortion of competition'.

The link between competition and economic efficiency is now generally recognised by governments throughout the world, and consumers too are increasingly aware that they can benefit from market mechanisms which work properly.

The Commission's powers and obligations under the Treaty give it a special responsibility in the establishment of a system of free competition. But in order to operate effectively the competition rules require the collaboration of the Member States, of business, and indeed of national courts: the Commission would like to see the national courts play a greater role, thereby helping to decentralise the enforcement of the competition rules. If there is to be successful collaboration of this kind the Commission will have to make a special effort to ensure transparency so that all those involved are sufficiently well informed.'[1]

1 See Commission XXI Report on Competition Policy, Introduction.

[13]

(h) 'Alongside the establishment of a common market, competition policy is one of the two great strategies by which the Treaty of Rome sets out to achieve the Community's fundamental objectives: the promotion of harmonious and balanced economic development throughout the Community, an improved standard of living, and closer relations between the Member States. Competition policy cannot, therefore, be pursued in isolation, as an end in itself, without reference to the legal, economic, political and social context.

Rapid changes in that context call for rigorous consistency and steadfastness in applying the competition rules, combined with greater flexibility in adapting to the new situation and staying in tune with the objectives which the Community has set itself for economic and social cohesion, industrial competitiveness, research and technological development, and the environment.

In addition to the completion of the internal market, the speed of technological change, and the globalisation of markets, there are two new factors which competition policy must take into account:

(a) the slowdown in economic growth, with its social consequences; and

(b) the application of the principle of subsidiarity.

These developments are combining to create an environment in which competition between firms is fiercer than ever, while the tendency to adopt a defensive and protectionist posture has never been so strong. At the same time, the Maastricht debate shows that the greatest possible clarity is needed in the Commission's efforts to ensure that competition is not distorted.'[1]

1 See Commission XXII Report on Competition Policy, Introduction.

[14]

(i) 'The link between Community objectives and competition policy is a two-way process. It is inconceivable that competition policy could be applied without reference to the priorities fixed by the Community. But it is also important to realise how an effective competition policy will help to attain these goals.

While this principle is not in dispute, the application of policy in practice will require careful consideration. In fact all the policy implications of the above mentioned major events have not yet been worked out and it is hoped that this Report will contribute towards the rich debate on how to achieve the correct balance in the application of competition policy and priorities which usually follows its launch. In this respect, this year's Report is a little more forward-looking than usual, in that in a by no means exhaustive summary, it suggests some of the ways in which competition policy may be adapted to meet the new Community priorities. The full details of these implications and the adaptation of policy to a rapidly changing world is an on-going and continuous process. Of course there are underlying principles that remain, and these are enshrined in the Treaty, but they cannot be applied mechanically without reference either to the context within which they have their impact or the main objectives and priorities of the Community.

This reference to the context within which competition policy is applied is not a new phenomenon, but stems from the fact that competition is an instrument of Community policy. Since the beginning of the Community, competition policy has helped pursue fundamental Community goals. It has helped create, for example, a common market, a harmonious development of economic conditions and an accelerated raising of the standards of living. This role received a further boost with the Single European Act establishing the programme for a real internal market, where increased competition was seen as the mechanism by which many gains of this programme would be realised once the fiscal, administrative and other barriers were eliminated. Its role was further enhanced with the Communication of 1990 on industrial policy in open and competitive markets that gave an important role to competition policy in improving productivity of European industry in a rapidly changing world with increasingly globalised markets.

The Maastricht Treaty has added new goals. *Inter alia,* it introduced and deepened industrial, cultural and environmental goals. It also made explicit the principle of subsidiarity. In fact these three objectives and the subsidiarity principle are discussed separately and in depth in this report. The White Paper clearly laid out the policies to achieve growth, competitiveness and, even more importantly, employment. The need for competition policy to achieve objectives and how these objectives affect the application of competition policy are also discussed. These developments do not devalue competition policy, rather they enhance it and give it renewed vigour and importance. A competition policy that did not have an impact on these policies or was not influenced by them would be marginalised and of less relevance.'[1]

1 See Commission XXIII Report on Competition Policy, Introduction. The reference to the 'White Paper' is to the 'White Paper on growth, competitiveness and employment: the challenges and ways forward into the 21st century' (COM(93) 700 final).

[15]

(j) '[T]he carrying out of the legislative programme on the internal market does not mean that no further efforts are required to achieve a genuine market without internal frontiers. In this respect, competition policy has two roles to play.

First, with the removal of regulatory trade barriers, the main obstacles to trade between Member States stem from the behaviour of firms or from practices by Member States wishing to grant privileges or aid to some of their enterprises. Economic operators may wish to avoid the consequences of the opening-up of markets, which bring them face to face with more intense competition from firms elsewhere. Competition policy is a key instrument in ensuring that the benefits resulting from the opening-up of markets are not thwarted by some. Secondly, competition policy can also be used to open up sectors that still remain closed despite the establishment of the internal market (for example, a large part of the energy sector and most of the telecommunications sector and postal services), with Member States having entrusted their operation to undertakings on which they have conferred exclusive or special rights.

Achieving a genuine single market therefore means tackling all the problems which in practice prevent the market from operating without impediment. This is an arduous task, since the obstacles to be removed are no doubt more covert than those resulting from legislative provisions. However, if the Union wishes to achieve the objectives mapped out in the EC Treaty, it must pursue its efforts in this area. From this point of view, competition policy is and must remain a priority for the Union.'[1]

1 See Commission XXIV Report on Competition Policy, Introduction.

[16]

(k) 'It is widely recognised that competition policy has a key role to play in ensuring that EU industry remains competitive.

Competition policy serves as an instrument to achieve the optimal allocation of resources, technical progress and the flexibility to adjust to a changing environment. In that respect, competition and competitiveness belong together. Experience shows that only those companies which are used to strong competition and perform well in open and dynamic markets will be able to function effectively on a wider scale — be it in other geographic areas or in a more global economy in general.

Competition policy and competitiveness policy are thus not contradictory but rather serve the same goals of creating the essential conditions for the development and maintenance of an efficient and competitive Community industry bringing better products and services to European citizens, and providing a stable economic environment.

While internal market integration shapes the economic context within which Community competition policy must be applied, it is also the case that the application of Community competition policy will help to reinforce the functioning of a single market. Three main areas of activity can be identified; anti-competitive agreements and practices, the regulated or monopolised sectors, and state aid. It is an essential consideration here that the Commission has at its disposal a set of interdependent competition policy instruments. The anti-trust rules, merger control, the policing of state aid and the rules of liberalisation, all serve the same objective of ensuring that competition in the internal market is not distorted.'[1]

1 See Commission XXV Report on Competition Policy, Introduction.

5. Objectives of competition policy: more recent statements

[17]

Even more recent statements of the Commission in its annual reports on competition policy have tended to focus on the objectives in relation to the general economic health of the EU and, in particular, in relation to Europe's competitiveness in the world at large. There is a marked shift of focus, therefore, away from competition policy as an instrument to achieve a single market.[1] These statements are often made with specific reference to the enlargement of the EU and the aim of extending the firm application of the competition rules to the new Member States.

1 See Commission White Paper on Modernisation, 1999 [1999] OJ C132/1, [1999] 5 CMLR 208, where the Commission noted: 'At the beginning the focus of activity was on establishing rules

on restrictive practices interfering directly with the goal of market integration ... The Commission has now come to concentrate more on ensuring effective competition by detecting and stopping cross-border cartels and maintaining competitive market structures.'

[18]

(a) 'The aim of competition policy, through its impact on the basic structures of the European economy, is to ensure that markets acquire or maintain the flexibility they need to allow scope for initiative and innovation and to allow an effective and dynamic allocation of society's resources. This structural action means that competition policy interacts with most other broadly based policies such as the development of the internal market, the policy on growth and competitiveness, the policy on cohesion, research and development policy, environmental policy and consumer protection.

Competition policy is thus both a Commission policy in its own right and an integral part of a large number of European Union policies and with them seeks to achieve the Community objectives set out in Article 2 of the Treaty, including the promotion of harmonious and balanced development of economic activities, sustainable and non-inflationary growth which respects the environment, a high level of employment and of social protection, the raising of the standard of living and quality of life, and economic and social cohesion.

In the final analysis, like all other Community policies, competition policy aims to enhance the economic prosperity of the European Union and the well-being of all its people.

If it is to perform its function fully, competition policy as a structural policy must work with and anticipate trends in the economy so as to ensure efficient operation of markets without acting unduly as a brake on their performance. It must in particular: – take account of globalization; – help to develop the full potential of the internal market; – modernize its instruments.'[1]

1 See Commission XXVI Report on Competition Policy, Introduction.

[19]

(b) '... improving the competitiveness of businesses both large and small, opening up markets, improving the allocation of resources, increasing consumer choice, etc.' are all 'traditional' objectives. Competition policy now has to start to take account of the newer challenges posed by monetary union, employment problems and enlargement.'[1]

1 See Commission XXVII Report on Competition Policy, Foreword.

[20]

(c) 'The first objective of competition policy is the maintenance of competitive markets. Competition policy serves as an instrument to encourage industrial efficiency, the optimal allocation of resources, technical progress and the flexibility to adjust to a changing environment. In order for the

Community to be competitive on worldwide markets, it needs a competitive home market ...

The second is the single market objective. An internal market is an essential condition for the development of an efficient and competitive industry. As the Community has progressively broken down government-erected trade barriers between Member States, companies operating in what they had regarded as 'their' national markets were, and are for the first time, exposed to competitors able to compete on a level playing field. There are two possible reactions to this: either to seek to compete on merit, looking to expand into other territories and benefit from the opportunities offered by a single market, or to erect private barriers to trade – to retrench and act defensively – in the hope of preventing market penetration. The Commission has used its competition policy as an active tool to prevent this, prohibiting, and fining heavily the parties to two main types of agreement: distribution and licensing agreements that prevent parallel trade between Member States, and agreements between competitors to keep out of one another's 'territories'... The aim is to prevent anticompetitive practices from undermining the single market's achievements.'[1]

1 See Commission XXIX Report on Competition Policy, Introduction, p 19.

[21]

(d) 'Competition policy is one of the pillars of the European Commission's action in the economic field. This action is founded on the principle, enshrined in the Treaty, of 'an open market economy with free competition'. It acknowledges the fundamental role of the market and of competition in guaranteeing consumer welfare, in encouraging the optimum allocation of resources and in granting economic agents the appropriate incentives to pursue productive efficiency, quality and innovation. However, the principle of an open market economy does not imply an attitude of blind faith or, possibly, indifference towards the operation of market mechanisms; on the contrary, it requires constant vigilance aimed at preserving those mechanisms. This is particularly true in the present context of markets evolving at a fast pace and becoming increasingly integrated at global level.'[1]

1 See Commission XXX Report on Competition Policy, Introduction, p 21.

[22]

(e) 'The virtues of effective competition on the market in delivering efficient allocation of resources and fostering innovation and technical development are widely recognised throughout the world. However, ensuring or creating the conditions which allow markets to function competitively constitutes an ongoing challenge both as regards the behaviour of actors on these markets and in view of obstacles created by State measures. Competition policy then serves a twofold aim: addressing market failures resulting from anticompetitive behaviour by market participants and from certain market structures, on the one hand, and contributing to an overall economic policy framework across economic sectors that is conducive to effective competition, on the other. In a world of continuing globalisation, competition advocacy within an integrated economic area, such as the European Union, necessarily needs to find also its external expression in order to provide for a level playing field in the international arena.'[1]

1 See Commission XXXII Report on Competition Policy, Introduction, p 19.

[23]

(f) 'EU competition policy plays an important role in achieving the competitiveness goals of the Lisbon agenda [of making Europe the most dynamic knowledge-based economy in the world]. It encompasses not only antitrust and merger rules, which are fundamental to any wellfunctioning market economy, but also the application of an efficient and firm State-aid discipline. In view of the world economic situation in general and efforts in Europe to encourage growth, it is essential that the interaction between the various policy instruments at the Commission's disposal be used to the best effect and that the improvement of the EU's competitiveness remains high on the Commission's agenda.'[1]

1 See Commission XXXIII Report on Competition Policy, Introduction, p 15. See also the 're-launch' of the Lisbon agenda, speech by Neelie Kroes, the competition commissioner to Bocconi University, Milan, 7 February 2005: http://www.europa.eu.int/comm/competition/speeches/index_speeches_by_the_commissioner.html.

[24]

The single market objective and competition policy are not yet entirely separate concepts, however.[1]

1 See discussion in J Baquero Cruz, *Between Competition and Free Movement: The Economic Constitutional Law of the European Community* (Hart, 2002).

[25]

In addition, the Commission has stressed one of the ultimate objectives of competition policy as being the promotion of the interests of consumers.[1] Indeed, there are indications that the Commission is moving towards the consumer welfare model of competition policy.[2]

1 See, for example, Commission XXXII Report on Competition Policy, Introduction, p 20, 'A more meaningful role for consumers'. See also Commission XXXIII Report on Competition Policy, Introduction, p 16, 'Competition Policy and the Consumer'. See also See Case C-7/97 *Oscar Bronner GmbH & Co KG v Mediaprint* [1998] ECR I-7791, [1999] 4 CMLR 112, Opinion of Advocate General Jacobs, para 58: 'The primary purpose of Article [82] is to prevent distortion of competition – and in particular to safeguard the interests of consumers – rather than to protect the position of particular competitors.'

2 See speech given by Mario Monti, as commissioner responsible for competition, in July 2001: 'the goal of competition policy, in all its aspects, is to protect consumer welfare by maintaining a high degree of competition in the common market. Competition should lead to lower prices, a wider choice of goods, and technological innovation, all in the interest of the consumer.' ('The Future for Competition Policy in the European Union', Merchants Taylor's Hall, London, 9 July 2001: http://www.europa.eu.int/comm/competition/speeches/index_speeches_by_the_commissioner.html).

B. IMPLEMENTATION OF THE RULES OF COMPETITION

[26]

The manner in which EC competition policy is implemented and enforced has recently undergone profound change. As of 1 May 2004, Regulation 17/62,[1] which had applied since 1962, was replaced by Council Regulation 1/2003.[2] This has been the key step in the modernisation of competition policy – a process which began in 1999 with the publication of the Commission White Paper on the subject.[3] There are other elements to the modernisation process.[4]

1 [1962] OJ Spec Ed 87.
2 [2003] OJ L1/1. Regulation 17/62 was repealed by Article 43 of Council Regulation 1/2003, with the exception of Article 8(3) which continues to apply to decisions adopted pursuant to Article 81(3) of the Treaty prior to the date of application of Council Regulation 1/2003 until the date of expiration of those decisions.
3 Commission White Paper on modernisation of the rules implementing Articles 81 and 82 of the EC Treaty [1999] OJ C132/1, [1999] 5 CMLR 208.
4 Some elements had already been implemented by 1 May 2004 – for example, the new vertical restraints regime (Commission Regulation 2790/99 [1999] OJ L336/21 and accompanying Guidelines [2000] OJ C291/1, and the new horizontal cooperation agreements regime (Commission Regulation 2658/2000 [2000] OJ L304/3 on the application of Article 81(3) to specialisation agreements and Commission Regulation 2659/2000 [2000] OJ L304/7 on its application to research and development agreements and accompanying Guidelines [2001] OJ C3/2. In addition, there has been the introduction of the replacement technology transfer block exemption – Regulation 772/2004 [2004] OJ L123/11 on Technology Transfer Agreements – and the new merger regulation controlling concentrations between undertakings (the EC Merger Regulation) (Council Regulation (EC) 139/2004 [2004] OJ L24/1). This replaced Regulation 4064/89 [1989] OJ L395/1.

[27]

The Commission summarised the three main elements of modernisation of the application of the competition rules as follows:

> the abolition of the system of notification and authorisation to be replaced by a directly applicable exception system; the development of decentralised application of the competition rules; and intensified *ex post* control.[1]

1 Commission White Paper on modernisation of the rules implementing Articles 81 and 82 of the EC Treaty [1999] OJ C132/1, [1999] 5 CMLR 208, para 138.

[28]

A key feature of Regulation 1/2003 is that it provides for the devolution of some of the powers of enforcement of the competition rules previously held by the Commission to the national competition authorities and the national courts of the Member States. Article 81(3) is made directly applicable. This change is intended, amongst other objectives, to free the Commission to pursue more serious cases of infringement of the competition rules as well as to encourage more private enforcement of the competition rules (as already occurs to a much greater degree in the United States).[1] In addition, the Regulation provides for the scrapping of the system of individual notification. In its place, Regulation 1/2003 provides for a system where: 'undertakings would have to make their own assessment of the compatibility of their restrictive practices with Community law, in the light of the legislation in force and the case law.'[2]

1 See Commission White Paper on modernisation of the rules implementing Articles 81 and 82 of the EC Treaty [1999] OJ C132/1, [1999] 5 CMLR 208.
2 Ibid, para 77.

1. Role of the Council

[29]
The role of the Council in competition matters is restricted to legislative activity. It has in this field no administrative or executive powers, other than certain powers to take decisions under Articles 87 and 88 of the EC Treaty.[1] Acting on a qualified majority on a proposal from the Commission and after consulting the European Parliament, the Council is obliged to adopt appropriate regulations or directives to give effect to the principles set out in Articles 81 and 82.[2]

1 These relate to State aids; see Vaughan, *Law of the European Union*, Section 29 ('State Aid', forthcoming).
2 EC Treaty, Article 83(1). For the matters to be covered by such regulations or directives, see Article 83(2).

[30]
The following regulations and decisions have previously been adopted by the Council to achieve these objects:

(a) Council Regulation (EEC) 17/62, implementing the rules of competition;[1]

(b) Council Regulation (EEC) 26/62, applying certain rules of competition to production of and trade in agricultural products;[2]

(c) Council Regulation (EEC) 141/62, exempting transport from the application of Council Regulation 17;[3]

(d) Council Regulation (EEC) 19/65 and Council Regulation (EEC) 2821/ 71 on the application of Article 85 [now 81](3) of the EC Treaty to certain categories of agreements and concerted practices;[4]

(e) Council Regulation (EEC) 1017/68, applying the competition rules to inland transport;[5]

(f) Council Regulation (EEC) 2988/74 concerning limitation periods and the enforcement of sanctions under the transport and competition rules;[6]

(g) Council Regulation (EEC) 4056/86 laying down detailed rules for the application of Articles 85 [now 81] and 86 [now 82] of the Treaty to maritime transport;[7]

(h) Council Regulation (EEC) 3975/87 laying down the procedure for the application of the rules on competition to undertakings in the air transport sector;[8]

(i) Council Regulation (EEC) 3976/87, as amended by Council Regulation (EEC) 2344/90, on the application of Article 85(3) [now 81(3)] of the Treaty to certain categories of agreements and concentrated practices in the air transport sector;[9]

(j) Council Regulation (EEC) 4064/89 on the control of concentrations between undertakings;[10]

(k) Council Regulation (EEC) 2342/90 on fares for scheduled air services; and Council Regulation (EEC) 2343/90 on access for air carriers to scheduled intra-Community air service routes and on the sharing of passenger capacity between air carriers on scheduled air services between Member States;[11]

(l) Council Regulations (EEC) 294/91 and 295/91 on air cargo services and common rules for a denied-boarding compensation system in scheduled air transport;[12]

(m) Council Regulation (EEC) 1534/91 on the application of Article 85(3) [now 81(3)] to certain categories of agreements, decisions and concerted practices in the insurance sector;[13]

(n) Council Regulation (EEC) 479/92 on the application of Article 85(3) [now 81(3)] to certain categories of agreements, decisions and concerted practices between liner shipping companies (consortia);[14]

(o) Council Regulation (EC) 304/95 on aid to shipbuilding;[15]

(p) Council Decision (EC, ECSC) 95/145 concerning the conclusion of the Agreement between the European Communities and the Government of the United States regarding the application of their competition laws;[16]

(q) Council Regulation 1/2003 – on the implementation of the rules on competition laid down in Articles 81 and 82 of the Treaty (the competition policy modernisation regulation);[17]

(r) Council Regulation 139/2004 – on the control of concentrations between undertakings (the EC Merger Regulation).[18]

1 Council Regulation (EEC) 17/62 (now repealed and replaced by Council Regulation 1/2003 ([2003] OJ L1/1)).
2 [1962] OJ 030/993.
3 [1962] OJ 124/2751. Repealed by Regulation 1/2003 [2003] OJ L1/1.
4 [1965] OJ P036/533 and [1971] OJ L285/46 respectively.
5 [1968] OJ L175/1.
6 [1974] OJ L319/1.
7 [1986] OJ L378/4. As to the application of the competition rules to shipping generally, see para [82]. Note, in particular, the Commission White Paper on review of Regulation 4056/86, suggesting the scrapping of the block exemption for liner conferences (2003/COMP/18). See also Commission Report, 'The Application of the Competition Rules to Liner Shipping', 26 October 2005 (http://europa.eu.int/comm/competition/antitrust/others/maritime/shipping_report_26102005.pdf).
8 [1987] OJ L374/1 – repealed (see COM(2003) 91 final; 2003/0038).
9 [1987] OJ L374/9, as amended. The amending Regulation 2344/90 [1990] OJ L217/15 is itself now no longer in force.
10 [1989] OJ L395/1 – repealed and replaced by the EC Merger Regulation (Regulation 139/2004) [2004] OJ L24/1.
11 [1990] OJ L217/1 – repealed by Regulation 2409/92 [1992] OJ L240/15); [1990] OJ L217/8 – repealed by Regulation 2408/92 [1992] OJ L240/8.
12 [1991] OJ L36/1 – repealed by Regulation 2408/92 [1992] OJ L240/8; [1991] OJ L36/5 – repealed by Regulation 261/2004 [2004] OJ L046/1.
13 [1991] OJ L143/1.
14 [1992] OJ L55/3.
15 [1995] OJ L332/1 (as amended by [1997] OJ L351/18).
16 [1995] OJ L95/51 (for corrigendum see [1995] OJ L131/1).

17 Regulation 1/2003 [2003] OJ L1/1.
18 Regulation 139/2004 [2004] OJ L24/1. This replaced Regulation 4064/89 [1989] OJ L395/1.

[31]
The Council has also adopted various directives and decisions in the air transport sector relevant to competition law.[1]

1 See Council Directive (EEC) 87/601 [1987] OJ L374/12 on fares for scheduled air services between Member States – repealed by Regulation (EEC) 2342/90 [1990] OJ L217/1; and Council Decision (EEC) 87/602 [1987] OJ L374/19 on sharing of passenger capacity and on access to scheduled air services routes – repealed by Regulation 2343/90 [1990] OJ L217/8. See also Council Regulation (EEC) 2299/89 [1989] OJ L220/1 on the code of conduct for computerised reservation systems.

2. General Treaty powers of the Commission

[32]
The general role of the Commission includes the obligation to ensure the proper functioning and development of the common market, and in particular to take decisions in the manner provided for in the EC Treaty and to exercise the powers conferred on it by the Council for the implementation of Council rules.[1] The Commission is given the specific duty to ensure the application of the principles laid down in Articles 81 and 82 and to investigate cases of suspected infringement of these principles and, if it finds there has been such an infringement, to propose appropriate measures to bring it to an end.[2] If the infringement is not brought to an end, the Commission in a reasoned decision may authorise Member States to take the measures, as determined by the Commission, necessary to remedy the situation.[3] The Commission Directorate-General responsible for competition policy was called DG IV and since 1999 has been called the Competition Directorate-General, or 'DG Comp', sub-divided into nine directorates.[4]

1 EC Treaty, Article 211.
2 EC Treaty, Article 85(1).
3 EC Treaty, Article 85(2).
4 DG Comp underwent reorganisation in line with the introduction of Council Regulation 1/2003. In particular, the previously separate Merger Task Force was incorporated into the other directorates.

3. Legislative powers of the Commission

[33]
The Council has granted to the Commission the power to legislate in a number of fields. Thus, the Commission is empowered:

(a) to adopt implementing provisions in the field of transport by rail, road and inland waterways under Council Regulation (EEC) 1017/68;[1]

(b) to grant block exemptions under Council Regulation (EEC) 19/65 and Council Regulation (EEC) 2821/71;[2]

(c) to adopt implementing provisions concerning the scope of the obligation of communication, the form, content and other details of complaints, applications and hearings under Council Regulation (EEC) 4056/86[3] (as amended by Council Regulation (EC) 1/2003, Article 38);

(d) to adopt regulations pursuant to Council Regulation (EEC) 3976/87[4] (as amended by Council Regulation (EC) 1/2003, Article 41);

(e) to adopt regulations pursuant to Council Regulation (EEC) 4064/89;[5]

(f) to adopt regulations pursuant to Council Regulation (EEC) 1534/91;

(g) to adopt regulations pursuant to Council Regulation (EEC) 479/92[6] (as amended by Council Regulation (EC) 1/2003, Article 42);

(h) to take such measures as may be appropriate in order to apply Council Regulation (EC)1/2003.[7]

The Commission also has its own legislative powers granted by the EC Treaty. Thus, in limited circumstances it may make directives or take decisions addressed to Member States.[8]

1 Council Regulation (EEC) 1017/68 [1968] OJ L175/1, Article 29, as amended. Note: Article 29 will be repealed with effect from 1 May 2007 (under Regulation 1/2003).

2 Council Regulation (EEC) 19/65, Article 1; Council Regulation (EEC) 2821/71, Article 1 (as amended by Council Regulation (EC) 1/2003, Article 40). The powers have been exercised in Commission Regulations (EEC) 67/67, 2779/72, 3604/82, 1983/83, 1984/83, 2349/84, 123/85, 417/85, 418/85, 4087/88, 556/89, 151/93 and 70/95. See also Commission Regulation (EC) 240/96 on the application of Article 81(3) to certain categories of technology transfer agreements (and see replacement technology transfer block exemption – Regulation 772/2004 [2004] OJ L123/11 on Technology Transfer Agreements) and Commission Regulation (EC) 1400/2002 on the application of Article 81(3) to categories of vertical agreements and concerted practices in the motor vehicle sector.

3 This power has been exercised in Commission Regulation (EEC) 4260/88, as amended by Commission Regulation (EC) 3666/93.

4 This power has been exercised in Commission Regulations (EEC) 2671/88, 2672/88, 2673/88, 4261/88, as amended by Commission Regulations (EC) 3666/93, 82/91, 83/91, 84/91, 1617/93, 3652/93.

5 This power has been exercised in Commission Regulation (EEC) 2367/90, now repealed and replaced by Commission Regulation (EC) 3384/94.

6 This power has been exercised in Commission Regulation (EC) 870/95.

7 Council Regulation (EC) 1/2003, Article 33.

8 EC Treaty, Article 86(3). This power has been exercised by Commission Directive (EEC) 80/723, requiring Member States to provide information to ensure that relations between public undertakings and Member States are more transparent. This Directive was upheld in Joined Cases 188-190/80 *France, Italy and United Kingdom v Commission* [1982] ECR 2545, [1982] 3 CMLR 144, ECJ. The Commission has also issued two directives relating to the telecommunications sector: Commission Directive (EEC) 88/301 [1988] OJ L131/73, [1991] 4 CMLR 922 on competition in the markets in telecommunications terminal equipment and Commission Directive (EEC) 90/388 [1990] OJ L192/10, [1991] 4 CMLR 932 on competition in the markets for telecommunications services.

4. Quasi-legislative powers of the Commission

[34]

In addition to legislative measures, the Commission issues notices and communications which, although not legally binding and although capable of being superseded or overruled generally or in a specific case, offer guidelines as to the Commission's views of the effect of the rules of competition in particular situations. These notices and communications are published in the Official Journal.

[35]
Other important sources of persuasive effect as to the Commission's attitude to general and specific applications of the rules of competition include the Commission's annual Report on Competition Policy (which includes also references to cases disposed of other than by final decision) and the Commission's Answers to Written Questions in the European Parliament. See paras [4]–[26] above for examples of Commission annual reports.

5. Administrative and executive powers and duties of the Commission

[36]
The administrative and executive powers and duties of the Commission in competition matters are dealt with in detail subsequently.[1]

1 See Vaughan, *Law of European Union,* Section 21B ('Competition – Procedures and Remedies), Chapter 1 ('EU Procedures').

2
SCOPE OF THE RULES OF COMPETITION

A. TERRITORIAL APPLICATION

1. The territory of the common market

[37]

The rules of competition only apply if trade between Member States is or may be affected and if there is a possibility of distortion of competition within the common market.[1] Both these matters may require consideration of the territorial application of the rules of competition. The territorial application of the EC Treaty for competition purposes comprises (although the position with regard to (c) and (d) is far from clear):

(a) the territories (presumably including the territorial waters and air space[2]) of all the Member States;[3]

(b) the French Overseas Departments;[4]

(c) Monaco, San Marino, Andorra,[5] Gibraltar, the Canary Islands, Ceuta, Melilla, Azores and Madeira;[6]

(d) the continental shelf adjacent to the Member States;[7] certainly it applies to products, such as oil, when won from the continental shelf adjacent to a Member State.[8]

Territories such as the Faeroe Islands, the Isle of Man, the Channel Islands and the Sovereign Base Areas in Cyprus are not within the common market for the purposes of the rules of competition.[9]

1 See EC Treaty, Article 81(1).

2 See the Commission's Memorandum concerning the applicability of the EC Treaty to the Continental Shelf 1970. For the rules as to State aids when applied to the continental shelf, see Commission VI Report on Competition Policy, points 21-221 (UK Offshore Installations), and Commission 9th Annual Report on Competition Policy, points 162-164 (UK Offshore Supplies). See also Answer to Written Question 489/73 [1974] OJ C49/3.

3 EC Treaty, Article 299(1) as amended by the Act of Accession 2003, Article 19; Act of Accession (1972), Article 26(1); Act of Accession (1979), Article 20; Adaptation Decision, Article 15(1); Act of Accession (1985), Article 24; Act of Accession (1994), Article 18. For the special position of the Aland Islands, see Act of Accession (1994), Article 28 (as substituted by Council Decision (EC, Euratom, ECSC) 95/1, Article 19) and Protocol 2; Act of Accession, 16 April 2003, Articles 2, 5(1), 53

4 EC Treaty, Article 299(2).

5 EC Treaty, Article 299(4).

6 Act of Accession (1972), Article 28; Act of Accession (1985), Article 25; Act of Accession (1994), Protocol 2. The extent to which the rules of competition apply to these countries as territories is far from clear.
7 See note 2 above.
8 See eg Case 174/84 *Bulk Oil (Zug) AG v Sun International Ltd* [1986] ECR 559, [1986] 2 CMLR 732, ECJ.
9 EC Treaty, Article 299(6); Act of Accession (1972), Article 26(3); Adaptation Decision, Article 15(2). See on other aspects, Opinion of Advocate-General Léger in Case C-293/02 *Jersey Produce Marketing Organisation v States of Jersey* (http://curia.eu.int/jurisp/cgi-bin/gettext.pl?lang=en&num=79949496C19020293&doc=T&ouvert=T&seance=CONCL).

2. *Treaties with third countries*

[38]
The Community has entered into many agreements with third countries which include references to the rules of competition.[1] It would seem that these provisions do not have direct effect and therefore cannot be relied upon by individuals.[2] The existence of such provisions and the procedures for reference to a joint committee do not exclude, in an appropriate case, the application of Articles 81and 82 of the EC Treaty.[3] The Community has also entered into two agreements with the United States regarding the application of their respective competition rules.[4] In addition, an EU–US merger working group has been established. This adopted guidelines in 2002 on 'best practices' to follow where there is an investigation in both the EU and the US in respect of the same transaction.[5]

1 See Agreement on the European Economic Area ([1994] OJ L1/3), as amended by the Protocol adjusting the EEA Agreement ([1994] OJ L1/572) (the original non-EC signatories were Austria, Finland (with the exclusion of the Aland Islands), Iceland, Liechtenstein, Norway, Sweden). On 1 May 2004, Cyprus, the Czech Republic, Estonia, Hungary, Latvia, Lithuania, Malta, Poland, Slovakia and Slovenia all joined the EEA. Norway, Iceland and Liechtenstein are the remaining non-EC signatories. Article 53 of the Agreement effectively reproduces EC Treaty, Article 81, and EEA Agreement, Article 54 does likewise with EC Treaty, Article 82. For a detailed account of these competition rules and their enforcement, see Norberg, *EEA Law: A Commentary on the EEA Agreement* (1993); see also Straiger, 'The competition rules of the EEA Agreement and their implementation' [1993] 1 ECLR 30. The competition provisions of the EFTA Treaties have been effectively superseded by the EEA Agreement, with the exception of Switzerland (see [1972] OJ L300/193). See also Agreements between the EC and Central and Eastern European Countries prior to their accession in 2004 (Hungary, 16 December 1991, [1993] OJ L347/2; Poland, 16 December 1991, [1993] OJ L348/2; Bulgaria, 8 March 1993, [1994] OJ L358/3; Czech Republic, 4 October 1993, [1994] OJ L360/2; Romania, 1 February 1994, [1994] OJ L357/2) and Free Trading Agreements with Latvia ([1994] OJ L374/2), Estonia ([1994] OJ L373/2), Lithuania ([1994] OJ L375/2). See Agreement between the EEC and Turkey, Article 16 (Ankara, 12 September 1963; [1964] OJ 3687); Agreement between the EEC and Canada, Article 2(2) (Ottawa, 6 July 1976; [1976] OJ L260/3). See also EC–Canada Cooperation Agreement ([1999] OJ L175/49; [1999] 5 CMLR 713); Interim Agreement between EC and Israel ([1996] OJ L71/2); EC–Japan Cooperation Agreement – see Commission Press Release IP/03/995, 10 July 2003.
2 Compare N March Hunnings in (1977) ELR 163 and (1978) ELR 278 with M Waelbroek (1978) ELR 27. See also JF Bellis, 'International Trade and EEC Competition' (1979) 16 CML Rev 647. In particular, such provisions do not appear to impose rights or obligations upon individuals, as opposed to contracting States, and do not prohibit such agreements or purchases but merely make them incompatible, and do not contain an equivalent of EC Treaty, Article 81(3). See also B Barack, *The Application of the Competition Rules of the EEC* (1981). For the likely position under the EEA Agreement, see Case T-115/94 *OPEL Austria v* Council, 22 January 1997, CFI.
3 See Commission Decision (EEC) 85/202 [1985] OJ L85/1, [1985] 3 CMLR 474 (*Re Wood Pulp*).

4 The first was concluded on 23 September 1991 ([1991] 4 CMLR 823). The agreement provides for the exchange of information and consultation on competition matters. It creates, inter alia, a 'positive comity' between the parties by allowing one party, where it believes that anti-competitive activities adverse to its important interests are carried out in the territory of the other party, to request that the other party's competition authorities initiate enforcement action. The Agreement also establishes a framework within which the parties may agree to coordinate their enforcement activities regarding anti-competitive activities that affect their interests as well as comity factors to be used in order to avoid conflicts over enforcement activities. The act whereby the Commission sought to conclude the Agreement was declared void by the ECJ on grounds of lack of competence: Case C-327/ 91 *France v Commission* [1994] ECR I-3641, [1994] 5 CMLR 517, ECJ. This position was rectified by the adoption of a joint decision of the Council and the Commission on 10 April 1995 ([1995] OJ L95/45), corrected in [1995] OJ L131/38.
The second agreement was concluded on 4 June 1998 (Agreement between the European Communities and the Government of the United States of America on the application of positive comity principles in the enforcement of their competition laws). This agreement focuses on the positive comity principle set out in Article V of the first agreement. It was approved by the Council and the Commission in a joint Decision of 29 May 1998 ([1998] OJ L173/26, [1999] 4 CMLR 502). It should be noted that mergers do not fall within the scope of this second agreement (Article II(4)).
Since then, the principle of positive comity has been relied on in *Sabre* (See Commission's XXX Report on Competition Policy (2000), point 453). See also Joined Cases T-191/98, T-212/98 to T-214/98 *Atlantic Container Line AB v Commission* [2003] ECR II 3275.
5 See http://europa.eu.int/comm/competition/mergers/others/.

3. Application to trade with third countries

[39]
The rules of competition may apply to agreements and practices relating to both imports into and exports from the Community provided that the necessary criteria for the application of the rules are satisfied.[1] With regard to exports, it is less likely that those criteria will be satisfied than in the case of imports, for there is less likely to be any or any significant effect within the common market,[2] although this will not always be the case,[3] particularly if there is a real possibility that the goods will be reimported into the Community.[4] With regard to imports, there is much more likelihood of an effect upon competition within the common markets.[5]

1 As to trade with third countries, see B Barack, *The Application of the Competition Rules of the EEC* (1981); JF Bellis 'International Trade and EEC Competition Law' (1979) 16 CML Rev 647.
2 For examples where export agreements or practices do not affect trade, see Commission Decision (EEC) 68/376 [1968] CMLR D78 (*Re Johs Rieckermann KG and. AEG-Elotherm GmbH Agreement*); Commission Decision (EEC) 69/202 [1970] CMLR D1 (*Re VVVF*); Commission Decision (EEC) 70/332 [1970] CMLR D19 (*Re Kodak*); Commission Decision (EEC) 70/488 [1970] CMLR D49 (*Re Omega Watches*); Commission Decision (EEC) 72/238 [1972] CMLR D45 (*Re A Raymond & Co and Nagoya Rubber Ltd Agreement*); Commission Decision (EEC) 75/494 [1975] 2 CMLR D40 (*Re Kabel- und Metaliwerke Neumeyer AG and Etablissements Luchaire SA Agreement*); Commission Decision (EEC) 78/253 [1978] 2 CMLR 397 (*Re Davide Campari-Milano SpA Agreement*); see also Commission XXI Competition Report, p 334 (*Re Igbel*). In Commission Decision (EEC) 88/541 [1988] OJ L301/68, [1989] 4 CMLR 610 (*BBC Brown Boveri/NGK*), an exclusive licence to market the product in question in a third country was considered by the Commission to have an effect within the Community since it amounted to an export ban from that third country to the Member States in which there was no intellectual property right protection.
3 See Joined Cases 40-48, 50,54-56, 111, 113, 114/73 *Coöperatieve vereniging Suiker Unie UA v* Commission [1975] ECR 1663 at 2010, [1976] 1 CMLR 295 at 477, ECJ; Commission Vth Report

on Competition Policy, point 35 (*Linoleum Export Cartel*); Commission Decision (EEC) 77/543 [1977] 2 CMLR D69 (*Re De Laval-Stork VOF Joint Venture*).
4 See Case C-306/96 *Javico International and Javico AG v Yves Saint Laurent Parfums SA* [1998] ECR I-1983. This applies in particular if the original export was to an EFTA country: Commission Decision (EEC) 75/94 [1975] 1 CMLR D31 (*Re Goodyear Italiana SpA*); Commission Decision (EEC) 75/494 [1975] 2 CMLR D40 (*Re Kabel- und Metaliwerke Neumeyer AG and Etablissements Luchaire SA Agreement*); Commission Decision (EEC) 76/159 [1976] 1 CMLR D61 (*Re SABA*); Commission Decision (EEC) 77/100 [1977] 1 CMLR D82 (*Re Junghans GmbH*).
5 See eg Case 22/71 *Béguelin Import Co v GL Import Export SA* [1971] ECR 949, [1972] CMLR 81, ECJ; Case 71/74 *Nederlandse Verenigning voor Fruit en Groentenimporthandel 'Frubo' v Commission* [1975] ECR 563, [1975] 2 CMLR 123, ECJ; Case 51/75 *EMI Records Ltd v CBS United Kingdom Ltd* [1976] ECR 811, [197612 CMLR 235, ECJ; Case 27/76 *United Brands Co v Commission* [1978] ECR 207, [1978] 1 CMLR 429, ECJ; Case 22/78 *Hugin Kassaregister AB v Commission* [1979] ECR 1869, [1979] 3 CMLR 345, ECJ; Commission Notice on Imports of Japanese Products ([1972] OJ C111/13); Commission Decision (EEC) 74/634 [1975] 1 CMLR D8 (*Re Franco-Japanese Ballbearings Agreement*); Commission Decision (EEC) 76/ 743 [1976] 2 CMLR D44 (*Re ReuterfBASF AG*); Commission Decision (EEC) 93/82 [1993] OJ L34/21 (*Re Cewal*). However, the de minimis provisions may exclude the application of the rules: Commission Decision (EEC) 72/238 [1972] CMLR D45 (*Re A Raymond & Co and Nagoya Rubber Ltd Agreement*). See, however, Commission Notice of 24 February 1989 [1989] OJ C45/4, [1989] 4 CMLR 413 (*Finnpap*), in which the Commission announced its intention not to take any action in respect of an exclusive marketing arrangement pursuant to which the Finnish Paper Mills Association ('Finnpap') is charged with the exclusive marketing in the Community of its members' newsprint production when Finnpap agreed to relax the exclusivity element of the arrangement.

[40]
The fact that certain conduct may relate only to the performance in a third country of a contract entered into in the territory of a Member State by parties within the jurisdiction of that Member State does not preclude the application of the rules of competition to other conduct occurring within the common market.[1]

1 Case 22/79 *Greenwich Film Production v SACEM* [1979] ECR 3275 at 3289, [1980] 1 CMLR 629 at 645, ECJ.

4. Extra-territorial jurisdiction

[41]
Articles 81 and 82 are silent as to whether they apply extra-territorially. Undertakings situated outside the European Community may be subject to Community rules of competition.[1] This jurisdiction has been treated differently by the Court of Justice, the Court of First Instance and the Commission.

1 This was first recognised in Case 22/71 *Béguelin Import Co v GL Import Export SA* [1971] ECR 949, [1972] CMLR 81, ECJ. As to the extra-territorial application of the rules of competition, see generally B Barack, *The Application of the Competition Rules of the EEC* (1981), and the bibliography there cited. It would seem clear that in an appropriate case the private law rights for individuals under Community law would have extra-territorial effect, so that individuals in a non-Community court or arbitral tribunal can rely on breaches of the Community rules of competition.

[42]
The Court of Justice has applied the theory of enterprise entity (also called the 'single economic entity doctrine').[1] This is dependent upon finding anti-competitive action within the Community.[2] When such action is effected by a subsidiary,[3] the holding company will be subject to Community law even though its seat is outside the

Community.[4] The conditions for the application of this doctrine are that the parent was actually exercising control[5] over the subsidiary and that this resulted in anti-competitive behaviour.[6] This has been applied by the Commission in prohibiting breaches of Articles 81 and 82 of the EC Treaty by multinational enterprises in relation to price fixing,[7] discriminatory pricing,[8] export bans,[9] refusal to supply,[10] exclusive or preferential supply[11] and acquisition of a company.[12] The same economic entity principles may now be applied so as to enable, for example, a claimant to bring an action in the English courts against a UK subsidiary of a foreign parent company that acted contrary to Article 81.[13]

1 Case 48/69 *Imperial Chemical Industries Ltd v Commission* (*'Dyestyffs'*) [1972] ECR 619, [1972] CMLR 557, ECJ; Case 52/69 *JR Geigy AG v Commission* [1972] ECR 787, [19721 CMLR 557, ECJ; Case 53/69 *Sandoz AG v Commission* [1972] ECR 845, [1972] CMLR 557, ECJ. See CS Kerse and N Khan, *EC Antitrust Procedure* (5th edn, 2005), para 7-004. For the interrelationship between the concept of enterprise entity and that of intra-enterprise conspiracy, see B Barack, *The Application of the Competition Rules of the EEC* (1981), p 74.

2 It therefore conforms with the territorial principle of international law: see I Brownlie, *Principles of Public International Law* (4th edn), Chapter XIV. See also B Barack, *The Application of the Competition Rules of the EEC* (1981). A finding of anti-competitive action was made in Case 48/69 *Imperial Chemical Industries Ltd v Commission* [1972] ECR 619, [1972] CMLR 557, ECJ; Case 6/72 *Europemballage Corpn and Continental Can Co Inc v Commission* [1973] ECR 215, [1973] CMLR 199, ECJ; Joined Cases 6,7/73 *Istituto Chemioterapico Italiano SpA and Commercial Solvents Corpn v Commission* [1974] ECR 223, [1974] 1 CMLR 309, ECJ. See also Case 27/76 *United Brands Co v Commission* [1978] ECR 207, [1978] 1 CMLR 429, ECJ; and Case 85/76 *Hoffmann-La Roche & Co AG v Commission* [1979] ECR 461, [1979] 3 CMLR 211, ECJ.

3 The question of whether or not a company is a subsidiary depends upon control, and a holding of 51 per cent may be sufficient: see Joined Cases 6, 7/73 *Istituto Chemioterapico Italiano SpA and Commercial Solvents Corpn v Commission* [1974] ECR 223, [1974] 1 CMLR 309, ECJ.

4 Case 48/69 *Imperial Chemical Industries Ltd v Commission* [1972] ECR 619 at 662, [1972] CMLR 557 at 629, ECJ.

5 Control is determined by an examination of ownership, managerial and administrative involvement, and the actual, or at least the possible, control which is exercised as a matter of fact: B Barack, *The Application of the Competition Rules of the EEC* (1981), p 54.

6 PJ Kuyper, 'European Community Law and Extra-territoriality: Some Trends and New Developments' (1984) 33 ICLQ 1013 at 1017; Case 6/72 *Europemballage Corpn and Continental Can Co Inc v Commission* [1973] ECR 215, [1973] CMLR 199, ECJ; Joined Cases 6,7/ 73 *Istituto Chemioterapico Italiano SpA and Commercial Solvents Corpn v Commission* [1974] ECR 223 at 253, 254, [1974] 1 CMLR 309 at 342-344, ECJ.

7 See eg Commission Decision (EEC) 69/243 [1969] CMLR D23 (*Re Aniline Dyes Cartel*). See also Commission Decision (EEC) 85/206 (*Re Aluminium Imports from Eastern Europe*) [1987] 3 CMLR 813.

8 See eg Commission Decision (EEC) 72/403 [1973] CMLR D2 (*Re Pittsburgh Corning Europe*); Commission Decision (EEC) 76/353 [1976] 1 CMLR D28 (*Re United Brands Co*).

9 See eg Commission Decision (EEC) 72/480 [1973] CMLR D43 (*Re WEA-Filipacchi Music SA*); Commission Decision (EEC) 76/915 [1977] 1 CMLR D61 (*Re Miller International Schaliplatten GmbH*); Commission Decision (EEC) 79/68 [1979] 1 CMLR 448 (*Re Kawasaki Motors*); Commission Decision (EEC) 80/256 [1980] 1 CMLR 457 (*Re Pioneer Hi-Fi Equipment*); Commission Decision (EEC) 80/1283 [1981] 2 CMLR 287 (*Re Johnson & Johnson*).

10 Commission Decision (EEC) 72/457 [1973] CMLR D50 (*Re Commercial Solvents*).

11 Commission Decision (EEC) 76/642 [1976] 2 CMLR D25 (*Re Vitamins*).

12 Commission Decision (EEC) 72/21 [1972] CMLR D11 (*Re Continental Can Co Inc*).

13 See *Provimi Ltd v Aventi Animal Nutrition SA* [2003] EWHC 961 (Comm), [2003] All ER (D) 59. Note: in *Amino Acids*, the Commission expressly cited the *Wood Pulp* judgment ([2001] OJ L 152/ 24, [2001] 5 CMLR 322, para 182). It should be noted that the fines were largely upheld on appeal – Case T-220/00 *Cheil Jedang Corpn v Commission*, 9 July 2003.

[43]
The Commission's view is that jurisdiction may also be exercised by applying the effects theory.[1] The conditions for the application of this doctrine are that acts of the undertaking should have a direct, immediate, reasonably foreseeable and substantial effect on competition between Member States.[2] This view was not accepted by the Court of Justice in the *Dyestuffs* case[3] despite a specific request to do so.[4] The Commission has subsequently reaffirmed its view.[5] In the *Wood Pulp* decision the Commission had assumed jurisdiction over undertakings by applying the effects doctrine where the enterprise entity doctrine was not an alternative.[6]

1 The Commission's approach was first expressed in Commission Decision (EEC) 64/233 [1964] CMLR 237 (*Re Grosfillex Sarl*): see 7th General Report on the Activities of the European Community (1964), point 67. As to the effects theory, see CSP Harding 'Jurisdiction in EEC Competition Law: Some Recent Developments' (1977) 11 Journal of World Trade 422, and B Barack, *The Application of the Competition Rules of the EEC* (1981), p 98. As to the effects theory in the United States, see *Restatement (Second) of Foreign Relations Law of the United States* S18 (1965), and *US v Aluminium Co of America* 148 F 2d 416 (1945).
2 Case 48/69 *Imperial Chemical Industries Ltd v Commission* [1972] ECR 619 at 693,694, [1972] CMLR 557 at 603,604, ECJ, per Mayras, Advocate General, whose opinion was influenced by the United States position, as to which see note 1.
3 Case 48/69 *Imperial Chemical Industries Ltd v Commission* [1972] ECR 619, [1972] CMLR 557, ECJ.
4 The request came both from the Commission and from Advocate General Mayras, both of whom favoured the effects theory.
5 See, in particular, Commission XI Report on Competition Policy, points 34-37; and generally CS Kerse and N Khan, *EC Antitrust Procedure* (5th edn, 2005) and A Jones and B Sufrin, *EC Competition Law* (2nd edn, 2004). See also Commission Decision (EEC) 74/634 [1975] 1 CMLR D8 (*Re Franco-Japanese Ballbearings Agreement*); Commission Decision (EEC) 75/77 [1975] 1 CMLR D83 (*Re French and Taiwanese Mushroom Packers*); Commission Decision (EEC) 77/129 [1977] 1 CMLR D44 (*Re Theal/ Watts*); Commission Decision (EEC) 78/252 [1978] 1 CMLR534 (*Re Vegetable Parchment*); Commission Decision (EEC) 79/90 [1979] 1 CMLR 464 (*Re White lead*).
6 Commission Decision (EEC) 85/202 [1985] OJ L85/1, [1985] 3 CMLR 474 (*Re Wood Pulp*), where the Commission fined 36 addressees, all of whom were outside the Community. Jurisdiction was assumed because the undertakings were exporting directly to or doing business within the Community. Some had branches, agencies or other establishments within the Community. It could be argued that certain judgments of the court give support to the effects theory: see eg Case 22/71 *Béguelin Import Co v GL Import Export SA* [1971] ECR 949, [1972] CMLR 81, ECJ, and Case 51/75 *EMI Records Ltd v CBS United Kingdom Ltd* [1976] ECR 811 at 848, [1976] 2 CMLR 235 at 266, ECJ. Similarly, in Commission Decision (EEC) 85/206 (*Re Aluminium Imports from Eastern Europe*) [1987] 3 CMLR 813, at para 14.6, the Commission assumed jurisdiction over undertakings outside the Community which traded into the territory, and, at para 14.7, asserted that such jurisdiction is not prohibited by international law.

[44]
In its judgment on the appeal from the Commission's decision in the *Wood Pulp* case, the Court of Justice again did not apply the effects doctrine. Instead, it held that on the facts of the case, the agreements in question had been implemented within the EEC by undertakings associated with the principal parties: whether subsidiaries, agents, sub-agents or branches within the Community.[1] Since the agreements had been implemented within the Community there was no need for the court to consider the place of the effects doctrine.[2]

1 It is worth noting that although the UK Government initially disputed the failure on the part of the ECJ to distinguish legally between a parent and a subsidiary company, this principle is now

incorporated into English (and other UK) law in the Competition Act 1998, s 60 (see Vaughan, *Law of the European Union*, Section 21B ('Competition – Procedures and Remedies'), Chapter 4 ('National Remedies').

2 See Joined Cases 89, 104, 114,116, 117,125-129/85 *Ahlström Osakeyhtio v Commission* [1988] ECR 5193, [1988] 4 CMLR 901, ECJ. For comment see in particular Van Gerven, 'The Wood Pulp Judgment' (1989) Fordham Corporate Law Institute Annual Proceedings, p 451 and especially p 470. See also Ferry, 'Towards Completing the Charm: The *Wood Pulp* judgment' (1989) 11 EIPR 19; Mann 'The Public International Law of Restrictive Trade Practices in the EuropeanCourt of Justice' (1989) 38 ICLQ 375.

[45]

The Court of Justice upholds the Commission's view that jurisdiction under the rules of competition is not affected by free trade agreements with third countries.[1]

1 See Joined Cases 89, 104, 114,116, 117, 125-129/85 *Ahlström Osakeyhtio v Commission* [1988] ECR 5193, [1988] 4 CMLR 901, ECJ, where the Court held that jurisdiction under Articles 81 and 82 was not affected by free trade agreements with Sweden, Finland, Norway and Portugal. Such agreements do not exclude the application of Articles 81 and 82. The Commission took a similar view in its Decision (EEC) 85/202 [1985] OJ L85/1, [1985] 3 CMLR 474 (*Re Wood Pulp*). See also Commission Decision (EEC) 86/398 (*Polypropylene*) [1986] OJ L230/1, [1988] 4 CMLR 347, on appeal Case 179/86 *Rhône-Poulenc SA v Commission* (Joined Cases T-1, 4,6-15/89 [1990] ECR II-637, [1991] ECR II-867, CFI), in which the Commission applied the same reasoning to undertakings established in EFTA countries.

[46]

In comparison with the ECJ's approach to the territorial scope of Articles 81 and 82, the Court of First Instance has taken a different approach in respect of the territorial scope of mergers. It has, while not expressly approving the effects doctrine, relied on the essential elements of it.[1]

1 See Case T-102/96 *Gencor Ltd v Commission* [1999] ECR II-753. See also the discussion in E Fox, 'The Merger Regulation and its Territorial Reach' [1999] ECLR 334, in particular at pp 335-6. See generally on the scope of the Merger Regulation (see Vaughan, *Law of the European Union*, Section 21C ('Competition – Mergers', forthcoming)).

5. Extra-territorial application

[47]

The application of Community competition law outside the Member States raises procedural problems in three areas:[1] discovery, service of process and enforcement.

1 See, generally, CS Kerse and N Khan, *EEC Antitrust Procedure* (5th edn, 2005), paras 3-030, 7-076; B Barack, *The Application of the Competition Rules of the EEC* (1981).

[48]

So far as discovery is concerned, the Commission may informally request information from enterprises situated wholly outside the Community.[1] It is undecided whether it can send a formal request.[2] If such an enterprise has a seat[3] in the Community any information in possession of the group may be obtained from that part of the enterprise.[4] Non-compliance with any such request could result in fines being imposed.[5] However, such fines are only enforceable against assets within the jurisdiction. The Commission may not carry out investigations outside the Community,[6] although it may request a Member State to conduct an investigation in a third country to the extent that the Member State has power to do so.[7] If the

Commission is carrying out an investigation in a new Member State and discovers relevant information relating to pre-accession infringements, the Commission is entitled to take that information into account even though at the time that information came into existence the Commission had no such jurisdiction.[8]

1 The Commission may by simple request or by decision require undertakings and associations of undertakings to provide all necessary information: Council Regulation (EC) 1/2003, Article 18(1) (formerly dealt with under Council Regulation (EEC) 17/62, Article 11(1)). The Commission is further empowered to carry out inspections under Article 20 of the same Regulation. An informal request poses no problems in international law because it is not coercive. If the undertaking is within the Community but the information is outside it, the request is enforceable against the undertaking (Commission Decision (EEC) 76/593 ([1976] OJ L192/27) (*Re CSV*)); Commission Decision (EEC) 78/24 [1978] 1 CMLR D63 (*Re Vereinigung Deutscher Freiformschmieden*), even though the law of the State where the information is situated makes disclosure unlawful (Commission Decision (EEC) 76/593 [1992] OJ L192/27 (*Re CSV*)).

2 When dealing with an undertaking situated outside the Community, the Commission may deal solely with the undertaking. The Court of Justice implicitly recognised the Commission's power to request information in such a situation in Case 27/76 *United Brands Co v Commission* [1978] ECR 207 at 302, [1978] 1 CMLR 429 at 503, ECJ.

3 This may be an associated company, subsidiary or holding company.

4 See eg Case 27/76 *United Brands Co v Commission* [1978] ECR 207 at 302, [1978] 1 CMLR 429 at 503, ECJ. This is based on the doctrine of enterprise entity.

5 If an undertaking supplies incorrect information, fails to supply information within a time limit imposed by a formal decision, or produces in an incomplete form books or other records required (under an inspection under Article 20 of Council Regulation (EC) 1/2003), a fine not exceeding 1% of the relevant entity's turnover in the preceding business year may be imposed: Council Regulation (EC) 1/2003, Article 23 (formerly under Regulation 17/62, Article 15(1)(b)).

6 The Commission has power to undertake all necessary investigations: Article 20 of Council Regulation (EC) 1/2003 (formerly dealt with under Regulation 17/62, Article 14(1)). However, this would be a clear breach of international law because it is an act of coercion. It may become possible if the Community makes treaties with non-Member countries. For example, under GATT (the forerunner to the WTO), the Commission has investigated breaches of the anti-dumping rules. See further Commission VIII Report on Competition Policy, Part 14. The Commission maintains contacts with various countries and bodies: see eg Commission XIV Report on Competition Policy, Chapter II. The fact that a group's headquarters is within the Community will not give the Commission jurisdiction to investigate outside the Community.

7 The Commission may request the competent authorities of Member States to carry out any investigations it considers necessary: Council Regulation (EC) 1/2003, Article 22 (formerly under Regulation 17/62, Article 13(1)). The exercise of such powers would depend upon the extra-territorial scope of any Member State's investigative powers relating to anti-trust rules.

8 See Case 97-99/87 *Dow Chemical Iberica SA v Commission* [1989] ECR 3165, [1991] 4 CMLR 410, paras 61-65.

[49]

So far as service of process is concerned, the Commission is required, where it is commencing proceedings under Articles 81 or 82, to inform the relevant undertakings before making those proceedings public. Notice must also be given of the objections that are being made.[1] A statement of objections may be served by post by sending it by registered post to an undertaking situated outside the Community.[2] The purpose of the statement is to give the undertaking concerned an opportunity of putting forward its defence and therefore it has no coercive effect.[3] It is immaterial that this method of service may be invalid by the law of the country to which the letter is sent.[4] A decision is properly served and thereby effective when it reaches the addressee and puts it in a position to take cognisance of it.[5] This may be done by service on the undertaking even when situated outside the Community,[6] or on a controlled subsidiary[7] or branch[8] within the Community, or probably through an independent agent acting under an obligation to inform the undertaking.[9] The Court of Justice has stated that irregularities in the procedure for notification of decisions are extraneous to that measure and cannot therefore invalidate it.[10]

1 See Articles 2(2) and 10 of Regulation 773/2004 [2004] OJ L123/18. This Regulation replaced Regulation 2842/98 on 1 May 2004.
2 Case 52/69 *JR Geigy AG v Commission* [1972] ECR 787 at 823, 824, [1972] CMLR 557 at 637, 638, ECJ
3 Case 52/69JR *Geigy AG v Commission* [1972] ECR 787 at 823, 824, [1972] CMLR 557 at 637, 638, ECJ; Case 6/72 *Europemballage Corpn and Continental Can Co Inc v Commission* [1973] ECR 215 at 239, 240, [1973] CMLR 199 at 219, 229, ECJ.
4 Case 52/69 *JR Geigy AG v Commission* [1972] ECR 787 at 823, [1972] CMLR 557 at 637, 638, ECJ.
5 See Case 6/72 *Europemballage Corpn and Continental Can Co Inc v Commission* [1973] ECR 215 at 241, [1973] CMLR 199 at 220, 221, ECJ, where the Court confirmed that the Commission need not use diplomatic channels. In Case 52/69 *JR Geigy AG v Commission* [1972] ECR 787, [1972] CMLR 557, ECJ, the Court rejected the argument that the company should be served in accordance with Swiss law.
6 See eg Commission Decision (EEC) 76/642 [1976] 2 CMLJR D25 (*Re Vitamins*).
7 See eg Case 48/69 *Imperial Chemical Industries Ltd v Commission* [1972] ECR 619, [1972] CMLR 557, ECJ; Case 52/69 *JR Geigy AG v Commission* [1972] ECR 787, [1972] CMLR 557, ECJ. This was done in eg Commission Decision (EEC) 76/353 [1976] 1 CMLR D28 (*Re United Brands Co*).
8 See Case 8/56 *Acciaierie Laminatoi Magliano Alpi SpA v High Authority* [1957-58] ECR 95, ECJ, a case under the ECSC Treaty, where it was held that service is effective if it reaches the inner structure of the addressee.
9 There is no decided case on the point. It is likely that such an obligation would have to be specified.
10 Case 48/69 *Imperial Chemical Industries Ltd v Commission* [1972] ECR 619 at 652, [1972] CMLR 557 at 620, ECJ; Case 52/69 *JR Geigy AG v Commission* [1972] ECR 787 at 825, [1972] CMLR 557 at 639, ECJ.

[50]

So far as enforcement is concerned, in an appropriate case where, it has jurisdiction, the Commission may order by decision an undertaking outside the Community to undertake action within,[1] although probably not outside,[2] the Community, or order an undertaking inside, but probably not outside, the Community to refrain from involvement in a practice outside, the Community.[3]

1 See eg Joined Cases 6, 7/73 *Istituto Chemioterapico Italiano SpA and Commercial Solvents Corpn v Commission* [1974] ECR 223, [1974] 1 CMLR 309, ECJ.
2 This would raise considerable difficulties (unless ancillary to action within the Community, as in Commission Decision (EEC) 72/21 [1972] CMLR D11 (*Re Continental Can Co Inc*), and Commission Decision (EEC) 72/457 [1973] CMLR D50 (*Re Commercial Solvents*)), for it would involve the exercise of extra-territorial coercive jurisdiction. The imposition of fines would not seem to be coercive: see Case 48/69 *Imperial Chemical Industries Ltd v Commission* [1972] ECR 619 at 695, [1972] CMLR 557 at 605, 606, ECJ, per Mayras, Advocate General.
3 This has never been done, but there is arguably authority for it in the Court's decision in Case 22/79 *Greenwich Film Production v SACEM* [1979] ECR 3275, [1980] 1 CMLR 629, ECJ.

[51]

The Commission may impose fines on the basis that it has jurisdiction and can serve a decision as outlined above.[1] Where more than one undertaking is involved, for example a parent and subsidiary, the Commission may make liability for payment joint and several, and may then seek to enforce against the undertaking located in the Community.[2] Decisions imposing a pecuniary obligation are enforceable in Member States under the EC Treaty.[3] The Commission has never attempted to enforce a fine in a non-Member State, and it is doubtful whether it has any power to do so.[4] The simplest route in such a situation is to serve the decision on the EU-based subsidiary of the parent in default, if such a subsidiary exists.[5]

1 Commission Decision (EEC) 78/252 [1978] 1 CMLR 534 (*Re Vegetable Parchment*); Commission Decision (EEC) 80/1283 [1981] 2 CMLR 287 (*Re Johnson & Johnson*).

2 See eg Joined Cases 6, 7/73 *Istituto Chemioterapico Italiano SpA and Commercial Solvents Corpn v Commission* [1974] ECR 223, [1974] 1 CMLR 309, ECJ. See also Commission Decision (EEC) 78/68 [1978] 1 CMLR D19 (*Re Hugin/Liptons*).

3 See EC Treaty, Article 256.

4 See Mann, 'Doctrine of Jurisdiction in International Law' [1964] 111 Recueil, and Mann 'Prerogative Rights of Foreign States and the Conflict of Laws' 40 Grotius 28. It is not thought that there have been any cases of such non-payment.

5 See, for example, Case 48/69 *ICI v Commission ('Dyestuffs')* [1972] ECR 619. The Commission first tried to serve the final decision on the non-EEC undertakings through diplomatic channels. Only when that proved to be unsuccessful did the Commission then serve the EEC subsidiaries.

B. PERSONAL APPLICATION

1. Meaning of 'undertaking'[1]

[52]

The EC Treaty does not define 'undertaking' for the purposes of the rules of competition.[2] The word has the same meaning for the purposes of both Articles 81 and 82. It is a much wider and looser concept than 'person'.[3] It is not dependent upon the precise legal characteristics of the entity or upon the way in which that entity is financed.[4] It would seem to be an essential characteristic of an undertaking that the activities pursued must be of an economic or commercial nature,[5] although this should be widely construed (see para [53] below). It is immaterial whether the undertaking supplies goods or services. The absence of a profit motive[6] or the absence of profits[7] is not relevant, provided that the objectives are economic or commercial. This is summarised by the following Commission statements:

> The functional concept of an undertaking in Article 85(1) [now Article 81(1)] covers any activity directed at trade in goods or services irrespective of the legal form of the undertaking and regardless of whether or not it is intended to earn profits.[8]
>
> [The] basic test is therefore whether the entity in question is engaged in an activity that is an economic one, involving the offering of goods or services on the market, which could at least in principle, be carried on by a private undertaking in order to make profits.[9]

1 See also Chapter 4, 'Abuse of a Dominant Position', paras [219] ff.

2 A helpful summary of the ECJ case law on this point is provided in the UK Competition Appeal Tribunal judgment in *Bettercare Group Limited v DGFT* [2002] CAT 7, [2002] Comp AR 299. The absence of a definition of 'undertaking' in the EC Treaty can be contrasted with the definitions given in the former ECSC Treaty, Article 80 and in the Euratom Treaty, Article 196(b). See Article 1 of Protocol 22 to the EEA Agreement for a definition of the term. See also

the discussion in Louri '"Undertaking"' as a Jurisdictional Element in EC Competition Rules' (2002) 29 LIEI 143.

3 Joined Cases 6, 7/73 *Istituto Chemioterapico Italiano SpA and Commercial Solvents Corpn v Commission* [1974] ECR 223 at 263, [1974] 1 CMLR 309 at 319, ECJ, per Warner, Advocate General.

4 See Case C-41/90 *Höfner and Elser v Macroton GmbH* [1991] ECR I-1979, [1993] 4 CMLR 306, para 21. See also, Case 32/65 *Italy v EEC Council and EEC Commission* [1966] ECR 389 at 418, 419, [1969] CMLR 39 at 52, ECJ per Roemer, Advocate General; Commission Decision (EEC) 86/398 [1986] OJ L230/1, [1988] 4 CMLR 347 (*Polypropylene*); the undertaking is an economic unit even if in law that economic unit consists of several different persons, natural or legal; see Case 170/83 *Hydrotherm Gerätebau GmbH v Compact de Dott Ing Mario Andreoli & CSAS* [1984] ECR 2999, [1985] 3 CMLR 224, ECJ; Commission Decision (EC) 94/601 [1994] OJ L243/1, [1994] 5 CMLR 547 (*Cartonboard*).
For further development of the point by the ECJ, see: *Poucet and Pistre v Assurances Generales de France* [1993] ECR I-637, para 17; Case 364/92 *SAT Fluggesellschaft v Eurocontrol* [1994] ECR 1-43, [1994] 5 CMLR 208 para 18, ECJ; Cases C-180-184/98, *Pavlov v Stichting Pensionenfonds Medische Specialisten* [2000] ECR I-6451, [2001] 4 CMLR 30, para 74; Case C-218/00, *Cisal di Batatistello Venanzio & Co v Istituto Nazionale per L'Assicurazione Contro Gli fortune Sul Lavoro (INAIL)* [2002] ECR I-691, [2002] 4 CMLR 833, para 22.
See also *Alpha Flight Services/Aeroports de Paris* [1998] OJ L230/10, [1998] 5 CMLR 611, paras 49-55, upheld on appeal Case T-128/98 [2000] ECR II-3929, [2001] 4 CMLR 1376, paras 120-126 and by the ECJ in Case C-82/01P [2002] ECR I-9297, [2003] 4 CMLR 609, paras 78-82; *Portugese Airports* [1999] OJ L69/31, [1999] 5 CMLR 103, para 12; *Ilmailulaitos/Luftfartsverket* [1999] OJ L69/24, [1999] 5 CMLR 90, paras 21-23.

5 Case 155/73 *Sacchi* [1974] ECR 409 at 430, [1974] 2 CMLR 177 at 204, ECJ. See also Commission Decision (EEC) 85/206 [1985] OJ L92/1, [1987] 3 CMLR 813 (*Re Aluminium Imports from Eastern Europe*); Case C-364/92 *SAT Fluggesellschaft v Eurocontrol* [1994] ECR I-43, [1994] 5 CMLR 208, ECJ. See also Case C-475/99 *Ambulanz Glöckner v Landkreis Süswestplaz* [2001] ECR 8089, [2002] 4 CMLR 726, para 19.

6 Joined Cases 209-215, 218/78 *Heintz van Landewyck Sàrl v Commission* [1980] ECR 3125, [1981] 3 CMLR 134, ECJ. See also Commission Decision (EEC) 81/1030 [1982] 1 CMLR 221 (*Re GVL*), and Case 7/82 *GVL v Commission* [1983] ECR 483, [1983] 3 CMLR 645, ECJ.

7 See eg Commission Decision (EEC) 83/546 [1984] 1 CMLR 694 (*Re Cast Iron and Steel Rolls*); Case C-244/94 *Fédération Française des Sociétés d'Assurances v Caisse Nationale d'Assurance Vieillesse Mutuelle Agricole* [1995] ECR I-4013, [1996] 4 CMLR 536, ECJ. See also Case C-67/96 *Albany International BV v Stichting Bedrijfspensioenfonds Textielindustrie* [1999] ECR I-5751, [2000] 4 CMLR 446.

8 See eg Commission Decision (EEC) 89/536 [1989] OJ L284/36, [1990] 4 CMLR 841 (Film purchases by German television stations).

9 Case C-67/96, *Albany International BV v Stichting Bedrijfspensioenfonds Textielindustrie* [1999] ECR I-5751, [2000] 4 CMLR 446, per Advocate-General Jacobs at para 311. See also Case C-475/99 *Ambulanz Glöckner v Landkreis Süswestplaz* [2001] ECR 8089, [2002] 4 CMLR 726. See also Case C-309/99 *Wouters v Alegemene Raad van de Nederlandse Order van Advocaten* [2002] ECR I-1577, [2002] 4 CMLR 913 in which the ECJ held that the competition rules in the Treaty: 'do not apply to activity which, by its nature, its aim and the rules to which it is subject does not belong in the sphere of economic activity... or which is connected with the exercise of the powers of a public authority.' (para 57)

[53]

An undertaking can be either a public[1] or a private body. The term has been held to encompass not only companies,[2] but also entities as diverse as partnerships,[3] mutual associations,[4] agricultural co-operatives,[5] performing rights societies,[6] cultural organisations,[7] sporting organisations[8] and sectoral social security schemes.[9] It has been held that professional bodies can also constitute undertakings.[10] Further examples include: a state-run employment agency,[11] independent customs agents,[12] the Spanish post office[13] and a public broadcasting institution.[14] A branch office however cannot be considered as an undertaking.[15]

1 For State-owned undertakings see eg Commission Statement [1976] 1 CMLR D89 (*Re British Broadcasting Corpn*), and Commission Decision (EEC) 82/861 [1983] 1 CMLR 457 (*Re British Telecommunications*), upheld on appeal in Case 41/83 *Italy v Commission* [1985] ECR 873, [1985] 2 CMLR 368, ECJ. The question as to whether a Member State itself may be regarded as an undertaking where it enters directly into a commercial agreement is unsettled. See eg French State/Suralmo, Commission IX Report on Competition Policy (1980), point 114. Where a local authority which enters a contract for concession acts in its capacity as public authority, it is not to be considered as an undertaking: Case 30/87 *Bodson v Pompes Funèbres des Regions Liberées Srl* [1988] ECR 2479, [1989] 4 CMLR 984, ECJ. An international organisation which operates, on behalf of the contracting States, a system of air control acting in the public interest and exercising public law powers, is not to be regarded as an undertaking: Case C-364/92 *SAT Fluggesellschaft mbH v Eurocontrol* [1994] ECR I-43, [1994] 5 CMLR 208, ECJ. An anti-pollution agency is not an undertaking because the activity in question 'is a task in the public interest which forms part of the essential functions of the State'. See Case C-343/95 *Diego Calì & Figli Srl v Servizi ecologici porto di Genova SpA (SEPG)* [1997] ECR I-1547 at para 22. See also discussion below at para [60], below.

2 In all their corporate forms, eg trust companies (Commission Decision (EEC) 79/253 [1979] 1 CMLR 650 (*Fides*)). As to partnerships, see Case 258/78 *Nungesser v Commission* [1982] ECR 2105, [1983] 1 CMLR 278) and note 3, below.

3 Commission Decision (EEC) 73/323 [1973] CMLR D250 (*Re William Prym-Werke KG and Beka Agreement*).

4 Commission Notice under Council Regulation (EEC) 17/62, Article 19(2), on *P & I Clubs* (OJ C9 11.1.85 p.11); *P&I Clubs* [1985] OJ L376/2, [1989] 4 CMLR 178.

5 Commission Decision (EEC) 80/234 [1980] 2 CMLR 402 (*Re Rennet*), confirmed in Case 61/80 *Cooperatieve Stremsel-en Kleurselfabriek v Commission* [1981] ECR 851, [1982] 1 CMLR 240, ECJ; Case C-250/92, *Gøttrup-Klim Grovvareforening v Dansk Landbrugs Grovvareselskab AmbA* [1994] ECR I-5641, [1996] 4 CMLR 191.

6 Commission Decision (EEC) 71/224 [1971] CMLR D35 (*Re GEMA*); Case 127/73 *Belgische Radio en Televisie (BRT) v SV SABAM* [1974] ECR 51 and 313, [1974] 2 CMLR 238, ECJ; Joined Cases 110, 241-242/88 *Lucazeau v Société des Auteurs, Compositeurs et Editeurs de Musique (SACEM)* [1989] ECR 2811, [1991] 4 CMLR 248, ECJ.

7 Joined Cases 43, 63/82 *VBVB and VBBB v Commission* [1984] ECR 19, [1985] 1 CMLR 27, ECJ.

8 Commission IX Report on Competition Policy, point 116 (*English Football League*). See also *Distribution of Package Tours during the 1990 World Cup* [1992] OJ L326/31, [1994] 5 CMLR 253, paras 43-58.

In a case concerning the 1998 Football World Cup in France, the French organisers were held by the Commission to be an undertaking and to have infringed the competition rules: *1998 World Cup Finals* [2000] OJ L5/55, [2000] 4 CMLR 963.

9 The original distinction was between schemes that were voluntary and those that were compulsory, the former constituting undertakings and the latter not: Case C-244/94 *Fedération Française des Societes d'Assurance v Caisse Nationale Vieillesse Mutuelle Agricole* [1995] ECR I-4013, [1996] 4 CMLR 536, ECJ; Joined Cases C-159, 160/91 *Poucet v Assurances Générales de France (AGF)* [1993] ECR I-637, ECJ. However, the situation is now more complex. In Case C-67/96, *Albany International BV v Stichting Bedrijfspensioenfonds Textielindustrie* [1999] ECR I-5751, [2000] 4 CMLR 446, the ECJ held that even though the sectoral pension fund in that case was compulsory, was a fund supplementing a small statutory pension and was non-profit making, it was still an undertaking. Similarly, in Cases C-180 to 184/98, *Pavlov v Stichting Pensionenfonds Medische Specialisten* [2000] ECR I-6451, [2001] 4 CMLR 30, the ECJ held that even though a sectoral pension fund was compulsory, it was an undertaking, since it was carrying out an economic activity. The decisive criterion in this context appears to be whether there is an economic relation between the contribution and the level of benefits or if the benefits and contributions are based on the principle of solidarity.

For a useful discussion on this point, see Winterstein 'Nailing the Jellyfish: Social Security and Competition Law' (1999) 20 ECLR 324.

10 See Case C-309/99 *Wouters v Alegemene Raad van de Nederlandse Order van Advocaten* [2002] ECR I-1577, [2002] 4 CMLR 913, in which the ECJ held that members of the Bar who offered legal services for a fee were involved in an economic activity and were, therefore, undertakings under the competition provisions. See also the DG Comp website: http://europa.eu.int/comm/competition/liberalization/conference/libprofconference.html in respect of the Commission's attitude to the liberal professions. See also Mario Monti 'Competition in Professional Services: New Light and New Challenges', 21 March 2003 (DG Comp website: 'Speeches of the Commissioner').

11 See Case C-41/90 *Höfner and Elser v Macroton GmbH* [1991] ECR I-1979, [1993] 4 CMLR 306; Case C-55/96 *Job Centre* [1997] ECR I-7119, [1998] 4 CMLR 708 (an Italian public placement office with an exclusive right to procure employment of employees in Italy was found to be an undertaking).

12 Case C-35/96, *Italy v Commission* [1998] ECR I-3851, [1998] 5 CMLR 889.

13 *Spanish Courier Services* [1990] OJ L233/19, [1991] 4 CMLR 560.

14 *Film Purchases by German Television Stations* [1989] OJ L284/96, [1990] 4 CMLR 841; Case 155/73, *Italy v Sacchi* [1974] ECR 409, [1974] 2 CMLR 177. See also *UEFA's Broadcasting Regulations* [2001] OJ L171/12, [2001] 5 CMLR 654, para 47.

15 See eg Commission Decision (EEC) 82/174 [1982] 2 CMLR 159 (*Re Fire Insurance*).

[54]

The following entities have been held not to be undertakings and so not subject to the competition rules: an air traffic control organisation;[1] a compulsory social security scheme,[2] a private body with public functions of anti-pollution surveillance and control;[3] a municipal authority granting exclusive concessions in the funeral business;[4] an institute providing workplace and work-related sickness insurance;[5] organisations (including government ministries) which run a national health system;[6] a group of sickness funds[7] and a public authority when conducting activities 'in the exercise of official authority'.[8]

1 Case C-364/92 *SAT Fluggesellschaft v Eurocontrol* [1994] ECR I-43, [1994] 5 CMLR 208. Here it was held that the activities being pursued were in the public interest and despite the fact that fees were collected (in the form of route charges), it was found that the air traffic control organisation was not an undertaking (see also discussion below, para [61], note 2).

2 Joined Cases C-159, 160/91 *Poucet v Assurances Générales de France (AGF)* [1993] ECR I-637.

3 Case C-343/95 *Diego Cali v SEPG* [1997] ECR I-1547, [1997] 5 CMLR 484 (see also discussion below, para [61], note 3).

4 Case 30/87 *Corinne Bodson v Pompes Funèbres des Regions Libérées SA* [1988] ECR 2479, [1989] 4 CMLR 984. The competition rules were held not to be applicable here as the body was carrying out an administrative public function (see also discussion below, para [61], note 2).

5 Case C-218/00 *Cisal di Battistello Venanzio v Istituto Nazionale per L'Assicurazione Contra Gli Infortuni Sul Lavoro (INAIL)* [2002] ECR I-691, [2002] 4 CMLR 833.

6 Case T-319/99 *FENIN v Commission* [2003] ECR II-357, [2003] 5 CMLR 34. This is on appeal to the ECJ (Case C-205/03P). In this case, the CFI stressed that it was the supply activities of the entity in question (here the supply of medical services), not the purchasing activities (the purchase of medicines and medical equipment) which should be the focus of the investigation as to whether it constituted an undertaking.

7 Cases C-264, 306, 354 and 355/01 *AOK Bundesverband v Ichthyol-Gesellschaft Cordes, Hermani* [2004] ECR, [2004] 4 CMLR 1261. The bodies were found to be involved in running a social security system: 'In this regard they fulfil an exclusively social function, which is founded on the principle of national solidarity and is entirely non-profit-making.' (para 51). See also Case C-67/96 *Albany International BV v Stichting Bedrijfspensioenfonds Textielindustrie* [1999] ECR I-5751, [2000] 4 CMLR 446 and the discussion at para [53], note 9 above.

8 Case C-343/95 *Cali e Figli* [1997] ECR I-1547, [1997] 5 CMLR 484, paras 16-17.

[55]
The Commission has also addressed the questions as to whether individuals[1] and groups of undertakings[2] might be regarded as undertakings for the purposes of Article 81(1) of the EC Treaty. An individual acting as an employee or purchasing goods or services as an end user is not an undertaking.[3]

1 An individual may be an undertaking for the purposes of Article 81(1) insofar as he engages in commercial or economic activity in his own right; eg Commission Decision (EEC) 76/29 [1976] 1 CMLR D14 (*Re AOIP/Beyrard*); Commission Decision (EEC) 76/743 [1976] 2 CMLR D44 (*Re Reuter/BASF AG*); Commission Decision (EEC) 78/516 [1978] 3 CMLR 306 (*Re UNITEL*); Commission Decision (EEC) 79/86 [1979] 1 CMLR 511 (*Re Vaessen/Moris*). See also Commission XII Report on Competition Policy, p 74 (*RAI/UNITEL*); the issue of agency has also recieved consideration from the ECJ since the mere description of an individual as agent is insufficient to prevent the application of Article 81: Commission Decision (EEC) 72/403 *Re Pittsburgh Coining Europe* [1973] CMLR D2; Joined Cases 40-48, 50, 54-56, 111, 113-114/73 *Suiker Unie v Commission* [1975] ECR 1663, [1976] 1 CMLR 295, ECJ; Commission Decision (EC) 93/438 [1993] OJ L203/27, [1995] 5 CMLR495 (*CNSD*) (customs agents classified as undertakings); Commission Decision (EC) 95/188 [1995] OJ L122/37, [1995] 5 CMLR 468 (*Coapi*) (industrial property agents classified as undertakings).

2 On the question as to whether separate corporate bodies within a group are themselves separate undertakings or whether the group itself constitutes the relevant undertaking, the Commission and the ECJ have applied the 'group economic unit' doctrine: see Joined Cases 15 and 16/74 *Centrafarm BV v Sterling Drug Inc and Winthrop* [1974] ECR 1147, [1974] 2 CMLR 480, ECJ; Commission Decision (EEC) 85/74 [1985] 1 CMLR 481 (*Peroxygen*); and Commission Decision (EC) 94/601 [1994] OJ L243/1, [1994] 5 CMLR 547 (*Cartonboard*). The group economic unit doctrine does not preclude the possibility that a subsidiary alone violates the competition rules, but agreements between companies in the same group will not be considered as agreements for the purposes of Article 81. For further details see para [129].

3 Case C-22/98, *Jean Claude Becu* [1999] ECR I-56656, [2001] 4 CMLR 968 – though note that an ex-employee who carries on a business would be considered to be an undertaking: *Reuter/BASF* [1976] OJ L254/40, [1976] 2 CMLR D44.

[56]
That an undertaking may be situated outside the Community does not make any difference to its existence as an undertaking.[1]

1 See eg Case 6/72 *Europemballage Corpn and Continental Can Co Inc v Commission* [1973] ECR 215, [1973] CMLR 199, ECJ.

[57]
An entity may be an undertaking for the purposes of some of the activities it performs, but not for others. The notion of an undertaking is therefore a relative concept.[1]

1 Per Advocate-General Jacobs in Case C-475/99 *Ambulanz Glöckner v Landkreis Süswestplaz* [2001] ECR 8089, [2002] 4 CMLR 726, para 72.

[58]
Special consideration has to be given to changes, in the course of the matters under investigation, of corporate structure and/or legal form[1] and the way it affects the existence of such undertakings, especially in order to determine the addressee of any decision as well as the undertaking responsible for the payment of any fine imposed.[2] The Commission considers that an undertaking responsible for an infringement which has transferred to another undertaking its activities in the sector concerned

with the infringement is not absolved from responsibility provided it still exists as a separate entity. Therefore, liability to fines does not follow the business transferred, unless the business transferred is held to constitute a separate undertaking. Where, however, an undertaking which committed an infringement has ceased to have a separate legal personality (on the occasion of a merger for instance), the successor of the original undertaking is responsible for the fine, even if the successor did not continue the unlawful activities, provided there is an economic and functional continuity between both undertakings. Therefore where the undertaking at fault remains separately identifiable in economic terms (no liquidation of the assets or the operating plants, same management and employment, etc) responsibility for infringement of the law is not extinguished upon the merger and rests with the undertaking which takes over.[3]

1 Commission Decision (EEC) 88/84 [1988] 4 CMLR 513 (*ARG Ltd and Unipart Group*). See also See Joined Cases 40-48, 50,54-56, 111, 113, 114/73 *Coöperatieve vereniging Suiker Unie UA v Commission* [1975] ECR 1663.

2 Commission Decision (EEC) 89/190 [1989] OJ L74/1, [1990] 4 CMLR 345 (*PVC*); Commission Decision (EEC) 89/191 [1989] OJ L74/21, [1990] 4 CMLR 382 (*LdPE*); Commission Decision (EEC) 85/74 [1985] OJ L35/1, [1985] 1 CMLR 481 (*Peroxygen Products*); and Commission Decision (EEC) 86/398 [1988] 4 CMLR 347 (*Polypropylene*), on appeal Joined Cases T-1, 4,6-15/89 *Rhône-Poulenc SA v Commission* [1991] ECR II-867, CFI.

3 See Case T-6/89 *Enichem Anic SpA v Commission of the European Communities* [1991] ECR II-1623 at paras 228-243, upheld on appeal. In the case of *Anic*, the legal person responsible for the operation of the undertaking when the infringement was committed continued to exist until the adoption of the Commission's decision and was held answerable for the infringement, whereas this was not the case for Saga Petrokjemi following its merger with Statoil.

[59]

Associations of undertakings are considered subsequently.[1]

1 See paras [105]–[107].

2. Public undertakings

[60]

Articles 81 and 82 of the EC Treaty apply to public undertakings, whether or not the undertakings come within the provisions of Article 86,[1] provided, of course, that they carry on the required economic or commercial activities. Examples of such public bodies or statutory entities include the British Broadcasting Corporation[2] (and British Telecom,[3] when it was State owned).

1 As to undertakings within EC Treaty, Article 86, see Chapter 5.

2 See Commission Statement [1976] 1 CMLR D89 (*Re British Broadcasting Corpn*).

3 See Commission Decision (EEC) 82/861 [1983] 1 CMLR 457 (*Re British Telecommunications*), on appeal in Case 41/83 *Italy v Commission* [1985] ECR 878, [1985] 2 CMLR 368, ECJ. In Commission Decision (EEC) 82/742 [1983] 1 CMLR 619 (*Re Amersham International Ltd and Buchler GmbH Joint Venture*), the Commission appears to have considered that Amersham International Ltd was an undertaking when it was originally a government agency rather than a commercial enterprise. See also the position of INRA in Commission Decision (EEC) 78/823 [1978] 3 CMLR 434 (*Re Maize seed*), on appeal in Case 258/78 LC *Nungesser KG v Commission* [1982] ECR 2015, [1983] 1 CMLR 278, ECJ. In Commission Decision (EEC) 85/206 (*Re Aluminium Imports from Eastern Europe*) [1987] 3 CMLR 813, the Commission stated in the context of a State trading organisation that whatever its precise status may be under the domestic law of its country of origin, and even where it is given no separate status from the State, an undertaking

which engages in the activity of trading is to be regarded as an undertaking for the purposes of EC Treaty, Article 81. See also Commission, IX Report on Competition Policy, pp 114, 115.

3. Member States

[61]

It is clear that State-owned corporations may be undertakings for the purposes of the EC Treaty, Articles 81 and 82.[1] It appears however that a distinction must be drawn between the activities conducted by such public undertakings. When conducting commercial activities, the bodies may be undertakings for the purposes of Articles 81 and 82, but when exercising public law powers the Member State would not be regarded as an undertaking.[2] Also, privately owned undertakings may exercise public law powers entrusted to them that fall outside the scope of Article 82.[3]

1 See para [60] above.
2 Case 30/87 *Bodson v Pompes Funèbres des Regions Libérées SA* [1988] ECR 2479, [1989] 4 CMLR 984, ECJ, in which the Court held that Article 81 did not apply to licensing arrangements between French municipalities acting in their capacity as public authorities and undertakings entrusted with the provision of a public service. In Joined Cases C-159, 160/91 *Poucet and Others v Assurances Générales de France and Others* [1993] ECR I-637, ECJ, the Court held that the management of a social security scheme based on the principle of national solidarity is not an economic activity within the meaning of Articles 81 and 82. Similarly, the Court held that Articles 82 and 86 are not applicable to an international organisation which operates a system of air control on behalf of the Contracting States exercising public law powers; the fact that charges were collected by that organisation does not imply that its activity has an economic nature, since the charges represented merely the consideration for the obligatory use of the air control system; see also Case C-364/92 *SAT Fluggesellschaft mbH v Eurocontrol* [1994] ECR I-43, [1994] 5 CMLR 208, ECJ. On the other hand, see Case C-41/90 *Höfner and Elser v Macrotron GmbH* [1991] ECR I-1979, [1993] 4 CMLR 595, ECJ, in which the Court regarded the German employment office as an undertaking; and Case C-179/90 *Merci Convenzionali Porto di Genoa v Siderurgica Gabrielli SpA* [1991] ECR I-5889, [1994] 4 CMLR 422, ECJ, in which the Court reached the same conclusion in respect of the Genoa port authority.
3 In Case 118/85 *Commission v Italy* [1987] ECR 2599, ECJ, the Court drew the distinction between the situation where the State acts in the exercise of official authority and that where it carries economic activities of an industrial and commercial nature. It held that it is of no importance whether the State acts through a body forming part of the state administration or a body on which it has conferred special or exclusive rights. In Case C-343/95, *Diego Cali v SEPG* [1997] ECR I-1547, [1997] 5 CMLR 484, the Court held that Article 82 did not apply to anti-pollution surveillance by a private company for the port authorities, even when port users must pay dues to finance the surveillance.

[62]

In addition to Articles 81 and 82, which are addressed to undertakings, the activities of the Member States are controlled under Articles 10, 86 and 96 of the EC Treaty. Article 10 requires Member States to abstain from any measure which could jeopardise the attainment of the objectives of the Treaty, and may be used in combination with the competition rules.[1] Article 86 provides that public undertakings are subject to the competition rules, subject to a narrowly interpreted exception, whilst para 3 of the Article enables the Commission to tailor a remedy in the form of a directive or decision.[2] Articles 96 and 97 provide power to eliminate distortions to competition caused by national laws.

1 Case 13/77 *GB-INNO-BM v Vereningning van Kleihandelaars in Tabak* [1977] ECR 2115, [1978] ECR 283, ECJ.

2 EC Treaty, Article 86 is considered in Chapter 5. The control of State aids as provided for in EC Treaty, Articles 88 and 89, which are of importance, is considered in Vaughan, *Law of the European Union*, Section 29 ('State Aid', forthcoming).

[63]

Since Articles 81 and 82 are addressed to undertakings, activity by Member States to persuade undertakings to enter into an anti-competitive agreement is no defence.[1]

1 Case 123/83 *Bureau National lnterprofessionnel du Cognac (BNIC) v Clair* [1985] ECR 391, [1985] 2 CMLR 430, ECJ, in which the Court stated that the fixing by a private trade association of minimum prices for cognac and the eaux de vie from which it is distilled infringed Article 85, although the association was set up at the request of the minister, who supervised its activities by appointing the chairman and sending a nominee to its meetings.

[64]

National law may itself be contrary to the EC Treaty, which takes priority, if the national law requires or favours the adoption of agreements contrary to Article 81 or reinforces their effect by making them binding on outsiders. This may be through a combination of Articles 10 and 81 of the Treaty when national measures support agreements which are incompatible with the Treaty[1] or merely an application of Article 10 when no such agreements are involved because they have been made superfluous by the existence of the national measures.[2] In this latter situation, where no bilateral action on the part of undertakings is involved, there remains some uncertainty in the Court as to the instances when it will invoke Article 10 to prohibit national measures.[3] The practice of the Commission is more precise in condemning governmental measures that protect one set of traders from competition by others as prohibited by Article 10 on the ground that such measures undermine the effect of the competition rules, even if citizens are not required to do anything that, in itself, infringes Articles 81 or 82. In particular sectors of industry, such as air transport, which are given special treatment in the EC Treaty, the same approach will apply provided that the undertakings involved are subject to the competition rules in the treaty.[4]

1 Case 136/86 *Bureau National lnterprofessionnel du Cognac (BNIC) v Aubert* [1987] ECR 4789, [1988] 4 CMLR 331, ECJ, in which the Court ruled that a ministerial order extending the effect of an anti-competitive agreement to all traders in eaux de vie from which cognac is distilled was, itself, forbidden by a combination of the then Articles 3(f), 5(2) and 85 (the latter two now being the renumbered Articles 10 and 81) and could not be relied upon as a basis for acting against a trader exceeding a marketing quota. See also, Case 311/ 85 *Vereniging van Vlaamse Reisbureaus v Sociale Dienst van de Plaatselijke en Gewestelijke Overheidsdiensten* [1987] ECR 3801, [1989] 4 CMLR 213, ECJ, in which the Court ruled that a trade association should not bring a private prosecution against a travel agent for sharing its commission with a customer, when this was prohibited by a royal decree that gave legal effect to the rules of professional conduct that forbade such price competition. In this case the government had not actively encouraged the restrictive agreement; Case 66/ 86 *Ahmed Saeed Flugreisen and Others v Zentrale zur Bekampfung unlauteren Wettbewerb eV* [1989] ECR 803, [1990] 4 CMLR 102, ECJ, in which the Court ruled that (in their renumbered form) Articles 10 and 82 as confirmed by Article 86(1) forbid national authorities from facilitating or approving tariff agreements that violate Article 81(1). See generally Advocate General Darmon in Case C-185/ 91 *Reiff* [1993] ECR I-5801, [1995] 5 CMLR 145, ECJ, for the application of the principle laid down in Case 13/77, *GB-INNO-BM v Verenigning van Kleihandelaars in Tabak* [1977] ECR 2115, [1978] ECR 283, ECJ; Case C-153/93, *Germany v Delta Schiffarts- und Speditionsgesellschaft mbH* [1994] ECR I-2517, [1996] 4 CMLR 21, ECJ; Case C-96/94, *Centro Servizi Spediporto Srl v Spedizione Marittima del Golfo Srl* [1995] ECR I-2883,

[1996] 4 CMLR 613, ECJ; Joined Cases C-140, 141, 142/94, *DIP SpA and others v Commune di Bassano del Grappa* [1995] ECR II-3257, [1996] 4 CMLR 157, ECJ.

2 Case 229/83 *Leclerc v Au Blé Vert* [1985] ECR 1, [1985] 2 CMLR 286, ECJ, in which, despite the absence of an agreement that infringed Article 81, the Court contemplated the application of the principle behind Article 10 (that Member States are not to detract, by means of national legislation, from the full and uniform application of Community law or from the effectiveness of its implementing measures, nor may they introduce or maintain in force measures, even of a legislative nature, which may render ineffective the competition rules applicable to undertakings) to the Lang Law in France which required publishers and importers of books to fix minimum retail prices for the books they publish or import, and made it illegal for retail sales to be made at a discount exceeding 5 per cent. The case was an Article 234 (ex Article 177) preliminary reference from the Court of Appeal at Poitiers, to the effect whether national legislation which renders agreements contrary to Article 81(1) superfluous was itself contrary to Article 10 of the EC Treaty. On the basis that the Commission had not defined its position on national systems of resale price maintenance for books, and the cultural arguments in support of such systems, the Court concluded that as Community law stood at the time, Article 10 combined with Article 81 (and the former Article 3(f)) were not themselves sufficiently defined to prevent the enactment of such national legislation; Case 267/86 *Van Eycke v ASPA* [1988] ECR 4769, [1990] 4 CMLR 330, ECJ, in which the Court ruled that Article 10 forbids governments to delegate to certain associations of private firms decisions as to rates of interest presumably since such favoured associations might operate in their own interests.

3 Case 231/83 *Cullet v Leclerc* [1985] ECR 305, [1985] 2 CMLR 524, ECJ, in which the Court held that Article 81 was not deprived of its effect in the instance of a law by which the French government fixed the minimum prices for petrol. The law, in the absence of inter-brand competition, was obviously anti-competitive. This case can be distinguished from Case 229/83 *Leclerc v Au Blé Vert* [1985] ECR 1, [1985] 2 CMLR 286. Where the product is heterogeneous, as are books, so that it is impossible for the government to control the price without leaving some discretion to the producers, Article 81 may be infringed. Where the product is homogeneous, such as petrol, national measures may apply both effectively and directly. In the latter case, Article 81 may not be infringed. The distinction does not seem to be based on either the extent to which competition has been eliminated by the measures (for in *Cullet* and *Van Eycke*, in which Article 81 was not infringed, price competition was eliminated but in *Au Blé Vert* price and other competition between different titles remained despite the State intervention), or on the extent to which public authorities have been involved (for in the *BNIC* cases, the prices were fixed under the supervision of the government whereas in *Au Blé Vert* discretion was left to the producers). Advocate General Mancini in *Van Eycke* based the distinction on different grounds: namely Article 81 will be infringed by such measures if they extend beyond the subject matter left to the jurisdiction of the Member States by the Treaty and thereby jeopardise the objectives of the Treaty.

4 See Joined Cases 209-213/84 *Ministère Public v Asjes* (*Nouvelles Frontières*) [1986] ECR 1425, [1986] 3 CMLR 173, ECJ, in which the Court ruled that governments must not enforce or favour the adoption of agreements contrary to Article 81(1) nor reinforce their effects. The case concerned French legislation making it a criminal offence not to submit air transport tariffs to the competent minister for approval or to depart from tariffs which have been approved. A ticket agency was prosecuted for selling air tickets at prices below those approved. The Court was asked for a preliminary ruling as to the compatibility of the French law with Community law. There was, however, at the material time no regulation implementing the competition rules in the EEC Treaty to the air transport sector. The Court assimilated the position to that prior to the entry into force of the former Regulation 17/62, so that the agreements had provisional validity unless and until the effects of the agreement were found by either the Commission under Article 85 or the competent national authorities under Article 84 to infringe Article 81.

[65]
The paucity of Commission decisions made on the basis of the combination of Articles 10 and 81 is matched by the rare use of the more specific provisions of Articles 96 and 97.

[66]
Articles 96 and 97 provide for the elimination of distortions to competition created by national law. Under the former Article, where the Commission finds that a difference between the provisions laid down by law, regulation or administrative action in Member States is distorting the conditions of competition in the common market and that the resultant distortion needs to be eliminated, it is to consult the Member States concerned. Should such consultation fail to result in an agreement eliminating the distortion in question, the Council shall then, on a proposal from the Commission, issue the necessary directives. Both the Council and Commission are given power to take any other appropriate measure provided for in the Treaty.[1] Where there is concern that the adoption or amendment of a provision laid down by law, regulation or administrative action may cause distortion falling within the meaning in Article 96, the Member State in question shall consult the Commission which after such consultation shall recommend to the state concerned such measures as may be appropriate to avoid the distortion feared.[2] Should the state concerned fail to comply with the Commission's recommendation, other Member States are not required themselves to take measures to eliminate the resultant distortion under Article 96; similarly, if the Member State which has ignored the Commission's recommendation is the only one to suffer detrimentally from the distortion in question, Article 96 will not apply.[3]

1 EC Treaty, Article 96.
2 EC Treaty Article 97(1). In Case C-134/94 *Esso Espanola v Communidad Autonoma de Canarias* [1995] ECR I-4223, [1996] 5 CMLR 154, ECJ, EC Treaty, Article 97(1) was said not to be directly effective (confirming Case 6/64 *Costa v ENEL* [1964] ECR 585, [1964] CMLR 425, ECJ).
3 EC Treaty, Article 97(2).

[67]
The Commission appears to give a very restrictive interpretation to these provisions. There must be cases of specific distortion before Article 96 may be invoked. By specific distortion the Commission appears to intend a situation in which a number of companies, or an industrial sector is at an advantage or disadvantage compared with other economic operators in the same country and there must be no comparable differences in treatment in other Member States.[1]

1 See the Commission's answer to Parliamentary question 360/80 ([1980] OJ C283/1). Mr Muntingh was concerned that German producers of potash were required to take expensive measures to minimise the pollution of rivers, which the French producers were not required to take. The Commission answered to the effect set out in the text, adding more specifically that as the German law on water resources applied not only to the potash industry but to industry as a whole and even to public bodies, there was no specific distortion in that case.

[68]
The Commission is tackling many such distortions through harmonisation provisions under Article 95 where possible. When there is no national law to be harmonised, however, the Commission may turn to Articles 96 and 97.

[69]
Member States may be involved in disputes relating to EC law in several other ways in addition to the question of the incompatibility of national legislation with competition law. There are four defences which raise the question either of State compulsion as the reason for the allegedly anti-competitive behaviour of the undertaking in question or of a relationship with the State which immunises the undertaking from the competition rules:

(a) Sovereign immunity: The Court of Justice has not supported the application of sovereign immunity as a defence to an action under Articles 81 or 82. The Commission however has recognised its existence as a defence in a competition law context, although it has not supported its application in any particular case.[1]

(b) Article 86(2): This Article provides that undertakings entrusted with the operation of services of general economic interest or having the character of a revenue-producing monopoly shall be subject to the rules contained in the EC Treaty, in particular the rules on competition insofar as the application of such rules does not obstruct the performance, in law or in fact, of the particular tasks assigned to them. The development of trade must not be affected to such an extent as would be contrary to the interests of the Community.

(c) State regulation of the market: The Court of Justice has accepted that where the relevant product and geographical market is so highly regulated that there was no latitude for competition, an undertaking adopting anti-competitive behaviour may not be in breach of Articles 81 or 82.[2] The plea will only succeed in extreme circumstances in which, in both fact and law, there is no competition capable of being affected.[3]

(d) Where the undertaking has been required to operate in an anti-competitive manner by State compulsion: The defence of State compulsion has not been rejected on principle by either the Commission or the court, although it has never succeeded.[4] The defence has been raised on the basis that the undertaking in question was required to act as it did by reason of the intervention of a public or quasi-public law body; alternatively the compulsion in question was a belief in the need to comply with the government's industrial or foreign policy. For the defence to succeed, it seems that the State must have made the conduct in question compulsory, with no opportunity for individual choice, and that such compulsion was based in laws.[5]

1 See Commission Decision (EEC) 85/206 [1985] OJ L92/1, [1987] 3 CMLR 813 (*Aluminium Products*), in which various Eastern European aluminium producers argued that Article 81 was inapplicable to them as, under socialist law, they had no separate status from the State. The Commission rejected the argument on the basis that they were carrying on commercial activities

to which the defence of sovereign immunity would never apply: claims of sovereign immunity should be confined to acts which are those of government and not of trade.
2 See Joined Cases 40-48, 50, 54-56, 111, 113-114/73 *Suiker Unie v Commission* [1975] ECR 1663, [1976] 1 CMLR 295, ECJ, in which in Italy the sugar industry was highly regulated in order that supply and demand be kept in balance so that for instance suppliers and customers were not allowed to negotiate with one another. The Court accepted that there was no competition capable of being distorted.
3 See Joined Cases 240-242, 261-262, 268-269/82 *Stichting Sigarettenindustrie and Others v Commission* [1985] ECR 3831, [1987] 3 CMLR 661, ECJ, which involved the imposition of a high ad valorem excise duty on cigarettes imposed by the Dutch authorities. To ensure that the correct duty had been paid cigarette packets were stamped stating the retail price, which was the price which had to be charged at retail level. This was combined with Dutch price controls which imposed maximum prices for goods. The Commission had accused many firms of price fixing under Article 81. The firms appealed to the Court of Justice arguing that the effect of the two regimes imposed by the Dutch authorities was to remove the possibility of price competition on the market. The Court rejected the arguments: the legislative regime did not prevent manufacturers setting different prices, even though the retail price was fixed, and it was unlikely that producers would have identical costs. Further, although the band in which prices could be charged was narrow this did not justify eliminating the risk of competition by horizontal price agreements. See also Case 260/82 *Nederlandse Sigarenwinkeliers Organisatie v Commission* [1985] ECR 3801, [1988] 4 CMLR 753, ECJ.
4 See Commission Decision (EEC) 76/684 [1976] OJ L231/24 (*Pabst and Richarz/BNIA*); Commission Decision (EEC) 82/896 [1982] OJ L379/1 (*AROW/BNIC*); Commission Decision (EEC) 85/202 [1985] OJ L85/1, [1985] 3 CMLR 474 (*Re Wood Pulp*), on appeal Joined Cases 89, 104, 114, 116, 117, 125-129/85 *Ahlström Oy v Commission* [1988] ECR 5193, [1988] 4 CMLR 901, ECJ; Commission Decision (EEC) 87/3 [1987] OJ L5/13 (*ENI/Montedison*); Commission Decision (EEC) 85/206 [1985] OJ L92/1, [1987] 3 CMLR 813 (*Aluminium Products*); Case 174/84 *Bulk Oil (Zug) AG v Sun International Ltd (No 2)* [1986] ECR 559, [1986] 2 CMLR 732, ECJ.
5 See in particular Commission Decision (EEC) 85/206 [1985] OJ L92/1, [1987] 3 CMLR 813 (*Aluminium Products*).

C. TEMPORAL APPLICATION

1. Time limits generally

[70]

There is no express provision in the EC Treaty setting out the time within which the Commission is required to act in enforcing the competition rules[1] and similarly no time bar precluding the Commission from taking a decision. The absence of such express limits may prove problematic where the Commission is empowered to make corrective or remedial orders.[2] It would be a matter for the Court of Justice to determine whether delay could preclude a particular decision, and this would presumably depend upon an evaluation of the laws of the various Member States.[3] In the enforcement of the rules of competition in national courts, particularly under the new regime,[4] national limitation periods will apply.[5]

1 Contrast the situation under the old ECSC Treaty, Article 35: see Joined Cases 109, 114/75 *National Carbonising Co Ltd v Commission* [1977] ECR 381, ECJ. Until recently it was the case that inaction by the Commission after it knew of anti-competitive conduct could preclude the Commission taking a decision and delay therefore would have an effect upon fines (even apart from the question of limitation): see CS Kerse and N Khan, *EEC Anti-Trust Procedure* (5th edn, 2005), p 317. However, the CFI recently ruled that in a system where complete limitation rules are in place (such as that in place by Regulation 2988/74 in force at the time of the judgment or currently Regulation 1/2003), there is no room for consideration of the Commission's duty to to exercise its power to impose fines within a reasonable period. See Case T-213/00 *CMA CGM v*

Commission [2003] ECR II-913, at paras 317-326. A voluntary reduction of the amount of the fine of €100,000 granted by the Commission was upheld by the CFI in the exercise of the Commission's discretion, but the Commission was not required to proceed to such a reduction. See also CS Kerse and N Khan, *EC Antitrust Procedure* (5th edn, 2005) at 7-057.

2 eg, interventions after the event by the Commission under Article 82 of the Treaty; in merger cases; and breaking up of joint ventures, under Article 81 of the Treaty. See, however, Articles 25 and 26 of Regulation 1/2003 imposing time limits on the Commission's power to impose and enforce penalties for contraventions of the competition rules – as to which, see below para [71].

3 See eg Case 51/69 *Farbenfabriken Bayer AG v Commission* [1972] ECR 745, ECJ.

4 Council Regulation (EC) 1/2003 [2004] OJ L1/1, applicable as of 1 May 2004.

5 See eg Case 33/76 *Rewe-Zentralfinanz v Landwirtschaftskammer für Saarland* [1976] ECR 1989, [1977] 1 CMLR 533, ECJ; Case 45/76 *Comet BV v Produktschap voor Siergewassen* [1976] ECR 2043, [1977] 1 CMLR 533, ECJ; Case 68/79 *Hans Just I/S v Danish Ministry for Fiscal Affairs* [1980] ECR 501, [1981] 2 CMLR 714, ECJ.

[71]

Delay in making a complaint to the Commission may be a factor in influencing the Commission to decline to take action[1] and this is certainly a factor in its determination whether to grant or refuse interim measures.

1 Council Regulation (EC) 1/2003 [2003] OJ L1/1, Article 7.

2. Limitation periods

[72]

The time limits in the application of the power of the Commission to impose fines or penalties or to enforce the collection of those fines or penalties are prescribed by regulation. The modernisation regulation[1] has seen the introduction of a number of time limits not present under the previous regime.[2] Until 30 April 2004, Regulation (EEC) 2988/74[3] governed limitation periods in proceedings and the enforcement of sanctions under, *inter alia*, the competition rules. As of 1 May 2004, that regulation is no longer to apply to the enforcement of the competition rules.[4]

1 Council Regulation (EC) 1/2003 [2003] OJ L1/1.

2 Council Regulation (EEC) 17/62 [1962] OJ Spec Ed 87.

3 [1974] OJ L319/1.

4 As set out in Council Regulation (EC) 1/2003 [2003] OJ L1/1, Article 37. Prior to Council Regulation (EEC) 2988/74, no limitation period was provided by Community law; eg Case 45/69 *Boehringer Mannheim GmbH v Commission* [1970] ECR 769, ECJ. But the requirement of legal certainty prevents the Commission from indefinitely delaying the exercise of its power to impose fines: Case 48/69 *ICI v Commission* [1972] ECR 619, [1972] CMLR 557, ECJ. Many of the issues concerning the proper interpretation of Council Regulation (EEC) 2988/74 were raised in Case T-328/94 *ICI v Commission* (*PVC II*) (at present before the CFI, see [1994] OJ C380/18).

[73]

Under the new regime, no fines[1] or periodic penalties[2] may be imposed[3] after three years in the case of infringements of provisions concerning requests for information or the conduct of inspections or after five years in the case of all other infringements.[4] Time begins to run on the day in which the infringement is committed, but, in the case of continuing or repeated infringements,[5] time begins to run on the day when the infringement ceases.[6] Any action by the Commission or by the competition authority of a Member State for the purpose of the investigation or proceedings in respect of an infringement shall interrupt the limitation period for the imposition of fines or periodic penalty payments with effect from the date of notification of that interruption to at least one of the undertakings involved in the infringement.[7] Each interruption starts time running afresh, but the maximum a limitation period can be extended by this route is to a period equal to twice the limitation period otherwise applicable.[8] That period can then be extended and the limitation period is suspended for so long as a decision of the Commission is the subject of proceedings pending before the Court of Justice.[9] With regard to the enforcement of fines or penalties, there is a limitation period of five years,[10] and time begins to run on the day on which the decision becomes final.[11] The limitation period can again be interrupted (by notification of a decision varying the original amount of the fine or periodic penalty payment or refusing an application for a variation or by any action of the Commission or of a Member State, acting at the request of the Commission, designed to enforced payment of the fine or periodic penalty payment)[12] and, again, each interruption starts time afresh.[13] The limitation period for the enforcement of penalties is suspended so long as time to pay is allowed or enforcement of payment is suspended pursuant to a decision of the ECJ.[14] The fact that the Commission cannot impose fines after expiration of the limitation periods does not mean that there can be no finding of infringement. Article 7(1) of the Modernisation Regulation expressly empowers the Commission to adopt decisions in relation to past infringements, if it has a legitimate interest in doing so. The mere declaration of the infringement would appear to be sufficient legitimate interest.[15]

1 The power to impose fines derives from Council Regulation (EC) 1/2003 [2003] OJ L1/1, Article 23.

2 The power to impose periodic penalties derives from Council Regulation (EC) 1/2003 [2003] OJ L1/1, Article 24.

3 This does not, however, prevent a decision being taken which does not impose a fine or a periodic penalty, or indeed a decision being taken which requires action by the undertaking in question.

4 Regulation 1/2003, Article 25(1).

5 For examples of continuing infringements, see Commission Decision (EEC) 77/129 [1977] 1 CMLRD44 (*Re Theal/ Watts*); Commission Decision (EEC) 82/897 [1983] 1 CMLR 412 (*Re Toltecs and Dorcet Trade Marks*); Commission Decision (EEC) 83/546 [1984] 1 CMLR 694 (*Re Cast Iron and Steel Rolls*).

6 Council Regulation (EEC) 2988/74, Article 1(2) (though note its repeal by Article 37 of Regulation 1/2003). The determination of the time when the infringement ceases may give rise to difficult questions of facts: eg Commission Decision (EEC) 84/405 [1985] 2 CMLR 108 (*Zinc Producer Group*); Commission Decision (EEC) 86/ 398 [1988] 4 CMLR 347 (*Polypropylene*). See also Commission Decision (EEC) 89/515 [1991] 4 CMLR 13 (*Re Welded Steel Mesh*).

7 Regulation 1/2003, Article 25(3).

8 Ibid, Article 25(5).

9 Ibid, Article 25(5) and (6).

10 Ibid, Article 26(1).

11 Ibid, Article 26(2).

12 Ibid, Article 26(3).

13 Ibid, Article 26(4).

14 Ibid, Article 26(5).

15 See the recent Commission decision in the choline chloride cartel of 9 December 2004 in case COMP/E-2/37.533. Although the American producers ceased their participation in the cartel more than five years before the first investigative action by the Commission and no fines could be imposed on them, the Commission decision was also addressed to them and declared their past infringement.

D. SECTORAL APPLICATION

[74]
The competition rules apply to all areas of economic activity. Some sectors have, however, been accorded special treatment.

1. Coal and steel

[75]
Until recently, the coal and steel industries (and the application of competition rules to them) were covered by the ECSC Treaty.[1] The ECSC Treaty expired on 23 July 2002. The EC Treaty now encompasses the coal and steel industries (it still expressly provides that its provisions do not affect the provisions of the ECSC Treaty[2]). The Commission has made clear that it does not intend to commence proceedings under the EC Treaty in respect of agreements which were authorised under the ECSC regime unless they were obviously not entitled to be exempted 'owing to substantial factual or legal developments'.[3] One effect of the expiry of the ECSC Treaty is that national competition authorities will now, for the first, time, have jurisdiction to apply competition rules in the coal and steel sectors.[4]

1 In particular, ECSC Treaty, Articles 65–67.
2 EC Treaty, Article 305(1).
3 Communication from the Commission concerning certain aspects of the treatment of competition cases resulting from the expiry of the ECSC Treaty ([2002] OJ C152/5), para 29.
4 Ibid, paras 4–5.

2. Nuclear energy

[76]
The EC Treaty provides that the provisions of that Treaty are not to derogate from the provisions of the Euratom Treaty.[1] Thus, certain agreements which relate to nuclear energy fall to be considered under the EC Treaty inasmuch as that consideration does not involve any derogation from the Euratom Treaty.[2] The Commission has shown an inclination to be lenient with cooperation agreements in the nuclear industry.[3]

1 EC Treaty, Article 305(2). See also Section 16 ('Agriculture').
2 See Commission Decision (EEC) 76/248 [1976] 2 CMLR Dl (*Re United Reprocessors GmbH*); Commission Decision (EEC) 76/249 [1976] 2 CMLR D15 (*Re KEWA*); Commission Decision (EEC) 82/742 [1983] 1 CMLR 619 (*Re Amersham International Ltd and Buchler GmbH Joint Venture*).
3 See, for example, Commission Decision (EEC) 76/248 [1976] 2 CMLR Dl (*Re United Reprocessors GmbH*); *GEC/Weir* [1977] OJ L327/26, [1978] 1 CMLR D42; *Scottish Nuclear, Nuclear Energy Agreement* [1991] OJ L178/31.

3. Agriculture[1]

[77]
The EC Treaty provides[2] that the rules of competition are to apply to production of or trade in agricultural products only to the extent determined by the Council.[3] The Council is granted a wide discretion for establishing a system of competition rules for the agricultural sector, the objectives[4] of the common agricultural policy[5] being the only limits it has to take into account. The Treaty thus makes it clear that with regard to agricultural products, priority must be given to the common agricultural policy and

to the objectives of that policy.[6] It should be noted that the competition provisions of the EEA agreement do not, however, apply to agricultural products, with the exception of certain limited processed agricultural goods.[7]

1 As to the operation of the competition rules in the agriculture sector generally, see Kapteyn and VerLoren van Themaat, *Introduction to the Law of the European Communities* (Kluwer Law International, 3rd edn, 1998), pp 1128 to 1171; Usher, *EC Agricultural Law* (OUP, 2nd edn, 2001); Cardwell, *The European Model of Agriculture* (OUP, 2003).
2 EC Treaty, Article 36. See further T Ottervanger on anti-trust and agriculture in Fordham Corporate Law Institute (1989), p 203.
3 ie, within the framework of EC Treaty, Article 37(2) and (3) and in accordance with the procedure there laid down.
4 As to these objectives, see ibid, Article 33.
5 Ibid, Article 36.
6 Case 139/79 *Maizena GmbH v Council* [1980] ECR 3393 at 3421, ECJ. See also *French Beef* ([2003] OJ L209/12). See, for the Commission's approach, Mario Monti 'The relationship between CAP and competition policy. Does EU competition law apply to agriculture?', COGECA Conference Helsinki Fair Trade, 13 November 2003: http://europa.eu.int/comm/competition/speeches/index_speeches_by_the_commissioner.html.
7 See Article 8(3) of the EEA Agreement. Fisheries are also excluded.

[78]

In 1962, the Council adopted Regulation 26, which applies the rules of competition[1] to, as well as certain provisions[2] relating to aids granted for,[3] production of or trade in agricultural products listed in Annex II of the Treaty. Two exceptions are however provided, and Article 2(1) of Regulation 26 exempts from the provisions of Article 81(1) to the Treaty agreements, decisions and concerted practices which form an integral part of a national market organisation or are necessary for the attainment of the objectives of the common agricultural policy set out in Article 33 of the Treaty.[4] Such exceptions are to be strictly construed.[5] Consequently, Article 82, which is not expressly mentioned, applies fully to these agreements. There is no derogation in respect of Article 82. Similarly agreements relating to products that do not appear in Annex II of the Treaty, are not exempted from the provisions of Article 81(1) of the Treaty, even if those products are substances ancillary to the production of other products which themselves come under that Annex.[6] Article 2 of Regulation 26 does not apply if the Commission finds that competition is excluded or that the objectives of Article 33 of the Treaty are jeopardised.[7]

1 Council Regulation (EEC) 26/62, Article 1, applies EC Treaty, Articles 81–86, and provisions implementing those Articles, to all agreements, decisions and practices referred to in Articles 81(1) and 82, which relate to the production of or trade in the products listed in Annex II. This is subject to Article 2 thereof.
2 ie EC Treaty, Article 88(1) and the first sentence of Article 88(3).
3 Council Regulation (EEC) 26/62, Article 4.
4 Council Regulation (EEC) 26/62, Article 2(1) expressly refers to decisions of farmers, farmers' associations and associations of such associations belonging to a single Member State which concern the production or sale of agricultural products or the use of joint facilities for the storage, treatment or processing of agricultural products and under which there is no obligation to charge identical prices. See Commission Decision (EEC) 85/76 [1985] OJ L35/35, [1985] 3 CMLR 101 (*Re Milchforderungsfonds*).
5 See Cases T-70/92 and T-71/92 *Florimex v Commission* [1997] ECR II-697, [1997] 5 CMLR 796, upheld on appeal inCase C-265/97P *VBA and Florimex v Commission* [2000] ECR I-2061, [2001] 5 CMLR 1343. See also Case C-266/97P *VBA and Florimex v Commission* [2000] ECR I-2135.

6 Case 61/80 *Coöperatieve Stremsel- en Kleurselfabriek v Commission* [1981] ECR 851, [1982] 1 CMLR 240, ECJ (*rennet and cheese*); Case 123/83 *Bureau National Interprofessionnel du Cognac (BNIC) v Clair* [1985] ECR 391, [1985] 2 CMLR 430, ECJ; Case 77/83 *CILFIT Srl v Ministero della Sanità* [1984] ECR 1257, ECJ; Case 136/86 *Bureau National Interprofessionnel du Cognac (BNIC) v* Aubert [1987] ECR 4789, [1988] 4 CMLR 331, ECJ. See also Commission Decision (EEC) 88/587 ([1988] OJ L316/43) (*Hudson Bay Dansk Pelsdyravlerforening*) and Case T-61/89 *Dansk Pelsdyrovlerforening v Commission* [1992] ECR II-1931, CFI; and, Case C-250/92, *Gøttrup-Klim Grovvareforening and Others v Dansk Landbrugs Grovvareselskab Amba* [1994] ECR I-5641, [1996] 4 CMLR 191, ECJ. The Commission has acknowleged that seeds come within Annex II (though it then held that neither of the Regulation 26/62 derogations was applicable): *Sicasov* ([1999] OJ L14/27) [1999] 4 CMLR 192, paras 65-69.

7 See Commission Decision (EEC) 85/76 [1985] OJ L35/35, [1985] 3 CMLR 101 (*Re Milchförderungsfonds*). See also Case 71/74 *Nederlandse Vereniging voor Fruit en Groentenimporthandel Frubo v Commission* [1975] ECR 563, [1975] 2 CMLR 123, ECJ, which emphasises that all the objectives must be achieved.

[79]

The Commission and, on appeal, the European Courts have sole jurisdiction to determine which agreements, decisions and practices fulfil the conditions of the exemptions under Article 2(1) of Regulation 26.[1] For this purpose, the Commission must consult with the Member States and hear the enterprises concerned and any other natural or legal person it considers appropriate. This evaluation shall be undertaken by the Commission either on its own initiative or at the request of a competent authority of a Member State or of an interested undertaking or association of undertakings.[2] Decisions shall be published.[3] The Commission, when evaluating agreements concerning agricultural products and their effect on competition, may take into account considerations such as the specific needs of agricultural co-operation.[4] The market situation in agriculture may be relevant on the question of any fines.[5] Under the old regime under Regulation 17/62, this administrative procedure could be combined with that of Regulation 17/62 and a single decision could reject the application of the exception of Article 2(1) of Regulation 26 and simultaneously determine the existence of an infringement of Article 81(1) of the Treaty in which case there was no need to comply with the requirements of Article 2(2) of Regulation 26.[6] Under Regulation 1/2003, the procedure should be the same. Where such an issue arises before a national court, the national court should probably stay proceedings until the Commission has reached a decision under Regulation 26. If the national court is satisfied that clearly an exemption would not be granted by the Commission, it can apply Article 81(1).[7]

1 Council Regulation (EEC) 26/62, Article 2(2). See Case 71/74 *Nederlandse Verenigning voor Fruit en groentenimporthandel Frubo v Commission* [1975] ECR 563, [1975] 2 CMLR 123, ECJ, and Case 177/78 *Pigs and Bacon Commission v McCarren & Co Ltd* [1979] ECR 2161 at 2215, [1979] 3 CMLR 389, ECJ; Case C-3l9/93 *Dijkstra v Friesland Coöperatie* [1995] ECR 1-4471, [1996] 5 CMLR 178, ECJ. However, in cases where Regulation 26, Article 1, applies, national courts have jurisdiction: see eg *Garden Cottage Foods Ltd v Milk Marketing Board* [1984] AC 130, [1983] 2 All ER 770, [1983] 3 CMLR 43, HL. See also Commission Decision (EEC) 85/76 [1985] OJ L35/35, [1985] 3 CMLR 101 (*Re Milchfarderungsfonds*).

2 Council Regulation (EEC) 26/62, Article 2(2). However, there is no need to consult the Member States if there is no doubt that Article 2(1) exceptions cannot apply: Case 71/74 *Nederlandse Vereniging voor Fruit en Groentenimporthandel 'Frubo' v Commission* [1975] ECR 563, [1975] 2 CMLR 123, ECJ.

3 Ibid, Articles 2(2) and (4).

4 Case 61/80 *Coöperatieve Stremsel- en Kleurselfabriek v Commission* [1981] ECR 851, [1982] 1 CMLR 240, ECJ.

5 Joined Cases 40-48, 50, 54-56, 111, 113-114/73 *Suiker Unie v Commission* [1975] ECR 1663, [1976] 1 CMLR 295, ECJ.

6 See Case 71/74 *Nederlandse Vereniging voor Fruit en Groentenimporthandel 'Frubo' v Commission* [1975] ECR 563 at 579-80, [1975] 2 CMLR 123, ECJ.

7 As the national court did in Commission Decision (EEC) 88/491 [1988] OJ L262/27 (*Bloemenveilingen Aalsmeer*).

[80]

The Commission and the Court of Justice have applied the rules of competition to agreements concerning agricultural products in many cases and although exemptions under Article 2(1) of Regulation 26 have often been sought, the Commission has seldom granted them. Where exemptions have been sought for practices which 'form an integral part of a national market' as defined by the Court of Justice,[1] the Commission has only ever rendered one positive decision.[2] In cases where the necessity of the practices for the attainment of the objectives of the common agricultural policy has been relied on, no exemptions were granted.[3]

1 Case 48/74 *Charmasson v Minister of Economic Affairs and Finance (Paris)* [1974] ECR 1383, [1975] 2 CMLR 208, ECJ.

2 For a positive decision see Commission Decision (EEC) 88/109 [1988] OJ L59/25, [1988] 4 CMLR 790 (*Re new potatoes*). For a negative decision see Commission Decision (EEC) 78/66 [1978] OJ L111/23, [1978] 1 CMLR D66 (*Re Cauliflowers*); Commission Decision (EEC) 80/183 [1980] OJ L39/64, [1980] 2 CMLR559 (*Re Tate & Lyle Refineries Ltd and Manbre Sugars Ltd (Cane sugar)*); Commission Decision (EEC) 85/76 [1985] OJ L35/35, [1985] 3 CMLR 101 (*Re Milchfarderungsfonds*). See also Case 231/78 *Commission v United Kingdom* [1979] ECR 1447, [1979] 2 CMLR 427 and Case 232/78 *Commission v France* [1979] ECR 2729, [1980] 1 CMLR 418. The Commission takes the view that where national market organisations have been replaced by a common organisation, an agreement between undertakings in that sector cannot be covered by this exception: Commission Decision (EEC) 86/596 [1986] OJ L348/50 (*Meldoc*).

3 See eg Joined Cases 40-48, 50,54-56, 111, 113-114/73 *Suiker Unie v Commission* [1975] ECR 1663, [1976] 1 CMLR 295, ECJ; Case 71/74 *Nederlandse Verenigning voor Fruit en Groentenimporthandel Frubo v Commission* [1975] ECR 563, [1975] 2 CMLR 123, ECJ; Commission Decision (EEC) 75/77 [1975] OJ L29/26, [1975] 1 CMLR D83 (*Re French and Taiwanese Mushroom Packers*). But see Commission Decision (EEC) 80/183 ([1980] OJ L39/64) (*Cane Sugar Supply Agreements*) where an exemption would have been granted if the agreement had affected trade in the common market. It was decided in Case 71/74 *Nederlandse Verenigning voor Fruit en Groentenimporthandel 'Frubo' v Commission* [1975] ECR 563, [1975] 2 CMLR 123 that it is not sufficient to show that the restrictive practice is necessary for the attainment of merely one of the objectives of the common agricultural policy.

[81]

Finally, whereas the Commission has considered in previous years that practices of farmers, farmers' associations and associations of such associations as stated in the second sentence of Article 2(1) of Regulation 26/62 were an exemption per se to the application of Article 81(1) of the Treaty,[1] the Commission has moved to a position that such exemption will only apply provided that one or both of the two exceptions provided for by the first sentence of Article 2(1) of Regulation 26/62 are satisfied.[2] Thus, an agreement concerning farmers and non-farmers cannot benefit from this exemption.[3] Excessively long agreements would not benefit from exemptions either.[4] To date the Commission has paid little attention to the particular characteristics of an agricultural cooperative.[5]

1 Commission Decision (EEC) 74/433 [1974] OJ L237/16 (*Frubo*).
2 Commission Decision (EEC) 85/76 [1985] OJ L35/35, [1985] 3 CMLR 101 (*Re Milch forderungsfonds*). The position of the Commission is difficult to accept and a ruling of the ECJ would have to be awaited for this question to be clarified: Commision Decision (EEC) 86/596 [1986] OJ L348/50 (*Meldoc*); Commission Decision (EEC) 88/491 [1988] OJ L262/27 (*Bloemenveilingen Aalsmeer*). See now Case C-319/93 *Dijkstra v Friesland Cooperatie* [1995] ECR I-4471, [1996] 5 CMLR 178, ECJ, where the ECJ considered the interrelationship of the first and second sentences of Regulation 26, Article 2.
3 Commission Decision (EEC) 78/66 [1978] OJ L1/23, [1978] 1 CMLR D66 (*Re Cauliflowers*).
4 Case C-399/93 *HG Oude Luttikhuis and Others v Verenigde Coöperatieve Melkindustrie Coberco BA* [1995] ECR I-4663, [1996] 5 CMLR 178, ECJ.
5 See Case 61/80 *Cooperatieve Stremsel- en Kleurselfabriek v Commission* [1981] ECR 851, [1982] 1 CMLR 240, where the Court did not have to take into account their particular characteristics (as argued for by the French Government in the French Court). See also Commission Decision (EEC) 88/587 [1988] OJ L316/43 (*Hudson Bay Dansk Pelsdyrovlerforening*) and Case T-61/89 *Dansk Pelsdyravlerforening v Commission* [1992] ECR II-1931, CFI.

4. Transport

[82]
The rules of competition apply to transport,[1] in respect of which sector the EC Treaty contains specific provisions.[2] Regulation 1017/68[3] applies the competition rules to transport by road, rail and inland waterways, Regulation 4056/86[4] applies to the maritime transport sector and Regulation 3975/87[5] applies to air transport. These Regulations all contained different procedural provisions. Procedural amendments brought about by the modernisation process which have relevance to the transport sector are set out in the amendment provisions of Regulation 1/2003.[6] These have the effect of making all transport sectors subject to the procedural requirements of Regulation 1/2003. There have been a number of findings of infringement in maritime transport under Regulation 4056/86,[7] but there are also instances of the Commission granting an exemption.[8] Significant reform of the block exemptions in the shipping sector is envisaged by the Commission. These proposals are summarised in a Commission Final Report on 'The Application of the Competition Rules to Liner Shipping'.[9]

1 Case 156/77 *Commission v Belgium* [1978] ECR 1881, ECJ. For the rules of competition in the transport sector, see Vaughan, *Law of the European Union,* Section 18 ('Transport', forthcoming).
2 Articles 70 to 80 EC.
3 [1968] OJ Spec Ed 302.
4 [1986] OJ L378/4; [1989] 4 CMLR 461. Note the Commission White Paper on a review of Regulation 4056/86 (COMP/2003/18). This proposes that the liner conference block exemption be repealed. See also Commission Regulation (EC) 870/95 on the application of Article 81(3) to certain categories of agreements, decisions and concerted practices between shipping companies ([1995] OJ L89/7), which came into force on 22 April 1995.
5 Regulation 3975/87 [1987] OJ L374/9, [1988] 4 CMLR 234, as amended by Regulation 2344/90 [1990] OJ L217/15.
6 Council Regulation (EC) 1/2003 [2003] OJ L1/1, [2003] 4 CMLR 551, Articles 36–43, in particular Article 36 amending Regulation (EEC) 1017/68, Article 38, amending the application of the competition rules to the maritime sector as set down in Regulation (EEC) 4056/86, and Article 39, amending Regulation 3975/87
7 *Trans-Atlantic Conference Agreement* [1999] OJ L95/1, [1999] 4 CMLR 1415 and on appeal to the CFI, Case T-191/99 *Atlantic Container Line v Commission* [2001] ECR II-3677. See also *Far East Trade and Tariff and Surcharges Agreement* [2000] OJ L268/1; *Greek Ferries* [1999] OJ L109/24,

[1999] 5 CMLR 47 and on appeal to the CFI, Cases T-56/99 etc *Marlines v Commission* [2003] ECR 0000.
8 See *P&O Stena Line* [1999] OJ L163/61, [1999] 5 CMLR 682, where the Commission granted an exemption for three years (extended in 2001 for six years (Commission XXXI Report on Competition Policy 2001, point 160)) to a joint venture providing cross-Channel ferry services.
9 Report of 26 October 2005 (http://europa.eu.int/comm/competition/antitrust/others/maritime/shipping_report_26102005.pdf). See especially p IX-220, regarding the impact of the repeal of the liner block exemption and the conclusion that repeal would lead to a decline in total transport prices for maritime container transport and an increase in innovation in the sector.

5. Telecommunications and broadcasting

[83]
The rules of competition also apply to telecommunications and broadcasting.[1]

1 For telecommunications and broadcasting, generally, and the rules of competition which apply to those sectors see Vaughan, *Law of the European Union,* Section 14 ('Electronic Communications').

6. Security and defence products

[84]
Under the EC Treaty, a Member State may take such measures as it considers necessary for the protection of the essential interests of its security which are connected with the production of or trade in arms, munitions and war material, although such measures must not adversely affect the conditions of competition in the common market regarding products which are not intended for specifically military purposes.[1] Provisions are made for the Council to draw up a list of products to which this applies,[2] but the list has not been published and is presumably secret.

1 EC Treaty, Article 296(1)(b). For an example of the interrelationship between military and non-military matters, see Commission IX Report on Competition Policy, p 72 (*France/Suralmo*); Commission Decision (EEC) 78/571 [1978] 2 CMLR758 (*SNPE/LEL*); Commission Decision (EEC) 78/921 [1979] 1 CMLR 403 (*WANO*); and Commission Notice [1990] OJ C239/2 (*GEC-Siemens/Plessey*), although the issue of the application of the rules on competition to defence products was left open in that case. See Commission XXIII Report on Competition Policy (1993), points 324-326, where the French Government successfully invoked Article 296(1)(b) to prevent notification of the manufacture of engines for missiles. It should be emphasised that Article 296(1) can only be invoked by Member States and not undertakings themselves. Similarly, see *British Aerospace/USEL* (Case IV/M.528, Decision of 24 December 1994) and *GEC/USEL* (Case IV/M.529, Decision of 7 December 1994).
2 See EC Treaty, Article 296(2), (3).

[85]
If measures so taken have the effect of distorting the conditions of competition in the common market, the Commission and the State concerned must examine how the measures can be adjusted to the rules laid down in the Treaty,[1] and the Commission or any Member State may bring the matter directly before the Court of Justice if it considers that another Member State is making improper use of the powers referred to above.[2]

1 EC Treaty, Article 298, 1st para
2 Ibid, 2nd para, which requires the Court to give its ruling in camera.

7. Banking and insurance

[86]

At various times it has been suggested that the rules of competition do not apply to banking and insurance because of the close connection of those sectors with capital movements, economic policy and the balance of payments.[1] However, it is now clear that the rules of competition apply not only to banking[2] and insurance[3] but also to related matters such as foreign exchange broking.[4]

1 See the arguments in Case 172/80 *Züchner v Bayerische Vereinsbank AG* [1981] ECR 2021, [1982] 1 CMLR 313, ECJ.

2 See Commission II Report on Competition Policy, p 58; Commission VIII Report on Competition Policy, pp 3l-36. Case 172/80 *Züchner v Bayerische Vereinsbank AG* [1981] ECR 2021, [1982] 1 CMLR 313, ECJ; Commission XIII Report on Competition Policy, p 59; Commission Decision (EEC) 85/77 [1985] 3 CMLR434 (*Re Uniform Eurocheques*); Commission Decision (EEC) 86/507 [1987] 2 CMLR 601 (*Irish Banks' Standing Committee*); Commission Decision (EEC) 87/13 [1989] 4 CMLR 149 (*Belgian Association of Banks*); Commission Decision (EEC) 87/103 [1989] 4 CMLR 238 (*ABI*); Commission Decision (EEC) 89/512 [1989] OJ L253/1 (*Dutch Banks*); Commission XXI Report on Competition Policy, paras 33-34 and p 335; Commission XXII Report on Competition Policy, p 417; Commission Decision (EEC) 92/212 [1992] OJ L95/50 (*Eurocheque: Helsinki Agreement*); Joined Cases T-39, 40/92 *Groupement des Cartes Bancaires 'CB' v Commission* [1994] ECR II-49, CFI. For a recent case of individual exemption under Article 85(3), see Commission Decision (EC) 96/ 454 [1996] OJ L188/37 (*BNP/Dresdner Bank*).

3 Commission Decision (EEC) 82/174 [1982] 2 CMLR 159 (*Re Fire Insurance*); Commission Decision (EEC) 84/191 [1984] 2 CMLR 484 (*Re Nuovo CEGAM*); Commission Decision (EEC) 85/75 [1985] 3 CMLR 246 (*Re Fire Insurance*), on appeal Case 45/85 *Verband der Sachversicherer eV v Commission* [1987] ECR 405, [1988] 4 CMLR 264, ECJ; Commission Decision (EEC) 85/615 [1985] OJ L376/15, [1989] 4 CMLR 178 (*P & I Clubs*); Commission II Report on Competition Policy, p 61 (*Inland Waterway Insurance*); Commission VI Report on Competition Policy, p 68 (*Transport Insurance*); Commission XIII Report on Competition Policy, p 59; Commission Decision (EEC) 90/ 22 [1990] OJ L13/34 (*TEKO*); and Commission Decision (EEC) 90/25 [1990] OJ L15/25 (*Concordato lncendio*); Commission Decision (EEC) 92/96 [1992] OJ L37/16 (*Assurpol*); Commission Decision (EEC) 93/3 [1993] OJ L4/26 (*Lloyd's Underwriters' Association and the Institute of London Underwriters*). See also Case 90/76 *Srl Ufficio van Ameyde v Srl Ufficio Centrale Italiano di Assistenza Automobilisti in Circolazione Internazionale* [1977] ECR 1091, [1978] 3 CMLR 478; Case 45/85 *Verband der Sachversicherer eV v Commission* [1987] ECR 405, [1988] 4 CMLR 264, ECJ; and Case 267/86 *Van Eycke v ASPA* [1988] ECR 4769, [1990] 4 CMLR 330, ECJ.

4 Commission VIII Report on Competition Policy, pp 35-36 (*Sarabex*) [1979] 1 CMLR 262.

[87]

The Commission has authority to issue block exemptions in respect of agreements which have as their object cooperation and harmonisation of certain practices in the insurance sector, namely agreements aiming at the establishment of common risk premium tariffs and common standard policy conditions, the common coverage of certain types of risks, the settlement of claims, the testing and acceptance of security devices and the keeping and handling of registers on aggravated risks.[1] The Commission adopted a block exemption in 1992.[2] This has now been replaced by a new block exemption.[3]

1 Council Regulation (EEC) 1534/91 [1991] OJ L143/1.

2 Commission Regulation (EEC) 3932/92 [1992] OJ L398/7. For cross-border credit transfers in banking, see Commission Notice [1995] OJ C251/3, [1995] 5 CMLR 551. Such transfers may fall within Article 81(1) and the Notice sets out guidance for exemption.

3 Regulation 358/2003 [2003] OJ L53/8, [2003] 4 CMLR 734. Note the new Member State exception in this Regulation.

8. Utilities

[88]

The privatisations that took place in many of the EU Member States from the 1980s onwards have created a new area of focus for the competition rules.[1] In sectors where a State-run service is opened to competition, the original provider will have a virtual or actual monopoly. A further feature is that policy considerations often dominate – in particular, the 'universal service obligation' – to ensure that even when the sector is open to competition a minimum service is still available to all. The Commission has played an increasingly important role in this area of application of the competition rules.[2]

1 For examples of application of competition rules to this area, see (1) on electricity: Council Directive 90/377/EEC [1990] OJ L185/16; Council Directive 90/547/EEC [1990] OJ L313/30; Council Directive 96/92/EC [1997] OJ L27/20 – establishing common rules for the internal market in electricity; and on the back of that legislation the application of competition policy by the Commission in, for example, the form of individual exemptions in Commission Decisions on *REN/Turbogas* [1996] OJ C118/7, [1996] 4 CMLR 881 and *ISAB Energy* [1996] OJ C138/3, [1996] 4 CMLR 889 where it approved long-term agreements for the supply of electricity; (2) on gas: Council Directive 90/337/EEC [1990] OJ L185/16 increasing the transparency of pricing of gas in the EU; Council Directive 91/296/EEC [1991] OJ L147/37 as amended by Council Directive 95/49/EC [1995] OJ L233/86; and Council Directive 98/30/EC [1998] OJ L204/1 establishing common rules for the storage, transmission and distribution of natural gas. The Commission has applied competition law in relation to a gas-interconnector built between Belgium and the UK (see Commission XXVth Report on Competition Policy (1995), point 82), and approving arrangements for use of the gas transport network in the UK in *British Gas Network Code* (see Commission XXVI Report on Competition Policy (1996), pp136-137)); (3) on post: see Case C-320/91 *Corbeau* [1993] ECR I-2533; [1995] 4 CMLR 621. In its judgment, the ECJ made clear that postal monopolies may be permitted under competition rules, but only so long as they meet certain requirements (see para 19 of the ECJ judgment), in particular, that the monopoly is not wider than that which is needed to maintain a universal service.

2 See, for example Commission Decision [1992] 5 CMLR 255 (*Sealink/B&I – Holyhead*) in relation to the 'essential facilities' doctrine. For a further discussion of this and of the application of the competition rules in the utilities sector, see Whish, *Competition Law* (5th edn, 2003), pp 667 et seq.

9. Electronic communications and e-commerce

[89]

For a discussion of the application of the competition rules to the electronic communications and e-commerce sectors, see Vaughan, *Law of the European Union*, Section 14 ('Electronic Communications').

10. Other sectors

[90]

The rules of competition also apply to cultural,[1] sporting[2] and professional service[3] sectors. It should be noted that there are particular exceptions to the application of the competition rules in the sporting sector where it is acknowledged that otherwise anti-competitive practices are sometimes necessary and of benefit to sport and to the wider public.[4] National competition authorities and courts will only intervene in the sports sector 'when it is necessary and in the interests of sports to do so'.[5] Further,

'... [s]port is subject to Community law only in so far as it constitutes an economic activity within the meaning of Article 2 EC'.[6] The Commission has expressly approved this limited application of the competition rules.[7]

1 Joined Cases 43, 63/82 *VBVB and VBBB v Commission* [1984] ECR 19, [1985] 1 CMLR 27, ECJ, concerning book publishing.

2 Commission IXth Report on Competition Policy, point 116 (*English Football League*). See also Advocate General Lena in Case C-415/93 *Union royale belge des sociétés de football association v Bosman* [1995] ECR I-4921, [1996] All ER (EC) 97, [1996] 1 CMLR 645, at para 261.

3 Case C-309/99 *Wouters v Algemene Raad van de Nederlandse Orde van Advocaten* [2002] ECR I-1577, [2002] 4 CMLR 913. See also *CNSD* [1993] OJ L203 (fixed fees for Italian customs agents) and *Belgian Architects Association* [2005] OJ L4 (recommended minimum fees), the full text of which can be found on the Commission's website.

4 See the discussion in Adam Lewis and Jonathan Taylor, *Sport: Law and Practice* (Butterworths, 2003) at pp 350 and 369 and, generally, pp 335-375. See also Brinckman and Vollebregt, 'The Marketing of Sport and its relation to EC Competition Law' [1998] ECLR 281; Kinsella and Daly, 'European Competition Law and Sports' (2001) 4(6) Sports Law Bulletin 7; and Beloff, 'The Sporting Exception in EC Competition Law" European Current Law Year Book 1999, p xi.

5 See Blackshaw, 'A Sporting Chance', European Lawyer (May 2002) 49.

6 See Case T-313/02 *Meca-Medina and Majcen v Commission* (30 September 2004) [2004] ECR 0000, [2004] 3 CMLR 60, para 37. See also Case 36/74 *Walrave and Koch* [1974] ECR 1405.

7 Commission press release, 'Limits to the application of Treaty competition rules to sport', 9 December 1999. See also Commission Decision letter of 27 June 2002 from Mario Monti to ENI (Case COMP/37.806) referring to the Court of Arbitration for Sport ruling in relation to UEFA rules in *AEK PAE and SK Slavia Praha v UEFA* CAS 98/2000 (Digest of CAS Awards II 1998-2000 (see p 36)). Note the repeated assertion that benefits derive to sport and the wider public from collective arrangements which might otherwise fall within the scope of the competition rules. See in relation to this point: *Hendry* [2002] UKCLR 5; *Greig v Insole* [1978] 3 All ER 449; Commission Decision of 23 July 2003 (*UEFA*) (2003) 2627; Commission XXXIII Report on Competition Policy (2003), p 25 (on joint selling arrangements between football clubs). This approach reflects that taken by the US courts in applying US anti-trust rules (see, for example, *National Collegiate Athletic Association v Board of Regents of University of Oklahoma* 104 S.Ct. 2948 (1984); *Molinas v National Basketball Association* 190 F.Supp 21 (DCNY 1961); *Deesen v Professional Golfers' Association* 358 F.2d 165 (9th Cir 1966); *Toscano v PGA Tour* 201 F.Supp.2d 1106 E.D.Cal. 2002); and *Morris Communications Corp v PGA Tour* 235 F.Supp.2d 1269 (M.D. Fla. 2002)).

3

AGREEMENTS, DECISIONS OF ASSOCIATIONS OF UNDERTAKINGS AND CONCERTED PRACTICES

A. INTRODUCTION

1. The prohibition of anti-competitive agreements and practices

[91]

Article 81(1) of the EC Treaty prohibits as incompatible with the common market:[1] all agreements[2] between undertakings,[3] decisions by associations of undertakings[4] and concerted practices[5] which may affect trade between Member States[6] and which have as their object or effect the prevention, restriction or distortion of competition[7] within the common market,[8] and in particular[9] those which:

(a) directly or indirectly fix purchase or selling prices or any other trading conditions;[10]

(b) limit or control production, markets, technical development or investment;[11]

(c) share markets or sources of supply;[12]

(d) apply dissimilar conditions to equivalent transactions with other trading parties, thereby placing them at a competitive disadvantage;[13]

(e) make the conclusion of contracts subject to acceptance by other parties of supplementary obligations which, by their nature or according to commercial usage, have no connection with the subject of such contracts.[14]

1 The words 'incompatible with the common market' do not add anything to the substantive scope of Article 81.
2 As to agreements, see para [98].
3 As to the meaning of 'undertaking', see para [52].
4 As to decisions by associations of undertakings, see para [105].
5 As to concerted practices, see para [108].
6 Ability to affect inter-State trade is discussed at para [155].
7 The prevention, restriction and distortion of competition are discussed at para [138].
8 For the geographical scope of application of the competition rules, see para [37].
9 The list is not exhaustive. For examples of the prevention, restriction or distortion of competition, see paras [138] and [178] ff.
10 EC Treaty, Article 81(1)(a).
11 Ibid, Article 81(1)(b).

12 Ibid, Article 81(1)(c).
13 Ibid, Article 81(1)(d).
14 Ibid, Article 81(1)(e).

[92]
Some forms of concerted behaviour may be capable of classification under more than one of the descriptions 'agreement', 'decision' or 'concerted practice'. If parties cooperate so as to bring about a restriction of competition, little will turn on the precise form that the cooperation takes. Thus, behaviour has been classified as amounting to both an agreement and a decision of an association of undertakings,[1] to both a concerted practice and a decision of an association of undertakings[2] and as constituting an agreement or at least a concerted practice.[3] The Commission's decision in *Wood Pulp*[4] simply used the term 'restrictive practices'; the Court of First Instance has held that the Commission is entitled to describe a sustained process of collusion, some of which amounted to an agreement and some to a concerted practice, as 'an agreement and a concerted practice' without separately classifying the elements of each.[5] However, the distinction can be of importance in determining who is liable for an infringement. The ECJ quashed the *Wood Pulp* decision[6] insofar as it found that price agreements concluded by the members of a trade association also constituted a decision by association, since it was not shown that the association had played any separate role in the implementation of the agreements.[7]

1 See eg Commission Decision (EEC) 78/670 [1978] OJ L224/29, [1978] 3 CMLR 524 (*GB Inno-BM/ FEDETAB*) (upheld on appeal in Joined Cases 209-215, 218/78 *Heintz van Landewyck Sari v Commission* [1980] ECR 3125, [1981] 3 CMLR 134, ECJ) and Commission Decision (EEC) 82/371 [1982] OJ L167/39, [1982] 2 CMLR 193 (*NAVEWA-ANSEAU*) (upheld on appeal in Joined Cases 96-102, 104, 105, 108, 110/82 *IAZ International Belgium NV v Commission* [1983] ECR 3369, [1984] 3 CMLR 276, ECJ).
2 Commission Decision (EEC) 82/174 [1982] OJ L80/36, [1982] 2 CMLR 159 (*Fire Insurance*).
3 Commission Decision (EEC) 69/243 [1969] OJ L195/11, [1969] CMLR D23 (*Aniline Dyes Cartel*) (upheld on appeal in Case 48/69 *Imperial Chemical Industries Ltd v Commission*) [1972] ECR 619, [1972] CMLR 557, ECJ). This is the position currently favoured by the Competition Appeal Tribunal in the UK. In *JJB Sports and Allsports v OFT* [2004] CAT 17, this was the case when a supplier received assurances or intimations about future pricing intentions from two retailers, and in each case passed those assurances or intimations on to the other retailer concerned. The CAT held (at para 655) that the supplier and the two retailers were properly to be regarded as parties to the same agreement or concerted practice. In *Argos and Littlewoods v OFT* [2004] CAT 24, the CAT found there to be two bilateral agreements or concerted practices between a toy manufacturer and each of two retailers and, although it stated that it was necessary to prove a tripartite agreement or concerted practice between all three players, the correct analysis was that the manufacturer and retailers were, in addition, parties to a tripartite concerted practice.
4 Commission Decision (EEC) 85/202 [1985] OJ L85/1, [1985] 3 CMLR 474.
5 Joined Cases T-1, 4, 6-15/89 *Rhone-Poulenc SA v Commission* [1991] ECR II-867, CFI.
6 Commission Decision (EEC) 85/202 [1985] OJ L85/1, [1985] 3 CMLR 474.
7 Joined Cases 89, 104, 114, 116, 117, 125-129/85 *Ahlström Osakeyhtio and Others v Commission* [1988] ECR 5193, [1980] 4 CMLR 901, ECJ.

[93]
Article 81(2) provides that agreements or decisions prohibited pursuant to Article 81[1] are automatically void.[2] It has, however, been held that as a matter of Community law only those elements of an agreement which infringe Article 81 are void, unless it is impossible to sever them from the rest; the consequences for other provisions of

the agreement are a matter for national law.[3] Further, just as the prohibition under Article 81(1) is itself of transient application, in play only so long as an agreement offends the provision, so too the nullity under Article 81(2) can be transient. Thus, if circumstances change and the agreement in question ceases to offend Article 81(1), it will cease to be void under Article 81(2).[4]

1 EC Treaty, Article 81(2) applies to an agreement or decision which is prohibited by Article 81(1) and not 'exempted' pursuant to Article 81(3). Article 81(2) does not provide that a concerted practice is void, presumably because concerted practices do not generally purport to give rise to legally binding obligations.

2 See Case 13/61 *Kiedinguerkoopbedrijf de Geus en Uitdenbogerd v Robert Bosch GmbH* [1962] ECR 45, [1962] CMLR 1, ECJ; Case 127/73 *Belgische Radio en Televisie (BRT) v SV SABAM* [1974] ECR 51, [1974] 2 CMLR 238, ECJ. Special rules apply to the agriculture and transport sectors; see Vaughan, *Law of the European Union*, Sections 16 ('Agriculture') and 18 ('Transport', forthcoming).

3 Case 56/65 *Sociéti Technique Minière v Maschinenbau Ulm GmbH* [1966] ECR 235, [1966] CMLR 357, ECJ; Case 319/82 *Société de Vente de Ciments et Betons de l'Est SA v Kerpen and Kerpen GmbH & Co KG* [1983] ECR 4173, [1985] 1 CMLR 511, ECJ; Case 10/86 *VAG France SA v Etablissements Magne* SA [1986] ECR 4071, [1988] 4 CMLR 98, ECJ.

4 *Passmore v Morland Plc* [1999] 3 All ER 1005, CA, per Chadwick LJ at 1014–15.

[94]

It is the duty of national courts to give effect to the rights created by Article 81.[1] English rules relating to illegality in contract apply to agreements which are void pursuant to Article 81.[2] An infringement of Article 81 may be actionable in England as a breach of statutory duty; and, if so, English law will give a remedy in damages as well as by injunction.[3] Participation in such an infringement may amount to a civil, but probably not a criminal,[4] conspiracy. In England and Wales at least, it is likely that an agreement held to infringe Article 81(1) will be illegal, not just void.[5]

1 Case 127/73 *Belgische Radio en Televisie (BRT) v SV SABAM* [1974] ECR 51, [1974] 2 CMLR 238, ECJ. See also Case C-126/97 *Eco Swiss China Time Ltd v Benetton* [1999] ECR I-3055, [2000] 5 CMLR 816 and Case C-453/99 *Courage Ltd v Crehan* [2001] ECR I-6297, [2001] 5 CMLR 28, para 21. National courts have an obligation to apply Article 81(2) and declare an agreement void if it offends Article 81(1).

2 *Chemidus Wavin Ltd v Societe pour la Transformation et l'Exploitation des Résines Industrielles SA* [1977] FSR 181, [1978] 3 CMLR 514, CA.

3 *Garden Cottage Foods Ltd v Milk Marketing Board* [1976] 2 CMLR 387, per Walton J; affirmed in [1978] 3 CMLR 514, CA; [1983] AC 130, [1983] 2 All ER 770, [1983] 3 CMLR 43, HL. See also Case C-453/99 *Courage Ltd v Crehan* [2001] ECR I-6297, [2001] 5 CMLR 28 and *Arkin v Borchard Lines Ltd* [2003] EWHC 687. In the latter case there was no dispute that there would be an entitlement to damages if there was a finding of a breach of Articles 81 or 82.

4 Criminal Law Act 1977, s 5(1).

5 See *Gibbs Mew plc v Gemmell* [1998] Eu LR 588, CA. See also the discussion on this point and on the impact of a finding of illegality on the right to damages in R Whish, *Competition Law* (5th edn, 2003) at p 291. See also Case C-453/99 *Courage v Crehan* [2001] ECR I-6297, [2001] 5 CMLR 1058.

[95]

The Commission has power to make final and interim orders for the termination of infringements,[1] enforced by periodic penalty payments in default,[2] and to impose fines in respect of breaches of Article 81 committed intentionally or negligently.[3]

1 Council Regulation (EC) 1/2003, Article 7 (the relevant provision was previously to be found in Council Regulation (EEC) 17/62, Article 3). Many of the cases cited were decided under the previous regime and should be read with reference to Regulation 17/62. See also Case 792/79R *Camera Care Ltd v Commission* [1980] ECR 119, [1980] 1 CMLR 334, ECJ.
2 Council Regulation (EC) 1/2003, Article 24 (these powers were formerly found in Council Regulation (EEC) 17/62, Article 16).
3 Ibid, Article 23 (formerly Regulation 17, Article 15).

2. Exemption

[96]
Article 81(3)[1] provides that Article 81(1) may be declared inapplicable in the case of any agreement or category of agreements between undertakings, any decision or category of decisions by associations of undertakings or any concerted practice or category of concerted practices which contributes to improving the production or distribution of goods or to promoting technical or economic progress while allowing consumers a fair share of the resulting benefit and which does not impose on the undertakings concerned restrictions which are not indispensable to the attainment of these objectives or afford such undertakings the possibility of eliminating competition in respect of a substantial part of the products in question.

1 EC Treaty, Article 81(3) is discussed at paras [197]–[218].

[97]
Until 2004, this exemption could be granted either individually by a decision of the Commission or in the form of a 'block exemption' in respect of a category of agreements, decisions or concerted practices by regulation.[1] Since 1 May 2004, however, it has not been possible to obtain individual exemptions in this way. Block exemptions remain, though. Prior to the implementation of Regulation 17/62, the national courts of the Member States had jurisdiction (deriving from Article 84 of the EC Treaty) to rule on the admissibility of agreements, decisions and concerted practices under Article 81 (and on abuse of a dominant position under Article 82). Under Regulation 17/62, Article 9(1), however, the Commission was given exclusive jurisdiction to grant individual exemption. Power to grant block exemption in respect of particular categories of agreements etc was conferred on the Commission by a number of Council regulations. Even under the Regulation 17 regime, if the validity of an agreement was in issue in proceedings before a national court, the court had to consider whether the agreement benefited from an exemption regulation and had to have regard to the possibility of an exemption being granted.[2] Now, however, the role of national courts and national competition authorities has been greatly expanded. Prior notification to the Commission is no longer available to parties wishing to obtain an individual exemption. Instead exemption under Article 81(3) on an individual basis may now be obtained by the compatibility of an agreement with Article 81(1) being raised as an issue before a national court or national competition authority and that body applying Article 81(3) on an individual basis.

1 Exemption of a category (or block) of agreements, etc is commonly known as 'block exemption'. The existing block exemption regulations are described generally at para [203].
2 See Case C-234/89 *Delimitis v Henninger Bräu AG* [1991] ECR I-935, [1992] 5 CMLR 210, ECJ. See also for information on the background to these changes, A Jones and B Sufrin, *EC Competition Law* (2nd edn, 2004), pp 101-105, 180-186 and 232-252.

B. AGREEMENTS, DECISIONS AND CONCERTED PRACTICES

1. Agreements

[98]

The essence of an agreement within the meaning of Article 81 is that one party voluntarily undertakes to limit its freedom of action with regard to the other.[1] '[T]he concept of an agreement within the meaning of Article 85(1) of the Treaty, as interpreted by the case-law, centres around the existence of a concurrence of wills between at least two parties, the form in which it is manifested being unimportant so long as it constitutes the faithful expression of the parties' intention.'[2] It is not necessary that the agreement should be a binding contract in civil law. The characterisation of the agreement in national law is irrelevant,[3] as is the fact that the agreement may be condoned at a national level.[4]

1 Commission Decision (EEC) 74/634 [1974] OJ L343/19, [1975] 1 CMLR D8 (*Franco-Japanese Ballbearings Agreement*); Commission Decision (EEC) 89/515 [1991] 4 CMLR13 (*Re Welded Steel Mesh*), on appeal Case T-141/89 *Trefileurope Sales Sarl v Commission* [1995] ECR II-791, CFI.
2 See Case T-41/96 *Bayer AG v Commission* [2000] ECR II-3383, [2001] 4 CMLR 126, para 69, affirmed on appeal Cases C-2 and 3/01P [2004] 4 CMLR 653.
3 Case 8/72 *Vereeniging van Cementhandelaren v Commission* [1972] ECR 977, [1973] CMLR 7, ECJ; Commission Decision (EEC) 74/634 [1974] OJ L343/19, [1975] 1 CMLR D8 (*Franco-Japanese Ballbearings Agreement*); Joined Cases 209-215, 218/78 *Van Landewyck v Commission* [1980] ECR 3125 at 3249, 3250, [1981] 3 CMLR 134 at 225, ECJ; Case 123/83 *Bureau National Interprofessionnel du Cognac v Clair* [1985] ECR 391, [1985] 2 CMLR 430, ECJ; Case C-277/87 *Sandoz prodotti Farmaceutici SpA v Commission* [1990] ECR I-45, ECJ.
4 Cases 240–2, 261 and 262/82 *SSI v Commission* [1985] ECR 3831, [1987] 3 CMLR 661. See also (in respect of associations of undertakings) Case 123/83 *BNIC v Clair* [1985] ECR 391, [1985] 2 CMLR 430 and Case C-309/99 *Wouters v Alegemene Raad van de Nederlandse Order van Advocaten* [2002] ECR I-577, [2002] 4 CMLR 913 (regarding an association of undertakings, some of whose members were government appointees).

[99]

The following have been held to be agreements within the meaning of Article 81: a gentlemen's agreement;[1] an agreement drawn up but never signed but nevertheless applied by both parties;[2] an understanding which was never reduced to writing at all;[3] an oral agreement;[4] the joint composition of a circular by a committee of dealers and approval of the circular by a manufacturer;[5] intimation of agreement to the circular by the addressees returning a countersigned copy;[6] the adoption of common rules;[7] an agreement between two trading associations on behalf of their members;[8] recognition by a trade association of a non-member undertaking in return for the non-member agreeing to comply with the association's rules;[9] assent to a decision of an association of undertakings by a member undertaking;[10] standard terms of sale used by a manufacturer;[11] and a compromise of litigation,[12] though the status of consent orders is unclear.[13] A number of separate but identical agreements between manufacturers and a management consultant for the purpose of appointing the management consultant to supervise an anti-competitive agreement between the manufacturers have been held to constitute a single agreement caught by Article 81.[14]

1 Case 41/69 *ACF Chemiefarma NV v Commission* [1970] ECR 661, ECJ.
2 Commission Decision (EEC) 79/934 [1979] OJ L286/32, [1979] 3 CMLR 684 (*BP Kemi*).

3 Commission Decision (EEC) 82/506 [1982] OJ L232/1, [1982] 3 CMLR 702 (*Stichting Sigarettenindustrie Agreements*). See also Commission Decision (EEC) 82/853 [1982] OJ L354/28, [1983] 1 CMLR 497 (*National Panasonic (UK) Ltd*) (a relationship between a manufacturer and its dealers 'under which the terms and conditions of supply were clearly understood').
4 Commission Decision (EEC) 77/129 [1977] OJ L39/19, [1977] 1 CMLR D44 (*Theal/Watts*); Case 28/77 *Tepea BV v Commission* [1978] ECR 1391, [1978] 3 CMLR 392, ECJ.
5 Commission Decision (EEC) 78/155 [1978] OJ L46/33, [1978] 2 CMLR 126 (*BMW Belgium NV and Belgian BMW Dealers*); Joined Cases 32, 36-82/78 *BMW Belgium SA v Commission* [1979] ECR 2435, [1980] 1 CMLR 370, ECJ.
6 Joined Cases 32, 36-82/78 *BMW Belgium SA v Commission* [1979] ECR 2435, [1980] 1 CMLR 370, ECJ.
7 Commission Decision (EEC) 74/292 [1974] OJ L160/1, [1974] 2 CMLR D50 (*European Glass Manufacturers*); Commission Decision (EEC) 75/497 [1975] OJ L228/3, [1975] 2 CMLR D20 (*Virgin Aluminium Producers IFTRA Rules*).
8 Commission Decision (EEC) 74/433 [1974] OJ L237/16, [1974] 2 CMLR D89 (*FRUBO*) (on appeal Case 71/74 *Nederlandse Vereniging voor Fruit en Groentenimporthandel v Commission* [1975] ECR 563, [1975] 2 CMLR 123, ECJ); Commission Decision (EEC) 82/123 [1982] OJ L54/36, [1982] 2 CMLR 344 (*VBBB and VBVB Agreement*) (on appeal Joined Cases 43,63/82 *VBVB and VBBB v Commission* [1984] ECR 19, [1985] 1 CMLR 27, ECJ); Commission Decision (EEC) 82/371 [1982] OJ L167/39, [1982] 2 CMLR 193 (*NAVE WAANSEALI*) (on appeal Joined Cases 96-102, 104, 105, 108, 110/82 *IAZ International Belgium NV v Commission* [1983] ECR 3369, [1984] 1 CMLR276, ECJ); Commission Decision (EEC) 82/506 [1982] OJ L232/1, [1982] 3 CMLR 702 (*Stichting Sigarettenindustrie Agreements*); Case 123/83 *BNIC v Clair* [1985] ECR 391, [1985] 2 CMLR 430; see also Case 67/63 *Société Rhinane d'Exploitation et de Manutention v High Authority* [1964] ECR 151, [1964] CMLR 350, ECJ.
9 Commission Decision (EEC) 78/59 [1978] 2 CMLR 194 (*Centraal Bureau voor do Rijwielhandel*).
10 Joined Cases 209-215, 218/78 *Van Landewyck Sar v Commission* [1980] ECR 3125, [1981] 3 CMLR 134, ECJ.
11 Commission Decision (EEC) 77/66 [1977] OJ L16/8, [1977] 1 CMLR D35 (*Gerofabriek NV*); Commission Decision (EEC) 78/922 [1978] OJ L322/26, [1979] 1 CMLR 81 (*Zanussi SpA Guarantee*) (standard form of manufacturer's guarantee to be passed on to the customer); Commission Decision (EEC) 79/68 [1979] 1 CMLR 448 (*Kawasaki Motors*) (export ban); Commission Decision (EEC) 80/1283 [1980] OJ L377/16, [1981] 2 CMLR 287 (*Johnson & Johnson*) (export ban contained in price list); Case C-277/87 *Sandoz Prodotti Farmaceutici SpA v Commission* [1990] ECR I-45, ECJ, [1989] 4 CMLR 628 (inclusion on invoices sent after delivery of goods of clause prohibiting export; term invalid in domestic law for want of formality; it was held that course of dealing implied tacit acceptance of clause by purchasers, and that invalidity in domestic law was irrelevant).
12 Commission Decision (EEC) 78/193 [1978] OJ L60/19, [1978] 2 CMLR 100 (*Penney's Trade Mark*); Case 35/83 *BAT Cigaretten-Fabriken GmbH v Commission* [1985] ECR 363, [1985] 2 CMLR 470, ECJ. In Case 65/86 *Bayer AG v Süllhafer* [1988] ECR 5249, [1990] 4 CMLR 182, the Court of Justice rejected the Commission's submission that an agreement resolving a genuine dispute is compatible with Article 81. The result of the Court's decision is that (where the effects of the agreement are appreciable and inter-State trade may be affected) it is very difficult to make a valid compromise of, eg, patent litigation. Such agreements inevitably include an agreement by at least one party to refrain from conduct which he previously asserted a right to carry on. The only way in which it can be ascertained whether the agreement truly restricts competition is by trying the original action, the cost of which the parties have sought to avoid in making the settlement.
13 In Case 258/78 *LC Nungesser KG v Commission* [1982] ECR 2015, [1983] 1 CMLR 278, ECJ the Court held that Article 81 applied to a form of judicial settlement under the German Code of Civil Procedure where settlements reached under that procedure were, as a matter of German law, still subject to rules analogous to those of illegality of contract. Both in that case and in *Bayer v Süllhafer*, note 12 above, the Court reserved its position on 'whether and to what extent a settlement reached before a national court which constitutes a judicial act may be invalid for breach of Community competition rules'. The meaning of these words is opaque.

14 Commission Decision (EEC) 80/1334 [1980] OJ L383/19, [1982] 2 CMLR 61 (*Italian Cast Glass*).

[100]

Agreements designed to provide for better working conditions do not fall within the scope of Article 81(1). The Court's reasoning is that, in this instance, the employment and social protection aims of the Treaty trump the competition aims.[1]

1 Case C-67/96 *Albany International BV v Stichting Bedrijfspensioenfonds Textielindustrie* [1999] ECR I-5751, [2000] 4 CMLR 446. See paras 46 to 64 in particular. This has been the subject of criticism: see Van den Bergh and Camesasca, 'Irreconcilable Principles? The Court of Justice Exempts Collective Labour Agreements from the Wrath of Antitrust' (2000) 25 EL Rev 492. See also Boni and Manzini, 'National Social Legislation and EC Antitrust Law' (2001) 24 World Competition 239 and Case C-222/98 *Van der Woude v Stichting Beatrixoord* [2000] ECR I-7111, [2001] 4 CMLR 93. See generally, A Jones and B Sufrin, *EC Competition Law* (2nd edn, 2004), p 131. Contrast the Court's approach to the professions: Cases C-180/98 *Pavel Pavlov v Stichting Pensioenfonds Medische Specialisten* [2000] ECR I-6451, [2001] 4 CMLR 30, paras 67-70; Case C-309/99 *Wouters v Alegemene Raad van de Nederlandse Order van Advocaten* [2002] ECR I-577, [2002] 4 CMLR 913.

[101]

The subjective intentions of the parties are not relevant in assessing whether they have entered into an agreement restrictive of competition.[1] In a number of cases, a policy determined unilaterally by one undertaking has been held to have received a sufficient measure of assent by another undertaking to fall within Article 81.[2] Parties cannot evade liability under Article 81 by showing that they never intended to implement or abide by the terms of the agreement in question.[3]

1 See Joined Cases 29,30/83 *Compagnie Royale Asturienne des Mines SA and Rheinzink GmbH v Commission* [1984] ECR 1679, [1985] 1 CMLR 688, ECJ. See generally on unilateral conduct, paras [122] ff.

2 See, for example, Case 32/78 *BMW v Commission* [1979] ECR 2435, [1980] 1 CMLR 370 and Case C-338/00P *Volkswagen v Commission* [2003] ECR I-9189, [2004] 4 CMLR 351. In the latter case, the ECJ affirmed the CFI's finding that: 'a call by a motor vehicle manufacturer to its authorised dealers is not a unilateral act which falls outside the scope of Article 81(1) but is an agreement within the meaning of that provision if it forms part of a set of continuous business relations governed by a general agreement drawn up in advance.'

3 Commission Decision of 24 July 2002 relating to a proceeding pursuant to Article 81 of the EC Treaty (*Industrial and medical gases*) [2003] OJ L84/1. See, in particular, para 351.

[102]

An agreement between companies which, though separate entities in civil law, form part of the same economic unit and certain agreements between principals and their agents does not fall within Article 81.[1]

1 See paras [129]–[132].

[103]

Both 'horizontal' and 'vertical' agreements fall to be considered under Article 81(1).

[104]

Once an agreement is found to have been reached, the form it takes is irrelevant.[1] An agreement covering several activities will be seen as a number of different agreements – one in respect of each activity – unless it can be shown that the activities are intimately linked and form one business arrangement.[2]

1 Case T-41/96 *Bayer AG v Commission* [2000] ECR II-3383, [2001] 4 CMLR 126, para 69, affirmed on appeal in Cases C-2 and 3/01P [2004] 4 CMLR 653.
2 See Commission Notice: Guidelines on the effect on trade concept [2004] OJ C101/81.

2. Decisions by associations of undertakings

[105]
Article 81 applies to the behaviour of associations, typically trade associations,[1] which by their rules of membership or by decisions taken within the association are liable to affect the commercial behaviour of their members.[2] It is irrelevant that the association is constituted as a non-profit-making body and does not itself trade. Article 81 also applies to decisions by an association of associations of undertakings.[3] A group of companies which form a single economic unit is not an association of undertakings.[4]

1 For other examples of 'associations', see Case C-250/92 *Gottrup-Klim Grovvareforening v Dansk Landbrugs Grovvaresel-skab AmbA* [1994] ECR I-5641, [1996] 4 CMLR 191 (agricultural cooperative); Case 123/83 *BNIC v Clair* [1985] ECR 391, [1985] 2 CMLR 430 (statutory body with a public role); and Case C-309/99 *Wouters v Alegemene Raad van de Nerderlandse Order van Advocaten* [2002] ECR I-577, [2002] 4 CMLR 913 (professional body).
2 See Commission Decision (EEC) 70/333 [1970] OJ L148/9, [1970] CMLR D25 (*ASPA*); Commission Decision (EEC) 72/390 [1972] OJ L26, [1972] CMLR D130 (*Belgian Central Heating Agreement*); Case 8/72 *Vereeniging van Cementhandelaren v Commission* [1972] ECR 977, [19731 CMLR 7, ECJ; Commission Decision (EEC) 74/433 [1974] OJ L237/16, [1974] 3 CMLR D89 (*FRUBO*) (on appeal Case 71/74 *Nederlandse Vereniging voor Fruit en Groentenimporthandel Commission* [1975] ECR 563, [1975] 2 CMLR 123, ECJ); Commission Decision (EEC) 76/684 [1976] OJ L231/24, [1976] 2 CMLR D63 (*Pabst & Richarz/BNIA*); Commission Decision (EEC) 78/59 [1978] 2 CMLR 194 (*Centraal Bureau voor do Rijwielhandel*); Commission Decision (EEC) 78/670, [1978] OJ L224/29, [1978] 3 CMLR 524 (*GB Inno-BM/FEDETAB*) (on appeal Joined Cases 209-215, 218/78 *Van Landewyck Sarl v Commission* [1980] ECR 3125, [1981] 3 CMLR 134, ECJ); Commission Decision (EEC) 80/ 257 [1980] OJ L62/28, [1980] 3 CMLR 193 (*Rolled Steel*) (a decision on the identical wording of the former ECSC Treaty, Article 65); Commission Decision (EEC) 80/917 [1980] OJ L260/24, [1980] 3 CMLR 429 (*National Sulphuric Acid Association*); Commission Decision (EEC) 82/123 [1982] OJ L54/36, [1982] 2 CMLR 344 (*VBBB and VBVB Agreement*) (on appeal in Joined Cases 43, 63/82 *VBVB and VBBB v Commission* [1984] ECR 19, [1985] 1 CMLR 27, ECJ); Commission Decision (EEC) 82/371 [1982] OJ L167/39, [1982] 2 CMLR 193 (*NAVEWA-ANSEAU*) (on appeal in Joined Cases 96-102, 104, 105, 108, 110/82 *IAZ International Belgium NV v Commission* [1983] ECR 3369, [1984] 3 CMLR 276, ECJ); Commission Decision (EEC) 82/896 [1982] OJ L379/1, [1983] 2 CMLR 240 (*AROW/BNIC*); Commission Decision (EEC) 85/76 [1985] OJ L35/35, [1985] 3 CMLR101 (*Milchforderungsfonds*); Commission Decision (EEC) 85/202 [1985] OJ L85/1, [1985] CMLR 474 (*Wood Pulp*) (on appeal Joined Cases 89, 104, 114, 116, 117, 125-129/85 *Ahlström Osakeyhtio and Others v Commission* [1988] ECR 5193, [1988] 4 CMLR 901, ECJ); Commission Decision (EEC) 86/ 499 [1985] OJ L291/46 (*VIFKA*); Commission Decision (EEC) 85/ 563 [1985] OJ L369/28, [1988] 4 CMLR 138 (*London Sugar Futures Market Ltd*); Commission Decision (EEC) 85/564 [1985] OJ L369/28, [1988] 4 CMLR143 (*London Cocoa Terminal Market Association Ltd*); Commission Decision (EEC) 85/565 [1985] OJ L369/31, [1988] 4 CMLR 155 (*Coffee Terminal Market Association of London Ltd*); Commission Decision (EEC) 85/566 [1985] OJ L369/34, [1988] 4 CMLR 149 (*London Rubber Terminal Market Association Ltd*) Commission Decision (EEC) 85/75 [1985] OJ L35/20, [1985] 3 CMLR 246 (*Fire Insurance*) (on appeal Case 45/85 *Verband der Sachversicherer BV v Commission* [1987] ECR 405, [1988] 4 CMLR 264, ECJ); Commission Decision (EEC) 87/13 [1987] OJ L7/27, [1989] 4 CMLR 141 (*Belgische Vereniging der Banken*); Commission Decision (EEC) 89/44 [1989] OJ L26/12 (*Publishers Association – Net Book Agreements*) (see Case T-66/89 *Publishers Association v Commission* [1992] 5 CMLR 120, CFI and on appeal Case C-360/92P [1995] ECR I-23, [1995] 5 CMLR33, ECJ); Commission Decision (EEC) 91/128 [1991] OJ L60/19 (*Sippa*); Commission Decision (EEC) 92/568 [1992] OJ L366/47

(*Distribution of railway tickets*); Commission Decision (EEC) 93/3 [1993] OJ L004/1 (*Lloyd's Underwriters Association*).
See also Joined Cases 209-215, 218/78 *Heintz van Landewyck Sàrl v Commission* [1980] ECR 3125, [1981] 3 CMLR 134, ECJ.
3 Commission Decision (EEC) 71/337 [1971] OJ L227/26, [1973] CMLR D135 (*Cematex*); Commission Decision (EEC) 77/722 [1977] OJ 1299/18, [1977] 2 CMLR D43 (*BPICA*); Commission Decision (EEC) 85/76 [1985] OJ L35/35, [1985] 3 CMLR 101 (*Milchforderungsfonds*).
4 See Joined Cases 228, 229/82 *Ford of Europe Inc and Ford Werke AG v Commission* [1984] ECR 1129 at 1160, [1984] 1 CMLR 649 at 672, ECJ.

[106]

The decision taken by the association need not be legally binding on the members, at least if it is intended to coordinate their conduct.[1] The constitution and general regulations of such an association may be a decision by the association.[2] The decision need not be taken by all the member undertakings at a general meeting, but may be taken by the management.[3] No formality is required for the taking of the decision; consequently the conduct of the association may amount to a decision.[4]

1 Commission Decision (EEC) 74/433 [1974] OJ L237/16, [1974] 2 CMLR D89 (*FRUBO*); Commission Decision (EEC) 80/257 [1980] 3 CMLR 193 (*Rolled Steel*); Commission Decision (EEC) 82/371 [1982] OJ L167/39, [1982] 2 CMLR 193 (*NAVEWA-ANSEALT*) (upheld on appeal); Commission Decision (EEC) 85/75 [1985] OJ L35/20, [1985] 3 CMLR 246 (*Fire Insurance*) (upheld on appeal in Case 45/85 *Verband den Sachversicherer eV v Commission* [1987] ECR 405, [1988] 4 CMLR 264, ECJ).
2 Commission Decision (EEC) 70/333 [1970] CMLR D25 (*ASPA*); Commission Decision (EEC) 78/59 [1978] OJ L20/18, [1978] 2 CMLR 194 (*Centraal Bureau voor de Rijwielhandel*). See also Commission Decision (EEC) 80/234 [1980] OJ L151/19, [1980] 2 CMLR 402 (*Rennet*) (on appeal in Case 61/80 *Cooperatieve Stremsel- en Kleurselfabriek v Commission* [1981] ECR 851, [1982] 2 CMLR 240, ECJ), where the rules of a cooperative were treated as an agreement between undertakings; and Commission Decision (EEC) 80/1071 [1980] OJ L318/1, [1981] 2 CMLR 498 (*IMA Rules*).
3 See eg Commission Decision (EEC) 71/337 [1973] CMLR D135 (*Cematex*).
4 Commission Decision (EEC) 80/257 [1980] 3 CMLR 193 (*Rolled Steel*).

[107]

Article 81 also applies to agreements between such associations[1] which do not require to be analysed as agreements between the member undertakings, although this analysis has also been used.[2] Agreements reached within the framework of a trade association are likely to be regarded as agreements within the meaning of Article 81.[3] Such an agreement will probably only be regarded as also involving a decision by the association if the association itself played a part in its implementation.[4]

1 Case 67/63 *Société Rhinane d'Exploitation et de Manutention v High Authority* [1964] ECR 151, [1964] CMLR 350, ECJ, a decision on the identical wording of ECSC Treaty, Article 65; Case 71/74 *Nederlandse Vereniging voor Fruit en Groentenimporthandel v Commission* [1975] ECR 563, [1975] 2 CMLR 123, ECJ; Commission Decision (EEC) 82/371 [1982] OJ L167/39, [1982] 2 CMLR 193 (*NAVEWA-ANSEAU*) (affirmed on appeal).
2 Commission Decision (EEC) 72/390 [1972] CMLR D130 (*Belgian Central Heating Agreement*); Commission Decision (EEC) 74/433 [1974] OJ L237/16, [1974] 2 CMLR D89 (*FRUBO*).
3 Case 123/83 *Bureau National Interprofessionnel du Cognac v Clam* [1985] ECR 391, [1985] 2 CMLR 430, ECJ; Case 136/86 *Bureau National Interprofessionnel du Cognac v Aubert* [1987] ECR 4789, [1988] 4 CMLR 331, ECJ.

4 See Joined Cases 89,104,114,116,117,125-129/85 *Ahlström Osakeyhtio v Commission* [1988] ECR 5193 at 5245, [1988] 4 CMLR 901 at 942-943, ECJ.

3. Concerted practices

[108]

Undertakings may restrict competition by concerted behaviour which falls short of an agreement. A common example of such behaviour is the mutual exchange between competitors of information such as sales figures, prices, discounts or other terms of supply which leads them to align their terms of supply, even though they do not agree with each other what their terms of supply will be.[1] Other loose forms of cooperation between undertakings have been held to amount to concerted practices.

1 As to concerted practices and pricing behaviour, see further paras [108] ff. For a general discussion of concerted practices see the second opinion of Advocate General Darmon in Joined Cases 89, 104, 114, 116, 117, 125-129/85 *Ahlström Osakeyhtio and Others v Commission* [1993] ECR I-1307, [1993] 4 CMLR 407, ECJ.

[109]

A concerted practice has been defined by the Court of Justice as a form of coordination between undertakings which, without having reached agreement properly so called, knowingly substitutes practical cooperation between them for the risks of competition. The criteria of coordination and co-operation required do not require an actual plan; they must be understood in the light of the concept inherent in the competition provisions of the EC Treaty, namely that each trader must determine independently the policy which he intends to adopt on the common market and the conditions which he intends to offer to his customers. This requirement of independence does not deprive traders of the right to adapt themselves intelligently to the existing or anticipated conduct of their competitors, but it does strictly preclude any direct or indirect contact between them, the object or effect of which is to create conditions of competition which do not correspond to the normal conditions of the market in question.[1]

1 Case 172/80 *Zuchner v Bayerische Vereinsbank AG* [1981] ECR 2021 at 2031, 2032, [1982] 1 CMLR 313 at 324, 325, ECJ, substantially repeating statements of the principle in Case 48/69 *Imperial Chemical Industries Ltd v Commission* [1972] ECR 619, [1972] CMLR 557, ECJ, and Joined Cases 40-48, 50, 54-56, 111, 113, 114/73 *Cooperatieve vereniging Suiker Unie UA v Commission* [1975] ECR 1663, [1976] 1 CMLR 295, ECJ.

[110]

A concerted practice is thus a distinct form of infringement of Article 81, distinguished from an agreement by the absence of an agreement or 'plan'. The distinction between a concerted practice and an agreement can be important. In addition to showing that entities have acted in concert (a requirement in proving both an agreement and a concerted practice), if a concerted practice is to be held to exist, there must also be proof of 'subsequent conduct on the market and a relationship of cause and effect between the two [the concertation and the practice]'.[1] Thus, there is an additional element that must be proved by the party bringing the challenge (be it a national court or competition authority or private individual).

1 Case C-199/92P *Hüls AG v Commission* [1999] ECR I-4287, [1999] 5 CMLR 1016, para 161. See this and other appeals from *Polypropylene* [1986] OJ L230/1, [1988] 4 CMLR 347, for example,

Case C-51/92P, SA *Hercules NV v Commission* [1999] ECR I-4235, [1999] 5 CMLR 976. See also for a useful summary of the law in this area Commission Decision (*Interbrew and Alken-Maes Belgian Beer*) [2003] OJ L200/1, in particular paras 222 to 227.

[111]

The Commission will sometimes rely on the concept of a concerted practice in cases where a restriction of competition can be readily observed but the Commission does not have evidence of an agreement.[1] The approach of the Commission and the Court of Justice is to infer that undertakings have acted in concert where it is clear that the conditions prevailing upon a particular market are not the result of free competition. Although the concept of a concerted practice pre-supposes contact between the parties, if the behaviour of the undertakings is clearly such as could only result from the parties acting in concert, it will be inferred that such contact has taken place, even where direct evidence of it is scanty. The inference cannot properly be drawn, however, if another explanation of the behaviour is possible.[2]

1 eg in Commission Decision (EEC) 69/243 [1969] CMLR D23 (*Aniline Dyes Cartel*) (upheld on appeal in Case 48/69 *Imperial Chemical Industries Ltd v Commission* [1972] ECR 619, [1972] CMLR 557, ECJ), the Commission stated that the increases in price which it found were at the very least the effect of concerted practices within the meaning of Article 81 of the EC Treaty, and that there was therefore no need to examine whether the increases were the result of an agreement. See also Commission Decision (EEC) 79/90 [1979] OJ L21/16, [1979] 1 CMLR 464 (*White lead*); Commission Decision (EEC) 80/182 [1980] 2 CMLR285 (*Floral Dungemittelverkaufsgesellschaft MbH*); Commission Decision (EEC) 82/367 [1982] OJ L161/18, [1982] 2 CMLR 233 (*Hasselblad*) (on appeal in Case 86/82 *Hasselblad (GB) Ltd v Commission* [1984] ECR 883, [1984] 1 CMLR 559, ECJ); and Commission Decision (EEC) 85/74 [1985] OJ L35/1, [1985] 1 CMLR 481 (*Penoxygen Products*).

2 Case 48/69 *Imperial Chemical Industries Ltd v Commission* [1972] ECR 619 at 659, [1972] CMLR 557 at 626, ECJ. For a discussion of the question of proof of a concerted practice, see the Opinion of Advocate General Slynn in Joined Cases 100-103/80 *Musique Diffussion Française SA and Others v Commission* [1983] ECR 1825, [1983] 3 CMLR 221, ECJ. In its second judgment in *Ahlström* of 31 March 1993 (Joined Cases C-89, 104, 114, 116-117, 125-129/85 *Ahlström Osakeyhtio and Others v Commission* [1993] ECR I-1307, [1993] 4 CMLR 407, ECJ), the ECJ quashed the Commission's finding of concerted practices regarding the pricing of wood pulp on the grounds that concertation was not the 'only plausible explanation' of the undertakings' pricing behaviour. See also Case T-30/91 *Solvay v Commission* [1995] ECR II-1775 at II-1805 to II-1810, [1995] All ER (EC) 600, [1996] 5 CMLR 57, CFI. In the German banks cartel regarding the passage to the Euro (Cases T-44, 54, 56 & 60-61/02 *Dresdner Bank ea v Commission*, 14 October 2004), although there was at least one meeting between the parties, there was uncertainty as to whether an agreement had been reached. As the applicants were successful in putting forward an alternative convincing interpretation of the document on which the Commission had based its infringement decision, the Court annulled the decision. It should also be noted however that this was the first time where the CFI gave default judgment (as the Commission failed to submit a defence within the prescribed time limit).

[112]

Concerted behaviour between companies which form a single economic unit is not a concerted practice within the meaning of Article 81.[1]

1 Joined Cases 228, 229/82 *Ford of Europe Inc and Ford Werke AG v Commission* [1984] ECR 1129 at 1160, [1984] 1 CMLR 649 at 672, ECJ and paras [129]–[132].

[113]
Similar or identical behaviour does not of itself amount to a concerted practice, since it may be the result of each undertaking's independent reaction to the conditions of the market. As already mentioned above,[1] there is no concerted practice where undertakings independently adapt themselves to the existing or anticipated conduct of their competitors. Nor is there a concerted practice unless a participant's uncertainty as to the future attitude of its competitors is lessened.[2] Cases of parallel behaviour raise two interrelated issues: (a) what forms of contact between undertakings give rise to a concerted practice; and (b) when is it appropriate to infer that such forms of contact have taken place?

1 See para [109].
2 Joined Cases 89, 104, 114, 116, 117, 125-129/85 *Ahlström Osakeyhtio and Others v Commission* [1993] ECR I-1307, [1993] 4 CMLR 407, ECJ; Case T-30/91 *Solway v Commission* [1995] ECR II-1775 at II-1807, [1995] All ER (EC) 600, [1996] 5 CMLR 57, CFI.

[114]
The Court of Justice has indicated that for a concerted practice to exist, it is sufficient that there has been direct or indirect contact between the undertakings with the object or effect either of influencing each other's behaviour on the market or of disclosing to each other the course of conduct contemplated by each.[1] Undertakings are engaged in a concerted practice if they adopt a practice as the result not of a decision taken by each in isolation, but of a mutual understanding that each will adopt the practice.[2]

1 Joined Cases 40-48, 50, 54-56, 111, 113, 114/73 *Cooperatieve vereniging Suiker Unie UA v Commission* [1975] ECR 1663 at 1942, [1976] 1 CMLR 295 at 425, ECJ.
2 Case 48/69 *Imperial Chemical Industries Ltd v Commission* [1972] ECR 619, [1972] CMLR 557, ECJ. See also Joined Cases 40-48, 50, 54-56, 111, 113, 114/73 *Cooperatieve vereniging Suiker Unie UA v Commission* [1975] ECR 1663 at 1942, [1976] 1 CMLR 295 at 425, ECJ.

[115]
An element of reciprocity appears to be required,[1] so that there is either reciprocal disclosure of the parties' intentions or, possibly, such disclosure by one party in circumstances where other parties have given him to understand that they will act in a certain way in consequence of disclosure. The sort of information whose disclosure is likely to give rise to a concerted practice is information which is: (a) not obtainable (or not readily obtainable) from the market; and (b) of a sort likely to affect decisions or prices or other terms of supply.[2]

1 See the second opinion of Advocate General Darmon in Joined Cases 89, 104, 114, 116, 117, 125-129/85 *Ahlström Osakeyhtio and Others v Commission* [1993] ECR I-1307, [1993] 4 CMLR 407, ECJ.
2 The exchange of information is considered further at para [119] below.

[116]
A concerted practice may be proved either by evidence of exchanges of information or by evidence of 'unnatural' parallel behaviour, or by a combination of the two. Thus, where banks throughout a Member State imposed uniform percentage rates of charge for money transfers between Member States, the court indicated that it was a question of fact whether:

(a) there had been contacts or exchanges of information between the banks as to the charges currently levied by each or to be levied in the future; and

(b) the uniform rate of charge could be the result of the free play of competition.[1]

1 Case 172/80 *Züchner v Bayerische Vereinsbank AG* [1981] ECR 2021, [1982] 1 CMLR 313, ECJ.

[117]

In a clear case, concertation will be inferred simply from behaviour. Thus where several undertakings simultaneously raised their prices for the same product by identical amounts (something which would not have happened as a result of normal market forces), they were found to have engaged in a concerted practice;[1] but the inference is only permissible if no other explanation than one of a concerted practice is possible.[2] Parallel behaviour is not to be treated as demonstrating participation in a concerted practice without an analysis of the circumstances of each alleged participant and reasons being given for rejecting any other explanation of its behaviour.[3] The Commission must disclose to an undertaking documents in its possession that are capable of substantiating an alternative explanation.[4]

1 Case 48/69 *Imperial Chemical Industries Ltd v Commission* [1972] ECR 619, [1972] CMLR 557, ECJ.

2 Joined Cases 40-48, 50, 54-56, 111, 113, 114/73 *Cooperatieve vereniging Suiker Unie UA v Commission* [1975] ECR 1663 at 1964, 1965, 1972, 1975, [1976] 1 CMLR 295 at 442, 448, 450, ECJ; Joined Cases 29, 30/83 *Compagnie Royale Asturienne des Mines SA and Rheinzink GmbH v Commission* [1984] ECR 1679 at 1702, [1985] 1 CMLR 688 at 711, ECJ; Case 395/87 *Ministère public v Tournier* [1989] ECR 2521, [1991] 4 CMLR 248, ECJ; Joined Cases 110, 241, 242/88 *Lucazeau and Others v Société des Auteurs, Compositeurs et Editeurs de Musique (Sacem) and Others* [1989] ECR 2811, [1991] 4 CMLR 248, ECJ. See also Cases T-68, 77,78/89 *Società Italiano Vetro SpA and Others v Commission* [1992] ECR II-1403, [1992] 5 CMLR 302, CFI, where the Court of First Instance analysed in detail the grounds upon which the Commission had concluded (in Commission Decision (EEC) 89/93 [1989] OJ L33/44 (*Italian Flat Glass*) that a concerted practice had been engaged in, and largely rejected the Commission's conclusions. In Joined Cases C-89, 104, 114, 116-117, 125-129/85 *Ahlström Osakeyhtio v Commission* [1993] ECR I-1307, [1993] 4 CMLR 407, ECJ, the Court similarly rejected the Commission's conclusion that concerted practices were to be inferred from parallel price announcements by suppliers of wood pulp.

3 Per Advocate General Darmon in Joined Cases C-89, 104, 114, 116-117, 125-129/85 *Ahlström Osakeyhtio v Commission* [1993] ECR I-1307, [1993] 4 CMLR 407, ECJ.

4 Case T-36/91 *ICI v Commission* [1995] ECR II-1847, CFI.

[118]

A concerted practice need not necessarily consist of the adoption of parallel or similar behaviour. Thus where manufacturers and their national distributors cooperate in measures to track down and/or eliminate parallel imports, they can be guilty of a concerted practice.[1] It has been indicated that if an undertaking alters its behaviour as a result of complaints from a competitor, they are engaged in a concerted practice.[2] Undertakings which continued to observe the terms of an agreement after it had ended were found to be engaged in a concerted practice.[3]

1 Case 28/77 *Tepea BV v Commission* [1978] ECR 1391 at 1416, [1978] 3 CMLR 392 at 415, ECJ; Commission Decision (EEC) 79/68 [1979] 1 CMLR 448 (*Kawasaki Motors*); Commission Decision (EEC) 80/256 [1980] OJ L60/21, [1980] 1 CMLR 457 (*Pioneer Hi-Fi Equipment*) (upheld in part on appeal in Joined Cases 100-103/80 *Musique Diffusion Française SA and Others v Commission* [1983] ECR 1825, [1983] 3 CMLR 221, ECJ); Commission Decision (EEC) 82/367 [1982] OJ L161/

18, [1982] 2 CMLR 233 (*Hasselblad*) (on appeal in Case 86/ 82 *Hasselblad (GB) Ltd v Commission* [1984] ECR 883, [1984] 1 CMLR 559, ECJ); Commission Decision (EEC) 92/261 [1992] OJ L131/32, (*Newitt/Dunlop Slazenger*) (on appeal Case T-43/92 *Dunlop Slazenger v Comission* [1994] ECR II-441, [1994] 5 CMLR 201, CFI).

2 Joined Cases 40-48, 50, 54-56, 111, 113, 114/73 *Cooperatieve vereniging Suiker Unie UA v Commission* [1975] ECR 1663 at 1962, [1976] 1 CMLR 295 at 440, ECJ.

3 Commission Decision (EEC) 779/90 [1979] OJ L21/16, [1979] 1 CMLR 464 (*White lead*); Commission Decision (EEC) 79/934 [1986] OJ L286/32, [1979] 3 EMLR 684 (*BP Kemi*); Commission Decision (EEC) 85/74 [1985] OJ L35/1, [1985] 1 CMLR 481 (*Peroxygen Products*).

4. *Exchange of information*

[119]

The compilation of statistics of the performance of a particular sector of industry is unobjectionable, even where these are broken down by individual product. However, where statistics relating to sales by individual undertakings are exchanged, and a fortiori where details of terms of supply are revealed, it will be inferred that the purpose of the exchange is to facilitate co-ordination of the marketing strategy of the undertakings involved and thereby reduce competition.[1] The exchange of such information will be regarded as the subject of an agreement[2] or a concerted practice.[3] The fact that it would be possible to collect such information from sources in the public domain is irrelevant; to do so would be more time-consuming and the fact that undertakings are spontaneously avoiding this procedure is evidence of solidarity and mutual influence between them.[4] Even if the statistics published by a trade association are in an unobjectionable form, the Commission will be suspicious if it finds that undertakings are supplying to the trade association more detailed information than is necessary for compiling the statistics, such as copies of invoices[5] or statistics on prices or sales figures.[6]

1 See generally, Case C-7/95P *John Deere Ltd v Commission* [1998] ECR I-3111, [1998] 5 CMLR 311.

2 Case T-34/92 *Fiatagri v Commission* [1994] ECR II-905, CFI; Case T-35/92 *John Deere Ltd v Commission* [1994] ECR II-957, CFI. See also Case T-29/92 *SPO and Others v Commission* [1995] ECR II-289, CFI.

3 Joined Cases 40-48, 50, 54-56, 111, 113, 114/73 *Cooperatieve vereniging Suiker Unie UA v Commission* [1975] ECR 1663 at 1962, 1963, [1975] 1 CMLR 295 at 441, ECJ; Commission Decision (EEC) 77/592 [1977] OJ L242, [1977] 2 CMLR D28 (*VNP and COBELPA*); Commission Decision (EEC) 78/252 [1978] OJ L70/54, [1978] 1 CMLR 534 (*Vegetable Parchment*); Commission Decision (EEC) 79/90 [1979] 1 CMLR 464 (*White lead*); Commission Decision (EEC) 79/934 [1979] OJ L286/32, [1979] 3 CMLR 684 (*BP Kemi*).

4 Commission Decision (EEC) 77/592 [1977] OJ L242, [1977] 2 CMLR D28 (*VNP and COBELPA*). In *Rhône-Poulenc v Commission* [1991] ECR II-0867, members of the polypropylene cartel were found to communicate with each other, *inter alia*, through unilateral announcements in the trade press.

5 Commission Decision (EEC) 78/252 [1978] 1 CMLR 534 (*Vegetable Parchment*).

6 Commission Decision (EC) 2001/418, [2001] OJ L152 (*Amino Acids*).

[120]

The exchange between a manufacturer and his appointed dealers of price lists, the names of customers and the serial numbers of equipment sold will be contrary to the rules of competition if it is designed to help the distributors prevent parallel imports.[1]

1 Commission Decision (EEC) 82/367 [1982] OJ L161/18, [1982] 2 CMLR 233 (*Hasselblad*) (on appeal in Case 86/82 *Hasselblad (GB) Ltd v Commission* [1984] ECR 883, [1984] 1 CMLR 559, ECJ);

see also Commission Decision (EEC) 92/261 [1992] OJ L131/32 (*Newitt/Dunlop Slazenger*) (on appeal Case T-43/92 *Dunlop Slazenger v Commission* [1994] ECR II-441, [1994] 5 CMLR 201, CFI).

[121]

The 1968 Notice[1] which previously covered exchange of information has now been replaced by the Commission Guidelines on horizontal cooperation agreements.[2] However, these Guidelines expressly do not cover information agreements.[3] Despite this, there is nothing in them to suggest that the guidance set out in the previous Notice is not still applicable.

1 Commission Notice concerning agreements, decisions and concerted practices in the field of cooperation between enterprises [1968] OJ C75/3, [1968] CMLR D5.
2 Guidelines on the applicability of Article 81 of the EC Treaty to horizontal cooperation agreements [2001] OJ C3/2, [2001] 4 CMLR 819.
3 Ibid, para 10.

5. Application of Article 81 to 'unilateral' conduct

[122]

Unlike Article 82, which applies to the unilateral conduct of an undertaking in a dominant position,[1] Article 81 applies only to concerted behaviour. Thus, for example, the mere charging of different prices to different customers is not in itself contrary to Article 81 in the absence of an agreement to do so, since Article 81 only prohibits behaviour which results from an agreement, decision or concerted practice and not the unilateral behaviour of an undertaking.[2] There are, however, situations in which conduct which might appear to be adopted unilaterally will be held to be, or to evidence, an infringement of Article 81. It should be noted, though, that the situations in which the Court will uphold the application of the Article 81(1) prohibition to such apparently unilateral behaviour has recently been curtailed in a number of judgments which distinguish earlier rulings. The development of the Court's approach to this area is set out in the following paragraphs.

1 Abuse of dominant position is discussed below at paras [219] ff.
2 Case T-102/92 *Viho v Commission* [1995] ECR II-17, CFI, upheld on appeal in Case C-73/95P *Viho v Commission* [1996] ECR I-5457, [1997] 4 CMLR 419, [1997] All ER (EC) 163, ECJ. This confirms that an entity may act in an anti-competitive manner and yet not be caught by Article 81 (if that act is unilateral) or Article 82 (if the entity is not in a dominant position). See also on this point Case T-41/96 *Bayer AG v Commission* [2000] ECR II-3383, [2001] 4 CMLR 126, para 179 – upheld by the Court of Justice, Cases C-2 and 3/01P *Bunderverband der Arzneimittel-Importeure EV and Commission v Bayer AG* [2004] 4 CMLR 653.

[123]

The principal situation where the Court will hold that there is an agreement despite a party acting in an apparently unilateral manner is where another party has assented to that act to a sufficient degree for that act to become a term of an agreement or a concerted practice.[1] The Commission has, however, sometimes not imposed a fine where an entity has only assented due to its weaker economic position and in fact has acted against its own economic interest.[2] It is interesting to note that in *Courage v Crehan*,[3] the first reported UK case on damages for breach of competition law, the claimant was a party to the illegal agreement. His claim was however successful as it was held that the agreement was in reality imposed on him.

1 See for example Case 32/78 *BMW v Commission* [1979] ECR 2435, [1980] 1 CMLR 370.

2 See *Volkswagen* [1998] OJ L124/60, [1998] 5 CMLR 33 (note the unsuccessful appeal in Case C-338/00P *Volkswagen AG v Commission* [2004] 4 CMLR 351). Other indications of the Commission's acceptance of the difficult position dealers and suppliers are placed in include: EC Regulation 1400/02 on the application of Article 81(3) of the Treaty to categories of vertical agreements and concerted practices in the motor vehicle sector [2002] OJ L203/30 (the motor vehicles block exemption)
3 *Courage v Crehan* [2004] ECC 28.

[124]
It is irrelevant to the application of Article 81 which party took the initiative in inserting any particular provision in an agreement and it is unnecessary to show that the parties had a shared anti-competitive purpose;[1] accordingly, if a term which restricts competition is included in contractual documentation, it will be treated as a term of an agreement falling within Article 81(1), even though the other party has not expressly assented to it or has ignored it.[2] Thus a term included in standard conditions of sale[3] or other documentation relating to a transaction[4] and, at least where there is a course of dealing, upon invoices[5] can fall within Article 81(1). In *Sandoz,*[6] Article 81 was held to have been infringed by the inclusion on invoices of words prohibiting the export of the goods to other Member States, even where the term was invalid in domestic law for want of the necessary formality and had never been sought to be enforced. It was no defence that the words were included in error and did not reflect the supplier's intentions.

1 See Joined Cases 29, 30/83 *Compagnie Royale Asturienne des Mines SA and Rheinzink GmbH v Commission* [1984] ECR 1679, [1985] 1 CMLR 688, ECJ.
2 See Joined Cases 29, 30/83 *Compagnie Royale Asturienne des Mines SA and Rheinzink GmbH v Commission* [1984] ECR 1679, [1985] 1 CMLR 688, ECJ; Case C-277/87 *Sandoz prodotti farmaceutici SpA v Commission* [1990] ECR I-45, ECJ.
3 See para [99], note 11.
4 Commission Decision (EEC) 78/922 [1978] OJ 1322/26, [1979] 1 CMLR 81 (*Zanussi SpA Guarantee*).
5 Case C-277/87 *Sandoz Prodotti Farmaceutici SpA v Commission* [1990] ECR I-45, ECJ; Commission Decision (EEC) 92/261 [1992] OJ L131/32 (*Newitt/Dunlop Slazenger*).
6 Case C-277/87 *Sandoz Prodotti Farmaceutici SpA v Commission* [1990] ECR I-45, ECJ. See also Commission Decision (EEC) 91/153 [1991] OJ L75/57 (*Vichy*).

[125]
Even where it is not reflected in any written term, a policy adopted by a supplier which colours the contractual relations between him and his dealers may be regarded as having been assented to by the dealers so as to constitute a term of an agreement or a concerted practice. Thus, for example, where a manufacturer adopts a selective distribution policy which involves not merely appointing only dealers with the requisite qualifications but also limiting the numbers of dealers, that policy may be taken to have been assented to by the dealers who are appointed so as to fall within Article 81. In *AEG,*[1] the Court of Justice rejected the contention that such a policy amounted only to unilateral conduct; it held that the manufacturer's policy formed part of the contractual relations between the manufacturer and the dealers since the admission of a dealer required his tacit or express acceptance of the policy. As a result, the manufacturer's systematic refusal to appoint additional dealers, in pursuance of the policy, was conduct carried out in the context of his agreements with the authorised distributors and was contrary to Article 81. In the second *Ford*

decision,[2] the Court held that Ford's refusal to supply right hand drive cars to its dealers in Germany was not a unilateral act, exempt from the prohibition in Article 81, but rather formed part of the contractual relations between Ford and the German dealers.

1 Case 107/82 *AEG-Telefunken AG v Commission* [1983] ECR 3151, [1984] 3 CMLR 325, ECJ.
2 Joined Cases 25, 26/84 *Ford-Werke AG and Ford of Europe Inc v Commission* [1985] ECR 2725, [1985] 3 CMLR 528, ECJ.

[126]

The Court did not find it necessary in *AEG* or *Ford* to look for proof of the assent by the dealers. In *AEG*,[1] such assent could possibly be inferred from the fact that, in order for a system of selective distribution to function, not only the manufacturer but also the authorised dealers must refrain from supplying unauthorised dealers. In *Ford*,[2] it is hard to see that dealers had any option whether or not to assent to a policy which was not in their interests. The Court's decision on this point conflicts somewhat with the first *Ford* decision[3] and was arguably unnecessary to the resolution of the issue in the case. The issue was whether the Commission could lawfully refuse exemption to Ford's distribution agreements on account of this policy. It was not necessary to hold that the policy itself infringed Article 81(1) in order to uphold the Commission's decision. In *Dunlop Slazenger*,[4] the CFI described it as settled case law that, when a producer chooses to organise the distribution of its products by a network of authorised distributors who are guaranteed exclusive or selective distribution, such a distribution system will be permitted under Community competition law only on condition that *inter alia* no prohibition on the resale of the products in question within the distribution network is imposed in fact or in law on the authorised distributors. Such stipulations, the effect of which is to partition national markets and in so doing to thwart the objective of achieving a common market, are inherently contrary to Article 81(1) of the Treaty; it rejected the contention that this was unilateral conduct falling outside Article 81. The CFI found evidence of tacit agreement or acceptance, but it is not clear that such evidence was essential to its reasoning.

1 Case 107/82 *AEG-Telefunken A-G v Commission* [1983] ECR 3151, [1984] 3 CMLR 325, ECJ.
2 Joined Cases 25, 26/84 *Ford-Werke AG and Ford of Europe Inc v Commission* [1985] ECR 2725, [1985] 3 CMLR 528, ECJ.
3 Joined Cases 228, 229/82 *Ford of Europe Inc and Ford Werke AG v Commission* [1984] ECR 1129, [1984] 1 CMLR 649, ECJ.
4 Case T-43/92 *Dunlop Slazenger v Commission* [1994] ECR II-441, CFI

[127]

However, the CFI and the Court have more recently displayed a change in their approach to the application of the Article 81(1) prohibition to unilateral conduct. The CFI has held that there must be evidence of a 'concurrence of wills' if there is to be a finding that apparently unilateral conduct is integral to an agreement.[1] In *Bayer AG v Commission* the Commission had found that an export ban adopted by Bayer to prevent parallel imports of pharmaceuticals breached Article 81. Bayer appealed against this finding and against the fine imposed. At the appeal hearing, the CFI found, contrary to the Commission, that there was not an agreement. The CFI focused on 'apparently unilateral conduct', which conduct is carried out with at least tacit acquiescence of the other party,[2] but noted that, in this case, there had not been any acquiescence or assent to Bayer's acts.[3] The CFI distinguished *AEG* and *Ford* on the grounds that they were cases where there had been express or tacit acceptance of the relevant acts.[4] The CFI's judgment was upheld in the Court of Justice. This new approach of the CFI and Court of Justice, which questions more rigorously the Commission's application of Article 81(1), has been maintained since.[5] The present situation is therefore that clear evidence will be needed of acquiescence in cases of otherwise unilateral conduct.

1 Case T-41/96 *Bayer AG v Commission* [2000] ECR II-3383, [2001] 4 CMLR 126.
2 Ibid, paras 66-71.
3 Ibid, paras 72-185.
4 Cases C-2 and 3/01P *Bunderverband der Arzneimittel-Importeure EV and Commission v Bayer AG* [2004] 4 CMLR 653. In particular, the CFI pointed out that, in itself, the act of the dealer joining the supplier's distribution network constituted acquiescence. See generally on this point, A Jones and B Sufrin, *EC Competition Law* (2nd edn, 2004), pp 134 et seq.
5 See, for example, Case T-208/01 *Volkswagen v Commission* [2004] 4 CMLR 727; Case T-67/01 *JCB Service v Commission* [2004] 4 CMLR 1346.

[128]
Arrangements regarding consumer guarantees have been held to fall within Article 81. In *Zanussi*[1] a manufacturer of domestic electrical appliances required his dealers to supply the purchaser with a card entitling the purchaser to the manufacturer's guarantee. It was a term of the guarantee that it would lapse if the appliance was used in a Member State other than that in which it was first supplied, thus putting at a disadvantage parallel importers who bought appliances in one country for resale in another. This restriction of competition was held to result from an agreement between the manufacturer and the dealers relating to the passing on of the guarantee documentation. The contract of guarantee itself could not fall within Article 81 as it was not an agreement between undertakings. In *ETA v DK Investment*,[2] it was a term of distribution agreements for electronic watches that the consumer was covered by a manufacturer's guarantee. The watches were supplied in packages containing a card addressed to customers offering the guarantee. The manufacturer brought proceedings against a parallel importer to restrain him from selling watches with the guarantee card on the grounds that the guarantee only applied where the watch was sold to the customer by an authorised dealer. The Court of Justice held that an agreement with authorised dealers to offer a consumer guarantee, 'by virtue of which' the guarantee was withheld from customers of parallel distributors, was contrary to Article 81. The lapsing of the guarantee in cases where watches passed through the hands of unauthorised distributors was thus treated as a term of the distribution agreements, though it was not expressly set out.

1 Commission Decision (EEC) 78/922 [1978] OJ L322/26, [1979] 1 CMLR 81 (*Zanussi SpA Guarantee*).
2 Case 31/85 *ETA Fabriques d'Ebauches SA v DK Investment SA* [1985] ECR 3933, [1986] 2 CMLR 674, ECJ. Note that provisions relating to guarantees may be compatible with Article 81 if the product is the subject of a lawful system of selective distribution: Case C-376/ 92 *Metro SB-Grofimankte GmbH and Co KG v Cartier SA* [1994] ECR I-15, [1994] 5 CMLR 331, ECJ.

6. Concerted behaviour between companies in the same group and agreements between principals and agents

[129]

Article 81 does not apply to agreements or concerted practices between a parent and a subsidiary company if the two form a single economic unit within which the subsidiary has no real freedom to determine its course of action on the market and the agreements or practices are concerned merely with the internal allocation of tasks as between them.[1] The same is true of an agreement between two subsidiaries which form part of a single economic unit.[2] This rule reflects the fact that Article 81 is concerned with concerted behaviour between separate economic operators. Its legal basis has been described as being either: (1) that because there is no potential for competition between companies under the same control, an agreement purporting to restrict competition between them cannot have any genuine anti-competitive effect;[3] (2) that a group of companies under the same control is only one 'undertaking';[4] or (3) that there is no agreement where there is only one directing will.[5]

1 Case 48/69 *ICI v Commission* [1972] ECR 619, ECJ; Joined Cases 15/74 and 16/74 *Centrafarm BV v Sterling Drug Inc and Winthrop* [1974] ECR 1147 at 1167, [1974] 2 CMLR 480 at 507, ECJ; Case 30/87 *Bodson v Pompes funebres des regions libérées SA* [1988] ECR 2479, [1989] 4 CMLR 984, ECJ; Case 66/86 *Ahmed Saeed Flugreisen v Zentrale zur Bekampfung unlauteren Wettbewerbs BV* [1989] ECR 803 at 848-849, [1990] 4 CMLR 102 at 134, ECJ. See also Case C-73/95P *Viho Europe BV v Commission* [1996] ECR I-5457, [1997] 4 CMLR 419.
See also WPJ Wils, 'The Undertaking as Subject of EC Competition Law and the Imputation of Infringements to Natural or Legal Persons' (2000) 25 EL Rev 99.
See further Notice on Agreements of Minor Importance [2001] OJ C368/13, [2002] 4 CMLR 699 and Article 11 of Regulation 2790/1999 [1999] OJ L336/1, [2000] 4 CMLR 398.

2 Case 30/87 *Bodson v Pompes funebres des regions libérées SA* [1988] ECR 2479, [1989] 4 CMLR 984, ECJ. See also Commission Decision (EEC) 79/934 [1979] OJ L286/32, [1979] 3 CMLR 684 (*BP Kemi*), where the sale by one wholly-owned subsidiary of products provided by another wholly-owned subsidiary was equated to a sale by the latter.

3 Case 22/71 *Béguelin Import Co v GL Import Export SA* [1971] ECR 949, [1972] CMLR 81, ECJ; Commission Decision (EEC) 69/195 [1969] OJ L165/12, [1969] CMLR D36 (*Christiani and Nielsen NV*).

4 Case 22/71 *Béguelin Import Co v GL Import Export SA* [1971] ECR 949, [1972] CMLR 81, ECJ, per Advocate General Dutheillet de Lamothe; Joined Cases 6, 7/73 *Istituto Chemioterapico Italiano SpA and Commercial Solvents Corpn v Commission* [1974] ECR 223, [1974] 1 CMLR 309, ECJ, per Advocate General Warner; Case T-11/89 *Shell v Commission* [1992] ECR II-757, CFI; Commission Decision (EEC) 78/68 [1978] OJ L22/23, [1978] 1 CMLR D19 (*Hugin/Liptons*) (revised on other grounds in Case 22/78 *Hugin Kassaregister AB v Commission* [1979] ECR 1869, [1979] 3 CMLR 345, ECJ). See also Case 170/83 *Hydrotherm Gerätebau GmbH v Compact de Dott Ing Mario Andreoli & CSAS* [1984] ECR 2999, [1985] 3 CMLR224, ECJ (companies under common control are one undertaking for the purpose of Commission Regulation (EEC) 67/67).

5 Case 48/69 *Imperial Chemical Industries Ltd v Commission* [1972] ECR 619, [1972] CMLR 557, ECJ; Commission Decision (EEC) 70/332 [1970] OJ L147/24, [1970] CMLR D19 (*Kodak*).

[130]

The decisive criterion is, however, whether the subsidiary is free to determine its commercial strategy; this is a question of fact, dependent on, for example, the degree of control exercised by the parent over the subsidiary's board of directors and over the business of the subsidiary (in areas such as marketing and investment) and the amount of profit the parent takes from the subsidiary. The mere fact of belonging to a group of companies is not decisive; account must be taken of the nature of the relationship between the companies and in particular whether they pursue the same strategy, determined by the parent company.[1] A 'deadlock' joint venture, of which two independent parents have joint control, will not be regarded as forming part of the same economic unit as either parent.[2] Where a parent has a majority shareholding, it will be presumed that the subsidiary is not independent.[3] However, it appears that where, despite having a controlling shareholding, a parent company leaves a subsidiary or subsidiaries free to determine their own commercial strategy, an agreement between them will be subject to Article 81.[4] It has been suggested that guidance as to what constitutes a single economic unit in the context of Article 81 may be obtained from an analysis of Article 3(3) of the EC Merger Regulation, which provides that even a minority shareholder and a subsidiary may constitute a single economic unit if that shareholder has the 'possibility of exercising decisive influence' over the affairs of the subsidiary.[5]

1 Case 30/87 *Bodson v Pompes funebres des regions libérées SA* [1988] ECR 2479, [1989] 4 CMLR 984, ECJ. See also Commission Decision (EEC) 69/195 [1969] CMLR D36 (*Christiani and Nielsen NV*); Commission Decision (EEC) 70/332 [1970] CMLR D19 (*Kodak*).
2 Commission Decision (EEC) 91/335, [1991] OJ L185/23 (*Gosme/Martell – DMP*).
3 Opinion of AG Warner in Cases 6 and 7/73 *Istituto Chemioterapico Italiano SpA and Commercial Solvents Corp v Commission* [1974] ECR 223, [1974] 1 CMLR 309.
4 Case 30/87 *Bodson v Pompes Funebres des Regions Liberées SA* [1988] ECR 2479, [1989] 4 CMLR 984, ECJ.
5 See R Whish, *Competition Law* (5th ed, 2003), pp 88-89.

[131]
The European Court's judgments indicate that, for an agreement between companies within the same economic unit to fall outside Article 81, the agreement must be concerned merely with the internal allocation of tasks as between the companies, but it is unclear whether and in what circumstances Article 81 could apply to such an agreement on the grounds that it went beyond the internal allocation of tasks and had repercussions on the competitive position of outsiders. In *Centrafarm v Sterling Drug Inc*,[1] Advocate General Trabucchi expressed the view that Article 81 does so apply. In continuing to refer, both in *Centrafarm* and in subsequent decisions, to agreements concerned merely with the internal allocation of tasks, the Court appears to have intended at least to leave the possibility open. The Commission has also stated the view that Article 81 does so apply: see the Commission's IVth Report on Competition Policy, point 52. However, the contrary view appears to have been assumed by the Commission and the Court of Justice in the first *Ford* case,[2] where an agreement between companies in the Ford group not to supply right hand drive cars to dealers in Germany was assumed not to be an agreement, decision of an association of undertakings or concerted practice within the meaning of Article 81. It is difficult to give a clear meaning to the concept of an agreement 'concerned merely with the internal allocation of tasks', and it would be anomalous if behaviour between two arms of the same concern could ever be caught by Article 81 if the arms have separate legal personality, given that Article 81 could not apply to an 'agreement' between two divisions of a single corporate entity. In *Viho v Commission*,[3] the Court of First Instance regarded it as irrelevant whether the effects of agreements between a parent company and subsidiaries controlled by it went beyond the internal allocation of tasks within the group.

1 Case 15/74 *Centrafarm BV v Sterling Drug Inc* [1974] ECR 1147 at 1180, [1974] 2 CMLR 480 at 550-502, ECJ.
2 Joined Cases 228, 229/82 *Ford of Europe Inc and Ford Werke AG v Commission* [1984] ECR 1129 at 1180, [1984] 1 CMLR 672, ECJ.
3 Case T-102/92 *Viho v Commission* [1995] ECR II-17, CFI, upheld on appeal in Case C-73/95P *Viho v Commission* [1997] All ER (EC) 163, ECJ.

[132]
By similar reasoning, Article 81 has been held not to apply to agreements between a principal and his agent; where the agent is a 'true' agent (through whom the principal contracts directly with customers) he forms part of the principal's undertaking.[1] This principle does not apply to agents, such as travel agents, who supply a distinct service to the public.[2] The Commission has set out Guidelines on the issue,[3] which provide assistance in ascertaining whether an agreement is a 'true' agency agreement or not – the key factor being the commercial risk borne by the agent.[4] This risk must be assessed on a case by case basis.[5] The Guidelines provide that agreements preventing the agent from acting as an agent or distributor of undertakings which compete with the principal (non-compete provisions) may infringe Article 81(1) where they lead to foreclosure on the relevant market.[6]

1 Joined Cases 40-48, 50, 54-56, 111, 113, 114/73 *Cooperatieve vereniging Suiker Unie UA v Commission* [1975] ECR 1663, [1976] 1 CMLR 295, ECJ. See also Cases C-73/95P *Viho Europe BV v Commission* [1996] ECR I-5457, [1997] 4 CMLR 419.
2 Case 311/85 *VZW Vereniging van Vlaamse Reisbureaus v VZW Sociale Dienst van de Plaatselijke en Gewestelijke Overheidsdiensten* [1987] ECR 3801, [1989] 4 CMLR 213, ECJ.
3 Commission Guidelines on Vertical Restraints [2000] OJ C291/1, [2000] 5 CMLR 1074. These replace Commission Notice on exclusive dealing contracts with commercial agents [1962] OJ L39/2921.
4 Ibid, para 13.
5 Ibid, para 16. See, for an example of the application of these Guidelines, Case T-325/01 *Daimler Chrysler v Commission* (appeal pending) with reference to Case C-266/93 *Bundeskartellamt v Volkswagen AG and VAG Leasing GmbH* [1995] ECR I-3477.
6 Ibid, para 19.

C. THE OBJECT OR EFFECT OF PREVENTING, RESTRICTING OR DISTORTING COMPETITION

1. Introduction

[133]
Article 81(1) applies to concerted behaviour which may affect trade between Member States and has as its object or effect the prevention, restriction or distortion of competition within the common market. The application of these criteria involves considering an agreement, decision or concerted practice (which, for brevity, will be referred to here as 'an agreement') against the background of competitive conditions that would prevail and the inter-State trade that would take place in its absence. Article 81(1) does not apply to an agreement unless its effects, both upon competition and upon inter-state trade, are 'appreciable', that is, not de minimis. The Commission has produced a series of Notices (the most recent in 2001[1]) in respect of appreciable effect on competition and a set of Guidelines (in 2004[2]) in respect of appreciable effect on trade between Member States. These are dealt with below.[3]

1 Commission Notice on Agreements of Minor Importance which do not appreciably restrict competition under Article 81(1) [2001] OJ C368/13.
2 Commission Notice: Guidelines on the effect on trade concept contained in Articles 81 and 82 [2004] OJ C101/81.
3 See paras [155] ff.

[134]
In order for Article 81 to apply, it is not necessary that individual provisions of the agreement should both prevent, restrict or distort competition and be capable of affecting inter-State trade. The question whether an agreement is capable of affecting inter-State trade is to be answered by looking at the agreement as a whole. If the agreement is capable of affecting inter-State trade, then Article 81 applies to any provision of the agreement which prevents, restricts or distorts competition, even though that provision viewed in isolation would not be capable of affecting inter-state trade.[1] Nevertheless, in considering the possible application of Article 81 to an agreement it is usually most convenient to consider first whether any provisions of the agreement prevent, restrict or distort competition and, if that is the case, to proceed to consider whether the agreement is capable of affecting inter-State trade. For that reason, this section of the title discusses the prevention, restriction or distortion of competition and the following section[2] discusses the extent to which an agreement may affect trade between Member States.

1 Case 193/83 *Windsurfing International Inc v Commission* [1986] ECR 611 at 664, [1986] 3 CMLR 489 at 541, ECJ.
2 See paras [155] ff.

2. *Object or effect*

[135]
The requirements of 'object or effect' of restricting competition are alternative and not cumulative. The words are to be read disjunctively. In applying Article 81 of the EC Treaty to an agreement, the first step is to consider the object of the agreement in the light of its economic context in order to see whether its intended effect is appreciably[1] to restrict competition. 'Competition' means the competition which would exist in the absence of the agreement.[2] It is not necessary at this stage to consider what the effects of the agreement actually are.[3] An agreement may therefore be caught by Article 81 before it has come into effect.[4] An agreement can be contrary to Article 81(1), whether or not the restrictive provision is complied with[5] or enforced,[6] or whether or not the attempt to restrict competition succeeds.[7] If the analysis of the intended effects of the agreement does not disclose an appreciable restriction of competition, the actual effects of the agreement or practice should then be considered in order to see whether the agreement or practice in fact appreciably restricts competition.[8]

1 See para [178].
2 Case 56/65 *Société Technique Minière v Maschinenbau Ulm GmbH* [1966] ECR 235, [1966] 1 CMLR 357, ECJ; Case 99/79 *Lancôme SA v Etos* BV [1980] ECR 2511, [1981] 2 CMLR 164, ECJ; Case 31/80 *L'Oreal NV v De Nieuwe AMCK PVBA* [1980] ECR 377S, [1981] 2 CMLR 235, ECJ; Case 42/84 *Remia BV v Commission* [1985] ECR 2545, [1987] 1 CMLR1, ECJ; Case 31/85 *ETA Fabriques d'Ebauches SA v DK Investment* SA [1985] ECR 3933, [1986] 2 CMLR 674, ECJ; Cases T-374, 375, 384 and 388/94 *European Night Services v Commission* [1998] ECR II-3141, [1998] 5 CMLR 718, para 136.

3 Joined Cases 56, 58/64 *Consten and Grundig v EEC Commission* [1966] ECR 299, [1966] CMLR 418, ECJ; Case 123/83 *BNIC v Clair* [1985] ECR 391, ECJ; Case 45/85 *Verband der Sachversicherer eV v Commission* [1987] ECR 405, [1988] 4 CMLR 264, ECJ (where the Court said expressly that the same principles applied to decisions of associations of undertakings as to agreements); Joined Cases T-39, 40/92 *Groupement des Cartes Bancaires 'CB' v Commission* [1994] ECR II-49, CFI.
4 Commission Decision (EEC) 72/480 [1972] OJ L308/52, [1973] CMLR D43 (*WEA-Fili pacchi Music SA*); Commission Decision (EEC) 74/634 [1974] OJ L343/19, [1975] 1 CMLR D8 (*Franco-Japanese Ballbearings Agreement*); Commission Decision (EEC) 75/77 [1975] OJ L29/26, [1975] 1 CMLR D83 (*French and Taiwanese Mushroom Packers*); Commission Decision (EEC) 75/497 [1975] 2 CMLR D20 (*Virgin Aluminium Producers*).
5 Case T-141/89 *Trefileurope Sales v Commission* [1995] ECR II-791, CFI; Case T-142/89 *Boel v Commission* [1995] ECR II-867, CFI.
6 Case T-43/92 *Dunlop Slazenger v Commission* [1994] ECR II-441, [1994] 5 CMLR 201, at para 61, CFI. See also Case C-277/87 *Sandoz prodottifarmaceutici SpA v Commission* [1990] ECR I-45, ECJ (a clause on a sales invoice prohibiting export had the object of restricting competition and it was therefore irrelevant that the clause was included in error and not enforced and was not shown to have had an effect on the behaviour of purchasers).
7 See export restrictions placed on Schiltz in Commission Decision (EEC) 82/866 [1982] OJ L362/40, [1983] 2 CMLR 285 (*Rolled Zinc Products*) (on appeal in Joined Cases 29, 30/83 *Compagnie Royale Asturienne des Mines SA and Rheinzink GmbH v Commission* [1984] ECR 1679, [1985] 1 CMLR 688, ECJ).
8 Case 56/65 *Société Technique Minière v Maschinenbau Ulm GmbH* [1966] ECR 235, [1966] 1 CMLR 357, ECJ; Case C-234/89 *Delimitis v Henninger Bräu AG* [1991] ECR I-935, [1992] 5 CMLR 210, ECJ.

[136]

The question whether an agreement has the object of preventing, restricting or distorting competition is a question of interpretation of the foreseeable effects of the agreement, not of the subjective intentions of the parties. Thus the Court of Justice has held that it is not necessary to inquire which of the two contracting parties took the initiative in inserting any particular clause or to verify that the parties had a common intent at the time when the agreement was concluded; it is rather a question of examining the aims pursued by the agreement as such, in the light of the economic context in which the agreement is to be applied.[1] Article 81 will apply whether the parties had a common purpose or one or more of them was apathetic or unwilling.[2] A clause prohibiting exports to other Member States infringes Article 81 whether or not it is complied with.[3]

1 Joined Cases 29, 30/83 *Compagnie Royale Asturienne des Mines SA and Rheinzink GmbH v Commission* [1984] ECR 1679 at 1703, 1704, [1985] 1 CMLR 688 at 712, ECJ.
2 Case T-141/89 *Trefileurope Sales v Commission* [1995] ECR II-791, CFI (no defence that undertaking participated reluctantly). For a further example of the imposition of a restriction of competition upon an unwilling party, see the passages concerning Schiltz in Commission Decision (EEC) 82/866 [1982] OJ L362/40, [1983] 2 CMLR 285 (*Rolled Zinc Products*) (on appeal Joined Cases 29, 30/83 *Compagnie Royale Asturienne des Mines SA and Rheinzink GmbH v Commission* [1984] ECR 1679, [1985] 1 CMLR 688, ECJ). See also Case 277/87 *Sandoz prodottifarmaceutici SpA v Commission* [1990] ECR I-45, ECJ.
3 Case T-66/92 *Herlitz v Commission* [1994] ECR II-531, [1995] 5 CMLR 458, at para 40, CFI; Case T-77/92 *Parker Pen v Commission* [1994] ECR II-549, [1995] 5 CMLR 435, at para 55, CFI.

[137]

In assessing the effects of an agreement upon competition, the agreement must be viewed in its economic and legal context taking into account all relevant facts, including the legislation of Member States[1] or other agreements.[2] Thus, an agreement may infringe Article 81(1) where one of the parties is able to obstruct parallel imports by means of the combined effect of the agreement and the provisions of national law governing import formalities[3] or intellectual property rights.[4] Where undertakings are multi-nationals, operating on a world scale, their relationship outside the Community may be relevant.[5] An agreement may have the object or effect of distorting competition, both where the parties are actual competitiors and where they are potential competitors.[6]

1 Joined Cases 56, 58/64 *Etablissements Consten SARL and Grundig-Verkaufs-GmbH v EEC Commission* [1966] ECR 299 at 343, [1966] CMLR 418 at 473, 474, ECJ.
2 Case 23/67 *Brasserie de Haecht SA v Wilkin* [1967] ECR 407, [1968] CMLR 26, ECJ. See also Case C-234/89 *Delimitis v Henninger Bräu AG* [1991] ECR I-935, [1992] 5 CMLR 210, ECJ.
3 Case 8/74 *Procureur du Roi v Dassonville* [1974] ECR 837, [1974] 2 CMLR 436, ECJ.
4 Joined Cases 56, 58/64 *Etablissements Consten SARL and Grundig-Verkaufs-GmbH v EEC Commission* [1966] ECR 299, [1966] CMLR 418, ECJ; Case 258/78 *LC Nungesser KG v Commission* [1982] ECR 2015, [1983] 1 CMLR 278, ECJ.
5 Joined Cases 142, 156/84 *British American Tobacco Co Ltd and RJ Reynolds Industries Inc v Commission* [1987] ECR 4487, [1988] 4 CMLR 24, ECJ.
6 Thus, EC Treaty, Article 85 applies, for example, to joint research and development agreements which restrict the potential competition that might have existed between the parties if they had developed the new product separately.

3. *Prevention, restriction or distortion of competition*

[138]
An agreement may prevent, restrict or distort competition within the meaning of Article 81(1) not only as between the parties to the agreement but also as between one of them and third persons.[1] Article 81(1) thus applies both to agreements between actual or potential competitors, referred to as 'horizontal' agreements, and to agreements between a supplier and an acquirer of goods or services, referred to as 'vertical' agreements. Examples of both types of restriction are given below.

1 Joined Cases 56, 58/64 *Etablissements Consten SARL and Grundig-Verkaufs-GmbH v EEC Commission* [1966] ECR 299, [1966] CMLR 418, ECJ. See also Case 31/85 *ETA Fabriques d'Ebauches SA v DK Investment SA* [1985] ECR 3933 at 3944, [1986] 2 CMLR 674 at 684, ECJ.

[139]
Article 81(1) is not infringed unless competition is 'appreciably' prevented, restricted or distorted; this 'de minimis rule' is discussed later.[1] Similarly, Article 81(1) is not infringed where there would be no possibility of any appreciable competition even in the absence of the agreement. This may be the case, for example, where owing to extensive government regulation the scope for competition is minimal or non-existent.[2] For the same reason a term of an agreement by which producers of natural cement undertook not to switch to production of artificial cement was held not to restrict competition when for practical reasons it had become impossible for the manufacturers to set up production of artificial cement.[3] Where two undertakings partially merged[4] their activities in a joint venture, their ancillary agreement not to compete with the joint venture was held not to fall within Article 81(1) where one of the parties had ceased to be in a position to compete and the other would have no commercial interest in doing so.[5] A possible reason why Article 81 does not apply to agreements between a parent and its subsidiary is that there is no pre-existing possibility of competition between them.[6]

1 See paras [178] ff.
2 Joined Cases 40-48, 50, 54-56, 111, 113, 114/73 *Cooperatieve vereniging Suiker Unie UA v Commission* [1975] ECR 1663 at 1923, 1924, [1976] 1 CMLR 295 at 411, ECJ; Joined Cases 209-215, 218/78 *Heintz van Landewyck Sar v Commission* [1980] ECR 3125 at 3261, 3262, [1981] 3 CMLR 134 at 234, ECJ.
3 Commission Decision (EEC) 69/152 [1969] OJ L122/8, [1969] CMLR D15 (*Cement Makers' Agreement*). The parties also undertook restrictions upon their sales of natural cement. These were held not to restrict competition appreciably in view of the small proportion of cement production accounted for by natural cement, which was an obsolete product.
4 As to mergers, see Vaughan, *Law of the European Union*, Section 21C ('Competition – Mergers', forthcoming).
5 Commission Decision (EEC) 75/95 [1975] 1 CMLR D68 (*SHV and Chevron Oil Europe Inc*). Article 81(1) will apply where the parties accept restrictions of competition in an area in which they remain potential competitors: see eg Commission Decision (EEC) 78/251 [1978] OJ L70/47, (*SOPELEM, Vickers Ltd and Microscopes Nachet SA Agreement*) [1978] 2 CMLR 146.
6 See para [129].

[140]
Article 81(1) applies to an agreement which prevents, restricts or distorts competition in the supply or acquisition of goods or services within the common market,[1] irrespective of the nationality or location of the parties.[2] It may therefore apply to an agreement relating to imports into the Community from non-Member countries.[3] It may also apply to an agreement relating to exports from the Community if either there is a likelihood of goods being reimported into the Community or, possibly, if the agreement has 'upstream' effects on competition within the common market.[4]

1 The territory of the common market is defined in para [37] above.
2 The nationality or location of the parties may be relevant to the power of the Commission to enforce the rules of competition: see paras [39] above.
3 See para [39] above and Joined Cases 89, 104, 114, 116, 117, 125-129/85 *Ahlström Osakeyhtio v Commission* [1988] ECR 5193, [1988] 4 CMLR 901, ECJ; Commission Decision (EEC) 91/ 301 [1991] OJ L152/54 (*Ansac*); Case T-37/92 *BEUC v Commission* [1994] ECR II-285, [1995] 4 CMLR 167, CFI.
4 See para [39] above.

4. Horizontal agreements

[141]
An important category of agreements restricting competition consists of those between actual or potential competitors, whether manufacturers of or dealers in goods or providers of services. Such 'horizontal' restrictions of competition may arise, in particular, where the parties undertake restrictions upon their activities or where, by co-operation, or by the exchange of sensitive information, they weaken competitive conditions between themselves. Competition is likely to be prevented, restricted or distorted where the direct or indirect effect of the agreement is to hamper one or more of the parties in the free and independent pursuit of a commercial activity which it formerly pursued or might, but for the agreement, have pursued.

[142]
The Commission has conducted an overhaul of the rules in this area.[1] There are now block exemptions[2] and Commission Guidelines on horizontal cooperation agree-

ments.[3] Horizontal agreements are dealt with in detail in Vaughan, *Law of the European Union,* Section 21F ('Competition – Horizontal Agreements').

1 Commission's XXVI Report on Competition Policy (1997), paras 46 and 47, announcing a review of policy on horizontal agreements – a review brought about in part by the imminent expiry of the block exemptions on specialisation agreements (Regulation 417/85 [1985] OJ L53/1) and R&D agreements (Regulation 418/85 [1985] OJ L53/5).
2 Regulation 2658/2000 [2000] OJ L304/3 on specialisation agreements and Regulation 2659/2000 [2000] OJ L304/7 on R&D agreements.
3 Commission Notice: Guidelines on horizontal cooperation agreements [2000] OJ C3/2.

5. Vertical agreements

[143]

For an agreement to fall within Article 81, it is not necessary that the parties should be actual or potential competitors or that the agreement should prevent, restrict or distort competition between the parties themselves. It was established at an early stage that Article 81 also applies to an agreement between parties not in competition with one another, typically between a supplier and an acquirer of goods or services, if the agreement prevents, restricts or distorts competition between one or both of the parties and third persons.[1] This will be the case where the supplier is restricted in supplying competitors of the acquirer, the acquirer is restricted as to how he may use or dispose of the goods or services acquired or the competitive situation as between (usually) the acquirer and third parties is distorted to the detriment of the third parties.

1 Joined Cases 56, 58/64 *Etablissements Consten SARL and Grundig-Venkaufs-GmbH v EEC Commission* [1966] ECR 299, [1966] CMLR 418, ECJ; Case 32/65 *Italy v EEC Council and EEC Commission* [1966] ECR 389, [1969] CMLR 39, ECJ. In Case C-234/89 *Delimitis v Henninger Bräu AG* [1991] ECR I-935, [1992] 5 CMLR 210, ECJ, the Court indicated that beer supply agreements, under which brewers obtain guaranteed outlets in return for financial advantages given to resellers, might not have the object of restricting competition, in which case it was necessary to analyse the market in order to determine whether they had that effect.

[144]

The Court of Justice has stated as a general principle that clauses in contracts of sale restricting the buyer's freedom to use the goods supplied in accordance with his own economic interests are restrictions of competition.[1] The same is true where a supplier accepts restrictions upon his freedom to supply goods or services to other acquirers and a substantial body of law has developed concerning exclusive and selective distribution agreements for goods, franchising and licences of intellectual property rights.[2]

1 Case 319/82 *Societe Vente de Ciments et Betons de l'Est SA v Kerpen and Kerpen GmbH & Co KG* [1983] ECR 4173, [1985] 1 CMLR 511, ECJ.
2 See Vaughan, *Law of the European Union,* Section 21E ('Competition – Intellectual Property', forthcoming).

[145]

An agreement which does not place restrictions on a party's commercial freedom ought not to be regarded as one which prevents, restricts or distorts competition on the grounds simply that it is onerous or commercially disadvantageous. In *Bayer AG and Maschinenfabrik Hennecke GmbH v Heinz Sullhofer,*[1] the Court of Justice held that a 'no-challenge' clause in a agreement in settlement of patent litigation, prohibiting the licensee from challenging the validity of a patent was not contrary to Article 81(1) where the licence was free of royalty and the licensee did not therefore 'suffer from the competitive disadvantage involved in the payment of royalties' or where the licence related to a technically outdated process which the licensee did not in fact use. This might suggest that in other circumstances such a clause could restrict competition to the extent that, by being precluded from seeking the revocation of a patent, the licensee remained subject to the obligation to pay royalties. It is submitted, however, that the court was merely indicating that the 'no-challenge' clause (a provision which is generally a prohibited restriction of competition) had no adverse effects in these circumstances, rather than advancing the general proposition that the mere adverse financial effect of an unjustified drain upon an undertaking's resources will normally be a restriction of competition. Such a proposition is not supported by any other decision of the court and seems to be contradicted by the subsequent decision in *Ottung v Weilbach A/S and Thomas Schmidt A/S*.[2]

1 Case 65/86 *Bayer AG and Maschinenfabrik Hennecke GmbH v Heinz Süllhofer* [1988] ECR 5249 [1990] 4 CMLR 182, ECJ.

2 Case 320/87 *Ottung v Klee and Weilbach A/S and Thomas Schmidt A/S* [1989] ECR 1177, [1990] 4 CMLR 915, ECJ.

[146]

An agreement can be contrary to Article 81 where it artificially *improves* the competitive position of one of the parties vis-à-vis third parties. Thus, Article 81 was infringed where a manufacturer limited the terms of his manufacturer's guarantee so that it did not apply to products bought outside the territory in which they were used[1] or to products not bought from an approved dealer.[2] The Court of Justice stated in the *ETA* case that the crucial element to be taken into consideration was the effect of withholding the guarantee upon the competitive position of parallel importers. An agreement will not prevent, restrict or distort competition within the meaning of Article 81 merely because one party rather than another has succeeded in concluding it; generally speaking the agreement must place a restriction on one or both parties, such as a provision for exclusivity, or must work to the disadvantage of a class of persons, such as parallel importers, whose interests are regarded as coinciding particularly closely with the interests protected by the competition rules. Any term imposed on a buyer which is calculated to discourage trade in the goods between Member States is likely to amount to a restriction of competition, and a clause prohibiting exports to other Member States is, by its very nature, a restriction of competition.[3]

1 Commission Decision (EEC) 78/922 [1978] OJ L322/26, [1979] 1 CMLR 81 (*Zanussi SpA Guarantee*).

2 Case 31/85 *ETA Fabriques d'Ebauches SA v DK Investment* SA [1985] ECR 3933, [1986] 2 CMLR674, ECJ; see para [125] above.

3 Case 19/77 *Miller v Commission* [1978] ECR 131, [1978] 2 CMLR 334, at para 7, ECJ; Joined Cases C-89, 104, 114, 116, 117 and 125-129/85 *Ahlström v Commission* [1993] ECR I-1307, [1993] 4 CMLR 407, at para 176, ECJ; Case T-66/92 *Henlitz v Commission* [1994] ECR II-531, [1995] 5 CMLR 458, at para 29, CFI; Case T-77/92 *Parker Pen v Commission* [1994] ECR II-549, [1995] 5 CMLR 435, at para 37, CFI.

[147]
The Commission has adopted a new block exemption on vertical restraints – Regulation 2790/2000.[1] It has also published Guidelines on Vertical Restraints.[2] These and detailed analysis of vertical restraints are covered in Vaughan, *Law of the European Union,* Section 21E ('Competition – Vertical Agreements', forthcoming).

1 [1999] OJ L336/21.
2 [2000] OJ C291/1.

6. Restrictions necessary for the promotion of competition

[148]
The judgment of the Court of Justice in *Grundig* established that the principle of freedom of competition under Article 81 of the EC Treaty 'concerns the various stages and manifestations of competition'[1] and that if an agreement restricted competition in one respect it was no defence that it might increase competition in another respect. The case concerned an agreement between a German manufacturer and his French distributor under which the parties sought to protect the distributor from competition by parallel imports.[2] The court held that the agreement did not escape from Article 81(1) merely because it might increase competition in France between Grundig products and products of other makes.

1 Joined Cases 56, 58/64 *Etablissements Consten SARL and Grundig-Verkaufs-GmbH v EEC Commission* [1966] ECR 299 at 342, [1966] CMLR 418 at 473, ECJ.
2 ie Grundig products bought in other territories and imported into France.

[149]
However, the Court has also indicated that a restriction of competition will not be contrary to Article 81(1) if it is necessary in the interest of an overall enhancement of competition. *Technique Minière,* decided shortly before *Grundig,* concerned an exclusive distributorship where the distributor was not protected from parallel imports. The agreement could be said to involve restrictions of competition, in that the manufacturer undertook not to appoint other distributors in the territory or to sell there himself. The Court stated that 'it may be doubted that there is an interference with competition if the said agreement seems really necessary for the penetration of a new area by an undertaking'.[1] The Court developed this reasoning in the *Maize Seed* case, which concerned an exclusive licence of plant breeder's rights for maize. It found that an undertaking established in another Member State which was not certain that it would not encounter competition from other licensees for the territory granted to it, or from the owner of the right himself, might be deterred from accepting the risk of cultivating and marketing the product. Such a result would be damaging to the dissemination of new technology and would prejudice competition in the Community between the new product and similar existing products. In those circumstances the grant of an open exclusive licence (ie where the only restrictions were upon the appointment of other licensees for the same territory and upon the licensor selling there himself) was not in itself incompatible with Article 81(1).[2]

1 Case 56/65 *Societé Technique Minière v Maschinenbau Ulm GmbH* [1966] ECR 235 at 250, [1966] CMLR 357 at 375, ECJ (the translations differ slightly).
2 Case 258/78 *LC Nungesser KG v Commission* [1982] ECR 2015 at 2069, [1983] 1 CMLR 278 at 353, ECJ.

[150]

The Court retreated somewhat from this position in its subsequent judgment in *Pronuptia*[1] concerning franchising. While the Court held that certain provisions protecting the know-how communicated to the franchisee and requiring him to conform to the franchised method and style of trading were not within Article 81(1), provisions (such as the allocation of sales territories) restricting competition between the franchisees were within Article 81(1). Departing from its reasoning in *Maize Seed*,[2] the Court held that the fact that franchisees would not take the franchise at all, unless protected from the establishment of another of the same franchises in the same locality, was only relevant to the possible application of Article 81(3).

1 Case 161/84 *Pronuptia de Paris GmbH, Frankfurt am Main v Pronuptia de Paris Irmgard Schillgalis* [1986] ECR 353, [1986] 1 CMLR 414, ECJ.
2 Case 258/78 *LC Nungesser KG v Commission* [1982] ECR 2015 at 2069, [1983] 1 CMLR 278.

[151]

Reasoning similar to that in *Technique Minière*[1] appeared again in *Delimitis*,[2] where the Court suggested that beer supply agreements, under which a brewer obtains the exclusive right to supply beer to an outlet in return for financial advantages given to the reseller such as the provision of a loan or premises at a favourable rent, might not have the object of restricting competition and that it was necessary to analyse the market in order to establish whether they had that effect. The underlying reasoning appears to be that such agreements facilitate the existence of a greater number of outlets and the mere fact that those outlets are tied to one brewer does not necessarily make the retail market less competitive.

1 Case 56/65 *Société Technique Minière v Maschinenbau Ulm GmbH* [1966] ECR 235, [1966] CMLR 357, ECJ.
2 Case C-234/89 *Delimitis v Henninger Bräu AG* [1991] ECR I-935, [1992] 5 CMLR 210, ECJ. See also *Brasserie de Haecht SA v Wilkin (No 1)* [1967] ECR 407, [1968] CMLR 26.

[152]

The Court has stated that Article 81(1) requires 'workable competition', that is to say the degree of competition necessary to ensure the observance of the basic requirements and the attainment of the objectives of the Treaty, in particular the creation of a single market achieving conditions similar to those of a domestic market. In accordance with this requirement the nature and intensiveness of competition may vary to an extent dictated by the products or services in question and the economic structure of the relevant market sectors. Applying this principle, the Court held that a system of selective distribution,[1] under which a manufacturer only supplies dealers selected on the basis of objective criteria of quality, is not contrary to Article 81(1), provided there is sufficient competition between brands and the criteria are such as relate to the quality of service to the consumer.[2] The Court adopted analogous reasoning in another case concerning a licence of plant breeder's rights,[3] where it held that a prohibition on the sale of basic seed[4] fell outside Article 81(1) since a breeder must be entitled to restrict propagation to growers whom he has selected as licensees. The judgment in *Wouters* has cast doubt on the CFI's approach to this area in the earlier *Metropole* case. It now appears that the preferred view is that consideration of whether or not a particular arrangement constitutes an infringement of Article 81(1) is a wider task than the CFI indicated in *Metropole*. Thus, arrangements which are apparently anti-competitive may well, if found to be necessary, be held not to constitute an infringement of Article 81 at all.[5]

1 See, generally, Case C-309/99 *Wouters v Algemene Raad van de Nederlandse Orde van Advocaten* [2002] ECR I-1577, [2002] All ER (EC) 193, [2002] 4 CMLR 913, ECJ; Case T-112/99 *Métropole Télévision v Commission* [2001] ECR II-2459, [2001] 5 CMLR 1236; and Case C-250/92 *Gøttrup-Klim Grovvareforeninger v Dansk Landburgs Grovvareselskab AmbA* [1994] ECR I-5641, [1996] 4 CMLR 191.
2 Case 26/76 *Metro SB-Grosmarkte GmbH & Co KG v Commission* [1977] ECR 1875 at 1904, [1978] 2 CMLR 1 at 33, 34, ECJ.
3 Case 27/87 *Erauw-Jacquéry SPRL v La Hesbignonne* [1988] ECR 1919, [1988] 4 CMLR 576, ECJ.
4 ie, seed intended to be sown in order to grow plants for seed rather than for cultivation.
5 See, for a helpful discussion on this point, *RCA and ART v OFT* [2005] CAT 29, paras 160 to 167.

[153]

The Court has held that in applying Article 81(1) to covenants restricting competition in the sale of a business it is necessary to consider how competition would function without such clauses. Since a business could not be effectively transferred if the vendor remained in competition with the business after the transfer, and since such transfers ultimately contribute to increasing the number of competitors in a market and therefore have beneficial effects on competition, covenants restricting competition which are limited to what is necessary for an effective transfer are not contrary to Article 81(1).[1]

1 Case 42/84 *Remia BV and Verenigde Bedrijven Nutricia NV v Commission* [1985] ECR 2545, [1987] 1 CMLR 1, ECJ. Note that these kind of cases are now dealt with under the EC Merger Regulation regime, Regulation 139/2004 [2004] OJ L24/1.

[154]

The extent to which a restriction on commercial behaviour may fall outside Article 81 on any of the above grounds remains uncertain. No clear governing principle emerges from the decisions. The cases have been ones in which, unlike the position in *Grundig*,[1] restrictions have been accepted as operating in the overall interest of competition,[2] but the circumstances have varied. In the case of sales of a business the restriction is an intrinsic part of the transaction, without which the buyer could not acquire the goodwill of the business at all. The *Delimitis* judgment[3] suggests that exclusive agreements which promote inter-brand competition may not have the object of restricting competition (though they may have that effect). Thirdly, restrictions have fallen outside Article 81 because it was judged unreasonable to expect a party to enter into a generally desirable transaction without the protection of such a restriction;[4] however, the court's treatment of the territorial protection of franchisees in the *Pronuptia*[5] judgment shows that it remains unclear to what extent this consideration is relevant to the application of Article 81(1). The CFI's treatment of ancillary restraints in *Métropole Télévision (M6)*[6] may prove helpful in this area. If a restraint is a minor part of major operation and is directly related and necessary to it, then that restraint may fall outside the scope of Article 81, if the main operation itself falls outside Article 81.

1 Joined Cases 56, 58/64 *Consten and Grundig v EEC Commission* [1966] ECR 299, [1966] CMLR 418, ECJ.
2 It may also have been relevant that the *Grundig* agreement gave absolute territorial protection, contrary to a basic principle of EC Treaty, Article 81. In Case 258/78 *LC Nungesser KG v Commission* [1982] ECR 2015, [1983] 1 CMLR278, ECJ, the Court was careful to confine the principle of necessity to 'open' agreements.
3 Case C-234/89 *Delimitis v Henninger Bräu AG* [1991] ECR I-935, [1992] 5 CMLR 210, ECJ.
4 Commission Decision (EEC) 68/317 [1968] OJ L201/1, [1968] CMLR D23 (*Alliance de Constructeurs Français de Machines-Outils*) appears to have been decided on a similar principle.
5 Case 161/84 *Pronuptia de Paris GmbH, Frankfurt am Main v Pronuptia de Paris Irmgard Schiligalis* [1986] ECR 353, [1986] 1 CMLR 414, ECJ.
6 See paras 103–106 of Case T-112/99 *Métropole Télévision (M6) v Commission* [2001] ECR II-2459, [2001] 5 CMLR 1236.

D. EFFECT ON TRADE BETWEEN MEMBER STATES[1]

1. Introduction

[155]

The requirement that to fall within Article 81 an agreement[2] must be one which may affect trade between Member States is intended to define the boundary between the areas respectively covered by Community law and national law; it is only to the extent that an agreement may affect trade between Member States that the restrictions of competition caused by the agreement fall within Article 81.[3] It is only necessary to show that an agreement is capable of having an effect on inter-State trade, not that it has had or is having such an effect. However, as with the restriction of competition, the effect must not be insignificant. It is not necessary to show that the restrictions in the agreement are themselves capable of affecting interstate trade if the agreement as a whole is capable of having such an effect.[4] The Commission has published Guidelines on how to determine the effect of an arrangement on trade.[5]

1 See also Chapter 4, 'Abuse of Dominant Position', paras [311] to [313].
2 In this section the term 'agreement' is again used to describe an agreement, decision by an association of undertakings or concerted practice.
3 Joined Cases 56, 58/64 *Etablissements Consten SARL and Grundig-Verkaufs-GmbH v EEC Commission* [1966] ECR 299, [1966] CMLR 418, ECJ; Case 56/65 *Societé Technique Minière v Maschinenbau Ulm GmbH* [1966] ECR 235, [1966] CMLR 357, ECJ.
4 Case 193/83 *Windsurfing International Inc v Commission* [1986] ECR 611, [1986] 3 CMLR 489, ECJ. In Case 27/87 *Erauw-Jacquery SPRL v La Hesbignonne SC* [1988] ECR 1919, [1988] 4 CMLR 576, ECJ, the Court held that an agreement fell within Article 81(1) where the provision restricting competition was 'related to another provision in the same agreement which restricts the licensee from exporting seed for propagation'. It is not clear whether the Court was thereby indicating a requirement for some form of link between the provision restricting competition and the provision capable of affecting trade. See also Commission Decision (EEC) 89/515 [1989] OJ L260/1, [1991] 4 CMLR 13 (*Welded Steel Mesh*).
5 Commission Notice: Guidelines on the effect on trade concept contained in Articles 81 and 82 of the Treaty [2004] OJ C101/81.

[156]

For these purposes, the term trade has a wide scope.[1] It includes all commercial and business transactions,[2] including the provision of services,[3] and extends, for example, to banking,[4] insurance[5] and telecommunications.[6] It is likely that it includes most if not all activities undertaken for reward. It is not limited to trade engaged in by any of the parties to the agreement or practice, nor to trade in the goods or services to which the restrictions of competition apply. Thus, for example, an agreement imposing restrictions on the sale of a raw material may affect trade between Member States if the finished product is the subject of such trade even if the raw material is not.[7] Trade between Member States includes supply of goods within a group of companies for sale in another Member State.[8]

1 Case 172/80 *Ztichner v Bayerische Vereinsbank AG* [1981] ECR 2021, [1982] 1 CMLR 313, ECJ.
2 The Court of First Instance has held that it includes any form of economic activity: see Case T-66/92 *Herlitz v Commission* [1994] ECR II-531 at para 32, [1995] 5 CMLR 458.
3 Commission Decision (EEC) 81/1030 [1981] OJ L370/49, [1982] 1 CMLR 221 (*GVL*). On the application of the competition rules to a franchise agreement concerning the provision of services, see Commission Decision (EEC) 88/604 [1988] OJ L332/38 (*Service-Master*).
4 Case 172/80 *Züchner v Bayerische Vereinsbank AG* [1981] ECR 2021, [1982] 1 CMLR 313, ECJ. See also Case 267/86 *Van Eycke v ASPANV* [1988] ECR 4769, [1990] 4 CMLR 330, ECJ.
5 Commission Decision (EEC) 85/75 [1985] OJ L35/20, [1985] 3 CMLR 246 (*Fire Insurance*) upheld on appeal in Case 45/85 *Verband der Sachversicherer eV v Commission* [1987] ECR 405, [1988] 4 CMLR 264, ECJ.
6 Commission Decision (EEC) 82/861 [1982] OJ L360/36, [1983] 1 CMLR 457 (*British Telecommunications*), upheld on appeal in Case 41/83 *Italy v Commission* [1985] ECR 873, [1985] 2 CMLR 368, ECJ.
7 Case 123/83 *Bureau National Interprofessional du Cognac v Clair* [1985] ECR 391, [1985] 2 CMLR 430, ECJ; Case 136/86 *Bureau National Interprofessionnel du Cognac v Aubert* [1987] ECR 4789, [1988] 4 CMLR 331, ECJ. See also Joined Cases 6, 7/73 *Istituto Chemioterapico Italiano SpA and Commercial Solvents Corpn v Commission* [1974] ECR 223, [1974] 1 CMLR 309, ECJ.
8 See Case 240/82 *Stichting Sigarettenindustrie v Commission* [1985] ECR 3831 at para 49, [1987] 3 CMLR 661, ECJ; Case T-7/93 *Langnese-Iglo GmbH v Commission* [1995] ECR II-1533 at II-1579, [1995] 5 CMLR 602, CFI.

[157]

The Court of Justice has held that an agreement is one which may affect trade between Member States if it is possible to foresee with a sufficient degree of probability on the basis of a set of objective factors of law and fact that it may have an influence, direct or indirect, actual or potential, on the pattern of trade between Member States, thus rendering more difficult the interpenetration of trade which the EC Treaty is intended to create and harming the attainment of the objectives of a single market between Member States.[1]

1 This definition is found, with slight variations of wording, in several judgments, including Joined Cases 56,58/64 *Etablissements Consten SARL and Grundig-Verkaufs-GmbH v EEC Commission* [1966] ECR 299, [1966] CMLR 418, ECJ; Case 56/65 *Société Technique Minière v Maschinenbau Ulm GmbH* [1966] ECR 235, [1966] CMLR 357, ECJ; Case 5/69 *Völk v Vervaecke* [1969] ECR 295, [1969] CMLR 273, ECJ; Case 1/71 *Cadillon SA v Höss, Maschinenbau KG* [1971] ECR 351, [1971] CMLR 420, ECJ; Joined Cases 209-215, 218/78 *Heintz van Landewyck Sàrl v Commission* [1980] ECR 3125, [1981] 3 CMLR 134, ECJ; Case 61/80 *Cooperatieve Streinsel- en Kleurselfabriek v Commission* [1981] ECR 851 at 867, [1982] 1 CMLR 240 at 257, ECJ; Case 126/80 *Salonia v Poidomani* [1981] ECR 1563, [1982] 1 CMLR 64, ECJ; Case 27/87 *Erauw-Jacquery SPRL v La Hesbignonne SC* [1988] ECR 1919, [1988] 4 CMLR 576, ECJ.

[158]

The Court has also indicated that the interpretation and application of the requirement of ability to affect inter-State trade must be based on the purpose of the requirement, which is to define, in the context of the law governing competition, the boundary between the areas respectively covered by Community law and the laws of the Member States. Community law covers any agreement or any practice which is capable of constituting a threat to freedom of trade between Member States in a manner which might harm the attainment of the objectives of a single market between the Member States, in particular by partitioning the national markets or by affecting the structure of competition within the common market. On the other hand conduct, the effects of which are confined to the territory of a single Member State, is governed by the national legal order.[1] However, an agreement operating in one Member State alone may have effect on inter-State trade.[2]

1 Case 22/78 *Hugin Kassaregister AB v Commission* [1979] ECR 1869, [1979] 3 CMLR 345, ECJ.
2 See para [166] below.

[159]

The objectives of the Treaty are not satisfied simply by the volume of trade between Member States; trade must take place in conditions of undistorted competition.[1] Thus in *Grundig* the court rejected the argument that the distribution agreement in question was calculated to increase the volume of Grundig equipment imported into France and was therefore compatible with Article 81. The court ruled that the fact that an agreement encourages an increase, even a large one, in the volume of trade between States is not sufficient to exclude the possibility that the agreement may 'affect' trade in a manner harmful to the objectives of the Treaty.[2] Since the agreement in question prevented parallel imports between France and other Member States, it fell within Article 81. It seems therefore that references to harm to the objectives of the treaty add little if anything to the definition, since an effect on trade between Member States resulting from the prevention, restriction or distortion of competition will almost inevitably be contrary to those objectives. It is not the practice of the Commission[3] or the Court of Justice[4] to consider whether a given effect on trade between Member States is harmful or beneficial to the objectives of the Treaty.

1 See Joined Cases 43, 63/82 *VBVB and VBBB v Commission* [1984] ECR 19 at 82, [1985] 1 CMLR 27 at 56, ECJ, per Advocate General Verloren Van Themaat.
2 Joined Cases 56, 58/64 *Etablissements Consten SARL and Grundig-Verkaufs-GmbH v EEC Commission* [1966] ECR 299 at 341, [1966] CMLR 418 at 471,472, ECJ.
3 Although the Commission has sometimes described particular agreements as particularly serious infringements of Article 81 of the EC Treaty on the ground that they are calculated to partition national markets, it has also regarded the requirement of effect on trade between Member States as satisfied by a mere alteration in the flow of such trade. See eg Commission Decision (EEC) 77/160 [1977] OJ L048/32, [1977] 1 CMLR D67 (*Vacuum Interrupters Ltd*).
4 In Joined Cases 43,63/82 *VBVB and VBBB v Commission* [1984] ECR 19, [1985] 1 CMLR 27, ECJ, the association of Dutch book publishers and the association of Flemish book publishers had set up uniform marketing arrangements, including resale price maintenance at uniform levels, over the whole of the Dutch-speaking territory of the Netherlands and Belgium. The associations argued that their agreement furthered the interests of the Community by making the Belgian-Dutch border irrelevant. Advocate General Verloren Van Themaat rejected that argument on the grounds that the agreement also prevented parallel imports (apparently following in this respect Joined Cases 56, 58/64 *Etablissements Consten SARL and Grundig-Verkaufs-GmbH v EEC Commission* [1966] ECR 299, [1966] CMLR 418, ECJ), but the Court stated simply that 'the agreement indisputably affects trade between Member States' without considering whether the effect was unfavourable.

2. Agreements which 'may' affect inter-State trade

[160]

Article 81(1) does not require proof that an agreement or practice has *in fact* appreciably affected inter-State trade (which in the majority of cases would moreover be difficult to establish for legal purposes), but merely requires that it be established that such agreements or practices are capable of having that effect.[1]

1 Case 19/77 *Miller International Schallplatten GmbH v Commission* [1978] ECR 131, [1978] 2 CMLR 334, ECJ.

[161]

So, for example, where Dutch cheese producers undertook the obligation to purchase rennet exclusively from a Dutch cooperative, thereby precluding themselves buying rennet in other Member States, it was no answer that all Dutch cheese producers had traditionally bought Dutch rennet and would continue to do so even if the obligation did not exist; it was sufficient that rennet was available in other Member States.[1] Where a producer of records and tape recordings of songs in German included an export prohibition in its contracts of sale, it was no answer that the music in question was intended for a German-speaking public and was only of marginal interest to the public in other Member States, or that none of the purchasers of the music were interested in exporting it.[2] It was sufficient to establish that there was at least a small demand for the music in other Member States, to draw an inference from the fact that the producer had thought it worthwhile inserting the clause and to note that the producer had an interest in preventing the re-importation of the recordings into Germany, which would threaten the higher price levels prevailing there. The Court added that arguments based on the current situation cannot sufficiently establish that clauses prohibiting exports are not such as to affect trade between Member States, even if it were possible to establish beyond reasonable doubt the accuracy of such general statements, since that situation may vary from one year to the next in terms of changes in the conditions or composition of the market, both in the common market as a whole and on the various national markets.[3]

1 Case 61/80 *Coöperatieve Stremsel- en Kleurselfabriek v Commission* [1981] ECR 851, [1982] 1 CMLR 240, ECJ.
2 Case 19/77 *Miller International Schallplatten GmbH v Commission* [1978] ECR 131, [1978] 2 CMLR 334, ECJ. See also Commission Decision (EEC) 80/182 ([1980] OJ L39/51) [1980] 2 CMLR 285 (*Floral Dungemittelverkaufsgesellschaft mbH*).
3 See also Case T-66/92 *Herlitz v Commission* [1994] ECR II-531 at para 34, [1995] 5 CMLR 458, CFI; Case T-77/92 *Parker Pen v Commission* [1994] ECR II-549 at para 59, [1995] 5 CMLR 435, CFI.

[162]

Although Article 81 requires that the effect on inter-State trade should be not merely hypothetical but foreseeable on the basis of objective factors,[1] the range of circumstances in which such an effect has been held to be foreseeable is very wide. However, a restriction on exporting goods outside the Community will not affect trade between Member States where by reason of the incidence of transport costs and customs duties there is little likelihood that the product would ever be re-imported so as to become the subject of inter-state trade.[2] The refusal of a manufacturer situated outside the Community to supply spare parts for the repair of his machines to undertakings in the Community which do not belong to his distribution network is not capable of affecting trade between Member States where even in the absence of the refusal there would be no trade in the parts between Member States.[3] It has sometimes been held that an agreement or practice will not appreciably affect inter-state trade where there is little or no cross-frontier trade, but much will depend upon the circumstances. Thus, in *Dutch Banks*,[4] the Commission held that certain arrangements between the banks were not capable of appreciably affecting trade between Member States since they affected the terms of supply of services (such as the hire of safe deposits) that were unlikely to be used by customers from other Member States. It is likely that arrangements that purport to forbid inter-State transactions will only fall outside Article 81 if entered into between very small undertakings, because competition policy frowns on such arrangements. On the other hand, it may be that arrangements (such as those in *Dutch Banks*) that only affect the *terms* of potential transactions with third parties will fall outside Article 81, even if made between larger undertakings, if the types of transaction potentially affected are unlikely to occur to an appreciable extent across inter-state borders.

1 See para [135] above.
2 See para [39] above and the cases there cited. Such a restriction could, how ever, affect trade between Member States if it affected inter-State trade in the goods before their export.
3 Case 22/78 *Hugin Kassaregister AB v Commission* [1979] ECR 1869, [1979] 3 CMLR 345, ECJ.
4 Commission Decision (EEC) 89/512 ([1989] OJ L253/1) (*Dutch Banks*).

3. Agreements which limit, or affect the terms of, cross-border transactions

[163]
Where the restrictions of competition relate to the terms on which goods or services are traded between parties in different Member States, the agreement will inescapably affect trade between Member States.[1] Agreements in which the parties agree not to make imports or exports, or to do so only to a limited extent, affect trade between Member States. Thus where manufacturers situated in different Member States agreed not to supply in each other's markets except at agreed prices, to agreed customers and subject to agreed quotas, their behaviour clearly affected trade between Member States by inhibiting the interpenetration of markets.[2] An agreement by a purchaser situated in a Member State to resell only in the same Member State[3] or only outside the common market[4] is capable of affecting trade between Member States, as is an agreement to purchase only from a domestic source.[5]

1 See eg Joined Cases 43, 63/82 *VBVB and VBBB v Commission* [1984] ECR 19, [1985] 1 CMLR 27, ECJ.
2 Commission Decision (EEC) 83/546 [1983] OJ L317/1, [1984] 1 CMLR 694 (*Cast Iron and Steel Rolls*).
3 Case 19/77 *Miller International Schallplatten GmbH v Commission* [1978] ECR 131, [1978] 2 CMLR 334, ECJ.
4 Joined Cases 29, 30/83 *Compagnie Royale Asturienne des Mines SA and Rheinzink GmbH v Commission* [1984] ECR 1679, [1985] 1 CMLR 688, ECJ.
5 Case 61/80 *Coöperatieve Stremsel- en Kleurselfabriek v Commission* [1981] ECR 851, [1982] 1 CMLR 240, ECJ.

[164]
A decision of an association of undertakings which affected the terms on which insurance was offered was held capable of affecting inter-State trade on the grounds, inter alia, that it affected the terms on which insurance was offered by local insurance companies which were subsidiaries of insurers based elsewhere in the Community.[1] The provision of insurance through a local subsidiary was regarded as being in effect an inter-State transaction.

1 Case 45/85 *Verband der Sachversicherer v Commission* [1987] ECR 405, [1988] 4 CMLR 264, ECJ.

[165]
Trade between Member States is also capable of being affected by an agreement or practice designed to hinder imports or exports by third persons, such as where a manufacturer assigns a trade mark to his distributor for the purpose of enabling the distributor to block parallel imports under national trade mark law,[1] or where a manufacturer and his distributors take concerted action to track down and eliminate parallel imports.[2]

1 See eg Joined Cases 56, 58/64 *Etablissements Consten SARL and Grundig-Verkaufs-GmbH v EEC Commission* [1966] ECR 299, [1966] CMLR 418, ECJ; Case 28/77 *Tepea BV v Commission* [1978] ECR 1391, [1978] 3 CMLR 392, ECJ.
2 See eg Joined Cases 100-103/80 *Musique Diffusion Française SA and Others v Commission* [1983] ECR 1825, [1983] 3 CMLR 221, ECJ; Case 86/82 *Hasselbiad (GB) Ltd v Commission* [1984] ECR 883, [1984] 1 CMLR 559, ECJ.

4. Partitioning of national markets

[166]
A very important category of agreements and practices which may affect inter-State trade is those which limit the access of suppliers in other Member States to a particular national market; such an agreement may be capable of affecting inter-State trade even though the parties to it are situated in the same Member State. It has been held that an agreement restrictive of competition which extends over the whole territory of a Member State may by its very nature have the effect of reinforcing the partitioning of the market on national lines, and thus affect trade between Member States,[1] because such agreements tend to hinder penetration of the national market from other Member States. A covenant by the vendor of a business not to sell competing goods in the Member State in which the business is situated is also capable of affecting inter-State trade by preventing the vendor selling goods imported from other Member States.[2] Inter-State trade has also been held to be affected where the majority of the dealers in a particular product in a Member State are members of a cartel;[3] the result is that foreign producers wishing to penetrate the market may only either supply the members of the cartel, who will not market the product competitively, or supply the minority of non-members.

1 Case 8/72 *Vereeniging van Cementhandelaren v Commission* [1972] ECR 977, [1973] CMLR 7, ECJ; Case 73/74 *Groupement des fabricants de papiers peints de Belgique v Commission* [1975] ECR 1491, [1976] 1 CMLR 589, ECJ; Case 126/80 *Salonia v Poidomani* [1981] ECR 1563, [1982] 1 CMLR 64, ECJ; Case 42/84 *Remia BV v Commission* [1985] ECR 2545, [1987] 1 CMLR 1, ECJ.
2 Case 42/84 *Remia BV v Commission* [1985] ECR 2545, [1987] 1 CMLR1, ECJ.
3 See eg Commission Decision (EEC) 72/22 [1972] OJ L13/34, [1973] CMLR D16 (*Ver eeniging van Cementhandelaren*) (*on appeal in Case 8/72 Vereeniging van Cementhandelaren v Commission*

[1972] ECR 977, [1973] CMLR 7, ECJ); *Commission Decision* (EEC) 75/358 [1975] OJ L159/22, [1975] 2 CMLR Dl (*Stoves and Heaters*).

[167]

A national cartel of manufacturers has also been held to be capable of affecting inter-State trade although it related only to the marketing of products manufactured in the same Member State, where the market was capable of being served by imports since, in order for parties to such an agreement to maintain their market share, it was necessary for them to protect themselves against outside competition and there was evidence that such defensive measures had been agreed.[1]

1 Case 246/86 *Société Cooperative des Asphalteurs Belges (Belasco) v Commission* [1989] ECR 2117, [1991] 4 CMLR 96, ECJ.

[168]

Vertical agreements such as, for example, exclusive distribution agreements are capable of affecting inter-State trade by restricting the ability of distributors and dealers to handle competing, imported goods. Whether the effects of such an agreement will be appreciable will depend in particular upon the degree of prevalence of such agreements in a particular sector.[1] A nationwide system of selective distribution is liable to affect trade between Member States in that dealers outside the system are prevented from importing or exporting the products in question.[2]

1 See para [167] below.
2 Commission Decision (EEC) 76/159 [1976] OJ L28/19, [1976] 1 CMLR D61 (*SABA*).

5. Network effect

[169]

An agreement which, taken in isolation, is not capable of appreciably affecting inter-State trade may fall within Article 81 if it is one of a number of similar agreements in existence over the territory of a Member State whose cumulative effect is to hinder penetration of the market. This situation, sometimes referred to as 'network effect', arises in the case of agreements tying retail dealers to particular suppliers, commonly in the case of petrol and alcoholic beverages.

[170]

The Court of Justice has held[1] that, in order for an agreement to fall within Article 81 as a result of network effect, two main conditions must be satisfied: (1) the overall effect of the class of agreements to which the agreement under consideration belongs must be to partition the national market by making it impossible or difficult for suppliers from other Member States to penetrate the market; and (2) the supplier who is party to the agreement under consideration must himself contribute substantially to the overall effect.

1 Case C-234/89 *Delimitis v Henninger Bräu AG* [1991] ECR I-935, [1992] 5 CMLR 210, ECJ. See also Case 23/67 *Brasserie de Haecht v Wilkin SA* [1967] ECR 407, [1968] CMLR 26, ECJ; Case 47/76 *De Norre v NV Brouwerij Concordia* [1977] ECR 65, [1977] 1 CMLR 378, ECJ; Case 31/80 *L'Orial NV v De Nieuwe AMCK PVBA* [1980] ECR 3775, [1981] 2 CMLR 235, ECJ; Case 311/85 *VZW Vereniging van Vlaamse Reisbureaus v* VZW *Sociale Dienst van de Plaatselijke en Gewestelijke Overheidsdiensten* [1987] ECR 3801, [1989] 4 CMLR 213, ECJ.

[171]
As regards the first condition, the relevant factors include the extent (both as regards number of outlets and volumes of product) to which the retail market in question is covered by tie agreements and the extent to which a new competitor can enter the market by acquiring an existing supplier, supplying to an intermediary wholesaler or opening new retail outlets. It is relevant to the whole 'economic and legal context' of the agreement, including the extent to which access to the market is hindered by other types of agreement.[1]

1 See Case T-7/93 *Langnese-Iglo v Commission* [1995] ECR II-1533, [1995] 5 CMLR 602, CFI (effects of the exclusion agreements relating to ice cream reinforced by existence of other agreements relating to the use of loaned freezer cabinets).

[172]
The second condition principally concerns the market share of the supplier in question, the number of outlets tied to it and the length of the ties.

[173]
The Commission recognises the impact that a network effect can have on a market and provides for stricter application of the competition rules in situations where such a network effect applies.[1]

1 Commission Notice on Agreements of Minor Importance which do not appreciably restrict competition under Article 81 [2001] OJ C368/13, para 8.

6. Altering the pattern of inter-State trade

[174]
An agreement or practice is capable of affecting trade between Member States whenever it brings about a state of affairs in which the flow of trade between Member States follows a different course from that which it would have followed in the absence of the agreement. Thus where a manufacturer situated outside the common market appointed a single exclusive distributor for the whole of the Community, the agreement was held to be capable of affecting inter-state trade in that the product would be available to dealers in the common market only through the exclusive distributor and his sub-distributors and not by direct purchase from the manufacturer.[1] By similar reasoning, a marketing joint venture between a Community-based undertaking and an undertaking from outside the common market, covering the whole territory of the Community, was liable to affect trade between Member States in that production and marketing would proceed in a different manner and from different places than in the absence of the agreement.[2] Where two undertakings in the same Member State, each of which had the potential to develop a certain new product, formed a joint venture to develop the product together, the Commission held that inter-State trade was capable of being affected in that exports to other Member States would start earlier and form a different pattern, the two undertakings would not be competitors in inter-State trade in the product, and other manufacturers would have more difficulty in penetrating the home market. A reciprocal licence of intellectual property between parties in the same Member State was held to be capable of affecting trade between Member States where the agreement related to intellectual property protected in several Member States.[3] An

agreement limiting the volume of motor cars to be exported from Japan to the United Kingdom was liable to interfere with the natural movement of trade; it was irrelevant that the agreement did not primarily concern inter-State trade.[4]

1 Commission Decision (EEC) 75/74 [1975] OJ L29/11, [1975] 1 CMLR D62 (*Europair International SA and Duro-Dyne Corpn Agreement*).
2 Commission Decision (EEC) 77/543 [1977] OJ L215/11, [1977] 2 CMLR D69 (*De Laval Stork VOF Joint Venture*).
3 Case 65/86 *Bayer AG v Süllhofer* [1988] ECR 5249, [1990] 4 CMLR 182, ECJ.
4 Case T-37/92 *Bureau Européen des Unions des Consommateurs (BEUC) and National Consumer Council v Commission* [1994] ECR II-285, [1995] 4 CMLR 167, CFI (since the forseeable effect of the agreement was to increase demand for cars imported from other Member States, the judgment is a further indication that effects on inter-State trade need not be adverse).

[175]
Where Italian manufacturers of cast glass, whose sales extended to the whole of the Community, agreed quotas for their sales on their home market, the agreement was held to be liable to affect trade between Member States in that the limits placed on their home sales affected their capacity to export.[1] Where a large number of producers of wood pulp, all situated outside the Community, fixed prices in concert, their behaviour was held to be apt to have an appreciable effect on trade between Member States by bringing about an artificially uniform price throughout the common market and thus impairing the structure of competition throughout the Community. In addition, the uniformity of price prevented cross-supplies between Member States which would probably otherwise have arisen by reason of differences in demand, exchange rates and transport costs.[2]

1 Commission Decision (EEC) 80/1334 [1980] OJ L383/19, [1982] 2 CMLR 61 (*Italian Cast Glass*).
2 Commission Decision (EEC) 85/202 [1985] OJ L85/1, [1985] 3 CMLR 474 (*Wood Pulp*), on appeal Joined Cases 89, 104, 114, 116, 117 and 125-129/85 *Ahlström Osakeyhtio and Others v Commission* [1993] ECR I-1307, [1993] 4 CMLR 407, ECJ; Advocate General Darmon considered that the concerted practices were capable of affecting inter-State trade on the grounds that practices affecting the price of wood pulp were likely to affect the cost of paper, in which there was inter-State trade (second opinion delivered 7 July 1992, paras 518, 519). The Court agreed with the Advocate General: Joined Cases 89, 104, 114, 116, 117, 125-129/85 *Ahlström Osakeyhtio v Commission* [1993] ECR I-1307, [1993] 4 CMLR 407, at para 142, ECJ.

[176]
It has been held that agreements between travel agents in the same Member State might affect inter-State trade where the travel agents sold travel organised by tour operators in other Member States, where travel was sold to customers residing in other Member States or where the travel was to other Member States.[1]

1 Case 311/85 *VZW Vereniging van Vlaamse Reis bureaus v VZW Sociale Dienst van de Plaatsel ijke en Gewestelijke Overheidsdiensten* [1987] ECR 3801, [1989] 4 CMLR 213, ECJ. See also Commission Decision (EEC) 92/521 [1992] OJ L326/31 (*1990 World Cup Package*).

[177]
In a number of cases decided under Article 82, the Court of Justice has held that an abuse of dominant position is one that may affect trade between Member States if it alters the competitive structure within the common market.[1] The Commission has sometimes adopted the same approach under Article 81. Where there were no other manufacturers and few potential manufacturers of a product in the common market,

a research and development joint venture between two potential manufacturers affected the structure of competition within the common market and was thus held to be capable of affecting trade between Member States.[2]

1 See Chapter 4.
2 Commission Decision (EEC) 77/160 [1977] 1 CMLR D67 (*Vacuum Interrupters Ltd*).

E. THE REQUIREMENT OF 'APPRECIABLE' EFFECT ON COMPETITION AND ON TRADE BETWEEN MEMBER STATES

1. An appreciable effect on competition

[178]
The Court of Justice has held that an agreement falls outside the prohibition in Article 81(1) where it has only an insignificant effect on the markets, taking into account the weak position which the parties have in the product market in question.[1] Thus, for example, an exclusive dealing agreement, even if it creates absolute territorial protection,[2] may escape the prohibition laid down in Article 81(1) because, in view of the weak position of the parties on the market, it is not capable of hindering the attainment of the objectives of a single market between Member States.[3]

1 Case 5/69 *Völk v Vervaecke* [1969] ECR 295, [1969] CMLR 273, ECJ; Case 1/71 *Cadillon SA v Höss, Maschinenbau KG* [1971] ECR 351, [1971] CMLR 420, ECJ. See also Case T-66/89 *Publishers Association v Commission* [1992] ECR II-1995, [1992] 5 CMLR 120, CFI; Case T-77/92 *Parker Pen v Commission* [1994] ECR II-549, [1995] 5 CMLR 435, CFI.
2 ie seeks to protect the distributor from competition by parallel imports.
3 Case 1/71 *Cadillon SA v Höss, Maschinenbau KG* [1971] ECR 351 at 356, [1971] CMLR 420 at 429, ECJ.

[179]
This de minimis rule applies where the parties to the agreement or practice, and consequently the products affected by it, account for an insignificant proportion of the relevant market. The de minimis rule is of considerable practical importance in excluding the application of the competition rules to small undertakings, and the Commission has given guidance on it by a series of notices, the most recent in 2001.[1] These notices are not binding, but the Commission describes them as persuasive for national courts and national competition authorities.[2] The Commission has applied the rule to joint buying or selling agreements by groups of small purchasers or retailers, where in each case the volume of goods involved represented a very small fraction of such trade.[3]

1 Commission Notice on Agreements of Minor Importance which do not Appreciably Restrict Competition under Article 81(1) [2001] OJ C368/13, [2002] 4 CMLR 699. This has replaced earlier Notices. See below in relation to the fact that the 2001 Notice relates only to appreciable effects on competition, not to appreciable effects on trade between Member States. Under the previous *de minimis* notices, the Commission set out what constitutes an 'appreciable effect on trade'. In the 2001 Notice, however, the Commission addresses only the issue of whether an agreement 'appreciably restricts competition'. The issue of appreciable effect on trade is left to the Commission Guidelines on the effect on trade concept contained in Articles 81 and 82 of the Treaty [2004] OJ C101/81.
2 Commission Notice of 3 September 1986, para 6. See, however, Case 1/71 *Cadillon SA v Häss, Maschinenbau KG* [1971] ECR 351 at 361, [1971] CMLR 420 at 427, ECJ, per Advocate General

Dutheillet de Lamothe; Case 126/80 *Salonia v Poidomani* [1981] ECR 1563 at 1588, 1589, [1982] 1 CMLR Mat 71, 72, ECJ, per Advocate General Reischl.
3 Commission Decision (EEC) 68/318 [1968] OJ L201/4, [1968] CMLR D28 (*SOCEMAS*); Commission Decision (EEC) 72/23 [1972] OJ L13/14, [1972] CMLR D83 (*SAFCO*); Commission Decision (EEC) 75/482 [1975] OJ L212/23, [1975] 2 CMLR D14 (*Intergroup Trading BV*).

[180]
In cases covered by the Notice, the Commission will not institute proceedings either upon application or on its own initiative, and, where undertakings assume in good faith that an agreement is covered by the Notice, the Commission will not impose fines. The Notice expressly provides that it is intended to give guidance to the national courts and national competition authorities of the Member States (though accepting that it does not bind them). This is significant in the context of those bodies increased powers under Regulation 1/2003.[1]

1 Commission Notice on Agreements of Minor Importance [2001] OJ C368/13, [2002] 4 CMLR 699, para 4.

[181]
Agreements between undertakings which affect trade between Member States do not appreciably restrict competition within the meaning of Article 81(1) if:

(a) in the case of an agreement between competitors on any of the relevant markets, the aggregate market share held by the parties to the agreement does not exceed 10 per cent on any of the relevant markets affected by the agreement;

(b) in the case of an agreement between non-competitors on any of the relevant markets, the market share held by each of the parties to the agreement does not exceed 15 per cent on any of the relevant markets affected by the agreement.

If there is doubt as to which category an agreement falls into, the 10 per cent threshold applies.[1]

1 Commission Notice on Agreements of Minor Importance [2001] OJ C368/13, [2002] 4 CMLR 699, para 7.

[182]
Where competition in a market is restricted by the cumulative effect of agreements for the sale of goods or services entered into by different suppliers or distributors, the usual thresholds under para 7 of the Notice are reduced to 5 per cent for agreements between both competitors and non-competitors. The Commission states that a cumulative foreclosure effect is unlikely to exist if less than 30 per cent of the relevant market is covered by parallel agreements or networks of agreements having similar effects.[1]

1 Commission Notice on Agreements of Minor Importance [2001] OJ C368/13, [2002] 4 CMLR 699, para 8.

[183]
As to undertakings which have previously come within the thresholds set out in the Notice growing so as to exceed them, the Commission Notice provides that agreements are not restrictive of competition if the market shares do not exceed the

thresholds of 10, 15 and 5 per cent of paras 7 and 8 of the Notice during two successive calendar years by more than two percentage points.[1]

1 Commission Notice on Agreements of Minor Importance [2001] OJ C368/13, [2002] 4 CMLR 699, para 9.

[184]
As to how the relevant market and thus the share of that market are defined for the purposes of the Notice, reference should be made to the Commission's Notice on the subject.[1]

1 Commission Notice on the definition of the relevent market for the purposes of Community competition law [1997] OJ C372/5, [1998] 4 CMLR 177.

[185]
Paragraphs 7, 8 and 9 of the Notice do not apply to agreements containing hardcore restrictions, being:[1]

(a) as regards agreements between competitors, restrictions which have as their object:
  (i) the fixing of prices when selling products to third parties;
  (ii) the limitation of output or sales;
  (iii) the allocation of markets or customers;
(b) as regards agreements between non-competitors, restrictions which have as their object:
  (i) the fixing of or imposition of minimum sale prices;
  (ii) the restriction of the territory into which, or the customers to whom, the buyer may sell.

1 Commission Notice on Agreements of Minor Importance [2001] OJ C368/13, [2002] 4 CMLR 699, para 9.

[186]
Though the requirement of appreciable effect is an important feature of the competition rules from the point of view of small undertakings, its operation is likely to be confined to cases where the effects of the agreement both as between the parties and as regards third persons can be seen to be slight. If an agreement affects competition, it is no defence for an individual participant to say that his own position or the market was too weak for his participation to make a difference.[1] Care must therefore be taken in applying the *de minimis* rule, especially in circumstances not covered by the Commission's Notice. The European Court has indicated that an undertaking with a 5 per cent market share is sufficiently large for its behaviour to be, in principle, capable of affecting inter-State trade.[2] The *de minimis* rule has been held not to apply in the case of a market divided among a large number of brands where the party's share, although small in percentage terms, was amongst the largest market shares held.[3] It is may be doubtful whether the rule would apply where the volume of goods affected by an agreement or practice was large, even if it only amounted to a small share of the relevant market.[4] Where a manufacturer imposed terms restrictive of competition in respect of a number of his products, the fact that

trade between Member States in one of those products was insignificant did not entitle him to claim the benefit of the de minimis rule in respect of that product; the court held that the rule did not apply where a large undertaking was the sole producer of the product.[5] If market share is only slightly above the relevant threshold set out in the Notice, there is a heavier onus to show that the agreement in question has an appreciable effect on competition and trade.[6]

1 Case T-6/89 *Enichem SpA v Commission* [1991] ECR II-1623, CFI; Case T-143/89 *Ferriere Nord SpA v Commission* [1995] ECR II-917, CFI.

2 Case 19/77 *Miller International Schallplatten GmbH v Commission* [1978] ECR 131, [1978] 2 CMLR 334, ECJ; Case 107/82 *AEG- Telefunken v Commission* [1983] ECR 3151, [1984] 3 CMLR 325, ECJ.

3 Joined Cases 100-103/80 *Musique Diffusion Française SA and Others v Commission* [1983] ECR 1825 at 1900, 1901, [1983] 3 CMLR 221 at 329,330, ECJ.

4 It was on the basis of the volumes of trade involved that Advocate General Slynn found the effects of the concerted practice to be appreciable in Joined Cases 100-103/80 *Musique Diffusion Française SA and Others v Commission* [1983] ECR 1825 at 1943, [1983] 3 CMLR 221 at 301, 302, ECJ. However, the explanatory memorandum accompanying the consultation draft of a new Commission Notice on minor agreements ([1997] OJ C29/3) states that this will only be so where particularly serious restrictions of competition are involved.

5 Case 30/78 *Distillers Co Ltd v Commission* [1980] ECR 2229 at 2265, [1980] 3 CMLR 121 at 167, 168, ECJ (the product was Pimm's).

6 See Cases T-374, 375, 384 and 388/94 *European Night Services v Commission* [1998] ECR II-3141, [1998] 5 CMLR 718.

[187]

Where three French fertiliser manufacturers coordinated their exports to Germany, where they had only 2 per cent of the market, their behaviour was held not to be de minimis. The French manufacturers were large producers, accounting for about 10 per cent of the Community production, and had surplus capacity; the German fertiliser market was dominated by three producers. The Commission found that relatively small quantities of imports would have an appreciable effect on market conditions in Germany and accordingly that a restriction of competition in relation to such imports would have appreciable effects.[1] In the case of a supplier outside the Community, its total (worldwide) production capacity and turnover may be more relevant than its share of the Community market in assessing the influence its conduct may have on that market.[2]

1 Commission Decision (EEC) 80/182 [1980] OJ L39/51, [1980] 2 CMLR 285 (*Floral Dungemittelverkaufsgesellschalt mbH*).

2 Per Advocate General Darmon in Joined Cases 89, 104, 114, 116, 117, 125-129/85 *Ahlström Osakeyhtio v Commission* [1993] ECR I-1307, [1993] 4 CMLR 407, at para 509, ECJ.

2. An appreciable effect on trade between Member States

[188]

For the Article 81(1) prohibition to apply to an agreement, that agreement must appreciably affect trade between Member States. If it does not, it will be the subject of the application of purely national competition rules. The Commission has published guidelines to assist in ascertaining whether an agreement has an appreciable effect on trade between Member States.[1]

1 Commission Guidelines on the effect on trade concept contained in Articles 81 and 82 of the Treaty [2004] OJ C101/81.

[189]
The Guidelines state: 'The concept of 'trade' is not limited to traditional exchanges of goods and services across borders. It is a wider concept, covering all cross-border economic activity including establishment. This interpretation is consistent with the fundamental objective of the Treaty to promote free movement of goods, services, persons and capital.'[1]

1 The Guidelines expressly cite Case C-309/99 *Wouters v Algemene Raad van de Nederlandse Order van Advocaten* [2002] ECR I-1577, para 95, [2002] 4 CMLR 913. See also Case 56/65 *Société La Technique Minière Ulm v Maschinenbau* [1966] ECR 235, [1966] CMLR 357.

[190]
In addition to the Guidelines, the ECJ and CFI have made extensive comment in the case law on the concept of appreciable effect on trade.[1] The Guidelines are stated to be without prejudice to this and to any further interpretation by those courts.[2]

1 Due to the fact that the previous *de minimis* notices dealt with appreciable effect on competition and trade together, much of the case law similarly addresses the two issues in conjunction. Reference should therefore be had to the section above on 'Appreciable effect on competition'.
2 Commission Guidelines on the effect on trade concept contained in Articles 81 and 82 of the Treaty [2004] OJ C101/81, para 5.

[191]
The Commission's view, in principle, is that agreements are not capable of appreciably affecting trade between Member States when the following cumulative conditions are met:[1]

(a) the aggregate market share of the parties on any relevant market within the Community affected by the agreement does not exceed 5 per cent; and

(b) (i) in the case of horizontal agreements, the aggregate annual Community turnover of the undertakings concerned in the products covered by the agreement does not exceed €40 million;

(ii) in the case of agreements concerning joint buying of products the relevant turnover shall be the parties' combined purchases of the products covered by the agreement;

(iii) in the case of vertical agreements, the aggregate annual Community turnover of the supplier in the products covered by the agreement does not exceed €40 million;

(iv) in the case of licence agreements the relevant turnover shall be the aggregate turnover of the licencees in the products incorporating the licensed technology and the licensor's own turnover in such products;

(v) in cases involving agreements concluded between a buyer and several suppliers the relevant turnover shall be the buyer's combined purchases of the products covered by the agreements.

1 Commission Guidelines on the effect on trade concept contained in Articles 81 and 82 of the Treaty [2004] OJ C101/81, para 52.

[192]

As with the Commission Notice on Agreements of Minor Importance, leeway is given to undertakings that might find themselves expanding so as to exceed the thresholds. The Guidelines provide that so long as the turnover set out above is not exceeded for more than two years, the Commission will continue to apply the same presumption that the agreement in question does not appreciably affect trade between Member States.[1]

1 Commission Guidelines on the effect on trade concept contained in Articles 81 and 82 of the Treaty [2004] OJ C101/81, para 52.

[193]

Where an agreement by its very nature is capable of affecting trade between Member States, for example, because it concerns imports and exports or covers several Member States, there is a 'rebuttable positive presumption' that such effects on trade are appreciable when the turnover of the parties exceeds €40 million. It can also often be presumed that effects are appreciable where the 5 per cent threshold is exceeded.[1] It should be noted that these 'rebuttable presumptions' will now assume great significance with the competition rules being enforced in the national courts of the Member States.[2]

1 Commission Guidelines on effect on trade concept contained in Articles 81 and 82 of the Treaty [2004] OJ C101/81, para 53.
2 See the discussion in A Jones and B Sufrin, *EC Competition Law* (2nd ed, 2004) at p 176. This is particularly so bearing in mind that Article 3 of Regulation 1/2003 provides that whenever a national court or competition authority of a Member State applies national competition rules, it must also apply Articles 81 and 82 if the agreement in question affects trade between Member States.

[194]

Restrictions imposed upon small undertakings at the behest of large undertakings may have appreciable effects. Where a very large German undertaking entered into an agreement with a small undertaking which restricted imports by the small undertaking into Germany, trade between Member States was held to be appreciably affected since the German market was dominated by large undertakings and the placing of restrictions upon even a small importer was serious.[1] Action by a manufacturer to prevent a dealer from effecting parallel imports appreciably affected both competition and trade between Member States, irrespective of the volumes involved, where there were only six producers in the Community and only one in Germany and the behaviour was intended to maintain the isolation of the German market.[2] An agreement by an inventor not to compete with the business he had sold appreciably restricted competition and was capable of appreciably affecting inter-State trade where, but for the restriction, the inventor could have made his invention available to others, from whom there would be likely to have been a substantial demand.[3] Purely national banking agreements are not capable of affecting trade between Member States.[4]

1 Commission Decision (EEC) 82/897 [1982] OJ L379/19, [1983] 1 CMLR 412 (*Toltecs and Dorcet Trade Marks*) (upheld on appeal in Case 35/83 *BAT Cigaretten-Fabriken GmbH v Commission* [1985] ECR 363, [1985] 2 CMLR 470, ECJ). The volume handled by the importer (0.17 tonnes) was

a very small fraction of the German market (2,500 tonnes). The point was not considered on the appeal.

2 Joined Cases 29, 30/83 *Compagnie Royale Asturienne des Mines SA and Rheinzink GmbH v Commission* [1984] ECR 1679, [1985] 1 CMLR 688, ECJ.

3 Commission Decision (EEC) 76/743 [1976] OJ L254/40, [1976] 2 CMLR D44 (*Renter BASF*).

4 Case C-215/96 *Carlo Bagnasco v BPN* [1999] ECR I-135, [1999] 4 CMLR 624; Commission Decision [1999] OJ L271/28, [2000] 4 CMLR 137 (*Dutch Banks*). See also the Commission Guidelines on effect on trade concept [2004] OJ C101/81, para 60.

[195]
The Court of Justice has indicated that the factors relevant to deciding whether an exclusive dealing agreement falls within Article 81 are, in particular: the nature and quantity, restricted or otherwise, of the products covered by the agreement; the standing of the grantor and of the grantee of the concession on the market in the products concerned; whether the agreement stands alone or is one of a series of agreements; and the extent to which any openings are left for other dealings in the products concerned in the form of re-exports or parallel imports.[1]

1 See Case 56/65 *Société Technique Minière v Maschinenbau Ulm GmbH* [1966] ECR 235, [1966] CMLR 357, ECJ; Case 22/71 *Béguelin Import Co v GL Import Export SA* [1971] ECR 949, [1972] CMLR 81, ECJ.

[196]
The Court has held that any restriction of competition deriving from arrangements created pursuant to the requirements of the national law of a Member State derives from the national law of the Member State, not from the agreement itself.[1]

1 Case C-198/01 *Consorzio Industrie Fiammiferi v Autorita Garante della Concorrenza e del Mercato*, 9 September 2003. Note: the national law must require the arrangement to be created, not just promote such an arrangement (see Cases T-191 and 212-214/98 *Atlantic Container Line v Commission*, 30 September 2003, para 1130).

F. EXEMPTION

1. Introduction

[197]
Once an agreement has been found to come within the scope of Article 81(1), it will be 'prohibited'[1] and will be declared 'automatically void'[2] unless it comes within the exception under Article 81(3). Article 81(3) allows account to be taken of the fact that the agreement in question, though prima facie anti-competitive, may contribute 'to improving the production or distribution of goods or to promoting technical or economic progress'.[3] The Commission has stated that while some consideration of the pro- and anti-competitive elements of an agreement can take place while interpreting Article 81(1), the full consideration of these factors (the application of the so-called 'rule of reason') must take place under Article 81(3).[4]

1 Article 81(1)

2 Article 81(2)

3 Article 81(3)

4 Commission White Paper on the Modernisation of the Rules Implementing Articles 81 and 82 of the EC Treaty [1999] OJ C132/1, paras 56 and 57, [1999] 5 CMLR 208.

[198]

A key feature of Regulation 1/2003 is that it provides for the devolution of some of the powers of enforcement of the competition rules previously held exclusively by the Commission to the national competition authorities and the national courts of the Member States. This change is intended, amongst other objectives, to free the Commission to pursue more serious cases of infringement of the competition rules as well as to encourage more private enforcement of the competition rules (as already occurs to a much greater degree in the United States).[1] Of greatest significance is the devolution of the power to apply Article 81(3). Regulation 1/2003 provides for the scrapping of the former system of individual notification and of exemption being granted on an individual basis by the Commission under Article 9(1) of Regulation 17. In its place, Regulation 1/2003 provides for a system where 'undertakings would have to make their own assessment of the compatibility of their restrictive practices with Community law, in the light of the legislation in force and the case law'.[2] Thus, consideration of the application of Article 81 can now be undertaken by the Commission or by national competition authorities or national courts. Application of Article 81(3) therefore occurs on an individual basis (though not as an 'individual exemption' in the manner of the previous regime), when considered by the Commission or by national courts or competition authorities or by way of the block exemptions. Regulation 1/2003 does not affect the validity and legal nature of the block exemptions.[3]

1 See Commission White Paper on modernisation of the rules implementing Articles 81 and 82 of the EC Treaty [1999] OJ C132/1, [1999] 5 CMLR 208.
2 Ibid, para 77.
3 Commission's Guidelines on the application of Article 81(3) of the Treaty [2004] OJ C101/97, para 2.

2. Exemption under Article 81(3)

[199]

(a) Individual application of Article 81(3): Regulation 1/2003 has removed the system of individual notification to and exemption by the Commission. There is therefore no longer any 'individual exemption'. Instead, the power to apply the competition rules has been devolved to the national courts and competition authorities to be applied on a case by case basis.[1] Article 81(3) is now therefore directly applicable.[2] National courts and national competition authorities are obliged, when considering whether an agreement comes within the Article 81(1) prohibition, to consider in addition the Article 81(3) exception. In addition, the Commission still has to apply and consider Article 81(3) in all cases where it intends to adopt a decision that there is a finding of infringement under Article 81 and that it should be brought to an end as well as on findings of non-applicability.[3]

1 Regulation 1/2003 [2003] OJ L1/1, Articles 5 and 6.
2 Ibid, Article 1(1) and (2).
3 Ibid, Articles 9 and 10.

[200]

(b) Block exemption: The alternative manner in which an agreement may avoid the Article 81(1) prohibition is for it to be drafted in such a way as to come within one of the block exemptions adopted by the Council and the Commission. These exemptions relate to:

(a) agreements on rail, road and inland waterway transport;[1]

(b) unfair pricing practices in maritime transport (liner conferences);[2]

(c) vertical agreements;[3]

(d) specialisation agreements;[4]

(e) research and development agreements;[5]

(f) passenger transit consultations and slot allocations at airports;[6]

(g) agreements relating to computerised reservation systems;[7]

(h) agreements in the insurance sector;[8]

(i) agreements between liner shipping companies;[9]

(j) vertical agreements and concerted practices in the motor vehicle sector;[10]

(k) technology transfer agreements.[11]

1 Regulation 1017/68 [1968] OJ L175/1.
2 Regulation 4057/86 [1986] OJ L378/14.
3 Regulation 2790/1999 [1999] OJ L336/21, [2000] 4 CMLR 398.
4 Regulation 2659/2000 [2000] OJ L304/3, [2001] 4 CMLR 800.
5 Regulation 2659/2000 [2000] OJ L304/7, [2001] 4 CMLR 808.
6 Regulation 1617/93 [1993] OJ L155/18, as amended by Regulation 1523/96 [1996] OJ L190/11. See also Regulation 411/2004 [2004] OJ L68/1.
7 Regulation 3652/93 [1993] OJ L333/37.
8 Regulation 358/2003 [2003] OJ L53/8, [2003] 4 CMLR 734. Note the new Member State exception in this Regulation.
9 Regulation 823/2000 [2000] OJ L100/24.
10 Regulation 1400/2002 [2002] OJ L203/30, [2002] 5 CMLR 777.
11 Regulation 772/2004 [2004] OJ L123/18.

3. The conditions for exemption

[201]
Article 81(3) provides that Article 81(1) may be 'declared inapplicable' in the case of agreements, decisions or concerted practices, or categories of agreements, decisions or concerted practices which satisfy each of four cumulative conditions. This procedure is usually referred to as 'exemption'. In summary, there are two positive conditions for exemption, namely:

(a) that the agreement[1] contributes to improving the production or distribution of goods or to promoting technical or economic progress; and

(b) that it allows consumers a fair share of the resulting benefit;

and two negative conditions, namely:

(a) that the agreement does not impose restrictions which are not indispensable to the attainment of these objectives; and

(b) that it does not afford the possibility of eliminating competition in respect of a substantial part of the products in question.

1 The term 'agreement' is again used in this section to refer to agreements, decisions of associations of undertakings and concerted practices.

[202]
Though the wording of Article 81(3) suggests that it principally envisages agreements relating to goods, it is equally applicable in the services sector and the concept of improving production or distribution has been applied by analogy to improvements in the supply of services.[1] The Court of First Instance has held[2] that in principle there is no category of agreement, decision or concerted practice that is incapable of receiving exemption, provided that all the conditions of Article 81(3) are satisfied.

1 See eg Recital 7 of the previously applicable Commission Regulation (EEC) 4087/88 granting block exemption to certain franchise agreements regarding goods or services (now replaced by the Vertical Agreements block exemption under Regulation 2790/1999 [1999] OJ L336/21, [2000] 4 CMLR 398). Individual exemptions were granted for a service franchise (Commission Decision (EEC) 88/604 [1988] OJ L332/38 (*ServiceMaster*)) and for agreements in the banking (eg Commission Decision (EEC) 85/77 [1985] OJ L35/43, [1985] 3 CMLR 434 (*Uniform Eurocheques*)), insurance (eg Commission Decision (EEC) 92/96 [1992] OJ L37/16 (*Assurpol*)), transport (eg Commission Decision (EEC) 91/408 [1991] OJ L258/18 (*IATA Passenger Agency Programme*)) and telecommunications (eg Commission Decision (EEC) 91/562 [1991] OJ L306/22 (*Eirpage*)) sectors
2 Case T-17/93 *Matra Hachette v Commission* [1994] ECR II-595 at para 85. See also Commission Decision (EC) 1995/695 [1999] OJ L275/17, in particular, paras 65-76, [2000] 4 CMLR 704 (*Reims II*) and Commission Decision (EC) 2002/914 [2002] OJ L318/17, para 79, [2003] 4 CMLR 283 (*Visa International – Multilateral Interchange Fee*).

[203]
In considering an agreement which falls within Article 81(1), it is sensible to consider next whether the agreement is of a type in respect of which a block exemption regulation has been adopted. Where that is the case, the relevant regulation will spell out in more detail the conditions that the Commission regards as requiring to be fulfilled in order for agreements of that type to be eligible for the application of Article 81(3).

[204]
The four conditions for exemption are cumulative.[1] Each must be satisfied and the relevant body considering Article 81(3) (be it the Commission or the national court or competition authority) will consider each of them separately, though they overlap to some extent. For example, an agreement which contributes to improving the production or distribution of goods is likely for that reason to work to the benefit of consumers, and an agreement which brings about a substantial elimination of competition from the affected market is unlikely to be regarded as improving conditions on that market in the sense required by the first condition.

1 Joined Cases 43, 63/82 *VBVB and VBBB v Commission* [1984] ECR 19, [1985] 1 CMLR 27, ECJ; Case T-66/89 *Publishers Association v Commission* [1992] ECR II-1995, [1992] 5 CMLR 120, CFI; Case T-17/93 *Matra Hachette Commission* [1994] ECR II-595, CFI. See also Cases T-528, 542, 543 and 546/93 *Métropole Télévision SA v Commission* [1996] ECR II-649; [1996] 5 CMLR 386, CFI; Cases T-185/00 *Métropole Télévision SA (M6) v Commission* [2002] ECR II-3805, [2003] 4 CMLR 707.

[205]
The conditions are expressed in general terms and leave a considerable margin of discretion.[1] The whole surrounding circumstances are relevant, including conduct of the parties outside the agreement.[2] The burden of proof in showing that the conditions for exemption are fulfilled lies on the parties seeking exemption.[3]

1 See Joined Cases 56, 58/64 *Etablissements Consten SARL and Grundig-Verkaufs-GmbH v EEC Commission* [1966] ECR 299, [1966] CMLR 418, 474, ECJ; Case 42/84 *Remia BV v Commission* [1985] ECR 2545, [1987] 1 CMLR 1, ECJ; Case T-17/93 *Matra Hachette v Commission* [1994] ECR II-595, CFI.
2 See Case 26/76 *Metro SB-Grossmarkte GmbH & Co KG v Commission* [1977] ECR 1875, [1978] 2 CMLR 1, ECJ; Case 75/84 *Metro SB-Grofimarkte GmbH & Co KG v Commission* [1986] ECR 3021, [1987] 1 CMLR 118, ECJ; Joined Cases 25,26/84 *Ford-Werke AG and Ford of Europe Inc v Commission* [1985] ECR 2725, [1985] 3 CMLR 528, ECJ.
3 Joined Cases 43, 63/82 *VBVB and VBBB v Commission* [1984] ECR 19, [1985] 1 CMLR 27, ECJ; Case 42/84 *Remia BV v Commission* [1985] ECR 2545, [1987] 1 CMLR 1, ECJ; Case T66/89 *Publishers Association v Commission* [1992] ECR II-1995, [1992] 5 CMLR 120, CFI.

[206]
The Commission has published guidelines on the application of Article 81(3)[1] and these are considered below in the discussion of the four conditions.

1 Guidelines on the application of Article 81(3) [1997] OJ C101/97.

[207]
(a) The first condition: improvement of the production or distribution of goods or contribution to technical or economic progress: The main positive requirement for an agreement to qualify for exemption is that it should be beneficial to the Community interest (not just to the parties themselves) by improving the production of goods, improving the distribution of goods, contributing to technical progress or contributing to economic progress. In the application of this condition, improvements in the supply of services should be treated as being analogous to improvements in the production or distribution of goods,[1] though agreements in the services sector may also be regarded as contributing to economic or technical progress.[2] An agreement may satisfy more than one of these alternative requirements and though the Commission has often specified which of the four limbs of the first condition is satisfied, in some decisions it has not stated precisely which of the four applies.[3]

1 See Cases 56/64 and 58/64 *Consten and Grundig v Commission* [1966] ECR 299 at 348, [1966] CMLR 418 at 478. See also Commission Decisions (EEC) 91/408 [1991] OJ L258/18 (*IATA Passenger Agency Programme*) at para 57; 91/481 [1991] OJ L258/29 (*IATA Cargo Agency Programme*) at para 51 (agreements held to 'contribute to improving the distribution of the air transport product'); 92/96 [1992] OJ L37/16 (*Assurpol*) ('the production of the insurance product is improved'); and 93/50 [1993] OJ L20/23, [1994] 5 CMLR 226, para 22 (*Astra*).
2 See, for example, Commission Decision (EEC) 89/95 [1989] OJ L36/16 (*Uniform Eurocheques*) (contributing to the security of the Eurocheque system held to promote economic progress); Commission Decision (EEC) 91/562 [1991] OJ L306/22 (*Eirpage*) (nationwide paging system enabled businesses to expand their activities geographically and thereby contributed to economic progress).
3 See, for example, Commission Decision (EEC) 85/77 [1985] OJ L35/43, [1985] 3 CMLR 434 (*Uniform Eurocheques*) (the Eurocheque system held simply to 'contribute to improving payment facilities within the common market'). More than one of the limbs may apply: see eg Commission Decision (EEC) 88/330 [1988] OJ L150/35 (*Bayer/BP Chemicals*) ('rationalising ... production activities, improving technical efficiency and product quality').

[208]
Improvements in the production of goods may occur through specialisation or research and development, both of which are covered by block exemption

regulations.[1] The Commission has been prepared to grant exemption, for example, to research and development agreements between very large undertakings, including those with the largest market shares in the world, if it is satisfied that the joint research and development is necessary in order to bring a desirable new product onto the market more quickly and that the other conditions for exemption are satisfied.[2] The Commission has been sympathetic to the position of undertakings in the Community facing competition on the world market from even larger competitors.[3] Other situations which have been regarded as contributing to an improvement in the production of goods include restructuring or rationalisation in industries affected by overcapacity or outmoded technology.[4]

1 Regulation 2659/2000 [2000] OJ L304/3, [2001] 4 CMLR 800 and Regulation 2659/2000 [2000] OJ L304/7, [2001] 4 CMLR 808 respectively.
2 For example, Commission Decision (EEC) 91/38 [1992] OJ L19/25 (*KSB/Goulds/Lowara/1TT*) (research and development agreement between the world's largest producers, exemption granted); Case T-17/93 *Matra Hachette v Commission* [1994] ECR II-595, CFI (joint ventures between Ford and Volkswagen, exemption upheld).
3 For example, Commission Decision (EEC) 90/46 [1990] OJ L32/19 (*Alcatel Espace/ ANT Nachrich tentechnik*).
4 For example, Commission Decision (EEC) 88/87 [1988] OJ L50/18 (*Enichem/ICD*); Commission Decision (EEC) 88/330 ([1988] OJ L150/35) (*Bayer/BP Chemicals*).

[209]

Improvements in the distribution of goods may be achieved by vertical agreements, which are also the subject of block exemption regulations.[1] It is rare that agreements between competitors will be regarded as improving the distribution of goods[2] and the Commission has, for example, refused exemption to joint selling arrangements.[3]

1 See Regulation 2790/1999 [1999] OJ L336/21, [2000] 4 CMLR 398 and Regulation 1400/2002 [2002] OJ L203/30, [2002] 5 CMLR 777.
2 Selective distribution agreements for motor vehicles are covered by Regulation 1475/95.
3 See, for example, Commission Decision (EEC) 80/182 [1990] OJ L39/51, [1980] 2 CMLR 285 (*Floral Dungemittelverkaufsgesellschaft GmbH*) ('no evidence ... that there are difficulties in planning production, storage, carriage and resale which could not be solved individually'). Distribution by one party of the other's production was, exceptionally, granted exemption in the wider context of a restructuring agreement in *Bayer/BP Chemicals*. Agreements regarding the running of trade fairs have been held to improve the distributions of goods; see Commission Decision (EEC) 91/128 [1991] OJ L60/19 (*Sippa*).

[210]

There are few, if any, agreements that have been held to contribute to technical or economic progress which have not also been, or could not also have been considered to improve the production or distribution of goods or the supply of services. Research and development agreements[1] and rationalisation[2] have both been held to improve the production of goods. Agreements which improve the provision of insurance[3] and the security of the Eurocheque system[4] have been held to contribute to economic progress. Similarly, improvements in efficiency in terms of costs or quality (for example, from the creation of new or improved products) will come within this condition.[5]

1 Commission Decision (EEC) 91/38 [1992] OJ L19/25 (*KSB/Goulds/Lowara/ITT*). See also the preamble to Commission Regulation (EEC) 418/85 ('co-operation in research and development and in the exploitation of the results generally promotes technical and economic progress ...').

2 Commission Decision (EEC) 88/330 [1988] OJ L150/35 (*Bayer/BP Chemicals*).
3 For example, Commission Decision (EEC) 84/191 [1984] OJ L99/29, [1984] 2 CMLR 484 (*Nuovo CEGAM*).
4 Commission Decision (EEC) 89/95 [1989] OJ L36/16 (*Uniform Eurocheques*).
5 Commission Guidelines on the application of Article 81(3) [2004] OJ C101/97, paras 59-72.

[211]
While some judgments and Commission Decisions showed an increasing tendency towards in interpreting this condition in a broad manner, considering factors of wider Community interest,[1] the favoured view now appears to be that the condition should be interpreted on narrower economic grounds.[2] This preference has arisen from the practical effect of implementing Regulation 1/2003 – it is the courts and competition authorities of the Member States which are now applying Article 81(3). It could possibly lead to confusion in the application of the competition rules if wider Community issues were considered and ruled upon at a national level as opposed to the simple economic questions that a narrow interpretation of this condition raises. The Commission itself has lent support to this view with its statement in the White Paper on modernisation of the competition rules that: Article 81(3) is intended 'to provide a legal framework for the economic assessment of restrictive practices and not to allow the application of the competition rules to be set aside because of political considerations'.[3] The matter is not entirely resolved, however, and socio-political and environmental factors, for example, have continued to play a part in the consideration of Article 81(3).[4]

1 See, for example Case 26/76 *Metro v Commission* [1977] ECR 1875, [1978] 2 CMLR 1 and Case 42/84 *Remia BV and Vernigde Bedrijven Nutricia NV v Commission* [1994] ECR 2545, [1987] 1 CMLR 1, para 42. See also Commission Decision (EEC) 94/296 [1994] OJ L131/15, [1995] 4 CMLR 646, paras 27-28 (*Stichting Baksteen*).
2 See the discussion in R Whish, *Competition Law* (5th edn, 2003), at p 155.
3 White Paper on modernisation of the rules implementing Articles 81 and 82 of the EC Treaty [1999] OJ C132/1, [1999] 5 CMLR 208, para 57.
4 See, for example, Commission Decision 2000/475 [2000] OJ L187/47, [2000] 5 CMLR 635 (*CECED*), where the Commission exempted an agreement restricting the import of less environmentally friendly washing machines. Note that this decision is no longer in force.

[212]
(b) The second condition: consumers receive a fair share of the resulting benefit: The Commission Guidelines provide extensive guidance to this condition.[1] The basic principle is that the pass-on benefits must at least compensate consumers for any actual or likely negative impact caused to them by the restriction of competition which has been found under Article 81(1). Thus, the net effect must be neutral from the point of view of those directly affected or likely to be affected.[2]

1 Commission Guidelines on the application of Article 81(3) [2004] OJ C101/97, paras 83-104
2 Ibid, para 85.

[213]
The concept of a 'fair share' of the benefit resulting from the improvement is qualitative rather than quantitative. It does not require the evaluation of the proportion of the benefits which consumers will derive, but it is rather concerned with ensuring: (a) that the agreement will produce benefits more widely than merely

for the parties themselves; and (b) that the benefits which the agreement might be expected to produce for those having dealings with the parties will indeed reach them. The word 'consumers' has been given a meaning analogous to 'customers' and it is not necessary to demonstrate that the benefits will be passed right to the final consumer.[1] Where an agreement produces an improvement in production or distribution or contributes to economic or technical progress, the Commission has often been prepared to accept that the inherent benefits will be passed on to customers as a result of the effect of competition in the market.[2]

1 See, for example, Commission Decision (EEC) 83/390 [1983] OJ L224/45 [1983] 3 CMLR 709 (*Rockwell/Iveco*) (benefits of joint venture for production of truck axles would be passed to truck manufacturers); Commission Decision (EEC) 88/330 [1988] OJ L150/35 (*Bayer/BP Chemicals*) (benefits for customers in the polyethylene processing industry).
2 See Commission Decision (EEC) 88/330 [1988] OJ L150/35 (*Bayer/BP Chemicals*) (benefits of wider product range and lower costs fairly shared by customers 'provided that workable competition is maintained, as is the case here').

[214]

The onus is on the parties to mount a positive case to show that consumers will be in a better position as a result of the agreement than without it. Exemption will be refused if consumers may be in no worse a position in the absence of the agreement. It is not necessary for it to be shown that the agreement will be detrimental to their interests.[1] However it is not necessary at this stage to assess whether consumers might benefit equally from, for example, attempts by the parties to penetrate the market individually;[2] that consideration goes only to whether the restrictions are indispensable.[3]

1 See Commission Decision (EEC) 91/130 [1991] OJ L63/32 (*Screensport/EBUMembers*).
2 Case T-17/93 *Matra Hachette v Commission* [1994] ECR II-595.
3 As to which, see below at para [215].

[215]

(c) The third condition: no restrictions that are not indispensable: This condition is dealt with in the Commission Guidelines.[1] The Guidelines set out a two-stage test. First, the restrictive agreement must be reasonably necessary in order to achieve the efficiencies. Secondly, the individual restrictions of competition that flow from the agreement must also be reasonably necessary for the attainment of the efficiencies. A restriction will be regarded as 'indispensable' provided that it is both conducive to and necessary for the achievement of the benefits expected to result from the agreement.[2] This will be the case where the restrictive provision is inherent in bringing about a beneficial structure of, for instance, production or distribution. The restrictions in a manufacturing joint venture agreement may be indispensable where any attempt by the parties to penetrate the market individually would be at a loss.[3]

1 Commission Guidelines on the application of Article 81(3) [2004] OJ C101/97, paras 73-82.
2 See, for example, Commission Decision 1999/421 [1999] OJ L161/61, [2000] 5 CMLR 646 (*P&O Stena Line*) where an exemption was granted in relation to a joint venture combining the ferry services of the two parties on one ferry route. For a recent example of consideration of this point, see Cases T-374, 375, 384, 388/94 *European Night Services v Commission* [1998] ECR II-3141, [1998] 5 CMLR 718, CFI.
3 Case T-17/93 *Matra Hachette v Commission* [1994] ECR II-595, CFI.

[216]
On the other hand, restrictions designed to bring about absolute territorial protection, whether by restricting the manufacturer or other distributors from supplying purchasers in the distributor's territory or by hampering the activities of parallel importers, will generally not be indispensable. Note, however, the block exemptions that qualify even this.[1] The block exemption regulations provide a guide as to restrictions that are unlikely to be regarded as indispensable.

1 See, for example, the Technology Transfer Agreements block exemption – Regulation 772/2004 [2004] OJ L123/18.

[217]
It is rare that an agreement that satisfies the other conditions for exemption will be rejected on the grounds of containing an unnecessary restriction, since the parties are very likely to agree to abandon the restriction in the interest of gaining exemption. However, in *Publishers' Association*,[1] the Commission refused exemption to the Net Book Agreement on the grounds that, even if resale price maintenance for books improved their distribution, it was not necessary to that end for publishers to operate uniform conditions of sale. The Commission's decision was upheld by the Court of First Instance[2] but annulled on appeal to the Court of Justice.[3]

1 Commission Decision (EEC) 89/44 [1989] OJ L22/12 (*Publishers Association/Net Book Agreements*).
2 Case T-66/89 *Publishers Association v Commission* [1992] ECR II-1995, [1992] 5 CMLR 120, CFI.
3 Case C-360/92P *Publishers Association v Commission* [1995] ECR I-23, [1995] 5 CMLR 33, ECJ.

[218]
(d) The fourth condition: competition not to be substantially eliminated: The Commission sets out guidance as to the requirements of this condition in its Guidelines.[1] In order to qualify for exemption, an agreement must not afford the parties the possibility of eliminating competition 'in respect of a substantial part of the products in question'. This requires an analysis of the 'relevant market', that is to say the market comprising the goods or services affected by the agreement and the goods or services which are interchangeable with, or compete with, them.[2] The geographical scope of the relevant market has also to be considered. Having defined the relevant market consideration then has to be given to the share of it accounted for by the parties to the agreement and the severity of the restrictions of competition caused by the agreement. The fourth condition does not require it to be shown that competition is in fact eliminated but that the agreement provides the possibility of eliminating it. This will be the case where, for example, the parties account for a very high proportion of the market and the restrictions relate to price competition.[3] In practice it is unlikely that an agreement will at the same time satisfy the first three conditions for exemption and fail the fourth, but where it is, for example, doubtful whether an agreement contributes to improving distribution, the fact that the agreement gives rise to the possibility of eliminating competition will be decisive against it.[4] For the fourth condition to be satisfied, it is necessary to show that at least a 'workable' level of competition will subsist.[5]

1 Commission Guidelines on the application of Article 81(3) [2004] OJ C101/97, paras 105-116.
2 Ibid, para 116 for illustrations of how to calculate the relevant market.

3 Cases 209-215, 218/78 *Heintz van Landewyck Sàrl v Commission* [1980] ECR 3125, [1981] 3 CMLR 134, ECJ. Large market shares are not in themselves fatal.
4 Cases 209-215, 218/78 *Heintz van Landewyck Sàrl v Commission* [1980] ECR 3125, [1981] 3 CMLR 134, ECJ.
5 See Commission Decision (EEC) 88/330 [1988] OJ L150/35 (*Bayer/BP Chemicals*).

4

ABUSE OF DOMINANT POSITION

A. THE PROHIBITION

1. Prohibition of abuse of dominant position

[219]

Any abuse[1] by one or more undertakings[2] of a dominant position[3] within the common market or in a substantial part of it[4] is prohibited[5] as incompatible with the common market[6] insofar as it may affect trade between Member States.[7] Such abuse may, in particular, consist in:[8]

(1) directly or indirectly imposing unfair purchase or selling prices or other unfair trading conditions;[9]

(2) limiting production, markets or technical development to the prejudice of consumers;[10]

(3) applying dissimilar conditions to equivalent transactions with other trading parties, thereby placing them at a competitive disadvantage;[11]

(4) making the conclusion of contracts subject to acceptance by the other parties of supplementary obligations which, by their nature or according to commercial usage, have no connection with the subject of such contracts.[12]

1 For the meaning of 'abuse', see paras [270]–[310]. In relation to Article 82 EC generally, the Commission is presently engaged in an internal review of its policy and has indicated that a comprehensive reassessment of its approach may result from a review of current economic thinking. See the speech of the Director General of DG Competition at the Fordham Corporate Law Institute, 23 October 2003 (http://europa.eu.int/comm/competition/speeches/text/sp2003_040_en.pdf) and *Anti-trust reform in Europe,* at the IBA/European Commission conference 11 March 2005 (http://europa.eu.int/comm/competition/speeches/text/sp2005_003_en.pdf) although the Commissioner responsible for competition stated in a speech at the Fordham Corporate Law Institute on 23 September 2005, *Preliminary Thoughts on a Policy Review of Article 82 EC,* that a radical change in enforcement policy is not envisaged. In addition, the Chief Economist of DG Competition commissioned a report from the Economic Advisory Group for Competition Policy (EAGCP) on 'an economic approach to Article 82' which was published on 21 July 2005 (http://europa.eu.int/comm/competition/publications/studies/eagcp_july_21_05.pdf). The report argues in favour of an economic-based approach to Article 82, in a way similar to Article 81 and merger control. It supports an effects-based rather than a form-based approach to competition policy. Such an approach focuses on the presence of anti-competitive effects that harm consumers, and is based on the examination of each specific case, based on sound economics and grounded on facts. The report argues that the competition authority's investigation should be led by the

question: what is the nature of the competitive harm involved in that case? The Commission has said that it will issue in 2006 working papers on dominance and some of the major abuses: predation, bundling, refusals to deal and loyalty rebates. Guidelines on Article 82 are due to be published at the same time. See also Sinclair, *Abuse of Dominance at a Crossroads – Potential Effect. Object and Appreciability under Article 82 EC* [2004] ECLR 491 and Furse, *Abusive Dynamics* [2005] ECLR 199.
2 For the meaning of 'undertaking', see paras [265].
3 For the meaning of 'dominant position', see paras [229] ff.
4 As to what constitutes the common market, see para [247].
5 As to the prohibition, see para [220].
6 These words appear to add nothing to the prohibition.
7 See paras [311], [312] for trade between Member States under Article 82 EC. As to trade between Member States under Article 81 EC, see paras [155] ff.
8 These are examples and not an exhaustive list. See, eg, Case 6/72 *Europemballage Corpn Co Inc v Commission* [1973] ECR 215, [1973] CMLR 199, para 26, ECJ; Cases C-395/96P etc *Compagnie Maritime Belge Transports SA v Commission* [2000] ECR I-1365, [2000] CMLR 1076, para 112.
9 EC Treaty, Article 82(a). See paras [279]–[281]. This provision, unlike Article 81(1)(a), makes reference to 'unfair' prices or other trading conditions. It is not thought that there is any significance in this.
10 Ibid Article 82(b). See para [304], [305]. This provision, unlike Article 81(1)(b), does not include 'control' or 'investment' and includes 'to the prejudice of consumers' but it is not thought that there is any importance to be drawn from these differences.
11 EC Treaty, Article 82(c).
12 Ibid Article 82(d).

2. The prohibition

[220]

Whereas Article 81(2) of the EC Treaty declares that all agreements or decisions prohibited pursuant to Article 81 are automatically void,[1] Article 82 prohibits any abuse of a dominant position but does not of itself entail nullity. There would seem to be no fundamental difference in these concepts, for infringements of Articles 81 and 82 both give a potential liability to fines and orders as to past and future conduct[2] and to damages,[3] and both create rights for individuals which national courts must protect.[4]

1 See para [93].
2 See paras [72] and [95] ff.
3 See paras [94] ff. See, *Yeheskel Arkin v (1) Borchard Lines Ltd and others and (2) Zim Israel Navigation Co Ltd and Others* [2003] EuLR 287 (Colman J). See also the right to claim damages under s 47A of the Competition Act 1998 where there has been a regulatory finding of abuse of a dominant position.
4 See Case C-453/99 *Courage Ltd v Bernard Crehan* [2001] ECR I-6297.

3. Structure of Article 82

[221]

According to the wording of Article 82 of the EC Treaty the conduct prohibited must fulfil three basic requirements: the existence of a dominant position, the improper exploitation of that position; and the possibility that this may affect trade between Member States.[1]

1 Case 24/67 *Parke, Davis & Co v Probel* [1968] ECR 55, [1968] CMLR 47, ECJ; Case 40/70 *Sirena Srlv Eda Srl* [1971] ECR 69, [1971] CMLR 260, ECJ. See also Case 247/86 *Société alsacienne et lorraine de telecommunications et d'electronique (Alsatel) v Novasam SA* [1988] ECR 5987, [1990] 4

CMLR 434, ECJ; Case T-158/00 *ARD v Commission* [2003] ECR II-3825, para 204, CFI; Case T-203/01 *Michelin v Commission* [2004] 4 CMLR 18, para 237, CFI.

[222]
Article 82 does not prohibit dominance, only its abuse. An undertaking in a dominant position is obliged, where appropriate, to modify its conduct so as not to impair effective competition on the market regardless of whether the Commission has adopted a decision to that effect.[1] Similarly, obtaining or strengthening a dominant position, individually or collectively, is not of itself prohibited by Article 82.[2]

1 Case 322/81 *Michelin* v *Commission* [1983] ECR 3461, para 57, ECJ; Case C-250/92 *Gottrup-Klim v Dansk Landbrugs Grovvareselskab AmbA* [1994] ECR I-5641, [1996] 4 CMLR 191, para 49, ECJ; Case T-51/89 *Tetra Pak* v *Commission* [1990] ECR II-309, para 23, CFI; and Joined Cases T-125/97 and T-127/97 *Coca-Cola* v *Commission* [2000] ECR II-1733, para 80, CFI; Case C-12/03P *Commission v Tetra-Laval BV* (unreported, judgment of 15 February 2005), ECJ, para 56.
2 Case T-17/93 *Matra Hachette v Commission* [1994] ECR II-595, paras 123-4, CFI. See Case C-250/99 *Gottrup-Klim v Dansk Landbrugs Grovvareselskab AmbA* [1994] ECR I-5641, [1996] 4 CMLR 191, para 49, ECJ. As to mergers, see Vaughan, *Law of the European Union*, Section 21C ('Competition – Mergers', forthcoming).

4. Interpretation of Article 82

[223]
Article 82 of the EC Treaty must be interpreted having regard to its spirit, general scheme and wording, as well as having regard to the systems and objectives of the Treaty.[1] The general objective of Article 3(1)(g)[2] EC is made specific in the rules on competition in the Treaty, and this includes Article 82.[3] It follows that Article 82 must be interpreted in the light of Articles 2 and 3(1)(g) EC to ensure a harmonious, balanced and sustainable development of economic activities and to ensure that competition within the internal market is not distorted, let alone eliminated.[4]

1 Case 6/72 *Europemballage Corpn and Continental Can Co Inc v Commission* [1973] ECR 215, [1973] CMLR 199, ECJ; Joined Cases 6, 7/73 *Istituto Chemioterapico Italiano SpA and Commercial Solvents Corpn v Commission* [1974] ECR 223, [1974] 1 CMLR 309, ECJ; Case 27/76 *United Brands Co v Commission* [1978] ECR 207, [1978] 1 CMLR 429, ECJ; Case 85/76 *Hoffmann-La Roche & Co AG v Commission* [1979] ECR 461, [1979] 3 CMLR 211, ECJ; Case 322/ 81 *Nederlandsche Banden-Industrie Michelin NV v Commission* [1983] ECR 3461, [1985] 1 CMLR 282, ECJ; Case 30/87 *Bodson v Pompes funèbres des regions libérées SA* [1988] ECR 2479, [1989] 4 CMLR 984, ECJ; and Case 247/86 *Société alsacienne et lorraine de telecommunications et d'electronique (Alsatel) v Novasam SA* [1988] ECR 5987, [1990] 4 CMLR 434, ECJ.
2 As to EC Treaty, Article 3(1)(g), see para [311], note 1.
3 Case 13/77 *GB-INNO-BM NV v Vereniging van de Kleinhandelaars in Tabak (ATAB)* [1977] ECR 2115, [1978] 1 CMLR 283, ECJ.
4 See the cases cited at note 1. The words 'balanced and sustainable' were added to Article 2 by the Treaty of Amsterdam. The recitals to the Treaty refer to 'fair competition'.

[224]
Article 82 may not be interpreted as creating distinct areas of application according to the level of the economy at which the affected undertakings operate. There is no distinction between whether the affected undertakings operate at the same level of the economic process or between non-competing persons operating at different levels: no distinction can be made where the Treaty does not make any distinction.[1]

1 Joined Cases 56, 58/64 *Etablissements Consten SARL and Grundig-Verkaufs-GmbH v Commission* [1966] ECR 299, [1966] CMLR 418, ECJ.

5. Interrelationship with Article 81

[225]

Articles 81 and 82 of the EC Treaty are complementary in that they seek to achieve a common general objective of maintaining effective competition[1] on different levels although they constitute independent legal instruments addressing different sitiuations.[2] Articles 81 and 82 may not be interpreted in such a way that they contradict each other, because they seek to achieve the same objective.[3] If a large market share were obtained as a result of an agreement to share markets, such an agreement falls to be considered under Article 81. If that allocation were carried out by a number of undertakings belonging to the same group, then Article 82 could be applicable.[4]

1 As to effective competition, see Case 13/60 *Geitling Ruhrkohlen-Verkaufsgesellschaft mbH v High Authority* [1962] ECR 83, [1962] CMLR 113, ECJ. Effective competition means workable competition, not perfect competition, which involves an examination of realistic commercial options having regard to the market affected: see Case C-250/92 *Gottrup Klim v Danske Landbrugs* [1994] ECR I-5641 and Case T-374/94 *European Night Ferries* [1998] ECR II-3141.
2 Case T-51/89 *Tetra Pak v Commission* [1990] ECR II-309.
3 Case 6/72 *Europemballage Corpn and Continental Can Co Inc v Commission* [1973] ECR 215, [1973] CMLR 199, ECJ. See also Case T-51/89 *Tetra Pak Rausing SA v Commission* [1990] ECR II-309, [1991] 4 CMLR 334, CFI.
4 Case 247/82 *Société alsacienne et lorraine de telecommunications et d'electronique* (*Alsatel*) *v Novasam SA* [1988] ECR 5987, [1990] 4 CMLR 434, ECJ. As to collective dominance, see para [266] below.

[226]

In the case of agreements between undertakings, where one of the undertakings is in a dominant position or they are jointly in a dominant position,[1] it may be necessary to consider not only Article 81 but also Article 82.[2] In such a situation, Article 82 would probably apply where the dominant undertaking could be said to have used its economic power in such a way that competition is distorted,[3] but probably would not apply where there was nothing to indicate such use of economic power and the parties merely enter into normal reciprocal obligations. The Commission is entitled, in an appropriate case, to proceed under Article 81 or Article 82[4] or both.[5]

1 As to collective dominance, see para [266] below.
2 See eg Commission Decision (EEC) 78/921 [1978] OJ L322/26, [1979] 1 CMLR 403 (*WANO Schwarzpulver GmbH*), which involved a joint venture agreement, and which was decided under Article 81 EC, but which could probably have been decided under Article 82. See further Case 66/82 *Ahmed Saeed Flugreisen v Zentrale zur Bekampfung unlauteren Wettbewerbs eV* [1989] ECR 803, [1990] 4 CMLR 102, ECJ, in which the Court declared that Articles 81 and 82 may be applied simultaneously to agreements between a firm which is dominant and its competitors where the former has succeeded in making the latter participate in the concerted and abusive behaviour. The Court named as examples of abusive agreements: those fixing excessively low prices, because they tend to exclude third parties from the market; those fixing excessively high prices, because they tend to exploit the ultimate consumers; and those fixing a single price for the product since they tend to eliminate all price competition. See Commission Decision (EEC) 89/113 [1989] OJ L43/27 (*Decca Navigator System*); and Commission Decision (EEC) 89/93 [1989] OJ L33/44 (*Italian Fiat Glass*) in which the Commission found that an allegedly dominant firm had by its agreements with competitors infringed both Articles 81 and 82; but see Joined Cases T-68, *77,*

78/89 *Societa Italiano Vetro SpA v Commission* [1992] ECR II-1403, [1992] 5 CMLR 302, CFI. See also Commission Decision (EEC) 92/163 [1992] OJ L72/1 (*Tetra Pak II*), upheld by the CFI in Case T-83/91 *Tetra Pak International SA v Commission* [1994] ECR II-755, CFI, and further upheld by the ECJ in Case C-333/94P *Tetra Pak International SA v Commission* [1996] ECR I-5951, ECJ. See also Case C-393/92 *Municipality of Almelo and Others v Energiebedrijfl Ijsselmij* [1994] ECR I-1477, ECJ.

3 eg loyalty rebates (see paras [283]–[286]) and requirements contracts (see para [290]). See also Commission Decision (EEC) 92/163 [1992] OJ L72/1 (*Tetra Pak II*) (upheld on appeal, see note 2).

4 See Case 81/76 *Hoffmann-La Roche & Co AG v Commission* [1979] ECR 461 at 550, 551, [1979] 3 CMLR 211 at 297, 298, ECJ, and the Opinion of Reischl, Advocate General, at 562 and at 221.

5 Case 66/82 *Ahmed Saeed Flugreisen v Zentrale zur Bekampfung unlauteren Wettbewerbs eV* [1989] ECR 803, [1990] 4 CMLR 102, ECJ. See further Commission Decision (EEC) 92/213 [1992] OJ L96/34 (*British Midland v Air Lingus*), where the Commission acted under both Articles 81 and 82. The same would apply in proceedings before a national court.

[227]

Behaviour which falls within the prohibition of Article 81(1) but which is covered by a block exemption or, in some situations, an individual exemption under Article 81(3) may nevertheless be an abuse of a dominant position depending on the relevant market circumstances.[1]

1 See Case C-395 and 396/96 P *Compagnie Maritime Belge Transports SA v Commission* [2000] ECR I-1365, [2000] CMLR 1076, paras 33 and 131, ECJ where the Court rejected the argument that because a practice was covered by the block exemption in relation to maritime transport it could not amount to a breach of Article 82 until the benefit of that exemption was withdrawn; also Case 26/76 *Metro SB-Grossmarkte GmbH & Co KG v Commission* [1977] ECR 1875, [1978] 2 CMLR 1, ECJ; Case 75/84 *Metro SB-Grossmarkte GmbH & Co KG v Commission* [1986] ECR 3021, [1987] 1 CMLR 118, ECJ, where in the field of selective distribution the court ruled that behaviour might fall to be considered under Article 81(1) or Article 82 depending on the market circumstances; Joined Cases 110, 241, 242/88 *Lucazeau v Société des auteurs, compositeurs et éditeurs de musique* (*SACEM*) [1989] ECR 2811, [1991] 4 CMLR 248, ECJ, where the Court considered that an agreement between the sole copyright management society in a Member State and the discotheques in that State to pay the former a blanket royalty on the whole repertoire might be prohibited by Article 81(1) and be a breach of Article 82 if excessive; Commission Decision (EEC) 88/501 [1988] OJ L272/27, [1990] 4 CMLR 47 (*Tetra Pak I*), in which the Commission considered that the acquisition of an exclusive patent licence to advanced technology by a firm in a dominant position on the relevant market constituted an abuse of Article 82, although such behaviour fell within the scope of Commission Regulation (EEC) 2349/84 [1984] OJ L219/15 on block exemption for patent licences (since superseded by Regulation 240/96). In the light of the market conditions, the Commission withdrew the application of the block exemption to the firm until the exclusive nature of the licence was dropped at which point Article 82 was also held no longer to be infringed. The decision was approved in Case T-51/89 *Tetra Pak Rausing SA v Commission* [1990] ECR II-309, [1991] 4 CMLR 334, CFI, where the Court ruled that whilst the grant of exemption cannot preclude the application of Article 82, in applying that article, the Commission must take account, wherever the factual and legal circumstances have altered, of the earlier findings made when exemption was granted under Article 81(3). See also Case C-310/93P *BPB Industries Plc and British Gypsum Ltd v Commission* [1995] ECR I-825, ECJ, in particular paras 63-69 of the Opinion of the Advocate General.

[228]

Despite the apparent structural differences between Articles 81 and 82, the approaches used for the assessment of business conduct under Articles 81(3) and 82 are similar.[1] Conduct will not be abusive if the relevant firm can adduce evidence objectively to justify its behaviour which would otherwise be abusive, just as in Article 81(3) the undertakings must satisfy the criteria that the agreement, concerted practice or decision improves production, distribution or more generally, technical or commercial progress. Further, the allegedly dominant firm can adduce evidence to show that effects on other undertakings in the relevant product market are not such as to prevent them from being able to compete or enter the market, just as in Article 81(3) the undertakings must satisfy the Commission that consumers have an equal share in the resulting benefits, and that the agreement does not substantially eliminate competition in the relevant market.[2] There may be a difference, however, on the burden of proof.[3]

1 Commission Decision (EEC) 85/609 [1985] OJ L374/1, [1986] 3 CMLR 273 (*ECS/AKZO*); Commission Decision (EEC) 87/500 [1987] OJ L286/36, [1988] 4 CMLR 67 (*BBI/ Boosey & Hawkes*); Commission Decision (EEC) 88/138 [1988] OJ L65/19, [1989] 4 CMLR 677 (*Hilti*); Commission Decision (EEC) 88/518 [1988] OJ L284/41, [1990] 4 CMLR 196 (*British Sugar/Napier Brown*); Commission Decision (EEC) 88/501 [1988] OJ L272/27, [1990] 4 CMLR 47 (*Tetra Pak 1*); Commission Decision (EEC) 88/589 [1988] OJ L317/47 (*London European/Sabena*); Commission Decision (EEC) 89/22 [1989] OJ L10/50, [1990] 4 CMLR 464 (*BPB Industries plc*), on appeal in Case C-310/93P *BPB Industries Plc and British Gypsum Ltd v Commission* [1995] ECR I-865, ECJ; Commission Decision (EEC) 89/205 [1989] OJ L78/43, [1989] 4 CMLR 757 (*Magill*), on appeal in Case T-76/89 *Independent Television Publications Ltd v Commission* [1991] ECR II-575, [1991] 4 CMLR 745, CFI, and further in Joined Cases C-241, 242/91 *Independent Television Publications (1TP) and Radio Telefís Éireann (RTE) v Commission* [1995] ECR I-743, [1995] 4 CMLR 718, ECJ.
2 In Case 85/76 *Hoffmann-La Roche & Co AG v Commission* [1979] ECR 461, [1979] 3 CMLR 211, ECJ, the Court suggested that the application of Article 81(3) would most likely have led to the same result as the application of Article 82. In Case 172/80 *Zuchner v Bayerische Vereinsbank* [1981] ECR 2021, [1982] 1 CMLR 313, ECJ, the Court observed that Article 82 deals with the abuse of a dominant position and does not cover the existence of concerted practices, to which the provisions of Article 81 solely apply. See on objective justification and abuse, further paras [275].
3 See, Article 2 of Regulation 1/2003 which states the pre-existing case law in relation the burden of proof. It is logical from the structure of Article 82 that the legal burden of proof to establish abuse should remain on the person so alleging, and that an undertaking which relies on objective justification (and proportionality) should only have the evidential burden of adducing the necessary facts, leaving it to be rebutted to the necessary standard of proof (see, for example, *Marks & Spencers Ltd, v Commissioners for Customs & Excise* [1999] EuLR 450 at 480-482 and the ECJ cases relied on; see also *Genzyme Ltd v OFT* [2004] CompAR 358, paras 576-581). See *RCA/ BHB v OFT* [2005] CAT 29 paras 132-133 (CAT). On the other hand, Advocate General Jacobs in Case C-53/03 *Syfait* (Opinion of 28 October 2004) arguably casts some doubt on that view (see para 72). In *Wireless Group v RJAR* (ChD, 16 December 2004) at para 48 Lloyd J says the burden is on the person alleging abuse to show an absence of justification. On the standard of proof, see B Vesterdoff, *Standard of Proof in Merger Cases* [2005] European Competition Journal, p 3, and *Napp Pharmaceuticals Holdings Ltd v DG of Fair Trading* [2002] CAT 5, para 110 and *JJB Sports plc and Allsports Ltd v OFT* [2004] CAT 17.

B. DOMINANT POSITION

1. Meaning of 'dominant position'

[229]
The EC Treaty does not define 'dominant position'. However, the Court of Justice has declared that a dominant position relates to a position of economic strength enjoyed by an undertaking which enables it to prevent effective competition being maintained on the relevant market[1] by giving it the power to behave to an appreciable extent independently of its competitors, customers and ultimately of its consumers.[2] 'Consumers' includes all firms who deal with the dominant undertaking

including purchasers, sellers, users, distributors and ultimate consumers, depending on the context. Dominance relates to the economic power to impede the maintenance of effective competition[3] and the power to determine conduct without taking account of competitive products.[4] Dominance also includes situations where other firms (which purchase from it or sell to it) have no real alternative but to deal with the dominant firm or where other firms are in a position of economic dependance on the dominant firm.[5] Such dominance may arise not only as a result of economic considerations, but by reason of legislation.[6] It can also cover purchasers with the requisite market power and thus includes independence from suppliers as well as consumers.[7]

1 As to the relevant market, see paras [234]–[244].
2 Case 27/76 *United Brands Co v Commission* [1978] ECR 207, [1978] 1 CMLR 429, ECJ; Case 85/76 *Hoffmann-La Roche & Co AG v Commission* [1979] ECR 461, [1979] 3 CMLR 211, ECJ; Case 31/80 *L'Oreal NV v De Nieuwe AMCK PVBA* [1980] ECR 3775, [1981] 2 CMLR 235, ECJ; Case 322/81 *Nederlandsche Banden-Industrie Michelin NV v Commission* [1983] ECR 3461, [1985] 1 CMLR 282, ECJ. See also Case 247/86 *Société alsacienne et lorraine de telecommunications et d'electronique (Alsatel) v Novasam SA* [1988] ECR 5987, [1990] 4 CMLR 434, ECJ; Case 30/87 *Bodson v Pompes funèbres des regions libérées SA* [1988] ECR 2479, [1989] 4 CMLR 984, ECJ; Case T-30/89 *Hilti AG v Commission* [1991] ECR 11-1439, [1990] 4 CMLR 602, CFI, subsequently upheld on appeal to the ECJ in Case C-53/92P *Hilti AG v Commission* [1994] ECR 1-667, ECJ; Case T-128/98 *Aéroports de Paris v Commission* [2000] ECR II-3929, para 147, ECJ; Case C-418/01 *IMS Health GmbH & Co. OHG v NDC Health GmbH & Co. KG* [2004] 4 CMLR 1543, para 189, ECJ.
3 Case 40/70 *Sirena Srl v Eda Srl* [1971] ECR 69, [1971] CMLR 260, ECJ; Case 78/70 *Deutsche Grammophon Gesellschaft mbH v Metro-SB-Grossmarkte GmbH & Co KG* [1971] ECR 487, [1971] CMLR 631, ECJ; Joined Cases 40-48, 50, 54-56, 111, 113, 114/73 *Coöperatieve vereniging Suiker Unie UA v Commission* [1975] ECR 1663, [1976] 1 CMLR 295, ECJ.
4 Case 22/78 *Hugin Kassaregister AB v Commission* [1979] ECR 1869, [1979] 3 CMLR 345, ECJ.
5 Case 298/83 *CICCE v Commission* [1985] ECR 1105 [1986] 1 CMLR 486, ECJ; *Radio Telefís Éireann (RTE) v Commission* [1991] ECR II-485, [1991] 4 CMLR 586, CFI, upheld in Joined Cases C-241, 242/91 *Independent Television Publications (ITP) and Radio Telefís Éireann (RTE) v Commission* [1995] ECR I-743, [1995] 4 CMLR 718, ECJ.
6 See for example Case 155/73 *Sacchi* [1974] ECR 409, [1974] 2 CMLR 177, ECJ; Case 26/75 *General Motors Continental NV v Commission* [1975] ECR 1367, [1976] 1 CMLR 95, ECJ; Case 13/77 *GB-INNO-BM NV v Vereniging van de Kleinhandeiaars in Tabak (ATAB)* [1977] ECR 2115, [1978] 1 CMLR 283, ECJ; Case 41/83 *Italy v Commission* [1985] ECR 873, [1985] 2 CMLR 368, ECJ; Case 226/84 *British Leyland plc v Commission* [1986] ECR 3263, [1987] 1 CMLR 85, ECJ; Case 311/84 *Centre belge d'études de marché - Telémarketing (CBEM) SA v Compagnie Luxembourgeoise de telédiffusion SA* [1985] ECR 3261, [1986] 2 CMLR 558, ECJ; Case C-260/89 *Elliniki Radiofonia Tileorasi v Kouvelas* [1991] ECR I-2925, [1994] 4 CMLR 540, ECJ.
7 See, for example, *GEMA* [1971] CMLR D35 and *Eurofirma* [1993] CMLR D217.

2. Determination of dominant position

[230]

In order to carry out the economic evaluation to determine the existence of a dominant position, it is necessary to determine the relevant product market[1] and the relevant geographical market[2] before assessing the economic strength of the undertaking on these markets.[3] It is probably also necessary, at least in some cases, to consider the temporal market.[4] Such an evaluation will require a thorough investigation of the factual circumstances of the undertaking concerned, its actual and potential competitors and of the market place.[5] Currently, the starting point in any such investigation should be the Commission Notice on the definition of the relevant market for the purposes of Community competition law.[6]

1 As to the relevant product market, see paras [234] ff.
2 As to the geographical market, see paras [245] ff.
3 See eg the structure of the decision in Case 27/76 *United Brands Co v Commission* [1978] ECR 207, [1978] 1 CMLR 429, ECJ.
4 As to the temporal market, see para [248].
5 See *Felixstowe Dock and Rly Co and European Ferries Ltd v British Transport Docks Board* [1976] 2 Lloyd's Rep 656 at 664, [1976] 2 CMLR 655 at 667, CA, per Scarman LJ. See also V Korah, 'Concept of a Dominant Position within the meaning of article 82' (1980) 17 CML Rev 395, where the author criticises the approach of the Court of Justice in Case 27/76 *United Brands Co v Commission* [1978] ECR 207, [1978] 1 CMLR 429, ECJ.
6 [1997] OJ C372. The Commission Notice states that '[f]irms are subject to three main sources of competitive constraints: demand substitutability, supply substitutability and potential competition. From an economic point of view, for the definition of the relevant market, demand substitution constitutes the most immediate and effective disciplinary force on the suppliers of a given product, in particular in relation to their pricing decisions' (para 13); see also XXVIIth Report on Competition Policy (1997), point 44. The Notice was relied on by the ECJ in Case T-346/02 *Cableuropa and Others v Commission* [2003] ECR II-4251 para 115, CFI. Compare also in this respect, the OFT's Guidelines on Abuse of a Dominant Position (OFT 402, December 2004) and on Market Definition (OFT 403, December 2004).

[231]
The Commission Notice makes clear (para 6) that its interpretation of the relevant market is without prejudice to the interpretation which may be given by the Court of Justice or the Court of First Instance.

[232]
The purpose of the Notice is to provide guidance as to how the Commission applies the concepts of relevant product and geographic market (para 1). The Notice refers (at para 2) to market definition as a tool to 'identify and define the boundaries of competition between firms'. The main purpose of market definition is to identify in a systematic way the competitive constraints that the undertakings involved face. The objective of defining a market in both its product and geographic dimension is to identify those actual competitors of the undertakings involved that are capable of constraining their behaviour and of preventing them from behaving independently of an effective competitive pressure (para 3). The Commission calculates market shares from this perspective.

[233]
As the Notice points out (at para 4), the definition of the relevant market in both its product and geographic dimensions often has a decisive influence on the assessment of a competition case. A further objective of the Notice is to render more transparent the Commission's approach to market definition, in the hope that increased transparency will also result in companies and their advisors being able to better anticipate the possibility that the Commission would raise competition concerns in an individual case. It is also intended that companies should be in a better position to understand what sort of information the Commission considers relevant for the purposes of market definition (para 5).

3. *Relevant product market*

[234]

(a) Importance of the relevant product market: The definition of 'the relevant product market'[1] is of fundamental significance,[2] for the possibility of competition can only be judged in the context of the market comprising the totality of the products which, with respect to their characteristics, are particularly suitable for satisfying constant needs and are only to a limited extent interchangeable with other products.[3] Moreover, since the determination of the relevant market is useful in assessing whether the undertaking concerned is in a position to prevent effective competition from being maintained and to behave to an appreciable extent independently of its competitors or service providers, the competitive conditions and the structure of supply and demand on the market must also be taken into consideration.[4] Failure to define the product market correctly could affect the validity of any finding in relation to a dominant position.[5]

1 For the definition, see para [235].
2 See eg Case 40/70 *Sirena Srl v Eda Srl* [1971] ECR 69, [1971] CMLR 260, ECJ; Case 78/70 *Deutsche Grammophon Gesellschaft mbH v Metro-SB-Grossmarkte GmbH & Co KG* [1971] ECR 487, [1971] CMLR 631, ECJ; Joined Cases 6, 7/73 *Istituto Chemioterapico Italiano SpA and Commercial Solvents Corpn v Commission* [1974] ECR 223, [1974] 1 CMLR 309, ECJ; Case 22/78 *Hugin Kassaregister AB v Commission* [1979] ECR 1829, [1979] 2 CMLR 345, ECJ; Case 31/80 *L'Oréal NV v De Nieuwe AMCK PVBA* [1980] ECR 3775, [1981] 2 CMLR 235, ECJ; Case 322/81 *Nederiandsche Banden-Industrie Michelin NV v Commission* [1983] ECR 3461, [1981] 1 CMLR 282, ECJ; Case 66/82 *Ahmed Saeed Flugreisen v Zentrale zur Bekämpfling unlauteren Wettbewerbs eV* [1989] ECR 803, [1990] 4 CMLR 102, ECJ; and Case 30/87 *Bodson v Pompes funebres des regions libérées SA* [1988] ECR 2479, [1989] 4 CMLR 984, ECJ.
3 Case 6/72 *Europemballage Corpn and Continental Can Co Inc v Commission* [1973] ECR 215, [1973] CMLR 199, ECJ; Case 31/80 *L'Oréal NV v De Nieuwe AMCK PVBA* [1980] ECR 3775, [1981] 2 CMLR 235, ECJ; Case 322/81 *Michelin* v *Commission* [1983] ECR 3461, para 37, ECJ See also Joined Cases T-68, 77, 78/89 *Società Italiano Vetro SpA v Commission* [1992] ECR 11-1403, [1992] 5 CMLR 302, CFI; Case T-65/96 *Kish Glass* v *Commission* [2000] ECR II-1885, para 62, CFI, confirmed on appeal by order of the ECJ in Case C-241/00P *Kish Glass* v *Commission* [2001] ECR I-7759.
4 Case C-418/01 *IMS Health GmbH & Co OHG v NDC Health GmbH & Co KG* [2004] 4 CMLR 1543 para 91, ECJ.
5 Case 6/72 *Europemballage Corpn and Continental Can Co Inc v Commission* [1973] ECR 215, [1973] CMLR 199, ECJ. At least, this would be so unless the undertaking would still be in a dominant position if the market had been correctly defined, which would be the case if the market had been defined too widely. The normal situation is that the undertaking concerned alleges that the Commission has defined the market too narrowly, and alleges that, if the market had been defined properly, the undertaking would not be in a dominant position. On appeal, it is not for the court to carry out its own analysis of the market but to verify the correctness of the Commission's findings and its reasoning: Joined Cases T-68, 77, 78/89 *Società Italiano Vetro SpA v Commission* [1992] ECR II-1403, [1992] 5 CMLR 302, CFI. See also the CAT's criticism of the OFT's findings of the relevant market in *RCA/BHB v OFT* [2005] CAT 29 at paras 135-150, and in particular the need for empirical evidence to carry out a proper economic evaluation of the product and the market and the need for a counterfactual.

[235]

(b) Meaning of 'the relevant product market': The 'relevant product market' means the market for a particular product which is sufficiently differentiated from other product markets so that it is only to a limited extent interchangeable with them and either not exposed to competition from other products or only exposed to such competition in a way which is hardly perceptible.[1] If there is competition between two products, and if that competition is affected by their price and intrinsic advantages to the consumer, it would be wrong to define the product market so as to encompass only one of those products.[2] This would be so even though for some users there would be no possibility of interchanging the products. The concept of a relevant market implies that there can be effective competition between the products in that market, and presupposes that there is a sufficient degree of interchangeability between all the products forming part of the same market insofar as a specific use of such products is concerned.[3]

1 Case 27/76 *United Brands Co v Commission* [1978] ECR 207, [1978] 1 CMLR 429, ECJ. See also Case T-69/89 *Radio Telefís Éireann v Commission* [1991] ECR II-485, [1991] 4 CMLR 586, CFI; Case T-70/89 *British Broadcasting Corpn and BBC Enterprises Ltd v Commission* [1991] ECR II-535, [1991] 4 CMLR 669, CFI; Case T-76/89 *Independent Television Publications Ltd v Commission* [1991] ECR II-575, [1991] 4 CMLR 745, CFI, in which the markets for weekly broadcast listings and for the television magazines in which they are published were held to constitute submarkets for television programme information in general, the lists of programmes for a 24-hour period published in newspapers being only substitutable to a limited extent for the advance information on all the week's programmes, upheld on appeal by the ECJ in Joined Cases C-241, 242/91 *Independent Television Publications (ITP) and Radio Telefís Éireann (RTE) v Commission* [1995] ECR I-743, [1995] 4 CMLR 718, ECJ; also Case T-504/93 *Tiercé Ladbroke v Commission* [1997] ECR II-923, para 81.

2 Joined Cases 19, 20/74 *Kali und Salz AG v Commission* [1975] ECR 499, [1975] 2 CMLR 154, ECJ, a case under EEC Treaty, Article 81, where the rival products were straight potash fertiliser and compound potash fertiliser. The same would apply to complementary foods, complementary products which are used or consumed together (eg knives and forks) or produced together. On complementary products, see OFT Guidelines on Market Definition and the CAT's reliance on this in *RCA/BHB v OFT* [2005] CAT 29 at para 149.

3 Case 85/76 *Hoffmann-La Roche & Co AG v Commission* [1979] ECR 461, [1979] 3 CMLR 211, ECJ; Case 247/86 *Société alsacienne et lorraine de telecommunications et d'electronique (Alsatel) v Novasam SA* [1988] ECR 5987, [1990] 4 CMLR 434, ECJ.

[236]

(c) Particular factors in determining the relevant product market

(i) General factors: Products may constitute a distinct market not only by reason of their use, but also by reason of their particular characteristics, which makes the products specially suitable for such use.[1] It may be possible to distinguish a market in raw materials from the market for derivatives.[2] In certain cases markets can legitimately be defined in very narrow terms; for example, in relation to services for a particular make of product,[3] or in relation to spare parts for a particular make of product,[4] or in the management of secondary exploitation rights in copyright material,[5] or in the market for replacement tyres for heavy vehicles,[6] or in the supply of information relating to national type-approval certification[7] or in relation to a particular air route,[8] or port,[9] or in relation to a product's design for use in conjunction with a particular make of another product.[10] Narrow markets may also arise in relation to luxury goods where the perceived prestige of a product means that it is readily substitutable with a very small number of other similar products[11] or in relation to products which are hardly substitutable at all in the eyes of the relevant consumer.[12] It is possible that in certain exceptional conditions the relevant market could consist only of each undertaking and its own customers.[13] The cases before the

ECJ and CFI indicate that the relevant product market is to be defined by reference to the facts in any given case, taking into account the whole economic context, which may include, notably: (a) the objective characteristics of the products; (b) the degree of substitutability or interchangeability between the products, having regard to their relative prices and intended use; (c) the competitive conditions; (d) the structure of the supply and demand; and (e) the attitudes of consumers and users. The key element is that of a competitive constraint: do the other products alleged to form part of the same market act as a competitive constraint on the conduct of the allegedly dominant firm. Contemporary evidence as to how the allegedly dominant undertaking itself views its competitors, and vice versa, may, depending on the particular circumstances, be of decisive importance when it comes to defining the market in any given case.[14]

1 Case 6/72 *Europemballage Corpn and Continental Can Co Inc v Commission* [1973] ECR 215, [1973] CMLR 199, ECJ; Case 27/76 *United Brands v Commission* [1978] ECR 207, para 31, ECJ

2 Joined Cases 6, 7/73 *Istituto Chemioterapico Italiano SpA and Commercial Solvents Corpn v Commission* [1974] ECR 223, [1974] 1 CMLR 309, ECJ.

3 Case 26/75 *General Motors Continental NV v Commission* [1975] ECR 1367, [1976] 1 CMLR 95, ECJ; Case 226/84 *British Leyland plc v Commission* [1986] ECR 3263, [1987] 1 CMLR 185, ECJ.

4 Case 22/78 *Hugin Kassaregister AB v Commission* [1979] ECR 1869, [1979] 3 CMLR 345, ECJ. In Case C-53/92P *Hilti AG v Commission* [1994] ECR I-667, [1994] 4 CMLR 614, ECJ, the ECJ emphasised that *Hugin* was not intended to lay down the criteria for distinguishing the market in consumables from that for equipments. See also the complaint in *Pelikan/Hyocena* (XXVth Report on Competition Policy, paras 86 to 87), where the Commission stated that each market for spare parts of consumables would have to be looked at individually to establish dominance.

5 Case 7/82 *GVL v Commission* [1983] ECR 483, [1983] 3 CMLR 645, ECJ.

6 Case 322/81 *Nederlandsche Banden-Industrie Michelin NV v Commission* [1983] ECR 3461, [1985] 1 CMLR 282, ECJ.

7 Commission Decision (EEC) 84/379 [1984] OJ L207/11, [1984] 3 CMLR 92 (*BL*).

8 Case 66/86 *Ahmed Saeed Flugreisen v Zentraie zur Bekiimpfung unlauteren Wettbewerbs eV* [1989] ECR 803, [1990] 4 CMLR 102, ECJ. See also Commission Decison (EEC) 92/213 [1992] OJ L96/34 (*British Midland v Aer Lingus*), where the relevant product market was the Dublin-London Heathrow route; Commission Decision (EC) 95/364 [1995] OJ L216/8, [1996] 4 CMLR 232 (*Brussels Airport*) (on appeal to the ECJ in Case C-291/95 *Belgium v Commission*), where the market for services linked to airport infrastructure for which a fee was payable at Zaventem airport constituted a relevant market.

9 Case C-179/90 *Merci Convenzionali Porto di Genova SpA v Siderurgica Gabrielli SpA* [1991] ECR I-5009, [1994] 4 CMLR 422, ECJ; Case C-18/93 *Corsica Ferries* [1994] ECR I-1783, ECJ; Commission Decision (EC) 94/19 [1994] OJ L15/8, [1995] 4 CMLR 84 (*Sea Containers/Stena Sealink*); Commission Decision (EC) 94/119 [1994] OJ L55/2, [1994] 5 CMLR 457(Port of Rødby); *Irish Continental Group v CCI Morlaix* (Case IV/35.388) [1995] 5 CMLR 177.

10 Case T-30/89 *Hilti AG v Commission* [1990] ECR II-163, [1990] 4 CMLR 602, CFI, upheld on appeal in Case C-53/92P *Hilti AG v Commission* [1994] ECR I-667, ECJ.

11 *Charles Jourdain* [1989] OJ L35/31, [1989] 4 CMLR 591; *Yves Saint Laurent* ([1992] OJ L12/24) [1993] 4 CMLR 120; *Parfums Givenchy SA* [1992] OJ L236/11, [1993] 5 CMLR 579.

12 For example the 'blind pass' tickets (that is, where the consumer did not know at the time of purchase which teams he would be seeing, eg buying semi-final tickets at the beginning of the tournament), held to constitute a separate product market in *Football World Cup 1998* [2000] OJ L5/55, [2000] 4 CMLR 963.

13 See Commission Decision (EEC) 77/327 ([1977] OJ L117/1) [1977] 2 CMLR l (*ABG Oil Companies*), which was not considered on appeal in Case 77/77 *Benzine en Petroleum Handelsmaatschappij BV v Commission* [1978] ECR 1513, [1978] 3 CMLR 174, ECJ.

14 *Aberdeen Journals v Director General of Fair Trading (No 1)* [2002] UKCLR 167, paras 96-104, CAT.

[237]

Where distortions to the market are created by the behaviour of the undertaking in question, these will be ignored in order objectively to assess the relevant market.[1] The relevant market in which dominance is to be tested need not be the relevant market in which the alleged abuse is committed.[2] The CFI held in *British Airways v Commission* that an abuse of a dominant position committed on the dominated product market may well infringe Article 82 even where the effects are only felt in a separate market on which the undertaking concerned does not hold a dominant position provided that separate market is sufficiently closely connected to the first.[3]

1 Commission Decision (EEC) 89/113 [1989] OJ L43/27 (*Decca Navigator System*).
2 Commission Decision (EEC) 85/609 [1985] OJ L374/1, [1986] 3 CMLR 273 (*ECS/AKZO*); Case 62/86 *AKZO Chemie v Commission* [1991] ECR I-3359, [1993] 5 CMLR 215, ECJ, in which the alleged abuse took place in one market where the firm in question was not dominant in order to prevent another firm, active on that market, from penetrating the market on which the relevant firm was dominant as a competitor. See also Commission Decision (EEC) 88/589 [1988] OJ L317/47 (*London European/Sabena*) in which the relevant market was that in which the relevant firm was considered dominant and abusive, although the intention was to affect the relevant firm's position on a different product market. See also Case T-83/91 *Tetra Pak International SA v Commission* [1994] ECR II-755, CFI, upheld on appeal to the ECJ in Case C-333/94P *Tetra Pak International SA v Commission* [1996] ECR I-5951, ECJ.
3 Case T-219/99 [2004] 4 CMLR 19, para 127, CFI; see also to that effect, Joined Cases 6/73 and 7/73 *Istituto Chemioterapico Italiano and Commercial Solvents* v *Commission* [1974] ECR 223, para 22, ECJ and Case 311/84 *CBEM* [1985] ECR 3261, para 26, ECJ. See the judgment of the English High Court in *Claritas (UK) Ltd v (1) Post Office (2) Postal Preference Service Ltd* [2001] UKCLR 2 holding that (i) in principle the dominated market and the market affected by the abuse had to be the same; (ii) to extend the concept of abuse to another market required a close link between the two markets; and (iii) any extension to related markets had to be circumscribed to ensure that it was extended only where an undertaking had a responsibility under Article 82 EC with regard to its conduct in those other markets.

[238]

In its Notice, the Commission sets out the process for defining the relevant product market including in particular the need to obtain all available relevant information and states that it does not follow a rigid hierarchy of different sources of information[1] and sets out the process of gathering information.[2] The Notice sets out the type of evidence which it considers relevant to assess whether products are demand substitutes:

(1) Evidence of substitution in the recent past: 'When available, this sort of information will normally be fundamental for market definition'. The Notice suggests that 'launches of new products in the past can also offer useful information, when it is possible to precisely analyse which products lost sales to the new product'.

(2) Quantitative tests consisting of various econometric and statistical approaches of that have specifically have been designed for the purpose of delineating markets: Estimates of elasticities and cross-price elasticities for the demand of a product, tests based on similarity of price movements over time, the analysis of causality between price series and similarity of price levels and/or their convergence (where capable of withstanding rigorous scrutiny).

(3) Views of customers and competitors: According to the Notice, the Commission will often contact the main customers and competitors of the companies involved in its enquiries, to gather their views on the boundaries of the product market as well as most of the factual information it requires to reach a conclusion on the scope of the market and '[r]easoned answers of customers and competitors as to what would happen if relative prices for the candidate products would increase in the candidate geographic area by a small amount (for instance of 5%–10%)' will be taken into account when sufficiently backed by factual evidence.

(4) Consumer preferences and marketing studies: The Notice warns that the 'methodology followed in consumer surveys carried out ad-hoc by the undertakings involved or their competitors ... will usually be scrutinized with utmost care' since '[u]nlike pre-existing studies, they have not been prepared in the normal course of business for the adoption of business decisions'.

(5) Barriers and costs associated with switching demand to potential substitutes: The Notice notes that these barriers or obstacles might have a wide range of origins, and in its decisions, the Commission has been confronted with 'regulatory barriers or other forms of State intervention, constraints arising in downstream markets, need to incur specific capital investment or loss in current output in order to switch to alternative inputs, the location of customers, specific investment in production process, learning and human capital investment, retooling costs or other investments, uncertainty about quality and reputation of unknown suppliers, and others'.

(6) Different categories of customers and price discrimination: the extent of the product market might be narrowed in the presence of distinct groups of customers: The Notice notes that a 'distinct group of customers for the relevant product may constitute a narrower, distinct market when such group could be subject to price discrimination. This will usually be the case when two conditions are met: (a) it is possible to identify clearly which group an individual customer belongs to at the moment of selling the relevant products to him, and (b) trade among customers or arbitrage by third parties should not be feasible'.[3]

1 Notice, paras 25-27, 33-34.
2 Ibid, para 37-43.
3 Ibid, paras 44-55.

[239]

(ii) Economic factors: An examination limited only to the objective characteristics of the relevant products cannot be sufficient: the competitive conditions and the structure of supply and demand on the market must also be taken into consideration.[1] Thus it will be necessary to consider supply and demand factors separately.[2] As the Commission Notice states, demand substitution will normally be the most important factor.

1 Case 322/81 *Nederiandsche Banden-Industrie Michelin NV v Commission* [1983] ECR 3461, [1981] 1 CMLR 282, ECJ.

2 See for example Commission Decision (EEC) 88/501 [1988] OJ L272/27, [1990] 4 CMLR 47 (*Tetra Pak I*), on appeal Case T-51/89 *Tetra Pak Rausing SA v Commission* [1990] ECR II-309, [1991] 4 CMLR 334, CFI; Case T-30/89 *Hilti AG v Commission* [1991] ECR II-1439, [1992] 4 CMLR 16, CFI, subsequently upheld on appeal to the ECJ in Case C-53/92P *Hilti AG v Commission* [1994] ECR I-667, ECJ.

[240]
Demand-side substitutability: The assessment of demand substitution entails a determination of the range of products which are viewed as substitutes by the consumer. The Commission Notice suggests the SSNIP test[1] as a means of examining this. This test involves postulating a small but significant non-transitory increase in price (eg, 5–10 per cent) and evaluating the likely reactions of customers to that increase. This approach implies that starting from the type of products that the undertakings involved sell and the area in which they sell them, additional products and areas will be included into or excluded from the market definition depending on whether competition from these other products and areas affect or restrain sufficiently the pricing of the parties' products in the short term.[2] It thus follows that identifying the wrong starting point by choosing the wrong product or mis-specifying the product can lead to the wrong questions about market definition being asked and the wrong market definition being identified.

1 'SSNIP' stands for Small but Significant and Non-transitory Increase in Price.
2 Commission Notice on the definition of the relevant market for the purposes of Community competition law [1997] OJ C372, paras 15-18. See further the analysis of price cross-elasticity in Case 6/72 *Europembaliage Corpn and Continental Can Co Inc v Commission* [1973] ECR 215, [1973] CMLR 199, ECJ; Case 27/76 *United Brands Co v Commission* [1978] ECR 207, [1978] 1 CMLR 429, ECJ. See also Case 322/81 *Nederlandsche Banden-Industrie Michelin NV v Commission* [1983] ECR 3461, [1985] 1 CMLR 282, ECJ. See also Case T-30/89 *Hilti AG v Commission* [1990] ECR II-163, [1990] 4 CMLR 602, CFI.

[241]
The question to be answered is whether the parties' customers would switch to readily available substitutes or to suppliers located elsewhere in response to the hypothetical long-term 5–10 per cent increase in the products and areas being considered. If substitution would be enough to make the price increase unprofitable because of the resulting loss of sales, additional substitutes and areas are included in the relevant market. This would be done until the set of products and geographic areas is such that small, permanent increases in relative prices would be profitable. The equivalent analysis is applicable in cases concerning buying power, where the starting point would then be the supplier and the price test allows to identify the alternative distribution channels or outlets for the supplier's products.[1]

1 Commission Notice on the definition of the relevant market for the purposes of Community competition law [1997] OJ C372, paras 15-18. See also Commission Decison (EEC) 88/138 [1988] OJ L65/19, [1989] 4 CMLR 677 (*Hilti*), Case T-30/89 *Hilti AG v Commission* [1990] ECR II-163, [1990] 4 CMLR 602, CFI, upheld on appeal in Case C-53/92P *Hilti AG v Commission* [1994] ECR I-667, ECJ. See the CAT's criticism of the OFT's approach to the application of the SSNIP test, and the need for empirical evidence in *RCA/BHB v OFT* [2005] CAT 29, paras 135-150.

[242]
As the Commission notes at para 19 of the Notice, there are limits to the usefulness of the SSNIP or 'hypothetical monopolist test' as it is sometimes called. In a monopoly

situation, the dominant undertaking may already be charging the highest price that its customers will bear and if the price increased even by a small margin they may cease buying from it at all. Thus, the SSNIP test may indicate a high degree of substitutability and a wider market than in fact exists. In such cases alternative methods of determining market power must be considered, ignoring any distortive effects the conduct of the dominant firm has itself created.[1] Equally there may be limitations in the use of economic or econometric techniques because no or insufficient reliable data is available. Survey data may be inconclusive because of the hypothetical nature of the question or the difficulty of obtaining sufficiently informed responses. In addition, the particular market circumstances may themselves create their own dynamics. For example, a product which might not appear, in the abstract, to be directly substitutable for another product may turn out to be in fact a significant competitor because of the particular circumstances of the local market at the time in question.[2]

1 The Supreme Court in the United States was criticized for making this error in *United States v EI du Pont de Nemour and Co* 351 US 377 (1956) in Landes and Posner, 'Market Power in Antitrust Cases' (1981) 94 Harvard Law Review 937, 960-961 (following which the error became known as 'the Cellophane Fallacy'). See further, Whish, *Competition Law* (5th edn, 2003), pp 30-32 and Bishop and Walker, *The Economics of EC Competition Law* (2nd edn, 2002) at pp 98-104.
2 *Aberdeen Journals v Director General of Fair Trading* [2002] UKCLR 167, para 102, CAT. Equally, extreme customer loyalty (eg supporters of a particular team) may also distort the result of such analysis. In fact the SNIPP test has been used relatively rarely by the Commision even in merger cases (some 11% of all cases; see Copenhagen Economics (2004) Enterprise Paper No 15, Brussels, European Commission). In the vast majority of cases the Commission and courts rely on simple factual arguments, in particular regarding demand substitution, rather than advanced economic methodology.

[243]
Supply-side substitutability: The Commission Notice states at paras 20–23 that supply-side substitutability may also be taken into account when defining markets in those situations in which its effects are 'equivalent to those of demand substitution in terms of effectiveness and immediacy'. This requires that suppliers be able to switch production to the relevant products and market them in the short term without incurring significant additional costs or risks in response to small and permanent changes in relative prices. When these conditions are met, the additional production that is put on the market will have a disciplinary effect on the competitive behaviour of the companies involved. Such an impact in terms of effectiveness and immediacy is equivalent to the demand substitution effect.[1]

1 On supply-side substitutability, see in particular Case 322/82 *Michelin v Commission* [1983] ECR 3461, [1985] 3 CMLR 282, para 41 and Case 22/78 *Hugin v Commission* [1979] ECR 1869, [1979] 3 CMLR 345.

[244]
Potential competition: The Commission Notice states (at para 24) that a further source of competitive constraint, potential competition, is not taken into account when defining markets. This is because the conditions under which potential competition will actually represent an effective competitive constraint depend on the analysis of specific factors and circumstances related to the conditions of entry. If required, this analysis is only carried out at a subsequent stage, 'in general once the position of the

companies involved in the relevant market has already been ascertained, and when such position gives rise to concerns from a competition point of view'.

4. Relevant geographic market

[245]
The geographic market to be taken into account involves an economic assessment of the area in which all the undertakings concerned are involved in the supply and demand of products or services, in which the conditions of competition are sufficiently homogeneous and which can be distinguished from neighbouring areas because the conditions of competition are appreciably different in those areas.[1] In its Notice on market definition, the Commission states that it will take 'a preliminary view of the scope of the geographic market on the basis of broad indications regarding the distribution of market shares of the parties and their competitors as well as a preliminary analysis of pricing and price differences at national and EU or EEA level'. According to the Commission, this initial view is used as a 'working hypothesis to focus the Commission's enquiries for the purposes of arriving at a precise geographic market definition'.[2] In order to determine whether a geographical market meets such conditions, it is relevant to consider the proportion of business carried on by the undertaking concerned in the territory in relation to the total business in that territory.[3] The Commission will also, in an appropriate case, take into account the continuing process of EU market integration.[4] In its Notice, the Commission sets out the type of evidence which it considers relevant to reach a conclusion as to the geographic market: past evidence of diversion of orders to other areas, basic demand characteristics, view of customers and competitors, current geographic patterns of purchasers, trade flows/patterns of shipments and barriers and associated switching costs to divert orders to companies in other areas (paras 44–55).

1 Case T-504/93 *Tierce Ladbroke v Commission* [1997] ECR II-923 at para 102.

2 Commission Notice on the definition of relevant market for the purposes of Community competition law [1997] OJ C372/5, paras 8 and 28-32, see also Joined Cases C-68/94 and C-30/95 *France and Others* v *Commission* [1998] ECR I-1375, para 143, ECJ. The Notice has been applied by the Commission in *Alpha Flight Services/Aeroports de Paris* [1998] OJ L230/10, [1998] 5 CMLR 611; *Flughafen Frankfurt/Main* [1998] OJ L72/30, [1998] 4 CMLR 779; *Van den Bergh Foods* [1998] OJ L246/1, [1998] 5 CMLR 530; *WorldCom/MCI* [1999] OJ L116/1, [1999] 5 CMLR 876; *MCI WorldCom/Sprint*, Decision of 28 June 2000, COMP/M.1741, available at http://europa.eu.int/comm/competition/mergers/cases.

3 Joined Cases 40-48, 50, 54-56, 111, 113, 114/73 *Coöperatieve vereniging Suiker Unie UA v Commission* [1975] ECR 1663, [1976] 1 CMLR 295, ECJ. See Case 247/86 *Societe alsacienne et lorraine de telecommunications et d'électronique (Alsatel) v Novasam SA* [1988] ECR 5987, [1990] 4 CMLR 434, ECJ, where because of the structure of the telecommunications market in France, the Court ruled that the economic strength of the undertaking in question could only be assessed by considering its provision of telecommunication services in the State as a whole and could not be restricted to regions; see also Case T-83/91 *Tetra Pak International SA v Commission* [1994] ECR II-755, CFI, upheld on appeal to the ECJ in Case C-333/94P *Tetra Pak International SA v Commission* [1996] ECR I-595, [1996] 1All ER (EC) 4, ECJ.

4 Commission Notice, para 32.

[246]
To fall within the prohibition, an abuse must be of a dominant position within the common market or in a substantial part of it.[1] Accordingly, the territory within which

the economic power of the undertaking must be considered is that part of the territory of the common market which constitutes the relevant geographical market.[2] However, in order to determine the power of the undertaking within that market, it may be relevant to consider its operations, if any, outside the common market in relation to factors such as supply, transportation, research, technical knowledge and selling methods,[3] or the fact that the dominant undertaking belongs to a group with worldwide activities.[4] There must be a clear delimitation of a substantial part of the common market in which the undertaking may be able to engage in conduct which hinders effective competition, and it must be an area in which the objective conditions of competition for the product in question are the same for all traders.[5]

1 EC Treaty, Article 82. For 'substantial part' see para [247] below.
2 See Case 27/76 *United Brands Co v Commission* [1978] ECR 207 at 281, [1978] 1 CMLR 429 at 489, ECJ.
3 Case 27/76 *United Brands Co v Commission* [1978] ECR 207 at 278-281, [1978] 1 CMLR 429 at 487, 489, ECJ.
4 Case 322/81 *Nederlandsche Banden-Industrie Michelin NV v Commission* [1983] ECR 3461 at 3510, [1981] 1 CMLR 282 at 327, ECJ.
5 Case 27/76 *United Brands Co v Commission* [1978] ECR 207, para 44, [1978] 1 CMLR 429, ECJ. In Case T-83/91 *Tetra Pak International SA v Commission* [1994] ECR II-755, CFI, the relevant geographic market was the whole of the Community for the products in question owing to stable intra-Community demand, the possibility of cross-border supplies and ease of transport between Member States.

5. Substantial part of the common market

[247]

In order to determine whether an area is large enough to amount to a substantial part of the common market, it is necessary to consider the volume of production and consumption of the product, as well as the habits and economic opportunities of vendors and purchasers. It is also necessary to consider factors such as freight rates in relation to the value of the product.[1] Member States will usually be 'substantial parts' of the common market.[2] A single facility has been held on several occasions to amount to a substantial part of the common market[3] and even an air or ferry route may also do so.[4] Each situation will depend upon an evaluation of the particular economic circumstances in issue.

1 Joined Cases 40-48, 50, 54-56, 111, 113, 114/73 *Coöperatieve vereniging Suiker Unie UA v Commission* [1975] ECR 1663, [1976] 1 CMLR 295, ECJ.
2 (Belgium and Luxembourg) Joined Cases 40-48, 50, 54-56, 111, 113, 114/73 *Coöperatieve vereniging Suiker Unie UA v Commission* [1975] ECR 1663 at 1976, 1977, [1976] 1 CMLR 295 at 451,452, ECJ; (Belgium) Case 26/75 *General Motors Continental NV v Commission* [1975] ECR 1367, [1976] 1 CMLR 95, ECJ. See also Case C-18/88 *Régie des Télégraphes et des Téléphones v SA GB-INNO-BN* [1991] ECR I-5941, ECJ; (Southern Germany) Joined Cases 40-48, 50, 54-56, 111, 113, 114/73 *Coöperatieve vereniging Suiker Unie UA v Commission* [1975] ECR 1663 at 1991-1993, [1976] 1 CMLR 295 at 463-465, ECJ; (Germany) Case 7/82 *GVL v Commission* [1983] ECR 483, [1983] 3 CMLR 645, ECJ. See also Case C-41/90 *Hofner v Macrotron GmbH* [1991] ECR I-1979, [1993] 4 CMLR 306, ECJ; (UK) Commission Decision (EEC) 82/821 [1982] OJ L360/36, [1983] 1 CMLR 457 (*British Telecommunications*); *Commission Decision* (EEC) 84/379 [1984] OJ L207/11, [1984] 3 CMLR 92 (*BL*); (Great Britain) Commission Decision (EEC) 78/68 [1978] OJ L22/23, [1978] 1 CMLR 19 (*Hugin/Liptons*); (Netherlands) Case 322/81 *Nederlandsche Banden-Industrie Michelin NV v Commission* [1983] ECR 3461, [1985] 1 CMLR 282, ECJ; (Greece) Case C-260/89 *Eliiniki Radiofonia Tileorasi v Kouvelas* [1991] ECR I-2925, [1994] 4 CMLR 540, ECJ; (Ireland and

Northern Ireland) Case T-69/89 *Radio Telefís Éireann v Commission* [1991] ECR II-481, [1991] 4 CMLR 582, CFI; Case T-70/89 *British Broadcasting Corpn and BBC Enterprises Ltd v Commission* [1991] ECR II-535, [1991] 4 CMLR 669, CFI; Case T-76/89 *Independent Television Publications Ltd v Commission* [1991] ECR II-575, [1991] 4 CMLR 745, CFI. Note, however, the English High Court in *Cutsforth v Mansfield Inns* [1986] 1 WLR 558, QB, where Sir Neil Lawson said 'nor, in my judgment, is the area of the North of England in which the defendants operate a "substantial part" of the common market (taken as a whole)'.

3 See Case C-179/90 *Merci Convenzionali Porto di Genova SpA v Siderurgica Gabrielli SpA* [1991] ECR I-5889, [1994] 4 CMLR 422, ECJ, where the Court ruled that the port of Genoa could be a substantial part of the common market because of its large traffic and the prominent part it plays in respect of maritime imports and exports; Case C-18/93 *Corsica Ferries* [1994] ECR 1-1783, ECJ (pilot services in Genoa); Commission Decision (EC) 94/119 [1994] OJ L55/52, [1994] 5 CMLR 457 (*Port of Rødby*); Commission Decision (EC) 95/364 [1995] OJ L216/8, [1996] 4 CMLR 232 (*Brussels Airport*) (11th busiest airport in the Community constitutes a 'substantial part of the common market'); Case C-163/99 *Portugal v Commission* (*Portuguese Airports*) [2001] ECR I-2613, ECJ; *Ilmailulaitos/Luftfartsverket* Commission Decision [1999] OJ L69/24, [1999] 5 CMLR 90; *Spanish Airports* [2000] OJ L208/36, [2000] 5 CMLR 967.

4 Case 66/86 *Ahmed Saeed* [1989] ECR 803 regarding a route taken by scheduled flights.

6. *The temporal market*

[248]

Article 82 EC relates to the position occupied by the undertaking in question at the time when the alleged abuse occurs.[1] However, a temporary situation which gives rise to an exceptional situation of dominance is unlikely to be sufficiently long term so as to create a dominant position,[2] nor would short-term factors which create a particularly narrow product market or a particularly small geographical market, for it is the long-term economic power which is important. On the other hand, regular seasonal factors may be relevant; thus a product available all the year round will not normally be in the same product market as a seasonal product.[3]

1 Joined Cases 40-48, 50, 54-56, 111, 113, 114/73 *Coöperatieve vereniging Suiker Unie UA v Commission* [1975] ECR 1663 at 1993, [1976] 1 CMLR 295 at 465, ECJ.

2 Case 77/77 *Benzine en Petroleum Handelsmaatschappij BV v Commission* [1978] ECR 1513, [1978] 3 CMLR 174, ECJ.

3 Case 27/76 *United Brands Co v Commission* [1978] ECR 207, [1978] 1 CMLR 429, ECJ.

7. *Assessment of market power*

[249]

(a) Economic strength generally: A dominant position, which enables an undertaking to prevent or restrict competition, derives from a combination of several factors which, when taken separately, are not necessarily determinative. A decision will involve consideration of the structure of the undertaking concerned and its competitive position in the market.[1] The economic strength[2] required is such that the undertaking is enabled to prevent effective competition being maintained in the relevant market, and such as to enable the undertaking to have an appreciable influence on the conditions under which competition will develop and to act largely in disregard of such competition, so long as such competition does not operate to its detriment.[3] An undertaking does not need to have eliminated all opportunity for competition to be in a dominant position,[4] and it may be in a dominant position even though it faces active competition from other undertakings,[5] or from partially interchangeable products.[6] Countervailing power of others in the market may negate dominance in certain cases.[7]

1 Case 27/76 *United Brands Co v Commission* [1978] ECR 207, [1978] 1 CMLR 429, ECJ; Case T-30/89 *Hilti AG v Commission* [1990] ECR II-163, [1990] 4 CMLR 602, CFI.
2 For a detailed discussion of the economic factors involved, Bishop and Walker, *The Economics of EC Competition* (2nd edn, 2002), chapter 3.
3 Case 27/76 *United Brands Co v Commission* [1978] ECR 207, [1978] 1 CMLR 429, ECJ; Case 85/76 *Hoffmann-La Roche & Co AG v Commission* [1979] ECR 461, [1979] 3 CMLR 211, ECJ; Case 322/81 *Nederlandsche Banden-Industrie Michelin NV v Commission* [1983] ECR 3461, [1985] 1 CMLR 282, ECJ; Case 311/84 *Centre belge d'études de marché – Télemarketing (CBEM) SA v Compagnie luxembourgeoise de télediffusion SA* [1985] ECR 3261, [1986] 2 CMLR 558, ECJ. See also Commission Decision (EEC) 89/113 [1989] OJ L43/27 (*Decca Navigator Systems*).
4 Case 27/76 *United Brands Co v Commission* [1978] ECR 207, [1978] 1 CMLR 429, ECJ; Case 85/76 *Hoffmann-La Roche & Co AG v Commission* [1979] ECR 461, [1979] 3 CMLR 211, ECJ; Case T-203/01 *Michelin* v *Commission* [2004] 4 CMLR 18, para 239, CFI; Case T-65/98 *Van den Bergh Foods* v *Commission* [2003] ECR II-4653, paras 149 and 160, CFI; and Case T-219/99 *British Airways* v *Commission* [2004] 4 CMLR 19, para 293, CFI; Case T-201/04 *Microsoft v Commission* [2005] 4 CMLR 406, para 383, CFI.
5 Case 27/76 *United Brands Co v Commission* [1978] ECR 207, [1978] 1 CMLR 429, ECJ.
6 Case 322/81 *Nederlandsche Banden-Industrie Michelin NV v Commission* [1983] ECR 3461, [1981] 1 CMLR 282, ECJ. Thus, the fact that individuals may be able to obtain a type approval by personal application will not prevent a dominant position being obtained by a motor manufacturer, when the application is exceptional and subject to strict conditions: Case 226/84 *British Leyland plc v Commission* [1986] ECR 3263, [1987] 1 CMLR 85, ECJ.
7 Case T-68/89 *SIV v Commission (Italian Flat Glass)* [1992] ECR II-1403, [1992] 5 CMLR 302; Case C-250/92 *Gottrup Klim v Dansk Landbrugs* [1994] ECR I-5641, [1996] 4 CMLR 191, para 32.

[250]

The economic strength of an undertaking is not measured by its profitability, for an undertaking may be in a dominant position even though it makes losses, at least in the short and medium term. A reduced profit margin or even losses for a time are not incompatible with a dominant position, just as large profits may be compatible with a situation where there is effective competition.[1]

1 Case 27/76 *United Brands Co v Commission* [1978] ECR 207, [1978] 1 CMLR 429, ECJ. See also Case 322/81 *Nederiandsche Banden-Industrie Michelin NV v Commission* [1983] ECR 3461, [1985] 1 CMLR 282, ECJ. See also, Case C-497/99P *Irish Sugar v Commission* [2001] ECR I-5333, where the undertaking was dominant despite making losses over a substantial period.

[251]

Although it will normally be the case that a dominant undertaking will be a producer or supplier of goods or services, it may be a purchaser.[1]

1 See Commission Communication in *Eurofima* [1973] CMLR D217 (Commission 3rd Report on Competition Policy, points 68, 69). See also Memorandum to the railway companies reminding them of the obligations under Article 82 both on purchasers of goods and services and the obligations whether on buyer or seller not to discriminate between suppliers or customers in different Member States or to set out to obtain goods or services exdusively in their country or from their own suppliers (XXth Report on Competition Policy, para 115).

[252]

(b) Economic strength and market share: The primary consideration in order to determine economic strength is market share.[1] Very large market shares are highly significant evidence of the existence of a dominant position.[2] A very large market share may be important evidence of a dominant position, but this factor taken separately may not be decisive but may be taken into consideration together with other factors.[3] For example, a market share of 90 per cent in the Southern German market and some 85 per cent in the Belgian market for sugar were held to be dominant positions,[4] as well as a share of between 70–80 per cent of the relevant market.[5] In other cases smaller shares have been held to justify the finding of a dominant position.[6] The Commission has stated that a dominant position could be said to exist if a market share of 40–45 per cent is reached (particularly if there is a large gap between that share and the share of its nearest rival),[7] although a dominant position cannot be ruled out in respect of a market share between 20 and 40 per cent.[8] On the other hand, a 5–10 per cent share of a market for highly technical products which appear to the majority of consumers to be readily interchangeable normally rules out the existence of a dominant position,[9] as does a 1 per cent share in such a market.[10] Especially large market shares may create a situation in which the undertaking in question has a position of special responsibility ('superdominance').

1 Case 27/76 *United Brands Co v Commission* [1978] ECR 207, [1978] 1 CMLR 429, ECJ. Cf Case 26/76 *Metro SB-Grossmarkte GmbH & Co KG v Commission* [1977] ECR 1875 at 1902, [1978] 2 CMLR 1 at 32, ECJ. See also Case 62/82 *Akzo Chemie v Commission* [1991] ECR I-3359, [1993] 5 CMLR 215, ECJ.

2 Case 85/76 *Hoffmann-La Roche & Co AG v Commission* [1979] ECR 461, [1979] 3 CMLR 211, ECJ. In interim relief cases, where expedition is of critical importance, the Commission has considered that very high market share suffices to demonstrate dominance: *ECS/AKZO* [1983] OJ L252/13, [1983] 3 CMLR 694; see also *NDC Health/IMS Health (Interim Measures)* [2002] OJ L59/18, [2002] 4 CMLR 111, paras 57-62.

3 Case 247/86 *Société alsacienne et lorraine de telecommunications et d'electronique (Alsatel) v Novasam SA* [1988] ECR 5987, [1990] 4 CMLR 434, ECJ.

4 Joined Cases 40-48, 50, 54-56, 111, 113, 114/73 *Coöperatieve vereniging Suiker Unie UA v Commission* [1975] ECR 1663 at 1978, 1994, [1976] 1 CMLR 295 at 452, 465, ECJ. See also Commission Decision (EEC) 91/299 [1991] OJ L152/21 (*Soda-ash – Solvay*), and Commission Decision (EEC) 91/300 [1991] OJ L152/40 (*Soda-ash – ICI*), where the respective shares of the markets were 70 per cent for Solvay in Continental Western Europe and over 90 per cent for ICI in the United Kingdom (indicative of dominance) (on appeal in Case T-32/91 *Solvay v Commission* [1995] ECR II-1825, [1996] 5 CMLR 91, CFI, on appeal Case C-287/95P *Commission v Solvay* [2000] ECR I-2391 and, Case T-37/91 *ICI v Commission* [1995] ECR II-1901, CFI). See further Commission Decision (EEC) 92/163 ([1992] OJ L72/1) (*Tetra Pak II*), upheld on appeal to the CFI in Case T-83/91 *Tetra Pak International SA c Commission* [1994] ECR II-755, ECJ, further upheld in Case C333/94 P *Tetra Pak International SA v Commission* [1996] ECR I-5951, ECJ.

5 Case T-30/89 *Hilti AG v Commission* 11990] ECR II-163, [1990] 4 CMLR 602, CFI.

6 In Case 27/76 *United Brands Co v Commission* [1978] ECR 207, [1978] 1 CMLR 429, ECJ, a market share of 40-45 per cent was, with the other factors, sufficient to establish a dominant position where the next largest competitor had a 10-15 per cent share. See also Case 62/82 *Akzo Chemie v Commission* [1991] ECR I-3359, [1993] 5 CMLR 215, ECJ.

7 See Commission 10th Report on Competition Policy, point 150. See Case C-250/92 *Gottrup Klim v Dansk Landbrugs* [1994] ECR I-5641, [1996] 4 CMLR 191, where in relation to market shares of 32 to 36 per cent, the ECJ said that 'while an undertaking which holds market shares of that size may, depending on the strength and number of its competitors, be considered to be in a dominant position, those market shares cannot on their own constitute conclusive evidence of the existence of a domonant position' (para 48). In Case T-219/99 *British Airways v Commission* [2004] 4 CMLR 19, the CFI upheld the decision of the Commission in *Virgin/British Airways* [2000] OJ L30/1, [2000] 4 CMLR 999 which for the first time found a dominant position where the undertaking concerned held less than 40% of the relevant market – here, BA held 39.7% of the market in the UK air travel agency services market.

8 See Commission 9th Report on Competition Policy, point 22.
9 Case 26/76 *Metro SB-Grossmärkte GmbH & Co KG v Commission* [1977] ECR 1875, [1978] 2 CMLR 1, ECJ.
10 Case 210/81 *Demo-Studio Schmidt v Commission* [1983] ECR 3045, [1984] 1 CMLR 63, ECJ.

[253]

The Commission has provided guidance as to how to calculate market share. In the Notice on market definition the Commission begins by stating that a total market size and market shares for each supplier can be calculated on the basis of their sales of the relevant products on the relevant area. In practice, the total market size and market shares are often available from market sources, ie, companies' estimates, studies commissioned to industry consultants and/or trade associations. When this is not the case, or also when available estimates are not reliable, the Commission will usually ask each supplier in the relevant market to provide its own sales in order to calculate total market size and market shares. If sales are usually the reference to calculate market shares, there are nevertheless other indications that, depending on the specific products or industry in question, can offer useful information such as, in particular, capacity, the number of players in bidding markets, units of fleet as in aerospace, or the reserves held in the case of sectors such as mining. As a rule of thumb, according to the Commission, both volume sales and value sales provide useful information. In cases of differentiated products, sales in value and their associated market share will usually be considered to better reflect the relative position and strength of each supplier.[1]

1 Commission Notice on the definition of relevant market for the purposes of Community competition law [1997] OJ C372/5, paras 53 to 55.

[254]

(c) Economic strength and resources and technology: The resources of an undertaking and its methods of supply, production, research, packaging, transportation, selling and displaying its product are relevant factors in evaluating economic strength.[1] The technological lead of an undertaking is also a relevant matter.[2] Similarly, great financial resources or reserves,[3] economies of scale[4] or a strong distribution system[5] may be further factors in determining dominance. On the other hand, the high quality of a product is a factor of competition, and does not by itself give rise to a dominant position,[4] at least in the ordinary case.[6] However, a very strong reputation for quality may indicate dominance.[7] The fact that an undertaking produces a wider range of products than its competitors will be irrelevant, at least when each product represents a distinct product market.[8]

1 Case 27/76 *United Brands Co v Commission* [1978] ECR 207, [1978] 1 CMLR 429, ECJ.
2 Case 85/76 *Hoffmann-La Roche & Co AG v Commission* [1979] ECR 461, [1979] 3 CMLR 211, ECJ. See also Commission Decision (EEC) 88/501 [1988] OJ L272/27, [1990] 4 CMLR 47 (*Tetra Pak I*).
3 Case 6/72 *Europembailage Corpn and Continental Can Co Inc v Commission* [1973] ECR 215, [1973] CMLR 199, ECJ. See also Case 322/81 *Nederlandsche Banden-Industrie Michelin NV v Commission* [1983] ECR 3461, [1985] 1 CMLR 282, ECJ; Case 30/87 *Bodson v Pompes funèbres des regions libérées SA* [1988] ECR 2479, [1989] 4 CMLR 984, ECJ. But this will not always be the case, see Case 85/76 *Hoffmann-La Roche & Co AG v Commission* [1979] ECR 461, [1979] 3 CMLR 211, ECJ.
4 Case 27/76 *United Brands Co v Commission* [1978] ECR 207, [1978] 1 CMLR 429, ECJ; see also Case C-310/93P *BPB Industries Plc and British Gypsum Ltd v Commission* [1995] ECR I-865, ECJ.

5 Case 27/76 *United Brands Co v Commission* [1978] ECR 207, [1978] 1 CMLR 429, ECJ; Case 85/76 *Hoffmann-La Roche & Co AG v Commission* [1979] ECR 461, [1979] 3 CMLR 211, ECJ.
6 Case 26/76 *Metro SB-Grossmarkte GmbH & Co KG v Commission* [1977] ECR 1875, [1978] 2 CMLR 1, ECJ.
7 An exception could be when it can be shown that the high quality product forms a distinct product market: *Michelin* [2002] OJ L143/1, [2002] 5 CMLR 388, paras 91-94.
8 Case 85/76 *Hoffmann-La Roche & Co AG v Commission* [1979] ECR 461, [1979] 3 CMLR 211, ECJ. But see Commission Decision (EEC) 89/22 [1989] OJ L10/50, [1990] 4 CMLR 464 (*BPB Industries plc*) and Commission Decision (EEC) 93/82 [1993] OJ L34/20 (*Cewal*); see also the fresh Decision in Cewal, 30 April 2004, (2004 Report on Competition Policy, 17 June 2005 (SEC(2005) 805 final)) after the ECJ reduced the fines imposed in the earlier Decision.

[255]
(d) Economic strength and behaviour: In determining a dominant position it may be necessary to consider the behaviour of the undertaking concerned. Thus it may be relevant in determining the existence of a dominant position to take account of the facts put forward as acts amounting to abuses, without necessarily having to acknowledge (at least at that stage of the legal analysis of the conduct under review) that they are abuses.[1] Such behaviour may consist of a policy in granting rebates[2] or in its treatment of competitors[3] and its own attitude to its market position.[4]

1 Case 27/76 *United Brands Co v Commission* [1978] ECR 207 at 278, [1978] 1 CMLR429 at 487, ECJ. Thus, in Case T-30/89 *Hilti AG v Commission* [1990] ECR 11-163, [1990] 4 CMLR 602, the CFI endorsed the Commission's argument that it was highly improbable that a non-dominant supplier would act as Hilti did (with regard to reliance upon patent and copyright protection) since effective competition would usually ensure that the adverse consequences of such behaviour would outweigh any benefits. The Commission held in the second *Michelin* decision that the undertaking's behaviour was strong evidence that a dominant position existed [2002] OJ L143/1, [2002] 5 CMLR 388, paras 197-199).
2 *Michelin* [2002] OJ L143/1, [2002] 5 CMLR 388, paras 197-199.
3 Case T-30/89 *Hilti AG v Commission* [1990] ECR II-163, [1990] 4 CMLR 602, CFI.
4 *BBI/Boosey & Hawkes* [1987] OJ L282/36, [1988] 4 CMLR 67).

[256]
(e) Economic strength and prices: The fact that customers may continue to buy more products from an undertaking, even though its prices may be substantially higher, may be determinative of a dominant position.[1] However, the fact that prices charged are neither an abuse nor even particularly high does not lead to the conclusion that an undertaking with a large market share is not in a dominant position.[2]

1 Case 27/76 *United Brands Co v Commission* [1978] ECR 207 at 285, [1978] 1 CMLR 429 at 491, ECJ.
2 Case 322/81 *Nederlandsche Banden-Industrie Michelin NV v Commission* [1983] ECR 3461, [1985] 1 CMLR 282, ECJ.

[257]
The fact that an undertaking is compelled by the pressure of its competitors' price reductions to lower its own prices is in general incompatible with that independent conduct which is the hallmark of a dominant position.[1]

1 Case 85/76 *Hoffmann-La Roche & Co AG v Commission* [1979] ECR 461, [1979] 3 CMLR 211, ECJ. However, the contrary is the case if the reductions are the result of a price policy deliberately and freely adopted.

[258]
(f) Economic strength and consumers: The fact that consumers may be dependant upon an undertaking for supplies of a particular product may also be indicative of a dominant position held by that undertaking.[1]

1 See eg Commisison Decision (EEC) 87/500 ([1987] OJ L282/36) [1988] 4 CMLR 67 (*BBI/Boosey & Hawkes*), where Boosey & Hawkes' brass instruments were the 'automatic first choice of all the top brass bands'. See also *Zoja/CSC – ICI* [1972] OJ L299/51; Commission Decision (EEC) 77/327 [1977] OJ L117/1, [1977] 2 CMLR Dl (*ABG Oil Companies*); and Commission Decision (EEC) 78/68 [1978] OJ L22/23, [1978] 1 CMLR D19 (*Hugin/ Liptons*). See also the findings that commercial dependence or obligatory dealings demonstrated dominance in Case T-229/94 *Deutsche Bahn v Commission* [1997] ECR II-1689, [1998] 4 CMLR 220, para 57 and the Commission's Decision in *Virgin/British Airways* [2000] OJ L30/1, [2000] 4 CMLR 999 and in *Michelin* [2002] OJ L143/1, [2002] 5 CMLR 388, paras 200-207.

[259]
(g) Economic strength and other competitors: A dominant position cannot be decisive if it has not been proved that competitors from other sectors are not in a position to enter the market, by simple adaption, with sufficient strength to create a serious counterweight.[1] The relevant market shares of competitors, particularly the next largest, is a significant factor in the determination of a dominant position.[2] The existence in the market of other undertakings, of comparable economic strength and in a position to be able to compete, negatives the existence of a dominant position;[3] but it would be otherwise if the competitors each have proportionately a much smaller share.[4]

1 Case 6/72 *Europemballage Corpn and Continental Can Co Inc v Commission* [1973] ECR 215 at 248, [1973] CMLR 199 at 227, ECJ.
2 Case 85/76 *Hoffmann-La Roche & Co AG v Commission* [1979] ECR 461, [1979] 3 CMLR 211, ECJ; Case 322/81 *Nederlandsche Banden-Industrie Michelin NV v Commission* [1983] ECR 3461, [1985] 1 CMLR 282, ECJ, where the relative shares were 57-65 per cent for Michelin and 4-8 per cent for the main competitors.
3 Case 51/75 *EMI Records Ltd v CBS United Kingdom Ltd* [1976] ECR 811, [1976] 2 CMLR 235, ECJ; Case 86/75 *EMI Records Ltd v CBS Grammofon A/S* [1976] ECR 871, [1976] 2 CMLR 235, ECJ; Case 96/75 *EMI Records Ltd v CBS Schalipiatten GmbH* [1976] ECR 913, [1976] 2 CMLR 235, ECJ.
4 Case 27/76 *United Brands Co v Commission* [1978] ECR 207, [1978] 1 CMLR 429, ECJ.

[260]
(h) Economic strength and duration: In evaluating the economic strength of an undertaking in relation to exclusive contracts, account must be taken of the duration of the obligations undertaken.[1] With regard to other competitors, consideration must be given to the length of time over which the competition has existed;[2] but, on the other hand, the fact that an undertaking has retained its market share over a period is not by itself evidence of a dominant position, for such a situation may well arise from effective competitive behaviour.[3] If there is a dominant position, then retention of the market share may be evidence that this position is being maintained.[4] However, it may be necessary to consider issues of dominance in the short and medium term, particularly when considering technological lead or consumer preferences, for that may correspond more to economic reality.[5]

1 Case 78/70 *Deutsche Grammophon Gesellschaft mbH v Metro-SB-Grossmarkte GmbH & Co KG* [1971] ECR 487, [1971] CMLR 631, ECJ.

2 Case 27/76 *United Brands Co v Commission* [1978] ECR 207, [1978] 1 CMLR 429, ECJ.
3 Case 85/76 *Hoffmann-La Roche & Co AG v Commission* [1979] ECR 461, [1979] 3 CMLR 211, ECJ.
4 Ibid.
5 Commission Decision (EEC) 92/163 [1992] OJ L72/1 (*Tetra Pak II*), upheld on appeal by the CFI in Case T-83/91 *Tetra Pak International SA v Commission* [1994] ECR II-755, CFI, further upheld in Case C-333/94P *Tetra Pak International SA v Commission* [1996] ECR I-5951, ECJ.

[261]
(i) Economic strength and intellectual property rights: The existence of patent or other intellectual property rights may,[1] but not necessarily will, make an undertaking dominant.[2] Intellectual property rights may contribute to the existence of a dominant position,[3] although mere ownership of them cannot confer such a position.[4]

1 Joined Cases C-241, 242/91P *Independent Television Publications (ITP) and Radio Telefís Éireann (RTE) v Commission* [1995] ECR I-743, [1995] 4 CMLR 718, ECJ. A dominant position was assumed on the basis of the holding of the intellectual property rights in Case C-418/01 *IMS Health v Commission* [2004] 4 CMLR 1543, ECJ and in Case 201/04 *Microsoft v Commission* [2005] 4 CMLR 406, CFI (interim relief).
2 Case 311/84 *Centre belge d'études de marché-telemarketing (CBEM) SA v Compagnie luxembourgeoise de telediffusion SA* [1985] ECR 3261, [1986] 2 CMLR 558, ECJ; Case C-41/90 *Hofner and Elser v Macrotron* [1991] ECR I-1979, [1993] 4 CMLR 306, at para 28, ECJ; Case C-260/89 *ERT v DEP* [1991] ECR I-2925, [1994] 4 CMLR 540, at para 31, ECJ; Case C-179/90 *Merci Convenzionali Porto di Genova SpA v Siderurgica Gabrielli SpA* [1991] ECR I-5889, [1994] 4 CMLR 422, at para 14, ECJ; Case C-320/91 *Corbeau* [1993] ECR I-2533, [1995] 4 CMLR 621, at para 9, ECJ; Commission Press Release of 16 May 1995, IP(95) 492, [1995] 4 CMLR 703 (*Port of Roscoff*); Case W/35/388, Commission Decision of 16 May 1995 [1995] 5 CMLR 177 (*Irish Continental Group v CCI Morlaix*); Commission Decision (EC) 94/19 [1994] OJ L15/5, [1995] 4 CMLR 84 (*Sea Containers/Stena Sealink: Interim Measures*); Commission Decision (EC) 94/119 [1994] OJ L55/52, [1994] 5 CMLR 451 (*Euro-port A/S Denmark*); Case C-323/93 *Société Agricole du Centre d'Insemination do la Crespelle v Cooperative d'élevage et d'insémination Artificielle du Département de La Mayenne* [1994] ECR I-5077, ECJ; Case C-18/93 *Corsica Ferries Italia Srl v Corpo dei Piloti del Porto di Genova* [1994] ECR I-1783, ECJ. See also Case 26/75 *General Motors Continental NV v Commission* [1975] ECR 1367, [1976] 1 CMLR 95, ECJ; Joined Cases 40-48, 50, 54-56, 11 1, 113, 114/73 *Cooperatieve vereniging Suiker Unie LIA v Commission* [1975] ECR 1663, [1976] 1 CMLR 295 at 456, ECJ; Case 78/70 *Deutsche Grammophon Geseilschaft mbH v Metro-SB-Grossmärkte GmbH & Co KG* [1971] ECR 487, [1971] 1 CMLR 631, at para 17, ECJ; Case 40/70 *Sirena v Eda* [1971] ECR 69, [1971] CMLR 260, at para 16, ECJ; Joined Cases C-241, 242/91P *Independent Television Publications (ITP) and Radio Telefís Éireann (RTE) v Commission* [1995] ECR I-743, [1995] 4 CMLR 718, ECJ; but cf *British Leyland v Armstrong* [1986] RPC 279 at 305, CA (overruled on other grounds); *Chiron Corpn v Murex Diagnostics Ltd* [1993] FSR 324, ChD (affirmed on other grounds in [1994] FSR 187, [1994] 1 CMLR 410, CA).
3 Case 24/67 *Parke, Davis & Co v Probe* [1968] ECR 55, [1968] CMLR 47, ECJ (patent); Case T-30/89 *Hilti v Commission* [1991] ECR II-1439, [1992] 4 CMLR 16, at para 93, CFI (patent); Case 27/76 *United Brands Co v Commission* [1978] ECR 207 at 280, 281, [1978] 1 CMLR 429 at 488, 489, ECJ (trade mark); Joined Cases C-241, 242/91P *Independent Television Publications (ITP) and Radio Telefís Éireann (RTE) v Commission* [1995] ECR I-743, [1995] 4 CMLR 718, ECJ, at para 47 (copyrights); Commission Press Release, IP(94) 653 of 17 July 1994 [1994] 5 CMLR 143 (*Microsoft*) (copyrights); Commission Decision (EEC) 72/21 [1972] CMLR D11 at D29, D30 (*Re Continental Can Co Inc*) (knowhow) (annulled on other grounds in Case 6/72 *Europemballage Corpn and Continental Can Co Inc v Commission* [1973] ECR 215, [1973] CMLR 199, ECJ); Commission Press Release, IP(84) 291 of 2 August 1984 [1984] 3 CMLR 147 (*IBM*) (copyright and confidential information); cf Case 238/87 *Volvo AB v Erik Veng (UK) Ltd* [1988] ECR 6211, [1989] 4 CMLR 122, ECJ, and, Case 53/87 *CICRA v Renault* [1988] ECR 6039, [1990] 4 CMLR 265, ECJ, where the point was left open.

4 Case 51/75 *EMI Records Ltd v CBS United Kingdom Ltd* [1976] ECR 811, [1976] 2 CMLR 235, ECJ; Joined Cases C-241, 242/91P *Independent Television Publications (ITP) and Radio Telefís Éireann (RTE) v Commission* [1995] ECR I-743, [1995] 4 CMLR 718, at para 46, ECJ.

[262]

Depending on the circumstances, the relevant market may be in the supply of certain products[1] or information[2] subject to an intellectual property right, or in the service of managing certain intellectual property rights[3] or in the grant of licences under such rights,[4] or possibly in the rights themselves.[5] There may be a separate relevant market in spare parts for, or consumables used in, equipment supplied by a particular undertaking;[6] or in information about equipment[7] or services,[8] supplied by a particular undertaking. The spare parts, consumables or information may be subject to intellectual property rights belonging to the supplier of the principal goods or services, which may as a result have a dominant position in such a market.[9] However, it was held that a manufacturer did not have a dominant position where it licensed its copyrights in the designs of spare parts for its products and did not retain for itself a major share of the market in such parts.[10]

1 Case 40/70 *Sirena Sriv Edo Srl* [1971] ECR 69, [1971] CMLR 260, ECJ; Case 78/70 *Deutsche Grammophon Geselisthaft mbH v Metro-SB-Grossmarkte GmbH & Co KG* [1971] ECR 487, [1971] CMLR 631, ECJ; Case 51/75 *EMI Records Ltd v CBS United Kingdom Ltd* [1976] ECR 811, [1976] 2 CMLR 235, ECJ; Case 27/76 *United Brands Co v Commission* [1978] ECR 207, [1978] 1 CMLR 429, ECJ; Case T-30/89 *Hilti AG v Commission* [1991] ECR II-1439, CFI, [1994] 4 CMLR, ECJ; *British Leyland Motor Corpn Ltd v Armstrong Patents Co Ltd* [1984] FSR 591, [1984] 3 CMLR 102, CA (reversed on other grounds [1986] RPC 279, HL); *Chiron Corpn v Murex Diagnostics Ltd* [1994] FSR 187, [1994] 1 CMLR 410, CA; *Intergraph v Solid Systems* [1993] FSR 617, ChD.

2 Joined Cases C-241, 242/91P *Independent Television Publications (ITP) and Radio Telefis Eireann (RTE) v Commission* [1995] ECR I-743, [1995] 4 CMLR 718, at para 47, ECJ. See also Case 26/75 *General Motors Continental NV v Commission* [1975] ECR 1367, [1976] 1 CMLR 95, ECJ; Case 226/84 *British Leyland plc v Commission* [1986] ECR 3263, [1987] 1 CMLR 185, ECJ.

3 See the collecting society cases discussed at paras [286] ff. See also Case C-179/90 *Merci Convenzionali Porto di Genova SpA v Siderurgica Gabrielli SpA* [1991] ECR I-5889, [1994] 4 CMLR 422, ECJ.

4 Case C-418/01 *IMS Health v Commission* [2004] 4 CMLR 1543, ECJ; Case 201/04 *Microsoft v Commission* [2005] 4 CMLR 406, CFI (interim relief); Commission Decision (EEC) 71/224 [1971] CMLR 135 (*Re GEMA*); Commission Decision (EEC) 82/204 [1982] 2 CMLR 482 (*Re GEMA Statutes*); Commission 24th Report on Competition Policy, para 284 (*Shell/Montecatini*). Cf *British Leyland Motor Corpn Ltd v Armstrong Patents Co Ltd* [1984] FSR 591, [1984] 3 CMLR 102, CA (reversed on other grounds [1986] RPC 279, HL).

5 See Commission Decision (EEC) 93/403 [1995] 4 CMLR 56 (*Re EBU/Eurovision System*) (a decision under Article 81); but cf *British Leyland v Armstrong* [1984] FSR 591, [1984] 3 CMLR 102, CA (reversed on other grounds in [1986] RPC 279, HL).

6 Case C-53/92P *Hilti AG v Commission* [1994] ECR I-667, [1994] 4 CMLR 614, ECJ (consumables). In Case 22/78 *Hugin Kassaregister AB v Commission* [1979] ECR 1869, [1979] 3 CMLR 345, ECJ, and Case 238/87 *Volvo AB v Erik Veng (UK) Ltd* [1988] ECR 6211, [1989] 4 CMLR 122, ECJ, the ECJ found it unnecessary to decide the point in relation to spare parts. However, it is thought that the principle established in *Hilti* in relation to consumables applies also to spare parts.

7 Case 26/75 *General Motors Continental NV v Commission* [1975] ECR 1367, [1976] 1 CMLR 95, ECJ; Case 226/84 *British Leyland plc v Commission* [1986] ECR 3263, [1987] 1 CMLR 185, ECJ).

8 Joined Cases C-241, 242/91P *Independent Television Publications (ITP) and Radio Telefís Éireann (RTE) v Commission* [1995] ECR I-743, [1995] 4 CMLR 718 at para 47, ECJ.

9 See cases cited at notes 6-8.

10 *British Leyland Motor Corpn Ltd v Armstrong Patents Co Ltd* [1984] FSR 591, [1984] 3 CMLR 102, CA (reversed on other grounds [1986] RPC 279, HL); criticised by JDC Turner, 'Euro-defences misunderstood' (1984) Eur Int Prop Rev 320.

[263]

(j) Economic strength and future entrants: A dominant position is not diminished by the existence of other potential manufacturing processes of an experimental nature or practised on a small scale.[1] It would be otherwise if other potential manufacturing processes were a real substitute.[2] In considering future entrants, consideration should be given to the size of capital investment required and the other practical and financial barriers to entering into the market.[3] For example, the very large advertising expenditure necessary to break into some markets has been held to be a substantial barrier to entry.[4]

1 Joined Cases 6, 7/73 *Istituto Cheinioterapico Italiano SpA and Commercial Solvents Corpn v Commission* [1974] ECR 223, [1974] 1 CMLR 309, ECJ.
2 Ibid. See also Case 6/72 *Europemballage Corpn and Continental Can Co Inc v Commission* [1973] ECR 215, [1973] CMLR 199, ECJ; Commission Decision (EEC) 93/252 [1993] OJ L116/21 (*Gillette*).
3 Case 27/76 *United Brands Co v Commission* [1978] ECR 207, [1978] 1 CMLR 429, ECJ. See also Commission Decision (EEC) 84/379 [1984] OJ L207/11, [1984] 3 CMLR 92 (*BL*).
4 Commission Decision [1992] OJ L356/1, [1993] 4 CMLR M17 (*Nestle/Perrier*) (soft drinks), Commission Decision [1994] OJ L352/32 (*Proctor & Gamble/VP Schickendanz*) (sanitary protection) ; Commission Decision [1996] OJ L/183/1 (*Kimberly-Clark/Scott Paper*) (toilet tissue).

[264]

A firm holds a dominant position where it can hinder the emergence of any effective competition because any potential competitors are in a position of economic dependence upon it.[1]

1 Case T-69/89 *Radio Telefís Éireann v Commission* [1991] ECR II-485, [1991] 4 CMLR 586, CFI; Case T-70/89 *British Broadcasting Corpn and BBC Enterprises Ltd v Commission* [1991] ECR II-535, [1991] 4 CMLR 669, CFI; Case T-76/89 *Independent Television Publications Ltd v Commission* [1991] ECR II-575, [1991] 4 CMLR 745, CFI; upheld by the ECJ in Joined Cases C-241, 242/91P *RTE v Commission* [1995] ECR I-743, [1995] 4 CMLR 718, ECJ.

8. Undertakings

[265]

(a) One or more undertakings: Undertakings[1] which together hold a dominant position and whose behaviour is characterised by united action must be regarded as an economic unit and are jointly and severally liable.[2] A principal and an agent may also be regarded as an economic unit, but it is otherwise if the agent performs tasks which are normally undertaken by an independent dealer.[3] If several distinct undertakings act in a concerted fashion, such conduct falls to be dealt with under Article 81, and not Article 82.[4]

1 Undertakings have the same meaning as under Article 81; see para [52] above.
2 Joined Cases 6, 7/73 *Istituto Chemioterapico Italiano SpA and Commercial Solvents Corpn v Commission* [1974] ECR 223, [1974] 1 CMLR 309, ECJ.
3 Joined Cases 40-48, 50, 54-56, 111, 113, 114/73 *Cooperatieve vereniging Suiker Linie UA v Commission* [1975] ECR 1663 at 1996-2000, [1976] 1 CMLR 295 at 467-470, ECJ. The Court has applied Article 82 to groups of undertakings when they form an economic unit and hold a dominant position on the relevant market: see Case 75/84 *Metro-SB-Grossmarkte GmbH & Co KG v Commission* [1986] ECR 3021, [1987] 1 CMLR 118, ECJ; Case 66/86 *Ahmed Saeed Flugreisen v*

Zentrale zur Bekampfung unlauteren Wettbewerbs eV [1989] ECR 803, [1990] 4 CMLR 102, ECJ; Case 247/86 *Societe alsacienne et lorraine de telecommunications et d'electronique (Alsatel) v Novasam SA* [1988] ECR 5987, [1990] 4 CMLR 434, ECJ; Case 30/87 *Bodson v Pompes funèbres des regions libérées SA* [1988] ECR 2479, [1989] 4 CMLR 984, ECJ; Case C- 393/92 *Municipality of Almelo and Others v Energiebedrijf Ijsselmij* [1994] ECR I-1477, ECJ; Commission Decision (EC) 94/119 [1994] OJ L55/52, [1994] 5 CMLR 457 (*Port of Rødby*); Joined Cases C-140, 142/94 *DIP SpA* [1995] ECR I-3257, [1996] 4 CMLR 157, ECJ.

4 Case 172/80 *Zuchner v Bayerische Vereinsbank AG* [1981] ECR 2021, [1982] 1 CMLR 313, ECJ.

[266]

In principle, a collective dominant position can fall to be considered under Article 82, for Article 82 provides that 'one or more undertakings' in a dominant position may abuse a dominant position, but that situation would only arise where the undertakings are united by such economic ties that the ties are sufficient to create a joint or collective dominant position, and this is required to be strictly proved.[1]

1 Joined Cases T-68, 77, 78/89 *Società Italiano Vetro SpA v Commission* [1992] ECR II-1403, [1992] 5 CMLR 302, CFI, where the allegation of joint dominance was not proved. However, to establish joint dominance the court emphasised that it is not sufficient to 'recycle' the facts establishing an infringement of Article 81. In Joined Cases T-24/93 *Compagnie Maritime Belge Transport v Commission* [1996] ECR II-1201, CFI, the court did not hold that the Commission had only 'recycled' but had sufficiently established that each of the requirements of Article 82 was met. This judgment was upheld by the ECJ in Case 395/96P [2000] ECR I-1365, [2000] 4 CMLR 1076, ECJ. The Commission has applied the doctrine of joint dominance in Commission Decision (EEC) 92/262 [1992] OJ L134/1 (*French–West African Shipowners Committees*); Commission Decision (EEC) 93/82 [1993] OJ L34/20 (*Cewal*) also the fresh Decision in Cewal, 30 April 2004 (2004 Report on Competition Policy, 17 June 2005 (SEC(2005) 805 final)) after the ECJ reduced the fines imposed in the earlier Decision and Commission Decision (EEC) 94/119 [1994] OJ L55/52, [1994] 5 CMLR 457 (*Port of Rødby*). There can also be national collective dominance: Case T-228/97 *Irish Sugar v Commission* [1999] ECR II-2969.

[267]

(b) Public enterprises: In referring to abuses of a dominant position, Article 82 of the EC Treaty is not exclusively concerned with the activities of private enterprise. It extends to public bodies[1] as well as to undertakings granted specific powers by statute or by public authorities.[2] It also extends to undertakings subject to official authorisation[3] or State supervision,[4] and to undertakings which are non-profit-making.[5] It is nevertheless important to determine that that the public or private body is engaged in an economic activity. Otherwise it will not amount to an undertaking and will not be the subject of the competition rules.[6] Where the activities are such that they have traditionally formed part of the State's activities or fulfil a social function then they fall outside the competition rules.[7] Where a Member State has enacted or maintained in force a measure in respect of public undertakings which is contrary to the rules contained in the EC Treaty, Article 86 EC must be considered.[8]

1 Case 155/73 *Sacchi* [1974] ECR 409, [1974] 2 CMLR 177, ECJ. See also Commission Decision (EEC) 82/86 [1982] OJ L360/36, [1983] 1 CMLR 457 (*British Telecommunications*), upheld on appeal in Case 41/83 *Italy v Commission* [1985] ECR 873, [1985] 2 CMLR 368, ECJ. See also Case C-41/90 *Hofner v Macrotron GmbH* [1991] ECR 1-1979, [1993] 4 CMLR 306, ECJ.

2 Case 127/73 *Belgische Radio en Televisie (BRT) v SV SABAM* [1974] ECR 51 and 313, [1974] 2 CMLR 238, ECJ; Case 26/75 *General Motors Continental NV v Commission* [1975] ECR 1367, [1976] 1 CMLR 95, ECJ; Case 90/76 *Van Ameyde v Srl Ufficio Centrale Italiano di Assistenza Assicurativa*

Automobilisti [1977] ECR 1091, [1977) 2 CMLR 478, ECJ; Case 13/77 *GB-INNO-BM NV v ATA* [1977] ECR 2115, [1978] 1 CMLR 283, ECJ; Case 311/84 *Centre belge d'etudes de marché - Telémarketing (CBEM) SA v Compagnie luxembourgeoise de telediffusion SA* [1985] ECR 3261, [1986] 2 CMLR 558, ECJ; Case T-69/89 *Radio Telefís Éireann v Commission* [1991] ECR II-485, [1991] 4 CMLR 586, CFI; Case T-70/89 *British Broadcasting Corpn and BBC Enterprises Ltd v Commission* [1991] ECR II-535, [1991] 4 CMLR 669, CFI; Case T-76/89 *Independent Television Publications Ltd v Commission* [1991] ECR II-575, [1991] 4 CMLR 745, CFI, on appeal Joined Cases C-241, 242/91P *Independent Television Publications (ITP) and Radio Telefís Éireann (RTE) v Commission* [1995] ECR I-743, [1995] 4 CMLR 718, ECJ; Case C-475/99 *Ambulanz Glockner v Landkreis Sudwestpfalz* [2001] ECR 8089, [2001] 4 CMLR 30, ECJ.

3 Case 7/82 *GVL v Commission* [1983] ECR 483, [1983] 3 CMLR 645, ECJ.

4 Case T-128/98 *Aeroports de Paris v Commission* [2000] ECR II-3929, CFI.

5 Case 127/73 *Belgische Radio en Televisie (BRT) v SV SABAM* [1974] ECR 51 and 313, [1974] 2 CMLR 238, ECJ; Case 7/82 *GVL v Commission* [1983] ECR 483, [1983] 3 CMLR 645, ECJ; Case C-67/96 *Albany International BV v Stichting Bedrijspensioenfonds Textilindustrie* [1999] ECR I-5751, [2000] 4 CMLR 446, ECJ.

6 So, for example, in Case C-343/95 *Diego Cali & Figli v Servizi Ecologici Porto di Genova* [1997] ECR I-1547, ECJ, the court held that Article 86 did not apply to anti-pollution surveillance by a private company for the port authorities.

7 As to the meaning of undertaking generally see paras [52] ff and [326] ff below.

8 As to EC Treaty, Article 86, see paras [314] ff.

[268]

(c) Member States: Whilst Article 82 of the EC Treaty is directed at undertakings, the Treaty imposes a duty upon Member States not to enact or maintain in force any measure which could deprive Article 82 of its effectiveness.[1] Member States may not enact measures enabling undertakings to escape from the prohibition contained in Article 82, and the fact that conduct by an undertaking may be encouraged or facilitated by a Member State even by legislation is no defence if the undertaking otherwise abuses its dominant position.[2] The fact that the absence or limitation of competition on the relevant market was created or encouraged by legislative provisions or regulations does not preclude the application of Article 82.[3]

1 EC Treaty, Article 86(1). See for example Case C-41/90 *Hofner v Macrotron GmbH* [1991] ECR I-1979, [1993] 4 CMLR 306, ECJ; Case C-323/93 *Société Agricole du Centre d'Insémination de la Crespelle v Cooperative d'Elevage et d'Insemination Artificielle du Département de la Mayenne* [1994] ECR I-5077, ECJ; Case C-475/99 *Ambulanz Glockner v Landkreis Sudwestpfalz* [2001] ECR 8089, [2001] 4 CMLR 30, ECJ; Case C-209/98 *Enterprenorforeningens Affals Miljosektion (FFAD) acting for Sydhavnens Sten & Grus ApS v Kobenhavns Kommune* [2000] ECR I-3743, [2001] 2 CMLR 936; Case C-203/96 *Chemische Afvalstoffen Dusseldorp BV and Others v Minister van Volkshuisvesting, Ruimtelijke Ordening en Milieubeheer* [1998] ECR I-4075, [1998] 3 CMLR 873, ECJ.

2 Case 13/77 *GB-INNO-BM NV v Vereniging van de Kleinhandelaars in Tabak (ATAB)* [1977] ECR 2115, [1978] 1 CMLR 283, ECJ.

3 Case 311/84 *Centre belge d'études de marché – Telemarketing (CBEM) SA v Compagnie luxembourgeoise de telediffusion SA* [1985] ECR 3261, [1986] 2 CMLR 558, ECJ. See also Case 78/70 *Deutsche Grammophon Gesellschaft mbH v Metro-SB-Grosmarkte GmbH & Co KG* [1971] ECR 487, [1971] CMLR 631, ECJ; Case 26/75 *General Motors Continental NV v Commission* [1975] ECR 1367, [1976] 1 CMLR 95, ECJ; Case 155/73 *Sacchi* [1974] ECR 409, [1974] 2 CMLR 177, ECJ; Case 226/84 *British Leyland plc v Commission* [1986] ECR 3263, [1987] 1 CMLR 185, ECJ; see also Case 30/87 *Bodson v Pompes Funèbres des Regions Libérées SA* [1988] ECR 2479, [1989] 4 CMLR 984, ECJ. See also Case C-41/90 *Hofner v Macrotron GmbH* [1991] ECR I-1979, [1993] 4 CMLR 306, ECJ.

[269]

Nevertheless, Article 82 does not apply to distortions of competition caused by activities of Member States,[1] and it does not, at least as a general rule, apply to a charge for the purpose of financing national aids.[2] Nor does it relate to national price-freeze rules.[3]

1 Case 231/83 *Cullet v Centre Leclerc Toulouse* [1985] ECR 305, [1985] 2 CMLR 524, ECJ; Case 229/83 *Association des Centres distributeurs Edouard Leclerc v Au BléVert Sàrl* [1981] ECR 1, [1981] 2 CMLR 282, ECJ. See also Commission 10th Report on Competition Policy, para 13. But see Case C-260/89 *Elliniki Radiofonia Tileorasi v Kouvelas* [1991] ECR I-2925, [1994] 4 CMLR 540, ECJ; Case C-41/90 *Hofner v Macrotron GmbH* [1991] ECR I-1979, [1993] 4 CMLR 306, ECJ, and Case C-179/90 *Merci Convenzionali Porto di Genova SpA v Siderurgica abrielli SpA* [1991] ECR I-5889, [1994] 4 CMLR 422, ECJ. See also Case C-18/88 *Regie des Télégraphes et des Téléphones v SA GB-INNO-BN* [1991] ECR I-5941, ECJ; Case C-320/91 *Corbeau* [1993] ECR I-2533, [1995] 4 CMLR 621, ECJ.

2 Case 2/73 *Riseria Luigi Geddo v Ente nazionale Risi* [1973] ECR 825, [1974] 1 CMLR 13, ECJ; Case 94/74 *Industria Gomma Articoli Var v Ente Nazionale per la Cellulosa e per la Carta* [1975] ECR 699, [1976] 2 CMLR 37, ECJ.

3 Case 5/79 *Procureur General v Buys* [1979] ECR 3203, [1980] 2 CMLR 493, ECJ.

C. ABUSE

1. Meaning of 'abuse'

[270]

The concept of abuse is an objective concept, and covers practices relating to the behaviour of the dominant undertaking which are likely to affect the structure of the market,[1] where competition has already been weakened, and which, through recourse to methods different from those governing normal competition in products or services on the basis of transactions of commercial operators, have the effect of hindering the maintenance or development of the level of competition still existing on the market.[2] Whilst the finding that a dominant position exists does not in itself imply any reproach to the undertaking concerned, it has a special responsibility, irrespective of the causes of that position, not to allow its conduct to impair genuine undistorted competition on the common market.[3]

1 See also *Compagnie Maritime Belge Transports SA v Commission* [2000] ECR I-1365, para 37.

2 Case 85/76 *Hoffmann-La Roche & Co AG v Commission* [1979] ECR 461, [1979] 3 CMLR 211, ECJ; Case 31/80 *L'Oreal NV v De Nieuwe AMCK PVBA* [1980] ECR 3775, [1981] 2 CMLR 235, ECJ; Case 322/81 *Nederlandsche Banden-Industrie Michelin NV v Commission* [1983] ECR 3461, [1985] 1 CMLR 282, ECJ. See also Case 66/86 *Ahmed Saeed Flugreisen v Zentrale zur Bekampfung unlauteren Wettbewerbs eV* [1989] ECR 803, [1990] 4 CMLR 102, ECJ; Commission Decision (EEC) 85/609 [1986] OJ L374/1, [1986] 3 CMLR 273 (*ECS/AKZO*); and Commission Decision (EEC) 88/589 [1988] OJ L317/47 (*London European/Sabena*).

3 Case 322/81 *Michelin v Commission* [1983] ECR 3461, para 57, and Case T-228/97 *Irish Sugar v Commission* [1999] ECR II-2969, para 112.

[271]

Similarly, whilst the fact that an undertaking is in a dominant position cannot deprive it of its entitlement to protect its own commercial interests when they are attacked, and whilst such an undertaking must be allowed the right to take such reasonable steps as it deems appropriate to protect those interests, such behaviour cannot be allowed if its purpose is to strengthen that dominant position and thereby abuse it.[1]

1 Case T-219/99 *British Airways v Commission* [2004] 4 CMLR 19, para 243; Case T-65/89 *BPB Industries and British Gypsum* v *Commission* [1993] ECR II-389, para 69; Joined Cases T-24/93 to T-26/93 and T-28/93 *Compagnie Maritime Belge Transports and Others* v *Commission* [1996] ECR II-1201, para 107). See also, *Claymore Dairies Ltd and Arla Foods UK plc v OFT* [2005] CAT 30, paras 185-188 where the CAT set out the relevant considerations at para 188.

[272]
A dominant firm may, by virtue of its 'special responsibility' be deprived of the right to follow a course of conduct that would not necessarily be objectionable if that course of conduct were followed by a non-dominant undertaking.[1] It is not necessary for the dominant undertaking to be a competitor or even act in the same field as the undertaking affected: all that is necessary is for competition to be impaired.[2] It is not necessary that the abuse should take place in the same market where the dominant position exists; it is sufficient that connecting links exist between the two markets.[3]

1 Case T-83/91 *Tetra Pak International SA v Commission* [1994] ECR II-755, para137; Case T-111/96 *ITT Promedia NV v Commission* [1998] ECR II-2937, para 139; Case T-65/98 *Van den Bergh Foods Ltd v Commission* [2004] 4 CMLR 663, para 159 ECJ; *Genzyme Ltd v OFT* [2004] CompAR 358 at para 484, CAT.
2 See eg Case 7/82 *GVL v Commission* [1983] ECR 483, [1983] 3 CMLR 645, ECJ.
3 Case T-219/99 *British Airways v Commission* [2004] 4 CMLR 19, para 127 CFI; *De Poste-La Poste* [2002] OJ L61/32, [2002] 4 CMLR 1426, paras 36-51; Case C-310/93 *British Gypsum v Commission* [1995] ECR I-865, ECJ. See also Joined Cases 6, 7/73 *Instituto Chemioterapico Italiano SpA and Commercial Solvents Corpn v Commission* [1974] ECR 223, [1974] 1 CMLR 309, ECJ; Case 5/85 *Akzo Chemie NV c Commission* [1986] ECR 2585, [1987] 3 CMLR 716, ECJ; Case T-83/91 *Tetra Pak International SA v Commission* [1994] ECR II-755, CFI.

2. Fault

[273]
The finding of an abuse is not dependent on fault.[1] However, the particular reprehensible way in which a dominant undertaking conducts itself in relation to its competitors might make conduct which could otherwise be acceptable into prohibited conduct.[2]

1 Case 6/72 *Europemballage Corpn and Continental Can Co Inc v Commission* [1973] ECR 215 at 246, [1973] CMLR 199 at 224, ECJ.
2 Joined Cases 40-48, 50, 54-56, 111, 113, 114/73 *Coöperatieve vereniging Suiker Unie UA v Commission* [1975] ECR 1663 at 1983, [1976] 1 CMLR 295 at 457, ECJ, where the Court emphasised the 'extremely hard-hearted way' in which the dominant undertaking conducted itself in a situation of unforeseen difficulties.

3. Causation

[274]
It is not necessary that there should be any causal connection between the dominant position and the abuse: conduct may be an abuse regardless of the means and procedure by which it is achieved.[1]

1 Case 6/72 *Europemballage Corpn and Continental Can Co Inc v Commission* [1973] ECR 215 at 245, [1973] CMLR 199 at 225, ECJ.

4. Objective justification

[275]

In order to amount to an abuse, the exploitation of the dominant position must be improper.[1] Accordingly, conduct which would otherwise be prohibited can be defended if evidence can be adduced to show that the conduct can be objectively justified,[2] provided the conduct is proportionate to the situation, taking into account the economic strength of the relevant undertakings.[3] However, it is not objective justification to prove that the conduct was encouraged or facilitated by legislation of a Member State,[4] or that the Community has adopted measures which reduce effective competition and which to some extent partition national markets, at least so long as the measures leave a residual field for competition.[5] If national legislation compels an undertaking to act in a certain way, however, the undertaking cannot be exposed to penalties under Article 82 EC.[6] The grant of an individual or block exemption under Article 81(3) cannot by itself render inapplicable the prohibition of abusive conduct under Article 82.[7]

1 Case T-219/99 *British Airways* v *Commission* [2004] 4 CMLR 19, para 290-292, CFI; Case 24/67 *Parke, Davis & Co v Probel* [1968] ECR 55, [1968] CMLR 47, ECJ; Case 40/70 *Sirena Srl v Edo Srl* [1971] ECR 69, [1971] CMLR 260, ECJ. For consideration of the justification advanced, see eg Commission Decision (EEC) 84/379 ([1984] OJ L207/11) [1984] 3 CMLR 92 (*BL*), on appeal Case 226/84 *British Leyland plc v Commission* [1986] ECR 3263, [1987] 1 CMLR 185, ECJ.

2 See eg Case 27/76 *United Brands Co v Commission* [1978] ECR 207, [1978] 1 CMLR 429, ECJ. As to the policy of quality, see Case 27/76, above, at 289 and at 494; as to protecting commercial interests if they are attacked, see Case 27/76, above, at 293 and at 496; and as to customers placing orders which are out of the ordinary, see Case 27/76, above, at 292 and at 496. The dominant undertaking cannot, however, be obliged to damage its own business or risk its own existence in the long term in order to keep a competitor alive: see Commission Decision (EEC) 76/185 [1976] OJ L35/6, [1976] 1 CMLR 82 (*National Carbonising Co Ltd*) (see also Joined Cases 109, 114/75 *National Carbonising Co Ltd v Commission* [1977] ECR 381, ECJ) (proceedings under the ECSC Treaty but equally applicable to the EC Treaty). In respect of conduct which can be objectively justified see also Commission Decision (EEC) 88/518 [1988] OJ L284/41, [1990] 4 CMLR 196 (*British Sugar/Napier Brown*); as to pricing below fixed cost and just covering, therefore, variable costs when such price is the highest price the market will take and thereby maximising profit see Commission Decision (EEC) 89/113 [1989] OJ L43/27 (*Decca Navigator System*); as to refusal to give access to facilities which are essential to activity on the relevant market see Case 311/84 *Centre belge d'études de marché – Telemarketing (CBEM) SA v Compagnie luxembourgeoise de telediffusion SA* [1985] ECR 3261, [1986] 2 CMLR 558, ECJ; Case 41/83 *Italy v Commission* [1985] ECR 873, [1985] 2 CMLR 368, ECJ; see also Case C-18/88 *Régie des Télégraphes et des Téléphones v SA GB-INNO-BM* [1991] ECR I-5941, ECJ, and also Commission Decision (EEC) 88/589 [1988] OJ L317/47 (*London European/Sabena*). See also Case 77/77 *Benzine en Petroleum Handelsmaatschappij BV v Commission* [1978] ECR 1513, [1978] 3 CMLR 174, ECJ (refusal to supply occasional customer in time of shortage objectively justified); Commission Decision (EEC) 88/518 [1988] OJ L284/41, [1990] 4 CMLR196 (*British Sugar/Napier Brown*) (refusal to supply longstanding customer when latter entered relevant market as competitor may be justified if action taken is reasonably necessary and no more); and see also Commission Decision (EEC) 89/22 [1989] OJ L10/50, [1990] 4 CMLR464 (*BPB Industries plc*) (refusal to supply longstanding customer in time of shortage when latter proved disloyal by seeking supplies elsewhere). As to burden of proof, see para [228], note 3 above.

3 Case 27/76 *United Brands Co v Commission* [1978] ECR 207 at 293, [1978] 1 CMLR 429 at 496,497, ECJ.

4 Case 13/77 *GB-INNO-BM NV v Vereniging van de Kleinhandelaars in Tabak (ATAB)* [1977] ECR 2115, [1978] 1 CMLR 283, ECJ. See also Case C-260/89 *Elliniki Radiofonia Tileorasi v Kouvelas*

[1991] ECR I-2925, [1994] 4 CMLR540, ECJ, and, Case C-41/90 *Hofner v Macrotron GmbH* [1991] ECR I-1979 [1993] 4 CMLR 306, ECJ.
5 Joined Cases 40-48, 50, 54-56, 111, 113, 114/73 *Coöperatieve vereniging Suiker Unie UA v Commission* [1975] ECR 1663 at 1913-1915, [1976] 1 CMLR 295 at 403,404, ECJ.
6 *CIF v Autorita Garante della Concorrenza e del Mercato* [2003] ECR I-8055, paras 53-54.
7 Case T-51/89 *Tetra Pak Rausing SA v Commission* [1990] ECR II-309, [1991] 4 CMLR 334, CFI.

[276]
The Commission (or the OFT) does not have to deal in its decision with all possible objective justifications for a particular course of conduct that could be, but have not been, raised by the dominant undertaking. The concept of objective justification does not fall to be applied in terms of benefits which accrue to the dominant undertaking but in terms of the general interest which Article 82 (and in the UK, the Chapter II prohibition of the Competition Act 1998) is designed to protect.[1]

1 *Genzyme Ltd v OFT* [2004] CompAR 358 at paras 577-578, CAT.

[277]
As to concerns of product safety and reliability, where there are rules which penalise the sale of dangerous products and the use of misleading claims as to the characteristics of products, and there are authorities empowered to enforce those laws; a dominant undertaking may not take steps on its own initiative to eliminate products which it, rightly or wrongly, regards as dangerous or inferior to its own products.[1]

1 Case T-30/89 *Hilti AG v Commission* [1990] ECR II-163, [1990] 4 CMLR 602, CFI, upheld on appeal in Case C-53/92P *Hilti AG v Commission* [1994] ECR I-667, ECJ.

5. The list of abuses in Article 82 EC

[278]
The list of abuses set out in Article 82 of the EC Treaty[1] is not exhaustive.[2] The examples are not limited to practices which directly cause damage to consumers, but include also those which are detrimental to them indirectly through their impact on an effective competition structure. An abuse may fall under one or more of the examples, or even under none of the examples, yet still fall under the prohibition in Article 82.

1 See EC Treaty, Article 82(a)-(d).
2 Joined Cases 6, 7/73 *Istituto Chemioterapico Italiano SpA and Commercial Solvents Corpn v Commission* [1974] ECR 223, [1974] 1 CMLR 309, ECJ; Case 6/72 *Europemballage Corpn and Continental Can Co Inc v Commission* [1973] ECR 215, [1973] CMLR 199, ECJ.

6. Pricing

[279]
An abuse of a dominant position may consist in directly or indirectly imposing unfair purchase or selling prices.[1] This will be so even though the level of those prices is fixed by contract specifications which form part of the conditions of the concession.[2] A price may be unfair if it is excessively high[3] or excessively low.[4] Applying the EC case law, the CAT held in *Aberdeen Journals Ltd v OFT (Aberdeen Journals No 2)* that the question whether a certain pricing practice by a dominant undertaking is to be regarded as abusive is a matter to be looked at in the round taking particularly into

account whether: (a) the dominant undertaking has had 'recourse to methods different from those which condition normal competition in products and services on the basis of the transactions of commercial operators'; and (b) such conduct has the effect of weakening or distorting competition.[5]

1 EC Treaty, Article 82(a). Cf Article 81(1)(a), and para [91] ff. For a review of the case law, see P Oliver, 'The Concept of "Abuse" of a Dominant Position under Article 82 EC: Recent Developments in relation to Pricing' (2005) 2 European Competition Journal 315. See generally DL Parrott, 'Pricing Policy and Community Rules on Competition and Free Movement of Goods' (1981) Yearbook of European Law. Case 24/67 *Parke, Davis & Co v Probel* [1968] ECR 55, [1968] CMLR 47, ECJ; Case 40/70 *Sirena Slav Edo Srl* [1971] ECR 69, [1971] 1 CMLR 260, ECJ; Case 78/70 *Deutsche Grammophon Gesellschaft mbH v Metro-SBGrossmarkte GmbH & Co KG* [1971] ECR 487, [1971] CMLR 631, ECJ; Case 26/75 *General Motors Continental NV v Commission* [1975] ECR 1367, [1976] 1 CMLR 95, ECJ.

2 Case 30/87 *Bodson v Pompes funèbres des regions libérées SA* [1988] ECR 2479, [1989] 4 CMLR 984, ECJ.

3 See eg Case 26/75 *General Motors Continental NV v Commission* [1975] ECR 1367, [1976] 1 CMLR 95, ECJ; Commission Decision (EEC) 84/379 [1984] OJ L207/11, [1984] 3 CMLR 92 (*BL*) and on appeal Case 226/84 *British Leyland plc v Commission* [1986] ECR 3263, [1987] 1 CMLR 185, ECJ.

4 See Commission Decision (EEC) 83/462 [1983] OJ L252/13, [1983] 3 CMLR 694 (*ECS/AKZO*) and Commission Decision (EEC) 93/82 [1993] OJ L34/20 (*Cewal*) also the fresh Decision in Cewal, 30 April 2004 (2004 Report on Competition Policy, 17 June 2005 (SEC(2005) 805 final)) after the ECJ reduced the fines imposed in the earlier Decision. See also the allegations in the English High Court in *Chelmkalm Motors Ltd v Esso Petroleum Co Ltd* [1979] 1 CMLR 73, ChD. An unfairly low price might also be dictated by a dominant buyer. See also Case 298/83 *Comité des Industries Cinématographiques des Communautes Européennes v Commission* [1985] ECR 1105, [1986] 1 CMLR 486, ECJ.

5 *Aberdeen Journals Ltd v OFT* [2003] CompAR 67 at para 350, CAT, followed in *Claymore Dairies Ltd and Arla Foods UK plc v OFT* [2005] CAT 30, para 189.

[280]

(a) Predatory pricing: Pricing below average variable costs by a dominant firm is normally to be regarded as abusive.[1] 'Variable costs' are those which vary with the output produced. It may be an abuse by a dominant undertaking to price between average variable cost and average total cost, if the intention is to eliminate a competitor.[2] Total costs are variable costs plus fixed costs including, where appropriate, a share of general overheads. Pricing between average variable cost and average total cost is likely to be abusive when undertaken in anticipation of competitive entry or in order to undercut a new entrant.[3] When assessing the allegation of predation, the time over which the costs are assessed is relevant since the longer the time period taken the more likely it is that costs will be classified as 'variable' rather than 'fixed'.[4]

1 Case 62/86 *Akzo Chemie BV v Commission* [1991] ECR I-3359, [1993] 5 CMLR 215, para 71, ECJ; Case C-333/94P *Tetra Pak International SA v Commission* [1996] ECR I-5951, para 41.See also *Wanadoo*, Commission Decision of 16 July 2003 (COMP/38.233). See, as to the procedure in investigating an allegation of predatory pricing, *Claymore Dairies Ltd and Arla Foods UK plc v OFT* [2005] CAT 30, para 208 where the CAT criticised the OFT for a failure properly the identify and verify costs (paras 216, 227-231, 259). For an analysis of predatory pricing and 'fighting ships', see P Oliver, 'The Concept of "Abuse" of a Dominant Position under Article 82 EC: Recent Developments in relation to Pricing' (2005) 2 European Competition Journal 315, 322-325.

2 As to the requirement of intent to eliminate a competitor and the evidence necessary to support such a finding, see *Claymore Dairies Ltd and Arla Foods UK plc v OFT* [2005] CAT 30, paras 270-271.
3 Case 62/86 *Akzo Chemie BV v Commission* [1991] ECR I-3359, [1993] 5 CMLR 215, para 71 ECJ; Case C-333/94 P *Tetra Pak International SA v Commission* [1996] ECR I-5951, para 41. See also the Commission Decision in *B2/Telia* (2004 Report on Competition Policy, 17 June 2005, para 48). See, in relation to a finding of predatory pricing by a 'super dominant' undertaking, *Napp Pharmaceutical Holdings Ltd v Director General Fair Trading* [2002] CompAR 13, CCAT.
4 *Aberdeen Journals Ltd v OFT* [2003] CompAR 67 at para 353-356, CAT (quoted extensively in *Claymore Dairies Ltd and Arla Foods UK plc v OFT* [2005] CAT 30 at para 189 which in particular deals with the position of determining the costs (paras 208-240) allocating the costs (paras 241-256) average variable costs (paras 257-260) and issues of intent (paras 269-282)).

[281]
(b) Margin squeeze: An undertaking in a dominant position, with the ability to set its own prices of its products, may be bound to supply customers dependent on it at prices which allow the customers a reasonable margin, sufficient to enable them to stay in business in the long term, and may be under such an obligation even though the customer is a competitor.[1]

1 See Commission Decision (EEC) 76/185 [1976] OJ L35/2, [1976] 1 CMLR D82 (*National Carbonising Co Ltd*); also *British Sugar/Napier Brown* [1988] OJ L284/41 where the Commission found that there was an insufficient margin for a sugar merchant as efficient as British Sugar to survive, based on its own costs which showed it operating at a loss. Margin squeeze was one of a number of anti-competitive practices aimed at driving Napier Brown out of the market. In Case T-5/97 *Industrie des Poudres Sphériques v Commission* [2000] ECR II-3755, the CFI defined a price squeeze as arising where a vertically integrated dominant firm supplies an input to rivals at prices 'at such level that those who purchase it do not have a sufficient profit margin on the processing to remain competitive on the market for the processed product'. The CFI suggested that this might occur where the prices for the upstream product were abusive or where the prices for the derived product were predatory. In *Deutsche Telekom* ([2003] OJ L263/9) the undertaking was found to have created a margin squeeze in circumstances where it charged competitors more for 'unbundled broadband access' at the wholesale level than it charged its subscribers for access at the retail level. The case is currently on appeal to the CFI. In *Deutsche Telekom,* the Commission said that a margin squeeze would occur where 'the spread between DT's retail and wholesale prices is either negative or at least insufficient to cover DT's own downstream costs'. DT would have been unable to offer its own retail services without incurring a loss if it had had to pay the wholesale access price. As a consequence the profit margins of competitors would be squeezed, even if they were just as efficient as DT. Significantly, the Commission stated that 'by proving the existence of a margin squeeze, the Commission has done enough to establish the existence of an abuse', without having to consider the effects on the market. For margin squeeze in the UK context, see *Genzyme Ltd v OFT* [2004] CompAR 358, CAT.

[282]
(c) Dissimilar conditions for equivalent transactions and price discrimination: It is an abuse of a dominant position for a dominant undertaking to apply dissimilar conditions (including prices) to equivalent transactions with other trading parties, thereby placing them at a competitive disadvantage.[1] It would amount to an application of dissimilar conditions for a dominant undertaking to discriminate in favour of national products as compared with products from other Member States,[2] or to discriminate between users.[3] The application of differential discounts to comparable situations will amount to the application of dissimilar conditions if this

arises as a result of the application of unequal criteria and there are no legitimate commercial reasons capable of justifying these differences of treatment.[4]

1 EC Treaty, Article 82(c). Cf Article 81(1)(d), and paras [91] ff; see also Case T-229/94 *Deutsche Bahn v Commission* [1997] ECR II-1689; Case T-219/99 *British Airways v Commission* [2004] 4 CMLR 19, paras 233-240, CFI. See also *R v Competition Commission, Director General of Telecommunications, ex p T-Mobile and Others* [2003] EWHC 1555 (Admin) for a discussion of price discrimination.

2 Case 155/73 *Sacchi* [1974] ECR 409, [1974) 2 CMLR 177, ECJ. See also Case 7/82 *GVL v Commission* [1983] ECR 483, [1983] 3 CMLR 645, ECJ and Case C-260/89 *Elliniki Radiofonia Tileorasi v Kouvelas* [1991] ECR I-2925, [1994] 4 CMLR 540, ECJ.

3 Commission Decision (EEC) 82/861 [1982] OJ L360/36, [1983] 1 CMLR 457 (*British Telecommunications*) upheld on appeal in Case 41/83 *Italy v Commission* [1985] ECR 873, [1985] 2 CMLR 368, ECJ.

4 Case 322/81 *Nederlandsche Banden-Industrie Michelin NV v Commission* [1983] ECR 3461, [1985] 1 CMLR 282, ECJ, where it was not established that there were unequal criteria or no legitimate justification. See Case 311/84 *Centre beige d'etudes de marché – Telemarketing (CBEM) SA v Compagnie luxembourgeoise de telediffusion SA* [1985] ECR 3261, [1986] 2 CMLR 558, ECJ; Commission Decision (EEC) 88/589 [1988] OJ L317/47 (*London European/Sabena*); and Commission Decision (EEC) 88/518 [1988] OJ L284/41 [1990] 4 CMLR 196 (*British Sugar/Napier Brown*).

[283]

(d) Prices with a tying effect: An annual fidelity or loyalty rebate,[1] designed to prevent customers from obtaining supplies from competing undertakings, resulting in different net prices being charged to two customers buying the same quantity, would amount to the application[2] of dissimilar conditions.[3] The same would apply in the case of a policy of differing prices.[4] In order to assess whether a system of discounts amounts to an abuse, it is necessary to consider all the circumstances in which the discount is given. In particular it is necessary to consider the criteria and conditions for the grant of the discount, and to consider whether the discount tends, by means of a benefit not justified by any economic service, to take away or restrict the buyer's freedom to choose his sources of supply, to restrict access to the market to competitors, to apply dissimilar conditions to equivalent transactions with other trading parties or to strengthen a dominant position by distorted competition.[5] Thus, a discount system (even where the discount is a very low percentage), based on sales targets to be achieved by dealers, operated by a company in a very substantial dominant position, where the discounts were subject to variations and were not published, and where the system was backed up by a network of commercial representatives, amounted to an abuse of a dominant position because it limited the choices open to dealers as regards suppliers and made access to the market more difficult for competitors.

1 See AL Morris, 'Requirements Contracts and their Treatment under the EC Treaty' 6 ELR 269-271.

2 ie within the meaning of EC Treaty, Article 82(c).

3 Case T-219/99 *British Airways v Commission* [2004] 4 CMLR 19, paras 227-300, CFI. See Case T-203/01 *Michelin v Commission* [2004] 4 CMLR 18, CFI. See also *Napp Pharmaceutical Holdings Ltd v Director General Fair Trading* [2002] CompAR 13, CCAT for pricing policies (including discriminatory pricing) having a tie-in effect in the UK. See also, Joined Cases 40-48, 50, 54-56, 111, 113, 114/73 *Coöperatieve vereniging Suiker Unie UA v Commission* [1975] ECR 1663 at 2004, [1976] 1 CMLR 295 at 472, ECJ; Case 85/76 *Hoffmann-La Roche & Co AG v Commission* [1979] ECR 461, [1979] 3 CMLR 211, ECJ; Case 322/81 *Nederlandsche Banden-Industrie Michelin NV v*

Commission [1983] ECR 3461, [1985] 1 CMLR 282, ECJ. This is in contradistinction to a quantity discount, linked solely to the volume of purchases from the manufacturer concerned.

4 Case 27/76 *United Brands Co v Commission* [1978] ECR 207 at 294-299, [1978] 1 CMLR 429 at 498-501, ECJ; Case T-83/91 *Tetra Pak International SA v Commission* [1994] ECR II-755, ECJ; Case C-18/93 *Corsica Ferries* [1994] ECR I-1783, ECJ (differing charge for piloting services based on nationality contrary to Article 82).

5 Case 322/81 *Nederlandsche Banden-Industrie Michelin NV v Commission* [1983] ECR 3461, [1985] 1 CMLR 282, ECJ.

[284]
Similarly, a dominant undertaking which makes selective offers to certain purchasers who are customers of its main competitor, as against its own customers, discriminates contrary to Article 82, where the customers are in comparable situations.[1]

1 Case 62/86 *Akzo Chemie BV v Commission* [1991] ECR I-3359, [1993] 5 CMLR 215, ECJ.

[285]
The prohibition on dissimilar prices is not avoided by the inclusion of a so-called 'English clause', namely a clause enabling a customer to retain the benefit of a fidelity rebate, even if the customer has bought from a competitor at a cheaper price, provided the customer notified the dominant undertaking of the cheaper price, and if the dominant undertaking failed to reduce its price to the lower price. Such a clause does not remedy the anti-competitive elements of the fidelity rebate and is itself an abuse, for it enables the dominant undertaking to obtain information about market conditions, which is of great value for the carrying out of its market strategy.[1]

1 Case 85/76 *Hoffmann-La Roche & Co AG v Commission* [1979] ECR 461, [1979] 3 CMLR 211, ECJ. See also Case C-393/92 *Municipality of Almelo and Others v Energiebedrijf Ijsselmij* [1994] ECR I-1477, ECJ; Case T-32/91 *Solvay v Commission* [1995] ECR II-1825, [1996] 5 CMLR 91, CFI, and Case T-37/91 *ICI v Commission* [1995] ECR II-1901, CFI (which having been annulled and the decisions retaken in December 2000 are still under appeal in the CFI: Case T-57/01 and T-66/01).

[286]
(e) Excessively high pricing: Exceptionally, an excessively high price charged by a dominant undertaking may amount to an abuse.[1] An excessively high price is one which is excessive in relation to the economic value of the product or service. This excess can be determined objectively if it is possible to compare the selling price and the cost of production.[2] Very high prices and very high profitability by a dominant undertaking might indicate prima facie an infringement of Article 82 EC.[3] However, in *BHB Enterprises Ltd. v Victor Chandler (International) Ltd*,[4] the English High Court rejected the notion of a *per se* rule whereby, where a dominant undertaking charges prices greatly in excess of the cost of production, there is in principle an abuse of its dominant position. Under such a rule the prices charged by an undertaking enjoying a dominant position in a particular market must be compared with the price he would have been able to charge had there been competition. If he charges more than he would have charged in a competitive market, he is abusing his dominant position.[5] Laddie J held, in reliance on the Opinion of the Advocate General in *Bronner*, that

> we still live in a free market economy where traders are allowed to run their businesses without undue interference. What Article 82 and section

> 18 of the Act are concerned with is unfair prices, not high prices. In determining whether a price is unfair it is necessary to consider the impact on the end consumer and all of the market conditions ...[6]

Laddie J also suggested that in 'a case where unfair pricing is alleged, assessment of the value of the asset both to the vendor and the purchaser must be a crucial part of the assessment. VCI's approach does not take into account value at all. It simply relates prices to the cost of acquisition or creation'.[7] Laddie J's judgment was subsequently examined in *Attheraces Ltd v BHB Ltd and BHB Enterprises Ltd*,[8] where the Vice-Chancellor held that: 'If and to the extent that Laddie J may have considered that a comparison of cost and price was irrelevant then I disagree with him.'[9] The better view, it is suggested, is that in examining potentially excessive pricing, a comparison between the production costs and the price should be the first, but not the sole determinative step, in the exercise.[10]

1 Competition regulators are generally reluctant to interfere with prices absent other anti-competitive conduct, see Whish, *Competition Law* (5th edn, 2003), p 195; see further the references to the importance of freedom of contract at paras 53, 56, 58-62 of the Opinion of AG Jacobs in Case C-7/97 *Oscar Bronner* [1998] ECR I-7791 and in *BHB Enterprises Ltd v Victor Chandler (International) Ltd* [2005] EWHC 1047 (Ch) per Laddie J at para 56. For an analysis of the case-law on excessive pricing, see P Oliver, 'The Concept of "Abuse" of a Dominant Position under Article 82 EC: Recent Developments in relation to Pricing' (2005) 2 European Competition Journal 315, 318-322.

2 *Deutsche Post AG – Interception of cross-border mail* [2001] OJ L331/40, [2002] 4 CMLR 598; Case 26/75 *General Motors Continental NV v Commission* [1975] ECR 1367, [1976] 1 CMLR 95, ECJ; Case 27/76 *United Brands Co v Commission* [1978] ECR 207, [1978] 1 CMLR 429, ECJ. See also Case 226/84 *British Leyland plc v Commission* [1986] ECR 3263, [1987] 1 CMLR 185, ECJ (in which excessive pricing was combined with discriminatory pricing); Case 53/87 *Consorzio italiano della componentistica di ricambio per autoveicoli v Regie nationale des usines Renault* [1988] ECR 6039, [1990] 4 CMLR 265, ECJ (in which the Court suggested, obiter, that the exercise of an exclusive right by the proprietor of an intellectual property right may be prohibited by Article 82 if it involves the fixing of prices for the protected product at an unfair level). See also Case T-30/89 *Hilti AG v Commission* [1990] ECR II-163, [1990] 4 CMLR 602, CFI, upheld on appeal in Case C-53/92P *Hilti AG v Commission* [1994] ECR I-667, ECJ. In Case 24/67 *Parke, Davis v Probel* [1968] ECR 55, [1968] CMLR 47, ECJ, the Court had said that a higher sales price for a product protected by an intellectual property right as compared with that of the unprotected product does not necessarily constitute an abuse; in Case 40/70 *Sirena Srl v Edo Srl* [1971] ECR 69, [1971] CMLR 260, ECJ, the Court stated that such high pricing, if unjustified by objective criteria, and if particularly high, may be a determining factor (ground 17); Joined Cases 110, 241, 242/88 *Lucazeau v Société des auteurs, compositeurs et editeurs de musique (SACEM)* [1989] ECR 2811, [1991] 4 CMLR 248, ECJ, where a dominant undertaking imposes scales of fees for its services which are appreciably higher than those charged in other Member States and where the comparison of the fee levels has been made on a consistent basis, that difference is indicative of an abuse: in such a case it is for the undertaking concerned to justify the difference by reference to objective dissimilarities between the situations in the respective Member States; and see Case 30/87 *Bodson v Pompes funèbres des regions libérees SA* [1988] ECR 2479, [1989] 4 CMLR 984, ECJ and Case 66/86 *Ahmed Saeed Flugreisen v Zentrale zur Bekampfung unlauteren Wettbewerbs eV* [1989] ECR 803, [1990] 4 CMLR 102, ECJ, for other factors to be taken into account in determining whether prices are excessive.

3 Commission Communication on *Sterling Airways* (10th Report on Competition Policy, points 136-138).

4 [2005] EWHC 1047 (Ch).

5 Paragraph 47.

6 Paragraph 56.

7 Paragraph 56.

8 [2005] EWHC 1553 (Ch).
9 Paragraph 49.
10 Case 27/76 *United Brands Co v Commission* [1978] ECR 207, [1978] 1 CMLR 429, ECJ, para 252; *Napp Pharmaceutical Holdings Ltd v DG of Fair Trading* [2002] CompAR 13, CCA, paras 390-392 and 402.

[287]
The fact that the price of a product sold by a dominant firm is higher than the price of a parallel import does not of itself prove abuse; however, if the difference is unjustified by any objective criteria and if it is particularly marked, it may be a determining factor in such an abuse.[1]

1 Case 24/67 *Parke, Davis & Co v Probel* [1968] ECR 55, [1968] CMLR 47, ECJ; Case 40/70 *Sirena Srl v Edo Srl* [1971] ECR 69, [1971] CMLR 260, ECJ; Case 78/70 *Deutsche Grammophon Gesellschaft mbH v Metro-SB-Grossmarkte GmbH & Co KG* [1971] ECR 487, [1971] CMLR 631, ECJ.

[288]
Charging an excessive price[1] for a certificate of conformity essential for the import of a motor car may constitute abuse of a dominant position where it has the effect of curbing parallel imports of motor cars by neutralising their price advantage, or by leading to unfair trade.[2]

1 ie excessive in relation to the economic value of the service provided.
2 Case 26/75 *General Motors Continental NV v Commission* [1975] ECR 1367, [1976] 1 CMLR 95, ECJ; Commission Decision (EEC) 84/379 [1984] OJ L207/11, [1984] 3 CMLR92 (*BL*). 'Unfair trade' here means unfair trade in the sense of EC Treaty, Article 82(c). See *BHB Enterprises Ltd v Victor Chandler (International) Ltd* [2005] EWHC 1047 (Ch) per Laddie J at para 46 ff and Case 226/84 *British Leyland plc v Commission* [1986] ECR 3263, [1987] 1 CMLR 185, ECJ.

7. Conditions with tying effects

[289]
(a) 'Bundling': The 'bundling' together by a dominant undertaking, in one inclusive price, of separate but ancillary products or services may constitute an abuse where the effect is to eliminate or substantially weaken competition in the supply of those ancillary products or services.[1]

1 Case T-201/04 *Microsoft v Commission* [2005] 4 CMLR 406, CFI, 22 December 2004, paras 23-24, Commission Decision (EEC) 88/518 [1988] OJ L284/41, [1990] 4 CMLR 196 (*British Sugar/Napier Brown*). See *Genzyme Ltd v OFT* [2004] CompAR 358 at para 533, CAT.

[290]
(b) Requirements contracts: A requirement contract is a contract by which a purchaser agrees to take, or a seller agrees to supply, a certain percentage (which may be 100 per cent) of the requirements of the purchase for a particular product.[1] An undertaking which is in a dominant position on a market and which ties purchasers (even if it does so at their request) by an obligation or promise on their part to obtain all or most of their requirements exclusively from the dominant undertaking abuses its dominant position within the meaning of Article 82 of the EC Treaty whether the obligation in question is stipulated without further qualification or whether it is undertaken in consideration of the grant of a rebate.[2]

1 See AL Morris, 'Requirements Contracts and their Treatment under the EC Treaty' 6 ELR 266-269.

2 Case 85/76 *Hoffmann-La Roche & Co AG v Commission* [1979] ECR 461, [1979] 3 CMLR 211, ECJ. See also Joined Cases 40-48, 50, 54-56, 111, 113, 114/73 *Cooperatieve vereniging Suiker Unie v Commission* [1975] ECR 1663 at 1999, [1976] 1 CMLR 295 at 468, 469, ECJ; and the Commission Communication in *Soda Ash* (11th Report on Competition Policy, paras 73-76), where the Commission accepted (in place of long-term exclusive contracts) medium-term fixed-quantity contracts which it did not consider infringed the EC Treaty. See also Case 62/86 *Akzo Chemie BV v Commission* [1991] ECR I-3359, [1993] 5 CMLR215, ECJ; Commission Decision (EEC) 89/22 [1989] OJ L10/50, [1990] 4 CMLR 464 (*BPB/British Gypsum*); on appeal the ECJ held that exclusive supply agreements which could be terminated by the customers without notice were nevertheless abusive by virtue of the pressure brought to bear on the latter by the loyalty rebates applied by the supplier: Case C-310/93P *BPB Industries Plc and British Gypsum Ltd v Commission* [1995] ECR I-865, ECJ; Case T-83/91 *Tetra Pak International SA v Commission* [1994] ECR II-755, CFI. See also Commission Decision (EEC) 91/299 [1991] OJ L152/21 (*Soda-ash – Solvay*) and Commission Decision (EEC) 91/300 [1991] OJ L152/40 (*Soda-ash*), on appeal in Case T32/91 *Solvay v Commission* [1995] ECR II-1825, [1996] 5 CMLR 91, CFI, and, Case T-37/91 *ICI v Commission* [1995] ECR II-1901, CFI (which decisions having been annulled and the decisions retaken in December 2000 are still under appeal in the CFI in Cases T-57/01 and T-66/01).

8. Requiring supplementary obligations

[291]

It is an abuse for a dominant undertaking to make the conclusion of contracts subject to acceptance by the other parties of supplementary obligations which, by their nature or according to commercial usage, have no connection with the subject of such contracts.[1] Restrictions placed on the users of certain telephone services may amount to enforcing supplementary obligations with no connection with the subject of the contract if the supplementary obligations arise out of a desire to protect the revenue of other undertakings.[2] Similarly, making supply of a product conditional upon certain terms, such as the dominant undertaking having control of its further processing or marketing,[3] or that certain export instructions be accepted,[4] is an abuse.[5]

1 EC Treaty, Article 82(d). Cf Article 81(1)(e), and para [91]; and cf the Patents Act 1977, s 44(1). See also Case T-83/91 *Tetra Pak International SA v Commission* [1994] ECR II-755, CFI.
2 Commission Decision (EEC) 82/861 [1982] OJ L360/36, [1983] 1 CMLR 457 (*British Telecommunications*), upheld on appeal in Case 41/83 *Italy v Commission* [1985] ECR 873, [1985] 2 CMLR 368, ECJ.
3 Commission Communication dated 18 November 1983 in *Stik Strip BV v Polaroid Nederland and Polaroid UK* [1984] 1 CMLR 132.
4 Joined Cases 40-48, 50, 54-56, 111, 113, 114/73 *Coöperatieve vereniging Suiker Unie UA v Commission* [1975] ECR 1663 at 1964, [1976] 1 CMLR 295 at 442, ECJ.
5 In the same way that making supply of a product conditional upon certain terms, tying unwanted products to the market product with no objective justification is an abuse; see Joined Cases 110, 241, 242/88 *Lucazeau v Société des auteurs, compositeurs et editeurs de musique (SACEM)* [1989] ECR 2811, [1991] 4 CMLR 248, ECJ; and Case T-30/89 *Hilti AG v Commission* [1990] ECR II-163, [1990] 4 CMLR 602, CFI, upheld by the ECJ in Case C-53/ 92P [1994] ECR I-667, [1994] 4 CMLR 614, ECJ.

9. Refusal to deal

[292]

An undertaking in a dominant position may abuse that position by refusing to supply an existing customer,[1] if it thereby risks eliminating competition on the part of that customer.[2] It is the same if the dominant undertaking refuses to deal except on condition that certain export restrictions be accepted.[3] It is clear that an existing customer includes a longstanding customer,[4] but the position of an occasional customer may be different.[5] With regard to a long-standing customer, there is an obligation to continue supplying provided the customer abides by regular commercial practice and does not place orders which are out of the ordinary.[6] However, in a period of shortage an occasional customer is not entitled to require the same treatment as traditional customers with long-term contracts.[7] In certain situations there may be an obligation to supply a customer placing a much larger order than it has done before, and it could still be an abuse if the dominant undertaking made supply conditional on having control of its further processing or marketing.[8] A refusal to supply could be construed from the introduction of a selective distribution system by a dominant undertaking where the distributors have not been selected on the basis of objective criteria applied.[9] It would also be an abuse for a dominant undertaking to refuse to deal with persons on the basis of foreign nationality or foreign residence, at least where there is no realistic alternative undertaking.[10] An undertaking holding a dominant position on a given market, which reserved to itself or to an undertaking belonging to the same group, without any objective necessity, an ancillary activity which could be carried out by a third undertaking in the context of its activities in a similar but separate market, with the risk of eliminating all competition by that undertaking, would be abusing its dominant position within the meaning of Article 82 of the EC Treaty.[11]

1 See C Vajda, 'Article 86 and a Refusal to Supply' [1981] E Comp L Rev 97. For a consideration of this matter in English and United States competition law, see T Sharpe 'Refusal to Supply' (1983) 99 LQR 36. See also D Ridyard, 'Essential facilities and the obligation to supply competitors under UK and EC Competition law' [1996] ECLR 438.

2 Joined Cases 6, 7/73 *Istituto Chemioterapico Italiano SpA and Commercial Solvents Corpn v Commission* [1974] ECR 223, [1974] 1 CMLR 309, ECJ.

3 Joined Cases 40-48, 50, 54-56, 111, 113, 114/73 *Coöperatieve vereniging Suiker Unie UA v Commission* [1975] ECR 1663 at 1983, [1976] 1 CMLR 295 at 456, ECJ.

4 Case 27/76 *United Brands Co v Commission* [1978] ECR 207, [1978] 1 CMLR 429, ECJ.

5 Case 77/77 *Benzine en Petroleum Handelsmaatschappij BV v Commission* [1978] ECR 1513, [1978] 3 CMLR 174, ECJ. See, however, Commission Decision (EEC) 84/379 [1984] OJ L207/11, [1984] 3 CMLR 92 (*BL*), on appeal Case 226/84 *British Leyland plc v Commission* [1986] ECR 3263, [1987] 1 CMLR 185, ECJ.

6 Case 27/76 *United Brands Co v Commission* [1978] ECR 207, [1978] 1 CMLR 429, ECJ.

7 Case 77/77 *Benzine en Petroleum Handelsmaatschappij BV v Commission* [1978] ECR 1513, [1978] 3 CMLR 174, ECJ.

8 Commission Communication dated 18 November 1983 in *Stik Strip BV v Polaroid Nederland and Polaroid UK* [1984] 1 CMLR 132.

9 Case 126/80 *Salonia v Poidomani* [1981] ECR 1563, [1982] 1 CMLR 64, ECJ.

10 Case 311/84 *Centre belge d'études de marché – Télémarketing (CBEM) SA v Compagnie luxembourgeoise de télédiffusion SA* [1985] ECR 3261, [1986] 2 CMLR 558, ECJ.

11 Case 7/82 *GVL v Commission* [1983] ECR 483, [1983] 3 CMLR 645, ECJ.

[293]

In the same way that an undertaking in a dominant position may abuse that position by refusing to deal, except on condition that certain export restrictions be accepted, so may the dominant undertaking if, in the absence of intellectual property rights, an inferior product is sold and the effect is to separate the markets and therefore eliminate competition.[1]

1 See Commission Decision (EEC) 89/113 [1989] OJ L43/27 (*Decca Navigator System*). See also generally on refusal to deal Case 311/84 *Centre belge d'études de marché – Telemarketing (CBEM) SA v Compagnie luxembourgeoise de rédiffusion SA* [1985] ECR 3261, [1986] 2 CMLR 558, ECJ; Commission Decision (EEC) 88/589 [1988] OJ L317/47 (*London European/Sabena*); Commission Decision (EEC) 88/518 [1988] OJ L284/41, [1990] 4 CMLR 196 (*British Sugar/Napier Brown*); Commission Decision (EEC) 89/22 [1989] OJ L10/50, [1990] 4 CMLR 464 (*BPB Industries plc*) (where a disloyal customer was distinguished from an occasional customer); but compare Commission Decision (EEC) 87/500 [1987] OJ L286/36, [1988] 4 CMLR 67 (*BBI/Boosey & Hawkes*) (in which subject to a condition of proportionality or objective necessity in the activity of the dominant firm combined with a refusal to deal, the latter's behaviour may be justified if it is the only means of preserving a competitive position).

[294]
The right to choose one's trading partners and freely to dispose of one's property are generally recognised principles in the laws of the Member States, in some cases with constitutional status. Accordingly, as a matter of Community law, incursions on those rights require careful justification.[1]

1 See, paras 58 and 62 of the Opinion of AG Jacob in Case C-7/97 *Oscar Bronner* [1998] ECR I-7791, relied on in *BHB Enterprise Ltd v Victor Chandler (International) Ltd* referred to at para [286] above.

10. Refusal to supply competitors and essential facilities

[295]
Similarly, it is an infringement of Article 82 EC for an undertaking in a dominant position to refuse to supply a competitor in a downstream market where the effect of such refusal would be to eliminate all competition in the downstream market.[1] It may also be an abuse to refuse to supply as an exclusionary tactic against a customer trying to enter an upstream market in competition with the supplier.[2]

1 Joined Cases 6, 7/73 *Istituto Chemioterapico Italiano Spa and Commercial Solvents Corpn v Commission* [1974] ECR 223, [1974] 309, ECJ.
2 *BBI/Boosey & Hawkes: Interim Measures* [1987] OJ L286/36, [1988] 4 CMLR 67; *NDC Health/IMS Health: Interim Measures* [2002] OJ L59/18, [2002] 4 CMLR 111.

[296]
The essential facilities doctrine is not independent of, but rather stems from, the case law in relation to refusals to supply.[1] On the basis of dicta of the ECJ,[2] the Commission has developed the notion that a dominant undertaking that owns or controls a facility or infrastructure which is necessary to provide services to customers in a downstream market and itself uses the facility to compete in such market,[3] may not refuse access to its competitors in that market or grant them access to the facility at terms less favourable than those it gives to its operation.[4] It seems that it is irrelevant whether the competitor seeking access to the facility is a new customer or an existing one.[5]

1 On the 'essential facilities' doctrine in US antitrust law see Areeda, 'Essential Facilities: an Epithet in Need of Limiting Principles' (1990) 58 Antitrust Law Journal 841; and *United States v Terminal Railroad Association of St Louis* 224 US 383 (1912); *Gamco Inc v Providence Fruit and Produce Building* 194 F.2d 484 (1st Cir 1952); and *Alaska Airlines v United Airlines et al* 948 F.2d 536 (9th Cir 1991). See also Doherty, 'Just what are Essential Facilities?' (2001) 38 CML Rev 397; see also *R v Dover Harbour Board, ex p Peter Gilder & Sons and Another* (1995) The Times, 17 April.

2 Joined Cases 6, 7/73 *Istituto Chemioterapico Italiano Spa and Commercial Solvents Corpn v Commission* [1974] ECR 223, [1974] CMLR 309, ECJ; and, in particular, Case 311/84 *Centre Belge d'études do marché – Telemarketing (CBEM) SA v Compagnie luxembourgeoise de télediffusion SA* [1985] ECR 3261, [1986] 2 CMLR 558, ECJ.
3 There would not seem to be any particular reason why the dominant undertaking would have to use the facility itself (see for example the *Dover* case at note 1). See also *Irish Continental Group v CCI Morlaix* (Case IV/35.388) [1995] 5 CMLR 177, where the refusal to grant access to the Port of Roscoff by CCI Morlaix, the managers of the port, was considered abusive, notwithstanding the 5 per cent stake held by CCI Morlaix in Brittany Ferries, the principal user of the port.
4 See Commission Decision (EEC) 88/589 [1988] OJ L317/47, [1989] 4 CMLR 662 (*London European/Sabena*) (on a refusal to grant access to a computer reservation system); Commission Decision (EEC) 92/213 [1992] OJ L96/34, [1993] 5 CMLR 352 (*British Midland v Aer Lingus*) (on a refusal to interline with a competing airline); Commission Decision of 11 June 1992 in Case IV/34.174 (*B&I v Sealink: Interim Measures*) [1992] 5 CMLR 255 (concerning the unfair organisation of the ferry schedules in Holyhead harbour); Commission Decision (EC) 94/19 [1994] OJ L15/8, [1995] 4 CMLR84 (*Sea Containers v Sealink: Interim Measures*) (on a failure to offer access to Holyhead harbour on non-discriminatory terms); see also Commission Decision (EC) 94/119 [1994] OJ L55/52, [1994] 5 CMLR 457 (*Port of Rødby*) (where the Danish government refused to allow a company to build a new commercial port near Rødby and subsequently refused it access to the facilities of that port. For a discussion of these cases see Glasi, 'The essential facilities doctrine in EC anti-trust law' (1994) ECLR 306.
5 See, in particular, Commission Decision (EEC) 92/213 [1992] OJ L96/34, [1993] 5 CMLR 352 (*British Midland v Aer Lingus*); Commission Decision (EC) 95/364 [1995] OJ L216, [1996] 4 CMLR 232 (*Brussels Airport*).

[297]
The essential facilities doctrine must be treated with some care since there are often good economic reasons to limit its application. In particular, the risk that third parties may obtain a 'free ride' on the fruits of an undertakings investment may deter such undertakings from making such investments in the future.[1] The Community Courts have refused to apply the essential facilities doctrine in *Tierce Ladbroke v Commission*[2] (the refusal to supply did not eliminate competition in the downstream market), *European Night Services*[3] and *Oscar Bronner*[4] (the product or service refused cannot be considered essential unless that is no real or potential substitute).

1 See, the Opinion of Advocate General Jacobs in Case C 7-97 *Oscar Bronner* [1998] ECR I-7791, paras 56-58.
2 Case T-504/93 *Tierce Ladbroke v Commission* [1997] ECR II-923.
3 Case T-374/94 *European Night Services v Commission* [1998] ECR II-3141.
4 Case C-7/97 *Oscar Bronner* [1998] ECR I-7791.

11. Abuse and intellectual property rights

[298]
The ECJ has developed in this area a particular jurisprudence in relation to intellectual property rights. The exercise of an intellectual property owner's rights (including refusal to grant a licence), even if it is the act of an undertaking holding a dominant position, cannot in itself constitute abuse of a dominant position.[1] The conduct of the owner of an intellectual property right which enjoys a dominant position can however be reviewed under Article 82 and, in exceptional circumstances, the exercise of the exclusive rights afforded by the right in question may be abusive.[2]

1 Case C-418/01 *IMS Health GmbH v NDC Health GmbH* [2004] 4 CMLR 1543, ECJ, para 34; Case 238/87 *Volvo* [1988] ECR 6211, para 8, and Case T-69/89 *RTE v Commission* [1991] ECR II-485, upheld by the ECJ in [1995] ECR I-743, para 49.
2 Case 102/77 *Hoffmann-La Roche & Co AG v Centrafarm Vertriebsgesellschaft Pharmazeutischer Erzeugnisse mbH* [1978] ECR 1139, [1978] 3 CMLR 217, ECJ (trade mark); Joined Cases C241, 242/91P *Independent Television Publications (ITP) and Radio Telefís Éireann (RTE) v Commission* [1995] ECR I-743, [1995] 4 CMLR 718, ECJ (copyright).

[299]
The ECJ held that such exceptional circumstances were present in the case giving rise to the judgment in *Magill*, in which the conduct of the television channels in a dominant position which gave rise to the complaint consisted in their relying on the copyright conferred by national legislation on the weekly listings of their programmes in order to prevent another undertaking from publishing information on those programmes together with commentaries, on a weekly basis.[1]

1 In Joined Cases C241, 242/91P *Independent Television Publications (ITP) and Radio Telefís Éireann (RTE) v Commission* [1995] ECR I-743, [1995] 4 CMLR 718, ECJ (*Magill*), the exceptional circumstances were constituted by the fact that the refusal in question concerned a product (information on the weekly schedules of certain television channels), the supply of which was indispensable for carrying on the business in question (the publishing of a general television guide), in that, without that information, the person wishing to produce such a guide would find it impossible to publish it and offer it for sale (*Magill*, para 53), the fact that such refusal prevented the emergence of a new product for which there was a potential consumer demand (para 54), the fact that it was not justified by objective considerations (para 55), and was likely to exclude all competition in the secondary market (para 56).

[300]
In order for the refusal by an undertaking which owns a copyright to give access to a product or service indispensable for carrying on a particular business to be treated as abusive, it is sufficient that three cumulative conditions be satisfied, namely, that that refusal is preventing the emergence of a new product for which there is a potential consumer demand, that it is unjustified and such as to exclude any competition on a secondary market.[1] In order to determine whether a product or service is indispensable for enabling an undertaking to carry on business in a particular market, it must be determined whether there are products or services which constitute alternative solutions, even if they are less advantageous, and whether there are technical, legal or economic obstacles capable of making it impossible or at least unreasonably difficult for any undertaking seeking to operate in the market to create, possibly in cooperation with other operators, the alternative products or services. In order to accept the existence of economic obstacles, it must be established, at the very least, that the creation of those products or services is not economically viable for production on a scale comparable to that of the undertaking which controls the existing product or service.[2]

1 Case C-418/01 *IMS Health GmbH v NDC Health GmbH* [2004] 4 CMLR 1543, ECJ, para 38
2 Ibid, para 28.

[301]
The exercise of intellectual property rights to prevent the importation of products infringing those rights does not constitute an abuse, if done by a dominant undertaking,[1] nor does the acquisition by a dominant undertaking of an exclusive

licence per se constitute an abuse, for it is necessary to consider the surrounding circumstances.[2]

1 Case 51/75 *EMI Records Ltd v CBS United Kingdom Ltd* [1976] ECR 811, [1976] 2 CMLR 235, ECJ; Case 86/75 *EMI Records Ltd v CBS Grammofon A/S* [1976] ECR 871, [1976] 2 CMLR 235, ECJ; Case 96/75 *EMI Records Ltd v CBS Schallplatten GmbH* [1976] ECR 913, [1976] 2 CMLR 235, ECJ (trade mark cases).
2 Case T-51/89 *Tetra Pak Rausing SA v Commission* [1990] ECR II-309, [1991] 4 CMLR 334, CFI.

[302]

A higher price for a patented product when compared with that of an unpatented product from another Member State, does not necessarily constitute an abuse,[1] but it may be a determining factor if the price is particularly high and unjustified by any objective criteria.[2] In certain circumstances the compulsory assignment of rights may be an abuse if the dominant undertaking imposes obligations which are not absolutely necessary or which encroach unfairly upon the rights of third persons.[3]

1 Case 24/67 *Parke, Davis & Co v Probel* [1968] ECR 55, [1968] CMLR 47, ECJ.
2 Case 40/70 *Sirena Srl v Edo Srl* [1971] ECR 69, [1971] CMLR 260, ECJ; Case 78/70 *Deutsche Grammophon Gesellschaft GmbH v Metro-SB-Grofimärkte GmbH & Co KG* [1971] ECR 487, [1971] CMLR 631, ECJ.
3 Case 127/73 *Belgische Radio en Televisie (BRT) v SV SABAM* [1974] ECR 313, [1974] 2 CMLR 238, ECJ.

[303]

The following are further examples of possible abuses by a dominant undertaking with intellectual property rights: to start various proceedings for infringements and to suspend those proceedings only on condition that the defendant enters into restrictive agreements and remains party to such agreements;[1] to register a trade mark when the dominant undertaking knows, or ought to know, that that mark is already used by a competitor;[2] to require a contractor to grant to the dominant undertaking unlimited rights resulting from the development under the contract, and to do so for no additional remuneration;[3] to run a society for the management of composers copyrights in such a way as to partition the common market and thereby restrict the freedom to provide services which constitutes one of the objectives of the treaty,[4] and needlessly to protract proceedings for the grant of patent licences of right by demanding a fee approximately six times higher than the figure ultimately awarded by the Comptroller of Patents.[5] With regard to the exclusive rights to manufacture and market spare parts at a manufacturer who holds the registered designs for those parts, conduct which could constitute abuse would be the arbitrary refusal to supply spare parts to independent repairers, the fixing of prices for spare parts or an unfair level or a decision to stop producing spare parts for a particular model still in wide circulation, but in the ordinary event the refusal to grant a licence, even for a reasonable royalty, will not be an abuse.[6] With regard to copyright, the exercise of the right to exclude third parties from reproducing the copyright material is abusive where it prevents the emergence of a new product which would satisfy a potential consumer demand and for which there is no substitute, where such conduct is not otherwise justified and where, by thus exercising the copyright, the owner reserves to himself an ancifiary market; such conduct goes beyond what is permitted as necessary to fulfil the essential function of the copyright and infringes Article 82.[7]

1 Commission Communication in *Zip-fasteners Market* (7th Report on Competition Policy, point 31.2).
2 Commission Communication in *Osram/Airam* (11th Report on Competition Policy, point 97).
3 Commission Communication in *Eurofima* [1973] 1 CMLR D217 (3rd Report on Competition Policy, points 68, 69).
4 Case 22/79 *Greenwich Film Production v SACEM* [1979] ECR 3275, [1980] 1 CMLR 629, ECJ; Case 7/82 *GVL v Commission* [1983] ECR 483, [1983] 3 CMLR 645, ECJ.
5 Case T-30/89 *Hilti AG v Commission* [1990] ECR II-163, [1990] 4 CMLR 602, CFI.
6 Case 238/87 *Volvo AB v Erik Veng (UK) Ltd* [1988] ECR 6211, [1988] 4 CMLR 122, ECJ; Case 53/87 *Consorzio italiano della componentistica di ricambio per autoveicoli v Régie nationale des usines Renault* [1988] ECR 6039, [1990] 4 CMLR 265, ECJ.
7 Joined Cases C-241, 242/91P *RTE v Commission* [1995] ECR 1-743, [1995] 4 CMLR 718, ECJ; the ECJ also ruled that, notwithstanding the fact that the protection of intellectual property rights is a matter for national laws, the imposition by the Commission of compulsory licensing as a remedy for the infringement described above is not ultra vires the then applicable Regulation 17/62, Article 3, and, on the facts of the case, is in compliance with the principle of proportionality. It must be noted that the copyright in question in this case covered a mere compilation of unsophisticated information, which is the result of a very limited creative effort and which would not generally qualify for intellectual property protection in other European systems of law. It may be questioned whether the position would have been the same had the copyright covered a more valuable set of information deriving from substantial investment such as, for instance, complex computer software.

12. Limiting production, markets or technical development

[304]

An abuse of dominant position may consist in limiting production, markets or technical development to the prejudice of consumers.[1] The limitation of markets to the prejudice of consumers can occur in many ways. Examples of such abuse by a dominant undertaking include compelling dealers to channel exports to specific destinations or consignments and requiring similar restrictions to be placed upon their customers;[2] the grant of a loyalty rebate, for this can reduce the opportunities of competitors selling their products;[3] preventing the emergence of a new product which would satisfy a potential consumer demand and which has no substitute;[4] and forbidding distributors from reselling the product in certain circumstances or by withdrawing supplies from a long-standing customer who abides by regular commercial practice, if the orders placed are not out of the ordinary.[5] Other examples which could amount to such an abuse include an exclusive purchase agreement between the largest producer and the largest consumer of a particular product,[6] and a selective distribution system operated by a dominant undertaking if the distributors are not selected on objectively justifiable criteria,[7] or when the dominant undertaking excludes other undertakings from the market.[8]

1 EC Treaty, Article 82(b). Cf Article 81(1)(b), and paras [91] ff, and note that Article 82(b) does not include the words 'or control' and 'or investment', and adds 'to the prejudice of consumers'. It is doubtful whether these differences have any particular significance in the light of the broad interpretation given to 'abuse'. See for express reference to the risk of limiting technical development: Case T-201/04 *Microsoft v Commission* [2005] 4 CMLR 406, CFI, para 20.
2 Joined Cases 40-48, 50, 54-56, 111, 113, 114/73 *Coöperatieve vereniging Suiker Unie UA v Commission* [1975] ECR 1663 at 1983, [1976] 1 CMLR 295 at 457, ECJ.
3 Joined Cases 40-48, 50, 54-56, 111, 113, 114/73 *Coöperatieve vereniging Suiker Unie UA v Commission* [1975] ECR 1663 at 2004, [1976] 1 CMLR 295 at 472, ECJ; Case C-393/92 *Municipality of Almelo and Others v Energiebedrijf Ijsselmij* [1994] ECR I-1477, ECJ.

4 Joined Cases C-241, 242/91P *Independent Television Publications (ITP) and Radio Telefís Éireann (RTE) v Commission* [1995] ECR 1-743, [1995] 4 CMLR 718, ECJ.
5 Case 27/76 *United Brands Co v Commission* [1978] ECR 207, [1978] 1 CMLR 429, ECJ.
6 Commission 7th Report on Competition Policy, point 131 (*Billiton and Metal & Thermit*).
7 Case 126/80 *Salonia v Poidomani* [1981] ECR 1563, [1982] 1 CMLR 64, ECJ.
8 Case 90/76 *Van Ameyde v Srl Ufficio Centrale Italiano diAssistenza Assicurativa Automobilisti* [1977] ECR 1091, [1977] 2 CMLR 478, ECJ.

[305]
The limitation of the provision of services may also amount to an abuse of a dominant position, where an undertaking has been entrusted with an exclusive right but is manifestly not in a position to satisfy the demand for that service and where the effective exercise of those activities has been rendered impossible by provisions of law.[1]

1 See C-41/90 *Hofner v Macrotron GmbH* [1991] ECR I-1979, [1993] 4 CMLR 306, ECJ. See also Commission Decision (EEC) 90/16 [1990] OJ L10/47 (*NEDS Express Deliveries*).

13. Restricting parallel trade between Member States

[306]
It is an abuse for an undertaking in a dominant position to use that position to restrict trade between Member States.[1] Even if an undertaking in a dominant position may not be under an obligation to facilitate imports or exports, once it had allowed such a trade to develop, it is an abuse for that undertaking to act or omit to act so as to inhibit such trade.[2] Moreover, such an undertaking cannot rely on its selection distribution system (even if exempted by the Commission) to create barriers to parallel trade.[3]

1 See generally Case 26/75 *General Motors Continental NV v Commission* [1975] ECR 1367, [1976] 1 CMLR 95, ECJ; Case 102/77 *Hoffmann-La Roche & Co AG v Centrafarm Vertriebsgesellschaft Pharmazeutischer Erzeugnisse mbH* [1978] ECR 1139, [1978] 3 CMLR 217, ECJ. See also Commission Decision (EEC) 75/74 [1975] OJ L29/11 (*Duro-Dyne – Europair*).
2 See *Deutsche Post AG – Interception of cross border mail* [2001] OJ L331/40, [2002] 4 CMLR 598; Case T-139/98 *Amministrazione Autonoma dei Monopoli dello Stato v Commission* [2001] ECR II-3413.
3 Case 226/84 *British Leyland plc v Commission* [1986] ECR 3263, [1987] 1 CMLR 185, ECJ.

14. Other unfair trading conditions

[307]
An abuse of a dominant position may consist in directly or indirectly imposing other unfair trading conditions.[1] The fact that an undertaking entrusted with the exploitation of copyrights and occupying a dominant position imposes on its members obligations which are not absolutely necessary for the attainment of its object and, thus, which encroach unfairly upon a member's freedom, may constitute an abuse by imposing unfair trading conditions.[2] It would be an abuse for an undertaking with monopoly rights to impose unfair conditions on users of its services,[3] or for a purchaser in a dominant position to insist that it should have unlimited rights to all inventions of its supplier, under contracts made with it, and an unlimited right to grant licences to third persons, without any additional payment.[4] Other examples of unfair trading conditions would include tying of supplies of certain goods to the sale of other goods,[5] inducing distributors not to fulfil export

orders,[6] frustrating the grant of licences of right,[7] preventing a licensor from using the licensed trade-mark[8] and refusal to honour guarantees.[9] Binding users to the dominant undertaking so as to limit competition by the use of contractual obligations, such as prohibitions on modifying machines, exclusive maintenance and repair services, exclusive supply of spare parts and the obligation to use only products supplied by the dominant undertaking.[10]

1 EC Treaty, Article 82(a). Cf Article 81(1)(a), and paras [91] ff.
2 Case 127/73 *Belgische Radio en Televisie (BRT) v SV SABAM* [1974] ECR 313, [1974] 2 CMLR 238, ECJ.
3 Case 155/73 *Sacchi* [1974] ECR 409, [1974] 2 CMLR 177, ECJ.
4 Commission Communication in *Eurofima* [1973] CMLR D217 (3rd Report on Competition Policy, points 68, 69).
5 See Case T-30/89 *Hilti AG v Commission* [1990] ECR II-163, [1990] 4 CMLR 602, CFI, upheld on appeal in Case C-53/92P [1994] ECR I-667, [1994] 4 CMLR 614, ECJ; Commission Decision (EEC) 88/518 [1988] OJ L284/41, [1990] 4 CMLR 196 (*British Sugar Napier Brown*).
6 Case T-30/89 *Hilti v Commission* [1990] ECR II-163 [1992] 4 CMLR 16, upheld on appeal in Case C-53/92P (see note 5).
7 Case T-30/89 *Hilti v Commission* [1990] ECR II-163 [1992) 4 CMLR 16, CFI, upheld on appeal in Case C-53/92P [1994] ECR 667, [1994] 4 CMLR 614, ECJ.
8 Commission Decision of 4 June 1992, 22nd Commission Report on Competition policy (*Chiquita/Fiffes*); 8th Commission Report on Competition Policy, para 125 (*Bayer/Tanabe*).
9 Case T-30/89 *Hilti v Commission* [1990] ECR II-163, [1992] 4 CMLR 16, CFI, upheld on appeal in Case C-53/92P [1994] ECR 667, [1994] 4 CMLR 614, ECJ.
10 Commission Decision (EEC) 92/163 [1992] OJ L72/1 (*Tetra Pak II*), upheld on appeal by the CFI in Case T-83/91 *Tetra Pak International SA v Commission* [1994] ECR II-755, and by the ECJ in Case C-333/94P [1996] ECR I-5951.

15. Other abuses

[308]

The list of potential abuses grows with the case law of the CFI and ECJ. It could be an abuse for a dominant undertaking to place unfair economic pressure on its dealers[1] or competitors.[2] It could also be an abuse for a dominant undertaking having monopoly or virtual monopoly power, to grant exclusive rights to one undertaking and so to exclude any other undertaking from entering into that market.[3] The acquisition of an exclusive licence by a dominant undertaking though not per se an abuse, could constitute an abuse if it has an anti-competitive effect.[4] An undertaking can abuse its dominant position through vexatious litigation.[5] It may be an abuse for a dominant undertaking to purchase a competitor's product and replace it on the shop shelf with its own.[6]

1 Joined Cases 40-48, 50, 54-56, 111, 113, 114/73 *Coöperatieve vereniging Suiker Unie UA v Commission* [1975] ECR 1663 at 1964, [1976] 1 CMLR 295 at 442, ECJ, where the Court emphasised the 'extremely hard-hearted way' in which this was done in a situation of unforeseen difficulties.
2 Case 62/86 *Akzo Chemie BV v Commission* [1991] ECR I-3359, [1993] 5 CMLR 215, ECJ.
3 See Commission Communications in *Football League TV* (Commission 9th Report on Competition Policy, point 116). It would seem that in such a situation of extreme market power there could be a positive duty to deal with all comers, and to do so on equal terms. In this respect, a comparison should be made with the US law on 'bottleneck' monopolies: see for example *US v Terminal RR Assu* 224 US 383, *Associated Press v US* 326 US 1, *Otter Tail Power Co v US* 410 US 366.
4 Case T-51/89 *Tetra Pak Rausing SA v Commission* [1990] ECR II-309, [1991] 4 CMLR 334, CFI.

5 Case T-111/96 *ITT Promedia NV v Commission* [1998] ECR II-2937.
6 Case T-228/97 *Irish Sugar v Commission* [1999] ECR II-2969, upheld on appeal Case C-497/99P *Irish Sugar v Commission* [2001] ECR I-5333.

16. Duration of abuse

[309]
It would seem that in certain situations conduct which could have become an abuse if it had been continued would not be an abuse if it was quickly terminated. Thus where conduct was terminated immediately upon complaints being received and the dominant undertaking reimbursed the complainants, and did so before the Commission commenced investigations, the conduct was not regarded as an abuse.[1] Less than total and immediate compliance will not prevent the conduct amounting to an abuse.[2]

1 Case 26/75 *General Motors Continental NV v Commission* [1975] ECR 1367, [1976] 1 CMLR 95, ECJ.
2 Case 226/84 *British Leyland plc v Commission* [1986] ECR 3263, [1987] 1 CMLR 185, ECJ.

17. Abuse and mergers

[310]
Abuse may occur if an undertaking in a dominant position strengthens such position in such a way that the degree of dominance so reached substantially fetters competition. This strengthening may occur if an undertaking thereby obtains a position so dominant that the objectives of the EC Treaty are circumvented by an alteration to the supply structure which seriously endangers the consumer's freedom of action in the market, and such a situation exists if practically all competition is eliminated, or if the only other undertakings left in the market are those whose behaviour depends on the dominant undertaking.[1]

1 Case 6/72 *Europemballage Corpn and Continental Can Co Inc v Commission* [1973] ECR 215, [1973] CMLR 199, ECJ; Joined Cases 142, 156/84 *British American Tobacco Co Ltd and R J Reynolds Industries Inc v Commission* [1986] ECR 1899, [1987] 2 CMLR 551, ECJ. See also Commission Decision (EEC) 93/252 [1993] OJ L116/21 (*Gillette*). See also Commission Decision (EEC) 88/501 [1988] OJ L272/27, [1990] 4 CMLR 47 (*Tetra Pak I*), on appeal Case T-51/89 *Tetra Pak Rausing SA v Commission* [1990] ECR II-309, [1991] 4 CMLR 334, CFI. See, Cases C-12/03P *Commission v Tetra Laval* [2005] 4 CMLR 8 where the ECJ dismissed the Commission's appeal against the judgment of the CFI in Case T-5/02 *Tetra Laval v Commission* [2002] ECR II-4381, by which the CFI annulled Commission Decision 2001/124/EC of 30 October 2001 declaring a concentration to be incompatible with the common market and the EEA Agreement (Case No COMP/M.2416 – *Tetra Laval/Sidel*). The CFI concluded that the Commission had failed to fulfil its obligation to establish that the potential leveraging by the merged entity would lead to the creation or strengthening of a dominant position on the relevant markets. As regards the Commission's claim that '[Tetra's] current dominant position in carton packaging' would be strengthened by the elimination of a source of constraints on competition from neighbouring markets as a result of the elimination of competition, the CFI held that the Commission had to prove that strengthening, which cannot be inferred automatically from the fact that there is a dominant position. It found that the Commission had failed to provide such proof (paras 15 and 16 of the ECJ's judgment).

D. AFFECTING TRADE BETWEEN MEMBER STATES

1. Inter-State trade

[311]

The requirement in the prohibition on abuse of dominant positions that trade between Member States be affected[1] is intended to define the sphere of application of Community law in relation to national law.[2] It also means that Article 82 of the EC Treaty covers not only abuse which may directly prejudice consumers but also abuse which indirectly prejudices them by impairing the effective competitive structure as envisaged by Article 3(1)(g),[3] or has such a potential.[4] Trade between Member States is affected if the conduct has the effect of diverting the movement of goods from their normal commercial channels, taking into account the economic and technical factors peculiar to the sector in question,[5] or if the competitive structure within the Community is distorted.[6] In establishing whether conduct can be regarded as adversely affecting inter-State trade, it is not necessary to establish specifically what effects the conduct has at present on the value of such trade for it is sufficient that the conduct may affect such trade.[7]

1 EC Treaty, Article 82. As to trade, see para [37], [77] and [155]. See, in particular, the Commission Notice Guidelines on the effect of trade concept contained in Articles 81 and 82 EC.
2 Joined Cases 6, 7/73 *Istituto Chemioterapico italiano SpA and Commercial Solvents Corpn v Commission* [1974] ECR 223, [1974] 1 CMLR 309, ECJ; Case 85/76 *Hoffmann-La Roche & Co AG v Commission* [1979] ECR 461, [1979] 3 CMLR 211, ECJ; Joined Cases 253/78 and 1-3/79 *Procureur do la République v Giry and Guerlain SA* [1980] ECR 2327, [1981] 2 CMLR 99, ECJ; Case 22/79 *Greenwich Film Production v SACEM* [1979] ECR 3275, [1980] 1 CMLR 629, ECJ; Case 7/82 *GVL v Commission* [1983] ECR 483, [1983] 3 CMLR 645, ECJ. See also Case T-69/89 *Radio Telefís Éireann v Commission* [1991] ECR II-485, [1991] 4 CMLR 586, CFI; Case T-70/89 *British Broadcasting Corpn and BBC Enterprises Ltd v Commission* [1991] ECR II-535, [1991] 4 CMLR 669, CFI; Case T-76/89 *Independent Television Publications Ltd v Commission* [1991] ECR II-575, [1991] 4 CMLR 745, CFI.
3 Joined Cases 6, 7/73 *Istituto Chemioterapico Italiano SpA and Commercial Solvents Corpn v Commission* [1974] ECR 223, [1974] 1 CMLR 309, ECJ. As to EC Treaty, Article 3(1)(g), see para [184], note 1.
4 Case 322/81 *Nederlandsche Banden-Industrie Michelin NV v Commission* [1983] ECR 3461, [1985] 1 CMLR 282, ECJ and Case C-41/90 *Hofner v Macroton GmbH* [1991] ECR I-1979, [1993] 3 CMLR 306, ECJ.
5 Case 22/78 *Hugin Kassaregister AB v Commission* [1979] ECR 1869, [1979] 3 CMLR 345, ECJ. See eg Commission Decision (EEC) 84/379 [1984] OJ L207/11, [1984] 3 CMLR 92 (*BL*).
6 Joined Cases 6, 7/73 *Istituto Chemioterapico Italiano SpA and Commercial Solvents Corpn v Commission* [1974] ECR 223, [1974] 1 CMLR 309, ECJ; Case 30/87 *Bodson v Pompes funèbres des regions libérées SA* [1988] ECR 2479, [1989] 4 CMLR 984, ECJ.
7 Case 226/84 *British Leyland plc v Commission* [1986] ECR 3263, [1987] 1 CMLR 185, ECJ; Case 322/81 *Nederlandsche Banden-Industrie Michelin NV v Commission* [1983] ECR 3461, [1985] 1 CMLR 282, ECJ; Case 30/87 *Bodson v Pompes funèbres des regions libérées SA* [1988] ECR 2479, [1989] 4 CMLR 984, ECJ; Case T-69/89 *Radio Telefís Éireann v Commission* [1991] ECR II-485, [1991] 4 CMLR 586, CFI; Case T-70/89 *British Broadcasting Corpn and BBC Enterprises Ltd v Commission* [1991] ECR II-535, [1991] 4 CMLR 669, CFI; Case T-76/89 *Independent Television Publications Ltd v Commission* [1991] ECR II-575, [1991] 4 CMLR 745, CFI.

[312]

Trade between Member States would be affected if, for example, the management of the undertaking is conducted in such a way as to partition the common market and thereby to restrict the freedom to provide services which is one of the objectives of the Treaty,[1] or by charging different prices in different countries,[2] or by protecting national production.[3] If a competitor in the Community is likely to be eliminated, it does not matter whether the conduct will affect that competitor's exports from the Community or its trade within the Community,[4] or whether the behaviour relates to trade between Member States.[5] In addition, in relation to contracts concerning third countries, it is necessary to consider all the activities of the dominant undertaking in question and not only those particular contracts in isolation, in order to determine whether trade between Member States is affected by the conduct in question.[6] Trade is equally affected when the holder of a dominant position in a Member State obstructs access to the market by competitors, and it makes no difference whether the conduct is confined to a single Member State, as long as it is capable of affecting patterns of trade and competition in the common market.[7] Trade between Member States would also be affected if provisions in contracts between a dominant supplier and customers had the effect of restricting imports from other Member States, thus partitioning the market.[8] On the other hand, trade would not be affected if the products in question would not normally be the subject matter of interstate trade, even if the market conditions were absolutely free.[9]

1 Case 22/79 *Greenwich Film Production v SACEM* [1979] ECR 3275, [1980] 1 CMLR 629, ECJ; Case 7/82 *GVL v Commission* [1983] ECR 483, [1983] 3 CMLR 645, ECJ.
2 Case 85/76 *Hoffmann-La Roche & Co AG v Commission* [1979] ECR 461, [1979] 3 CMLR 211, ECJ.
3 Case 126/80 *Salonia v Poidomani* [1981] ECR 1563, [1982] 1 CMLR 64, ECJ.
4 Joined Cases 6, 7/73 *Istituto Chemioterapico Italiano SpA and Commercial Solvents Corpn v Commission* [1974] ECR 223, [1974] 1 CMLR 309, ECJ; Case 22/79 *Greenwich Film Production v SACEM* [1979] ECR 3275, [1980] 1 CMLR 629, ECJ.
5 Case 27/76 *United Brands Co v Commission* [1978] ECR 207, [1978] 1 CMLR 429, ECJ.
6 Case 22/79 *Greenwich Film Production v SACEM* [1979] ECR 3275, [1980] 1 CMLR 629, ECJ.
7 Case 322/81 *Nederlandsche Banden-Industrie Michelin NV v Commission* [1983] ECR 3461, [1985] 1 CMLR 282, ECJ. Case T-30/89 *Hilti AG v Commission* [1990] ECR II-163, [1990] 4 CMLR 602, CFI.
8 Case 247/86 *Société alsacienne et lorraine de telecommunications et d'électronique (Alsatel) v Novasam SA* [1988] ECR 5987, [1990] 4 CMLR 434, ECJ.
9 Case 22/78 *Hugin Kassaregister AB v Commission* [1979] ECR 1869, [1979] 3 CMLR 345, ECJ.

2. Trade and other activities

[313]
The requirement in the prohibition on abuse of dominant position, that trade be affected,[1] does not mean that Article 82 of the EC Treaty is restricted to trade and industrial activities.[2] Article 82 has been applied to many services, such as telephone and telex services,[3] employee agencies,[4] insurance,[5] banking,[6] copyright collecting societies,[7] television advertising,[8] type approvals for motor cars,[9] film distribution[10] and newspaper distribution,[11] funeral services,[12] and port activities.[13]

1 EC Treaty, Article 82.
2 Joined Cases 6, 7/73 *Istituto Chemioterapico Italiano SpA and Commercial Solvents Corpn v Commission* [1974] ECR 223, [1974] 1 CMLR 309, ECJ.
3 Commission Decision (EEC) 82/861 [1982] OJ L360/36, [1983] 1 CMLR 457 (*British Telecommunications*), upheld on appeal in Case 41/83 *Italy v Commission* [1985] ECR 873, [1985] 2 CMLR 368, ECJ.
4 Case C-41/90 *Hofner v Macroton GmbH* [1991] ECR I-1979, [1993] 3 CMLR 306, ECJ.

5 Case 90/76 *Van Ameyde v Srl Ufficio Centrale Italiano di Assistenza Assicurativa Automobilisti* [1977] ECR 1091, [1977] 2 CMLR 478, ECJ.
6 Case 172/80 *Zuchner v Bayerische Vereinsbank AG* [1981] ECR 2021, [1982] 1 CMLR 313, ECJ.
7 Case 7/82 *GVL v Commission* [1983] ECR 483, [1983] 3 CMLR 645, ECJ.
8 Case 155/73 *Sacchi* [1974] ECR 409, [1974] 2 CMLR 177, ECJ.
9 Case 26/75 *General Motors Continental NV v Commission* [1975] ECR 1367, [1976] 1 CMLR 95, ECJ and Case 226/84 *British Leyland plc v Commission* [1986] ECR 3263, [1987] 1 CMLR 185, ECJ.
10 Case 22/79 *Greenwich Film Production v SACEM* [1979] ECR 3275, [1980] 1 CMLR 629, ECJ.
11 Case 126/80 *Salonia v Poidomani* [1981] ECR 1563, [1982] 1 CMLR 64, ECJ.
12 Case 30/87 *Bodson v Pompes funèbres des regions libérées SA* [1988] ECR 2479, [1989] 4 CMLR 984, ECJ.
13 Case C-179/90 *Merci Convenzionali Porto di Genova Spa v Siderurgica Gabrielli SpA* [1991] ECR 1-5889, [1994] 4 CMLR 422, ECJ; Case C-18/93 *Corsica Ferries* [1994] ECR I-1783, ECJ; Commission Decision (EC) 94/19 [1994] OJ L15/8, [1995] 4 CMLR 84 (*Containers/Stena Sealink*); *Commission Decision* (EC) 94/119 [1994] OJ L55/52, [1994] 5 CMLR 457 (*Port of Rødby*); Irish *Continental Group v CCI Mortaix* (Case IV/35.388) [1995] 5 CMLR 177.

5
STATE INVOLVEMENT AND THE APPLICATION OF THE RULES ON COMPETITION

A. ARTICLE 86

1. The provisions of Article 86

[314]
Article 86 provides:

> (1) In the case of public undertakings and undertakings to which Member States grant special or exclusive rights, Member States shall neither enact nor maintain in force any measure contrary to the rules contained in the Treaty, in particular to those rules provided for in Article 12 and Articles 81 to 89.
>
> (2) Undertakings entrusted with the operation of services of general economic interest or having the character of a revenue-producing monopoly shall be subject to the rules contained in this Treaty, in particular to the rules on competition, in so far as the application of such rules does not obstruct the performance, in law or in fact, of the particular tasks assigned to them. The development of trade must not be affected to such an extent as would be contrary to the interests of the Community.
>
> (3) The Commission shall ensure the application of the provisions of this Article and shall, where necessary, address appropriate directives or decisions to Member States.

[315]
Each sub-paragraph of Article 86 performs a different function. The Article applies to particular types of undertakings having links with the State which enable the State to play a part in determining the conditions under which those undertakings carry out their economic activities.[1]

(1) Article 86(1) contains a prohibition addressed to Member States, setting out the duty of Member States not to take measures in its relationships with public undertakings or undertakings to which Member States have granted

special or exclusive rights, which are detrimental to the effective application of the Treaty rules on, amongst other things, competition.

(2) Article 86(2) provides a limited exemption for certain types of undertakings from the application of the Treaty rules including, once again, the competition rules. Article 86(2) applies to those undertakings falling within Article 86(1), as well as to undertakings entrusted with the operation of services of general economic interest and to undertakings having the character of a revenue producing monopoly.

(3) Article 86(3) gives the Commission powers to take individual decisions, and to adopt specific legislation, to ensure that Member States comply with the provisions of Article 86. These powers, particularly the power to adopt legislation, have been used extensively by the Commission to liberalise certain industries throughout the Community and, in particular, to bring about liberalisation in the telecommunications industry.

1 Also international organisations: see Case C-364/92 *SAT Fluggesellschaft mbH v Eurocontrol* [1994] ECR I-43, [1994] 5 CMLR 208, ECJ (although the Court held that the functions carried out by Eurocontrol were not economic activities).

2. The purpose of Article 86 and the relevance of Articles 3(g) and 10 of the Treaty

[316]
Article 86(1) ensures that there is no possibility of avoiding the application of the Treaty rules by virtue of State interference in the economic activities of an undertaking. It ensures, in particular, that the rules on competition are respected. The obligations in Article 86 stem ultimately from Article 3(g) of the EC Treaty which states that the 'activities of the Community shall include ... (g) a system ensuring that competition in the internal market is not distorted'.[1] The Commission's powers in Article 86(3) to control State interference in economic activities in individual cases, and to introduce legislation prohibiting certain types of State interference in individual fields, similarly arise from Article 3(g) of the Treaty.

1 In Case 13/77 *NV GB-INNO-BM v ATAB* [1977] ECR 2115, [1978] 1 CMLR 283, ECJ, the Court referred in paras 28 and 29 to the general objectives of the Treaty as excluding any national system of regulation which hinders trade within the Community, and to the fact that the general obligation in Article 3(g) is 'made specific' in several Treaty provisions concerning the rules on competition. Article 86 is one such provision. See also Case T-54/99 *Maxmobil v Commission* [2002] ECR II-313 at para 52 (on appeal Case C-141/02P *Commission v T-Mobil Austria*, 22 February 2005).

[317]
Article 86(2) recognises that, in some cases, the full application of the Treaty rules needs to be tempered so that legitimate objectives pursued by States can be achieved. The Treaty rules, including the competition rules contained in Articles 81 and 82, would normally apply with full force to the types of undertakings described in Article 86 (although the competition rules do not apply to the State itself). Article 86(2) relaxes the normal application of the Treaty in the case of such undertakings in certain situations. It is capable of being invoked not only by undertakings but also by

Member States themselves in relation to the measures they have enacted or maintained in force which would otherwise fall within Article 86(1).[1]

1 Case C-203/96 *Chemische Afvalstoffen Dusseldorp BV and Others v Minister van Volkshuisvesting, Ruimtelijke Ordening en Milieubeheer* [1998] ECR I-4075, [1998] 3 CMLR 873, ECJ.

[318]

The Court of Justice has held that the obligations of Member States under Article 86(1) are the specific application of a general duty which binds Member States in Article 10 of the EC Treaty.[1] Under Article 10 EC Member States must take all appropriate measures, whether general or particular, to ensure fulfilment of the obligations arising out of the EC Treaty or resulting from action taken by the institutions of the Community, must facilitate the achievement of the Community's task and must abstain from any measure which could jeopardise the attainment of the objectives of the Treaty.

1 See eg Case 13/77 *NV GB-INNO-BM v ATAB* [1977] ECR 2115; [1978] 1 CMLR 283, ECJ; Case C-260/89 *Elliniki Radiophonia Tileorasi (ERT) v DEP* [1991] ECR I-2925, [1994] 4 CMLR 540, ECJ; Case C-320/91 *Corbeau* [1993] ECR I-2533, [1995] 4 CMLR 621, ECJ.

[319]

In the first years of the application of Article 86(1) it was suggested that that there was no relevant distinction between Member States' obligations under Article 86(1) and their obligations under Article 10. If correct, this would have limited the practical importance of Article 86(1) as a separate provision, and would have made it unnecessary to consider whether not the conditions of Article 86(1) were met or whether the undertakings in question needed to enjoy special or exclusive rights.[1] The Court of Justice has nevertheless in practice applied Article 86(1) over many years mainly in conjunction with Article 82 without resorting to the independent use of Article 10. The Court of Justice has explained that Article 10 cannot be applied independently whenever the situation is governed by a specific provision of the Treaty such as Article 86(1).[2] However, Article 10 has been used frequently in conjunction with Article 81.[3]

1 See the previous edition of this title at para 19.137.
2 Case C-323/93 *Société Agricole du Centre d'Insémination de la Crespelle v Cooperative d'Elevage et d'Insemination Artificielle du Département de la Mayenne* [1994] ECR I-5077, ECJ at para 15; Joined Cases C-78/90 to C-83/90 *Compagnie Commerciale de l'Ouest and Others* [1992] ECR I-1847 at para 19.
3 See paras [380] to [387] below.

3. Balancing competing interests

[320]

In Article 86 cases a balance has to be struck between the freedom of Member States to make political, social and economic choices about the conditions under which economic activities are to be carried out on the one hand, and the goal of ensuring the universal application of the Treaty rules on the other. The degree to which Member States are free to make such choices is central to Article 86.[1]

1 D Edward and M Hoskins, 'Article 90: Deregulation and EC Law. Reflections Arising from the XVI FIDE Conference' (1995) 32 CMLRev 157.

[321]
At one end of the spectrum, the activities of Member States, even where they are carried out by private-law entities on Member States' behalf, fall outside the field of economic activity altogether. Such activities have traditionally been reserved to and have been carried out by Member States. The bodies carrying out those activities are not undertakings. They are therefore not subject to Article 86, nor to the other competition provisions of the Treaty. A number of Article 86 cases have turned on whether the State involvement in question fell within the sphere of economic activity at all. At the opposite end of the spectrum, certain economic activities have been been the subject of Community legislation to liberalise certain industries using Article 86(3). In those areas State freedom of action has been very significantly curtailed, with the Commission deciding on the extent to which exclusive or special rights may be conferred in a particular industry. In between these two extremes lie those cases where the State pursues its objectives by granting exclusive or special rights to undertakings, or by entrusting them with specific tasks, and, in doing so, protects them from the normal rigours of competition to a greater or lesser degree.

4. Requirement to apply Article 86(1) in conjunction with another Treaty provision

[322]
Article 86(1) can only apply in conjunction with one or more other articles of the Treaty. It cannot apply on its own. There are no limits as to which other Treaty articles can be used in conjunction with Article 86(1). However, Article 86(1) refers 'in particular' to Article 12 (non-discrimination) and to Articles 81 to 89 (competition and State aid rules). The emphasis given to these articles shows the significance Article 86(1) has for competition law, as does its position in the Treaty. Article 86 occupies a position between the competition rules applying to private undertakings (Articles 81 and 82) and the rules relating to State intervention in the form of State aids (Articles 87 to 89).

[323]
Although this section concentrates on competition law, Article 86 has also been applied in conjunction with other Treaty articles. Examples include Article 28 on free movement of goods,[1] Article 39 on free movement of workers,[2] Article 43 on freedom of establishment[3] and Article 49 on freedom to provide services.[4]

1 Case C-18/88 *RTT v GB-Inno-BM* [1991] ECR I-5941, ECJ.
2 Case C-179/90 *Merci Convenzionali Porto di Genova SpA v Siderurgica Gabrielli SpA* [1991] ECR I-5889, [1994] 4 CMLR 422, ECJ.
3 Case 33/74 *Van Binsbergen v Bestuur van de Bedrijfsvereniging voor de Metaalnijverheid* [1974] ECR 1299, ECJ
4 Case 2/74 *Reyners v Belgium* [1974] ECR 631; Case 13/76 *Dona v Montera* [1976] ECR 1333; Case C-260/89 *Elliniki Radiophonia Tileorasi (ERT) v DEP* [1991] ECR I-2925, [1994] 4 CMLR 540, ECJ.

5. Article 86 and direct effect

[324]
Article 86(1) has direct effect only when it is read together with another provision of the Treaty also having direct effect.[1] Individuals therefore have the right to rely upon those provisions as against other parties, including other individuals.[2] Courts must

give effect to those provisions as part of Community law.[3] The result is that any national law or measure which infringes Article 86 will be held to be inapplicable. It may be possible to sever those infringing parts of the law or measure from the remainder which does not infringe Article 86.[4]

1 See Case C-179/90 *Merci Convenzionali Porto di Genova SpA v Siderurgica Gabrielli SpA* [1991] ECR I-5889, [1994] 4 CMLR 422, ECJ at para 23; Case C-242/95 *GT-Link A/S v Danske Staatsbaner (DSB)* [1997] ECR I-4449, [1997] 5 CMLR 601, ECJ at para 57, Case C-22/98 *Becu* [1999] ECR I-5665, [2001] 4 CMLR 968 at para 21; Case C-258/98 *Giovanni Carra* [2000] ECR I-4217 at para 11.

2 Case C-41/90 *Hofner & Elser v Macroton* [1991] ECR I-1979, [1993] 4 CMLR 396, ECJ in which Article 86(1) was relied upon as a defence in proceedings between individual parties.

3 Case 155/73 *Sacchi* [1974] ECR 409, [1974] 2 CMLR 177, ECJ; Case C-18/88 *RTT v GB-Inno-BM* [1991] ECR I-5941, ECJ; Case C-179/90 *Merci Convenzionali Porto di Genova SpA v Siderurgica Gabrielli SpA* [1991] ECR I-5889, [1994] 4 CMLR 422, ECJ; Case C-67/96 *Albany International BV v Stichting Bedrijspensioenfonds Textilindustrie* [1999] ECR I-5751, [2000] 4 CMLR 446, ECJ, Advocate General Jacobs at para 472.

4 See para 480 of the Advocate General's Opinion in Case C-67/96 *Albany International BV v Stichting Bedrijspensioenfonds Textilindustrie* [1999] ECR I-5751, [2000] 4 CMLR 446, ECJ.

B. ARTICLE 86(1)

1. Article 86(1) only applies to certain types of undertaking

[325]

(a) General: Article 86 only applies to those undertakings with a qualifying connection with a Member State, namely 'public undertakings' and undertakings to which a Member State has granted 'special or exclusive rights'. These concepts are not defined anywhere in the Treaty. In order to interpret them it is therefore necessary to look at the case law of the Court of Justice and at other provisions, in particular, Commission legislation on related subjects.

[326]

(b) The meaning of 'undertaking': Articles 86(1) and 86(2) refer in several places to 'undertakings'. The word 'undertaking' bears the same meaning in those paragraphs as that given to it by the case-law relating to other Treaty articles.[1] 'Undertaking' is a Community law concept to be interpreted by the Court of Justice, and not by national courts according to their own rules. An entity's legal status under national rules and the way in which it is financed do not affect the question of whether it is an undertaking for the purposes of the Treaty.[2] The Court of Justice has consistently adopted a functional approach to the task of identifying an undertaking. Whether an entity is an 'undertaking' is determined entirely by reference to whether or not it is engaged in an economic activity. Those who perform work for undertakings have been classified as workers and not therefore as undertakings in their own right.[3] It is not necessary for the body carrying out the activities to have a separate legal identity from the State for Article 86(1) to apply. It is enough that the activity is being carried out by a public authority.[4]

1 As to the meaning of undertaking under Article 81, see paras [52]–[58] above.

2 See Case C-41/90 *Hofner & Elser v Macroton* [1991] ECR I-1979, [1993] 4 CMLR 396, ECJ at para 21; Joined Cases C-159/91 and C-160/91 *Poucet and Pistre* [1993] ECR I-637, at para 17; Case C-343/95 *Diego Cali* [1997] ECR I-1547 at paras 16, 18; Case C-67/96 *Albany International BV v Stichting Bedrijspensioenfonds Textilindustrie* [1999] ECR I-5751, [2000] 4 CMLR 446, ECJ at para

77; Case C-475/99 *Ambulanz Glockner v Landkreis Sudwestpfalz* [2001] ECR 8089, [2002] 4 CMLR 726, ECJ at para 19; Joined Cases C-180/98 to C-184/98 *Pavlov and Others* [2000] ECR I-6451 at para 74, Joined Cases C-189/02P, C-205/02P, C-208/02P and C-213/02P *Dansk Rørindustri* [2005] ECR I-000 at para 112. Cases-264/01, 06/01, 354/01 and 355/01 *AOK Bundesverband v Ichthyol-Gesellschaft Cordes, Hermani & Co* [2004] ECR I-2493 (Advocate General Jacobs at point 25).

3 Case C-22/98 *Becu* [1999] ECR I-5665, [2001] 4 CMLR 968, ECJ at paras 26, 30.

4 Case 118/85 *Commission v Italy* [1987] ECR 2599, ECJ at paras 8 and 10.

[327]
The question of whether an entity is in fact an 'undertaking' arises frequently in Article 86 cases. Where the activities in question are such that they have traditionally formed part of a State's public functions or fulfil a purely social function, then the entity will normally fall outside the definition of an undertaking and Article 86 will not apply. An entity can be regarded as an undertaking for some parts of its activities whilst the rest of its activities fall outside the competition rules.[1]

1 See Cases-264/01, 06/01, 354/01 and 355/01 *AOK Bundesverband v Ichthyol-Gesellschaft Cordes, Hermani & Co* [2004] ECR I-2493 at para 58; for example, the Amministrazione Autonoma dei Monopoli di Stato in Case 118/85 *Commission v Italy* [1987] ECR 2599, at para 7 of the judgment and the Bundesanstalt für Arbeit in Case C-41/90 *Hofner & Elser v Macroton* [1991] ECR I-1979, [1993] 4 CMLR 396, ECJ; see also the Advocate General's Opinion in Case C-475/99 *Ambulanz Glockner v Landkreis Sudwestpfalz* [2001] ECR 8089, [2002] 4 CMLR 726, ECJ at para 72; and Case T-128/1998 *Aeroports de Paris v Commission* [2000] ECR II-3929 at para 108.

[328]
(c) Cases where the activity is not economic: In a number of Article 86 cases particular activities have been held to be typically associated with the exercise of a public authority's powers and to fall outside the definition of 'undertaking'. For example, the Court has held that the activities of a company which had been granted an exclusive concession to carry out pollution surveillance in the port of Genoa were activities connected with the protection of the environment and therefore typically those of a public authority.[1] Similarly, it has held that an international organisation, which established and collected charges levied on users of air navigation services as a result of multilateral agreements and paid the charges (less a collection fee) to the States which had signed those agreements, was not an undertaking. The control and supervision of air space was held to be typically associated with the powers of a public authority.[2] The test applied by the Court of Justice is whether the activity in question is connected by its nature, its aims and the rules to which it is subject with the exercise of powers which are typically those of a public authority.

1 Case C-343/95 *Diego Cali* [1997] ECR I-1547 at para 23.

2 Case C-364/92 *SAT Fluggesellschaft mbH v Eurocontrol* [1994] ECR I-43, [1994] 5 CMLR 208, ECJ at paras 30, 31.

[329]
Certain organisations running compulsory social security schemes have been held not to be undertakings.[1] The Spanish National Health Service was not an undertaking.[2] Nor was a body operating a system of compulsory insurance for workers against accidents at work and occupational diseases.[3] In *AOK* the Court held that German sickness funds providing statutory health insurance were not undertakings because they fulfilled an exclusively social function and were entirely

non-profit making.[4] Similarly, the task of authorising others to carry out certain activities is unlikely to amount to carrying on an economic activity.[5] The activity of authorising the opening of tobacco outlets and controlling their number and distribution is not an economic activity.[6]

1 Case C-159-160/91 *Poucet and Pistre v Assuramces Generales de France* [1993] ECR I-637.

2 Case T-319/99 *FENIN* [2003] ECR II-351; appealed to the ECJ in Case C-205/03P (the Advocate General's Opinion was delivered on 10 November 2005).

3 Case C-218/00 *Cisal di Battistello Venanzio & C. Sas and Instituto nazionale per l'assicurazione contro gli infortuni sul lavoro (INAIL)* [2002] ECR I-691, [2002] 4 CMLR 24, ECJ.

4 Cases-264/01, 06/01, 354/01 and 355/01 *AOK Bundesverband v Ichthyol-Gesellschaft Cordes, Hermani & Co* [2004] ECR I-2493.

5 Advocate General Jacobs in Case C-475/99 *Ambulanz Glockner v Landkreis Sudwestpfalz* [2001] ECR 8089, [2002] 4 CMLR 726, ECJ, took the view that a decision-making activity of granting or refusing an authorisation to perform public ambulance services was a typical administrative decision usually reserved for public authorities and not an economic activity. Cf Case C 41/83 *Italy v Commission* [1985] ECR 873 at paras 19 and 20.

6 See Case 387/93 *Banchero* [1995] ECR I-4663 at para 49.

[330]

(d) Cases where the activity is economic: In other cases the Court has held that the activities in question were economic in nature. Employment procurement and recruiting activities have been held to be economic activities.[1] In *Hofner and Elser* the Court said that the fact that such activities were normally entrusted to public agencies could not affect the economic nature of such activities. Similarly, the placement of employees in jobs has been held to be an economic activity and a public placement office has been classed as an undertaking.[2] A non-profit making sectoral pension fund has been held to be an undertaking,[3] as has an occupational pension fund with compulsory membership set up by a profession's representative body.[4] In each case the fund operated in some respects in the same manner as, and in competition with, authorised insurance companies, notwithstanding the fact that it also fulfilled a social function. The management and operation of airports in Paris for commercial fees has been held to be the carrying on of an economic activity. The existence of a system of special supervision of publicly owned property was not incompatible with the provision of economic services.[5]

1 See Case C-41/90 *Hofner & Elser v Macroton* [1991] ECR I-1979, [1993] 4 CMLR 396, ECJ at paras 21, 22.

2 See Case C-55/96 *Job Centre* [1997] ECR I-7140, [1998] 4 CMLR 708, ECJ at paras 21-25.

3 Case C-67/99 *Albany International BV v Stichting Bedrijspensioenfonds Textilindustrie* [1999] ECR I-5751, [2000] 4 CMLR 446 at paras 84 and 85; Joined Cases C-115/97 to C-117/97 *Brentjens* [1999] ECR I-6025 at paras 82-87.

4 Joined Cases C-180/98 to C-184/98 *Pavlov* [2000] ECR I-6451 at paras 115, 116.

5 Case T-128/98 *Aeroports de Paris v Commission* [2000] ECR II-3929 at paras 120, 125.

[331]

Performing waste management functions for a municipality is an economic activity.[1] In *Ambulanz Glockner* the Court held that non-profit making medical aid organisations to whom the operation of a medical ambulance service had been assigned by the administrative districts responsible for such services were undertakings, when they carried out the provision of emergency transport services and non-emergency patient transfer services.[2] The Court took into account the fact that such activities have not always been, and are not necessarily, carried on by such organisations or by public authorities.[3] Further, the fact that public service obligations carried out by medical aid organisations may be less competitive than comparable services provided by other operators not bound by such obligations did not preclude the activities being regarded as economic activities. The Advocate General in *Ambulanz Glockner* commented that it followed from Article 86(1) and (2) and Article 87 that public service obligations, special or exclusive rights, or State financing could not prevent an operator's activities from being regarded as economic activities.[4] Any activity which involves offering goods and services to the market has been held to be an economic activity.[5]

1 Case C-203/96 *Chemische Afvalstoffen Dusseldorp BV and Others v Minister van Volkshuisvesting, Ruimtelijke Ordening en Milieubeheer* [1998] ECR I-4075, [1998] ECR I-4075, ECJ; Case C-209/98 *Enterprenorforeningens Affals Miljosektion (FFAD) acting for Sydhavnens Sten & Grus ApS v Kobenhavns Kommune* [2000] ECR I-3743.
2 Case C-475/99 *Ambulanz Glockner v Landkreis Sudwestpfalz* [2001] ECR 8089, [2002] 4 CMLR 726, ECJ.
3 Ibid, para 20. See also Case C-55/96 *Job Centre* [1997] ECR I-7119, [1998] 4 CMLR 708, ECJ at para 22 where a similar point was made by the Court. See Advocate General Jacob's Opinion in Case C-475/99 *Ambulanz Glockner* at para 68 who suggested that part of the test was whether the goods or services could in principle be carried out by a private actor in order to make profits and his Opinion in Case C-67/99 *Albany International BV v Stichting Bedrijspensioenfonds Textilindustrie* [1999] ECR I-5751, [2000] 4 CMLR 446, ECJ at para 311. See also his Opinions in Cases-264/01, 06/01, 354/01 and 355/01 *AOK Bundesverband v Ichthyol-Gesellschaft Cordes, Hermani & Co* [2004] ECR I-2493 at para 27 and in Case C-222/04 *Misisterio dell'Economia e delle Finaze v Cassa di Risparmio di Firenze SPA and Others* (27 October 2005) at paras 78 and 79. For a detailed review of the principles see the Advocate General's Opinion in Case C-205/03P *FENIN* (10 November 2005) (judgment still awaited at the time of writing).
4 Case C-67/99 *Albany International BV v Stichting Bedrijspensioenfonds Textilindustrie* [1999] ECR I-5751, [2000] 4 CMLR 446, ECJ, Advocate General Jacob's Opinion at para 69.
5 See Case 118/85 *Commission v Italy* [1987] ECR 2599, Case C-35/96 *Commission v Italy* [1998] ECR I- 3851; Case T-513/93 *Consiglio Nazionale degli Spedizionieri Doganali v Commission* [2000] ECR II-1807; Joined Cases C-180/98 to C-184/98 *Pavlov and Others* [2000] ECR I-6451 at para 75; Case T-128/1998 *Aeroports de Paris v Commission* [2000] ECR II-3929 at para 107.

[332]
(e) **Public undertakings:** 'Public undertaking' is a Community concept,[1] which is not defined anywhere in the Treaty. A public undertaking is one owned by the State or one with which the State has strong contractual, financial or structural links, which enable it to exercise control over the undertaking's behaviour.[2] The State does not actually have to exercise the control it has; it is sufficient that it has the ability to do so. Nor does the control have to be direct. It may also arise indirectly, as for instance when control is exercised through entities which are themselves controlled by the State.

1 See para 9 of Advocate General Reichsl's Opinion in Case 188-190/80 *France, Italy and the UK v Commission* [1982] ECR 2545.
2 See the comments of the Advocate General in Case C-463/00 *Commission v Spain* [2003] ECR I-4581 at para 56: '... it may be inferred from a purposive interpretation that the distinction between public and private undertakings, for the purposes of the Treaty, cannot be based merely on the identity of its various shareholders, but depends on the opportunity available to the State to impose specific economic policies other than the pursuit of the greatest financial gain which characterises private business.'

[333]
'Public undertaking' was originally defined by the Commission in a different context in the Transparency Directive.[1] Article 2(1)(b) of the Transparency Directive defines a public undertaking as an undertaking over which the public authorities may exercise, directly or indirectly, a dominant influence by virtue of their ownership of it, their financial participation in it or the rules that govern it. The Article goes on to define what is required for a dominant influence to exist as follows: 'A dominant influence is to be presumed when the public authority holds the major part of the undertaking's subscribed capital, controls the majority of votes attached to the shares issued or can appoint more than half of the members of the undertaking's administrative, managerial or supervisory body.'[2] The Court of Justice subsequently upheld this definition in a case in which it was challenged by a number of Member States[3] and it has been applied by the Court.[4] The Commission applies the test contained in the Transparency Directive when determining whether a body is a 'public undertaking' for the purposes of Article 86.[5]

1 Commission Directive 80/723 [1980] OJ L195/35, as last amended by Commission Directive 2000/52/EC [2000] OJ L193/75.
2 Similar tests have been used in the public procurement context in order to establish the existence of a public body; namely whether or not the finance was wholly or mainly by another contracting authority, whether the body was subject to management supervision by another contracting authority or whether another contracting authority appointed more than half of the board of directors. However, the procurement rules are concerned with bodies established for the specific purpose of meeting needs in the general interest and not having an industrial or commercial character. They would presumably not therefore be classified as undertakings; see the comments of Advocate General Leger in Case C-44/96 *Mannesmann Anlagenbau Austria AG v Strohal Rotationsdruck GmbH* [1998] ECR I-73 at paras 67-69.
3 Cases 188-190/80 *France, Italy and the UK v Commission* [1982] ECR 2545.
4 Case 118/85 *Commission v Italy* [1987] ECR 2599.
5 See the Community Framework for State Aid in the form of public service compensation of 13 July 2005, DGCOMP/D(2005) 179 at footnote 4. For examples of the Commission applying this definition see *GSM Spain* [1997] OJ L76/19 where the Commission noted that the telecommunications company was a public undertaking within the meaning of Article 2 of the Transparency Directive and went on to list the reasons why the State exercised decisive influence over the company, concluding that the company constituted a public undertaking for the purposes of Article 86(1); and see also the recent Commission decision of 20 October 2004 on *German Restrictions on Mail Preparation* at para 42.

[334]
(f) Special or exclusive rights
(i) General: Article 86(1) applies to undertakings which have been granted 'special or exclusive rights'. Again no definition is given in the Treaty.

[335]
(ii) Exclusive rights: The concept of exclusive rights is more familiar that the concept of special rights. Exclusive rights to carry out an economic activity may be granted by the State to public or private undertakings. Where they have been granted to public undertakings Article 86(1) applies in any event, and it is unnecessary to consider separately the question of exclusive rights.[1] However, where the undertaking is a private one, it becomes necessary to consider the meaning of exclusive rights.

1 This was the view taken by the Advocate General in Case C-34/2001 to C-38/2001 *Enirisorse SpA v Ministero delle Finanze* [2003] ECR I-14243 at para 37.

[336]
An exclusive right exists where the State has granted to an undertaking through a legal instrument the sole right, or monopoly, to carry out an economic activity in a particular geographical area. The area can be the whole of a national territory, or part of it.[1] It may be necessary to analyse carefully the legal or regulatory provisions or a number of different instruments to determine whether or not an exclusive right has in fact been conferred, or what the precise extent of that right is.[2]

1 Cases where only a monopoly was conferred over only part of a national territory include Case C-323/93 *Société Agricole du Centre d'Insémination de la Crespelle v Cooperative d'Elevage et d'Insemination Artificielle du Département de la Mayenne* [1994] ECR I-5077, ECJ; Case C-179/90 *Merci Convenzionali Porto di Genova SpA v Siderurgica Gabrielli SpA* [1991] ECR I-5889, [1994] 4 CMLR 422, ECJ; Case 30/87 *Bodson v Pompes Funèbres des Regions Libérées SA* [1988] ECR 2479, [1989] 4 CMLR 984, ECJ; Case C-209/98 E*nterprenorforeningens Affals Miljosektion (FFAD) acting for Sydhavnens Sten & Grus ApS v Kobenhavns Kommune* [2000] ECR I-3743, [2001] 2 CMLR 936. In *La Crespelle* the national legislation not only provided for the authorisation of insemination centres in particular areas, but it also provided that each centre should have the exclusive right to serve a defined area. This created a series of exclusive rights and what the Court referred to as a series of contiguous territorially limited monopolies in the national territory.
2 In Joined Cases C-115/97 to C-117/97 *Brentjens* [1999] ECR I-6025 the Court held that the public authorities' decision to make affiliation to a sectoral pension fund compulsory involved granting that fund an exclusive right to collect and administer pension contributions.

[337]
The corollary of an exclusive right is that no one else is able to carry out the same activity in the same area. In order to qualify as an exclusive right, the ability to carry out an activity will entail the prevention of others from carrying out that same activity, giving the former a competitive advantage over those who have been excluded.[1] In some cases the prohibition on carrying out the same activity may be enforceable by administrative, or even criminal, penalties for encroaching on the monopoly.[2]

1 This is consistent with the approach of the Court in Case C-475/99 *Ambulanz Glockner v Landkreis Sudwestpfalz* [2001] ECR 8089, [2002] 4 CMLR 726, ECJ, in which the Court suggested in the context of special rights that there should be protection given to one undertaking which may substantially affect the ability of other undertakings to exercise the economic activity in question in the same geographical area under substantially equivalent conditions. See also Case 387/93 *Banchero* [1995] ECR I-4663 at where legislation reserved the retail sale of tobacco to authorised traders and merely laid down the conditions which needed to be met in order to obtain access to the market. No exclusive rights were granted because the rules did not confer on any outlet a particular advantage over its competitors. In Case 13/77 *NV GB-INNO_BM v ATAB* [1977] ECR 2115, [1978] 1 CMLR 283, ECJ at para 41 the Court doubted whether a legislative provision which allowed manufacturers and importers of certain products to fix compulsory selling prices to customers created either special or exclusive rights. It held that those producers and manufacturers who could qualify for such rights were an indefinite class and did not enjoy special, and certainly not exclusive, rights.
2 See Case C-320/91 *Corbeau* [1993] I-ECR-2533, [1995] 4 CMLR 621, ECJ; Case C-55/96 *Job Centre* [1997] ECR I-7140, [1998] 4 CMLR 708, ECJ.

[338]
Examples of exclusive rights include the rights granted in *Corsica Ferries* to local mooring groups to carry out mooring operations which prevented shipping companies from using their own staff to carry out such operations,[1] and the Belgian postal monopoly in *Corbeau,*[2] conferring on the Regie des Postes the exclusive right to collect, carry and distribute all correspondence of whatever nature in Belgium. In the Commission decision on *German Restrictions on Mail Preparation* the DPAG had a postal monopoly under German laws covering transport on a commercial basis of certain mail items.[3] In the *Job Centre* case only the public placement offices were allowed to carry out activities as intermediaries between supply and demand on the employment market.[4] In *Merci*[5] and in *Raso*[6] there were monopolies on the supply of labour to other undertakings also authorised to carry out dock work. In *FFAD* only three undertakings were allowed to receive building waste within the municipality of Copenhagen and process it.[7] The Court found that those three undertakings must therefore be regarded as having an exclusive right.[8] In *Dusseldorp*[9] the Netherlands Government argued that AVR Chemie did not have exclusive rights to incinerate dangerous waste in the Netherlands because there was no other undertaking in the Netherlands which was capable of treating waste oil to a sufficiently high standard.[10] The Court held that the documents showed that the AVR Chemie was designated as the sole end-processor for the incineration of dangerous waste and therefore had an exclusive right.[11]

1 Case C-266/96 *Corsica Ferries France SA v Gruppo Antichi Ormeggiatori del Porto di Genova* [1998] ECR I-3949.
2 Case C-320/91 *Corbeau* [1993] I-ECR-2533, [1995] 4 CMLR 621, ECJ.
3 Decision of 20 October 2004 at para 43
4 Case C-55/96 *Job Centre* [1997] ECR I-7140, [1998] 4 CMLR 708, ECJ.
5 Case C-179/90 *Merci Convenzionali Porto di Genova SpA v Siderurgica Gabrielli SpA* [1991] ECR I-5889, [1994] 4 CMLR 422, ECJ.
6 Case 163/96 *Silvano Raso* [1998] ECR I-533, [1998] 4 CMLR 737.
7 Case C-209/98 *Enterprenorforeningens Affals Miljosektion (FFAD) acting for Sydhavnens Sten & Grus ApS v Kobenhavns Kommune* [2000] ECR I-3743, [2001] 2 CMLR 936.
8 This is odd since none of them enjoyed the sole right to carry on the activity although they were one of a group of three who could do so. The explanation may be simply that the Court used the expression 'exclusive rights' as a short hand expression for 'special or exclusive rights'. There seems no doubt that the companies enjoyed 'special rights'.
9 Case C-203/96 *Chemische Afvalstoffen Dusseldorp BV and Others v Minister van Volkshuisvesting, Ruimtelijke Ordening en Milieubeheer* [1998] ECR I-4075, [1998] ECR I-4075, ECJ.
10 Ibid, see Advocate General's Opinion at para 97.
11 Ibid, see para 58 of the judgment.

[339]
It is important to distinguish between an exclusive right granted by a public authority which triggers the application of Article 86, and exclusive rights of different type, for instance exclusive distribution rights or licences, which are granted by a public entity carrying out economic activities.[1] Such an entity may be either the State or a public undertaking forming an integral part of the State. Article 81 applies to the latter situation rather than Article 86.[2]

1 The basis for distinguishing between the two situations is the nature of the function of the measure or regulation in question, and whether that function is properly to be categorised as an

activity of a public authority or a purely commercial or economic activity. See the discussion in Buendia Sierra, *Exclusive Rights and State Monopolies under EC Law* at para 1.36ff. He states at para 1.48 that the distinction is between those measures whose function is to organise a market (where the measure is of a regulatory nature with the State acting as a public authority) and a measure taken in the course of the normal exercise of an economic activity (where the measure lacks a regulatory character).

2 In Case 30/87 *Bodson v Pompes Funèbres des Regions Libérées SA* [1988] ECR 2479, [1989] 4 CMLR 984, ECJ exclusive concessions were granted by French local councils to certain private undertakings for the provision of funeral services. The Court of Justice held that Article 86(1) applied, and not Article 81, because the contracts were concluded by the local councils acting in their capacity as public authorities, not as undertakings (see para 18). In Case C-393/92 *Almelo* [1994] ECR I-1517 at para 31 the Court held that supply contracts concluded between regional electricity distributors and local distributors containing an exclusive purchasing clause were not subject to Article 86. The contracts were not concluded by the public authorities as such, but by regional distributors who held a public service concession from the public authorities. The contracts did not involve any transfer of that concession to the local distributors.

[340]

(iii) Special rights: 'Special rights' has a different meaning from exclusive rights. In *France v Commission*[1] part of the Court's reasoning in partially annulling the Commission's first Directive on telecommunications terminal equipment[2] was that the Directive, which required Member States to remove special rights from national monopoly holders, did not identify what special rights were.[3] The concept of special rights has not been defined in the Treaty. A definition was given in the Telecommunications Terminal Equipment Directive introduced following *France v Commission.*[4] A similar definition was inserted into the Telecommunications Services Directive[5] by the Telecommunications Full Competition Directive.[6] Articles 2(1)(b) and (c) of that Directive required Member States to withdraw all those measures which granted special rights 'which limit to two or more the number of undertakings authorized to provide such telecommunications services or to establish or provide such networks, otherwise than according to objective, proportional and non-discriminatory criteria' or 'which designate, other than according to objective, proportional and non-discriminatory criteria several competing undertakings to provide such telecommunications services or to establish or to provide such networks'. The Court subsequently laid down the following definition in a case concerned with the interpretation of the concept of special or exclusive rights in a number of telecommunications directives:[7] '... the exclusive or special rights in question must generally be taken to be rights which are granted by the authorities of a Member State to an undertaking or a limited number of undertakings otherwise than according to objective, proportional and non-discriminatory criteria and which substantially affect the ability of other undertakings to provide or operate telecommunications networks or to provide telecommunications services in the same geographical area under substantially equivalent conditions.'

1 Case C-202/88 *France v Commission* [1991] ECR I-1223.

2 Commission Directive (EEC) 88/301 on competition in the markets for telecommunications terminal equipment [1988] OJ L131/73, [1991] 4 CMLR 922. The Directive was adopted on 16 May 1988 under the Commission's powers in Article 86(3).

3 See Case C-202/88 *France v Commission* [1991] ECR I-1223, para 45. The Court also held that the mere existence of special or exclusive rights was not necessarily incompatible with the

Treaty. Such rights had to be assessed in the light of the different rules of the Treaty to which Article 86(1) refers, see ibid para 22.
4 Commission Directive 94/46 [1994] OJ L268/15; see recital 11.
5 Commission Directive 90/388/EEC on competition in the markets for telecommunications services [1990] OJ L192/10.
6 Commission Directive 96/19/EC amending Directive 90/388/EEC.
7 Case C-302/94 *British Telecommunications v Commission* [1996] ECR I-6417 at para 34.

[341]
However, in his Opinion in *Ambulanz Glockner*[1] Advocate General Jacobs expressed the view that whilst this definition may be used to define the concept of special or exclusive rights in Article 86(1), that part requiring that the rights be 'granted otherwise than according to objective, proportional and non-discriminatory criteria' was specifically designed to apply to the liberalisation process in the telecommunications sector. Therefore it was not, he said, relevant to the identification of special or exclusive rights for the purposes of applying Article 86(1) or (2).[2] The Court of Justice appears to have followed the Advocate General's test in its judgment in *Ambulanz Glockner*. It held that a system, under which provision of patient transport services was effectively reserved to particular organisations by the operation of a system of refusing permits to potential competitors on the basis that to grant them could have adverse effects on the operation and profitability of the public ambulance system, amounted to the grant of a special or exclusive right. The Court ruled that it was sufficient that protection was being conferred by a legislative measure on a limited number of undertakings which could substantially affect the ability of other undertakings to exercise the economic activity in question in the same geographical area under substantially equivalent conditions.[3]

1 Case C-475/99 *Ambulanz Glockner v Landkreis Sudwestpfalz* [2001] ECR 8089, [2002] 4 CMLR 726, ECJ.
2 Ibid, Advocate General's Opinion at paras 88-89. Cf *GSM Italy* (para 6) [1995] OJ L280/49 and *GSM Spain* (para 10) [1997] OJ L76/19.
3 Ibid, judgment, para 24.

2. The prohibited conduct under Article 86(1)

[342]
(a) Enact or maintain in force: Member States are not permitted to bring into effect a measure that contravenes the Treaty. It seems likely that the obligation not to 'maintain in force' requires Member States to review their previously enacted measures, which may not have breached the Treaty rules when they were enacted but do so following an alteration in conditions. Member States therefore have a continuing obligation to keep legal monopolies under review.[1]

1 See Case C-320/91 *Corbeau* [1993] ECR I-2533, [1995] 4 CMLR 621, ECJ; L Hancher, 'Casenote on Corbeau' (1994) 31 CMLRev 105. D Edward and M Hoskins, 'Article 90: Deregulation and EC Law. Reflections Arising from the XVI FIDE Conference' (1995) 32 CMLRev 157. In Case C-17/03 *Vereniging voor Energie, Milieu en Water v Directeur van de Dienst uitvoering en toezicht energie* (judgment of 7 June 2005) the Netherlands Director in charge of energy supply argued that Article 86(2) should be invoked to justify continuing with long-term supply contracts even after the company which had been granted special rights had completed the service of general economic interest assigned to it. The Court did not find it necessary to answer the question.

[343]

(b) Measures: 'Measures' has a wide meaning. It includes not only laws and regulations, but all forms of administrative practices, recommendations and agreements or decisions of Member States, so long as they affect a public undertaking or an undertaking given special or exclusive rights.[1] Measures of municipal authorities are included within Article 86(1).[2] In the two *GSM* cases[3] the Commission held that rules which made the grant of mobile licences subject to fees which were not also payable by the sole existing licence holder were measures contrary to Article 86. Similarly in *Connect Austria*, national legislation under which additional frequencies could be allocated to a public undertaking in a dominant position without the imposition of a separate fee, whereas the new entrant to the market had to pay a fee for its licence to use those frequencies, was a State measure which could breach Article 86(1).[4] In *Mobistar*[5] the Court clearly considered that tax measures applying to mobile phone infrastructures could be relevant measures.[6] A concession agreement giving an undertaking the exclusive right to perform funeral services was a measure.[7] In a case interpreting the word 'measure' under Article 28 of the Treaty the Court of Justice has held that measures do not need to have binding effect.[8]

1 See Case C-203/96 *Chemische Afvalstoffen Dusseldorp BV and Others v Minister van Volkshuisvesting, Ruimtelijke Ordening en Milieubeheer* [1998] ECR I-4075, [1998] 3 CMLR 873, ECJ at para 61 which refers to any law regulation or administrative provision. In that case the relevant measure was a Long Term Plan whereby a Member State required undertakings to deliver their waste for recovery, such as oil filters to a national undertaking on which it has conferred the exclusive right. In Case C-475/99 *Ambulanz Glockner v Landkreis Sudwestpfalz* [2001] ECR 8089, [2002] 4 CMLR 726, ECJ the relevant measure was a law which entitled an administrative district to refuse to authorise others who wished to provide ambulance services if it considered that to do so would affect the operation and profitability of the public ambulance services. Moreover, the administrative district had to consult those operating the public ambulance services to see whether they considered that there would be such an effect. In *Port of Rødby* [1994] OJ L55/52 a refusal to grant access to ferry terminal facilities was a State measure.

2 In Case C-209/98 *Enterprenorforeningens Affals Miljosektion (FFAD) acting for Sydhavnens Sten & Grus ApS v Kobenhavns Kommune* [2000] ECR I-3743, [2001] 2 CMLR 936 the measure in question was a municipal regulation adopted in Copenhagen establishing a system for waste recovery and processing and limiting those who could process the waste to a specific number even though others were sufficiently qualified to process the waste.

3 *GSM Italy* [1995] OJ L280/49 and *GSM Spain* [1997] OJ L76/19.

4 Case C-462/89 *Connect Austria Gesellschaft fur Telekommunikation GmbH v Telekom Control-Kommission and Mobilkom Austria* [2003] ECR I-5197 at para 87. Although not analysed by reference to Article 86, see Joined Cases C-327/03 and C-328/03 *Budesrepublik Deutshland v ISIS* (judgment of 20 October 2005) which concerned the interpretation of Article 11 of Directive 97/13/EC and the need to ensure undistorted competition between telephone operators by precluding legislation requiring new operators to pay charges to take over telephone numbers when the dominant incumbent operator had obtained a very large stock of numbers free of charge. See also Commission decisions in *Brussels National Airport* [1995] OJ L280/49, *Portuguese Airports* [1999] OJ L69/31 and Case C-163/99 *Portugal v Commission* [2001] ECR I-2613, *Spanish Airports* [2000] OJ L208/36.

5 Joined Cases C-544/03 and C-545/03 *Mobistar SA v Commune de Fleron; Belgacom Mobile SA v Commune de Schaerbeek* (judgment of 8 September 2005) at para 49.

6 The Court was considering the question of whether the measures were covered by Article 3c of Directive 90/388 added by Directive 96/2 (now superseded). However the reason for inclusion of Article 3c of the Directive was that such restrictions infringed Article 86 in conjunction with Article 82 of the Treaty and should be lifted by Member States.

7 Case 30/87 *Bodson v Pompes Funèbres des Regions Libérées SA* [1988] ECR 2479, [1989] 4 CMLR 984, ECJ.
8 Case 249/81 *Commission v Ireland* [1982] ECR 4005 at para 28.

[344]
(c) Article 82 in conjunction with Article 86(1): The main use of Article 86(1) by the Court has been in conjunction with Article 82 of the Treaty. Article 82 is of particular relevance because the grant of special or exclusive rights is capable in some circumstances of conferring a dominant position on an undertaking in a relevant market.[1] There are two possible situations. The first is where the relevant measure is the grant of the exclusive rights itself. The second is where the relevant measure favours an already dominant undertaking. In either case it is the role of the State in bringing about the situation giving rise to the abuse which leads to infringement of Article 86(1). Without a link with a State measure there is simply a breach of Article 82 for which the undertaking, but not the State, is liable.[2] Where the undertaking is obliged by State rules to act in an anti-competitive manner (eg, to apply anti-competitive tariffs) the undertaking will not be liable as it will be able to rely upon the defence of State compulsion.[3]

1 It will do so if the area in which special or exclusive rights are granted is a market in its own right.
2 The State is not liable for breaches of Article 82: see Case C-18/88 *RTT v GB-INNO-BM SA* [1991] ECR I-5973 at para 20; Case C-320/91 *Corbeau* [1993] ECR I-2533, [1995] 4 CMLR 621, ECJ.
3 See Joined Cases C-359/95P and C-379/95P *Commission v France v Ladbroke Racing* [1997] ECR I-6265 at para 33.

[345]
In certain circumstances the grant of exclusive rights giving rise to a dominant position can give rise to a breach of Article 86. In such cases, the Court asks, first, whether or not the exclusive rights have given rise to a dominant position and, secondly, whether there is an appropriate link between the grant of those rights and actual or potential abuses by the undertaking of its dominant position.

[346]
A legal monopoly granted by a State in a substantial part of the common market will give rise to a dominant position.[1] In *Dusseldorp* the Court held that the grant of exclusive rights for the incineration of dangerous waste on the territory of a Member State as a whole must be regarded as conferring on the undertaking concerned a dominant position in a substantial part of the common market.[2] Similarly, in *La Crespelle*[3] the grant of a series of territorially limited monopolies which together covered the entire territory of a Member State created a dominant position in a substantial part of the common market. The grant of exclusive rights to perform mooring services within particular Italian ports conferred a dominant position in a substantial part of the common market.[4] The grant of an exclusive right to manage a supplementary pension scheme in an industrial sector in a Member State was held to confer a dominant position within the meaning of Article 86.[5]

1 See eg Case 311/84 *CBEM* [1985] ECR 3261 at para 16; Case C-55/96 *Job Centre* [1997] ECR I-7140, [1998] 4 CMLR 708, ECJ at para 30.
2 Case C-203/96 *Chemische Afvalstoffen Dusseldorp BV and Others v Minister van Volkshuisvesting, Ruimtelijke Ordening en Milieubeheer* [1998] ECR I-4075, [1998] 3 CMLR 873, ECJ.

3 Case C-323/93 *Société Agricole du Centre d'Insémination de la Crespelle v Cooperative d'Elevage et d'Insemination Artificielle du Département de la Mayenne* [1994] ECR I-5077, ECJ at para 17; Case C-179/90 *Merci Convenzionali Porto di Genova SpA v Siderurgica Gabrielli SpA* [1991] ECR I-5889, [1994] 4 CMLR 422, ECJ at para 14; Case C-18/88 *RTT v GB-Inno-BM* [1991] ECR I-5941, ECJ at para 17.

4 Case C-266/96 *Corsica Ferries France SA v Gruppo Antichi Ormeggiatori del Porto di Genova* [1998] ECR I-3949 at paras 38 and 39; Case C-179/90 *Merci Convenzionali Porto di Genova SpA v Siderurgica Gabrielli SpA* [1991] ECR I-5889, [1994] 4 CMLR 422, ECJ at para 15; Case 163/96 *Silvano Raso* [1998] ECR I-533, [1998] 4 CMLR 737 at para 26.

5 Case C-67/96 *Albany International BV v Stichting Bedrijspensioenfonds Textilindustrie* [1999] ECR I-5751 at para 92.

[347]

The grant by the State of exclusive rights which give rise to a dominant position does not give rise in all cases to a breach of Article 86. The Court has therefore repeated frequently that the mere grant of such rights is not, by itself, a breach of Article 86.[1] However, the grant may be the relevant measure which infringes Article 86 in certain circumstances. These arise if the factual context is such that merely by exercising its exclusive rights the undertaking cannot avoid abusing its dominant position, or when such rights are liable to create a situation in which the undertaking is led or induced to commit abuses.[2]

1 Case C-475/99 *Ambulanz Glockner v Landkreis Sudwestpfalz* [2001] ECR 8089, [2002] 4 CMLR 726, ECJ at para 39; Case C-209/98 *Enterprenorforeningens Affals Miljosektion (FFAD) acting for Sydhavnens Sten & Grus ApS v Kobenhavns Kommune* [2000] ECR I-3743, [2001] 2 CMLR 936 at para 66; Case C-41/90 *Hofner & Elser v Macroton* [1991] ECR I-1979, [1993] 4 CMLR 396, ECJ at para 29.

2 Joined Cases C-115/97 to C-117/97 *Brentjens* [1999] ECR I-6025 at para 93; Case C-41/90 *Hofner & Elser v Macroton* [1991] ECR I-1979, [1993] 4 CMLR 396, ECJ at para 29; Case C-260/89 *Elliniki Radiophonia Tileorasi (ERT) v DEP* [1991] ECR I-2925, [1994] 4 CMLR 540, ECJ para 37; Case C-179/90 *Merci Convenzionali Porto di Genova SpA v Siderurgica Gabrielli SpA* [1991] ECR I-5889, [1994] 4 CMLR 422, ECJ at paras 16-17; Case C-323/93 *Société Agricole du Centre d'Insémination de la Crespelle v Cooperative d'Elevage et d'Insemination Artificielle du Département de la Mayenne* [1994] ECR I-5077, ECJ at para 18; Case 163/96 *Silvano Raso* [1998] ECR I-533, [1998] 4 CMLR 737 at para 27; Case C-55/96 *Job Centre* [1997] ECR I-7140, [1998] 4 CMLR 708, ECJ at para 31.

[348]

In *Dusseldorp*[1] the Court adopted a somewhat less demanding test. It stated that there will be a breach of Article 86 if a State adopts any measure 'which enables an undertaking on which it has conferred exclusive rights to abuse its dominant position'. There must be a causal link between the grant of the rights and the abuses in order for the State to bear responsibility.[2]

1 In Case C-203/96 *Chemische Afvalstoffen Dusseldorp BV and Others v Minister van Volkshuisvesting, Ruimtelijke Ordening en Milieubeheer* [1998] ECR I-4075, [1998] 3 CMLR 873, ECJ at para 61.

2 Case C-323/93 *Société Agricole du Centre d'Insémination de la Crespelle v Cooperative d'Elevage et d'Insemination Artificielle du Département de la Mayenne* [1994] ECR I-5077, ECJ.

[349]

It is not necessary to show that abuses of a dominant position have actually been committed. It may be enough that the measure in question could hypothetically lead the undertakings to commit abuses.[1]

1 Case 163/96 *Silvano Raso* [1998] ECR I-533, [1998] 4 CMLR 737 at para 31; Case C-18/88 *RTT v GB-Inno-BM* [1991] ECR I-5941, ECJ at paras 23-24. In *RTT* there was no allegation that there had been any actual abuse.

3. Particular examples of the grant of special or exclusive rights infringing Article 86(1) in conjunction with Article 82

[350]

(a) **Manifest inability to satisfy demand:** A State's decision to grant special or exclusive rights will infringe Article 86 where it can be shown that the undertaking to which those rights has been granted is manifestly unable to meet the demand for the services it has been entrusted with providing.[1] In such cases the undertaking in question cannot avoid abusing Article 82 EC. The Court has held that in such circumstances the Member State creates a situation where the provision of a service is limited contrary to Article 82(2)(b) of the Treaty.[2]

1 See Case C-41/90 *Hofner & Elser v Macrotron GmbH* [1991] ECR I-1979, [1993] 4 CMLR 396, ECJ at para 31.

2 Article 82(2)(b) states that an abuse of a dominant position may consist in 'limiting production, markets or technical development to the prejudice of consumers'. Public placement offices may well be unable to satisfy a significant portion of all requests for services on an extensive, differentiated and constantly changing market. It has been suggested by Advocate General Jacobs that a Member State may be held responsible only where there is 'system failure', that is to say, where the abuses are a direct consequence of its regulatory or decisional intervention, whereas undertakings with special or exclusive rights are alone responsible for any infringement of the competition rules attributable exclusively to them. If a medical aid organisation or an investment fund is manifestly not able to satisfy demand due to its own bad management or investment policy then, according to Advocate General Jacobs, Articles 86(1) and 82 will not be infringed (see para 148 of his Opinion in Case C-475/99 *Ambulanz Glockner v Landkreis Sudwestpfalz* [2001] ECR 8089, [2002] 4 CMLR 726, ECJ and para 412 of his Opinion in Case C-67/96 *Albany International BV v Stichting Bedrijspensioenfonds Textilindustrie* [1999] ECR I-5751, [2000] 4 CMLR 446, ECJ).

[351]

An abuse of Article 82 may consist in limiting the provision of a service to the prejudice of those seeking to use that service.[1] Where this has resulted from a State measure Article 86 is infringed.[2] In *Dusseldorp* the fact that the applicant was required to supply its waste to the national undertaking, which held the exclusive right to incinerate waste and could not export it, even though the quality of processing available in another Member State was comparable in quality, had the effect of restricting outlets.[3] In such cases the Court has sometimes gone on to examine whether the obligation to use a particular service could be justified on the grounds that the service was a service of general economic interest and satisfied the requirements of Article 86(2).[4]

1 Case C-55/96 *Job Centre* [1997] ECR I-711 9 at para 32; Case C-258/98 *Giovanni Carra* [2000] ECR I-4217.

2 Case C-203/96 *Chemische Afvalstoffen Dusseldorp BV and Others v Minister van Volkshuisvesting, Ruimtelijke Ordening en Milieubeheer* [1998] ECR I-4075, [1998] 3 CMLR 873, ECJ at para 64.

3 Ibid, see paras 62 and 63.

4 Ibid, see para 64. In Joined Cases C-115/97 to C-117/97 *Brentjens* [1999] ECR I-6025 the Court examined the question in the light of Article 86(2); namely whether the restriction of competition brought about by the decision to place the management of a sectoral pension

scheme with one insurer was justified as a task necessary for the performance of a particular social task of general interest. See further paras [361]–[374] below.

[352]
(b) Conflict of interest: Article 86(1) will be infringed where the grant of the exclusive rights creates a conflict of interest. The fact that the grant makes it likely that the undertaking would adopt a policy which favours its own interests is sufficient. For example, in *Raso*,[1] the scheme under which the dock-work company obtained the exclusive right to supply temporary workers to other dock-work companies with which it also competed on the market meant that the company would have a 'conflict of interest'. Merely by exercising its monopoly it would be able to distort in its favour the equal conditions of competition between the various operators on the market in dock-work services.[2] Similarly in *ERT*[3] a Greek radio and telephone company had exclusive rights both in relation to original broadcasting of programmes and the re-transmitting of programmes. It was held that where this was liable to create a situation where the company would be led to infringe Article 82 by adopting a discriminatory broadcasting policy which favoured its own programmes, Article 86 would be infringed.[4]

1 Case 163/96 *Silvano Raso* [1998] ECR I-533, [1998] 4 CMLR 737; see also the Commission's decision on *Italian Ports Legislation* [1997] OJ L301/17I.
2 Case 163/96 *Silvano Raso* [1998] ECR I-533, [1998] 4 CMLR 737, see paras 28 and 29.
3 Case C-260/89 *Elliniki Radiophonia Tileorasi (ERT) v DEP* [1991] ECR I-2925, [1994] 4 CMLR 540, ECJ
4 Ibid, see para 37. See the Advocate General in Case C-67/96 *Albany International BV v Stichting Bedrijspensioenfonds Textilindustrie* [1999] ECR I-5751, [2000] 4 CMLR 446, ECJ at para 448, although the Court reached a different conclusion on the question of whether there was a conflict of interest.

[353]
In the *Telecommunications Terminal Equipment* case[1] the relevant directive obliged Member States to ensure that decisions on regulatory and supervisory matters concerning terminal equipment was entrusted to a body independent of the undertaking operating the public network. Otherwise the body operating the network would have power to determine such questions at will and would be placed at an obvious advantage over its competitors.[2] In *RTT*[3] the undertaking which held a monopoly in the establishment and operation of the telephone network and which marketed terminal equipment was also entrusted with drawing up the specifications for terminal equipment and granting type-approvals for such equipment. The Court described this as being 'tantamount to conferring upon the monopoly undertaking the power to determine at will which terminal equipment may be connected to the public network, and thereby placing that undertaking at an obvious advantage over its competitors'. The Court held that Member States were precluded from granting such a power to an undertaking where that undertaking was itself competing with those operators on the market for that equipment.[4] In *Albany* the Court reached a different conclusion on the basis that the fund merely checked that the scheme which had been entered into by the employers fulfilled certain conditions and the system could not be regarded as likely to lead the fund to abuse that power.[5] In addition, because there were certain complex financial evaluations to be carried out it was reasonable not to confer the power of exemption on a separate body. However, it was

important that the exercise of the power was subject to review by the national courts.[6]

1 Case C-202/88 *France v Commission* [1991] ECR I-1223.
2 Ibid, see para 51.
3 Case C-18/88 *RTT v GB-INNO-BM SA* [1991] ECR I-5973
4 Ibid, see paras 25-28.
5 Case C-67/96 *Albany International BV v Stichting Bedrijspensioenfonds Textilindustrie* [1999] ECR I-5751, [2000] 4 CMLR 446, ECJ at para 116.
6 Ibid, see paras 120-121.

[354]
(c) Pricing cases: A Member State may infringe Article 86(1) if it creates a situation in which an undertaking enjoying exclusive rights is encouraged to charge excessive prices contrary to Article 82. In *Merci*[1] the Court concluded that the grant of an exclusive right to organise dock work induced the undertaking to demand payment for services which had not been requested, to charge disproportionate prices, to refuse to have recourse to modern technology and to grant price reductions. However, unlike the position in *Hofner*[2] the undertaking was able to avoid abusing its position in this way. In *GT-Link*[3] the port authority was guilty of price discrimination by waiving harbour dues for its own operations but imposing them on competitors. The Court imposed an obligation to maintain a system which ensured transparency in the operation of charges. In *Corsica Ferries*[4] the Court was concerned with port tariffs which included a supplement which it was argued was indispensable if a universal mooring service was to be maintained. The Court held that these were justified, applying Article 86(2).

1 Case C-179/90 *Merci Convenzionali Porto di Genova SpA v Siderurgica Gabrielli SpA* [1991] ECR I-5889, [1994] 4 CMLR 422, ECJ
2 See Case C-41/90 *Hofner & Elser v Macrotron GmbH* [1991] ECR I-1979, [1993] 4 CMLR 396, ECJ.
3 Case C-242/95 *GT-Link A/S v Danske Staatsbaner (DSB)* [1997] ECR I-4449.
4 Case C-266/96 *Corsica Ferries France SA v Gruppo Antichi Ormeggiatori del Porto di Genova* [1998] ECR I-3949.

[355]
The Commission has found price discrimination contrary to Articles 82 and 86 in a number of decisions concerning discriminatory transport fares,[1] airport landing fees[2] and port tariffs.[3] In the *German restrictions on mail preparation* decision[4] the Commission found that rules which applied dissimilar conditions to similar cases, that is to major senders of mail and self-provision intermediaries, infringed Article 86 in conjunction with Article 82 because it amounted to State-induced discrimination.

1 *Spanish Transport Fares* [1987] OJ L194/28.
2 *Brussels National Airport* [1995] OJ L216/8; *Portuguese Airports* [1999] OJ L69/31 upheld on appeal in case C-163/99 *Portugal v Commission* [2001] ECR I-2613; *Spanish Airports* [2000] OJ L208/36.
3 *Piloting tariffs in the port of Genoa* [1997] OJ L301/27.
4 Commission decision of 20 October 2004 at para 65.

[356]
However, in other cases no causal link was found between the State measure and the relevant pricing behaviour.[1] In *FFAD* the Court concluded that prices were

determined by competition between the three undertakings and that there was nothing to suggest that the municipal rules would necessarily lead the undertakings to abuse their dominant position.[2] In *La Crespelle* the complaint was that the insemination centres which had been granted exclusive rights charged excessive prices.[3] The question was whether the alleged excessive charging was the direct consequence of the national law. The law merely allowed insemination centres to require breeders who requested the centres to provide them with semen from other production centres to pay the additional cost entailed by that choice and allowed the centres to calculate the costs. The Court held that the provision did not lead the centres to charge the disproportionate costs and the grant of the rights was not therefore contrary to Article 86.[4]

1 As for the need for a causal link, see the comments of Advocate General Jacobs in Case C-203/96 *Chemische Afvalstoffen Dusseldorp BV and Others v Minister van Volkshuisvesting, Ruimtelijke Ordening en Milieubeheer* [1998] ECR I-4075, [1998] 3 CMLR 873, ECJ at para 101.
2 Case C-209/98 *Enterprenorforeningens Affals Miljosektion (FFAD) acting for Sydhavnens Sten & Grus ApS v Kobenhavns Kommune* [2000] ECR I-3743, [2001] 2 CMLR 936 at paras 71 and 82.
3 Case C-323/93 *Société Agricole du Centre d'Insémination de la Crespelle v Cooperative d'Elevage et d'Insemination Artificielle du Département de la Mayenne* [1994] ECR I-5077, ECJ.
4 Ibid, paras 21-22.

[357]
(d) Extension to ancillary markets: A measure which enables an undertaking holding a dominant position to reserve to itself an ancillary activity on a neighbouring market or to extend its dominant position will infringe Article 86. Undertakings which hold a monopoly in one market must not reserve to themselves, without any objective necessity, a separate market thereby eliminating competition.[1] Member States are prohibited from reaching the same result by virtue of a State measure.[2]

1 Case 311/84 *CBEM* [1985] ECR 3261.
2 See Case C-18/88 *RTT v GB-Inno-BM* [1991] ECR I-5941, ECJ at paras 20-21 and 25. In the Commission's *German Restrictions on Mail Preparation* decision (20 October 2004) at para 59 the Commission held that state measures which assisted the undertaking enjoying exclusive rights to extend its market power into a neighbouring market violated the principle of equal opportunities between different economic operators and were prohibited by Article 86, relying on *RTT* and the two *GSM* decisions, [1995] OJ L280/49 and [1997] OJ L 76/19. In those circumstances it held that the dominant undertaking could not avoid abusing its market power. DPAG was induced to extend its market power into the market for mail preparation services (see para 60).

[358]
In the *RTT* case the Court held that the unjustified extension of the monopoly in the operation of the telephone network to the market for supplying terminal equipment on which the undertaking was also competing infringed Article 82 and Article 86.[1] By the same reasoning the European Court has upheld provisions of Commission Directives (EEC) 88/301 and 90/388 which prohibited the granting to telecommunications network operators of exclusive rights regarding the provision of ancillary equipment and services.[2] In *Ambulanz Glockner* a law which enabled medical aid organisations to carry out not only emergency ambulance services but also non-emergency services, which could have been carried out by independent organisations, and which gave them certain advantages in doing so, infringed Article 86. The

Court held that the measure gave an advantage to the medical aid organisations which already had an exclusive right on the emergency transport market, and therefore limited markets contrary to Article 82(b) by reserving such markets to particular organisations.[3] Similarly requiring new entrants to a telecommunications market to make payments which an incumbent operator was not required to make was capable of extending the monopoly rights of the incumbents.[4]

1 Case C-18/88 *RTT v GB-Inno-BM* [1991] ECR I-5941, ECJ.
2 Case C-202/88 *France v Commission* [1991] I-ECR 1223; Joined Cases C-271, 281, 289/90 *Spain, Belgium and Italy v Commission* [1992] ECR I-5833.
3 Case C-475/99 *Ambulanz Glockner v Landkreis Sudwestpfalz* [2001] ECR 8089, [2002] 4 CMLR 726, ECJ at para 43.
4 *GSM Italy* [1995] OJ L280/49 and *GSM Spain* [1997] OJ L76/19. See also Joined Cases C-544/03 and C-545/03 *Mobistar SA v Commune de Fleron; Belgacom Mobile SA v Commune de Schaerbeek* (judgment of 8 September 2005) at para 49. For similar issues under Directive 97/13/EC see Joined Cases C-327/03 and C-328/03 *Budesrepublik Deutshland v ISIS* (judgment of 20 October 2005).

[359]
A case concerning the extent of an existing monopoly was *Corbeau.*[1] Private courier services were competing with the basic postal service by undercutting the basic postal rate in certain areas where they were able to do so. There was no suggestion that the State monopoly-holder, the Regie des Postes, had acted abusively. The Court's approach was to hold that the grant of exclusive rights would contravene Article 86(1), save to the extent that the legislation was necessary to enable the basic postal service to carry out its task and may therefore be justified under Article 86(2).[2] The Court reasoned that those entrusted with tasks of general economic interest may often need to offset profits from the more profitable parts of its business against the less profitable areas in order to carry out its universal service obligations in conditions of economic equilibrium. To this end, it may be justifiable to restrict competition from other undertakings in the economically profitable areas to prevent them from 'cherry picking'.[3] What was unacceptable was the exclusion of services which were dissociable from the service of general interest and which called for additional services not offered by the traditional postal services 'insofar as such specific services by their nature and the conditions in which they are provided do not compromise the economic equilibrium of the service of general economic interest performed by the holder of the exclusive right'.[4]

1 Case C-320/91 *Corbeau* [1993] ECR I-2533, [1995] 4 CMLR 621, ECJ.
2 For the different approaches which may be taken in considering the legality of a monopoly see D. Edward and M. Hoskins, 'Article 90: Deregulation and EC Law. Reflections Arising from the XVI FIDE Conference' (1995) 32 CMLRev 157.
3 Ibid, paras 17 and 18.
4 Ibid, para 19. It may be possible to analyse this case as concerning the illegality of reserving ancillary markets or services to a party holding a justifiable monopoly. However, the court itself did not analyse the case in this way.

[360]
(e) Refusal to supply: The Commission has held that there had been an infringement of Article 86 where a Danish port operator refused to allow a Swedish company the right to build a new port terminal or have access to the existing State-run terminal for

the purposes of operating an alternative ferry service.[1] This had the effect of denying essential facilities to a downstream operator and eliminating competition in the downstream market. In *Deutsche Post* the Court held that returning items of mail to origin unless the senders paid the full amount of internal postage without deducting the terminal dues corresponding to items of mail paid by other postal services constituted a refusal to sell which was contrary to Article 82 and therefore infringed Article 86.[2]

1 *Port of Rødby* [1994] OJ L55/52.
2 See Joined Cases C-147-8/97 *Deutsche Post AG v Gesellschaft fur Zahlungssysteme mbH (GZS) and Citicorp Kartenservice GmbH* [2000] ECR I-825 at paras 59-61.

C. ARTICLE 86(2)

1. Purpose

[361]
Article 86(2) provides for a limited exemption from the rules contained in the EC Treaty in the case of two specific categories of undertakings, whether public or private undertakings – namely those entrusted with services of general economic interest and revenue producing monopolies. The exemption applies only insofar as the application of the Treaty rules does not obstruct the performance of their tasks. Member States may also rely upon Article 86(2).[1] Article 86(2) seeks to reconcile the Member State's interest in using certain undertakings as an instrument of economic or fiscal and possibly even social policy with the Community's interest in ensuring compliance with the rules on competition and the internal market.[2]

1 Case C-203/96 *Chemische Afvalstoffen Dusseldorp BV and Others v Minister van Volkshuisvesting, Ruimtelijke Ordening en Milieubeheer* [1998] ECR I-4075, [1998] 3 CMLR 873, ECJ.
2 See Advocate General Jacobs in Case C-67/96 *Albany International BV v Stichting Bedrijspensioenfonds Textilindustrie* [1999] ECR I-5751, [2000] 4 CMLR 446, ECJ at para 436.

2. Undertakings having the character of a revenue producing monopoly

[362]
Revenue producing monopolies are undertakings upon which the State has conferred a monopoly over a particular economic activity for the purpose of raising revenue for the State. No such monopolies exist in the United Kingdom. Examples of revenue-producing monopolies in other Member States include monopolies over alcohol and tobacco. They usually constitute commercial monopolies as well and are subject to Article 31 of the EC Treaty which concerns State monopolies of a commercial character.[1]

1 For a recent example, see Case C-483/02 *Hanner* (judgment of 31 May 2005) at paras 32 to 37.

3. Undertakings entrusted with the operation of services of general economic interest

[363]
Since Article 86(2) 'permits, in certain circumstances, derogation from the rules of the Treaty, there must be a strict definition of those undertakings which can take advantage of it'.[1] Article 86(2) is to be restrictively interpreted.[2]

1 Case 127/73 *BRT v SV SABAM* [1974] ECR 313 at para 19; Case C-242/95 *GT-Link A/S v Danske Staatsbaner (DSB)* [1997] ECR I-4449, [1997] 5 CMLR 601, ECJ at para 50; Case 157/94 *Commission v Netherlands (Re Electricity Imports)* [1997] ECR I-5699, [1997] 5 CMLR 601 at para 37.

2 See eg Case C-242/95 *GT-Link A/S v Danske Staatsbaner (DSB)* [1997] ECR I-4449 at para 50, Case C-340/99 *TNT Traco SpA v Poste Italiane SpA* [2001] ECR I-4109 at para 56.

[364]

An undertaking will only fall within Article 86(2) if it has been *entrusted* with the operation of a service of general economic interest. There must have been an act of a public authority addressed to the undertaking in question.[1] This act need not take the form of legislation but may simply be an act or measure of a Member State, for example, the grant of a concession. The undertaking must have been placed by that act under certain obligations to carry out the activities in question.[2] Water supply companies set up by public authorities in order to secure regular supply and distribution of water under conditions to guarantee public health are undertakings which have been entrusted with the operation of services of general economic interest.[3]

1 Case 127/73 *BRT v SV SABAM* [1974] ECR 313 at paras 20-1.

2 See the Opinion of Advocate General Jacobs in Case C-203/96 *Chemische Afvalstoffen Dusseldorp BV and Others v Minister van Volkshuisvesting, Ruimtelijke Ordening en Milieubeheer* [1998] ECR I-4075, [1998] 3 CMLR 873, ECJ at para 103. The Commission's 2004 Report on Competition Policy (para 393) suggests that a public service assignment is required in order to define the respective obligations of the undertaking and of the State (national, regional or local authority). The assignment must specify the precise nature of the public service obligation, the undertaking and territory concerned, any exclusive rights assigned to the undertakings, the calculation and review of the public service compensation, including a reasonable profit and the arrangements for repaying overcompensation and for any intervention by the state in the event of under-compensation. See also para 2.3 of the Commission's draft Framework for State aid in the form of public compensation at http://europa.eu.int/comm/competition/state_aid/others/ which sets down the need for an instrument specifying the public service obligation.

3 *Re NAVENA-ANSEAU* [1982] OJ L167/39. See also [1982] OJ L325/20. The decision was upheld on appeal in Cases 96/82 *IAZ International Belgium SA v Commission* [1983] ECR 3369.

[365]

The mere fact that an undertaking operates such a service will not suffice. An undertaking to which the State has not assigned any task and which manages private interests is not within the definition.[1] Nor does the fact that an undertaking has satisfied various requirements to obtain an authorisation to carry out a task mean that it is entrusted with that activity. In *GVL*[2] the Court held that the mere fact that companies managing copyright and related rights has to be officially authorised, were subject to monitoring by the German Patent Office and were under certain duties to conduct themselves in a particular way, did not lead to the conclusion that those companies had been entrusted with a service of general economic interest within the meaning of Article 86(2). There is a distinction to be drawn between being entrusted with providing certain services and merely being subject to regulation and public supervision in relation to the way in which activities are carried out. Similarly, the fact that Member States gave express legal approval to the Eurocheque clearing system did not bring that activity within Article 86(2).[3]

1 Case 127/73 *BRT v SV SABAM* [1974] ECR 313 at para 23.

2 Case 7/82 *GVL v Commission* [1983] ECR 483 at paras 30-32. See also the Commission's *VTM* decision 97/606/EC, [1997] OJ L244/18 at para 14. (The decision was appealed on unrelated grounds and the appeal was dismissed: Case T-266/1997 *VTM v Commission* [1999] ECR II-2329.)
3 *Uniform Eurocheques* [1985] OJ L35/43

[366]

Public utilities will almost always amount to services of general economic interest. The Court has held that the following all constitute the provision of services of general economic interest: the provision of a public water supply,[1] a telecommunications system,[2] ensuring the navigability of a main waterway,[3] a public electricity supply,[4] national postal services,[5] employment placement services,[6] the operation of a non-viable air route for reasons of general interest,[7] the treatment of waste materials,[8] mooring services in ports,[9] the provision of supplementary pension schemes[10] and ambulance services.[11] On the other hand, the concept does not include the transfer of funds by a bank to foreign countries,[12] the loading, unloading and trans-shipment and storage of goods in a port,[13] the services of authors' rights societies,[14] nor the production and sale of telephones or terminal equipment.[15]

1 *Re NAVENA-ANSEAU* [1982] OJ L167/39. See also [1982] OJ L325/20. The decision was upheld on appeal in Cases 96/82 *IAZ International Belgium SA v Commission* [1983] ECR 3369.
2 *Re British Telecommunications* [1982] OJ L360/36, upheld on appeal in Case 41/83 *Italy v Commission* [1985] ECR 873; Case C-18/88 *RTT v GB-Inno-BM* [1991] ECR I-5941, ECJ.
3 Case 10/71 *Ministere Public de Luxembourg v Muller* [1971] ECR 723 at 730.
4 Case 155/73 *Sacchi* [1974] ECR 409, [1974] 2 CMLR 177, ECJ; Case C-393/92 *Gemeente Almelo and others v Energiebedrijf Ijsselmij NV* [1994] ECR I-4777.
5 Case C-320/91 *Corbeau* [1993] I-ECR-2533, [1995] 4 CMLR 621, ECJ. The performance of obligations flowing form the Universal Postal Convention also amount to services of general economic interest: see Joined Cases C-147-8/97 *Deutsche Post AG v Gesellschaft fur Zahlungssysteme mbH (GZS) and Citicorp Kartenservice GmbH* [2000] ECR I-825 at para 44.
6 See Case C-41/90 *Hofner & Elser v Macrotron GmbH* [1991] ECR I-1979, [1993] 4 CMLR 396, ECJ.
7 Case 66/86 *Ahmed Saeed Flugreisen v Zentrale zur Bekampfung unlauteren Wettbewerbs eV* [1989] ECR 803, [1990] 4 CMLR 102, ECJ. See also Case T-260/94 *Air Inter v Commission* [1997] ECR II-997.
8 Case C-209/98 *Enterprenorforeningens Affals Miljosektion (FFAD) acting for Sydhavnens Sten & Grus ApS v Kobenhavns Kommune* [2000] ECR I-3743, [2001] 2 CMLR 936; Case C-203/96 *Chemische Afvalstoffen Dusseldorp BV and Others v Minister van Volkshuisvesting, Ruimtelijke Ordening en Milieubeheer* [1998] ECR I-4075, [1998] 3 CMLR 873, ECJ.
9 Case C-266/96 *Corsica Ferries France SA v Gruppo Antichi Ormeggiatori del Porto di Genova* [1998] ECR I-3949.
10 Case C-67/96 *Albany International BV v Stichting Bedrijspensioenfonds Textilindustrie* [1999] ECR I-5751, [2000] 4 CMLR 446, ECJ [1999] ECR I-5751.
11 Case C-475/99 *Ambulanz Glockner v Landkreis Sudwestpfalz* [2001] ECR 8089, [2002] 4 CMLR 726, ECJ.
12 Case 172/80 *Zuchner* [1981] ECR I-2021, [1982] 1 CMLR 313, ECJ.
13 Case C-179/90 *Merci Convenzionali Porto di Genova SpA v Siderurgica Gabrielli SpA* [1991] ECR 1-5889, [1994] 4 CMLR 422, ECJ.
14 See Commission Decision (EEC) 71/224 [1971] CMLR D35 (*Re Gema*); Case 127/73 *BRT v SV SABAM* [1974] ECR 313, [1974] 2 CMLR 238, ECJ; Case 7/82 *GVL v Commission* [1983] ECR 483, [1983] 3 CMLR 645, ECJ.
15 Case-18/88 *RTT v SA GB-INNO-BM* [1991] ECR I-5941 at para 22.

[367]

The concept of services of general economic interest has been the subject of a series of recent papers from the Commission.[1] The 2001 Communication[2] defined SGEIs as 'market services which the Member States or the Community subject to specific public service obligations by virtue of a general interest criterion. This would tend to cover such things as transport networks, energy and communication'. Further definitions of 'services of general interest', 'services of general economic interest', 'public service' and 'public service obligations' are to be found in the Commission's White Paper of 2004.[3] The Commission has now adopted, in July 2005, a series of measures[4] whose aim is to provide legal certainty in the field of financing services of general economic interest, following on from the judgments of the Court in cases such as *Altmark*[5] and *Enirisorse*.[6] The measures comprise a Commission Decision, a Commission Framework and an amendment to the Commission Transparency Directive (80/723/EEC). The Commission's recent papers including the July 2005 Framework suggest that it considers that Member States have a wide margin of discretion regarding the nature of services which could be classified as being services of general economic interest or SGEIs.[7] The more traditional approach has been that application of Article 86(2) to particular areas of activity by Member States is a matter which the Commission is entitled to monitor, subject to the supervision of the Courts.[8] The courts are willing to hold that Member States have wrongly categorised activities as SGEIs in appropriate cases.[9] In either case, it seems that some degree of review will be undertaken. However, the extent of that review may be limited, following the more recent views expressed by the Commission and the Court.

1 Commission Communication on Services of General Economic Interest [1996] OJ C281/3, Commission Communication [2001] OJ C17/4, Report to the Laeken European Council on services of general interest COM(2001) 598 final, Commission Non-Paper on Services of General Economic Interest and State Aid at http://europa.eu.int/comm/competition/state_aid/others/, Green Paper on Services of general interest COM(2003) 270 final, White Paper on services of general interest. 12 May 2004, COM(2004) 374 final.

2 Communication on services of general economic interest [2001] OJ C17/4, Annex II.

3 White Paper on services of general interest, 12 May 2004, COM(2004) 374 final, Annex I.

4 See http://europe.eu.int/comm/competition/state_aid/others/action_plan/; See also Press release of 15 July 2005, IP/05/937. These measures are not discussed here as they concern the question of whether certain financial arrangements constitute State aid.

5 Case C-280/00 *Altmark Trans GmbH v Nahverkehrsgesellschaft Altmark GmbH* [2003] ECR I-7747.

6 Joined Cases C-34/01 to C-38/01 *Enirisorse SpA v Ministero delle Finanze* [2003] ECR I-14243.

7 See http://europea.eu.int/comm/competition/state_aid/others/action_plan/; Framework DGCOMP/D(2005) 179 at para 8. The passage suggests that the Commission's task is only to ensure that Article 86(2) is applied without manifest error as regards definition of SGEIs. See also Case 157/94 *Commission v Netherlands (Re Electricity Imports)* [1997] ECR I-5699, [1997] 5 CMLR 601 at para 40, where the Court stated that Member States cannot be precluded when determining what services of general economic interest to entrust to national undertakings from taking account of objectives pertaining to their national policy. Similarly, in Case C-16/2001 *GEMO* [2003] ECR I-13769 Advocate General Jacobs expressed the view that the Court's review of whether an activity amounted to a service of a general economic interest was only a 'marginal control', meaning that there is only a very limited degree of interference in the State's categorisation of the activity in order to eliminate abuse (see footnote 74 of the Opinion).

8 See to this effect Case 10/71 *Ministère Public du Luxembourg v Muller* [1971] ECR 723 at paras 14-15 and Case 41/83 *Italy v Commission* [1985] ECR 873 at para 30.

9 Case-18/88 *RTT v SA GB-INNO-BM* [1991] ECR I-5941 at para 22.

4. Obstruction of the performance of the tasks entrusted

[368]
Undertakings covered by Article 86(2) are subject to the rules of the Treaty unless it is established that the application of those rules would obstruct the performance of the task entrusted to them. Article 86(2) involves an appraisal, on the one hand, of the requirements of the particular task entrusted to the undertaking and, on the other hand, of the interests of the Community.

[369]
The Court has held that it is not necessary to show that the financial balance or economic viability of the undertaking is threatened in order to come within Article 86(2).[1] However, it has adopted varying approaches on the applicable test which must be satisfied by a party relying on Article 86(2).[2] In *Corbeau* the Court stated that the question to be considered was 'the extent to which a restriction on competition or even the exclusion of all competition from other economic operators is necessary in order to allow the holder of the exclusive right to perform its task of general economic interest and in particular to have the benefit of economically acceptable conditions'.[3] The Court held that it was for the national court to decide whether this criterion was met in that case. In a number of cases the Court has considered whether the fact that an undertaking was protected in some way from competition, preventing others from 'cherry picking' the more profitable elements of a service, could be justified by a need to ensure that an unprofitable aspect of providing a universal service was carried out under 'economically acceptable conditions'[3]. In *FFAD* the Court considered that environmental considerations meant that the undertaking could rely upon Article 86(2).[4] However, in relation to undertakings that are entrusted with SGEIs, it may be the case that some of their services are dissociable from the SGEI and the special protection they are afforded should not extend to these services.[5] Quite often an undertaking entrusted with a SGEI will be afforded a monopoly in a lucrative market to offset losses incurred in the provision of the SGEI. Although this may be acceptable under Community law,[6] in recent case law, the ECJ appears to have been more willing to scrutinise the extent to which cross-subsidisation is to be permitted. In *Ambulanz Glöckner*[7] the Court held that cross-subsidisation of the public service of emergency ambulance services with profitable non-emergency ambulance services will only fall under Article 86(2) if the undertaking entrusted with the SGEI in question is able to satisfy demand for ambulance services.

1 See Case 157/94 *Commission v Netherlands (Re Electricity Imports)* [1997] ECR I-5699 at para 52.
2 See comments of Advocate General Jacob in Case C-203/96 *Chemische Afvalstoffen Dusseldorp BV and Others v Minister van Volkshuisvesting, Ruimtelijke Ordening en Milieubeheer* [1998] ECR I-4075, [1998] 3 CMLR 873, ECJ describing the various different ways in which the test for obstruction under Article 86(2) has been formulated.
3 Case C-320/91 *Corbeau* [1993] ECR I-2533, [1995] 4 CMLR 621, ECJ at para 16. See also Case C-393/92 *Gemeente Almelo and Others v Energiebedrijf Ijsselmij NV* [1994] ECR I-4777 ; Case 66/86 *Ahmed Saeed Flugreisen v Zentrale zur Bekampfung unlauteren Wettbewerbs eV* [1989] ECR 803, [1990] 4 CMLR 102, ECJ; Case C-260/89 *Elliniki Radiophonia Tileorasi (ERT) v DEP* [1991] ECR I-2925, [1994] 4 CMLR 540, ECJ. However, in other cases the Court has decided for itself whether the conditions for the application of Article 86(2) were met: see See Case C-266/96 *Corsica Ferries France SA v Gruppo Antichi Ormeggiatori del Porto di Genova* [1998] ECR I-3949; Cases C67/96

Albany International BV v Stichting Bedrijspensioenfonds Textilindustrie [1999] ECR I-5751; Joined Cases C-147-8/97 *Deutsche Post AG v Gesellschaft fur Zahlungssysteme mbH (GZS) and Citicorp Kartenservice GmbH* [2000] ECR I-825.

4 Case C-209/98 *Enterprenorforeningens Affals Miljosektion (FFAD) acting for Sydhavnens Sten & Grus ApS v Kobenhavns Kommune* [2000] ECR I-3743, [2001] 2 CMLR 936.

5 See Case C-320/91 *Corbeau* [1993] ECR I-2533, [1995] 4 CMLR 621, ECJ at para 21.

6 See eg Cases C-147-148/97 *Deutsche Post* [2000] ECR I-825.

7 Case C-475/99 *Ambulanz Glockner v Landkreis Sudwestpfalz* [2001] ECR 8089, [2002] 4 CMLR 726, ECJ at para 65.

[370]

In other cases the Court has adopted a stricter approach requiring proof that the objective could not be equally achieved by other means and that without the contested measure the undertaking could not carry out its entrusted task.[1] This is to be contrasted with *Commission v Netherlands*[2] where the Court held that '[the] burden of proof cannot be so extensive as to require the Member State ... to ... prove positively that no other conceivable measure, which by definition would be hypothetical, could enable those tasks to be performed under the same conditions'. The Court has held that undertakings remain subject to the competition rules pursuant to Article 86(2) unless and to the extent to which it is shown that their application is incompatible with the discharge of their duties.[3]

1 See Case C-203/96 *Chemische Afvalstoffen Dusseldorp BV and Others v Minister van Volkshuisvesting, Ruimtelijke Ordening en Milieubeheer* [1998] ECR I-4075, [1998] 3 CMLR 873, ECJ. See also *Re NAVENA-ANSEAU* [1982] OJ L167/39. See also [1982] OJ L325/20. The decision was upheld on appeal in Cases 96/82 *IAZ International Belgium SA v Commission* [1983] ECR 3369. In that decision the Commission stated that it was 'not sufficient ... that compliance with the provisions of the treaty makes performance of the particular task more complicated. A possible limitation of the application of the rules on competition can be envisaged only in the event that the undertaking concerned has no other technically and economically feasible means of performing its particular task'. See also *British Telecommunications* [1982] OJ L360/36, upheld on appeal in Case 41/83 *Italy v Commission* [1985] ECR 873, where the Italian government argued (unsuccessfully) that BT's breach of Article 86 was unavoidable and therefore justified by reason of its pre-existing obligations under the International Telecommunication Union. Case T-260/94 *Air Inter v Commission* [1997] II-997. Case C-209/98 *Enterprenorforeningens Affals Miljosektion (FFAD) acting for Sydhavnens Sten & Grus ApS v Kobenhavns Kommune* [2000] ECR I-3743, [2001] 2 CMLR 936.

2 Case C-157/94 *Commission v Netherlands (Electricity Imports)* [1997] ECR I-5699 at para 58.

3 See Case 155/73 *Sacchi* [1974] ECR 409, [1974] 2 CMLR 177, ECJ at para 15; Case C-41/90 *Hofner & Elser v Macrotron GmbH* [1991] ECR I-1979, [1993] 4 CMLR 396, ECJ at para 24.

[371]

It is not necessary for water supply companies to discriminate in the issuing of conformity labels for washing machines,[1] for an agricultural research institute to restrict distribution of seeds,[2] or for telecommuncations network operators to enjoy exclusive rights to the supply of terminal equipment[3] or the right to approve equipment for connection to the network[4] or the exclusive right to provide ancillary communications services,[5] or for airline operators to maintain exclusivity on certain domestic air routes.[6] It seems that Article 86(2) does not permit Member States to adopt, for the protection of an entrusted undertaking, measures which restrict imports from other Member States contrary to Article 28.[7]

1 *Re NAVENA-ANSEAU* [1982] OJ L167/39. See also [1982] OJ L325/20. The decision was upheld on appeal in Cases 96/82 *IAZ International Belgium SA v Commission* [1983] ECR 3369.
2 *Maize Seed* OJ [1978] L 286/23, upheld on appeal in Case 258/78 *LC Nungesser KG v Commission* [1982] ECR 2015
3 Case C-202/88 *France v Commission* [1991] ECR I-1223.
4 Case-18/88 *RTT v SA GB-INNO-BM* [1991] ECR I-5941.
5 Joined Cases 271, 281, 289/90 *Spain, Belgium, Italy v Commission* [1992] ECR I-5833.
6 Case T-260/94 *Air Inter v Commission* [1997] ECR II-997.
7 Case 72/83 *Campus Oil v Minister for Industry and Energy* [1984] ECR 2727. See also Case C-483/02 *Hanner* (judgment of 31 May 2005)

5. No adverse effect on trade contrary to the interests of the Community

[372]
Article 86(2) contains a requirement that 'the development of trade must not be affected to such an extent as would be contrary to the interests of the Community'. This part of Article 86(2) has attracted little attention to date in the case law of the Court.[1] It appears to require more than simply an 'effect on trade between Member States'. It refers to a balancing exercise which appears to be similar in nature to that undertaken in Article 86(2) generally. It has been suggested in certain Advocate General's Opinions that it calls for proof that the measure in question has in fact had a substantial effect on intra-Community trade.[2]

1 It is referred to in Case C-157/94 *Commission v Netherlands* [1997] ECR I-5699 where the Court took the view that it was for the Commission to show that the exclusive right has affected inter-state trade in a manner contrary to the proviso. This appears to be a reversal of the normal burden of proof. One would expect the party relying on the defence to bear the burden of demonstrating the lack of any such effect.
2 See Advocate General Leger in Case C-483/02 *Hanner* (judgment of 31 May 2005) at para 143 and Advocate General Cosmas in his Joined Opinion in Case C-157/94 *Commission v Netherlands* [1997] ECR I-5699, Case C-158/94 *Commission v Italy* [1997] ECR I-5789, and Case C-159/94 *Commission v France* [1997] ECR I-5815 at para 126.

6. Direct effect

[373]
In the *BRT v SABAM*[1] and *Sacchi*[2] cases the Court held that Articles 81 and 82 of the Treaty are directly applicable to undertakings which fall within Article 86(2). Where Article 86(2) is relied upon as a defence to such actions the court is entitled to rule on the questions of whether the undertaking has been entrusted with the operation of a service of general economic interest. It may also rule on the question of whether the task would be obstructed. Earlier case law appeared to indicate that only the Commission could judge the obstruction question, but it is now clear that national courts are able to do so. The Court said expressly in *ERT*[3] that it was for the national court to verify any obstruction.

1 Case 127/73 *BRT v SV SABAM* [1974] ECR 313, ECJ.
2 Case 155/73 *Sacchi* [1974] ECR 409, [1974] 2 CMLR 177, ECJ.
3 Case C-260/89 *Elliniki Radiophonia Tileorasi (ERT) v DEP* [1991] ECR I-2925, [1994] 4 CMLR 540, ECJ.

[374]
If these were the only requirements of Article 86(2) it would be clear that national courts were competent to apply Article 86(2). However, the question of whether

national courts can rule upon the applicability of the proviso regarding adverse effect on trade contrary to the interests of the Community has not been decided, although there do not seem to be any good reasons why national courts could not make the assessment required under this provision. In any event it is not clear whether or not this proviso adds anything to the balancing exercise carried out under the other parts of Article 86(2). If not, it is unlikely to be an impediment to Article 86(2) having direct effect.

D. ARTICLE 86(3)

1. Powers of the Commission under Article 86(3)

[375]

The Commission has a specific duty under Article 86(3) to ensure that Article 86 is applied. This is in addition to its general duty to see that the provisions of the EC Treaty are observed contained in Article 211. The Court in *France v Commission*[1] held that the supervisory power conferred on the Commission in Article 86(3) over measures adopted by undertakings with which they have specific links referred to in Article 86 allowed it to specify particular obligations arising under the Treaty. Article 86(3) also confers specific to take action against existing infringements in the form of decisions addressed to Member States and to issue directives in areas where it considers that breaches of Articles 86(1) have occurred or might occur in the future.[2]

1 Case C-202/88 *France v Commission* [1991] ECR I-1223.
2 As to the basis upon which the Commission may choose to act either by a decision or a directive see Case C-163/1999 *Portuguese Republic v Commission* [2001] ECR I-2613 at paras 27-28. The Commission has also used Article 86(3) to adopt its Decision concerning the application of Article 86(2) of the Treaty to State aid in the form of public service compensation to undertakings carrying out serivces of general economic interest: see http://europe.eu.int/comm/competition/state_aid/others/action_plan/; See also Press release of 15 July 2005, IP/05/937.

[376]

(a) **Decisions:** The Commission's powers under Article 86(3) relate only to State measures and do not extend to conduct engaged in by undertakings on their own initiative.[1] A decision taken under Article 86(3) is binding in its entirety and the addressee must comply with it unless and until it obtains from the Court a suspension of the decision or a declaration that it is void.[2] Although no particular procedure applies to the taking of such decisions the Commission must comply with the basic procedural requirements of EC law, including the duty to give reasons[3] and the duty to respect a Member State's rights of defence.[4] The Commission's powers extend to indicating what measures a Member State to which a decision is addressed must adopt in order to comply with its obligations under Community law. The Court has held that the Commission enjoys a wide discretion as regards the action which it considers necessary for it to take and the means which it should adopt.[5]

1 Case C-202/88 *France v Commission* [1991] ECR I-1223 at 1272. However, the Commission has its general powers to act against undertakings falling within Articles 86(1) and (2) of the EC Treaty in the same way as it acts against undertakings breaching Articles 81 and 82 of the EC Treaty. Examples of such action include Decision (EEC) 82/861 [1982] OJ L360/36 (*Re British Telecommunications*), upheld on appeal in Case 41/83 *Italy v EC Commission* [1985] ECR 873, *Decision* (EEC) 76/684 [1976] 2 CMLR D63 (*Re Pabst & Richarz/BNIA*) and Decision (EEC) 78/823

[1978] OJ L286/23 (*Re Maize Seed*), substantially upheld on appeal in Case 258/78 *L C Nungesser KG v EC Commission* [1982] ECR 2015.
2 See Case 226/87 *EC Commission v Greece* [1988] ECR 3611 which concerned an action against Greece for failure to comply with a decision taken under Article 86(3) (then Article 90(3)), namely [1985] OJ L152/25 (*Greek Public Property Insurance*). The Court held that the Commission Decision was binding on Greece until set aside or suspended by the Court. Its validity could not therefore be challenged in the proceedings before the Court.
3 Case C-163/1999 *Portuguese Republic v Commission* [2001] ECR I-2613 at para 39.
4 See Cases C-48/90 and C-66/90 *Netherlands and Koninklijke PTT Nederland v Commission* [1992] ECR I-565. The Court quashed the Commission's Decision in *Dutch Express Delivery Services* ([1990] OJ L10/47) because of a number of procedural errors by the Commission.
5 Case C-163/1999 *Portuguese Republic v Commission* [2001] ECR I-2613 at para 20. There has been suggestion by the Commission in its September 2005 Communication on Professional Services (5 September 2005), COM(2005) 405 final, that the Commission should use Article 86(3) as the legal base where taking action in the case of professional services, rather than Articles 3(1)(g) and 10(2) read in conjunction with Article 81 (see para 23 of the Communication).

[377]
The Commission has taken decisions against State measures under Article 86(3) in a number of fields. Since its first decision 1985 it has take decisions against legislation in Greece requiring that all public property in Greece was insured by Greek public sector insurance companies,[1] against discriminatory transport fares[2] and against airport landing fees,[3] against charges applied to new entrants to telecommunications markets which did not apply to the incumbent,[4] against a Danish refusal to allow a Swedish group to build a new port terminal or have access to the existing port terminal with a view to operating a ferry service from the Port of Rødby,[5] against the Flemish government in respect of exclusive rights to broadcast television advertising,[6] against Italian employment practices in ports and port tariffs[7] and in respect of conditions applicable to postal services,[8] including most recently a decision in relation to mail preparation in Germany.[9]

1 *Greek Public Property Insurance* [1985] OJ L152/25.
2 *Spanish Transport Fares* [1987] OJ L194/28.
3 *Brussels National Airport (Zaventem)* [1995] OJ L216/8; *Portuguese Airports* [1999] OJ L69/31 upheld on appeal in Case C-163/99 *Portugal v Commission* [2001] ECR I-2613; *Spanish Airports* [2000] OJ L208/36.
4 *GSM Italy* [1995] OJ L280/49 and *GSM Spain* [1997] OJ L76/19.
5 *Port of Rødby* [1994] OJ L55/52.
6 *Flanders television advertising monopoly* [1997] OJ L244/18, upheld on appeal in Case T-266/97 *Vlaamse Televisie Maatschappij NV v Commission* [1999] ECR II-2329.
7 *Italian Ports Legislation* [1997] OJ L301/27; *Piloting tariffs in the port of Genoa* [1997] OJ L301/27.
8 *Dutch Express Delivery Services* [1990] OJ L10/47. See Cases C-48/90 and C-66/90 *Netherlands and Koninklijke PTT Nederland v Commission* [1992] ECR I-565 quashing the decision on appeal. *Spanish International Courier Services* [1990] OJ L233/19; *New Postal Services in Italy* [2001] OJ L63/59; *Mail Preparation in France* [2001] OJ L120/19.
9 *Mail Preparation in Germany* (decision of 20 October 2004) COMP/38.745. See section 4.1 of the 2004 Competition Report.

[378]
An individual may in some circumstances be entitled to bring an action for annulment under Article 230 of the EC Treaty against a decision of the Commission taken under Article 86(3) and addressed to a Member State provided that the

conditions laid down in Article 230 are satisfied.[1] However, an individual does not have standing to challenge a decision by the Commission to refuse to act on a complaint alleging infringement of Article 86 EC. The Court has held that the Commission is not obliged to bring proceedings and take a decision under Article 86(3) and individuals cannot therefore oblige the Commission take a specific decision.[2]

1 Case 107/95P *Bundesverband der Bilanzbuchhalter v Commission* [1997] ECR I-947 at para 24Case C-141/2002P *Commission v T Mobile Austria GmbH* (decision of 22 February 2005) at para 68.

2 Case C-141/2002P *Commission v T Mobile Austria GmbH* (decision of 22 February 2005) at paras 69-70.

[379]

(b) Directives: The Commission has the power to adopt directives under Article 86(3) without having to comply with specific procedures for creating legislation and without having to seek the agreement of Member States.[1] It has made extensive use of these powers in order to seek to liberalise the telecommunications market[2] as well as in other fields. It has also used directives in order to create obligations upon Member States to ensure that their financial relations with public undertakings are transparent.[3] Directives in each of these areas have been challenged, although unsuccessfully, by Member States claiming that the wrong legal base was used for their adoption.[4] It is not possible to use Article 86(3) for the purpose of achieving harmonisation and so Article 95 has been used as the legal base of a number of telecommunications directives including those adopted recently in 2002[5] to lay down the obligations of telecommunications service providers.

1 The fact that the Council also has power to lay down provisions which impinge on the sphere of application of Article 86 does not preclude the Commission from exercising its powers under Article 86 (see Case C-202/88 *France v Commission* [1991] ECR I-1223 at paras 19-21).

2 See Commission Directive (EEC) 88/301 [1988] OJ L131/73 on telecommunications terminal equipment, which required Member States to withdraw any special or exclusive rights granted to operators of public telecommunications networks to use such equipment. See also Commission Directive (EEC) 90/388 [1990] OJ L192/10 on telecommunications services. This Directive required the abolition first of all special or exclusive rights to provide telecommunications services other than voice telephony, and subsequently (by amendment) the abolition of such rights in relation to voice telephony.

3 Commission Directive 80/723 [1980] OJ L195/35, as last amended by Directive 2000/52/EC [2000] OJ L193/75.

4 Commission Directive (EEC) 88/301 [1988] OJ L131/73 was challenged in Case C-202/88 *France v Commission* [1991] ECR I-1223. The Court held that the Commission did have power to introduce the Directive and was entitled to specify in concrete terms the obligations which arise for Member States under Article 86(1) (see para 17). However, the provisions must relate to the duty of supervision imposed as a result of Article 86(3). The Court held that 'the subject matter of the power conferred on the Commission ... is different from and more specific than that of the powers conferred on the Council by either Article [95] or Article [83]' (see para 25). The Court annulled certain parts of the Directive, amongst other reasons because no specific definition of 'special rights' was given. Commission Directive (EEC) 88/301 [1988] OJ L131/73 was challenged in Joined Cases C-271, 281, 289/90 *Spain, Belgium and Italy v EC Commission* [1992] ECR I-5833 where the Court, following its judgment in *France v Commission,* also annulled part of the Directive in question. Commission Directive 80/723 [1980] OJ L195/35 was challenged unsuccessfully in Case 188/80 *France v Commission* [1982] ECR 2545; see also Case C-325/91 *France v Commission* [1993] ECR I-3283.

5 Directive 2002/19/EC on Access [2002] OJ L108/7, Directive 2002/20/EC on Authorisation [2002] OJ L108/21, Directive 2002/21/EC on a Common Regulatory framework [2002] OJ L108/33, Directive 2002/22/EC on Universal Services [2002] OJ L108/51.

E. ARTICLE 81 IN CONJUNCTION WITH ARTICLE 10

[380]
State involvement in the activities of undertakings affecting competition is not only subject to control under Article 86 of the Treaty. Such involvement may also infringe Article 81, read in conjunction with Article 10 and Article 3(g). Article 3(g) states that 'activities of the Community shall include ... (g) a system ensuring that competition in the internal market is not distorted'. Article 10 includes an obligation on Member States to 'abstain from any measure which could jeopardise the attainment of the objectives of the Treaty'.

[381]
It would certainly have been possible to construe Article 10 and Article 3(g), read together, as regulating generally the power of Member States to impose restrictions on the commercial behaviour of undertakings. Thus, it might have been possible to use Article 10 and Article 3(g) to strike down legislation or regulations introduced by Member States which had the same effects as an agreement between undertakings contrary to Article 81 (for example, the introduction of resale price maintenance). However, the Court has in fact adopted a much more limited approach to the use of these Articles. It views the purpose of these rules as being to ensure that Member States are not be able to shield private undertakings from the constraints imposed by Article 81,[1] and are unable to make ineffective the competition rules applicable to undertakings.[2] The duty of Member States is not to introduce or maintain in force measures, even of a legislative or regulatory nature, which may render ineffective the competition rules applicable to undertakings.[3]

1 Case 13/77 *NV GB-INNO-BM v ATAB* [1977] ECR 2115, [1978] 1 CMLR 283 at para 33. Advocate General Lenz in Case 311/85 *Vlaamse Reisbureaus* [1987] ECR 3801 explained that if Member States were permitted to restrict the sphere of application of the competition provisions of the EEC Treaty by means of legislative measures they would be able to determine unilaterally the scope of Community law (para 34 of his Opinion). As the Court has noted in Case C-198/01 *CIF v Autorita Garante della Concorrenza e del Mercato* [2003] ECR I-8055 at para 51, where undertakings are required by national legislation to engage in anti-competitive conduct they cannot be held accountable for infringement of Articles 81 and 82 EC (see Joined Cases C-359/95P and C-379/95P *Commission v France v Ladbroke Racing* [1997] ECR I-6265 at para 33). Where the national law merely encourages or makes it easier for undertakings to engage in 'autonomous anti-competitive conduct' those undertakings remain subject to Articles 81 and 82 (see para 56 of the judgment in *CIF*). The issue in the case was whether the national legislation which delegated power to allocate production between undertakings to a consortium precluded autonomous anti-competitive conduct by the undertakings. The Court held that this was for the national court to determine.

2 Case 267/86 *Van Eycke v ASPA NV* [1988] ECR 4769, [1990] 4 CMLR 330 at para 16.

3 See eg Case C-198/01 *CIF v Autorita Garante della Concorrenza e del Mercato* [2003] ECR I-8055 at para 45.

[382]
There are now two well-recognised circumstances in which Article 81 can be used in conjunction with Article 10. These were laid down originally by the Court in *Van*

Eycke,[1] a case decided in 1988. The Court has followed a consistent approach ever since and has repeated the formulation used in that case to describe the conditions under which these articles will be contravened. Article 81, in conjunction with Article 10, will therefore be infringed (a) where the state requires or favours the adoption of restrictive agreements, decisions or concerted practices or reinforces their effects, or (b) when the state deprives its regulations of their official character by delegating to private traders the responsibility for taking decisions affecting the economic sphere.

1 Case 267/86 *Van Eycke v ASPA NV* [1988] ECR 4769, [1990] 4 CMLR 330.

1. Requiring or favouring the adoption of anti-competitive agreements or reinforcing their effects

[383]

In many cases governments will consult affected areas of industry before adopting rules by legislation. They may set up advisory committees, or ask for draft reports on matters such as appropriate fee scales or other terms on which services are offered. In such situations there may only be a barely perceptible difference between cases where rules are made after consultation with industry and cases where rules give effect to an agreement made by industry. It is not contrary to Community law for a Member State to consult with representatives of an industry before adopting a statutory provision.[1] Nor does the fact that a State requires a professional or other organisation to produce a draft fee tariff mean that the tariff finally adopted does not have the character of legislation.[2] However, if representatives have met together within a framework set up by the Member State for the purpose of agreeing matters related to the supply of a product or service, or if the State creates a statutory obligation for them to meet and agree,[3] or if it approves agreements after they have been made,[4] then the Member State will have 'required or favoured' an agreement contrary to Articles 10 and 81.

1 Case 267/86 *Van Eycke v ASPA NV* [1988] ECR 4769, [1990] 4 CMLR 330 at para 19.
2 Case C-185/91 *Reiff* [1993] ECR I-5801 at paras 22, 23; Case C-266/96 *Corsica Ferries France SA v Gruppo Antichi Ormeggiatori del Porto di Genova* [1998] ECR I-3949 at para 52; Case C-35/99 *Arduino* [2002] ECR I-1529 at paras 36, and 41-43.
3 Case C-35/96 *CNSD* [1998] ECR I-3851 at paras 55-56.
4 Case 136/86 *BNIC v Aubert* [1987] ECR 4789.

[384]

A Member State reinforces an anti-competitive agreement if it incorporates that agreement, in whole or in part, in its own legislation or regulations, or if it requires or encourages compliance with the agreement on the part of undertakings.[1] A Member State could infringe Article 10 in conjunction with Article 81 either by introducing preferential treatment for compliance, or alternatively by imposing sanctions for non-compliance. In *Van Eycke* a Belgian man claimed that competition in savings interest rates between savings institutions had been eliminated as a result of government action. National legislation had restricted tax exemption for interest on savings accounts to those accounts which did not exceed the maximum interest rate levels fixed by legislation. It was clear that the legislation provided an inducement to comply with the maximum levels in question. However, the Court still found that the legislature had reserved to itself the ability to fix the maximum rates and not just adopted an agreement reached by undertakings. The Court did not consider that the legislation merely confirmed the method of restricting the yield on deposits of the maximum rates adopted under *pre-existing* agreements, decisions or practices. Without such a link to pre-existing anti-competitive agreements there was no infringement of Article 10 in conjunction with Article 81.[2] If the measure is purely a State measure unrelated to any anti-competitive agreement then there is no infringement.[3]

1 Case 267/86 *Van Eycke v ASPA NV* [1988] ECR 4769, [1990] 4 CMLR 330.
2 See also the views expressed by Advocate General Jacobs in Case C-67/96 *Albany International BV v Stichting Bedrijspensioenfonds Textilindustrie* [1999] ECR I-5751 at para 127 of his Opinion.
3 Case 231/83 *Cullet v Leclerc* [1985] ECR 305 (where the legislation introduced fixed minimum prices for petrol). It had been thought after Case 229/83 *Leclerc v Au Blé Vert* [1985] ECR 1 that Article 10 might be used to prohibit State measures which were contrary to the full effect of the rules on competition even where no concerted behaviour by undertakings is involved. The legislation in that case produced the same result as an agreement to observe minimum resale prices in that it required book publishers to stipulate retail prices which retailers were then obliged by law to observe. The Court did not actually find any infringement on the basis that there was no clear Community policy as regards price-fixing systems for books. The obligations of Member States were not therefore clear enough to suggest that they should not have enacted such legislation. In Case C-2/91 *Meng* [1993] ECR I-5751, Case C-185/91 *Reiff* [1993] ECR I-5801, and Case C-245/91 *Ohra* [1993] ECR I-5851 the Court implicitly rejected the *Au Blé Vert* approach and repeated the previous requirements set out in the case law. It is therefore consistently assumed that there needs to be some connection between the State measure and the private conduct of undertakings: see e.g Advocate General Leger in Case C-35/99 *Arduino* [2002] ECR I-1529 at paras 82 and para 88 for an alternative approach advocated by him and by Advocate General Jacobs in C-184/98 *Pavlov and Others* [2000] ECR I-6451 at paras 163-4.

[385]
Cases where a Member State has reinforced an agreement include the situation in *Asjes* where a Member State approved air tariffs previously agreed between undertakings.[1] In that case the State's approval had the effect of rendering those tariffs legally binding on all traders selling tickets for travel on the journeys to which the tariffs related. Similarly, Belgian rules making licences for travel agents conditional on observing particular commercial practices (which included only selling tickets at particular tariffs and not sharing commissions with customers or giving other rebates or discounts) reinforced the effects of anti-competitive agreements between tour operators and travel agents. The legislation gave the agreements a permanent character because the parties could no longer rescind them. The legislation also gave rise to various legal consequences and sanctions under Belgian law.[2] In another case cognac producers and retailers agreed a production quota between themselves within the framework of a national organisation, the BNIC.[3] National legislation extended the effects of the quota to the entire sector by decree and made the agreement, which was contrary to Article 81, binding. It made no difference to whether the agreement itself was found to be contrary to Article 81 that it was reached within the framework of a national organisation.

1 Cases 209-213/84 *Ministère Public v Asjes* [1986] ECR 1425. The action failed because there was no implementing regulation in the air transport sector at the relevant time, so that it was not possible for national courts to determine whether the agreements in question breached Article 81 (see para 68 of the judgment). However, in Case 66/86 *Ahmed Saeed Flugreisen v Zentrale zur Bekmpfung Unlauteren Wettbewerbs eV* [1989] ECR 803, [1990] 4 CMLR 102 a similar approval by

the authorities of air tariffs which the airlines had agreed between themselves was found to be contrary to Articles 3(g), 10 and 81. The Court stated at para 49 that Member States must restrain from taking any measure which might be construed as encouraging airlines to conclude tariff agreements contrary to the Treaty competition provisions.
2 Case 311/85 *Vlaamse Reisbureaus* [1987] ECR 3801.
3 Case 136/86 *BNIC v Aubert* [1987] ECR 4789.

[386]
The agreement between undertakings must be an anti-competitive one for the Member State's conduct to be caught by Article 81 in conjunction with Article 10. It must therefore be an agreement between economic agents and not publicly appointed representatives acting as such. If the agreement is reached by a committee which is mainly constituted by representatives of public authorities then there is no such agreement.[1] The position is otherwise, however, if the committee is made up solely of economic traders whose interests it protects.[2] Similarly, if the agreement is not contrary to Article 81 there is no question of any State measure which requires, favours or reinforces that agreement falling within Article 81 and Article 10.[3]

1 Case C-185/91 *Reiff* [1993] ECR I-5801 at para 17; Case C-96/94 *Centro Servizi Spediporto Srl v Spedizioni Marritima del Golfo* [1995] ECR I-2883 at paras 23-25; Joined Cases C-140/94, C-141/94 and C-142/94 *DIP SpA v Commune di Bassano del Grappa and others* [1995] ECR I-3257 at paras 17-19
2 See eg Case C-35/96 *CNSD* [1998] ECR I-3851 at paras 40 to 44; Joined Cases C-180/98 to C-184/98 *Pavlov and Others* [2000] ECR I-6451 at para 88.
3 Case C-266/96 *Corsica Ferries France SA v Gruppo Antichi Ormeggiatori del Porto di Genova* [1998] ECR I-3949 at paras 50, 51. In Case C-67/96 *Albany International BV v Stichting Bedrijspensioenfonds Textilindustrie* [1999] ECR I-5751 the agreement establishing a supplementary pension scheme contributed to an improvement in working conditions in a specific section and did not fall within Article 81 (see paras 61 to 64). It followed that action by the State to make affiliation compulsory for those who were not bound as parties to the agreement did not infringe Articles 3(g), 10 and 81 of the Treaty (see paras 66-70). See also Joined Cases C-180/98 to C-184/98 *Pavlov and Others* [2000] ECR I-6451 at paras 97-100 for reasoning to similar effect.

2. Delegating to private traders responsibility for taking decisions affecting the economic sphere

[387]
If a Member State delegates to private traders the responsibility to take decisions affecting the economic sphere, it deprives its own legislation of its official character and, according to the formulation in *Van Eycke*,[1] this is sufficient for Articles 10 and Article 81 to apply.[2] In *van Eycke*[3] itself the Court held that authorities in that case reserved to themselves the power to fix the maximum rates of interest on savings and did not delegate the responsibility to any private trader. The legislation therefore had an official character. Similarly in *DIP*[4] the mayor had the power to grant individual licences to private economic operators to run shops and had not delegated that power to the municipal committee. On the other hand, in *CNSD*[5] the national legislation had wholly relinquished to private operators (customs agents) the powers of the public authorities to set tariffs and therefore infringed Articles 81 and 10.

1 Case 267/86 *Van Eycke v ASPA NV* [1988] ECR 4769, [1990] 4 CMLR 330, at para 16.
2 Ibid at para 19

3 The rationale (although not discussed in any detail in the case law) appears to be that by delegating the State regulatory function to those who are actors in the market the State is providing for and authorising *in advance* an agreement, decision or concerted practice which, potentially at least, has restrictive effects on competition. Private traders cannot be said to be fulfilling a regulatory function, but will in general act in their own economic interests. In effect, the State has, by its legislation, put it out of its own power to regulate the market. This 'abandonment' by States of 'their prerogatives', as it was described in Case C-185/91 *Reiff* [1993] ECR I-5801 at para 24, to a number of undertakings will be contrary to Articles 3(g), 10 and 81. One of the questions which arises is does delegation to one enterprise to determine prices or other conditions unilaterally, without an agreement, decision or concerted practice, infringe these Articles? Advocate General Darmon in *Reiff* thought that the answer was no, on the basis that, because Article 81 is relied upon for the infringement, unilateral acts are excluded (see para 55). For a different view see Bacon in 'State Regulation of the Market and EC Competition Rules: Articles 85 and 86 Compared' [1997] 18 ECLR 283 at 284.

4 Joined Cases C-140/94, C-141/94 and C-142/94 *DIP SpA v Commune di Bassano del Grappa and others* [1995] ECR I-3257 at para 23.

5 Case C-35/96 *CNSD* [1998] ECR I-3851 at para 57.

Appendices

TREATY ESTABLISHING THE EC 199

REGULATION 1-2003 209

NOTICE ON MINOR AGREEMENTS 235

NOTICE ON DEFINITION OF RELEVANT MARKET 239

GUIDELINES ON EXEMPTION 251

GUIDELINES ON EFFECT ON TRADE 273

PART ONE

PRINCIPLES

Article 1

By this Treaty, the HIGH CONTRACTING PARTIES establish among themselves a EUROPEAN COMMUNITY.

Article 2

The Community shall have as its task, by establishing a common market and an economic and monetary union and by implementing common policies or activities referred to in Articles 3 and 4, to promote throughout the Community a harmonious, balanced and sustainable development of economic activities, a high level of employment and of social protection, equality between men and women, sustainable and non-inflationary growth, a high degree of competitiveness and convergence of economic performance, a high level of protection and improvement of the quality of the environment, the raising of the standard of living and quality of life, and economic and social cohesion and solidarity among Member States.

Article 3

1. For the purposes set out in Article 2, the activities of the Community shall include, as provided in this Treaty and in accordance with the timetable set out therein:

(a) the prohibition, as between Member States, of customs duties and quantitative restrictions on the import and export of goods, and of all other measures having equivalent effect;

(b) a common commercial policy;

(c) an internal market characterised by the abolition, as between Member States, of obstacles to the free movement of goods, persons, services and capital;

(d) measures concerning the entry and movement of persons as provided for in Title IV;

(e) a common policy in the sphere of agriculture and fisheries;

(f) a common policy in the sphere of transport;

(g) a system ensuring that competition in the internal market is not distorted;

(h) the approximation of the laws of Member States to the extent required for the functioning of the common market;

(i) the promotion of coordination between employment policies of the Member States with a view to enhancing their effectiveness by developing a coordinated strategy for employment;

(j) a policy in the social sphere comprising a European Social Fund;

(k) the strengthening of economic and social cohesion;

Reproduced from the Official Journal of the European Communities: C 324, 24/12/2002 P. 0040–0044

(l) a policy in the sphere of the environment;

(m) the strengthening of the competitiveness of Community industry;

(n) the promotion of research and technological development;

(o) encouragement for the establishment and development of trans-European networks;

(p) a contribution to the attainment of a high level of health protection;

(q) a contribution to education and training of quality and to the flowering of the cultures of the Member States;

(r) a policy in the sphere of development cooperation;

(s) the association of the overseas countries and territories in order to increase trade and promote jointly economic and social development;

(t) a contribution to the strengthening of consumer protection;

(u) measures in the spheres of energy, civil protection and tourism.

2. In all the activities referred to in this Article, the Community shall aim to eliminate inequalities, and to promote equality, between men and women.

Article 4

1. For the purposes set out in Article 2, the activities of the Member States and the Community shall include, as provided in this Treaty and in accordance with the timetable set out therein, the adoption of an economic policy which is based on the close coordination of Member States' economic policies, on the internal market and on the definition of common objectives, and conducted in accordance with the principle of an open market economy with free competition.

2. Concurrently with the foregoing, and as provided in this Treaty and in accordance with the timetable and the procedures set out therein, these activities shall include the irrevocable fixing of exchange rates leading to the introduction of a single currency, the ecu, and the definition and conduct of a single monetary policy and exchange-rate policy the primary objective of both of which shall be to maintain price stability and, without prejudice to this objective, to support the general economic policies in the Community, in accordance with the principle of an open market economy with free competition.

3. These activities of the Member States and the Community shall entail compliance with the following guiding principles: stable prices, sound public finances and monetary conditions and a sustainable balance of payments.

Article 5

The Community shall act within the limits of the powers conferred upon it by this Treaty and of the objectives assigned to it therein.

In areas which do not fall within its exclusive competence, the Community shall take action, in accordance with the principle of subsidiarity, only if and in so far as the objectives of the proposed action cannot be sufficiently achieved by the Member States and can therefore, by reason of the scale or effects of the proposed action, be better achieved by the Community.

Any action by the Community shall not go beyond what is necessary to achieve the objectives of this Treaty.

Article 6

Environmental protection requirements must be integrated into the definition and implementation of the Community policies and activities referred to in Article 3, in particular with a view to promoting sustainable development.

Article 7

1. The tasks entrusted to the Community shall be carried out by the following institutions:

— a EUROPEAN PARLIAMENT,

— a COUNCIL,

— a COMMISSION,

— a COURT OF JUSTICE,

— a COURT OF AUDITORS.

Each institution shall act within the limits of the powers conferred upon it by this Treaty.

2. The Council and the Commission shall be assisted by an Economic and Social Committee and a Committee of the Regions acting in an advisory capacity.

Article 8

A European system of central banks (hereinafter referred to as 'ESCB') and a European Central Bank (hereinafter referred to as 'ECB') shall be established in accordance with the procedures laid down in this Treaty; they shall act within the limits of the powers conferred upon them by this Treaty and by the Statute of the ESCB and of the ECB (hereinafter referred to as 'Statute of the ESCB') annexed thereto.

Article 9

A European Investment Bank is hereby established, which shall act within the limits of the powers conferred upon it by this Treaty and the Statute annexed thereto.

Article 10

Member States shall take all appropriate measures, whether general or particular, to ensure fulfilment of the obligations arising out of this Treaty or resulting from action taken by the institutions of the Community. They shall facilitate the achievement of the Community's tasks.

They shall abstain from any measure which could jeopardise the attainment of the objectives of this Treaty.

Article 11 (*)

1. Member States which intend to establish enhanced cooperation between themselves in one of the areas referred to in this Treaty shall address a request to the Commission, which may submit a proposal to the Council to that effect. In the event of the Commission not submitting a proposal, it shall inform the Member States concerned of the reasons for not doing so.

2. Authorisation to establish enhanced cooperation as referred to in paragraph 1 shall be granted, in compliance with Articles 43 to 45 of the Treaty on European Union, by the Council, acting by a qualified majority on a proposal from the Commission and after consulting the European Parliament. When enhanced cooperation relates to an area covered by the procedure referred to in Article 251 of this Treaty, the assent of the European Parliament shall be required.

A member of the Council may request that the matter be referred to the European Council. After that matter has been raised before the European Council, the Council may act in accordance with the first subparagraph of this paragraph.

3. The acts and decisions necessary for the implementation of enhanced cooperation activities shall be subject to all the relevant provisions of this Treaty, save as otherwise provided in this Article and in Articles 43 to 45 of the Treaty on European Union.

Article 11a (**)

Any Member State which wishes to participate in enhanced cooperation established in accordance with Article 11 shall notify its intention to the Council and to the Commission, which shall give an opinion to the Council within three months of the date of receipt of that notification. Within four months of the date of receipt of that notification, the Commission shall take a decision on it, and on such specific arrangements as it may deem necessary.

Article 12

Within the scope of application of this Treaty, and without prejudice to any special provisions contained therein, any discrimination on grounds of nationality shall be prohibited.

The Council, acting in accordance with the procedure referred to in Article 251, may adopt rules designed to prohibit such discrimination.

Article 13 (*)

1. Without prejudice to the other provisions of this Treaty and within the limits of the powers conferred by it upon the Community, the Council, acting unanimously on a proposal from the Commission and after consulting the European Parliament, may take appropriate action to combat discrimination based on sex, racial or ethnic origin, religion or belief, disability, age or sexual orientation.

2. By way of derogation from paragraph 1, when the Council adopts Community incentive measures, excluding any harmonisation of the laws and regulations of the Member States, to support action taken by the Member States in order to contribute to the achievement of the objectives referred to in paragraph 1, it shall act in accordance with the procedure referred to in Article 251.

(*) Article amended by the Treaty of Nice.
(**) Article inserted by the Treaty of Nice (former Article 11(3)).

Article 14

1. The Community shall adopt measures with the aim of progressively establishing the internal market over a period expiring on 31 December 1992, in accordance with the provisions of this Article and of Articles 15, 26, 47(2), 49, 80, 93 and 95 and without prejudice to the other provisions of this Treaty.

2. The internal market shall comprise an area without internal frontiers in which the free movement of goods, persons, services and capital is ensured in accordance with the provisions of this Treaty.

3. The Council, acting by a qualified majority on a proposal from the Commission, shall determine the guidelines and conditions necessary to ensure balanced progress in all the sectors concerned.

Article 15

When drawing up its proposals with a view to achieving the objectives set out in Article 14, the Commission shall take into account the extent of the effort that certain economies showing differences in development will have to sustain during the period of establishment of the internal market and it may propose appropriate provisions.

If these provisions take the form of derogations, they must be of a temporary nature and must cause the least possible disturbance to the functioning of the common market.

Article 16

Without prejudice to Articles 73, 86 and 87, and given the place occupied by services of general economic interest in the shared values of the Union as well as their role in promoting social and territorial cohesion, the Community and the Member States, each within their respective powers and within the scope of application of this Treaty, shall take care that such services operate on the basis of principles and conditions which enable them to fulfil their missions.

PART TWO

CITIZENSHIP OF THE UNION

Article 17

1. Citizenship of the Union is hereby established. Every person holding the nationality of a Member State shall be a citizen of the Union. Citizenship of the Union shall complement and not replace national citizenship.

2. Citizens of the Union shall enjoy the rights conferred by this Treaty and shall be subject to the duties imposed thereby.

COMMON RULES ON COMPETITION, TAXATION AND APPROXIMATION OF LAWS

CHAPTER 1

RULES ON COMPETITION

SECTION 1

RULES APPLYING TO UNDERTAKINGS

Article 81

1. The following shall be prohibited as incompatible with the common market: all agreements between undertakings, decisions by associations of undertakings and concerted practices which may affect trade between Member States and which have as their object or effect the prevention, restriction or distortion of competition within the common market, and in particular those which:

(a) directly or indirectly fix purchase or selling prices or any other trading conditions;

(b) limit or control production, markets, technical development, or investment;

(c) share markets or sources of supply;

(d) apply dissimilar conditions to equivalent transactions with other trading parties, thereby placing them at a competitive disadvantage;

(e) make the conclusion of contracts subject to acceptance by the other parties of supplementary obligations which, by their nature or according to commercial usage, have no connection with the subject of such contracts.

2. Any agreements or decisions prohibited pursuant to this article shall be automatically void.

3. The provisions of paragraph 1 may, however, be declared inapplicable in the case of:

— any agreement or category of agreements between undertakings,

Reproduced from the Official Journal of the European Communities: C 325, 24/12/2002 P. 0064–0066

— any decision or category of decisions by associations of undertakings,

— any concerted practice or category of concerted practices,

which contributes to improving the production or distribution of goods or to promoting technical or economic progress, while allowing consumers a fair share of the resulting benefit, and which does not:

(a) impose on the undertakings concerned restrictions which are not indispensable to the attainment of these objectives;

(b) afford such undertakings the possibility of eliminating competition in respect of a substantial part of the products in question.

Article 82

Any abuse by one or more undertakings of a dominant position within the common market or in a substantial part of it shall be prohibited as incompatible with the common market in so far as it may affect trade between Member States.

Such abuse may, in particular, consist in:

(a) directly or indirectly imposing unfair purchase or selling prices or other unfair trading conditions;

(b) limiting production, markets or technical development to the prejudice of consumers;

(c) applying dissimilar conditions to equivalent transactions with other trading parties, thereby placing them at a competitive disadvantage;

(d) making the conclusion of contracts subject to acceptance by the other parties of supplementary obligations which, by their nature or according to commercial usage, have no connection with the subject of such contracts.

Article 83

1. The appropriate regulations or directives to give effect to the principles set out in Articles 81 and 82 shall be laid down by the Council, acting by a qualified majority on a proposal from the Commission and after consulting the European Parliament.

2. The regulations or directives referred to in paragraph 1 shall be designed in particular:

(a) to ensure compliance with the prohibitions laid down in Article 81(1) and in Article 82 by making provision for fines and periodic penalty payments;

(b) to lay down detailed rules for the application of Article 81(3), taking into account the need to ensure effective supervision on the one hand, and to simplify administration to the greatest possible extent on the other;

(c) to define, if need be, in the various branches of the economy, the scope of the provisions of Articles 81 and 82;

(d) to define the respective functions of the Commission and of the Court of Justice in applying the provisions laid down in this paragraph;

(e) to determine the relationship between national laws and the provisions contained in this section or adopted pursuant to this article.

Article 84

Until the entry into force of the provisions adopted in pursuance of Article 83, the authorities in Member States shall rule on the admissibility of agreements, decisions and concerted practices and on abuse of a dominant position in the common market in accordance with the law of their country and with the provisions of Article 81, in particular paragraph 3, and of Article 82.

Article 85

1. Without prejudice to Article 84, the Commission shall ensure the application of the principles laid down in Articles 81 and 82. On application by a Member State or on its own initiative, and in cooperation with the competent authorities in the Member States, which shall give it their assistance, the Commission shall investigate cases of suspected infringement of these principles. If it finds that there has been an infringement, it shall propose appropriate measures to bring it to an end.

2. If the infringement is not brought to an end, the Commission shall record such infringement of the principles in a reasoned decision. The Commission may publish its decision and authorise Member States to take the measures, the conditions and details of which it shall determine, needed to remedy the situation.

Article 86

1. In the case of public undertakings and undertakings to which Member States grant special or exclusive rights, Member States shall neither enact nor maintain in force any measure contrary to the rules contained in this Treaty, in particular to those rules provided for in Article 12 and Articles 81 to 89.

2. Undertakings entrusted with the operation of services of general economic interest or having the character of a revenue-producing monopoly shall be subject to the rules contained in this Treaty, in particular to the rules on competition, in so far as the application of such rules does not obstruct the performance, in law or in fact, of the particular tasks assigned to them. The development of trade must not be affected to such an extent as would be contrary to the interests of the Community.

3. The Commission shall ensure the application of the provisions of this Article and shall, where necessary, address appropriate directives or decisions to Member States.

I

(Acts whose publication is obligatory)

COUNCIL REGULATION (EC) No 1/2003
of 16 December 2002
on the implementation of the rules on competition laid down in Articles 81 and 82 of the Treaty
(Text with EEA relevance)

THE COUNCIL OF THE EUROPEAN UNION,

Having regard to the Treaty establishing the European Community, and in particular Article 83 thereof,

Having regard to the proposal from the Commission ([1]),

Having regard to the opinion of the European Parliament ([2]),

Having regard to the opinion of the European Economic and Social Committee ([3]),

Whereas:

(1) In order to establish a system which ensures that competition in the common market is not distorted, Articles 81 and 82 of the Treaty must be applied effectively and uniformly in the Community. Council Regulation No 17 of 6 February 1962, First Regulation implementing Articles 81 and 82 (*) of the Treaty ([4]), has allowed a Community competition policy to develop that has helped to disseminate a competition culture within the Community. In the light of experience, however, that Regulation should now be replaced by legislation designed to meet the challenges of an integrated market and a future enlargement of the Community.

(2) In particular, there is a need to rethink the arrangements for applying the exception from the prohibition on agreements, which restrict competition, laid down in Article 81(3) of the Treaty. Under Article 83(2)(b) of the Treaty, account must be taken in this regard of the need to ensure effective supervision, on the one hand, and to simplify administration to the greatest possible extent, on the other.

(3) The centralised scheme set up by Regulation No 17 no longer secures a balance between those two objectives. It hampers application of the Community competition rules by the courts and competition authorities of the Member States, and the system of notification it involves prevents the Commission from concentrating its resources on curbing the most serious infringements. It also imposes considerable costs on undertakings.

(4) The present system should therefore be replaced by a directly applicable exception system in which the competition authorities and courts of the Member States have the power to apply not only Article 81(1) and Article 82 of the Treaty, which have direct applicability by virtue of the case-law of the Court of Justice of the European Communities, but also Article 81(3) of the Treaty.

([1]) OJ C 365 E, 19.12.2000, p. 284.
([2]) OJ C 72 E, 21.3.2002, p. 305.
([3]) OJ C 155, 29.5.2001, p. 73.
(*) The title of Regulation No 17 has been adjusted to take account of the renumbering of the Articles of the EC Treaty, in accordance with Article 12 of the Treaty of Amsterdam; the original reference was to Articles 85 and 86 of the Treaty.
([4]) OJ 13, 21.2.1962, p. 204/62. Regulation as last amended by Regulation (EC) No 1216/1999 (OJ L 148, 15.6.1999, p. 5).

(5) In order to ensure an effective enforcement of the Community competition rules and at the same time the respect of fundamental rights of defence, this Regulation should regulate the burden of proof under Articles 81 and 82 of the Treaty. It should be for the party or the authority alleging an infringement of Article 81(1) and Article 82 of the Treaty to prove the existence thereof to the required legal standard. It should be for the undertaking or association of undertakings invoking the benefit of a defence against a finding of an infringement to demonstrate to the required legal standard that the conditions for applying such defence are satisfied. This Regulation affects neither national rules on the standard of proof nor obligations of competition authorities and courts of the Member States to ascertain the relevant facts of a case, provided that such rules and obligations are compatible with general principles of Community law.

(6) In order to ensure that the Community competition rules are applied effectively, the competition authorities of the Member States should be associated more closely with their application. To this end, they should be empowered to apply Community law.

(7) National courts have an essential part to play in applying the Community competition rules. When deciding disputes between private individuals, they protect the subjective rights under Community law, for example by awarding damages to the victims of infringements. The role of the national courts here complements that of the competition authorities of the Member States. They should therefore be allowed to apply Articles 81 and 82 of the Treaty in full.

(8) In order to ensure the effective enforcement of the Community competition rules and the proper functioning of the cooperation mechanisms contained in this Regulation, it is necessary to oblige the competition authorities and courts of the Member States to also apply Articles 81 and 82 of the Treaty where they apply national competition law to agreements and practices which may affect trade between Member States. In order to create a level playing field for agreements, decisions by associations of undertakings and concerted practices within the internal market, it is also necessary to determine pursuant to Article 83(2)(e) of the Treaty the relationship between national laws and Community competition law. To that effect it is necessary to provide that the application of national competition laws to agreements, decisions or concerted practices within the meaning of Article 81(1) of the Treaty may not lead to the prohibition of such agreements, decisions and concerted practices if they are not also prohibited under Community competition law. The notions of agreements, decisions and concerted practices are autonomous concepts of Community competition law covering the coordination of behaviour of undertakings on the market as interpreted by the Community Courts. Member States should not under this Regulation be precluded from adopting and applying on their territory stricter national competition laws which prohibit or impose sanctions on unilateral conduct engaged in by undertakings. These stricter national laws may include provisions which prohibit or impose sanctions on abusive behaviour toward economically dependent undertakings. Furthermore, this Regulation does not apply to national laws which impose criminal sanctions on natural persons except to the extent that such sanctions are the means whereby competition rules applying to undertakings are enforced.

(9) Articles 81 and 82 of the Treaty have as their objective the protection of competition on the market. This Regulation, which is adopted for the implementation of these Treaty provisions, does not preclude Member States from implementing on their territory national legislation, which protects other legitimate interests provided that such legislation is compatible with general principles and other provisions of Community law. In so far as such national legislation pursues predominantly an objective different from that of protecting competition on the market, the competition authorities and courts of the Member States may apply such legislation on their territory. Accordingly, Member States may under this Regulation implement on their territory national legislation that prohibits or imposes sanctions on acts of unfair trading practice, be they unilateral or contractual. Such legislation pursues a specific objective, irrespective of the actual or presumed effects of such acts on competition on the market. This is particularly the case of legislation which prohibits undertakings from imposing on their trading partners, obtaining or attempting to obtain from them terms and conditions that are unjustified, disproportionate or without consideration.

(10) Regulations such as 19/65/EEC (1), (EEC) No 2821/71 (2), (EEC) No 3976/87 (3), (EEC) No 1534/91 (4), or (EEC) No 479/92 (5) empower the Commission to apply Article 81(3) of the Treaty by Regulation to certain categories of agreements, decisions by associations of undertakings and concerted practices. In the areas defined by such Regulations, the Commission has adopted and may continue to adopt so called 'block' exemption Regulations by which it declares Article 81(1) of the Treaty inapplicable to categories of agreements, decisions and concerted practices. Where agreements, decisions and concerted practices to which such Regulations apply nonetheless have effects that are incompatible with Article 81(3) of the Treaty, the Commission and the competition authorities of the Member States should have the power to withdraw in a particular case the benefit of the block exemption Regulation.

(11) For it to ensure that the provisions of the Treaty are applied, the Commission should be able to address decisions to undertakings or associations of undertakings for the purpose of bringing to an end infringements of Articles 81 and 82 of the Treaty. Provided there is a legitimate interest in doing so, the Commission should also be able to adopt decisions which find that an infringement has been committed in the past even if it does not impose a fine. This Regulation should also make explicit provision for the Commission's power to adopt decisions ordering interim measures, which has been acknowledged by the Court of Justice.

(12) This Regulation should make explicit provision for the Commission's power to impose any remedy, whether behavioural or structural, which is necessary to bring the infringement effectively to an end, having regard to the principle of proportionality. Structural remedies should only be imposed either where there is no equally effective behavioural remedy or where any equally effective behavioural remedy would be more burdensome for the undertaking concerned than the structural remedy. Changes to the structure of an undertaking as it existed before the infringement was committed would only be proportionate where there is a substantial risk of a lasting or repeated infringement that derives from the very structure of the undertaking.

(13) Where, in the course of proceedings which might lead to an agreement or practice being prohibited, undertakings offer the Commission commitments such as to meet its concerns, the Commission should be able to adopt decisions which make those commitments binding on the undertakings concerned. Commitment decisions should find that there are no longer grounds for action by the Commission without concluding whether or not there has been or still is an infringement. Commitment decisions are without prejudice to the powers of competition authorities and courts of the Member States to make such a finding and decide upon the case. Commitment decisions are not appropriate in cases where the Commission intends to impose a fine.

(1) Council Regulation No 19/65/EEC of 2 March 1965 on the application of Article 81(3) (The titles of the Regulations have been adjusted to take account of the renumbering of the Articles of the EC Treaty, in accordance with Article 12 of the Treaty of Amsterdam; the original reference was to Article 85(3) of the Treaty) of the Treaty to certain categories of agreements and concerted practices (OJ 36, 6.3.1965, p. 533). Regulation as last amended by Regulation (EC) No 1215/1999 (OJ L 148, 15.6.1999, p. 1).

(2) Council Regulation (EEC) No 2821/71 of 20 December 1971 on the application of Article 81(3) (The titles of the Regulations have been adjusted to take account of the renumbering of the Articles of the EC Treaty, in accordance with Article 12 of the Treaty of Amsterdam; the original reference was to Article 85(3) of the Treaty) of the Treaty to categories of agreements, decisions and concerted practices (OJ L 285, 29.12.1971, p. 46). Regulation as last amended by the Act of Accession of 1994.

(3) Council Regulation (EEC) No 3976/87 of 14 December 1987 on the application of Article 81(3) (The titles of the Regulations have been adjusted to take account of the renumbering of the Articles of the EC Treaty, in accordance with Article 12 of the Treaty of Amsterdam; the original reference was to Article 85(3) of the Treaty) of the Treaty to certain categories of agreements and concerted practices in the air transport sector (OJ L 374, 31.12.1987, p. 9). Regulation as last amended by the Act of Accession of 1994.

(4) Council Regulation (EEC) No 1534/91 of 31 May 1991 on the application of Article 81(3) (The titles of the Regulations have been adjusted to take account of the renumbering of the Articles of the EC Treaty, in accordance with Article 12 of the Treaty of Amsterdam; the original reference was to Article 85(3) of the Treaty) of the Treaty to certain categories of agreements, decisions and concerted practices in the insurance sector (OJ L 143, 7.6.1991, p. 1).

(5) Council Regulation (EEC) No 479/92 of 25 February 1992 on the application of Article 81(3) (The titles of the Regulations have been adjusted to take account of the renumbering of the Articles of the EC Treaty, in accordance with Article 12 of the Treaty of Amsterdam; the original reference was to Article 85(3) of the Treaty) of the Treaty to certain categories of agreements, decisions and concerted practices between liner shipping companies (Consortia) (OJ L 55, 29.2.1992, p. 3). Regulation amended by the Act of Accession of 1994.

(14) In exceptional cases where the public interest of the Community so requires, it may also be expedient for the Commission to adopt a decision of a declaratory nature finding that the prohibition in Article 81 or Article 82 of the Treaty does not apply, with a view to clarifying the law and ensuring its consistent application throughout the Community, in particular with regard to new types of agreements or practices that have not been settled in the existing case-law and administrative practice.

(15) The Commission and the competition authorities of the Member States should form together a network of public authorities applying the Community competition rules in close cooperation. For that purpose it is necessary to set up arrangements for information and consultation. Further modalities for the cooperation within the network will be laid down and revised by the Commission, in close cooperation with the Member States.

(16) Notwithstanding any national provision to the contrary, the exchange of information and the use of such information in evidence should be allowed between the members of the network even where the information is confidential. This information may be used for the application of Articles 81 and 82 of the Treaty as well as for the parallel application of national competition law, provided that the latter application relates to the same case and does not lead to a different outcome. When the information exchanged is used by the receiving authority to impose sanctions on undertakings, there should be no other limit to the use of the information than the obligation to use it for the purpose for which it was collected given the fact that the sanctions imposed on undertakings are of the same type in all systems. The rights of defence enjoyed by undertakings in the various systems can be considered as sufficiently equivalent. However, as regards natural persons, they may be subject to substantially different types of sanctions across the various systems. Where that is the case, it is necessary to ensure that information can only be used if it has been collected in a way which respects the same level of protection of the rights of defence of natural persons as provided for under the national rules of the receiving authority.

(17) If the competition rules are to be applied consistently and, at the same time, the network is to be managed in the best possible way, it is essential to retain the rule that the competition authorities of the Member States are automatically relieved of their competence if the Commission initiates its own proceedings. Where a competition authority of a Member State is already acting on a case and the Commission intends to initiate proceedings, it should endeavour to do so as soon as possible. Before initiating proceedings, the Commission should consult the national authority concerned.

(18) To ensure that cases are dealt with by the most appropriate authorities within the network, a general provision should be laid down allowing a competition authority to suspend or close a case on the ground that another authority is dealing with it or has already dealt with it, the objective being that each case should be handled by a single authority. This provision should not prevent the Commission from rejecting a complaint for lack of Community interest, as the case-law of the Court of Justice has acknowledged it may do, even if no other competition authority has indicated its intention of dealing with the case.

(19) The Advisory Committee on Restrictive Practices and Dominant Positions set up by Regulation No 17 has functioned in a very satisfactory manner. It will fit well into the new system of decentralised application. It is necessary, therefore, to build upon the rules laid down by Regulation No 17, while improving the effectiveness of the organisational arrangements. To this end, it would be expedient to allow opinions to be delivered by written procedure. The Advisory Committee should also be able to act as a forum for discussing cases that are being handled by the competition authorities of the Member States, so as to help safeguard the consistent application of the Community competition rules.

(20) The Advisory Committee should be composed of representatives of the competition authorities of the Member States. For meetings in which general issues are being discussed, Member States should be able to appoint an additional representative. This is without prejudice to members of the Committee being assisted by other experts from the Member States.

(21) Consistency in the application of the competition rules also requires that arrangements be established for cooperation between the courts of the Member States and the Commission. This is relevant for all courts of the Member States that apply Articles 81 and 82 of the Treaty, whether applying these rules in lawsuits between private parties, acting as public enforcers or as review courts. In particular, national courts should be able to ask the Commission for information or for its opinion on points concerning the application of Community competition law. The Commission and the competition authorities of the Member States should also be able to submit written or oral observations to courts called upon to apply Article 81 or Article 82 of the Treaty. These observations should be submitted within the framework of national procedural rules and practices including those safeguarding the rights of the parties. Steps should therefore be taken to ensure that the Commission and the competition authorities of the Member States are kept sufficiently well informed of proceedings before national courts.

(22) In order to ensure compliance with the principles of legal certainty and the uniform application of the Community competition rules in a system of parallel powers, conflicting decisions must be avoided. It is therefore necessary to clarify, in accordance with the case-law of the Court of Justice, the effects of Commission decisions and proceedings on courts and competition authorities of the Member States. Commitment decisions adopted by the Commission do not affect the power of the courts and the competition authorities of the Member States to apply Articles 81 and 82 of the Treaty.

(23) The Commission should be empowered throughout the Community to require such information to be supplied as is necessary to detect any agreement, decision or concerted practice prohibited by Article 81 of the Treaty or any abuse of a dominant position prohibited by Article 82 of the Treaty. When complying with a decision of the Commission, undertakings cannot be forced to admit that they have committed an infringement, but they are in any event obliged to answer factual questions and to provide documents, even if this information may be used to establish against them or against another undertaking the existence of an infringement.

(24) The Commission should also be empowered to undertake such inspections as are necessary to detect any agreement, decision or concerted practice prohibited by Article 81 of the Treaty or any abuse of a dominant position prohibited by Article 82 of the Treaty. The competition authorities of the Member States should cooperate actively in the exercise of these powers.

(25) The detection of infringements of the competition rules is growing ever more difficult, and, in order to protect competition effectively, the Commission's powers of investigation need to be supplemented. The Commission should in particular be empowered to interview any persons who may be in possession of useful information and to record the statements made. In the course of an inspection, officials authorised by the Commission should be empowered to affix seals for the period of time necessary for the inspection. Seals should normally not be affixed for more than 72 hours. Officials authorised by the Commission should also be empowered to ask for any information relevant to the subject matter and purpose of the inspection.

(26) Experience has shown that there are cases where business records are kept in the homes of directors or other people working for an undertaking. In order to safeguard the effectiveness of inspections, therefore, officials and other persons authorised by the Commission should be empowered to enter any premises where business records may be kept, including private homes. However, the exercise of this latter power should be subject to the authorisation of the judicial authority.

(27) Without prejudice to the case-law of the Court of Justice, it is useful to set out the scope of the control that the national judicial authority may carry out when it authorises, as foreseen by national law including as a precautionary measure, assistance from law enforcement authorities in order to overcome possible opposition on the part of the undertaking or the execution of the decision to carry out inspections in non-business premises. It results from the case-law that the national judicial authority may in particular ask the Commission for further information which it needs to carry out its control and in the absence of which it could refuse the authorisation. The case-law also confirms the competence of the national courts to control the application of national rules governing the implementation of coercive measures.

(28) In order to help the competition authorities of the Member States to apply Articles 81 and 82 of the Treaty effectively, it is expedient to enable them to assist one another by carrying out inspections and other fact-finding measures.

(29) Compliance with Articles 81 and 82 of the Treaty and the fulfilment of the obligations imposed on undertakings and associations of undertakings under this Regulation should be enforceable by means of fines and periodic penalty payments. To that end, appropriate levels of fine should also be laid down for infringements of the procedural rules.

(30) In order to ensure effective recovery of fines imposed on associations of undertakings for infringements that they have committed, it is necessary to lay down the conditions on which the Commission may require payment of the fine from the members of the association where the association is not solvent. In doing so, the Commission should have regard to the relative size of the undertakings belonging to the association and in particular to the situation of small and medium-sized enterprises. Payment of the fine by one or several members of an association is without prejudice to rules of national law that provide for recovery of the amount paid from other members of the association.

(31) The rules on periods of limitation for the imposition of fines and periodic penalty payments were laid down in Council Regulation (EEC) No 2988/74 [1], which also concerns penalties in the field of transport. In a system of parallel powers, the acts, which may interrupt a limitation period, should include procedural steps taken independently by the competition authority of a Member State. To clarify the legal framework, Regulation (EEC) No 2988/74 should therefore be amended to prevent it applying to matters covered by this Regulation, and this Regulation should include provisions on periods of limitation.

(32) The undertakings concerned should be accorded the right to be heard by the Commission, third parties whose interests may be affected by a decision should be given the opportunity of submitting their observations beforehand, and the decisions taken should be widely publicised. While ensuring the rights of defence of the undertakings concerned, in particular, the right of access to the file, it is essential that business secrets be protected. The confidentiality of information exchanged in the network should likewise be safeguarded.

(33) Since all decisions taken by the Commission under this Regulation are subject to review by the Court of Justice in accordance with the Treaty, the Court of Justice should, in accordance with Article 229 thereof be given unlimited jurisdiction in respect of decisions by which the Commission imposes fines or periodic penalty payments.

(34) The principles laid down in Articles 81 and 82 of the Treaty, as they have been applied by Regulation No 17, have given a central role to the Community bodies. This central role should be retained, whilst associating the Member States more closely with the application of the Community competition rules. In accordance with the principles of subsidiarity and proportionality as set out in Article 5 of the Treaty, this Regulation does not go beyond what is necessary in order to achieve its objective, which is to allow the Community competition rules to be applied effectively.

(35) In order to attain a proper enforcement of Community competition law, Member States should designate and empower authorities to apply Articles 81 and 82 of the Treaty as public enforcers. They should be able to designate administrative as well as judicial authorities to carry out the various functions conferred upon competition authorities in this Regulation. This Regulation recognises the wide variation which exists in the public enforcement systems of Member States. The effects of Article 11(6) of this Regulation should apply to all competition authorities. As an exception to this general rule, where a prosecuting authority brings a case before a separate judicial

(1) Council Regulation (EEC) No 2988/74 of 26 November 1974 concerning limitation periods in proceedings and the enforcement of sanctions under the rules of the European Economic Community relating to transport and competition (OJ L 319, 29.11.1974, p. 1).

authority, Article 11(6) should apply to the prosecuting authority subject to the conditions in Article 35(4) of this Regulation. Where these conditions are not fulfilled, the general rule should apply. In any case, Article 11(6) should not apply to courts insofar as they are acting as review courts.

(36) As the case-law has made it clear that the competition rules apply to transport, that sector should be made subject to the procedural provisions of this Regulation. Council Regulation No 141 of 26 November 1962 exempting transport from the application of Regulation No 17 ([1]) should therefore be repealed and Regulations (EEC) No 1017/68 ([2]), (EEC) No 4056/86 ([3]) and (EEC) No 3975/87 ([4]) should be amended in order to delete the specific procedural provisions they contain.

(37) This Regulation respects the fundamental rights and observes the principles recognised in particular by the Charter of Fundamental Rights of the European Union. Accordingly, this Regulation should be interpreted and applied with respect to those rights and principles.

(38) Legal certainty for undertakings operating under the Community competition rules contributes to the promotion of innovation and investment. Where cases give rise to genuine uncertainty because they present novel or unresolved questions for the application of these rules, individual undertakings may wish to seek informal guidance from the Commission. This Regulation is without prejudice to the ability of the Commission to issue such informal guidance,

HAS ADOPTED THIS REGULATION:

CHAPTER I

PRINCIPLES

Article 1

Application of Articles 81 and 82 of the Treaty

1. Agreements, decisions and concerted practices caught by Article 81(1) of the Treaty which do not satisfy the conditions of Article 81(3) of the Treaty shall be prohibited, no prior decision to that effect being required.

2. Agreements, decisions and concerted practices caught by Article 81(1) of the Treaty which satisfy the conditions of Article 81(3) of the Treaty shall not be prohibited, no prior decision to that effect being required.

3. The abuse of a dominant position referred to in Article 82 of the Treaty shall be prohibited, no prior decision to that effect being required.

([1]) OJ 124, 28.11.1962, p. 2751/62; Regulation as last amended by Regulation No 1002/67/EEC (OJ 306, 16.12.1967, p. 1).

([2]) Council Regulation (EEC) No 1017/68 of 19 July 1968 applying rules of competition to transport by rail, road and inland waterway (OJ L 175, 23.7.1968, p. 1). Regulation as last amended by the Act of Accession of 1994.

([3]) Council Regulation (EEC) No 4056/86 of 22 December 1986 laying down detailed rules for the application of Articles 81 and 82 (The title of the Regulation has been adjusted to take account of the renumbering of the Articles of the EC Treaty, in accordance with Article 12 of the Treaty of Amsterdam; the original reference was to Articles 85 and 86 of the Treaty) of the Treaty to maritime transport (OJ L 378, 31.12.1986, p. 4). Regulation as last amended by the Act of Accession of 1994.

([4]) Council Regulation (EEC) No 3975/87 of 14 December 1987 laying down the procedure for the application of the rules on competition to undertakings in the air transport sector (OJ L 374, 31.12.1987, p. 1). Regulation as last amended by Regulation (EEC) No 2410/92 (OJ L 240, 24.8.1992, p. 18).

Article 2

Burden of proof

In any national or Community proceedings for the application of Articles 81 and 82 of the Treaty, the burden of proving an infringement of Article 81(1) or of Article 82 of the Treaty shall rest on the party or the authority alleging the infringement. The undertaking or association of undertakings claiming the benefit of Article 81(3) of the Treaty shall bear the burden of proving that the conditions of that paragraph are fulfilled.

Article 3

Relationship between Articles 81 and 82 of the Treaty and national competition laws

1. Where the competition authorities of the Member States or national courts apply national competition law to agreements, decisions by associations of undertakings or concerted practices within the meaning of Article 81(1) of the Treaty which may affect trade between Member States within the meaning of that provision, they shall also apply Article 81 of the Treaty to such agreements, decisions or concerted practices. Where the competition authorities of the Member States or national courts apply national competition law to any abuse prohibited by Article 82 of the Treaty, they shall also apply Article 82 of the Treaty.

2. The application of national competition law may not lead to the prohibition of agreements, decisions by associations of undertakings or concerted practices which may affect trade between Member States but which do not restrict competition within the meaning of Article 81(1) of the Treaty, or which fulfil the conditions of Article 81(3) of the Treaty or which are covered by a Regulation for the application of Article 81(3) of the Treaty. Member States shall not under this Regulation be precluded from adopting and applying on their territory stricter national laws which prohibit or sanction unilateral conduct engaged in by undertakings.

3. Without prejudice to general principles and other provisions of Community law, paragraphs 1 and 2 do not apply when the competition authorities and the courts of the Member States apply national merger control laws nor do they preclude the application of provisions of national law that predominantly pursue an objective different from that pursued by Articles 81 and 82 of the Treaty.

CHAPTER II

POWERS

Article 4

Powers of the Commission

For the purpose of applying Articles 81 and 82 of the Treaty, the Commission shall have the powers provided for by this Regulation.

Article 5

Powers of the competition authorities of the Member States

The competition authorities of the Member States shall have the power to apply Articles 81 and 82 of the Treaty in individual cases. For this purpose, acting on their own initiative or on a complaint, they may take the following decisions:

— requiring that an infringement be brought to an end,

— ordering interim measures,

— accepting commitments,

— imposing fines, periodic penalty payments or any other penalty provided for in their national law.

Where on the basis of the information in their possession the conditions for prohibition are not met they may likewise decide that there are no grounds for action on their part.

Article 6

Powers of the national courts

National courts shall have the power to apply Articles 81 and 82 of the Treaty.

CHAPTER III

COMMISSION DECISIONS

Article 7

Finding and termination of infringement

1. Where the Commission, acting on a complaint or on its own initiative, finds that there is an infringement of Article 81 or of Article 82 of the Treaty, it may by decision require the undertakings and associations of undertakings concerned to bring such infringement to an end. For this purpose, it may impose on them any behavioural or structural remedies which are proportionate to the infringement committed and necessary to bring the infringement effectively to an end. Structural remedies can only be imposed either where there is no equally effective behavioural remedy or where any equally effective behavioural remedy would be more burdensome for the undertaking concerned than the structural remedy. If the Commission has a legitimate interest in doing so, it may also find that an infringement has been committed in the past.

2. Those entitled to lodge a complaint for the purposes of paragraph 1 are natural or legal persons who can show a legitimate interest and Member States.

Article 8

Interim measures

1. In cases of urgency due to the risk of serious and irreparable damage to competition, the Commission, acting on its own initiative may by decision, on the basis of a *prima facie* finding of infringement, order interim measures.

2. A decision under paragraph 1 shall apply for a specified period of time and may be renewed in so far this is necessary and appropriate.

Article 9

Commitments

1. Where the Commission intends to adopt a decision requiring that an infringement be brought to an end and the undertakings concerned offer commitments to meet the concerns expressed to them by the Commission in its preliminary assessment, the Commission may by decision make those commitments binding on the undertakings. Such a decision may be adopted for a specified period and shall conclude that there are no longer grounds for action by the Commission.

2. The Commission may, upon request or on its own initiative, reopen the proceedings:

(a) where there has been a material change in any of the facts on which the decision was based;

(b) where the undertakings concerned act contrary to their commitments; or

(c) where the decision was based on incomplete, incorrect or misleading information provided by the parties.

Article 10

Finding of inapplicability

Where the Community public interest relating to the application of Articles 81 and 82 of the Treaty so requires, the Commission, acting on its own initiative, may by decision find that Article 81 of the Treaty is not applicable to an agreement, a decision by an association of undertakings or a concerted practice, either because the conditions of Article 81(1) of the Treaty are not fulfilled, or because the conditions of Article 81(3) of the Treaty are satisfied.

The Commission may likewise make such a finding with reference to Article 82 of the Treaty.

CHAPTER IV

COOPERATION

Article 11

Cooperation between the Commission and the competition authorities of the Member States

1. The Commission and the competition authorities of the Member States shall apply the Community competition rules in close cooperation.

2. The Commission shall transmit to the competition authorities of the Member States copies of the most important documents it has collected with a view to applying Articles 7, 8, 9, 10 and Article 29(1). At the request of the competition authority of a Member State, the Commission shall provide it with a copy of other existing documents necessary for the assessment of the case.

3. The competition authorities of the Member States shall, when acting under Article 81 or Article 82 of the Treaty, inform the Commission in writing before or without delay after commencing the first formal investigative measure. This information may also be made available to the competition authorities of the other Member States.

4. No later than 30 days before the adoption of a decision requiring that an infringement be brought to an end, accepting commitments or withdrawing the benefit of a block exemption Regulation, the competition authorities of the Member States shall inform the Commission. To that effect, they shall provide the Commission with a summary of the case, the envisaged decision or, in the absence thereof, any other document indicating the proposed course of action. This information may also be made available to the competition authorities of the other Member States. At the request of the Commission, the acting competition authority shall make available to the Commission other documents it holds which are necessary for the assessment of the case. The information supplied to the Commission may be made available to the competition authorities of the other Member States. National competition authorities may also exchange between themselves information necessary for the assessment of a case that they are dealing with under Article 81 or Article 82 of the Treaty.

5. The competition authorities of the Member States may consult the Commission on any case involving the application of Community law.

6. The initiation by the Commission of proceedings for the adoption of a decision under Chapter III shall relieve the competition authorities of the Member States of their competence to apply Articles 81 and 82 of the Treaty. If a competition authority of a Member State is already acting on a case, the Commission shall only initiate proceedings after consulting with that national competition authority.

Article 12

Exchange of information

1. For the purpose of applying Articles 81 and 82 of the Treaty the Commission and the competition authorities of the Member States shall have the power to provide one another with and use in evidence any matter of fact or of law, including confidential information.

2. Information exchanged shall only be used in evidence for the purpose of applying Article 81 or Article 82 of the Treaty and in respect of the subject-matter for which it was collected by the transmitting authority. However, where national competition law is applied in the same case and in parallel to Community competition law and does not lead to a different outcome, information exchanged under this Article may also be used for the application of national competition law.

3. Information exchanged pursuant to paragraph 1 can only be used in evidence to impose sanctions on natural persons where:

— the law of the transmitting authority foresees sanctions of a similar kind in relation to an infringement of Article 81 or Article 82 of the Treaty or, in the absence thereof,

— the information has been collected in a way which respects the same level of protection of the rights of defence of natural persons as provided for under the national rules of the receiving authority. However, in this case, the information exchanged cannot be used by the receiving authority to impose custodial sanctions.

Article 13

Suspension or termination of proceedings

1. Where competition authorities of two or more Member States have received a complaint or are acting on their own initiative under Article 81 or Article 82 of the Treaty against the same agreement, decision of an association or practice, the fact that one authority is dealing with the case shall be sufficient grounds for the others to suspend the proceedings before them or to reject the complaint. The Commission may likewise reject a complaint on the ground that a competition authority of a Member State is dealing with the case.

2. Where a competition authority of a Member State or the Commission has received a complaint against an agreement, decision of an association or practice which has already been dealt with by another competition authority, it may reject it.

Article 14

Advisory Committee

1. The Commission shall consult an Advisory Committee on Restrictive Practices and Dominant Positions prior to the taking of any decision under Articles 7, 8, 9, 10, 23, Article 24(2) and Article 29(1).

2. For the discussion of individual cases, the Advisory Committee shall be composed of representatives of the competition authorities of the Member States. For meetings in which issues other than individual cases are being discussed, an additional Member State representative competent in competition matters may be appointed. Representatives may, if unable to attend, be replaced by other representatives.

3. The consultation may take place at a meeting convened and chaired by the Commission, held not earlier than 14 days after dispatch of the notice convening it, together with a summary of the case, an indication of the most important documents and a preliminary draft decision. In respect of decisions pursuant to Article 8, the meeting may be held seven days after the dispatch of the operative part of a draft decision. Where the Commission dispatches a notice convening the meeting which gives a shorter period of notice than those specified above, the meeting may take place on the proposed date in the absence of an objection by any Member State. The Advisory Committee shall deliver a written opinion on the Commission's preliminary draft decision. It may deliver an opinion even if some members are absent and are not represented. At the request of one or several members, the positions stated in the opinion shall be reasoned.

4. Consultation may also take place by written procedure. However, if any Member State so requests, the Commission shall convene a meeting. In case of written procedure, the Commission shall determine a time-limit of not less than 14 days within which the Member States are to put forward their observations for circulation to all other Member States. In case of decisions to be taken pursuant to Article 8, the time-limit of 14 days is replaced by seven days. Where the Commission determines a time-limit for the written procedure which is shorter than those specified above, the proposed time-limit shall be applicable in the absence of an objection by any Member State.

5. The Commission shall take the utmost account of the opinion delivered by the Advisory Committee. It shall inform the Committee of the manner in which its opinion has been taken into account.

6. Where the Advisory Committee delivers a written opinion, this opinion shall be appended to the draft decision. If the Advisory Committee recommends publication of the opinion, the Commission shall carry out such publication taking into account the legitimate interest of undertakings in the protection of their business secrets.

7. At the request of a competition authority of a Member State, the Commission shall include on the agenda of the Advisory Committee cases that are being dealt with by a competition authority of a Member State under Article 81 or Article 82 of the Treaty. The Commission may also do so on its own initiative. In either case, the Commission shall inform the competition authority concerned.

A request may in particular be made by a competition authority of a Member State in respect of a case where the Commission intends to initiate proceedings with the effect of Article 11(6).

The Advisory Committee shall not issue opinions on cases dealt with by competition authorities of the Member States. The Advisory Committee may also discuss general issues of Community competition law.

Article 15

Cooperation with national courts

1. In proceedings for the application of Article 81 or Article 82 of the Treaty, courts of the Member States may ask the Commission to transmit to them information in its possession or its opinion on questions concerning the application of the Community competition rules.

2. Member States shall forward to the Commission a copy of any written judgment of national courts deciding on the application of Article 81 or Article 82 of the Treaty. Such copy shall be forwarded without delay after the full written judgment is notified to the parties.

3. Competition authorities of the Member States, acting on their own initiative, may submit written observations to the national courts of their Member State on issues relating to the application of Article 81 or Article 82 of the Treaty. With the permission of the court in question, they may also submit oral observations to the national courts of their Member State. Where the coherent application of Article 81 or Article 82 of the Treaty so requires, the Commission, acting on its own initiative, may submit written observations to courts of the Member States. With the permission of the court in question, it may also make oral observations.

For the purpose of the preparation of their observations only, the competition authorities of the Member States and the Commission may request the relevant court of the Member State to transmit or ensure the transmission to them of any documents necessary for the assessment of the case.

4. This Article is without prejudice to wider powers to make observations before courts conferred on competition authorities of the Member States under the law of their Member State.

Article 16

Uniform application of Community competition law

1. When national courts rule on agreements, decisions or practices under Article 81 or Article 82 of the Treaty which are already the subject of a Commission decision, they cannot take decisions running counter to the decision adopted by the Commission. They must also avoid giving decisions which would conflict with a decision contemplated by the Commission in proceedings it has initiated. To that effect, the national court may assess whether it is necessary to stay its proceedings. This obligation is without prejudice to the rights and obligations under Article 234 of the Treaty.

2. When competition authorities of the Member States rule on agreements, decisions or practices under Article 81 or Article 82 of the Treaty which are already the subject of a Commission decision, they cannot take decisions which would run counter to the decision adopted by the Commission.

CHAPTER V

POWERS OF INVESTIGATION

Article 17

Investigations into sectors of the economy and into types of agreements

1. Where the trend of trade between Member States, the rigidity of prices or other circumstances suggest that competition may be restricted or distorted within the common market, the Commission may conduct its inquiry into a particular sector of the economy or into a particular type of agreements across various sectors. In the course of that inquiry, the Commission may request the undertakings or associations of undertakings concerned to supply the information necessary for giving effect to Articles 81 and 82 of the Treaty and may carry out any inspections necessary for that purpose.

The Commission may in particular request the undertakings or associations of undertakings concerned to communicate to it all agreements, decisions and concerted practices.

The Commission may publish a report on the results of its inquiry into particular sectors of the economy or particular types of agreements across various sectors and invite comments from interested parties.

2. Articles 14, 18, 19, 20, 22, 23 and 24 shall apply *mutatis mutandis*.

Article 18

Requests for information

1. In order to carry out the duties assigned to it by this Regulation, the Commission may, by simple request or by decision, require undertakings and associations of undertakings to provide all necessary information.

2. When sending a simple request for information to an undertaking or association of undertakings, the Commission shall state the legal basis and the purpose of the request, specify what information is required and fix the time-limit within which the information is to be provided, and the penalties provided for in Article 23 for supplying incorrect or misleading information.

3. Where the Commission requires undertakings and associations of undertakings to supply information by decision, it shall state the legal basis and the purpose of the request, specify what information is required and fix the time-limit within which it is to be provided. It shall also indicate the penalties provided for in Article 23 and indicate or impose the penalties provided for in Article 24. It shall further indicate the right to have the decision reviewed by the Court of Justice.

4. The owners of the undertakings or their representatives and, in the case of legal persons, companies or firms, or associations having no legal personality, the persons authorised to represent them by law or by their constitution shall supply the information requested on behalf of the undertaking or the association of undertakings concerned. Lawyers duly authorised to act may supply the information on behalf of their clients. The latter shall remain fully responsible if the information supplied is incomplete, incorrect or misleading.

5. The Commission shall without delay forward a copy of the simple request or of the decision to the competition authority of the Member State in whose territory the seat of the undertaking or association of undertakings is situated and the competition authority of the Member State whose territory is affected.

6. At the request of the Commission the governments and competition authorities of the Member States shall provide the Commission with all necessary information to carry out the duties assigned to it by this Regulation.

Article 19

Power to take statements

1. In order to carry out the duties assigned to it by this Regulation, the Commission may interview any natural or legal person who consents to be interviewed for the purpose of collecting information relating to the subject-matter of an investigation.

2. Where an interview pursuant to paragraph 1 is conducted in the premises of an undertaking, the Commission shall inform the competition authority of the Member State in whose territory the interview takes place. If so requested by the competition authority of that Member State, its officials may assist the officials and other accompanying persons authorised by the Commission to conduct the interview.

Article 20

The Commission's powers of inspection

1. In order to carry out the duties assigned to it by this Regulation, the Commission may conduct all necessary inspections of undertakings and associations of undertakings.

2. The officials and other accompanying persons authorised by the Commission to conduct an inspection are empowered:

(a) to enter any premises, land and means of transport of undertakings and associations of undertakings;

(b) to examine the books and other records related to the business, irrespective of the medium on which they are stored;

(c) to take or obtain in any form copies of or extracts from such books or records;

(d) to seal any business premises and books or records for the period and to the extent necessary for the inspection;

(e) to ask any representative or member of staff of the undertaking or association of undertakings for explanations on facts or documents relating to the subject-matter and purpose of the inspection and to record the answers.

3. The officials and other accompanying persons authorised by the Commission to conduct an inspection shall exercise their powers upon production of a written authorisation specifying the subject matter and purpose of the inspection and the penalties provided for in Article 23 in case the production of the required books or other records related to the business is incomplete or where the answers to questions asked under paragraph 2 of the present Article are incorrect or misleading. In good time before the inspection, the Commission shall give notice of the inspection to the competition authority of the Member State in whose territory it is to be conducted.

4. Undertakings and associations of undertakings are required to submit to inspections ordered by decision of the Commission. The decision shall specify the subject matter and purpose of the inspection, appoint the date on which it is to begin and indicate the penalties provided for in Articles 23 and 24 and the right to have the decision reviewed by the Court of Justice. The Commission shall take such decisions after consulting the competition authority of the Member State in whose territory the inspection is to be conducted.

5. Officials of as well as those authorised or appointed by the competition authority of the Member State in whose territory the inspection is to be conducted shall, at the request of that authority or of the Commission, actively assist the officials and other accompanying persons authorised by the Commission. To this end, they shall enjoy the powers specified in paragraph 2.

6. Where the officials and other accompanying persons authorised by the Commission find that an undertaking opposes an inspection ordered pursuant to this Article, the Member State concerned shall afford them the necessary assistance, requesting where appropriate the assistance of the police or of an equivalent enforcement authority, so as to enable them to conduct their inspection.

7. If the assistance provided for in paragraph 6 requires authorisation from a judicial authority according to national rules, such authorisation shall be applied for. Such authorisation may also be applied for as a precautionary measure.

8. Where authorisation as referred to in paragraph 7 is applied for, the national judicial authority shall control that the Commission decision is authentic and that the coercive measures envisaged are neither arbitrary nor excessive having regard to the subject matter of the inspection. In its control of the proportionality of the coercive measures, the national judicial authority may ask the Commission, directly or through the Member State competition authority, for detailed explanations in particular on the grounds the Commission has for suspecting infringement of Articles 81 and 82 of the Treaty, as well as on the seriousness of the suspected infringement and on the nature of the involvement of the undertaking concerned. However, the national judicial authority may not call into question the necessity for the inspection nor demand that it be provided with the information in the Commission's file. The lawfulness of the Commission decision shall be subject to review only by the Court of Justice.

Article 21

Inspection of other premises

1. If a reasonable suspicion exists that books or other records related to the business and to the subject-matter of the inspection, which may be relevant to prove a serious violation of Article 81 or Article 82 of the Treaty, are being kept in any other premises, land and means of transport, including the homes of directors, managers and other members of staff of the undertakings and associations of undertakings concerned, the Commission can by decision order an inspection to be conducted in such other premises, land and means of transport.

2. The decision shall specify the subject matter and purpose of the inspection, appoint the date on which it is to begin and indicate the right to have the decision reviewed by the Court of Justice. It shall in particular state the reasons that have led the Commission to conclude that a suspicion in the sense of paragraph 1 exists. The Commission shall take such decisions after consulting the competition authority of the Member State in whose territory the inspection is to be conducted.

3. A decision adopted pursuant to paragraph 1 cannot be executed without prior authorisation from the national judicial authority of the Member State concerned. The national judicial authority shall control that the Commission decision is authentic and that the coercive measures envisaged are neither arbitrary nor excessive having regard in particular to the seriousness of the suspected infringement, to the importance of the evidence sought, to the involvement of the undertaking concerned and to the reasonable likelihood that business books and records relating to the subject matter of the inspection are kept in the premises for which the authorisation is requested. The national judicial authority may ask the Commission, directly or through the Member State competition authority, for detailed explanations on those elements which are necessary to allow its control of the proportionality of the coercive measures envisaged.

However, the national judicial authority may not call into question the necessity for the inspection nor demand that it be provided with information in the Commission's file. The lawfulness of the Commission decision shall be subject to review only by the Court of Justice.

4. The officials and other accompanying persons authorised by the Commission to conduct an inspection ordered in accordance with paragraph 1 of this Article shall have the powers set out in Article 20(2)(a), (b) and (c). Article 20(5) and (6) shall apply *mutatis mutandis*.

Article 22

Investigations by competition authorities of Member States

1. The competition authority of a Member State may in its own territory carry out any inspection or other fact-finding measure under its national law on behalf and for the account of the competition authority of another Member State in order to establish whether there has been an infringement of Article 81 or Article 82 of the Treaty. Any exchange and use of the information collected shall be carried out in accordance with Article 12.

2. At the request of the Commission, the competition authorities of the Member States shall undertake the inspections which the Commission considers to be necessary under Article 20(1) or which it has ordered by decision pursuant to Article 20(4). The officials of the competition authorities of the Member States who are responsible for conducting these inspections as well as those authorised or appointed by them shall exercise their powers in accordance with their national law.

If so requested by the Commission or by the competition authority of the Member State in whose territory the inspection is to be conducted, officials and other accompanying persons authorised by the Commission may assist the officials of the authority concerned.

CHAPTER VI

PENALTIES

Article 23

Fines

1. The Commission may by decision impose on undertakings and associations of undertakings fines not exceeding 1 % of the total turnover in the preceding business year where, intentionally or negligently:

(a) they supply incorrect or misleading information in response to a request made pursuant to Article 17 or Article 18(2);

(b) in response to a request made by decision adopted pursuant to Article 17 or Article 18(3), they supply incorrect, incomplete or misleading information or do not supply information within the required time-limit;

(c) they produce the required books or other records related to the business in incomplete form during inspections under Article 20 or refuse to submit to inspections ordered by a decision adopted pursuant to Article 20(4);

(d) in response to a question asked in accordance with Article 20(2)(e),

— they give an incorrect or misleading answer,

— they fail to rectify within a time-limit set by the Commission an incorrect, incomplete or misleading answer given by a member of staff, or

— they fail or refuse to provide a complete answer on facts relating to the subject-matter and purpose of an inspection ordered by a decision adopted pursuant to Article 20(4);

(e) seals affixed in accordance with Article 20(2)(d) by officials or other accompanying persons authorised by the Commission have been broken.

2. The Commission may by decision impose fines on undertakings and associations of undertakings where, either intentionally or negligently:

(a) they infringe Article 81 or Article 82 of the Treaty; or

(b) they contravene a decision ordering interim measures under Article 8; or

(c) they fail to comply with a commitment made binding by a decision pursuant to Article 9.

For each undertaking and association of undertakings participating in the infringement, the fine shall not exceed 10 % of its total turnover in the preceding business year.

Where the infringement of an association relates to the activities of its members, the fine shall not exceed 10 % of the sum of the total turnover of each member active on the market affected by the infringement of the association.

3. In fixing the amount of the fine, regard shall be had both to the gravity and to the duration of the infringement.

4. When a fine is imposed on an association of undertakings taking account of the turnover of its members and the association is not solvent, the association is obliged to call for contributions from its members to cover the amount of the fine.

Where such contributions have not been made to the association within a time-limit fixed by the Commission, the Commission may require payment of the fine directly by any of the undertakings whose representatives were members of the decision-making bodies concerned of the association.

After the Commission has required payment under the second subparagraph, where necessary to ensure full payment of the fine, the Commission may require payment of the balance by any of the members of the association which were active on the market on which the infringement occurred.

However, the Commission shall not require payment under the second or the third subparagraph from undertakings which show that they have not implemented the infringing decision of the association and either were not aware of its existence or have actively distanced themselves from it before the Commission started investigating the case.

The financial liability of each undertaking in respect of the payment of the fine shall not exceed 10 % of its total turnover in the preceding business year.

5. Decisions taken pursuant to paragraphs 1 and 2 shall not be of a criminal law nature.

Article 24

Periodic penalty payments

1. The Commission may, by decision, impose on undertakings or associations of undertakings periodic penalty payments not exceeding 5 % of the average daily turnover in the preceding business year per day and calculated from the date appointed by the decision, in order to compel them:

(a) to put an end to an infringement of Article 81 or Article 82 of the Treaty, in accordance with a decision taken pursuant to Article 7;

(b) to comply with a decision ordering interim measures taken pursuant to Article 8;

(c) to comply with a commitment made binding by a decision pursuant to Article 9;

(d) to supply complete and correct information which it has requested by decision taken pursuant to Article 17 or Article 18(3);

(e) to submit to an inspection which it has ordered by decision taken pursuant to Article 20(4).

2. Where the undertakings or associations of undertakings have satisfied the obligation which the periodic penalty payment was intended to enforce, the Commission may fix the definitive amount of the periodic penalty payment at a figure lower than that which would arise under the original decision. Article 23(4) shall apply correspondingly.

CHAPTER VII

LIMITATION PERIODS

Article 25

Limitation periods for the imposition of penalties

1. The powers conferred on the Commission by Articles 23 and 24 shall be subject to the following limitation periods:

(a) three years in the case of infringements of provisions concerning requests for information or the conduct of inspections;

(b) five years in the case of all other infringements.

2. Time shall begin to run on the day on which the infringement is committed. However, in the case of continuing or repeated infringements, time shall begin to run on the day on which the infringement ceases.

3. Any action taken by the Commission or by the competition authority of a Member State for the purpose of the investigation or proceedings in respect of an infringement shall interrupt the limitation period for the imposition of fines or periodic penalty payments. The limitation period shall be interrupted with effect from the date on which the action is notified to at least one undertaking or association of undertakings which has participated in the infringement. Actions which interrupt the running of the period shall include in particular the following:

(a) written requests for information by the Commission or by the competition authority of a Member State;

(b) written authorisations to conduct inspections issued to its officials by the Commission or by the competition authority of a Member State;

(c) the initiation of proceedings by the Commission or by the competition authority of a Member State;

(d) notification of the statement of objections of the Commission or of the competition authority of a Member State.

4. The interruption of the limitation period shall apply for all the undertakings or associations of undertakings which have participated in the infringement.

5. Each interruption shall start time running afresh. However, the limitation period shall expire at the latest on the day on which a period equal to twice the limitation period has elapsed without the Commission having imposed a fine or a periodic penalty payment. That period shall be extended by the time during which limitation is suspended pursuant to paragraph 6.

6. The limitation period for the imposition of fines or periodic penalty payments shall be suspended for as long as the decision of the Commission is the subject of proceedings pending before the Court of Justice.

Article 26

Limitation period for the enforcement of penalties

1. The power of the Commission to enforce decisions taken pursuant to Articles 23 and 24 shall be subject to a limitation period of five years.

2. Time shall begin to run on the day on which the decision becomes final.

3. The limitation period for the enforcement of penalties shall be interrupted:

(a) by notification of a decision varying the original amount of the fine or periodic penalty payment or refusing an application for variation;

(b) by any action of the Commission or of a Member State, acting at the request of the Commission, designed to enforce payment of the fine or periodic penalty payment.

4. Each interruption shall start time running afresh.

5. The limitation period for the enforcement of penalties shall be suspended for so long as:

(a) time to pay is allowed;

(b) enforcement of payment is suspended pursuant to a decision of the Court of Justice.

CHAPTER VIII

HEARINGS AND PROFESSIONAL SECRECY

Article 27

Hearing of the parties, complainants and others

1. Before taking decisions as provided for in Articles 7, 8, 23 and Article 24(2), the Commission shall give the undertakings or associations of undertakings which are the subject of the proceedings conducted by the Commission the opportunity of being heard on the matters to which the Commission has taken objection. The Commission shall base its decisions only on objections on which the parties concerned have been able to comment. Complainants shall be associated closely with the proceedings.

2. The rights of defence of the parties concerned shall be fully respected in the proceedings. They shall be entitled to have access to the Commission's file, subject to the legitimate interest of undertakings in the protection of their business secrets. The right of access to the file shall not extend to confidential information and internal documents of the Commission or the competition authorities of the Member States. In particular, the right of access shall not extend to correspondence between the Commission and the competition authorities of the Member States, or between the latter, including documents drawn up pursuant to Articles 11 and 14. Nothing in this paragraph shall prevent the Commission from disclosing and using information necessary to prove an infringement.

3. If the Commission considers it necessary, it may also hear other natural or legal persons. Applications to be heard on the part of such persons shall, where they show a sufficient interest, be granted. The competition authorities of the Member States may also ask the Commission to hear other natural or legal persons.

4. Where the Commission intends to adopt a decision pursuant to Article 9 or Article 10, it shall publish a concise summary of the case and the main content of the commitments or of the proposed course of action. Interested third parties may submit their observations within a time limit which is fixed by the Commission in its publication and which may not be less than one month. Publication shall have regard to the legitimate interest of undertakings in the protection of their business secrets.

Article 28

Professional secrecy

1. Without prejudice to Articles 12 and 15, information collected pursuant to Articles 17 to 22 shall be used only for the purpose for which it was acquired.

2. Without prejudice to the exchange and to the use of information foreseen in Articles 11, 12, 14, 15 and 27, the Commission and the competition authorities of the Member States, their officials, servants and other persons working under the supervision of these authorities as well as officials and civil servants of other authorities of the Member States shall not disclose information acquired or exchanged by them pursuant to this Regulation and of the kind covered by the obligation of professional secrecy. This obligation also applies to all representatives and experts of Member States attending meetings of the Advisory Committee pursuant to Article 14.

CHAPTER IX

EXEMPTION REGULATIONS

Article 29

Withdrawal in individual cases

1. Where the Commission, empowered by a Council Regulation, such as Regulations 19/65/EEC, (EEC) No 2821/71, (EEC) No 3976/87, (EEC) No 1534/91 or (EEC) No 479/92, to apply Article 81(3) of the Treaty by regulation, has declared Article 81(1) of the Treaty inapplicable to certain categories of agreements, decisions by associations of undertakings or concerted practices, it may, acting on its own initiative or on a complaint, withdraw the benefit of such an exemption Regulation when it finds that in any particular case an agreement, decision or concerted practice to which the exemption Regulation applies has certain effects which are incompatible with Article 81(3) of the Treaty.

2. Where, in any particular case, agreements, decisions by associations of undertakings or concerted practices to which a Commission Regulation referred to in paragraph 1 applies have effects which are incompatible with Article 81(3) of the Treaty in the territory of a Member State, or in a part thereof, which has all the characteristics of a distinct geographic market, the competition authority of that Member State may withdraw the benefit of the Regulation in question in respect of that territory.

CHAPTER X

GENERAL PROVISIONS

Article 30

Publication of decisions

1. The Commission shall publish the decisions, which it takes pursuant to Articles 7 to 10, 23 and 24.

2. The publication shall state the names of the parties and the main content of the decision, including any penalties imposed. It shall have regard to the legitimate interest of undertakings in the protection of their business secrets.

Article 31

Review by the Court of Justice

The Court of Justice shall have unlimited jurisdiction to review decisions whereby the Commission has fixed a fine or periodic penalty payment. It may cancel, reduce or increase the fine or periodic penalty payment imposed.

Article 32

Exclusions

This Regulation shall not apply to:

(a) international tramp vessel services as defined in Article 1(3)(a) of Regulation (EEC) No 4056/86;

(b) a maritime transport service that takes place exclusively between ports in one and the same Member State as foreseen in Article 1(2) of Regulation (EEC) No 4056/86;

(c) air transport between Community airports and third countries.

Article 33

Implementing provisions

1. The Commission shall be authorised to take such measures as may be appropriate in order to apply this Regulation. The measures may concern, *inter alia*:

(a) the form, content and other details of complaints lodged pursuant to Article 7 and the procedure for rejecting complaints;

(b) the practical arrangements for the exchange of information and consultations provided for in Article 11;

(c) the practical arrangements for the hearings provided for in Article 27.

2. Before the adoption of any measures pursuant to paragraph 1, the Commission shall publish a draft thereof and invite all interested parties to submit their comments within the time-limit it lays down, which may not be less than one month. Before publishing a draft measure and before adopting it, the Commission shall consult the Advisory Committee on Restrictive Practices and Dominant Positions.

CHAPTER XI

TRANSITIONAL, AMENDING AND FINAL PROVISIONS

Article 34

Transitional provisions

1. Applications made to the Commission under Article 2 of Regulation No 17, notifications made under Articles 4 and 5 of that Regulation and the corresponding applications and notifications made under Regulations (EEC) No 1017/68, (EEC) No 4056/86 and (EEC) No 3975/87 shall lapse as from the date of application of this Regulation.

2. Procedural steps taken under Regulation No 17 and Regulations (EEC) No 1017/68, (EEC) No 4056/86 and (EEC) No 3975/87 shall continue to have effect for the purposes of applying this Regulation.

Article 35

Designation of competition authorities of Member States

1. The Member States shall designate the competition authority or authorities responsible for the application of Articles 81 and 82 of the Treaty in such a way that the provisions of this regulation are effectively complied with. The measures necessary to empower those authorities to apply those Articles shall be taken before 1 May 2004. The authorities designated may include courts.

2. When enforcement of Community competition law is entrusted to national administrative and judicial authorities, the Member States may allocate different powers and functions to those different national authorities, whether administrative or judicial.

3. The effects of Article 11(6) apply to the authorities designated by the Member States including courts that exercise functions regarding the preparation and the adoption of the types of decisions foreseen in Article 5. The effects of Article 11(6) do not extend to courts insofar as they act as review courts in respect of the types of decisions foreseen in Article 5.

4. Notwithstanding paragraph 3, in the Member States where, for the adoption of certain types of decisions foreseen in Article 5, an authority brings an action before a judicial authority that is separate and different from the prosecuting authority and provided that the terms of this paragraph are complied with, the effects of Article 11(6) shall be limited to the authority prosecuting the case which shall withdraw its claim before the judicial authority when the Commission opens proceedings and this withdrawal shall bring the national proceedings effectively to an end.

Article 36

Amendment of Regulation (EEC) No 1017/68

Regulation (EEC) No 1017/68 is amended as follows:

1. Article 2 is repealed;
2. in Article 3(1), the words 'The prohibition laid down in Article 2' are replaced by the words 'The prohibition in Article 81(1) of the Treaty';
3. Article 4 is amended as follows:
   (a) In paragraph 1, the words 'The agreements, decisions and concerted practices referred to in Article 2' are replaced by the words 'Agreements, decisions and concerted practices pursuant to Article 81(1) of the Treaty';
   (b) Paragraph 2 is replaced by the following:

   '2. If the implementation of any agreement, decision or concerted practice covered by paragraph 1 has, in a given case, effects which are incompatible with the requirements of Article 81(3) of the Treaty, undertakings or associations of undertakings may be required to make such effects cease.'
4. Articles 5 to 29 are repealed with the exception of Article 13(3) which continues to apply to decisions adopted pursuant to Article 5 of Regulation (EEC) No 1017/68 prior to the date of application of this Regulation until the date of expiration of those decisions;
5. in Article 30, paragraphs 2, 3 and 4 are deleted.

Article 37

Amendment of Regulation (EEC) No 2988/74

In Regulation (EEC) No 2988/74, the following Article is inserted:

'*Article 7a*

Exclusion

This Regulation shall not apply to measures taken under Council Regulation (EC) No 1/2003 of 16 December 2002 on the implementation of the rules on competition laid down in Articles 81 and 82 of the Treaty (*).

(*) OJ L 1, 4.1.2003, p. 1.'

Article 38

Amendment of Regulation (EEC) No 4056/86

Regulation (EEC) No 4056/86 is amended as follows:

1. Article 7 is amended as follows:

   (a) Paragraph 1 is replaced by the following:

   '1. *Breach of an obligation*

   Where the persons concerned are in breach of an obligation which, pursuant to Article 5, attaches to the exemption provided for in Article 3, the Commission may, in order to put an end to such breach and under the conditions laid down in Council Regulation (EC) No 1/2003 of 16 December 2002 on the implementation of the rules on competition laid down in Articles 81 and 82 of the Treaty (*) adopt a decision that either prohibits them from carrying out or requires them to perform certain specific acts, or withdraws the benefit of the block exemption which they enjoyed.

   (*) OJ L 1, 4.1.2003, p. 1.'

   (b) Paragraph 2 is amended as follows:

   (i) In point (a), the words 'under the conditions laid down in Section II' are replaced by the words 'under the conditions laid down in Regulation (EC) No 1/2003';

   (ii) The second sentence of the second subparagraph of point (c)(i) is replaced by the following:

   'At the same time it shall decide, in accordance with Article 9 of Regulation (EC) No 1/2003, whether to accept commitments offered by the undertakings concerned with a view, *inter alia*, to obtaining access to the market for non-conference lines.'

2. Article 8 is amended as follows:

   (a) Paragraph 1 is deleted.

   (b) In paragraph 2 the words 'pursuant to Article 10' are replaced by the words 'pursuant to Regulation (EC) No 1/2003'.

   (c) Paragraph 3 is deleted;

3. Article 9 is amended as follows:

   (a) In paragraph 1, the words 'Advisory Committee referred to in Article 15' are replaced by the words 'Advisory Committee referred to in Article 14 of Regulation (EC) No 1/2003';

   (b) In paragraph 2, the words 'Advisory Committee as referred to in Article 15' are replaced by the words 'Advisory Committee referred to in Article 14 of Regulation (EC) No 1/2003';

4. Articles 10 to 25 are repealed with the exception of Article 13(3) which continues to apply to decisions adopted pursuant to Article 81(3) of the Treaty prior to the date of application of this Regulation until the date of expiration of those decisions;

5. in Article 26, the words 'the form, content and other details of complaints pursuant to Article 10, applications pursuant to Article 12 and the hearings provided for in Article 23(1) and (2)' are deleted.

Article 39

Amendment of Regulation (EEC) No 3975/87

Articles 3 to 19 of Regulation (EEC) No 3975/87 are repealed with the exception of Article 6(3) which continues to apply to decisions adopted pursuant to Article 81(3) of the Treaty prior to the date of application of this Regulation until the date of expiration of those decisions.

Article 40

Amendment of Regulations No 19/65/EEC, (EEC) No 2821/71 and (EEC) No 1534/91

Article 7 of Regulation No 19/65/EEC, Article 7 of Regulation (EEC) No 2821/71 and Article 7 of Regulation (EEC) No 1534/91 are repealed.

Article 41

Amendment of Regulation (EEC) No 3976/87

Regulation (EEC) No 3976/87 is amended as follows:

1. Article 6 is replaced by the following:

   '*Article 6*

   The Commission shall consult the Advisory Committee referred to in Article 14 of Council Regulation (EC) No 1/2003 of 16 December 2002 on the implementation of the rules on competition laid down in Articles 81 and 82 of the Treaty (*) before publishing a draft Regulation and before adopting a Regulation.

   (*) OJ L 1, 4.1.2003, p. 1.'

2. Article 7 is repealed.

Article 42

Amendment of Regulation (EEC) No 479/92

Regulation (EEC) No 479/92 is amended as follows:

1. Article 5 is replaced by the following:

   '*Article 5*

   Before publishing the draft Regulation and before adopting the Regulation, the Commission shall consult the Advisory Committee referred to in Article 14 of Council Regulation (EC) No 1/2003 of 16 December 2002 on the implementation of the rules on competition laid down in Articles 81 and 82 of the Treaty (*).

   (*) OJ L 1, 4.1.2003, p. 1.'

2. Article 6 is repealed.

Article 43

Repeal of Regulations No 17 and No 141

1. Regulation No 17 is repealed with the exception of Article 8(3) which continues to apply to decisions adopted pursuant to Article 81(3) of the Treaty prior to the date of application of this Regulation until the date of expiration of those decisions.

2. Regulation No 141 is repealed.

3. References to the repealed Regulations shall be construed as references to this Regulation.

Article 44

Report on the application of the present Regulation

Five years from the date of application of this Regulation, the Commission shall report to the European Parliament and the Council on the functioning of this Regulation, in particular on the application of Article 11(6) and Article 17.

On the basis of this report, the Commission shall assess whether it is appropriate to propose to the Council a revision of this Regulation.

Article 45

Entry into force

This Regulation shall enter into force on the 20th day following that of its publication in the *Official Journal of the European Communities.*

It shall apply from 1 May 2004.

This Regulation shall be binding in its entirety and directly applicable in all Member States.

Done at Brussels, 16 December 2002.

For the Council
The President
M. FISCHER BOEL

Commission Notice on agreements of minor importance which do not appreciably restrict competition under Article 81(1) of the Treaty establishing the European Community (*de minimis*) (1)

(2001/C 368/07)

(Text with EEA relevance)

I

1. Article 81(1) prohibits agreements between undertakings which may affect trade between Member States and which have as their object or effect the prevention, restriction or distortion of competition within the common market. The Court of Justice of the European Communities has clarified that this provision is not applicable where the impact of the agreement on intra-Community trade or on competition is not appreciable.

2. In this notice the Commission quantifies, with the help of market share thresholds, what is not an appreciable restriction of competition under Article 81 of the EC Treaty. This negative definition of appreciability does not imply that agreements between undertakings which exceed the thresholds set out in this notice appreciably restrict competition. Such agreements may still have only a negligible effect on competition and may therefore not be prohibited by Article 81(1) (2).

3. Agreements may in addition not fall under Article 81(1) because they are not capable of appreciably affecting trade between Member States. This notice does not deal with this issue. It does not quantify what does not constitute an appreciable effect on trade. It is however acknowledged that agreements between small and medium-sized undertakings, as defined in the Annex to Commission Recommendation 96/280/EC (3), are rarely capable of appreciably affecting trade between Member States. Small and medium-sized undertakings are currently defined in that recommendation as undertakings which have fewer than 250 employees and have either an annual turnover not exceeding EUR 40 million or an annual balance-sheet total not exceeding EUR 27 million.

4. In cases covered by this notice the Commission will not institute proceedings either upon application or on its own initiative. Where undertakings assume in good faith that an agreement is covered by this notice, the Commission will not impose fines. Although not binding on them, this notice also intends to give guidance to the courts and authorities of the Member States in their application of Article 81.

5. This notice also applies to decisions by associations of undertakings and to concerted practices.

6. This notice is without prejudice to any interpretation of Article 81 which may be given by the Court of Justice or the Court of First Instance of the European Communities.

II

7. The Commission holds the view that agreements between undertakings which affect trade between Member States do not appreciably restrict competition within the meaning of Article 81(1):

   (a) if the aggregate market share held by the parties to the agreement does not exceed 10 % on any of the relevant markets affected by the agreement, where the agreement is made between undertakings which are actual or potential competitors on any of these markets (agreements between competitors) (4); or

   (b) if the market share held by each of the parties to the agreement does not exceed 15 % on any of the relevant markets affected by the agreement, where the agreement is made between undertakings which are not actual or potential competitors on any of these markets (agreements between non-competitors).

   In cases where it is difficult to classify the agreement as either an agreement between competitors or an agreement between non-competitors the 10 % threshold is applicable.

(1) This notice replaces the notice on agreements of minor importance published in OJ C 372, 9.12.1997.

(2) See, for instance, the judgment of the Court of Justice in Joined Cases C-215/96 and C-216/96 *Bagnasco (Carlos) v Banca Popolare di Novara and Casa di Risparmio di Genova e Imperia* (1999) ECR I-135, points 34-35. This notice is also without prejudice to the principles for assessment under Article 81(1) as expressed in the Commission notice 'Guidelines on the applicability of Article 81 of the EC Treaty to horizontal cooperation agreements', OJ C 3, 6.1.2001, in particular points 17-31 inclusive, and in the Commission notice 'Guidelines on vertical restraints', OJ C 291, 13.10.2000, in particular points 5-20 inclusive.

(3) OJ L 107, 30.4.1996, p. 4. This recommendation will be revised. It is envisaged to increase the annual turnover threshold from EUR 40 million to EUR 50 million and the annual balance-sheet total threshold from EUR 27 million to EUR 43 million.

(4) On what are actual or potential competitors, see the Commission notice 'Guidelines on the applicability of Article 81 of the EC Treaty to horizontal cooperation agreements', OJ C 3, 6.1.2001, paragraph 9. A firm is treated as an actual competitor if it is either active on the same relevant market or if, in the absence of the agreement, it is able to switch production to the relevant products and market them in the short term without incurring significant additional costs or risks in response to a small and permanent increase in relative prices (immediate supply-side substitutability). A firm is treated as a potential competitor if there is evidence that, absent the agreement, this firm could and would be likely to undertake the necessary additional investments or other necessary switching costs so that it could enter the relevant market in response to a small and permanent increase in relative prices.

8. Where in a relevant market competition is restricted by the cumulative effect of agreements for the sale of goods or services entered into by different suppliers or distributors (cumulative foreclosure effect of parallel networks of agreements having similar effects on the market), the market share thresholds under point 7 are reduced to 5 %, both for agreements between competitors and for agreements between non-competitors. Individual suppliers or distributors with a market share not exceeding 5 % are in general not considered to contribute significantly to a cumulative foreclosure effect (1). A cumulative foreclosure effect is unlikely to exist if less than 30 % of the relevant market is covered by parallel (networks of) agreements having similar effects.

9. The Commission also holds the view that agreements are not restrictive of competition if the market shares do not exceed the thresholds of respectively 10 %, 15 % and 5 % set out in point 7 and 8 during two successive calendar years by more than 2 percentage points.

10. In order to calculate the market share, it is necessary to determine the relevant market. This consists of the relevant product market and the relevant geographic market. When defining the relevant market, reference should be had to the notice on the definition of the relevant market for the purposes of Community competition law (2). The market shares are to be calculated on the basis of sales value data or, where appropriate, purchase value data. If value data are not available, estimates based on other reliable market information, including volume data, may be used.

11. Points 7, 8 and 9 do not apply to agreements containing any of the following hardcore restrictions:

(1) as regards agreements between competitors as defined in point 7, restrictions which, directly or indirectly, in isolation or in combination with other factors under the control of the parties, have as their object (3):

(a) the fixing of prices when selling the products to third parties;

(b) the limitation of output or sales;

(c) the allocation of markets or customers;

(2) as regards agreements between non-competitors as defined in point 7, restrictions which, directly or indirectly, in isolation or in combination with other factors under the control of the parties, have as their object:

(a) the restriction of the buyer's ability to determine its sale price, without prejudice to the possibility of the supplier imposing a maximum sale price or recommending a sale price, provided that they do not amount to a fixed or minimum sale price as a result of pressure from, or incentives offered by, any of the parties;

(b) the restriction of the territory into which, or of the customers to whom, the buyer may sell the contract goods or services, except the following restrictions which are not hardcore:

— the restriction of active sales into the exclusive territory or to an exclusive customer group reserved to the supplier or allocated by the supplier to another buyer, where such a restriction does not limit sales by the customers of the buyer,

— the restriction of sales to end users by a buyer operating at the wholesale level of trade,

— the restriction of sales to unauthorised distributors by the members of a selective distribution system, and

— the restriction of the buyer's ability to sell components, supplied for the purposes of incorporation, to customers who would use them to manufacture the same type of goods as those produced by the supplier;

(c) the restriction of active or passive sales to end users by members of a selective distribution system operating at the retail level of trade, without prejudice to the possibility of prohibiting a member of the system from operating out of an unauthorised place of establishment;

(d) the restriction of cross-supplies between distributors within a selective distribution system, including between distributors operating at different levels of trade;

(1) See also the Commission notice 'Guidelines on vertical restraints', OJ C 291, 13.10.2000, in particular paragraphs 73, 142, 143 and 189. While in the guidelines on vertical restraints in relation to certain restrictions reference is made not only to the total but also to the tied market share of a particular supplier or buyer, in this notice all market share thresholds refer to total market shares.

(2) OJ C 372, 9.12.1997, p. 5.

(3) Without prejudice to situations of joint production with or without joint distribution as defined in Article 5, paragraph 2, of Commission Regulation (EC) No 2658/2000 and Article 5, paragraph 2, of Commission Regulation (EC) No 2659/2000, OJ L 304, 5.12.2000, pp. 3 and 7 respectively.

(e) the restriction agreed between a supplier of components and a buyer who incorporates those components, which limits the supplier's ability to sell the components as spare parts to end users or to repairers or other service providers not entrusted by the buyer with the repair or servicing of its goods;

(3) as regards agreements between competitors as defined in point 7, where the competitors operate, for the purposes of the agreement, at a different level of the production or distribution chain, any of the hardcore restrictions listed in paragraph (1) and (2) above.

12. (1) For the purposes of this notice, the terms 'undertaking', 'party to the agreement', 'distributor', 'supplier' and 'buyer' shall include their respective connected undertakings.

(2) 'Connected undertakings' are:

(a) undertakings in which a party to the agreement, directly or indirectly:

— has the power to exercise more than half the voting rights, or

— has the power to appoint more than half the members of the supervisory board, board of management or bodies legally representing the undertaking, or

— has the right to manage the undertaking's affairs;

(b) undertakings which directly or indirectly have, over a party to the agreement, the rights or powers listed in (a);

(c) undertakings in which an undertaking referred to in (b) has, directly or indirectly, the rights or powers listed in (a);

(d) undertakings in which a party to the agreement together with one or more of the undertakings referred to in (a), (b) or (c), or in which two or more of the latter undertakings, jointly have the rights or powers listed in (a);

(e) undertakings in which the rights or the powers listed in (a) are jointly held by:

— parties to the agreement or their respective connected undertakings referred to in (a) to (d), or

— one or more of the parties to the agreement or one or more of their connected undertakings referred to in (a) to (d) and one or more third parties.

(3) For the purposes of paragraph 2(e), the market share held by these jointly held undertakings shall be apportioned equally to each undertaking having the rights or the powers listed in paragraph 2(a).

COMMISSION NOTICE on the definition of relevant market for the purposes of Community competition law (97/C 372/03)

(Text with EEA relevance)

I. INTRODUCTION

1. The purpose of this notice is to provide guidance as to how the Commission applies the concept of relevant product and geographic market in its ongoing enforcement of Community competition law, in particular the application of Council Regulation No 17 and (EEC) No 4064/89, their equivalents in other sectoral applications such as transport, coal and steel, and agriculture, and the relevant provisions of the EEA Agreement (1). Throughout this notice, references to Articles 85 and 86 of the Treaty and to merger control are to be understood as referring to the equivalent provisions in the EEA Agreement and the ECSC Treaty.

2. Market definition is a tool to identify and define the boundaries of competition between firms. It serves to establish the framework within which competition policy is applied by the Commission. The main purpose of market definition is to identify in a systematic way the competitive constraints that the undertakings involved (2) face. The objective of defining a market in both its product and geographic dimension is to identify those actual competitors of the undertakings involved that are capable of constraining those undertakings' behaviour and of preventing them from behaving independently of effective competitive pressure. It is from this perspective that the market definition makes it possible inter alia to calculate market shares that would convey meaningful information regarding market power for the purposes of assessing dominance or for the purposes of applying Article 85.

3. It follows from point 2 that the concept of 'relevant market' is different from other definitions of market often used in other contexts. For instance, companies often use the term 'market' to refer to the area where it sells its products or to refer broadly to the industry or sector where it belongs.

4. The definition of the relevant market in both its product and its geographic dimensions often has a decisive influence on the assessment of a competition case. By rendering public the procedures which the Commission follows when considering market definition and by indicating the criteria and evidence on which it relies to reach a decision, the Commission expects to increase the transparency of its policy and decision-making in the area of competition policy.

5. Increased transparency will also result in companies and their advisers being able to better anticipate the possibility that the Commission may raise competition concerns in an individual case. Companies could, therefore, take such a possibility into account in their own internal decision-making when contemplating, for instance, acquisitions, the creation of joint ventures, or the establishment of certain agreements. It is also intended that companies should be in a better position to understand what sort of information the Commission considers relevant for the purposes of market definition.

6. The Commission's interpretation of 'relevant market' is without prejudice to the interpretation which may be given by the Court of Justice or the Court of First Instance of the European Communities.

Reproduced from the Official Journal of the European Communities: C 372, 9/12/1997 P. 0005–0013

II. DEFINITION OF RELEVANT MARKET

Definition of relevant product market and relevant geographic market

7. The Regulations based on Article 85 and 86 of the Treaty, in particular in section 6 of Form A/B with respect to Regulation No 17, as well as in section 6 of Form CO with respect to Regulation (EEC) No 4064/89 on the control of concentrations having a Community dimension have laid down the following definitions, 'Relevant product markets' are defined as follows:

> 'A relevant product market comprises all those products and/or services which are regarded as interchangeable or substitutable by the consumer, by reason of the products' characteristics, their prices and their intended use'.

8. 'Relevant geographic markets' are defined as follows:

> 'The relevant geographic market comprises the area in which the undertakings concerned are involved in the supply and demand of products or services, in which the conditions of competition are sufficiently homogeneous and which can be distinguished from neighbouring areas because the conditions of competition are appreciably different in those area'.

9. The relevant market within which to assess a given competition issue is therefore established by the combination of the product and geographic markets. The Commission interprets the definitions in paragraphs 7 an 8 (which reflect the case-law of the Court of Justice and the Court of First Instance as well as its own decision-making practice) according to the orientations defined in this notice.

Concept of relevant market and objectives of Community competition policy

10. The concept of relevant market is closely related to the objectives pursued under Community competition policy. For example, under the Community's merger control, the objective in controlling structural changes in the supply of a product/service is to prevent the creation or reinforcement of a dominant position as a result of which effective competition would be significantly impeded in a substantial part of the common market. Under the Community's competition rules, a dominant position is such that a firm or group of firms would be in a position to behave to an appreciable extent independently of its competitors, customers and ultimately of its consumers (3). Such a position would usually arise when a firm or group of firms accounted for a large share of the supply in any given market, provided that other factors analysed in the assessment (such as entry barriers, customers' capacity to react, etc.) point in the same direction.

11. The same approach is followed by the Commission in its application of Article 86 of the Treaty to firms that enjoy a single or collective dominant position. Within the meaning of Regulation No 17, the Commission has the power to investigate and bring to an end abuses of such a dominant position, which must also be defined by reference to the relevant market. Markets may also need to be defined in the application of Article 85 of the Treaty, in particular, in determining whether an appreciable restriction of competition exists or in establishing if the condition pursuant to Article 85 (3) (b) for an exemption from the application of Article 85 (1) is met.

12. The criteria for defining the relevant market are applied generally for the analysis of certain types of behaviour in the market and for the analysis of structural changes in the supply of products. This methodology, though, might lead to different results depending on the nature

of the competition issue being examined. For instance, the scope of the geographic market might be different when analysing a concentration, where the analysis is essentially prospective, from an analysis of past behaviour. The different time horizon considered in each case might lead to the result that different geographic markets are defined for the same products depending on whether the Commission is examining a change in the structure of supply, such as a concentration or a cooperative joint venture, or examining issues relating to certain past behaviour.

Basic principles for market definition

Competitive constraints

13. Firms are subject to three main sources or competitive constraints: demand substitutability, supply substitutability and potential competition. From an economic point of view, for the definition of the relevant market, demand substitution constitutes the most immediate and effective disciplinary force on the suppliers of a given product, in particular in relation to their pricing decisions. A firm or a group of firms cannot have a significant impact on the prevailing conditions of sale, such as prices, if its customers are in a position to switch easily to available substitute products or to suppliers located elsewhere. Basically, the exercise of market definition consists in identifying the effective alternative sources of supply for the customers of the undertakings involved, in terms both of products/services and of geographic location of suppliers.

14. The competitive constraints arising from supply side substitutability other then those described in paragraphs 20 to 23 and from potential competition are in general less immediate and in any case require an analysis of additional factors. As a result such constraints are taken into account at the assessment stage of competition analysis.

Demand substitution

15. The assessment of demand substitution entails a determination of the range of products which are viewed as substitutes by the consumer. One way of making this determination can be viewed as a speculative experiment, postulating a hypothetical small, lasting change in relative prices and evaluating the likely reactions of customers to that increase. The exercise of market definition focuses on prices for operational and practical purposes, and more precisely on demand substitution arising from small, permanent changes in relative prices. This concept can provide clear indications as to the evidence that is relevant in defining markets.

16. Conceptually, this approach means that, starting from the type of products that the undertakings involved sell and the area in which they sell them, additional products and areas will be included in, or excluded from, the market definition depending on whether competition from these other products and areas affect or restrain sufficiently the pricing of the parties' products in the short term.

17. The question to be answered is whether the parties' customers would switch to readily available substitutes or to suppliers located elsewhere in response to a hypothetical small (in the range 5 % to 10 %) but permanent relative price increase in the products and areas being considered. If substitution were enough to make the price increase unprofitable because of the resulting loss of sales, additional substitutes and areas are included in the relevant market. This would be done until the set of products and geographical areas is such that small, permanent increases in relative prices would be profitable. The equivalent analysis is applicable in cases

concerning the concentraiton of buying power, where the starting point would then be the supplier and the price test serves to identify the alternative distribution channels or outlets for the supplier's products. In the application of these principles, careful account should be taken of certain particular situations as described within paragraphs 56 and 58.

18. A practical example of this test can be provided by its application to a merger of, for instance, soft-drink bottlers. An issue to examine in such a case would be to decide whether different flavours of soft drinks belong to the same market. In practice, the question to address would be whether consumers of flavour A would switch to other flavours when confronted with a permanent price increase of 5 % to 10 % for flavour A. If a sufficient number of consumers would switch to, say, flavour B, to such an extent that the price increase for flavour A would not be profitable owing to the resulting loss of sales, then the market would comprise at least flavours A and B. The process would have to be extended in addition to other available flavours until a set of products is identified for which a price rise would not induce a sufficient substitution in demand.

19. Generally, and in particular for the analysis of merger cases, the price to take into account will be the prevailing market price. This may not be the case where the prevailing price has been determined in the absence of sufficient competition. In particular for the investigation of abuses of dominant positions, the fact that the prevailing price might already have been substantially increased will be taken into account.

Supply substitution

20. Supply-side substitutability may also be taken into account when defining markets in those situaitons in which its effects are equivalent to those of demand substitution in terms of effectiveness and immediacy. This means that suppliers are able to switch production to the relevant products and market them in the short term (4) without incurring significant additional costs or risks in response to small and permanent changes in relative prices. When these conditions are met, the additional production that is put on the market will have a disciplinary effect on the competitive behaviour of the companies involved. Such an impact in terms of effectiveness and immediacy is equivalent to the demand substitution effect.

21. These situations typically arise when companies market a wide range of qualities or grades of one product; even if, for a given final customer or group of consumers, the different qualities are not substitutable, the different qualities will be grouped into one product market, provided that most of the suppliers are able to offer and sell the various qualities immediately and without the significant increases in costs described above. In such cases, the relevant product market will encompass all products that are substitutable in demand and supply, and the current sales of those products will be aggregated so as to give the total value or volume of the market. The same reasoning may lead to group different geographic areas.

22. A practical example of the approach to supply-side substitutability when defining product markets is to be found in the case of paper. Paer is usually supplied in a range of different qualities, from standard writing paper to high quality papers to be used, for instance, to publish art books. From a demand point of view, different qualities of paper cannot be used for any given use, i.e. an art book or a high quality publication cannot be based on lower quality papers. However, paper plants are prepared to manufacture the different qualities, and production can be adjusted with negligible costs and in a short time-frame. In the absence of particular difficulties in distribution, paper manufacturers are able therefore, to compete for orders of the various qualities, in particular if orders are placed with sufficient lead time to allow for modification of production plans. Under such circumstances, the Commission would

not define a separate market for each quality of paper and its respective use. The various qualities of paper are included in the relevant market, and their sales added up to estimate total market galue and volume.

23. When supply-side substitutability would entail the need to adjust significantly existing tangible and intangible assets, additional investments, strategic decisions or time delays, it will not be considered at the stage of market definition. Examples where supply-side substitution did not induce the Commission to enlarge the market are offered in the area of consumer products, in particular for branded beverages. Although bottling plants may in principle bottle different beverages, there are costs and lead times involved (in terms of advertising, product testing and distribution) before the products can actually be sold. In these cases, the effects of supply-side substitutability and other forms of potential competition would then be examined at a later stage.

Potential competition

24. The third source of competitive constraint, potential competition, is not taken into account when defining markets, since the conditions under which potential competition will actually represent an effective competitive constraint depend on the analysis of specific factors and circumstances related to the conditions of entry. If required, this analysis is only carried out at a subsequent stage, in general once the position of the companies involved in the relevant market has already been ascertained, and when such position gives rise to concerns from a competition point of view.

III. EVIDENCE RELIED ON TO DEFINE RELEVANT MARKETS

The process of defining the relevant market in practice

Product dimension

25. There is a range of evidence permitting an assessment of the extent to which substitution would take place. In individual cases, certain types of evidence will be determinant, depending very much on the characteristics and specificity of the industry and products or services that are being examined. The same type of evidence may be of no importance in other cases. In most cases, a decision will have to be based on the consideration of a number of criteria and different items of evidence. The Commission follows an open approach to empirical evidence, aimed at making an effective use of all available information which may be relevant in individual cases. The Commission does not follow a rigid hierarchy of different sources of information or types of evidence.

26. The process of defining relevant markets may be summarized as follows: on the basis of the preliminary information available or information submitted by the undertakings involved, the Commission will usually be in a position to broadly establish the possible relevant markets within which, for instance, a concentration or a restriction of competition has to be assessed. In general, and for all practical purposes when handling individual cases, the question will usually be to decide on a few alternative possible relevant markets. For instance, with respect to the product market, the issue will often be to establish whether product A and product B belong or do not belong to the same product market. it is often the case that the inclusion of product B would be enough to remove any competition concerns.

27. In such situations it is not necessary to consider whether the market includes additional products, or to reach a definitive conclusion on the precise product market. If under the conceivable alternative market definitions the operation in question does not raise competition concerns, the question of market definition will be left open, reducing thereby the burden on companies to supply information.

Geographic dimension

28. The Commission's approach to geographic market definition might be summarized as follows: it will take a preliminary view of the scope of the geographic market on the basis of broad indications as to the distribution of market shares between the parties and their competitors, as well as a preliminary analysis of pricing and price differences at national and Community or EEA level. This initial view is used basically as a working hypothesis to focus the Commission's enquiries for the purposes of arriving at a precise geographic market definition.

29. The reasons behind any particular configuration of prices and market shares need to be explored. Companies might enjoy high market shares in their domestic markets just because of the weight of the past, and conversely, a homogeneous presence of companies throughout the EEA might be consistent with national or regional geographic markets. The initial working hypothesis will therefore be checked against an analysis of demand characteristics (importance of national or local preferences, current patterns of purchases of customers, product differentiation/brands, other) in order to establish whether companies in different areas do indeed constitute a real alternative source of supply for consumers. The theoretical experiment is again based on substitution arising from changes in relative prices, and the question to answer is again whether the customers of the parties would switch their orders to companies located elsewhere in the short term and at a negligible cost.

30. If necessary, a further check on supply factors will be carried out to ensure that those companies located in differing areas do not face impediments in developing their sales on competitive terms throughout the whole geographic market. This analysis will include an examination of requirements for a local presence in order to sell in that area the conditions of access to distribution channels, costs associated with setting up a distribution network, and the presence or absence of regulatory barriers arising from public procurement, price regulations, quotas and tariffs limiting trade or production, technical standards, monopolies, freedom of establishment, requirements for administrative authorizations, packaging regulations, etc. In short, the Commission will identify possible obstacles and barriers isolating companies located in a given area from the competitive pressure of companies located outside that area, so as to determine the precise degree of market interpenetration at national, European or global level.

31. The actual pattern and evolution of trade flows offers useful supplementary indications as to the economic importance of each demand or supply factor mentioned above, and the extent to which they may or may not constitute actual barriers creating different geographic markets. The analysis of trade flows will generally address the question of transport costs and the extent to which these may hinder trade between different areas, having regard to plant location, costs of production and relative price levels.

Market integration in the Community

32. Finally, the Commission also takes into account the continuing process of market integration, in particular in the Community, when defining geographic markets, especially in

the area of concentrations and structural joint ventures. The measures adopted and implemented in the internal market programme to remove barriers to trade and further integrate the Community markets cannot be ignored when assessing the effects on competition of a concentration or a structural joint venture. A situation where national markets have been artifically isolated from each other because of the existence of legislative barriers that have now been removed will generally lead to a cautious assessment of past evidence regarding prices, market shares or trade patterns. A process of market integration that would, in the short term, lead to wider geographic markets may therefore be taken into consideration when defining the geographic market for the purposes of assessing concentrations and joint ventures.

The process of gathering evidence

33. When a precise market definition is deemed necessary, the Commission will often contact the main customers and the main companies in the industry to enquire into their views about the boudaries of product and geographic markets and to obtain the necessary factual evidence to reach a conclusion. The Commission might also contact the relevant professional associations, and companies active in upstream markets, so as to be able to define, in so far as necessary, separate product and geographic markets, for different levels of production or distribution of the products/services in question. It might also request additional information to the undertakings involved.

34. Where appropriate, the Commission will address written requests for information to the market players mentioned above. These requests will usually include questions relating to the perceptions of companies about reactions to hypothetical price increases and their views of the boundaries of the relevant market. They will also ask for provision of the factual information the Commission deems necessary to reach a conclusion on the extent of the relevant market. The Commission might also discuss with marketing directors or other officers of those companies to gain a better understanding on how negotiations between suppliers and customers take place and better understand issues relating to the definition of the relevant market. Where appropriate, they might also carry out visits or inspections to the premises of the parties, their customers and/or their competitors, in order to better understand how products are manufactured and sold.

35. The type of evidence relevant to reach a conclusion as to the product market can be categorized as follows:

Evidence to define markets – product dimension

36. An analysis of the product characteristics and its intended use allows the Commission, as a first step, to limit the field of investigation of possible substitutes. However, product characteristics and intended use are insufficient to show whether two products are demand substitutes. Functional interchangeability or similarity in characteristics may not, in themselves, provide sufficient criteria, because the responsiveness of customers to relative price changes may be determinded by other considerations as well. For example, there may be different competitive contraints in the original equipment market for car components and in spare parts, thereby leading to a separate delineation of two relevant markets. Conversely, differences in product characteristics are not in themselves sufficient to exclude demand substitutability, since this will depend to a large extent on how customers value different characteristics.

37. The type of evidence the Commission considers relevant to assess whether two products are demand substitutes can be categorized as follows:

38. Evidence of substitution in the recent past. In certain cases, it is possible to analyse evidence relating to recent past events or shocks in the market that offer actual examples of substituion between two products. When available, this sort of information will normally be fundamental for market definition. If there have been changes in relative prices in the past (all else being equal), the reactions in terms of quantities demanded will be determinant in establishing substitutability. Launches of new products in the past can also offer useful information, when it is possible to precisely analyse which products have lost sales to the new product.

39. There are a number of quantitative tests that have specifically been designed for the purpose of delineating markets. These tests consist of various econometric and statistical approaches estimates of elasticities and cross-price elasticities (5) for the demand of a product, tests based on similarity of price movements over time, the analysis of causality between price series and similarity of price levels and/or their convergence. The Commission takes into account the available quantitative evidence capable of withstanding rigorous scrutiny for the purposes of establishing patterns of substitution in the past.

40. Views of customers and competitors. The Commission often contacts the main customers and competitors of the companies involved in its enquiries, to gather their views on the boundaries of the product market as well as most of the factual information it requires to reach a conclusion on the scope of the market. Reasoned answers of customers and competitors as to what would happen if relative prices for the candidate products were to increase in the candidate geographic area by a small amount (for instance of 5 % to 10 %) are taken into account when they are sufficiently backed by factual evidence.

41. Consumer preferences. In the case of consumer goods, it may be difficult for the Commission to gather the direct views of end consumers about substitute products. Marketing studies that companies have commissioned in the past and that are used by companies in their own decision-making as to pricing of their products and/or marketing actions may provide useful information for the Commission's delineation of the relevant market. Consumer surveys on usage patterns and attitudes, data from consumer's purchasing patterns, the views expressed by retailers and more generally, market research studies submitted by the parties and their competitors are taken into account to establish whether an economically significant proportion of consumers consider two products as substitutable, also taking into account the importance of brands for the products in question. The methodology followed in consumer surveys carried out ad hoc by the undertakings involved or their competitors for the purposes of a merger procedure or a procedure pursuant to Regulation No 17 will usually be scrutinized with utmost care. Unlike pre-existing studies, they have not been prepared in the normal course of business for the adoption of business decisions.

42. Barriers and costs associated with switching demand to potential substitutes. There are a number of barriers and costs that might prevent the Commission from considering two prima facie demand substitutes as belonging to one single product market. It is not possible to provide an exhaustive list of all the possible barriers to substitution and of switching costs. These barriers or obstacles might have a wide range of origins, and in its decisions, the Commission has been confronted with regulatory barriers or other forms of State intervention, constraints arising in downstream markets, need to incur specific capital investment or loss in current output in order to switch to alternative inputs, the location of customers, specific investment in production process, learning and human capital investment, retooling costs or other investments, uncertainty about quality and reputation of unknown suppliers, and others.

43. Different categories of customers and price discrimination. The extent of the product market might be narrowed in the presence of distinct groups of customers. A distinct group of customers for the relevant product may constitute a narrower, distinct market when such ha group could be subject to price discrimination. This will usually be the case when two conditions are met: (a) it is possible to identify clearly which group an individual customer belongs to at the moment of selling the relevant products to him, and (b) trade among customers or arbitrage by third parties should not be feasible.

Evidence for defining markets – geographic dimension

44. The type of evidence the Commission considers relevant to reach a conclusion as to the geographic market can be categorized as follows:

45. Past evidence of diversion of orders to other areas. In certain cases, evidence on changes in prices between different areas and consequent reactions by customers might be available. Generally, the same quantitative tests used for product market definition might as well be used in geographic market definition, bearing in mind that international comparisons of prices might be more complex due to a number of factors such as exchange rate movements, taxation and product differentiation.

46. Basic demand characteristics. The nature of demand for the relevant product may in itself determine the scope of the geographical market. Factors such as national preferences or preferences for national brands, language, culture and life style, and the need for a local presence have a strong potential to limit the geographic scope of competition.

47. Views of customers and competitors. Where appropriate, the Commission will contact the main customers and competitors of the parties in its enquiries, to gather their views on the boundaries of the geographic market as well as most of the factual information it requires to reach a conclusion on the scope of the market when they are sufficiently backed by factual evidence.

48. Current geographic pattern of purchases. An examination of the customers' current geographic pattern of purchases provides useful evidence as to the possible scope of the geographic market. When customers purchase from companies located anywhere in the Community or the EEA on similar terms, or they procure their supplies through effective tendering procedures in which companies from anywhere in the Community or the EEA submit bids, usually the geographic market will be considered to be Community-wide.

49. Trade flows/pattern of shipments. When the number of customers is so large that it is not possible to obtain through them a clear picture of geographic purchasing patterns, information on trade flows might be used alternatively, provided that the trade statistics are available with a sufficient degree of detail for the relevant products. Trade flows, and above all, the rationale behind trade flows provide useful insights and information for the purpose of establishing the scope of the geographic market but are not in themselves conclusive.

50. Barriers and switching costs associated to divert orders to companies located in other areas. The absence of trans-border purchases or trade flows, for instance, does not necessarily mean that the market is at most national in scope. Still, barriers isolating the national market have to identified before it is concluded that the relevant geographic market in such a case is national. Perhaps the clearest obstacle for a customer to divert its orders to other areas is the impact of transport costs and transport restrictions arising from legislation or from the nature of the relevant products. The impact of transport costs will usually limit the scope of the geographic market for bulky, low-value products, bearing in mind that a transport

disadvantage might also be compensated by a comparative advantage in other costs (labour costs or raw materials). Access to distribution in a given area, regulatory barriers still existing in certain sectors, quotas and custom tariffs might also constitute barriers isolating a geographic area from the competitive pressure of companies located outside that area. Significant switching costs in procuring supplies from companies located in other countries constitute additional sources of such barriers.

51. On the basis of the evidence gathered, the Commission will then define a geographic market that could range from a local dimension to a global one, and there are examples of both local and global markets in past decisions of the Commission.

52. The paragraphs above describe the different factors which might be relevant to define markets. This does not imply that in each individual case it will be necessary to obtain evidence and assess each of these factors. Often in practice the evidence provided by a susbset of these factors will be sufficient to reach a conclusion, as shown in the past decisional practice of the Commission.

IV. CALCULATION OF MARKET SHARE

53. The definition of the relevant market in both its product and geograhic dimensions allows the identification the suppliers and the customers/consumers active on that market. On that basis, a total market size and market shares for each supplier can be calculated on the basis of their sales of the relevant products in the relevant area. In practice, the total market size and market shares are often available from market sources, i.e. companies' estimates, studies commissioned from industry consultants and/or trade associations. When this is not the case, or when available estimates are not reliable, the Commission will usually ask each supplier in the relevant market to provide its own sales in order to calculate total market size and market shares.

54. If sales are usually the reference to calculate market shares, there are nevertheless other indications that, depending on the specific products or industry in question, can offer useful information such as, in particular, capacity, the number of players in bidding markets, units of fleet as in aerospace, or the reserves held in the case of sectors such as mining.

55. As a rule of thumb, both volume sales and value sales provide useful information. In cases of differentiated products, sales in value and their associated market share will usually be considered to better reflect the relative position and strength of each supplier.

V. ADDITIONAL CONSIDERATIONS

56. There are certain areas where the application of the principles above has to be undertaken with care. This is the case when considering primary and secondary markets, in particular, when the behaviour of undertakings at a point in time has to be analysed pursuant to Article 86. The method of defining markets in these cases is the same, i.e. assessing the responses of customers based on their purchasing decisions to relative price changes, but taking into account as well, constraints on substitution imposed by conditions in the connected markets. A narrow definition of market for secondary products, for instance, spare parts, may result when compatibility with the primary product is important. Problems of finding compatible secondary products together with the existence of high prices and a long lifetime of the primary products may render relative price increases of secondary products profitable. A different market definition may result if significant substitution between secondary products is

possible or if the characteristics of the primary products make quick and direct consumer responses to relative price increases of the secondary products feasible.

57. In certain cases, the existence of chains of substitution might lead to the definition of a relevant market where products or areas at the extreme of the market are not directly substitutable. An example might be provided by the geographic dimension of a product with significant transport costs. In such cases, deliveries from a given plant are limited to a certain area around each plant by the impact of transport costs. In principle, such an area could constitute the relevant geographic market. However, if the distribution of plants is such that there are considerable overlaps between the areas around different plants, it is possible that the pricing of those products will be constrained by a chain substitution effect, and lead to the definition of a broader geographic market. The same reasoning may apply if product B is a demand substitute for products A and C. Even if products A and C are not direct demand substitutes, they might be found to be in the same relevant product market since their respective pricing might be constrained by substitution to B.

58. From a practical perspective, the concept of chains of substitution has to be corroborated by actual evidence, for instance related to price interdependence at the extremes of the chains of substitution, in order to lead to an extension of the relevant market in an individual case. Price levels at the extremes of the chains would have to be of the same magnitude as well.

(1) The focus of assessment in State aid cases is the aid recipient and the industry/sector concerned rather than identification of competitive constraints faced by the aid recipient. When consideration of market power and therefore of the relevant market are raised in any particular case, elements of the approach outlined here might serve as a basis for the assessment of State aid cases.

(2) For the purposes of this notice, the undertakings involved will be, in the case of a concentration, the parties to the concentration; in investigations within the meaning of Article 86 of the Treaty, the undertaking being investigated or the complainants; for investigations within the meaning of Article 85, the parties to the Agreement.

(3) Definition given by the Court of Justice in its judgment of 13 February 1979 in Case 85/76, Hoffmann-La Roche [1979] ECR 461, and confirmed in subsequent judgments.

(4) That is such a period that does not entail a significant adjustment of existing tangible and intangible assets (see paragraph 23).

(5) Own-price elasticity of demand for product X is a measure of the responsiveness of demand for X to percentage change in its own price. Cross-prise elasticity between products X and Y is the responsiveness of demand for product X to percentage change in the price of product Y.

COMMUNICATION FROM THE COMMISSION

Notice

Guidelines on the application of Article 81(3) of the Treaty

(2004/C 101/08)

(Text with EEA relevance)

1. INTRODUCTION

1. Article 81(3) of the Treaty sets out an exception rule, which provides a defence to undertakings against a finding of an infringement of Article 81(1) of the Treaty. Agreements, decisions of associations of undertakings and concerted practices (1) caught by Article 81(1) which satisfy the conditions of Article 81(3) are valid and enforceable, no prior decision to that effect being required.

2. Article 81(3) can be applied in individual cases or to categories of agreements and concerted practices by way of block exemption regulation. Regulation 1/2003 on the implementation of the competition rules laid down in Articles 81 and 82 (2) does not affect the validity and legal nature of block exemption regulations. All existing block exemption regulations remain in force and agreements covered by block exemption regulations are legally valid and enforceable even if they are restrictive of competition within the meaning of Article 81(1) (3). Such agreements can only be prohibited for the future and only upon formal withdrawal of the block exemption by the Commission or a national competition authority (4). Block exempted agreements cannot be held invalid by national courts in the context of private litigation.

3. The existing guidelines on vertical restraints, horizontal cooperation agreements and technology transfer agreements (5) deal with the application of Article 81 to various types of agreements and concerted practices. The purpose of those guidelines is to set out the Commission's view of the substantive assessment criteria applied to the various types of agreements and practices.

4. The present guidelines set out the Commission's interpretation of the conditions for exception contained in Article 81(3). It thereby provides guidance on how it will apply Article 81 in individual cases. Although not binding on them, these guidelines also intend to give guidance to the courts and authorities of the Member States in their application of Article 81(1) and (3) of the Treaty.

5. The guidelines establish an analytical framework for the application of Article 81(3). The purpose is to develop a methodology for the application of this Treaty provision. This methodology is based on the economic approach already introduced and developed in the guidelines on vertical restraints, horizontal co-operation agreements and technology transfer agreements. The Commission will follow the present guidelines, which provide more detailed guidance on the application of the four conditions of Article 81(3) than the guidelines on vertical restraints, horizontal co-operation agreements and technology transfer agreements, also with regard to agreements covered by those guidelines.

6. The standards set forth in the present guidelines must be applied in light of the circumstances specific to each case. This excludes a mechanical application. Each case must be assessed on its own facts and the guidelines must be applied reasonably and flexibly.

7. With regard to a number of issues, the present guidelines outline the current state of the case law of the Court of Justice. However, the Commission also intends to explain its policy with regard to issues that have not been dealt with in the case law, or that are subject to interpretation. The Commission's position, however, is without prejudice to the case law of the Court of Justice and the Court of First Instance concerning the interpretation of Article 81(1) and (3), and to the interpretation that the Community Courts may give to those provisions in the future.

2. THE GENERAL FRAMEWORK OF ARTICLE 81 EC

2.1. The Treaty provisions

8. Article 81(1) prohibits all agreements between undertakings, decisions by associations of undertakings and concerted practices which may affect trade between Member States (6) and which have as their object or effect the prevention, restriction or distortion of competition (7).

9. As an exception to this rule Article 81(3) provides that the prohibition contained in Article 81(1) may be declared inapplicable in case of agreements which contribute to improving the production or distribution of goods or to promoting technical or economic progress, while allowing consumers a fair share of the resulting benefits, and which do not impose restrictions which are not indispensable to the attainment of these objectives, and do not afford such undertakings the possibility of eliminating competition in respect of a substantial part of the products concerned.

10. According to Article 1(1) of Regulation 1/2003 agreements which are caught by Article 81(1) and which do not satisfy the conditions of Article 81(3) are prohibited, no prior decision to that effect being required [8]. According to Article 1(2) of the same Regulation agreements which are caught by Article 81(1) but which satisfy the conditions of Article 81(3) are not prohibited, no prior decision to that effect being required. Such agreements are valid and enforceable from the moment that the conditions of Article 81(3) are satisfied and for as long as that remains the case.

11. The assessment under Article 81 thus consists of two parts. The first step is to assess whether an agreement between undertakings, which is capable of affecting trade between Member States, has an anti-competitive object or actual or potential [9] anti-competitive effects. The second step, which only becomes relevant when an agreement is found to be restrictive of competition, is to determine the pro-competitive benefits produced by that agreement and to assess whether these pro-competitive effects outweigh the anti-competitive effects. The balancing of anti-competitive and pro-competitive effects is conducted exclusively within the framework laid down by Article 81(3) [10].

12. The assessment of any countervailing benefits under Article 81(3) necessarily requires prior determination of the restrictive nature and impact of the agreement. To place Article 81(3) in its proper context it is appropriate to briefly outline the objective and principal content of the prohibition rule of Article 81(1). The Commission guidelines on vertical restraints, horizontal co-operation agreements and technology transfer agreements [11] contain substantial guidance on the application of Article 81(1) to various types of agreements. The present guidelines are therefore limited to recalling the basic analytical framework for applying Article 81(1).

2.2. The prohibition rule of Article 81(1)

2.2.1. *General remarks*

13. The objective of Article 81 is to protect competition on the market as a means of enhancing consumer welfare and of ensuring an efficient allocation of resources. Competition and market integration serve these ends since the creation and preservation of an open single market promotes an efficient allocation of resources throughout the Community for the benefit of consumers.

14. The prohibition rule of Article 81(1) applies to restrictive agreements and concerted practices between undertakings and decisions by associations of undertakings in so far as they are capable of affecting trade between Member States. A general principle underlying Article 81(1) which is expressed in the case law of the Community Courts is that each economic operator must determine independently the policy, which he intends to adopt on the market [12]. In view of this the Community Courts have defined 'agreements', 'decisions' and 'concerted practices' as Community law concepts which allow a distinction to be made between the unilateral conduct of an undertaking and co-ordination of behaviour or collusion between undertakings [13]. Unilateral conduct is subject only to Article 82 of the Treaty as far as Community competition law is concerned. Moreover, the convergence rule set out in Article 3(2) of Regulation 1/2003 does not apply to unilateral conduct. This provision applies only to agreements, decisions and concerted practices, which are capable of affecting trade between Member States. Article 3(2) provides that when such agreements, decisions and concerted practices are not prohibited by Article 81, they cannot be prohibited by national competition law. Article 3 is without prejudice to the fundamental principle of primacy of Community law, which entails in particular that agreements and abusive practices that are prohibited by Articles 81 and 82 cannot be upheld by national law [14].

15. The type of co-ordination of behaviour or collusion between undertakings falling within the scope of Article 81(1) is that where at least one undertaking vis-à-vis another undertaking undertakes to adopt a certain conduct on the market or that as a result of contacts between them uncertainty as to their conduct on the market is eliminated or at least substantially reduced [15]. It follows that co-ordination can take the form of obligations that regulate the market conduct of at least one of the parties as well as of arrangements that influence the market conduct of at least one of the parties by causing a change in its incentives. It is not required that co-ordination is in the interest of all the undertakings concerned [16]. Co-ordination must also not necessarily be express. It can also be tacit. For an agreement to be capable of being regarded as having been concluded by tacit acceptance there must be an invitation from an undertaking to another undertaking, whether express or implied, to fulfil a goal jointly [17]. In certain circumstances an agreement may be inferred from and imputed to an ongoing commercial relationship between the parties [18]. However, the mere fact that a measure adopted by an undertaking falls within the context of on-going business relations is not sufficient [19].

16. Agreements between undertakings are caught by the prohibition rule of Article 81(1) when they are likely to have an appreciable adverse impact on the parameters of competition on the market, such as price, output, product quality, product variety and innovation. Agreements can have this effect by appreciably reducing rivalry between the parties to the agreement or between them and third parties.

2.2.2. *The basic principles for assessing agreements under Article 81(1)*

17. The assessment of whether an agreement is restrictive of competition must be made within the actual context in which competition would occur in the absence of the agreement with its alleged restrictions [20]. In making this assessment it is necessary to take account of the likely impact of the agreement on inter-brand competition (i.e. competition between suppliers of competing brands) and on intra-brand competition (i.e. competition between distributors of the same brand). Article 81(1) prohibits restrictions of both inter-brand competition and intra-brand competition [21].

18. For the purpose of assessing whether an agreement or its individual parts may restrict inter-brand competition and/or intra-brand competition it needs to be considered how and to what extent the agreement affects or is likely to affect competition on the market. The following two questions provide a useful framework for making this assessment. The first question relates to the impact of the agreement on inter-brand competition while the second question relates to the impact of the agreement on intra-brand competition. As restraints may be capable of affecting both inter-brand competition and intra-brand competition at the same time, it may be necessary to analyse a restraint in light of both questions before it can be concluded whether or not competition is restricted within the meaning of Article 81(1):

(1) Does the agreement restrict actual or potential competition that would have existed without the agreement? If so, the agreement may be caught by Article 81(1). In making this assessment it is necessary to take into account competition between the parties and competition from third parties. For instance, where two undertakings established in different Member States undertake not to sell products in each other's home markets, (potential) competition that existed prior to the agreement is restricted. Similarly, where a supplier imposes obligations on his distributors not to sell competing products and these obligations foreclose third party access to the market, actual or potential competition that would have existed in the absence of the agreement is restricted. In assessing whether the parties to an agreement are actual or potential competitors the economic and legal context must be taken into account. For instance, if due to the financial risks involved and the technical capabilities of the parties it is unlikely on the basis of objective factors that each party would be able to carry out on its own the activities covered by the agreement the parties are deemed to be non-competitors in respect of that activity [22]. It is for the parties to bring forward evidence to that effect.

(2) Does the agreement restrict actual or potential competition that would have existed in the absence of the contractual restraint(s)? If so, the agreement may be caught by Article 81(1). For instance, where a supplier restricts its distributors from competing with each other, (potential) competition that could have existed between the distributors absent the restraints is restricted. Such restrictions include resale price maintenance and territorial or customer sales restrictions between distributors. However, certain restraints may in certain cases not be caught by Article 81(1) when the restraint is objectively necessary for the existence of an agreement of that type or that nature [23]. Such exclusion of the application of Article 81(1) can only be made on the basis of objective factors external to the parties themselves and not the subjective views and characteristics of the parties. The question is not whether the parties in their particular situation would not have accepted to conclude a less restrictive agreement, but whether given the nature of the agreement and the characteristics of the market a less restrictive agreement would not have been concluded by undertakings in a similar setting. For instance, territorial restraints in an agreement between a supplier and a distributor may for a certain period of time fall outside Article 81(1), if the restraints are objectively necessary in order for the distributor to penetrate a new market [24]. Similarly, a prohibition imposed on all distributors not to sell to certain categories of end users may not be restrictive of competition if such restraint is objectively necessary for reasons of safety or health related to the dangerous nature of the product in question. Claims that in the absence of a restraint the supplier would have resorted to vertical integration are not sufficient. Decisions on whether or not to vertically integrate depend on a broad range of complex economic factors, a number of which are internal to the undertaking concerned.

19. In the application of the analytical framework set out in the previous paragraph it must be taken into account that Article 81(1) distinguishes between those agreements that have a restriction of competition as their object and those agreements that have a restriction of competition as their effect. An agreement or contractual restraint is only prohibited by Article 81(1) if its object or effect is to restrict inter-brand competition and/or intra-brand competition.

20. The distinction between restrictions by object and restrictions by effect is important. Once it has been established that an agreement has as its object the restriction of competition, there is no need to take account of its concrete effects ([25]). In other words, for the purpose of applying Article 81(1) no actual anti-competitive effects need to be demonstrated where the agreement has a restriction of competition as its object. Article 81(3), on the other hand, does not distinguish between agreements that restrict competition by object and agreements that restrict competition by effect. Article 81(3) applies to all agreements that fulfil the four conditions contained therein ([26]).

21. Restrictions of competition *by object* are those that by their very nature have the potential of restricting competition. These are restrictions which in light of the objectives pursued by the Community competition rules have such a high potential of negative effects on competition that it is unnecessary for the purposes of applying Article 81(1) to demonstrate any actual effects on the market. This presumption is based on the serious nature of the restriction and on experience showing that restrictions of competition by object are likely to produce negative effects on the market and to jeopardise the objectives pursued by the Community competition rules. Restrictions by object such as price fixing and market sharing reduce output and raise prices, leading to a misallocation of resources, because goods and services demanded by customers are not produced. They also lead to a reduction in consumer welfare, because consumers have to pay higher prices for the goods and services in question.

22. The assessment of whether or not an agreement has as its object the restriction of competition is based on a number of factors. These factors include, in particular, the content of the agreement and the objective aims pursued by it. It may also be necessary to consider the context in which it is (to be) applied and the actual conduct and behaviour of the parties on the market ([27]). In other words, an examination of the facts underlying the agreement and the specific circumstances in which it operates may be required before it can be concluded whether a particular restriction constitutes a restriction of competition by object. The way in which an agreement is actually implemented may reveal a restriction by object even where the formal agreement does not contain an express provision to that effect. Evidence of subjective intent on the part of the parties to restrict competition is a relevant factor but not a necessary condition.

23. Non-exhaustive guidance on what constitutes restrictions by object can be found in Commission block exemption regulations, guidelines and notices. Restrictions that are black-listed in block exemptions or identified as hardcore restrictions in guidelines and notices are generally considered by the Commission to constitute restrictions by object. In the case of horizontal agreements restrictions of competition by object include price fixing, output limitation and sharing of markets and customers ([28]). As regards vertical agreements the category of restrictions by object includes, in particular, fixed and minimum resale price maintenance and restrictions providing absolute territorial protection, including restrictions on passive sales ([29]).

24. If an agreement is not restrictive of competition by object it must be examined whether it has restrictive effects on competition. Account must be taken of both actual and potential effects ([30]). In other words the agreement must have likely anti-competitive effects. In the case of restrictions of competition by effect there is no presumption of anti-competitive effects. For an agreement to be restrictive by effect it must affect actual or potential competition to such an extent that on the relevant market negative effects on prices, output, innovation or the variety or quality of goods and services can be expected with a reasonable degree of probability ([31]). Such negative effects must be appreciable. The prohibition rule of Article 81(1) does not apply when the identified anti-competitive effects are insignificant ([32]). This test reflects the economic approach which the Commission is applying. The prohibition of Article 81(1) only applies where on the basis of proper market analysis it can be concluded that the agreement has likely anti-competitive effects on the market ([33]). It is insufficient for such a finding that the market shares of the parties exceed the thresholds set out in the Commission's *de minimis* notice ([34]). Agreements falling within safe harbours of block exemption regulations may be caught by Article 81(1) but this is not necessarily so. Moreover, the fact that due to the market shares of the parties, an agreement falls outside the safe harbour of a block exemption is in itself an insufficient basis for finding that the agreement is caught by Article 81(1) or that it does not fulfil the conditions of Article 81(3). Individual assessment of the likely effects produced by the agreement is required.

25. Negative effects on competition within the relevant market are likely to occur when the parties individually or jointly have or obtain some degree of market power and the agreement contributes to the creation, maintenance or strengthening of that market power or allows the parties to exploit such market power. Market

power is the ability to maintain prices above competitive levels for a significant period of time or to maintain output in terms of product quantities, product quality and variety or innovation below competitive levels for a significant period of time. In markets with high fixed costs undertakings must price significantly above their marginal costs of production in order to ensure a competitive return on their investment. The fact that undertakings price above their marginal costs is therefore not in itself a sign that competition in the market is not functioning well and that undertakings have market power that allows them to price above the competitive level. It is when competitive constraints are insufficient to maintain prices and output at competitive levels that undertakings have market power within the meaning of Article 81(1).

26. The creation, maintenance or strengthening of market power can result from a restriction of competition between the parties to the agreement. It can also result from a restriction of competition between any one of the parties and third parties, e.g. because the agreement leads to foreclosure of competitors or because it raises competitors' costs, limiting their capacity to compete effectively with the contracting parties. Market power is a question of degree. The degree of market power normally required for the finding of an infringement under Article 81(1) in the case of agreements that are restrictive of competition by effect is less than the degree of market power required for a finding of dominance under Article 82.

27. For the purposes of analysing the restrictive effects of an agreement it is normally necessary to define the relevant market ([35]). It is normally also necessary to examine and assess, *inter alia*, the nature of the products, the market position of the parties, the market position of competitors, the market position of buyers, the existence of potential competitors and the level of entry barriers. In some cases, however, it may be possible to show anti-competitive effects directly by analysing the conduct of the parties to the agreement on the market. It may for example be possible to ascertain that an agreement has led to price increases. The guidelines on horizontal cooperation agreements and on vertical restraints set out a detailed framework for analysing the competitive impact of various types of horizontal and vertical agreements under Article 81(1) ([36]).

2.2.3. *Ancillary restraints*

28. Paragraph 18 above sets out a framework for analysing the impact of an agreement and its individual restrictions on inter-brand competition and intra-brand competition. If on the basis of those principles it is concluded that the main transaction covered by the agreement is not restrictive of competition, it becomes relevant to examine whether individual restraints contained in the agreement are also compatible with Article 81(1) because they are ancillary to the main non-restrictive transaction.

29. In Community competition law the concept of ancillary restraints covers any alleged restriction of competition which is directly related and necessary to the implementation of a main non-restrictive transaction and proportionate to it ([37]). If an agreement in its main parts, for instance a distribution agreement or a joint venture, does not have as its object or effect the restriction of competition, then restrictions, which are directly related to and necessary for the implementation of that transaction, also fall outside Article 81(1) ([38]). These related restrictions are called ancillary restraints. A restriction is directly related to the main transaction if it is subordinate to the implementation of that transaction and is inseparably linked to it. The test of necessity implies that the restriction must be objectively necessary for the implementation of the main transaction and be proportionate to it. It follows that the ancillary restraints test is similar to the test set out in paragraph 18(2) above. However, the ancillary restraints test applies in all cases where the main transaction is not restrictive of competition ([39]). It is not limited to determining the impact of the agreement on intra-brand competition.

30. The application of the ancillary restraint concept must be distinguished from the application of the defence under Article 81(3) which relates to certain economic benefits produced by restrictive agreements and which are balanced against the restrictive effects of the agreements. The application of the ancillary restraint concept does not involve any weighing of pro-competitive and anti-competitive effects. Such balancing is reserved for Article 81(3) ([40]).

31. The assessment of ancillary restraints is limited to determining whether, in the specific context of the main non-restrictive transaction or activity, a particular restriction is necessary for the implementation of that transaction or activity and proportionate to it. If on the basis of objective factors it can be concluded that without the restriction the main non-restrictive transaction would be difficult or impossible to implement, the restriction may be regarded as objectively necessary for its implementation and proportionate to it ([41]). If, for example, the main object of a franchise agreement does not restrict competition, then restrictions, which are necessary for the proper functioning of the agreement, such as obligations aimed at protecting the uniformity and reputation of the franchise system, also fall outside Article 81(1) ([42]). Similarly, if a joint venture is not in itself restrictive of competition, then restrictions that are necessary for the functioning of the agreement are

deemed to be ancillary to the main transaction and are therefore not caught by Article 81(1). For instance in *TPS* [43] the Commission concluded that an obligation on the parties not to be involved in companies engaged in distribution and marketing of television programmes by satellite was ancillary to the creation of the joint venture during the initial phase. The restriction was therefore deemed to fall outside Article 81(1) for a period of three years. In arriving at this conclusion the Commission took account of the heavy investments and commercial risks involved in entering the market for pay-television.

2.3. **The exception rule of Article 81(3)**

32. The assessment of restrictions by object and effect under Article 81(1) is only one side of the analysis. The other side, which is reflected in Article 81(3), is the assessment of the positive economic effects of restrictive agreements.

33. The aim of the Community competition rules is to protect competition on the market as a means of enhancing consumer welfare and of ensuring an efficient allocation of resources. Agreements that restrict competition may at the same time have pro-competitive effects by way of efficiency gains [44]. Efficiencies may create additional value by lowering the cost of producing an output, improving the quality of the product or creating a new product. When the pro-competitive effects of an agreement outweigh its anti-competitive effects the agreement is on balance pro-competitive and compatible with the objectives of the Community competition rules. The net effect of such agreements is to promote the very essence of the competitive process, namely to win customers by offering better products or better prices than those offered by rivals. This analytical framework is reflected in Article 81(1) and Article 81(3). The latter provision expressly acknowledges that restrictive agreements may generate objective economic benefits so as to outweigh the negative effects of the restriction of competition [45].

34. The application of the exception rule of Article 81(3) is subject to four cumulative conditions, two positive and two negative:

(a) The agreement must contribute to improving the production or distribution of goods or contribute to promoting technical or economic progress,

(b) Consumers must receive a fair share of the resulting benefits,

(c) The restrictions must be indispensable to the attainment of these objectives, and finally

(d) The agreement must not afford the parties the possibility of eliminating competition in respect of a substantial part of the products in question.

When these four conditions are fulfilled the agreement enhances competition within the relevant market, because it leads the undertakings concerned to offer cheaper or better products to consumers, compensating the latter for the adverse effects of the restrictions of competition.

35. Article 81(3) can be applied either to individual agreements or to categories of agreements by way of a block exemption regulation. When an agreement is covered by a block exemption the parties to the restrictive agreement are relieved of their burden under Article 2 of Regulation 1/2003 of showing that their individual agreement satisfies each of the conditions of Article 81(3). They only have to prove that the restrictive agreement benefits from a block exemption. The application of Article 81(3) to categories of agreements by way of block exemption regulation is based on the presumption that restrictive agreements that fall within their scope [46] fulfil each of the four conditions laid down in Article 81(3).

36. If in an individual case the agreement is caught by Article 81(1) and the conditions of Article 81(3) are not fulfilled the block exemption may be withdrawn. According to Article 29(1) of Regulation 1/2003 the Commission is empowered to withdraw the benefit of a block exemption when it finds that in a particular case an agreement covered by a block exemption regulation has certain effects which are incompatible with Article 81(3) of the Treaty. Pursuant to Article 29(2) of Regulation 1/2003 a competition authority of a Member State may also withdraw the benefit of a Commission block exemption regulation in respect of its territory (or part of its territory), if this territory has all the characteristics of a distinct geographic market. In the case of withdrawal it is for the competition authorities concerned to demonstrate that the agreement infringes Article 81(1) and that it does not fulfil the conditions of Article 81(3).

37. The courts of the Member States have no power to withdraw the benefit of block exemption regulations. Moreover, in their application of block exemption regulations Member State courts may not modify their scope by extending their sphere of application to agreements not covered by the block exemption regulation in question ([47]). Outside the scope of block exemption regulations Member State courts have the power to apply Article 81 in full (cf. Article 6 of Regulation 1/2003).

3. THE APPLICATION OF THE FOUR CONDITIONS OF ARTICLE 81(3)

38. The remainder of these guidelines will consider each of the four conditions of Article 81(3) ([48]). Given that these four conditions are cumulative ([49]) it is unnecessary to examine any remaining conditions once it is found that one of the conditions of Article 81(3) is not fulfilled. In individual cases it may therefore be appropriate to consider the four conditions in a different order.

39. For the purposes of these guidelines it is considered appropriate to invert the order of the second and the third condition and thus deal with the issue of indispensability before the issue of pass-on to consumers. The analysis of pass-on requires a balancing of the negative and positive effects of an agreement on consumers. This analysis should not include the effects of any restrictions, which already fail the indispensability test and which for that reason are prohibited by Article 81.

3.1. **General principles**

40. Article 81(3) of the Treaty only becomes relevant when an agreement between undertakings restricts competition within the meaning of Article 81(1). In the case of non-restrictive agreements there is no need to examine any benefits generated by the agreement.

41. Where in an individual case a restriction of competition within the meaning of Article 81(1) has been proven, Article 81(3) can be invoked as a defence. According to Article 2 of Regulation 1/2003 the burden of proof under Article 81(3) rests on the undertaking(s) invoking the benefit of the exception rule. Where the conditions of Article 81(3) are not satisfied the agreement is null and void, cf. Article 81(2). However, such automatic nullity only applies to those parts of the agreement that are incompatible with Article 81, provided that such parts are severable from the agreement as a whole ([50]). If only part of the agreement is null and void, it is for the applicable national law to determine the consequences thereof for the remaining part of the agreement ([51]).

42. According to settled case law the four conditions of Article 81(3) are cumulative ([52]), i.e. they must all be fulfilled for the exception rule to be applicable. If they are not, the application of the exception rule of Article 81(3) must be refused ([53]). The four conditions of Article 81(3) are also exhaustive. When they are met the exception is applicable and may not be made dependant on any other condition. Goals pursued by other Treaty provisions can be taken into account to the extent that they can be subsumed under the four conditions of Article 81(3) ([54]).

43. The assessment under Article 81(3) of benefits flowing from restrictive agreements is in principle made within the confines of each relevant market to which the agreement relates. The Community competition rules have as their objective the protection of competition on the market and cannot be detached from this objective. Moreover, the condition that consumers ([55]) must receive a fair share of the benefits implies in general that efficiencies generated by the restrictive agreement within a relevant market must be sufficient to outweigh the anti-competitive effects produced by the agreement within that same relevant market ([56]). Negative effects on consumers in one geographic market or product market cannot normally be balanced against and compensated by positive effects for consumers in another unrelated geographic market or product market. However, where two markets are related, efficiencies achieved on separate markets can be taken into account provided that the group of consumers affected by the restriction and benefiting from the efficiency gains are substantially the same ([57]). Indeed, in some cases only consumers in a downstream market are affected by the agreement in which case the impact of the agreement on such consumers must be assessed. This is for instance so in the case of purchasing agreements ([58]).

44. The assessment of restrictive agreements under Article 81(3) is made within the actual context in which they occur ([59]) and on the basis of the facts existing at any given point in time. The assessment is sensitive to material changes in the facts. The exception rule of Article 81(3) applies as long as the four conditions are fulfilled and ceases to apply when that is no longer the case ([60]). When applying Article 81(3) in accordance with these principles it is necessary to take into account the initial sunk investments made by any of the parties and the time needed and the restraints required to commit and recoup an efficiency enhancing investment. Article 81 cannot be applied without taking due account of such *ex ante* investment. The risk facing the parties and the sunk investment that must be committed to implement

the agreement can thus lead to the agreement falling outside Article 81(1) or fulfilling the conditions of Article 81(3), as the case may be, for the period of time required to recoup the investment.

45. In some cases the restrictive agreement is an irreversible event. Once the restrictive agreement has been implemented the *ex ante* situation cannot be re-established. In such cases the assessment must be made exclusively on the basis of the facts pertaining at the time of implementation. For instance, in the case of a research and development agreement whereby each party agrees to abandon its respective research project and pool its capabilities with those of another party, it may from an objective point of view be technically and economically impossible to revive a project once it has been abandoned. The assessment of the anti-competitive and pro-competitive effects of the agreement to abandon the individual research projects must therefore be made as of the time of the completion of its implementation. If at that point in time the agreement is compatible with Article 81, for instance because a sufficient number of third parties have competing research and development projects, the parties' agreement to abandon their individual projects remains compatible with Article 81, even if at a later point in time the third party projects fail. However, the prohibition of Article 81 may apply to other parts of the agreement in respect of which the issue of irreversibility does not arise. If for example in addition to joint research and development, the agreement provides for joint exploitation, Article 81 may apply to this part of the agreement if due to subsequent market developments the agreement becomes restrictive of competition and does not (any longer) satisfy the conditions of Article 81(3) taking due account of *ex ante* sunk investments, cf. the previous paragraph.

46. Article 81(3) does not exclude *a priori* certain types of agreements from its scope. As a matter of principle all restrictive agreements that fulfil the four conditions of Article 81(3) are covered by the exception rule (61). However, severe restrictions of competition are unlikely to fulfil the conditions of Article 81(3). Such restrictions are usually black-listed in block exemption regulations or identified as hardcore restrictions in Commission guidelines and notices. Agreements of this nature generally fail (at least) the two first conditions of Article 81(3). They neither create objective economic benefits (62) nor do they benefit consumers (63). For example, a horizontal agreement to fix prices limits output leading to misallocation of resources. It also transfers value from consumers to producers, since it leads to higher prices without producing any countervailing value to consumers within the relevant market. Moreover, these types of agreements generally also fail the indispensability test under the third condition (64).

47. Any claim that restrictive agreements are justified because they aim at ensuring fair conditions of competition on the market is by nature unfounded and must be discarded (65). The purpose of Article 81 is to protect effective competition by ensuring that markets remain open and competitive. The protection of fair conditions of competition is a task for the legislator in compliance with Community law obligations (66) and not for undertakings to regulate themselves.

3.2. **First condition of Article 81(3): Efficiency gains**

3.2.1. *General remarks*

48. According to the first condition of Article 81(3) the restrictive agreement must contribute to improving the production or distribution of goods or to promoting technical or economic progress. The provision refers expressly only to goods, but applies by analogy to services.

49. It follows from the case law of the Court of Justice that only objective benefits can be taken into account (67). This means that efficiencies are not assessed from the subjective point of view of the parties (68). Cost savings that arise from the mere exercise of market power by the parties cannot be taken into account. For instance, when companies agree to fix prices or share markets they reduce output and thereby production costs. Reduced competition may also lead to lower sales and marketing expenditures. Such cost reductions are a direct consequence of a reduction in output and value. The cost reductions in question do not produce any pro-competitive effects on the market. In particular, they do not lead to the creation of value through an integration of assets and activities. They merely allow the undertakings concerned to increase their profits and are therefore irrelevant from the point of view of Article 81(3).

50. The purpose of the first condition of Article 81(3) is to define the types of efficiency gains that can be taken into account and be subject to the further tests of the second and third conditions of Article 81(3). The aim of the analysis is to ascertain what are the objective benefits created by the agreement and what is the economic importance of such efficiencies. Given that for Article 81(3) to apply the pro-competitive effects flowing from the agreement must outweigh its anti-competitive effects, it is necessary to verify what is the link between the agreement and the claimed efficiencies and what is the value of these efficiencies.

51. All efficiency claims must therefore be substantiated so that the following can be verified:

(a) The *nature* of the claimed efficiencies;

(b) The *link* between the agreement and the efficiencies;

(c) The *likelihood* and *magnitude* of each claimed efficiency; and

(d) *How* and *when* each claimed efficiency would be achieved.

52. Letter (a) allows the decision-maker to verify whether the claimed efficiencies are objective in nature, cf. paragraph 49 above.

53. Letter (b) allows the decision-maker to verify whether there is a sufficient causal link between the restrictive agreement and the claimed efficiencies. This condition normally requires that the efficiencies result from the economic activity that forms the object of the agreement. Such activities may, for example, take the form of distribution, licensing of technology, joint production or joint research and development. To the extent, however, that an agreement has wider efficiency enhancing effects within the relevant market, for example because it leads to a reduction in industry wide costs, these additional benefits are also taken into account.

54. The causal link between the agreement and the claimed efficiencies must normally also be direct [69]. Claims based on indirect effects are as a general rule too uncertain and too remote to be taken into account. A direct causal link exists for instance where a technology transfer agreement allows the licensees to produce new or improved products or a distribution agreement allows products to be distributed at lower cost or valuable services to be produced. An example of indirect effect would be a case where it is claimed that a restrictive agreement allows the undertakings concerned to increase their profits, enabling them to invest more in research and development to the ultimate benefit of consumers. While there may be a link between profitability and research and development, this link is generally not sufficiently direct to be taken into account in the context of Article 81(3).

55. Letters (c) and (d) allow the decision-maker to verify the value of the claimed efficiencies, which in the context of the third condition of Article 81(3) must be balanced against the anti-competitive effects of the agreement, see paragraph 101 below. Given that Article 81(1) only applies in cases where the agreement has likely negative effects on competition and consumers (in the case of hardcore restrictions such effects are presumed) efficiency claims must be substantiated so that they can be verified. Unsubstantiated claims are rejected.

56. In the case of claimed cost efficiencies the undertakings invoking the benefit of Article 81(3) must as accurately as reasonably possible calculate or estimate the value of the efficiencies and describe in detail how the amount has been computed. They must also describe the method(s) by which the efficiencies have been or will be achieved. The data submitted must be verifiable so that there can be a sufficient degree of certainty that the efficiencies have materialised or are likely to materialise.

57. In the case of claimed efficiencies in the form of new or improved products and other non-cost based efficiencies, the undertakings claiming the benefit of Article 81(3) must describe and explain in detail what is the nature of the efficiencies and how and why they constitute an objective economic benefit.

58. In cases where the agreement has yet to be fully implemented the parties must substantiate any projections as to the date from which the efficiencies will become operational so as to have a significant positive impact in the market.

3.2.2. *The different categories of efficiencies*

59. The types of efficiencies listed in Article 81(3) are broad categories which are intended to cover all objective economic efficiencies. There is considerable overlap between the various categories mentioned in Article 81(3) and the same agreement may give rise to several kinds of efficiencies. It is therefore not appropriate to draw clear and firm distinctions between the various categories. For the purpose of these guidelines, a distinction is made between cost efficiencies and efficiencies of a qualitative nature whereby value is created in the form of new or improved products, greater product variety etc.

60. In general, efficiencies stem from an integration of economic activities whereby undertakings combine their assets to achieve what they could not achieve as efficiently on their own or whereby they entrust another undertaking with tasks that can be performed more efficiently by that other undertaking.

61. The research and development, production and distribution process may be viewed as a value chain that can be divided into a number of stages. At each stage of this chain an undertaking must make a choice between performing the activity itself, performing it together with (an)other undertaking(s) or outsourcing the activity entirely to (an)other undertaking(s).

62. In each case where the choice made involves cooperation on the market with another undertaking, an agreement within the meaning of Article 81(1) normally needs to be concluded. These agreements can be vertical, as is the case where the parties operate at different levels of the value chain or horizontal, as is the case where the firms operate at the same level of the value chain. Both categories of agreements may create efficiencies by allowing the undertakings in question to perform a particular task at lower cost or with higher added value for consumers. Such agreements may also contain or lead to restrictions of competition in which case the prohibition rule of Article 81(1) and the exception rule of Article 81(3) may become relevant.

63. The types of efficiencies mentioned in the following are only examples and are not intended to be exhaustive.

3.2.2.1. Cost efficiencies

64. Cost efficiencies flowing from agreements between undertakings can originate from a number of different sources. One very important source of cost savings is the development of new production technologies and methods. In general, it is when technological leaps are made that the greatest potential for cost savings is achieved. For instance, the introduction of the assembly line led to a very substantial reduction in the cost of producing motor vehicles.

65. Another very important source of efficiency is synergies resulting from an integration of existing assets. When the parties to an agreement combine their respective assets they may be able to attain a cost/output configuration that would not otherwise be possible. The combination of two existing technologies that have complementary strengths may reduce production costs or lead to the production of a higher quality product. For instance, it may be that the production assets of firm A generate a high output per hour but require a relatively high input of raw materials per unit of output, whereas the production assets of firm B generate lower output per hour but require a relatively lower input of raw materials per unit of output. Synergies are created if by establishing a production joint venture combining the production assets of A and B the parties can attain a high(er) level of output per hour with a low(er) input of raw materials per unit of output. Similarly, if one undertaking has optimised one part of the value chain and another undertaking has optimised another part of the value chain, the combination of their operations may lead to lower costs. Firm A may for instance have a highly automated production facility resulting in low production costs per unit whereas B has developed an efficient order processing system. The system allows production to be tailored to customer demand, ensuring timely delivery and reducing warehousing and obsolescence costs. By combining their assets A and B may be able to obtain cost reductions.

66. Cost efficiencies may also result from economies of scale, i.e. declining cost per unit of output as output increases. To give an example: investment in equipment and other assets often has to be made in indivisible blocks. If an undertaking cannot fully utilise a block, its average costs will be higher than if it could do so. For instance, the cost of operating a truck is virtually the same regardless of whether it is almost empty, half-full or full. Agreements whereby undertakings combine their logistics operations may allow them to increase the load factors and reduce the number of vehicles employed. Larger scale may also allow for better division of labour leading to lower unit costs. Firms may achieve economies of scale in respect of all parts of the value chain, including research and development, production, distribution and marketing. Learning economies constitute a related type of efficiency. As experience is gained in using a particular production process or in performing particular tasks, productivity may increase because the process is made to run more efficiently or because the task is performed more quickly.

67. Economies of scope are another source of cost efficiency, which occur when firms achieve cost savings by producing different products on the basis of the same input. Such efficiencies may arise from the fact that it is possible to use the same components and the same facilities and personnel to produce a variety of products. Similarly, economies of scope may arise in distribution when several types of goods are distributed in the same vehicles. For instance, a producer of frozen pizzas and a producer of frozen vegetables may obtain economies of scope by jointly distributing their products. Both groups of products must be distributed in refrigerated vehicles and it is likely that there are significant overlaps in terms of customers. By combining their operations the two producers may obtain lower distribution costs per distributed unit.

68. Efficiencies in the form of cost reductions can also follow from agreements that allow for better planning of production, reducing the need to hold expensive inventory and allowing for better capacity utilisation. Efficiencies of this nature may for example stem from the use of 'just in time' purchasing, i.e. an obligation on a supplier of components to continuously supply the buyer according to its needs thereby avoiding the need for the buyer to maintain a significant stock of components which risks becoming obsolete. Cost savings may also result from agreements that allow the parties to rationalise production across their facilities.

3.2.2.2. Qualitative efficiencies

69. Agreements between undertakings may generate various efficiencies of a qualitative nature which are relevant to the application of Article 81(3). In a number of cases the main efficiency enhancing potential of the agreement is not cost reduction; it is quality improvements and other efficiencies of a qualitative nature. Depending on the individual case such efficiencies may therefore be of equal or greater importance than cost efficiencies.

70. Technical and technological advances form an essential and dynamic part of the economy, generating significant benefits in the form of new or improved goods and services. By cooperating undertakings may be able to create efficiencies that would not have been possible without the restrictive agreement or would have been possible only with substantial delay or at higher cost. Such efficiencies constitute an important source of economic benefits covered by the first condition of Article 81(3). Agreements capable of producing efficiencies of this nature include, in particular, research and development agreements. An example would be A and B creating a joint venture for the development and, if successful, joint production of a cell-based tyre. The puncture of one cell does not affect other cells, which means that there is no risk of collapse of the tyre in the event of a puncture. The tyre is thus safer than traditional tyres. It also means that there is no immediate need to change the tyre and thus to carry a spare. Both types of efficiencies constitute objective benefits within the meaning of the first condition of Article 81(3).

71. In the same way that the combination of complementary assets can give rise to cost savings, combinations of assets may also create synergies that create efficiencies of a qualitative nature. The combination of production assets may for instance lead to the production of higher quality products or products with novel features. This may for instance be the case for licence agreements, and agreements providing for joint production of new or improved goods or services. Licence agreements may, in particular, ensure more rapid dissemination of new technology in the Community and enable the licensee(s) to make available new products or to employ new production techniques that lead to quality improvements. Joint production agreements may, in particular, allow new or improved products or services to be introduced on the market more quickly or at lower cost ([70]). In the telecommunications sector, for example, cooperation agreements have been held to create efficiencies by making available more quickly new global services ([71]). In the banking sector cooperation agreements that made available improved facilities for making cross-border payments have also been held to create efficiencies falling within the scope of the first condition of Article 81(3) ([72]).

72. Distribution agreements may also give rise to qualitative efficiencies. Specialised distributors, for example, may be able to provide services that are better tailored to customer needs or to provide quicker delivery or better quality assurance throughout the distribution chain ([73]).

3.3. Third condition of Article 81(3): Indispensability of the restrictions

73. According to the third condition of Article 81(3) the restrictive agreement must not impose restrictions, which are not indispensable to the attainment of the efficiencies created by the agreement in question. This condition implies a two-fold test. First, the restrictive agreement as such must be reasonably necessary in order to achieve the efficiencies. Secondly, the individual restrictions of competition that flow from the agreement must also be reasonably necessary for the attainment of the efficiencies.

74. In the context of the third condition of Article 81(3) the decisive factor is whether or not the restrictive agreement and individual restrictions make it possible to perform the activity in question more efficiently than would likely have been the case in the absence of the agreement or the restriction concerned. The question is not whether in the absence of the restriction the agreement would not have been concluded, but whether more efficiencies are produced with the agreement or restriction than in the absence of the agreement or restriction ([74]).

75. The first test contained in the third condition of Article 81(3) requires that the efficiencies be specific to the agreement in question in the sense that there are no other economically practicable and less restrictive means of achieving the efficiencies. In making this latter assessment the market conditions and business realities facing the parties to the agreement must be taken into account. Undertakings invoking the benefit of Article 81(3) are not required to consider hypothetical or theoretical alternatives. The Commission will not second guess the business judgment of the parties. It will only intervene where it is reasonably clear that there are realistic and attainable alternatives. The parties must only explain and demonstrate why such seemingly realistic and significantly less restrictive alternatives to the agreement would be significantly less efficient.

76. It is particularly relevant to examine whether, having due regard to the circumstances of the individual case, the parties could have achieved the efficiencies by means of another less restrictive type of agreement and, if so, when they would likely be able to obtain the efficiencies. It may also be necessary to examine whether the parties could have achieved the efficiencies on their own. For instance, where the claimed efficiencies take the form of cost reductions resulting from economies of scale or scope the undertakings concerned must explain and substantiate why the same efficiencies would not be likely to be attained through internal growth and price competition. In making this assessment it is relevant to consider, *inter alia*, what is the minimum efficient scale on the market concerned. The minimum efficient scale is the level of output required to minimise average cost and exhaust economies of scale ([75]). The larger the minimum efficient scale compared to the current size of either of the parties to the agreement, the more likely it is that the efficiencies will be deemed to be specific to the agreement. In the case of agreements that produce substantial synergies through the combination of complementary assets and capabilities the very nature of the efficiencies give rise to a presumption that the agreement is necessary to attain them.

77. These principles can be illustrated by the following hypothetical example:

A and B combine within a joint venture their respective production technologies to achieve higher output and lower raw material consumption. The joint venture is granted an exclusive licence to their respective production technologies. The parties transfer their existing production facilities to the joint venture. They also transfer key staff in order to ensure that existing learning economies can be exploited and further developed. It is estimated that these economies will reduce production costs by a further 5 %. The output of the joint venture is sold independently by A and B. In this case the indispensability condition necessitates an assessment of whether or not the benefits could be substantially achieved by means of a licence agreement, which would be likely to be less restrictive because A and B would continue to produce independently. In the circumstances described this is unlikely to be the case since under a licence agreement the parties would not be able to benefit in the same seamless and continued way from their respective experience in operating the two technologies, resulting in significant learning economies.

78. Once it is found that the agreement in question is necessary in order to produce the efficiencies, the indispensability of each restriction of competition flowing from the agreement must be assessed. In this context it must be assessed whether individual restrictions are reasonably necessary in order to produce the efficiencies. The parties to the agreement must substantiate their claim with regard to both the nature of the restriction and its intensity.

79. A restriction is indispensable if its absence would eliminate or significantly reduce the efficiencies that follow from the agreement or make it significantly less likely that they will materialise. The assessment of alternative solutions must take into account the actual and potential improvement in the field of competition by the elimination of a particular restriction or the application of a less restrictive alternative. The more restrictive the restraint the stricter the test under the third condition ([76]). Restrictions that are black listed in block exemption regulations or identified as hardcore restrictions in Commission guidelines and notices are unlikely to be considered indispensable.

80. The assessment of indispensability is made within the actual context in which the agreement operates and must in particular take account of the structure of the market, the economic risks related to the agreement, and the incentives facing the parties. The more uncertain the success of the product covered by the agreement, the more a restriction may be required to ensure that the efficiencies will materialise. Restrictions may also be indispensable in order to align the incentives of the parties and ensure that they concentrate their efforts on the implementation of the agreement. A restriction may for instance be necessary in order to avoid hold-up problems once a substantial sunk investment has been made by one of the parties. Once for instance a supplier has made a substantial relationship-specific

investment with a view to supplying a customer with an input, the supplier is locked into the customer. In order to avoid that *ex post* the customer exploits this dependence to obtain more favourable terms, it may be necessary to impose an obligation not to purchase the component from third parties or to purchase minimum quantities of the component from the supplier (77).

81. In some cases a restriction may be indispensable only for a certain period of time, in which case the exception of Article 81(3) only applies during that period. In making this assessment it is necessary to take due account of the period of time required for the parties to achieve the efficiencies justifying the application of the exception rule (78). In cases where the benefits cannot be achieved without considerable investment, account must, in particular, be taken of the period of time required to ensure an adequate return on such investment, see also paragraph 44 above.

82. These principles can be illustrated by the following hypothetical examples:

P produces and distributes frozen pizzas, holding 15 % of the market in Member State X. Deliveries are made directly to retailers. Since most retailers have limited storage capacity, relatively frequent deliveries are required, leading to low capacity utilisation and use of relatively small vehicles. T is a wholesaler of frozen pizzas and other frozen products, delivering to most of the same customers as P. The pizza products distributed by T hold 30 % of the market. T has a fleet of larger vehicles and has excess capacity. P concludes an exclusive distribution agreement with T for Member State X and undertakes to ensure that distributors in other Member States will not sell into T's territory either actively or passively. T undertakes to advertise the products, survey consumer tastes and satisfaction rates and ensure delivery to retailers of all products within 24 hours. The agreement leads to a reduction in total distribution costs of 30 % as capacity is better utilised and duplication of routes is eliminated. The agreement also leads to the provision of additional services to consumers. Restrictions on passive sales are hardcore restrictions under the block exemption regulation on vertical restraints (79) and can only be considered indispensable in exceptional circumstances. The established market position of T and the nature of the obligations imposed on it indicate this is not an exceptional case. The ban on active selling, on the other hand, is likely to be indispensable. T is likely to have less incentive to sell and advertise the P brand, if distributors in other Member States could sell actively in Member State X and thus get a free ride on the efforts of T. This is particularly so, as T also distributes competing brands and thus has the possibility of pushing more of the brands that are the least exposed to free riding.

S is a producer of carbonated soft drinks, holding 40 % of the market. The nearest competitor holds 20 %. S concludes supply agreements with customers accounting for 25 % of demand, whereby they undertake to purchase exclusively from S for 5 years. S concludes agreements with other customers accounting for 15 % of demand whereby they are granted quarterly target rebates, if their purchases exceed certain individually fixed targets. S claims that the agreements allow it to predict demand more accurately and thus to better plan production, reducing raw material storage and warehousing costs and avoiding supply shortages. Given the market position of S and the combined coverage of the restrictions, the restrictions are very unlikely to be considered indispensable. The exclusive purchasing obligation exceeds what is required to plan production and the same is true of the target rebate scheme. Predictability of demand can be achieved by less restrictive means. S could, for example, provide incentives for customers to order large quantities at a time by offering quantity rebates or by offering a rebate to customers that place firm orders in advance for delivery on specified dates.

3.4. Second condition of Article 81(3): Fair share for consumers

3.4.1. *General remarks*

83. According to the second condition of Article 81(3) consumers must receive a fair share of the efficiencies generated by the restrictive agreement.

84. The concept of '*consumers*' encompasses all direct or indirect users of the products covered by the agreement, including producers that use the products as an input, wholesalers, retailers and final consumers, i.e. natural persons who are acting for purposes which can be regarded as outside their trade or profession. In other words, consumers within the meaning of Article 81(3) are the customers of the parties to the agreement and subsequent purchasers. These customers can be undertakings as in the case of buyers of industrial machinery or an input for further processing or final consumers as for instance in the case of buyers of impulse ice-cream or bicycles.

85. The concept of *'fair share'* implies that the pass-on of benefits must at least compensate consumers for any actual or likely negative impact caused to them by the restriction of competition found under Article 81(1). In line with the overall objective of Article 81 to prevent anti-competitive agreements, the net effect of the agreement must at least be neutral from the point of view of those consumers directly or likely affected by the agreement ([80]). If such consumers are worse off following the agreement, the second condition of Article 81(3) is not fulfilled. The positive effects of an agreement must be balanced against and compensate for its negative effects on consumers ([81]). When that is the case consumers are not harmed by the agreement. Moreover, society as a whole benefits where the efficiencies lead either to fewer resources being used to produce the output consumed or to the production of more valuable products and thus to a more efficient allocation of resources.

86. It is not required that consumers receive a share of each and every efficiency gain identified under the first condition. It suffices that sufficient benefits are passed on to compensate for the negative effects of the restrictive agreement. In that case consumers obtain a fair share of the overall benefits ([82]). If a restrictive agreement is likely to lead to higher prices, consumers must be fully compensated through increased quality or other benefits. If not, the second condition of Article 81(3) is not fulfilled.

87. The decisive factor is the overall impact on consumers of the products within the relevant market and not the impact on individual members of this group of consumers ([83]). In some cases a certain period of time may be required before the efficiencies materialise. Until such time the agreement may have only negative effects. The fact that pass-on to the consumer occurs with a certain time lag does not in itself exclude the application of Article 81(3). However, the greater the time lag, the greater must be the efficiencies to compensate also for the loss to consumers during the period preceding the pass-on.

88. In making this assessment it must be taken into account that the value of a gain for consumers in the future is not the same as a present gain for consumers. The value of saving 100 euro today is greater than the value of saving the same amount a year later. A gain for consumers in the future therefore does not fully compensate for a present loss to consumers of equal nominal size. In order to allow for an appropriate comparison of a present loss to consumers with a future gain to consumers, the value of future gains must be discounted. The discount rate applied must reflect the rate of inflation, if any, and lost interest as an indication of the lower value of future gains.

89. In other cases the agreement may enable the parties to obtain the efficiencies earlier than would otherwise be possible. In such circumstances it is necessary to take account of the likely negative impact on consumers within the relevant market once this lead-time has lapsed. If through the restrictive agreement the parties obtain a strong position on the market, they may be able to charge a significantly higher price than would otherwise have been the case. For the second condition of Article 81(3) to be satisfied the benefit to consumers of having earlier access to the products must be equally significant. This may for instance be the case where an agreement allows two tyre manufacturers to bring to market three years earlier a new substantially safer tyre but at the same time, by increasing their market power, allows them to raise prices by 5 %. In such a case it is likely that having early access to a substantially improved product outweighs the price increase.

90. The second condition of Article 81(3) incorporates a sliding scale. The greater the restriction of competition found under Article 81(1) the greater must be the efficiencies and the pass-on to consumers. This sliding scale approach implies that if the restrictive effects of an agreement are relatively limited and the efficiencies are substantial it is likely that a fair share of the cost savings will be passed on to consumers. In such cases it is therefore normally not necessary to engage in a detailed analysis of the second condition of Article 81(3), provided that the three other conditions for the application of this provision are fulfilled.

91. If, on the other hand, the restrictive effects of the agreement are substantial and the cost savings are relatively insignificant, it is very unlikely that the second condition of Article 81(3) will be fulfilled. The impact of the restriction of competition depends on the intensity of the restriction and the degree of competition that remains following the agreement.

92. If the agreement has both substantial anti-competitive effects and substantial pro-competitive effects a careful analysis is required. In the application of the balancing test in such cases it must be taken into account that competition is an important long-term driver of efficiency and innovation. Undertakings that are not subject to effective competitive constraints – such as for instance dominant firms – have less incentive to maintain or build on the efficiencies. The more substantial the impact of the agreement on competition, the more likely it is that consumers will suffer in the long run.

93. The following two sections describe in more detail the analytical framework for assessing consumer pass-on of efficiency gains. The first section deals with cost efficiencies, whereas the section that follows covers other types of efficiencies such as new or improved products (qualitative efficiencies). The framework, which is developed in these two sections, is particularly important in cases where it is not immediately obvious that the competitive harms exceed the benefits to consumers or *vice versa* (84).

94. In the application of the principles set out below the Commission will have regard to the fact that in many cases it is difficult to accurately calculate the consumer pass-on rate and other types of consumer pass-on. Undertakings are only required to substantiate their claims by providing estimates and other data to the extent reasonably possible, taking account of the circumstances of the individual case.

3.4.2. *Pass-on and balancing of cost efficiencies*

95. When markets, as is normally the case, are not perfectly competitive, undertakings are able to influence the market price to a greater or lesser extent by altering their output (85). They may also be able to price discriminate amongst customers.

96. Cost efficiencies may in some circumstances lead to increased output and lower prices for the affected consumers. If due to cost efficiencies the undertakings in question can increase profits by expanding output, consumer pass-on may occur. In assessing the extent to which cost efficiencies are likely to be passed on to consumers and the outcome of the balancing test contained in Article 81(3) the following factors are in particular taken into account:

(a) The characteristics and structure of the market,

(b) The nature and magnitude of the efficiency gains,

(c) The elasticity of demand, and

(d) The magnitude of the restriction of competition.

All factors must normally be considered. Since Article 81(3) only applies in cases where competition on the market is being appreciably restricted, see paragraph 24 above, there can be no presumption that residual competition will ensure that consumers receive a fair share of the benefits. However, the degree of competition remaining on the market and the nature of this competition influences the likelihood of pass-on.

97. The greater the degree of residual competition the more likely it is that individual undertakings will try to increase their sales by passing on cost efficiencies. If undertakings compete mainly on price and are not subject to significant capacity constraints, pass-on may occur relatively quickly. If competition is mainly on capacity and capacity adaptations occur with a certain time lag, pass-on will be slower. Pass-on is also likely to be slower when the market structure is conducive to tacit collusion (86). If competitors are likely to retaliate against an increase in output by one or more parties to the agreement, the incentive to increase output may be tempered, unless the competitive advantage conferred by the efficiencies is such that the undertakings concerned have an incentive to break away from the common policy adopted on the market by the members of the oligopoly. In other words, the efficiencies generated by the agreement may turn the undertakings concerned into so-called 'mavericks' (87).

98. The nature of the efficiency gains also plays an important role. According to economic theory undertakings maximise their profits by selling units of output until marginal revenue equals marginal cost. Marginal revenue is the change in total revenue resulting from selling an additional unit of output and marginal cost is the change in total cost resulting from producing that additional unit of output. It follows from this principle that as a general rule output and pricing decisions of a profit maximising undertaking are not determined by its fixed costs (i.e. costs that do not vary with the rate of production) but by its variable costs (i.e. costs that vary with the rate of production). After fixed costs are incurred and capacity is set, pricing and output decisions are determined by variable cost and demand conditions. Take for instance a situation in which two companies each produce two products on two production lines operating only at half their capacities. A specialisation agreement may allow the two undertakings to specialise in producing one of the two products and scrap their second production line for the other product. At the same time the specialisation may allow the companies to reduce variable input and stocking costs. Only the latter savings will have a direct effect on the pricing and output decisions of the undertakings, as they will influence the marginal costs of production. The scrapping by each undertaking of one of their production lines will not reduce their variable costs and will not have an impact on their production costs. It follows that undertakings may have a direct incentive to pass on to consumers in the form of higher output and lower prices efficiencies that reduce marginal costs, whereas they have no such direct incentive with regard to efficiencies that reduce fixed costs. Consumers are therefore more likely to receive a fair share of the cost efficiencies in the case of reductions in variable costs than they are in the case of reductions in fixed costs.

99. The fact that undertakings may have an incentive to pass on certain types of cost efficiencies does not imply that the pass-on rate will necessarily be 100 %. The actual pass-on rate depends on the extent to which consumers respond to changes in price, i.e. the elasticity of demand. The greater the increase in demand caused by a decrease in price, the greater the pass-on rate. This follows from the fact that the greater the additional sales caused by a price reduction due to an increase in output the more likely it is that these sales will offset the loss of revenue caused by the lower price resulting from the increase in output. In the absence of price discrimination the lowering of prices affects all units sold by the undertaking, in which case marginal revenue is less than the price obtained for the marginal product. If the undertakings concerned are able to charge different prices to different customers, i.e. price discriminate, pass-on will normally only benefit price-sensitive consumers [88].

100. It must also be taken into account that efficiency gains often do not affect the whole cost structure of the undertakings concerned. In such event the impact on the price to consumers is reduced. If for example an agreement allows the parties to reduce production costs by 6 %, but production costs only make up one third of the costs on the basis of which prices are determined, the impact on the product price is 2 %, assuming that the full amount is passed-on.

101. Finally, and very importantly, it is necessary to balance the two opposing forces resulting from the restriction of competition and the cost efficiencies. On the one hand, any increase in market power caused by the restrictive agreement gives the undertakings concerned the ability and incentive to raise price. On the other hand, the types of cost efficiencies that are taken into account may give the undertakings concerned an incentive to reduce price, see paragraph 98 above. The effects of these two opposing forces must be balanced against each other. It is recalled in this regard that the consumer pass-on condition incorporates a sliding scale. When the agreement causes a substantial reduction in the competitive constraint facing the parties, extraordinarily large cost efficiencies are normally required for sufficient pass-on to occur.

3.4.3. *Pass-on and balancing of other types of efficiencies*

102. Consumer pass-on can also take the form of qualitative efficiencies such as new and improved products, creating sufficient value for consumers to compensate for the anti-competitive effects of the agreement, including a price increase.

103. Any such assessment necessarily requires value judgment. It is difficult to assign precise values to dynamic efficiencies of this nature. However, the fundamental objective of the assessment remains the same, namely to ascertain the overall impact of the agreement on the consumers within the relevant market. Undertakings claiming the benefit of Article 81(3) must substantiate that consumers obtain countervailing benefits (see in this respect paragraphs 57 and 86 above).

104. The availability of new and improved products constitutes an important source of consumer welfare. As long as the increase in value stemming from such improvements exceeds any harm from a maintenance or an increase in price caused by the restrictive agreement, consumers are better off than without the agreement and the consumer pass-on requirement of Article 81(3) is normally fulfilled. In cases where the likely effect of the agreement is to increase prices for consumers within the relevant market it must be carefully assessed whether the claimed efficiencies create real value for consumers in that market so as to compensate for the adverse effects of the restriction of competition.

3.5. Fourth condition of Article 81(3): No elimination of competition

105. According to the fourth condition of Article 81(3) the agreement must not afford the undertakings concerned the possibility of eliminating competition in respect of a substantial part of the products concerned. Ultimately the protection of rivalry and the competitive process is given priority over potentially pro-competitive efficiency gains which could result from restrictive agreements. The last condition of Article 81(3) recognises the fact that rivalry between undertakings is an essential driver of economic efficiency, including dynamic efficiencies in the shape of innovation. In other words, the ultimate aim of Article 81 is to protect the competitive process. When competition is eliminated the competitive process is brought to an end and short-term efficiency gains are outweighed by longer-term losses stemming *inter alia* from expenditures incurred by the incumbent to maintain its position (rent seeking), misallocation of resources, reduced innovation and higher prices.

106. The concept in Article 81(3) of elimination of competition in respect of a substantial part of the products concerned is an autonomous Community law concept specific to Article 81(3) ([89]). However, in the application of this concept it is necessary to take account of the relationship between Article 81 and Article 82. According to settled case law the application of Article 81(3) cannot prevent the application of Article 82 of the Treaty ([90]). Moreover, since Articles 81 and 82 both pursue the aim of maintaining effective competition on the market, consistency requires that Article 81(3) be interpreted as precluding any application of this provision to restrictive agreements that constitute an abuse of a dominant position ([91]) ([92]). However, not all restrictive agreements concluded by a dominant undertaking constitute an abuse of a dominant position. This is for instance the case where a dominant undertaking is party to a non-full function joint venture ([93]), which is found to be restrictive of competition but at the same time involves a substantial integration of assets.

107. Whether competition is being eliminated within the meaning of the last condition of Article 81(3) depends on the degree of competition existing prior to the agreement and on the impact of the restrictive agreement on competition, i.e. the reduction in competition that the agreement brings about. The more competition is already weakened in the market concerned, the slighter the further reduction required for competition to be eliminated within the meaning of Article 81(3). Moreover, the greater the reduction of competition caused by the agreement, the greater the likelihood that competition in respect of a substantial part of the products concerned risks being eliminated.

108. The application of the last condition of Article 81(3) requires a realistic analysis of the various sources of competition in the market, the level of competitive constraint that they impose on the parties to the agreement and the impact of the agreement on this competitive constraint. Both actual and potential competition must be considered.

109. While market shares are relevant, the magnitude of remaining sources of actual competition cannot be assessed exclusively on the basis of market share. More extensive qualitative and quantitative analysis is normally called for. The capacity of actual competitors to compete and their incentive to do so must be examined. If, for example, competitors face capacity constraints or have relatively higher costs of production their competitive response will necessarily be limited.

110. In the assessment of the impact of the agreement on competition it is also relevant to examine its influence on the various parameters of competition. The last condition for exception under Article 81(3) is not fulfilled, if the agreement eliminates competition in one of its most important expressions. This is particularly the case when an agreement eliminates price competition ([94]) or competition in respect of innovation and development of new products.

111. The actual market conduct of the parties can provide insight into the impact of the agreement. If following the conclusion of the agreement the parties have implemented and maintained substantial price increases or engaged in other conduct indicative of the existence of a considerable degree of market power, it is an indication that the parties are not subject to any real competitive pressure and that competition has been eliminated with regard to a substantial part of the products concerned.

112. Past competitive interaction may also provide an indication of the impact of the agreement on future competitive interaction. An undertaking may be able to eliminate competition within the meaning of Article 81(3) by concluding an agreement with a competitor that in the past has been a 'maverick' (95). Such an agreement may change the competitive incentives and capabilities of the competitor and thereby remove an important source of competition in the market.

113. In cases involving differentiated products, i.e. products that differ in the eyes of consumers, the impact of the agreement may depend on the competitive relationship between the products sold by the parties to the agreement. When undertakings offer differentiated products the competitive constraint that individual products impose on each other differs according to the degree of substitutability between them. It must therefore be considered what is the degree of substitutability between the products offered by the parties, i.e. what is the competitive constraint that they impose on each other. The more the products of the parties to the agreement are close substitutes the greater the likely restrictive effect of the agreement. In other words, the more substitutable the products the greater the likely change brought about by the agreement in terms of restriction of competition on the market and the more likely it is that competition in respect of a substantial part of the products concerned risks being eliminated.

114. While sources of actual competition are usually the most important, as they are most easily verified, sources of potential competition must also be taken into account. The assessment of potential competition requires an analysis of barriers to entry facing undertakings that are not already competing within the relevant market. Any assertions by the parties that there are low barriers to market entry must be supported by information identifying the sources of potential competition and the parties must also substantiate why these sources constitute a real competitive pressure on the parties.

115. In the assessment of entry barriers and the real possibility for new entry on a significant scale, it is relevant to examine, *inter alia*, the following:

(i) The regulatory framework with a view to determining its impact on new entry.

(ii) The cost of entry including sunk costs. Sunk costs are those that cannot be recovered if the entrant subsequently exits the market. The higher the sunk costs the higher the commercial risk for potential entrants.

(iii) The minimum efficient scale within the industry, i.e. the rate of output where average costs are minimised. If the minimum efficient scale is large compared to the size of the market, efficient entry is likely to be more costly and risky.

(iv) The competitive strengths of potential entrants. Effective entry is particularly likely where potential entrants have access to at least as cost efficient technologies as the incumbents or other competitive advantages that allow them to compete effectively. When potential entrants are on the same or an inferior technological trajectory compared to the incumbents and possess no other significant competitive advantage entry is more risky and less effective.

(v) The position of buyers and their ability to bring onto the market new sources of competition. It is irrelevant that certain strong buyers may be able to extract more favourable conditions from the parties to the agreement than their weaker competitors (96). The presence of strong buyers can only serve to counter a prima facie finding of elimination of competition if it is likely that the buyers in question will pave the way for effective new entry.

(vi) The likely response of incumbents to attempted new entry. Incumbents may for example through past conduct have acquired a reputation of aggressive behaviour, having an impact on future entry.

(vii) The economic outlook for the industry may be an indicator of its longer-term attractiveness. Industries that are stagnating or in decline are less attractive candidates for entry than industries characterised by growth.

(viii) Past entry on a significant scale or the absence thereof.

116. The above principles can be illustrated by the following hypothetical examples, which are not intended to establish thresholds:

Firm A is brewer, holding 70 % of the relevant market, comprising the sale of beer through cafés and other on-trade premises. Over the past 5 years A has increased its market share from 60 %. There are four other competitors in the market, B, C, D and E with market shares of 10 %, 10 %, 5 % and 5 %. No new entry has occurred in the recent past and price changes implemented by A have generally been followed by competitors. A concludes agreements with 20 % of the on-trade premises representing 40 % of sales volumes whereby the contracting parties undertake to purchase beer only from A for a period of 5 years. The agreements raise the costs and reduce the revenues of rivals, which are foreclosed from the most attractive outlets. Given the market position of A, which has been strengthened in recent years, the absence of new entry and the already weak position of competitors it is likely that competition in the market is eliminated within the meaning of Article 81(3).

Shipping firms A, B, C, and D, holding collectively more than 70 % of the relevant market, conclude an agreement whereby they agree to coordinate their schedules and their tariffs. Following the implementation of the agreement prices rise between 30 % and 100 %. There are four other suppliers, the largest holding about 14 % of the relevant market. There has been no new entry in recent years and the parties to the agreement did not lose significant market share following the price increases. The existing competitors brought no significant new capacity to the market and no new entry occurred. In light of the market position of the parties and the absence of competitive response to their joint conduct it can reasonably be concluded that the parties to the agreement are not subject to real competitive pressures and that the agreement affords them the possibility of eliminating competition within the meaning of Article 81(3).

A is a producer of electric appliances for professional users with a market share of 65 % of a relevant national market. B is a competing manufacturer with 5 % market share which has developed a new type of motor that is more powerful while consuming less electricity. A and B conclude an agreement whereby they establish a production joint venture for the production of the new motor. B undertakes to grant an exclusive licence to the joint venture. The joint venture combines the new technology of B with the efficient manufacturing and quality control process of A. There is one other main competitor with 15 % of the market. Another competitor with 5 % market share has recently been acquired by C, a major international producer of competing electric appliances, which itself owns efficient technologies. C has thus far not been active on the market mainly due to the fact that local presence and servicing is desired by customers. Through the acquisition C gains access to the service organisation required to penetrate the market. The entry of C is likely to ensure that competition is not being eliminated.

---

(1) In the following the term 'agreement' includes concerted practices and decisions of associations of undertakings.

(2) OJ L 1, 4.1.2003, p. 1.

(3) All existing block exemption regulations and Commission notices are available on the DG Competition web-site: http://www.europa.eu.int/comm/dgs/competition

(4) See paragraph 36 below.

(5) See Commission Notice on Guidelines on vertical restraints (OJ C 291, 13.10.2000, p. 1), Commission Notice on Guidelines on the application of Article 81 of the Treaty to horizontal cooperation agreements (OJ C 3, 6.1.2001, p. 2), and Commission Notice on Guidelines on the application of Article 81 of the Treaty to technology transfer agreements, not yet published.

(6) The concept of effect on trade between Member States is dealt with in separate guidelines.

(7) In the following the term 'restriction' includes the prevention and distortion of competition.

(8) According to Article 81(2) such agreements are automatically void.

(9) Article 81(1) prohibits both actual and potential anti-competitive effects, see e.g. Case C-7/95 P, John Deere, [1998] ECR I-3111, paragraph 77.

(10) See Case T-65/98, Van den Bergh Foods, [2003] ECR II . . ., paragraph 107 and Case T-112/99, Métropole télévision (M6) and others, [2001] ECR II-2459, paragraph 74, where the Court of First Instance held that it is only in the precise framework of Article 81(3) that the pro- and anti-competitive aspects of a restriction may be weighed.

(11) See note above.

(12) See e.g. Case C-49/92 P, Anic Partecipazioni, [1999] ECR I-4125, paragraph 116; and Joined Cases 40/73 to 48/73 and others, Suiker Unie, [1975] ECR page 1663, paragraph 173.

(13) See in this respect paragraph 108 of the judgment in Anic Partecipazioni cited in the previous note and Case C-277/87, Sandoz Prodotti, [1990] ECR I-45.

([14]) See in this respect e.g. Case 14/68, Walt Wilhelm, [1969] ECR 1, and more recently Case T-203/01, Michelin (II), [2003] ECR II . . ., paragraph 112.

([15]) See Joined Cases T-25/95 and others, Cimenteries CBR, [2000] ECR II-491, paragraphs 1849 and 1852; and Joined Cases T-202/98 and others, British Sugar, [2001] ECR II-2035, paragraphs 58 to 60.

([16]) See to that effect Case C-453/99, Courage v Crehan, [2001] ECR I-6297, and paragraph 3444 of the judgment in Cimenteries CBR cited in the previous note.

([17]) See in this respect Joined Cases C-2/01 P and C-3/01 P, Bundesverband der Arzneimittel-Importeure, [2004] ECR I . . ., paragraph 102.

([18]) See e.g. Joined Cases 25/84 and 26/84, Ford, [1985] ECR 2725.

([19]) See in this respect paragraph 141 of the judgment in Bundesverband der Arzneimittel-Importeure cited in note.

([20]) See Case 56/65, Société Technique Minière, [1966] ECR 337, and paragraph 76 of the judgment in John Deere, cited in note 9.

([21]) See in this respect e.g. Joined Cases 56/64 and 58/66, Consten and Grundig, [1966] ECR 429.

([22]) See in this respect e.g. Commission Decision in Elopak/Metal Box – Odin (OJ 1990 L 209, p. 15) and in TPS (OJ 1999 L 90, p. 6).

([23]) See in this respect the judgment in Société Technique Minière cited in note 20 and Case 258/78, Nungesser, [1982] ECR 2015.

([24]) See rule 10 in paragraph 119 of the Guidelines on vertical restraints cited in note above, according to which inter alia passive sales restrictions — a hardcore restraint — are held to fall outside Article 81(1) for a period of 2 years when the restraint is linked to opening up new product or geographic markets.

([25]) See e.g. paragraph 99 of the judgment in Anic Partecipazioni cited in note 12.

([26]) See paragraph 46 below.

([27]) See Joined Cases 29/83 and 30/83, CRAM and Rheinzink, [1984] ECR 1679, paragraph 26, and Joined Cases 96/82 and others, ANSEAU-NAVEWA, [1983] ECR 3369, paragraphs 23-25.

([28]) See the Guidelines on horizontal cooperation agreements, cited in note, paragraph 25, and Article 5 of Commission Regulation 2658/2000 on the application of Article 81(3) of the Treaty to categories of specialisation agreements (OJ L 304, 5.12.2000, p. 3).

([29]) See Article 4 Commission Regulation 2790/1999 on the application of Article 81(3) of the Treaty to categories of vertical agreements and concerted practices (OJ L 336, 29.12.1999, p. 21) and the Guidelines on Vertical Restraints, cited in note, paragraph 46 et seq. See also Case 279/87, Tipp-Ex, [1990] ECR I-261, and Case T-62/98, Volkswagen v Commission, [2000] ECR II-2707, paragraph 178.

([30]) See paragraph 77 of the judgment in John Deere cited in note 9.

([31]) It is not sufficient in itself that the agreement restricts the freedom of action of one or more of the parties, see paragraphs 76 and 77 of the judgment in Métropole television (M6) cited in note10. This is in line with the fact that the object of Article 81 is to protect competition on the market for the benefit of consumers.

([32]) See e.g. Case 5/69, Völk, [1969] ECR 295, paragraph 7. Guidance on the issue of appreciability can be found in the Commission Notice on agreements of minor importance which do not appreciably restrict competition under Article 81(1) of the Treaty (OJ C 368, 22.12.2001, p. 13) The notice defines appreciability in a negative way. Agreements, which fall outside the scope of the de minimis notice, do not necessarily have appreciable restrictive effects. An individual assessment is required.

([33]) See in this respect Joined Cases T-374/94 and others, European Night Services, [1998] ECR II-3141.

([34]) See note 32.

([35]) See in this respect Commission notice on the definition of the relevant market for the purposes of Community competition law (OJ C 372, 9.12.1997, p. 1).

([36]) For the reference in the OJ see note 5.

([37]) See paragraph 104 of the judgment in Métropole télévision (M6) and others, cited in note 10.

([38]) See e.g. Case C-399/93, Luttikhuis, [1995] ECR I-4515, paragraphs 12 to 14.

([39]) See in this respect paragraphs 118 et seq. of the Métropole television judgment cited in note 10.

([40]) See paragraph 107 of the judgment in Métropole télévision judgement cited in note 10.

([41]) See e.g. Commission Decision in Elopak/Metal Box – Odin cited in note 22.

([42]) See Case 161/84, Pronuptia, [1986] ECR 353.

([43]) See note 22. The decision was upheld by the Court of First Instance in the judgment in Métropole télévision (M6) cited in note 10.

([44]) Cost savings and other gains to the parties that arise from the mere exercise of market power do not give rise to objective benefits and cannot be taken into account, cf. paragraph 49 below.

([45]) See the judgment in Consten and Grundig, cited in note 21.

([46]) The fact that an agreement is block exempted does not in itself indicate that the individual agreement is caught by Article 81(1).

([47]) See e.g. Case C-234/89, Delimitis, [1991] ECR I-935, paragraph 46.

([48]) Article 36(4) of Regulation 1/2003 has, inter alia, repealed Article 5 of Regulation 1017/68 applying rules of competition to transport by rail, road and inland waterway. However, the Commission's case practice adopted under Regulation 1017/68 remains relevant for the purposes of applying Article 81(3) in the inland transport sector.

([49]) See paragraph 42 below.

([50]) See the judgment in Société Technique Minière cited in note 20.

([51]) See in this respect Case 319/82, Kerpen & Kerpen, [1983] ECR 4 173, paragraphs 11 and 12.

([52]) See e.g. Case T-185/00 and others, Métropole télévision SA (M6), [2002] ECR II-3805, paragraph 86, Case T-17/93, Matra, ECR [1994] II-595, paragraph 85; and Joined Cases 43/82 and 63/82, VBVB and VBBB, [1984] ECR 19, paragraph 61.

([53]) See Case T-213/00, CMA CGM and others, [2003] ECR II . . ., paragraph 226.

([54]) See to that effect implicitly paragraph 139 of the Matra judgment cited in note 52 and Case 26/76, Metro (I), [1977] ECR 1875, paragraph 43.

([55]) As to the concept of consumers see paragraph 84 below where it is stated that consumers are the customers of the parties and subsequent buyers. The parties themselves are not 'consumers' for the purposes of Article 81(3).

([56]) The test is market specific, see to that effect Case T-131/99, Shaw, [2002] ECR II-2023, paragraph 163, where the Court of First Instance held that the assessment under Article 81(3) had to be made within the same analytical framework as that used for assessing the restrictive effects, and Case C-360/92 P, Publishers Association, [1995] ECR I-23, paragraph 29, where in a case where the relevant market was wider than national the Court of Justice held that in the application of Article 81(3) it was not correct only to consider the effects on the national territory.

([57]) In Case T-86/95, Compagnie Générale Maritime and others, [2002] ECR II-1011, paragraphs 343 to 345, the Court of First Instance held that Article 81(3) does not require that the benefits are linked to a specific market and that in appropriate cases regard must be had to benefits 'for every other market on which the agreement in question might have beneficial effects, and even, in a more general sense, for any service the quality or efficiency of which might be improved by the existence of that agreement'. Importantly, however, in this case the affected group of consumers was the same. The case concerned intermodal transport services encompassing a bundle of, inter alia, inland and maritime transportation provided to shipping companies across the Community. The restrictions related to inland transport services, which were held to constitute a separate market, whereas the benefits were claimed to occur in relation to maritime transport services. Both services were demanded by shippers requiring intermodal transport services between northern Europe and South-East and East Asia. The judgment in CMA CGM, cited in note 53 above, also concerned a situation where the agreement, while covering several distinct services, affected the same group of consumers, namely shippers of containerised cargo between northern Europe and the Far East. Under the agreement the parties fixed charges and surcharges relating to inland transport services, port services and maritime transport services. The Court of First Instance held (cf. paragraphs 226 to 228) that in the circumstances of the case there was no need to define relevant markets for the purpose of applying Article 81(3). The agreement was restrictive of competition by its very object and there were no benefits for consumers.

([58]) See paragraphs 126 and 132 of the Guidelines on horizontal co-operation agreements cited in note 5 above.

([59]) See the Ford judgment cited in note 18.

([60]) See in this respect for example Commission Decision in TPS (OJ L 90, 2.4.1999, p. 6). Similarly, the prohibition of Article 81(1) also only applies as long as the agreement has a restrictive object or restrictive effects.

([61]) See paragraph 85 of the Matra judgment cited in note 52.

([62]) As to this requirement see paragraph 49 below.

([63]) See e.g. Case T-29/92, Vereniging van Samenwerkende Prijsregelende Organisaties in de Bouwnijverheid (SPO), [1995] ECR II-289.

([64]) See e.g. Case 258/78, Nungesser, [1982] ECR 2015, paragraph 77, concerning absolute territorial protection.

([65]) See in this respect e.g. the judgment in SPO cited in note 63.

([66]) National measures must, inter alia, comply with the Treaty rules on free movement of goods, services, persons and capital.

([67]) See e.g. the judgment in Consten and Grundig cited in note 21.

([68]) See in this respect Commission Decision in Van den Bergh Foods (OJ 1998 L 246, p. 1).

([69]) See in this respect Commission Decision in Glaxo Wellcome (OJ 2001 L 302, p. 1).

([70]) See e.g. Commission Decision in GEAE/P&W (OJ 2000 L 58, p. 16); in British Interactive Broadcasting/Open (OJ 1999 L 312, p. 1) and in Asahi/Saint Gobain (OJ 1994 L 354, page 87).

([71]) See e.g. Commission Decision in Atlas (OJ 1996 L 239, p. 23), and in Phoenix/Global One (OJ 1996 L 239, p. 57).

([72]) See e.g. Commission Decision in Uniform Eurocheques (OJ 1985 L 35, p. 43).

([73]) See e.g. Commission Decision in Cégétel + 4 (OJ 1999 L 88, p. 26).

([74]) As to the former question, which may be relevant in the context of Article 81(1), see paragraph 18 above.

([75]) Scale economies are normally exhausted at a certain point. Thereafter average costs will stabilise and eventually rise due to, for example, capacity constraints and bottlenecks.

([76]) See in this respect paragraphs 392 to 395 of the judgment in Compagnie Générale Maritime cited in note 57.

([77]) See for more detail paragraph 116 of the Guidelines on Vertical Restraints cited in note 5.

([78]) See Joined Cases T-374/94 and others, European Night Services, [1998] ECR II-3141, paragraph 230.

([79]) See Commission Regulation No 2790/1999 on the application of Article 81(3) of the Treaty on categories of vertical agreements and concerted practices (OJ 1999 L 336, page 21).

([80]) See in this respect the judgment in Consten and Grundig cited in note 21, where the Court of Justice held that the improvements within the meaning of the first condition of Article 81(3) must show appreciable objective advantages of such a character as to compensate for the disadvantages which they cause in the field of competition.

([81]) It is recalled that positive and negative effects on consumers are in principle balanced within each relevant market (cf. paragraph 43 above).

([82]) See in this respect paragraph 48 of the Metro (I) judgment cited in note 54.

([83]) See paragraph 163 of the judgment in Shaw cited in note 56.

([84]) In the following sections, for convenience the competitive harm is referred to in terms of higher prices; competitive harm could also mean lower quality, less variety or lower innovation than would otherwise have occurred.

([85]) In perfectly competitive markets individual undertakings are price-takers. They sell their products at the market price, which is determined by overall supply and demand. The output of the individual undertaking is so small that any individual undertaking's change in output does not affect the market price.

([86]) Undertakings collude tacitly when in an oligopolistic market they are able to coordinate their action on the market without resorting to an explicit cartel agreement.

([87]) This term refers to undertakings that constrain the pricing behaviour of other undertakings in the market who might otherwise have tacitly colluded.

([88]) The restrictive agreement may even allow the undertakings in question to charge a higher price to customers with a low elasticity of demand.

([89]) See Joined Cases T-191/98, T-212/98 and T-214/98, Atlantic Container Line (TACA), [2003] ECR II-. . ., paragraph 939, and Case T-395/94, Atlantic Container Line, [2002] ECR II-875, paragraph 330.

([90]) See Joined Cases C-395/96 P and C-396/96 P, Compagnie maritime belge, [2000] ECR I-1365, paragraph 130. Similarly, the application of Article 81(3) does not prevent the application of the Treaty rules on the free movement of goods, services, persons and capital. These provisions are in certain circumstances applicable to agreements, decisions and concerted practices within the meaning of Article 81(1), see to that effect Case C-309/99, Wouters, [2002] ECR I-1577, paragraph 120.

([91]) See in this respect Case T-51/89, Tetra Pak (I), [1990] ECR II-309, and Joined Cases T-191/98, T-212/98 and T-214/98, Atlantic Container Line (TACA), [2003] ECR II-. . ., paragraph 1456.

([92]) This is how paragraph 135 of the Guidelines on vertical restraints and paragraphs 36, 71, 105, 134 and 155 of the Guidelines on horizontal cooperation agreements, cited in note 5, should be understood when they state that in principle restrictive agreements concluded by dominant undertakings cannot be exempted.

([93]) Full function joint ventures, i.e. joint ventures that perform on a lasting basis all the functions of an autonomous economic entity, are covered by Council Regulation (EEC) No 4064/89 on the control of concentrations between undertakings (OJ 1990 L 257, p 13).

([94]) See paragraph 21 of the judgment in Metro (I) cited in note 54.

([95]) See paragraph 97 above.

([96]) See in this respect Case T-228/97, Irish Sugar, [1999] ECR II-2969, paragraph 101.

COMMISSION NOTICE

Guidelines on the effect on trade concept contained in Articles 81 and 82 of the Treaty

(2004/C 101/07)

(Text with EEA relevance)

1. INTRODUCTION

1. Articles 81 and 82 of the Treaty are applicable to horizontal and vertical agreements and practices on the part of undertakings which 'may affect trade between Member States'.

2. In their interpretation of Articles 81 and 82, the Community Courts have already substantially clarified the content and scope of the concept of effect on trade between Member States.

3. The present guidelines set out the principles developed by the Community Courts in relation to the interpretation of the effect on trade concept of Articles 81 and 82. They further spell out a rule indicating when agreements are in general unlikely to be capable of appreciably affecting trade between Member States (the non-appreciable affectation of trade rule or NAAT-rule). The guidelines are not intended to be exhaustive. The aim is to set out the methodology for the application of the effect on trade concept and to provide guidance on its application in frequently occurring situations. Although not binding on them, these guidelines also intend to give guidance to the courts and authorities of the Member States in their application of the effect on trade concept contained in Articles 81 and 82.

4. The present guidelines do not address the issue of what constitutes an appreciable restriction of competition under Article 81(1). This issue, which is distinct from the ability of agreements to appreciably affect trade between Member States, is dealt with in the Commission Notice on agreements of minor importance which do not appreciably restrict competition under Article 81(1) of the Treaty (1) (the *de minimis* rule). The guidelines are also not intended to provide guidance on the effect on trade concept contained in Article 87(1) of the Treaty on State aid.

5. These guidelines, including the NAAT-rule, are without prejudice to the interpretation of Articles 81 and 82 which may be given by the Court of Justice and the Court of First Instance.

2. THE EFFECT ON TRADE CRITERION

2.1. General principles

6. Article 81(1) provides that 'the following shall be prohibited as incompatible with the common market: all agreements between undertakings, decisions of associations of undertakings and concerted practices which may affect trade between Member States and which have as their object or effect the prevention, restriction or distortion of competition within the common market'. For the sake of simplicity the terms 'agreements, decisions of associations of undertakings and concerted practices' are collectively referred to as 'agreements'.

7. Article 82 on its part stipulates that 'any abuse by one or more undertakings of a dominant position within the common market or in a substantial part thereof shall be prohibited as incompatible with the common market insofar as it may affect trade between Member States.' In what follows the term 'practices' refers to the conduct of dominant undertakings.

8. The effect on trade criterion also determines the scope of application of Article 3 of Regulation 1/2003 on the implementation of the rules on competition laid down in Articles 81 and 82 of the Treaty (2).

9. According to Article 3(1) of that Regulation the competition authorities and courts of the Member States must apply Article 81 to agreements, decisions by associations of undertakings or concerted practices within the meaning of Article 81(1) of the Treaty which may affect trade between Member States within the meaning of that provision, when they apply national competition law to such agreements, decisions or concerted practices. Similarly, when the competition authorities and courts of the Member States apply national competition law to any abuse prohibited by Article 82 of the Treaty, they must also apply Article 82 of the Treaty. Article 3(1) thus obliges the competition authorities and courts of the Member States to also apply Articles 81 and 82 when they apply national competition law to agreements and abusive practices which may affect trade between Member States. On the other hand, Article 3(1) does not oblige national competition authorities and courts to apply national competition law when they apply Articles 81 and 82 to agreements, decisions and concerted practices and to abuses which may affect trade between Member States. They may in such cases apply the Community competition rules on a stand alone basis.

10. It follows from Article 3(2) that the application of national competition law may not lead to the prohibition of agreements, decisions by associations of undertakings or concerted practices which may affect trade between Member States but which do not restrict competition within the meaning of Article 81(1) of the Treaty, or which fulfil the conditions of Article 81(3) of the Treaty or which are covered by a Regulation for the application of Article 81(3) of the Treaty. Member States, however, are not under Regulation 1/2003 precluded from adopting and applying on their territory stricter national laws which prohibit or sanction unilateral conduct engaged in by undertakings.

11. Finally it should be mentioned that Article 3(3) stipulates that without prejudice to general principles and other provisions of Community law, Article 3(1) and (2) do not apply when the competition authorities and the courts of the Member States apply national merger control laws, nor do they preclude the application of provisions of national law that predominantly pursue an objective different from that pursued by Articles 81 and 82 of the Treaty.

12. The effect on trade criterion is an autonomous Community law criterion, which must be assessed separately in each case. It is a jurisdictional criterion, which defines the scope of application of Community competition law ([3]). Community competition law is not applicable to agreements and practices that are not capable of appreciably affecting trade between Member States.

13. The effect on trade criterion confines the scope of application of Articles 81 and 82 to agreements and practices that are capable of having a minimum level of cross-border effects within the Community. In the words of the Court of Justice, the ability of the agreement or practice to affect trade between Member States must be 'appreciable' ([4]).

14. In the case of Article 81 of the Treaty, it is the agreement that must be capable of affecting trade between Member States. It is not required that each individual part of the agreement, including any restriction of competition which may flow from the agreement, is capable of doing so ([5]). If the agreement as a whole is capable of affecting trade between Member States, there is Community law jurisdiction in respect of the entire agreement, including any parts of the agreement that individually do not affect trade between Member States. In cases where the contractual relations between the same parties cover several activities, these activities must, in order to form part of the same agreement, be directly linked and form an integral part of the same overall business arrangement ([6]). If not, each activity constitutes a separate agreement.

15. It is also immaterial whether or not the participation of a particular undertaking in the agreement has an appreciable effect on trade between Member States ([7]). An undertaking cannot escape Community law jurisdiction merely because of the fact that its own contribution to an agreement, which itself is capable of affecting trade between Member States, is insignificant.

16. It is not necessary, for the purposes of establishing Community law jurisdiction, to establish a link between the alleged restriction of competition and the capacity of the agreement to affect trade between Member States. Non-restrictive agreements may also affect trade between Member States. For example, selective distribution agreements based on purely qualitative selection criteria justified by the nature of the products, which are not restrictive of competition within the meaning of Article 81(1), may nevertheless affect trade between Member States. However, the alleged restrictions arising from an agreement may provide a clear indication as to the capacity of the agreement to affect trade between Member States. For instance, a distribution agreement prohibiting exports is by its very nature capable of affecting trade between Member States, although not necessarily to an appreciable extent ([8]).

17. In the case of Article 82 it is the abuse that must affect trade between Member States. This does not imply, however, that each element of the behaviour must be assessed in isolation. Conduct that forms part of an overall strategy pursued by the dominant undertaking must be assessed in terms of its overall impact. Where a dominant undertaking adopts various practices in pursuit of the same aim, for instance practices that aim at eliminating or foreclosing competitors, in order for Article 82 to be applicable to all the practices forming part of this overall strategy, it is sufficient that at least one of these practices is capable of affecting trade between Member States ([9]).

18. It follows from the wording of Articles 81 and 82 and the case law of the Community Courts that in the application of the effect on trade criterion three elements in particular must be addressed:

(a) The concept of 'trade between Member States',

(b) The notion of 'may affect', and

(c) The concept of 'appreciability'.

2.2. **The concept of 'trade between Member States'**

19. The concept of 'trade' is not limited to traditional exchanges of goods and services across borders ([10]). It is a wider concept, covering all cross-border economic activity including establishment ([11]). This interpretation is consistent with the fundamental objective of the Treaty to promote free movement of goods, services, persons and capital.

20. According to settled case law the concept of 'trade' also encompasses cases where agreements or practices affect the competitive structure of the market. Agreements and practices that affect the competitive structure inside the Community by eliminating or threatening to eliminate a competitor operating within the Community may be subject to the Community competition rules ([12]). When an undertaking is or risks being eliminated the competitive structure within the Community is affected and so are the economic activities in which the undertaking is engaged.

21. The requirement that there must be an effect on trade 'between Member States' implies that there must be an impact on cross-border economic activity involving at least two Member States. It is not required that the agreement or practice affect trade between the whole of one Member State and the whole of another Member State. Articles 81 and 82 may be applicable also in cases involving part of a Member State, provided that the effect on trade is appreciable ([13]).

22. The application of the effect on trade criterion is independent of the definition of relevant geographic markets. Trade between Member States may be affected also in cases where the relevant market is national or sub-national ([14]).

2.3. **The notion 'may affect'**

23. The function of the notion 'may affect' is to define the nature of the required impact on trade between Member States. According to the standard test developed by the Court of Justice, the notion 'may affect' implies that it must be possible to foresee with a sufficient degree of probability on the basis of a set of objective factors of law or fact that the agreement or practice may have an influence, direct or indirect, actual or potential, on the pattern of trade between Member States ([15]) ([16]). As mentioned in paragraph 20 above the Court of Justice has in addition developed a test based on whether or not the agreement or practice affects the competitive structure. In cases where the agreement or practice is liable to affect the competitive structure inside the Community, Community law jurisdiction is established.

24. The 'pattern of trade'-test developed by the Court of Justice contains the following main elements, which are dealt with in the following sections:

   (a) 'A sufficient degree of probability on the basis of a set of objective factors of law or fact',

   (b) An influence on the 'pattern of trade between Member States',

   (c) 'A direct or indirect, actual or potential influence' on the pattern of trade.

2.3.1. *A sufficient degree of probability on the basis of a set of objective factors of law or fact*

25. The assessment of effect on trade is based on objective factors. Subjective intent on the part of the undertakings concerned is not required. If, however, there is evidence that undertakings have intended to affect trade between Member States, for example because they have sought to hinder exports to or imports from other Member States, this is a relevant factor to be taken into account.

26. The words 'may affect' and the reference by the Court of Justice to 'a sufficient degree of probability' imply that, in order for Community law jurisdiction to be established, it is not required that the agreement or practice will actually have or has had an effect on trade between Member States. It is sufficient that the agreement or practice is 'capable' of having such an effect ([17]).

27. There is no obligation or need to calculate the actual volume of trade between Member States affected by the agreement or practice. For example, in the case of agreements prohibiting exports to other Member States there is no need to estimate what would have been the level of parallel trade between the Member States concerned, in the absence of the agreement. This interpretation is consistent with the jurisdictional nature of the effect on trade criterion. Community law jurisdiction extends to categories of agreements and practices that are capable of having cross-border effects, irrespective of whether a particular agreement or practice actually has such effects.

28. The assessment under the effect on trade criterion depends on a number of factors that individually may not be decisive ([18]). The relevant factors include the nature of the agreement and practice, the nature of the products covered by the agreement or practice and the position and importance of the undertakings concerned ([19]).

29. The nature of the agreement and practice provides an indication from a qualitative point of view of the ability of the agreement or practice to affect trade between Member States. Some agreements and practices are by their very nature capable of affecting trade between Member States, whereas others require more detailed analysis in this respect. Cross-border cartels are an example of the former, whereas joint ventures confined to the territory of a single Member State are an example of the latter. This aspect is further examined in section 3 below, which deals with various categories of agreements and practices.

30. The nature of the products covered by the agreements or practices also provides an indication of whether trade between Member States is capable of being affected. When by their nature products are easily traded across borders or are important for undertakings that want to enter or expand their activities in other Member States, Community jurisdiction is more readily established than in cases where due to their nature there is limited demand for products offered by suppliers from other Member States or where the products are of limited interest from the point of view of cross-border establishment or the expansion of the economic activity carried out from such place of establishment ([20]). Establishment includes the setting-up by undertakings in one Member State of agencies, branches or subsidiaries in another Member State.

31. The market position of the undertakings concerned and their sales volumes are indicative from a quantitative point of view of the ability of the agreement or practice concerned to affect trade between Member States. This aspect, which forms an integral part of the assessment of appreciability, is addressed in section 2.4 below.

32. In addition to the factors already mentioned, it is necessary to take account of the legal and factual environment in which the agreement or practice operates. The relevant economic and legal context provides insight into the potential for an effect on trade between Member States. If there are absolute barriers to cross-border trade between Member States, which are external to the agreement or practice, trade is only capable of being affected if those barriers are likely to disappear in the foreseeable future. In cases where the barriers are not absolute but merely render cross-border activities more difficult, it is of the utmost importance to ensure that agreements and practices do not further hinder such activities. Agreements and practices that do so are capable of affecting trade between Member States.

2.3.2. *An influence on the 'pattern of trade between Member States'*

33. For Articles 81 and 82 to be applicable there must be an influence on the 'pattern of trade between Member States'.

34. The term 'pattern of trade' is neutral. It is not a condition that trade be restricted or reduced ([21]). Patterns of trade can also be affected when an agreement or practice causes an increase in trade. Indeed, Community law jurisdiction is established if trade between Member States is likely to develop differently with the agreement or practice compared to the way in which it would probably have developed in the absence of the agreement or practice ([22]).

35. This interpretation reflects the fact that the effect on trade criterion is a jurisdictional one, which serves to distinguish those agreements and practices which are capable of having cross-border effects, so as to warrant an examination under the Community competition rules, from those agreements and practices which do not.

2.3.3. A *'direct or indirect, actual or potential influence' on the pattern of trade*

36. The influence of agreements and practices on patterns of trade between Member States can be 'direct or indirect, actual or potential'.

37. Direct effects on trade between Member States normally occur in relation to the products covered by an agreement or practice. When, for example, producers of a particular product in different Member States agree to share markets, direct effects are produced on trade between Member States on the market for the products in question. Another example of direct effects being produced is when a supplier limits distributor rebates to products sold within the Member State in which the distributors are established. Such practices increase the relative price of products destined for exports, rendering export sales less attractive and less competitive.

38. Indirect effects often occur in relation to products that are related to those covered by an agreement or practice. Indirect effects may, for example, occur where an agreement or practice has an impact on cross-border economic activities of undertakings that use or otherwise rely on the products covered by the agreement or practice ([23]). Such effects can, for instance, arise where the agreement or practice relates to an intermediate product, which is not traded, but

which is used in the supply of a final product, which is traded. The Court of Justice has held that trade between Member States was capable of being affected in the case of an agreement involving the fixing of prices of spirits used in the production of cognac ([24]). Whereas the raw material was not exported, the final product — cognac — was exported. In such cases Community competition law is thus applicable, if trade in the final product is capable of being appreciably affected.

39. Indirect effects on trade between Member States may also occur in relation to the products covered by the agreement or practice. For instance, agreements whereby a manufacturer limits warranties to products sold by distributors within their Member State of establishment create disincentives for consumers from other Member States to buy the products because they would not be able to invoke the warranty ([25]). Export by official distributors and parallel traders is made more difficult because in the eyes of consumers the products are less attractive without the manufacturer's warranty ([26]).

40. Actual effects on trade between Member States are those that are produced by the agreement or practice once it is implemented. An agreement between a supplier and a distributor within the same Member State, for instance one that prohibits exports to other Member States, is likely to produce actual effects on trade between Member States. Without the agreement the distributor would have been free to engage in export sales. It should be recalled, however, that it is not required that actual effects are demonstrated. It is sufficient that the agreement or practice be capable of having such effects.

41. Potential effects are those that may occur in the future with a sufficient degree of probability. In other words, foreseeable market developments must be taken into account ([27]). Even if trade is not capable of being affected at the time the agreement is concluded or the practice is implemented, Articles 81 and 82 remain applicable if the factors which led to that conclusion are likely to change in the foreseeable future. In this respect it is relevant to consider the impact of liberalisation measures adopted by the Community or by the Member State in question and other foreseeable measures aiming at eliminating legal barriers to trade.

42. Moreover, even if at a given point in time market conditions are unfavourable to cross-border trade, for example because prices are similar in the Member States in question, trade may still be capable of being affected if the situation may change as a result of changing market conditions ([28]). What matters is the ability of the agreement or practice to affect trade between Member States and not whether at any given point in time it actually does so.

43. The inclusion of indirect or potential effects in the analysis of effects on trade between Member States does not mean that the analysis can be based on remote or hypothetical effects. The likelihood of a particular agreement to produce indirect or potential effects must be explained by the authority or party claiming that trade between Member States is capable of being appreciably affected. Hypothetical or speculative effects are not sufficient for establishing Community law jurisdiction. For instance, an agreement that raises the price of a product which is not tradable reduces the disposable income of consumers. As consumers have less money to spend they may purchase fewer products imported from other Member States. However, the link between such income effects and trade between Member States is generally in itself too remote to establish Community law jurisdiction.

2.4. **The concept of appreciability**

2.4.1. *General principle*

44. The effect on trade criterion incorporates a quantitative element, limiting Community law jurisdiction to agreements and practices that are capable of having effects of a certain magnitude. Agreements and practices fall outside the scope of application of Articles 81 and 82 when they affect the market only insignificantly having regard to the weak position of the undertakings concerned on the market for the products in question ([29]). Appreciability can be appraised in particular by reference to the position and the importance of the relevant undertakings on the market for the products concerned ([30]).

45. The assessment of appreciability depends on the circumstances of each individual case, in particular the nature of the agreement and practice, the nature of the products covered and the market position of the undertakings concerned. When by its very nature the agreement or practice is capable of affecting trade between Member States, the appreciability threshold is lower than in the case of agreements and practices that are not by their very nature capable of affecting trade between Member States. The stronger the market position of the undertakings concerned, the more likely it is that an agreement or practice capable of affecting trade between Member States can be held to do so appreciably ([31]).

46. In a number of cases concerning imports and exports the Court of Justice has considered that the appreciability requirement was fulfilled when the sales of the undertakings concerned accounted for about 5 % of the market [32]. Market share alone, however, has not always been considered the decisive factor. In particular, it is necessary also to take account of the turnover of the undertakings in the products concerned [33].

47. Appreciability can thus be measured both in absolute terms (turnover) and in relative terms, comparing the position of the undertaking(s) concerned to that of other players on the market (market share). This focus on the position and importance of the undertakings concerned is consistent with the concept 'may affect', which implies that the assessment is based on the ability of the agreement or practice to affect trade between Member States rather than on the impact on actual flows of goods and services across borders. The market position of the undertakings concerned and their turnover in the products concerned are indicative of the ability of an agreement or practice to affect trade between Member States. These two elements are reflected in the presumptions set out in paragraphs and 53 below.

48. The application of the appreciability test does not necessarily require that relevant markets be defined and market shares calculated [34]. The sales of an undertaking in absolute terms may be sufficient to support a finding that the impact on trade is appreciable. This is particularly so in the case of agreements and practices that by their very nature are liable to affect trade between Member States, for example because they concern imports or exports or because they cover several Member States. The fact that in such circumstances turnover in the products covered by the agreement may be sufficient for a finding of an appreciable effect on trade between Member States is reflected in the positive presumption set out in paragraph below.

49. Agreements and practices must always be considered in the economic and legal context in which they occur. In the case of vertical agreements it may be necessary to have regard to any cumulative effects of parallel networks of similar agreements [35]. Even if a single agreement or network of agreements is not capable of appreciably affecting trade between Member States, the effect of parallel networks of agreements, taken as a whole, may be capable of doing so. For that to be the case, however, it is necessary that the individual agreement or network of agreements makes a significant contribution to the overall effect on trade [36].

2.4.2. *Quantification of appreciability*

50. It is not possible to establish general quantitative rules covering all categories of agreements indicating when trade between Member States is capable of being appreciably affected. It is possible, however, to indicate when trade is normally not capable of being appreciably affected. Firstly, in its notice on agreements of minor importance which do not appreciably restrict competition in the meaning of Article 81(1) of the Treaty (the *de minimis* rule) [37] the Commission has stated that agreements between small and medium-sized undertakings (SMEs) as defined in the Annex to Commission Recommendation 96/280/EC [38] are normally not capable of affecting trade between Member States. The reason for this presumption is the fact that the activities of SMEs are normally local or at most regional in nature. However, SMEs may be subject to Community law jurisdiction in particular where they engage in cross-border economic activity. Secondly, the Commission considers it appropriate to set out general principles indicating when trade is normally not capable of being appreciably affected, i.e. a standard defining the absence of an appreciable effect on trade between Member States (the NAAT-rule). When applying Article 81, the Commission will consider this standard as a negative rebuttable presumption applying to all agreements within the meaning of Article 81(1) irrespective of the nature of the restrictions contained in the agreement, including restrictions that have been identified as hardcore restrictions in Commission block exemption regulations and guidelines. In cases where this presumption applies the Commission will normally not institute proceedings either upon application or on its own initiative. Where the undertakings assume in good faith that an agreement is covered by this negative presumption, the Commission will not impose fines.

51. Without prejudice to paragraph below, this negative definition of appreciability does not imply that agreements, which do not fall within the criteria set out below, are automatically capable of appreciably affecting trade between Member States. A case by case analysis is necessary.

52. The Commission holds the view that in principle agreements are not capable of appreciably affecting trade between Member States when the following cumulative conditions are met:

(a) The aggregate market share of the parties on any relevant market within the Community affected by the agreement does not exceed 5 %, and

(b) In the case of horizontal agreements, the aggregate annual Community turnover of the undertakings concerned [39] in the products covered by the agreement does not exceed 40 million euro. In the case of agreements concerning the joint buying of products the relevant turnover shall be the parties' combined purchases of the products covered by the agreement.

In the case of vertical agreements, the aggregate annual Community turnover of the supplier in the products covered by the agreement does not exceed 40 million euro. In the case of licence agreements the relevant turnover shall be the aggregate turnover of the licensees in the products incorporating the licensed technology and the licensor's own turnover in such products. In cases involving agreements concluded between a buyer and several suppliers the relevant turnover shall be the buyer's combined purchases of the products covered by the agreements.

The Commission will apply the same presumption where during two successive calendar years the above turnover threshold is not exceeded by more than 10 % and the above market threshold is not exceeded by more than 2 percentage points. In cases where the agreement concerns an emerging not yet existing market and where as a consequence the parties neither generate relevant turnover nor accumulate any relevant market share, the Commission will not apply this presumption. In such cases appreciability may have to be assessed on the basis of the position of the parties on related product markets or their strength in technologies relating to the agreement.

53. The Commission will also hold the view that where an agreement by its very nature is capable of affecting trade between Member States, for example, because it concerns imports and exports or covers several Member States, there is a rebuttable positive presumption that such effects on trade are appreciable when the turnover of the parties in the products covered by the agreement calculated as indicated in paragraphs 52 and 54 exceeds 40 million euro. In the case of agreements that by their very nature are capable of affecting trade between Member States it can also often be presumed that such effects are appreciable when the market share of the parties exceeds the 5 % threshold set out in the previous paragraph. However, this presumption does not apply where the agreement covers only part of a Member State (see paragraph 90 below).

54. With regard to the threshold of 40 million euro (cf. paragraph 52 above), the turnover is calculated on the basis of total Community sales excluding tax during the previous financial year by the undertakings concerned, of the products covered by the agreement (the contract products). Sales between entities that form part of the same undertaking are excluded ([40]).

55. In order to apply the market share threshold, it is necessary to determine the relevant market ([41]). This consists of the relevant product market and the relevant geographic market. The market shares are to be calculated on the basis of sales value data or, where appropriate, purchase value data. If value data are not available, estimates based on other reliable market information, including volume data, may be used.

56. In the case of networks of agreements entered into by the same supplier with different distributors, sales made through the entire network are taken into account.

57. Contracts that form part of the same overall business arrangement constitute a single agreement for the purposes of the NAAT-rule ([42]). Undertakings cannot bring themselves inside these thresholds by dividing up an agreement that forms a whole from an economic perspective.

3. THE APPLICATION OF THE ABOVE PRINCIPLES TO COMMON TYPES OF AGREEMENTS AND ABUSES

58. The Commission will apply the negative presumption set out in the preceding section to all agreements, including agreements that by their very nature are capable of affecting trade between Member States as well as agreements that involve trade with undertakings located in third countries (cf. section 3.3 below).

59. Outside the scope of negative presumption, the Commission will take account of qualitative elements relating to the nature of the agreement or practice and the nature of the products that they concern (see paragraphs and above). The relevance of the nature of the agreement is also reflected in the positive presumption set out in paragraph 53 above relating to appreciability in the case of agreements that by their very nature are capable of affecting trade between Member States. With a view to providing additional guidance on the application of the effect on trade concept it is therefore useful to consider various common types of agreements and practices.

60. In the following sections a primary distinction is drawn between agreements and practices that cover several Member States and agreements and practices that are confined to a single Member State or to part of a single Member State. These two main categories are broken down into further subcategories based on the nature of the agreement or practice involved. Agreements and practices involving third countries are also dealt with.

3.1. Agreements and abuse covering or implemented in several Member States

61. Agreements and practices covering or implemented in several Member States are in almost all cases by their very nature capable of affecting trade between Member States. When the relevant turnover exceeds the threshold set out in paragraph above it will therefore in most cases not be necessary to conduct a detailed analysis of whether trade between Member States is capable of being affected. However, in order to provide guidance also in these cases and to illustrate the principles developed in section 2 above, it is useful to explain what are the factors that are normally used to support a finding of Community law jurisdiction.

3.1.1. *Agreements concerning imports and exports*

62. Agreements between undertakings in two or more Member States that concern imports and exports are by their very nature capable of affecting trade between Member States. Such agreements, irrespective of whether they are restrictive of competition or not, have a direct impact on patterns of trade between Member States. In Kerpen & Kerpen, for example, which concerned an agreement between a French producer and a German distributor covering more than 10 % of exports of cement from France to Germany, amounting in total to 350 000 tonnes per year, the Court of Justice held that it was impossible to take the view that such an agreement was not capable of (appreciably) affecting trade between Member States ([43]).

63. This category includes agreements that impose restrictions on imports and exports, including restrictions on active and passive sales and resale by buyers to customers in other Member States ([44]). In these cases there is an inherent link between the alleged restriction of competition and the effect on trade, since the very purpose of the restriction is to prevent flows of goods and services between Member States, which would otherwise be possible. It is immaterial whether the parties to the agreement are located in the same Member State or in different Member States.

3.1.2. *Cartels covering several Member States*

64. Cartel agreements such as those involving price fixing and market sharing covering several Member States are by their very nature capable of affecting trade between Member States. Cross-border cartels harmonise the conditions of competition and affect the interpenetration of trade by cementing traditional patterns of trade ([45]). When undertakings agree to allocate geographic territories, sales from other areas into the allocated territories are capable of being eliminated or reduced. When undertakings agree to fix prices, they eliminate competition and any resulting price differentials that would entice both competitors and customers to engage in cross-border trade. When undertakings agree on sales quotas traditional patterns of trade are preserved. The undertakings concerned abstain from expanding output and thereby from serving potential customers in other Member States.

65. The effect on trade produced by cross-border cartels is generally also by its very nature appreciable due to the market position of the parties to the cartel. Cartels are normally only formed when the participating undertakings together hold a large share of the market, as this allows them to raise price or reduce output.

3.1.3. *Horizontal cooperation agreements covering several Member States*

66. This section covers various types of horizontal cooperation agreements. Horizontal cooperation agreements may for instance take the form of agreements whereby two or more undertakings cooperate in the performance of a particular economic activity such as production and distribution ([46]). Often such agreements are referred to as joint ventures. However, joint ventures that perform on a lasting basis all the functions of an autonomous economic entity are covered by the Merger Regulation ([47]). At the level of the Community such full function joint ventures are not dealt with under Articles 81 and 82 except in cases where Article 2(4) of the Merger Regulation is applicable ([48]). This section therefore does not deal with full-function joint ventures. In the case of non-full function joint ventures the joint entity does not operate as an autonomous supplier (or buyer) on any market. It merely serves the parents, who themselves operate on the market ([49]).

67. Joint ventures which engage in activities in two or more Member States or which produce an output that is sold by the parents in two or more Member States affect the commercial activities of the parties in those areas of the Community. Such agreements are therefore normally by their very nature capable of affecting trade between Member States compared to the situation without the agreement ([50]). Patterns of trade are affected when undertakings switch their activities to the joint venture or use it for the purpose of establishing a new source of supply in the Community.

68. Trade may also be capable of being affected where a joint venture produces an input for the parent companies, which is subsequently further processed or incorporated into a product by the parent undertakings. This is likely to be the case where the input in question was previously sourced from suppliers in other Member States, where the parents previously produced the input in other Member States or where the final product is traded in more than one Member State.

69. In the assessment of appreciability it is important to take account of the parents' sales of products related to the agreement and not only those of the joint entity created by the agreement, given that the joint venture does not operate as an autonomous entity on any market.

3.1.4. *Vertical agreements implemented in several Member States*

70. Vertical agreements and networks of similar vertical agreements implemented in several Member States are normally capable of affecting trade between Member States if they cause trade to be channelled in a particular way. Networks of selective distribution agreements implemented in two or more Member States for example, channel trade in a particular way because they limit trade to members of the network, thereby affecting patterns of trade compared to the situation without the agreement (51).

71. Trade between Member States is also capable of being affected by vertical agreements that have foreclosure effects. This may for instance be the case of agreements whereby distributors in several Member States agree to buy only from a particular supplier or to sell only its products. Such agreements may limit trade between the Member States in which the agreements are implemented, or trade from Member States not covered by the agreements. Foreclosure may result from individual agreements or from networks of agreements. When an agreement or networks of agreements that cover several Member States have foreclosure effects, the ability of the agreement or agreements to affect trade between Member States is normally by its very nature appreciable.

72. Agreements between suppliers and distributors which provide for resale price maintenance (RPM) and which cover two or more Member States are normally also by their very nature capable of affecting trade between Member States (52). Such agreements alter the price levels that would have been likely to exist in the absence of the agreements and thereby affect patterns of trade.

3.1.5. *Abuses of dominant positions covering several Member States*

73. In the case of abuse of a dominant position it is useful to distinguish between abuses that raise barriers to entry or eliminate competitors (exclusionary abuses) and abuses whereby the dominant undertaking exploits its economic power for instance by charging excessive or discriminatory prices (exploitative abuses). Both kinds of abuse may be carried out either through agreements, which are equally subject to Article 81(1), or through unilateral conduct, which as far as Community competition law is concerned is subject only to Article 82.

74. In the case of exploitative abuses such as discriminatory rebates, the impact is on downstream trading partners, which either benefit or suffer, altering their competitive position and affecting patterns of trade between Member States.

75. When a dominant undertaking engages in exclusionary conduct in more than one Member State, such abuse is normally by its very nature capable of affecting trade between Member States. Such conduct has a negative impact on competition in an area extending beyond a single Member State, being likely to divert trade from the course it would have followed in the absence of the abuse. For example, patterns of trade are capable of being affected where the dominant undertaking grants loyalty rebates. Customers covered by the exclusionary rebate system are likely to purchase less from competitors of the dominant firm than they would otherwise have done. Exclusionary conduct that aims directly at eliminating a competitor such as predatory pricing is also capable of affecting trade between Member States because of its impact on the competitive market structure inside the Community (53). When a dominant firm engages in behaviour with a view to eliminating a competitor operating in more than one Member State, trade is capable of being affected in several ways. First, there is a risk that the affected competitor will cease to be a source of supply inside the Community. Even if the targeted undertaking is not eliminated, its future competitive conduct is likely to be affected, which may also have an impact on trade between Member States. Secondly, the abuse may have an impact on other competitors. Through its abusive behaviour the dominant undertaking can signal to its competitors that it will discipline attempts to engage in real competition. Thirdly, the very fact of eliminating a competitor may be sufficient for trade between Member States to be capable of being affected. This may be the case even where the undertaking that risks being eliminated mainly engages in exports to third countries (54). Once the effective competitive market structure inside the Community risks being further impaired, there is Community law jurisdiction.

76. Where a dominant undertaking engages in exploitative or exclusionary abuse in more than one Member State, the capacity of the abuse to affect trade between Member States will normally also by its very nature be appreciable. Given the market position of the dominant undertaking concerned, and the fact that the abuse is implemented in several Member States, the scale of the abuse and its likely impact on patterns of trade is normally such that trade between Member States is capable of being appreciably affected. In the case of an exploitative abuse such as price discrimination, the abuse alters the competitive position of trading partners in several Member States. In the case of exclusionary abuses, including abuses that aim at eliminating a competitor, the economic activity engaged in by competitors in several Member States is affected. The very existence of a dominant position in several Member States implies that competition in a substantial part of the common market is already weakened ([55]). When a dominant undertaking further weakens competition through recourse to abusive conduct, for example by eliminating a competitor, the ability of the abuse to affect trade between Member States is normally appreciable.

3.2. Agreements and abuses covering a single, or only part of a, Member State

77. When agreements or abusive practices cover the territory of a single Member State, it may be necessary to proceed with a more detailed inquiry into the ability of the agreements or abusive practices to affect trade between Member States. It should be recalled that for there to be an effect on trade between Member States it is not required that trade is reduced. It is sufficient that an appreciable change is capable of being caused in the pattern of trade between Member States. Nevertheless, in many cases involving a single Member State the nature of the alleged infringement, and in particular, its propensity to foreclose the national market, provides a good indication of the capacity of the agreement or practice to affect trade between Member States. The examples mentioned hereafter are not exhaustive. They merely provide examples of cases where agreements confined to the territory of a single Member State can be considered capable of affecting trade between Member States.

3.2.1. *Cartels covering a single Member State*

78. Horizontal cartels covering the whole of a Member State are normally capable of affecting trade between Member States. The Community Courts have held in a number of cases that agreements extending over the whole territory of a Member State by their very nature have the effect of reinforcing the partitioning of markets on a national basis by hindering the economic penetration which the Treaty is designed to bring about ([56]).

79. The capacity of such agreements to partition the internal market follows from the fact that undertakings participating in cartels in only one Member State, normally need to take action to exclude competitors from other Member States ([57]). If they do not, and the product covered by the agreement is tradable ([58]), the cartel risks being undermined by competition from undertakings from other Member States. Such agreements are normally also by their very nature capable of having an appreciable effect on trade between Member States, given the market coverage required for such cartels to be effective.

80. Given the fact that the effect on trade concept encompasses potential effects, it is not decisive whether such action against competitors from other Member States is in fact adopted at any given point in time. If the cartel price is similar to the price prevailing in other Member States, there may be no immediate need for the members of the cartel to take action against competitors from other Member States. What matters is whether or not they are likely to do so, if market conditions change. The likelihood of that depends on the existence or otherwise of natural barriers to trade in the market, including in particular whether or not the product in question is tradable. In a case involving certain retail banking services ([59]) the Court of Justice has, for example, held that trade was not capable of being appreciably affected because the potential for trade in the specific products concerned was very limited and because they were not an important factor in the choice made by undertakings from other Member States regarding whether or not to establish themselves in the Member State in question ([60]).

81. The extent to which the members of a cartel monitor prices and competitors from other Member States can provide an indication of the extent to which the products covered by the cartel are tradable. Monitoring suggests that competition and competitors from other Member States are perceived as a potential threat to the cartel. Moreover, if there is evidence that the members of the cartel have deliberately fixed the price level in the light of the price level prevailing in other Member States (limit pricing), it is an indication that the products in question are tradable and that trade between Member States is capable of being affected.

82. Trade is normally also capable of being affected when the members of a national cartel temper the competitive constraint imposed by competitors from other Member States by inducing them to join the restrictive agreement, or if their exclusion from the agreement places the competitors at a competitive disadvantage ([61]). In such cases the agreement either prevents these competitors from exploiting any competitive advantage that they have, or raises their costs, thereby having a negative impact on their competitiveness and their sales. In both

cases the agreement hampers the operations of competitors from other Member States on the national market in question. The same is true when a cartel agreement confined to a single Member State is concluded between undertakings that resell products imported from other Member States ([62]).

3.2.2. *Horizontal cooperation agreements covering a single Member State*

83. Horizontal cooperation agreements and in particular non-full function joint ventures (cf. paragraph 66 above), which are confined to a single Member State and which do not directly relate to imports and exports, do not belong to the category of agreements that by their very nature are capable of affecting trade between Member States. A careful examination of the capacity of the individual agreement to affect trade between Member States may therefore be required.

84. Horizontal cooperation agreements may, in particular, be capable of affecting trade between Member States where they have foreclosure effects. This may be the case with agreements that establish sector-wide standardisation and certification regimes, which either exclude undertakings from other Member States or which are more easily fulfilled by undertakings from the Member State in question due to the fact that they are based on national rules and traditions. In such circumstances the agreements make it more difficult for undertakings from other Member States to penetrate the national market.

85. Trade may also be affected where a joint venture results in undertakings from other Member States being cut off from an important channel of distribution or source of demand. If, for example, two or more distributors established within the same Member State, and which account for a substantial share of imports of the products in question, establish a purchasing joint venture combining their purchases of that product, the resulting reduction in the number of distribution channels limits the possibility for suppliers from other Member States of gaining access to the national market in question. Trade is therefore capable of being affected ([63]). Trade may also be affected where undertakings which previously imported a particular product form a joint venture which is entrusted with the production of that same product. In this case the agreement causes a change in the patterns of trade between Member States compared to the situation before the agreement.

3.2.3. *Vertical agreements covering a single Member State*

86. Vertical agreements covering the whole of a Member State may, in particular, be capable of affecting patterns of trade between Member States when they make it more difficult for undertakings from other Member States to penetrate the national market in question, either by means of exports or by means of establishment (foreclosure effect). When vertical agreements give rise to such foreclosure effects, they contribute to the partitioning of markets on a national basis, thereby hindering the economic interpenetration which the Treaty is designed to bring about ([64]).

87. Foreclosure may, for example, occur when suppliers impose exclusive purchasing obligations on buyers ([65]). In Delimitis ([66]), which concerned agreements between a brewer and owners of premises where beer was consumed whereby the latter undertook to buy beer exclusively from the brewer, the Court of Justice defined foreclosure as the absence, due to the agreements, of real and concrete possibilities of gaining access to the market. Agreements normally only create significant barriers to entry when they cover a significant proportion of the market. Market share and market coverage can be used as an indicator in this respect. In making the assessment account must be taken not only of the particular agreement or network of agreements in question, but also of other parallel networks of agreements having similar effects ([67]).

88. Vertical agreements which cover the whole of a Member State and which relate to tradable products may also be capable of affecting trade between Member States, even if they do not create direct obstacles to trade. Agreements whereby undertakings engage in resale price maintenance (RPM) may have direct effects on trade between Member States by increasing imports from other Member States and by decreasing exports from the Member State in question ([68]). Agreements involving RPM may also affect patterns of trade in much the same way as horizontal cartels. To the extent that the price resulting from RPM is higher than that prevailing in other Member States this price level is only sustainable if imports from other Member States can be controlled.

3.2.4. *Agreements covering only part of a Member State*

89. In qualitative terms the assessment of agreements covering only part of a Member State is approached in the same way as in the case of agreements covering the whole of a Member State. This means that the analysis in section 2 applies. In the assessment of appreciability, however, the two categories must be distinguished, as it must be taken into account that only part of a Member State is covered by the agreement. It must also be taken into account what proportion of the national territory is susceptible to trade. If, for example, transport costs or the operating radius of equipment render it economically unviable for undertakings from other Member States to serve the entire territory of another Member State, trade is capable of being affected if the agreement forecloses access to the part of the territory of a Member State that is susceptible to trade, provided that this part is not insignificant ([69]).

90. Where an agreement forecloses access to a regional market, then for trade to be appreciably affected, the volume of sales affected must be significant in proportion to the overall volume of sales of the products concerned inside the Member State in question. This assessment cannot be based merely on geographic coverage. The market share of the parties to the agreement must also be given fairly limited weight. Even if the parties have a high market share in a properly defined regional market, the size of that market in terms of volume may still be insignificant when compared to total sales of the products concerned within the Member State in question. In general, the best indicator of the capacity of the agreement to (appreciably) affect trade between Member States is therefore considered to be the share of the national market in terms of volume that is being foreclosed. Agreements covering areas with a high concentration of demand will thus weigh more heavily than those covering areas where demand is less concentrated. For Community jurisdiction to be established the share of the national market that is being foreclosed must be significant.

91. Agreements that are local in nature are in themselves not capable of appreciably affecting trade between Member States. This is the case even if the local market is located in a border region. Conversely, if the foreclosed share of the national market is significant, trade is capable of being affected even where the market in question is not located in a border region.

92. In cases in this category some guidance may be derived from the case law concerning the concept in Article 82 of a substantial part of the common market (70). Agreements that, for example, have the effect of hindering competitors from other Member States from gaining access to part of a Member State, which constitutes a substantial part of the common market, should be considered to have an appreciable effect on trade between Member States.

3.2.5. *Abuses of dominant positions covering a single Member State*

93. Where an undertaking, which holds a dominant position covering the whole of a Member State, engages in exclusionary abuses, trade between Member States is normally capable of being affected. Such abusive conduct will generally make it more difficult for competitors from other Member States to penetrate the market, in which case patterns of trade are capable of being affected (71). In Michelin (72), for example, the Court of Justice held that a system of loyalty rebates foreclosed competitors from other Member States and therefore affected trade within the meaning of Article 82. In Rennet (73) the Court similarly held that an abuse in the form of an exclusive purchasing obligation on customers foreclosed products from other Member States.

94. Exclusionary abuses that affect the competitive market structure inside a Member State, for instance by eliminating or threatening to eliminate a competitor, may also be capable of affecting trade between Member States. Where the undertaking that risks being eliminated only operates in a single Member State, the abuse will normally not affect trade between Member States. However, trade between Member States is capable of being affected where the targeted undertaking exports to or imports from other Member States (74) and where it also operates in other Member States (75). An effect on trade may arise from the dissuasive impact of the abuse on other competitors. If through repeated conduct the dominant undertaking has acquired a reputation for adopting exclusionary practices towards competitors that attempt to engage in direct competition, competitors from other Member States are likely to compete less aggressively, in which case trade may be affected, even if the victim in the case at hand is not from another Member State.

95. In the case of exploitative abuses such as price discrimination and excessive pricing, the situation may be more complex. Price discrimination between domestic customers will normally not affect trade between Member States. However, it may do so if the buyers are engaged in export activities and are disadvantaged by the discriminatory pricing or if this practice is used to prevent imports (76). Practices consisting of offering lower prices to customers that are the most likely to import products from other Member States may make it more difficult for competitors from other Member States to enter the market. In such cases trade between Member States is capable of being affected.

96. As long as an undertaking has a dominant position which covers the whole of a Member State it is normally immaterial whether the specific abuse engaged in by the dominant undertaking only covers part of its territory or affects certain buyers within the national territory. A dominant firm can significantly impede trade by engaging in abusive conduct in the areas or vis-à-vis the customers that are the most likely to be targeted by competitors from other Member States. For example, it may be the case that a particular channel of distribution constitutes a particularly important means of gaining access to broad categories of consumers. Hindering access to such channels can have a substantial impact on trade between Member States. In the assessment of appreciability it must also be taken into account that the very presence of the dominant undertaking covering the whole of a Member State is likely to make market penetration more difficult. Any abuse which makes it more difficult to enter the national market should therefore be considered to appreciably affect trade. The combination of the market position of the dominant undertaking and the anti-competitive nature of its conduct implies that such abuses have normally by their very nature an appreciable effect on trade. However, if the abuse is purely local in nature or

involves only an insignificant share of the sales of the dominant undertaking within the Member State in question, trade may not be capable of being appreciably affected.

3.2.6. *Abuse of a dominant position covering only part of a Member State*

97. Where a dominant position covers only part of a Member State some guidance may, as in the case of agreements, be derived from the condition in Article 82 that the dominant position must cover a substantial part of the common market. If the dominant position covers part of a Member State that constitutes a substantial part of the common market and the abuse makes it more difficult for competitors from other Member States to gain access to the market where the undertaking is dominant, trade between Member States must normally be considered capable of being appreciably affected.

98. In the application of this criterion regard must be had in particular to the size of the market in question in terms of volume. Regions and even a port or an airport situated in a Member State may, depending on their importance, constitute a substantial part of the common market (77). In the latter cases it must be taken into account whether the infrastructure in question is used to provide cross-border services and, if so, to what extent. When infrastructures such as airports and ports are important in providing cross-border services, trade between Member States is capable of being affected.

99. As in the case of dominant positions covering the whole of a Member State (cf. paragraph 95 above), trade may not be capable of being appreciably affected if the abuse is purely local in nature or involves only an insignificant share of the sales of the dominant undertaking.

3.3. Agreements and abuses involving imports and exports with undertakings located in third countries, and agreements and practices involving undertakings located in third countries

3.3.1. *General remarks*

100. Articles 81 and 82 apply to agreements and practices that are capable of affecting trade between Member States even if one or more of the parties are located outside the Community (78). Articles 81 and 82 apply irrespective of where the undertakings are located or where the agreement has been concluded, provided that the agreement or practice is either implemented inside the Community (79), or produce effects inside the Community (80). Articles 81 and 82 may also apply to agreements and practices that cover third countries, provided that they are capable of affecting trade between Member States. The general principle set out in section 2 above according to which the agreement or practice must be capable of having an appreciable influence, direct or indirect, actual or potential, on the pattern of trade between Member States, also applies in the case of agreements and abuses which involve undertakings located in third countries or which relate to imports or exports with third countries.

101. For the purposes of establishing Community law jurisdiction it is sufficient that an agreement or practice involving third countries or undertakings located in third countries is capable of affecting cross-border economic activity inside the Community. Import into one Member State may be sufficient to trigger effects of this nature. Imports can affect the conditions of competition in the importing Member State, which in turn can have an impact on exports and imports of competing products to and from other Member States. In other words, imports from third countries resulting from the agreement or practice may cause a diversion of trade between Member States, thus affecting patterns of trade.

102. In the application of the effect on trade criterion to the above mentioned agreements and practices it is relevant to examine, inter alia, what is the object of the agreement or practice as indicated by its content or the underlying intent of the undertakings involved (81).

103. Where the object of the agreement is to restrict competition inside the Community the requisite effect on trade between Member States is more readily established than where the object is predominantly to regulate competition outside the Community. Indeed in the former case the agreement or practice has a direct impact on competition inside the Community and trade between Member States. Such agreements and practices, which may concern both imports and exports, are normally by their very nature capable of affecting trade between Member States.

3.3.2. *Arrangements that have as their object the restriction of competition inside the Community*

104. In the case of imports, this category includes agreements that bring about an isolation of the internal market (82). This is, for instance, the case of agreements whereby competitors in the Community and in third countries share markets, e.g. by agreeing not to sell in each other's home markets or by concluding reciprocal (exclusive) distribution agreements (83).

105. In the case of exports, this category includes cases where undertakings that compete in two or more Member States agree to export certain (surplus) quantities to third countries with a view to co-ordinating their market conduct inside the Community. Such export agreements serve to reduce price competition by limiting output inside the Community, thereby affecting trade between Member States. Without the export agreement these quantities might have been sold inside the Community (84).

3.3.3. *Other arrangements*

106. In the case of agreements and practices whose object is not to restrict competition inside the Community, it is normally necessary to proceed with a more detailed analysis of whether or not cross-border economic activity inside the Community, and thus patterns of trade between Member States, are capable of being affected.

107. In this regard it is relevant to examine the effects of the agreement or practice on customers and other operators inside the Community that rely on the products of the undertakings that are parties to the agreement or practice (85). In Compagnie maritime belge (86), which concerned agreements between shipping companies operating between Community ports and West African ports, the agreements were held to be capable of indirectly affecting trade between Member States because they altered the catchment areas of the Community ports covered by the agreements and because they affected the activities of other undertakings inside those areas. More specifically, the agreements affected the activities of undertakings that relied on the parties for transportation services, either as a means of transporting goods purchased in third countries or sold there, or as an important input into the services that the ports themselves offered.

108. Trade may also be capable of being affected when the agreement prevents re-imports into the Community. This may, for example, be the case with vertical agreements between Community suppliers and third country distributors, imposing restrictions on resale outside an allocated territory, including the Community. If in the absence of the agreement resale to the Community would be possible and likely, such imports may be capable of affecting patterns of trade inside the Community (87).

109. However, for such effects to be likely, there must be an appreciable difference between the prices of the products charged in the Community and those charged outside the Community, and this price difference must not be eroded by customs duties and transport costs. In addition, the product volumes exported compared to the total market for those products in the territory of the common market must not be insignificant (88). If these product volumes are insignificant compared to those sold inside the Community, the impact of any re-importation on trade between Member States is considered not to be appreciable. In making this assessment, regard must be had not only to the individual agreement concluded between the parties, but also to any cumulative effect of similar agreements concluded by the same and competing suppliers. It may be, for example, that the product volumes covered by a single agreement are quite small, but that the product volumes covered by several such agreements are significant. In that case the agreements taken as a whole may be capable of appreciably affecting trade between Member States. It should be recalled, however (cf. paragraph 49 above), that the individual agreement or network of agreements must make a significant contribution to the overall effect on trade.

---

(1) OJ C 368, 22.12.2001, p. 13.

(2) OJ L 1, 4.1.2003, p. 1.

(3) See e.g. Joined Cases 56/64 and 58/64, Consten and Grundig, [1966] ECR p. 429, and Joined Cases 6/73 and 7/73, Commercial Solvents, [1974] ECR p. 223.

(4) See in this respect Case 22/71, Béguelin, [1971] ECR p. 949, paragraph 16.

(5) See Case 193/83, Windsurfing, [1986] ECR p. 611, paragraph 96, and Case T-77/94, Vereniging van Groothandelaren in Bloemkwekerijprodukten, [1997] ECR II-759, paragraph 126.

(6) See paragraphs 142 to 144 of the judgment in Vereniging van Groothandelaren in Bloemkwekerijprodukteten cited in the previous footnote.

(7) See e.g. Case T-2/89, Petrofina, [1991] ECR II-1087, paragraph 226.

(8) The concept of appreciability is dealt with in section 2.4 below.

(9) See in this respect Case 85/76, Hoffmann-La Roche, [1979] ECR p. 461, paragraph 126.

(10) Throughout these guidelines the term 'products' covers both goods and services.

(11) See Case 172/80, Züchner, [1981] ECR p. 2021, paragraph 18. See also Case C-309/99, Wouters, [2002] ECR I-1577, paragraph 95, Case C-475/99, Ambulanz Glöckner, [2001] ECR I-8089, paragraph 49, Joined Cases C-215/96 and 216/96, Bagnasco, [1999] ECR I-135, paragraph 51, Case C-55/96, Job Centre, [1997] ECR I-7119, paragraph 37, and Case C-41/90, Höfner and Elser, [1991] ECR I-1979, paragraph 33.

(12) See e.g. Joined Cases T-24/93 and others, Compagnie maritime belge, [1996] ECR II-1201, paragraph 203, and paragraph 23 of the judgment in Commercial Solvents cited in footnote.

(13) See e.g. Joined Cases T-213/95 and T-18/96, SCK and FNK, [1997] ECR II-1739, and sections 3.2.4 and 3.2.6 below.

(14) See section 3.2 below.

(15) See e.g. the judgment in Züchner cited in footnote 11 and Case 319/82, Kerpen & Kerpen, [1983] ECR 4173, Joined Cases 240/82 and others, Stichting Sigarettenindustrie, [1985] ECR 3831, paragraph 48, and Joined Cases T-25/95 and others, Cimenteries CBR, [2000] ECR II-491, paragraph 3930.

(16) In some judgments mainly relating to vertical agreements the Court of Justice has added wording to the effect that the agreement was capable of hindering the attainment of the objectives of a single market between Member States, see e.g. Case T-62/98, Volkswagen, [2000] ECR II-2707, paragraph 179, and paragraph 47 of the Bagnasco judgment cited in footnote 11, and Case 56/65, Société Technique Minière, [1966] ECR 337. The impact of an agreement on the single market objective is thus a factor which can be taken into account.

(17) See e.g. Case T-228/97, Irish Sugar, [1999] ECR II-2969, paragraph 170, and Case 19/77, Miller, [1978] ECR 131, paragraph 15.

(18) See e.g. Case C-250/92, Gøttrup-Klim [1994] ECR II-5641, paragraph 54.

(19) See e.g. Case C-306/96, Javico, [1998] ECR I-1983, paragraph 17, and paragraph 18 of the judgment in Béguelin cited in footnote 4.

(20) Compare in this respect the judgments in Bagnasco and Wouters cited in footnote 11.

(21) See e.g. Case T-141/89, Tréfileurope, [1995] ECR II-791, Case T-29/92, Vereniging van Samenwerkende Prijsregelende Organisaties in de Bouwnijverheid (SPO), [1995] ECR II-289, as far as exports were concerned, and Commission Decision in Volkswagen (II) (OJ L 264, 2.10.2001, p. 14).

(22) See in this respect Case 71/74, Frubo, [1975] ECR 563, paragraph 38, Joined Cases 209/78 and others, Van Landewyck, [1980] ECR 3125, paragraph 172, Case T-61/89, Dansk Pelsdyravler Forening, [1992] ECR II-1931, paragraph 143, and Case T-65/89, BPB Industries and British Gypsum, [1993] ECR II-389, paragraph 135.

(23) See in this respect Case T-86/95, Compagnie Générale Maritime and others, [2002] ECR II-1011, paragraph 148, and paragraph 202 of the judgment in Compagnie maritime belge cited in footnote 12.

(24) See Case 123/83, BNIC v Clair, [1985] ECR 391, paragraph 29.

(25) See Commission Decision in Zanussi, OJ L 322, 16.11.1978, p. 36, paragraph 11.

(26) See in this respect Case 31/85, ETA Fabrique d'Ébauches, [1985] ECR 3933, paragraphs 12 and 13.

(27) See Joined Cases C-241/91 P and C-242/91 P, RTE (Magill), [1995] ECR I-743, paragraph 70, and Case 107/82, AEG, [1983] ECR 3151, paragraph 60.

(28) See paragraph 60 of the AEG judgment cited in the previous footnote.

(29) See Case 5/69, Völk, [1969] ECR 295, paragraph 7.

(30) See e.g. paragraph 17 of the judgment in Javico cited in footnote 19, and paragraph 138 of the judgment in BPB Industries and British Gypsum cited in footnote 22.

(31) See paragraph 138 of the judgment in BPB Industries and British Gypsum cited in footnote 22.

(32) See e.g. paragraphs 9 and 10 of the Miller judgment cited in footnote 17, and paragraph 58 of the AEG judgment cited in footnote 27.

(33) See Joined Cases 100/80 and others, Musique Diffusion Française, [1983] ECR 1825, paragraph 86. In that case the products in question accounted for just above 3 % of sales on the national markets concerned. The Court held that the agreements, which hindered parallel trade, were capable of appreciably affecting trade between Member States due to the high turnover of the parties and the relative market position of the products, compared to those of products produced by competing suppliers.

(34) See in this respect paragraphs 179 and 231 of the Volkswagen judgment cited in footnote 16, and Case T-213/00, CMA CGM and others, [2003] ECR I-, paragraphs 219 and 220.

(35) See e.g. Case T-7/93, Langnese-Iglo, [1995] ECR II-1533, paragraph 120.

(36) See paragraphs 140 and 141 of the judgment in Vereniging van Groothandelaren in Bloemkwekerijprodukten cited in footnote 5.

(37) See Commission Notice on agreements of minor importance which do not appreciably restrict competition under Article 81(1) of the Treaty (OJ C 368, 22.12.2001, p. 13, paragraph 3).

(38) OJ L 107, 30.4.1996, p. 4. With effect from 1.1.2005 this recommendation will be replaced by Commission Recommendation 2003/361/EC concerning the definition of micro, small and medium-sized enterprises (OJ L 124, 20.5.2003, p. 36).

(39) The term 'undertakings concerned' shall include connected undertakings as defined in paragraph 12.2 of the Commission's Notice on agreements of minor importance which do not appreciably restrict competition under Article 81(1) of the Treaty establishing the European Community (OJ C 368, 22.12.2001, p. 13).

(40) See the previous footnote.

(41) When defining the relevant market, reference should be made to the notice on the definition of the relevant market for the purposes of Community competition law (OJ C 372, 9.12.1997, p. 5).

(42) See also paragraph 14 above.

(43) See paragraph 8 of the judgment in Kerpen & Kerpen cited in footnote 15. It should be noted that the Court does not refer to market share but to the share of French exports and to the product volumes involved.

(44) See e.g. the judgment in Volkswagen cited in footnote 16 and Case T-175/95, BASF Coatings, [1999] ECR II-1581. For a horizontal agreement to prevent parallel trade see Joined Cases 96/82 and others, IAZ International, [1983] ECR 3369, paragraph 27.

(45) See e.g. Case T-142/89, Usines Gustave Boël, [1995] ECR II-867, paragraph 102.

(46) Horizontal cooperation agreements are dealt with in the Commission Guidelines on the applicability of Article 81 of the EC Treaty to horizontal cooperation agreements (OJ C 3, 6.1.2001, p. 2). Those guidelines deal with the substantive competition assessment of various types of agreements but do not deal with the effect on trade issue.

(47) See Council Regulation (EC) No 139/2004 on the control of concentrations between undertakings (OJ L 24, 29.1.2004, p. 1).

(48) The Commission Notice on the concept of full-function joint ventures under the Merger Regulation (OJ C 66, 2.3.1998, p. 1) gives guidance on the scope of this concept.

(49) See e.g. the Commission Decision in Ford/Volkswagen (OJ L 20, 28.1.1993, p. 14).

(50) See in this respect paragraph 146 of the Compagnie Générale Maritime judgment cited in footnote 23 above.

(51) See in this respect Joined Cases 43/82 and 63/82, VBVB and VBBB, [1984] ECR 19, paragraph 9.

(52) See in this respect Case T-66/89, Publishers Association, [1992] ECR II-1995.

(53) See in this respect the judgment in Commercial Solvents cited in footnote 3, in the judgment in Hoffmann-La Roche, cited in footnote, paragraph 125, and in RTE and ITP cited in footnote, as well as Case 6/72, Continental Can, [1973] ECR 215, paragraph 16, and Case 27/76, United Brands, [1978] ECR 207, paragraphs 197 to 203.

(54) See paragraphs 32 and 33 of the judgment in Commercial Solvents cited in footnote 3.

(55) According to settled case law dominance is a position of economic strength enjoyed by an undertaking which enables it to prevent effective competition being maintained on the relevant market by affording it the power to act to an appreciable extent independently of its competitors, its customers and ultimately of the consumers, see e.g. paragraph 38 of the judgment in Hoffmann-La Roche cited in footnote 9.

(56) See for a recent example paragraph 95 of the Wouters judgment cited in footnote 11.

(57) See e.g. Case 246/86, Belasco, [1989] ECR 2117, paragraph 32-38.

(58) See paragraph 34 of the Belasco judgment cited in the previous footnote and more recently Joined Cases T-202/98 a.o., British Sugar, [2001] ECR II-2035, paragraph 79. On the other hand this is not so when the market is not susceptible to imports, see paragraph 51 of the Bagnasco judgment cited in footnote 11.

(59) Guarantees for current account credit facilities.

(60) See paragraph 51 of the Bagnasco judgment cited in footnote 11.

(61) See in this respect Case 45/85, Verband der Sachversicherer, [1987] ECR 405, paragraph 50, and Case C-7/95 P, John Deere, [1998] ECR I-3111. See also paragraph 172 of the judgment in Van Landewyck cited in footnote 22, where the Court stressed that the agreement in question reduced appreciably the incentive to sell imported products.

(62) See e.g. the judgment in Stichting Sigarettenindustrie, cited in footnote 15, paragraphs 49 and 50.

(63) See in this respect Case T-22/97, Kesko, [1999] ECR II-3775, paragraph 109.

(64) See e.g. Case T-65/98, Van den Bergh Foods, [2003] ECR II-. . ., and the judgment in Langnese-Iglo, cited in footnote 35 paragraph 120.

(65) See e.g. judgment of 7.12.2000, Case C-214/99, Neste, ECR I-11121.

(66) See judgment of 28.2.1991, Case C-234/89, Delimitis, ECR I-935.

(67) See paragraph 120 of the Langnese-Iglo judgment cited in footnote 35.

(68) See e.g. Commission Decision in Volkswagen (II), cited in footnote 21, paragraphs 81 *et seq.*

(69) See in this respect paragraphs 177 to 181 of the judgment in SCK and FNK cited in footnote 13.

(70) See as to this notion the judgment in Ambulanz Glöckner, cited in footnote 11, paragraph 38, and Case C-179/90, Merci convenzionali porto di Genova, [1991] ECR I-5889, and Case C-242/95, GT-Link, [1997] ECR I-4449.

(71) See e.g. paragraph 135 of the judgment in BPB Industries and British Gypsum cited in footnote.

(72) See Case 322/81, Nederlandse Banden Industrie Michelin, [1983] ECR 3461

(73) See Case 61/80, Coöperative Stremsel- en Kleurselfabriek, [1981] ECR 851, paragraph 15.

(74) See in this respect judgment in Irish Sugar, cited in footnote 17 paragraph 169.

(75) See paragraph 70 of the judgment in RTE (Magill) cited in footnote 27.

(76) See the judgment in Irish Sugar cited in footnote 17.

(77) See e.g. the case law cited in footnote 70.

(78) See in this respect Case 28/77, Tepea, [1978] ECR 1391, paragraph 48, and paragraph 16 of the judgment in Continental Can cited in footnote 53.

(79) See Joined Cases C-89/85 and others, Ahlström Osakeyhtiö (Woodpulp), [1988] ECR 651, paragraph 16.

(80) See in this respect Case T-102/96, Gencor, [1999] ECR II-753, which applies the effects test in the field of mergers.

(81) See to that effect paragraph 19 of the judgment in Javico cited in footnote 19.

(82) See in this respect Case 51/75, EMI v CBS, [1976] ECR 811, paragraphs 28 and 29.

(83) See Commission Decision in Siemens/Fanuc (OJ L 376, 31.12.1985, p. 29).

(84) See in this respect Joined Cases 29/83 and 30/83, CRAM and Rheinzinc, [1984] ECR 1679, and Joined Cases 40/73 and others, Suiker Unie, [1975] ECR 1663, paragraphs 564 and 580.

(85) See paragraph 22 of the judgment in Javico cited in footnote 19.

(86) See paragraph 203 of the judgment in Compagnie maritime belge cited in footnote 12.

(87) See in this respect the judgment in Javico cited in footnote 19.

(88) See in this respect paragraphs 24 to 26 of the Javico judgment cited in footnote 19.

Index

References are to paragraph number

Abuse of dominant position 219–313
- abuse
  - causation 274
  - duration 309
  - essential facilities 295–297
  - fault 273
  - intellectual property rights 298–304
  - limiting production, markets or technical development 304, 305
  - list in Article 82 278
  - meaning 270–272
  - mergers 310
  - objective justification 275–277
  - parallel trade between Member States, restricting 306
  - potential 308
  - refusal to deal 292, 293
  - refusal to supply 295–297
  - supplementary obligations, requiring 291
  - tying effects, conditions with 290
  - unfair trading conditions 307
- affecting trade between Member States
  - inter-State trade 311, 312
  - trade and other activities 313
- assessment of market power 249–264
- bundling 289
- dominant position
  - determination 230–233
  - meaning 225–228
- duration of abuse 309
- economic strength
  - behaviour 255
  - consumers 258
  - duration 260
  - future entrants 263, 264
  - generally 249–251
  - intellectual property rights 261, 262
  - market share 252, 253
  - other competitors 259
  - prices 256, 257
  - resources and technology 254
- effect of finding 220
- essential facilities 295–297
- intellectual property rights 298–304
- interpretation of provisions 223, 224
- interrelationship with Article 81 225–228
- limiting production, markets or technical development 304, 305
- list of potential abuses 308
- market power, assessment of 249–264
- meaning 219, 229
- parallel trade between Member States, restricting 306
- pricing 279–288. *See also* Pricing
- prohibition 219, 220
- refusal to deal 292, 293
- refusal to supply 295–297
- relevant geographic market 245, 246
- relevant product market
  - factors affecting determination 236–244
  - importance 234
  - meaning 235
- requirements contracts 290
- structure of Article 82 221, 222
- substantial part of the common market 247
- supplementary obligations 291
- temporal market 248
- tying effects, conditions with 289, 290
- undertakings
  - Member States 268, 269
  - one or more 265, 266
  - public enterprises 267
- unfair trading conditions 307

Administrative powers
- Commission 36

Agreements
- anti-competitive agreements and practices, prohibition of 98–104
- between companies 102
- characteristics 98
- essence of 98
- examples 99
- form 104
- horizontal 103
- meaning 98–104
- principals and agents 102
- several activities, covering 104
- subjective intentions of parties 101
- vertical 103
- working conditions, agreements for better 100

Agriculture
sectoral application 77–81
Anti-competitive agreements and practices, prohibition of
affecting trade between Member States 91
agreement, decision or concerted practice 92
agreements. *See* Agreements
appreciable effect 178–196
trade between Member States, effect on 188–196
Commission power's 95
concerted practices 108–118
agreement, decision or concerted practice 92
And see Concerted practices
prohibition 91
decisions
associations of undertakings 105–107
duty of national courts 94
effect on trade between Member States 155–177
agreements which limit, or affect the terms of, cross-border transactions 163–165
agreements which may affect inter-State trade 160–163
altering pattern of inter-State trade 174–177
generally 155–159
network effect 169–173
partioning of national markets 166–168
exchange of information 119–121
exemption 96, 97, 197–218
Article 81(3) 199, 200
block exemption 200
competition not to be substantially eliminated 218
conditions for exemption 201–218
consumers receive fair share of resulting benefit 212–214
generally 197, 198
improvement of the production or distribution or goods or contribution to technical or economic progress 207–211
indispensable, no restrictions that are not 215–217
individual exemption 199
generally 91–95
liability for infringement 92
meaning 178
object or effect of preventing, restricting or distorting competition 91, 133–154
generally 133, 134
horizontal agreements 141, 142
object or effect 135–137
prevention, restriction or distortion of competition 138–140
restrictions necessary for the promotion of competition 148–154
vertical agreements 143–147
unilateral conduct 122–128
void agreements 93
Appreciable effect **178–196**
trade between Member States, effect on 188–196

Banking
sectoral application 86, 87

Coal and steel
sectoral application 75
Commission
administrative powers 36
anti-competitive agreements and practices, prohibition of 95
duties 36
legislative powers 33
powers
administrative powers 36
executive 36
legislative 33
quasi-legislative 34, 35
treaty 32
quasi-legislative powers 34, 35
Reports on Competition Policy 4
State aid
decisions 376–378
directives 379
powers 375–379
treaty powers 32
Concerted practices **108–118**
See also Anti-competitive agreements and practices, prohibition of
agreement distinguished 110
cooperation 109
coordination 109
definition 109
direct or indirect contact 114
evidence of agreement, no 111
example 108
independence 109, 113
mutual understandings 114
parallel behaviour 118
prohibition 91
reciprocity 115

same group, between companies in 129–132
similar behaviour 118
single economic unit, companies forming 112
subsequent conduct on market 110
unnatural parallel behaviour 116

Council
implementation of rules of competition 29–31

Cultural sector
sectoral application 90

Deal, refusal to **292, 293**

Dominant position, abuse of. See Abuse of dominant position

E-commerce
sectoral application 89

EC Treaty
rules of competition in context of 2

Electronic communications
sectoral application 89

Exchange of information
anti-competitive agreements and practices, prohibition of 119–121

Exclusive rights
State aid 334, 335–339

Exemption
anti-competitive agreements and practices, prohibition of 96, 97, 197–218
Article 81(3) 199, 200
block exemption 200
conditions for exemption 201–218
consumers receive fair share of resulting benefit 212–214
generally 197, 198
improvement of the production or distribution or goods or contribution to technical or economic progress 207–211
indispensable, no restrictions that are not 215–217
individual exemption 199

Insurance
sectoral application 86, 87

Intellectual property rights
abuse of dominant position 298–304

Member States
undertakings 61–69

Pricing **279–288**
annual fidelity rebate 283
discrimination 282
dissimilar conditions for equivalent transactions 282
excessively high pricing 286–288
generally 279
loyalty rebate 283
margin squeeze 281
predatory 280
State aid 354–356
tying effect 283–285

Principals and agents
agreements 102

Professional services
sectoral application 90

Refusal to deal **292, 293**

Refusal to supply **360**

Relevant geographic market **245, 246**

Relevant product market
See also Abuse of dominant position
factors affecting determination 236–244
importance 234
meaning 235

Rules of competition
EC Treaty context 2
fair competition, promotion of 3
implementation 26–36
administrative powers of Commission 36
Council's role 29–31
duties of Commission 36
executive powers of Commission 36
generally 26–28
legislative powers of Commission 33
quasi-legislative powers of Commission 34, 35
Treaty powers of Commission 32
objectives 3–25
scope. *See* Scope of rules of competition
source 1
Treaty Establishing a Constitution for Europe 1

Scope of rules of competition **37–90**
personal application
See also Undertakings
Member States 61–69
public undertakings 53, 60
undertaking, meaning of 52–59
sectoral application
agriculture 77–81
banking 86, 87
broadcasting 83
coal and steel 75
cultural 90
e-commerce 89

electronic communications 89
generally 74
insurance 86, 87
nuclear energy 76
professional services 90
security and defence products 84, 85
sport 90
telecommunications 83
transport 82
utilities 88
temporal application
limitation periods 72, 73
time limits generally 70, 71
territorial application
application to trade with third countries 39, 40
extra-territorial application 47–51
extra-territorial jurisdiction 41–46
territory of common market 37
treaties with third countries 38

Sectoral application
agriculture 77–81
banking 86, 87
broadcasting 83
coal and steel 75
cultural sector 90
e-commerce 89
electronic communications 89
generally 74
insurance 86, 87
nuclear energy 76
professional services 90
security and defence products 84, 85
sporting sector 90
telecommunications 83
transport 82
utilities 88

Security and defence products
sectoral application 84, 85

Special rights
State aid 334, 340, 341

Sporting sector
sectoral application 90

State aid **314–387**
ancillary markets, extension to 357–359
anti-competitive agreements 383–386
Article 81 and Article 10 380–387
Article 86 314, 315
balancing competing interests 320, 321
Commission
directives 379
powers 375–379
conflict of interest 352, 353
delegating responsibility for decisions affecting economic sphere to private traders 387
direct effect 324
exclusive rights 334, 335–339
exemption 361–374
adverse effect on trade contrary to Community interests, no 372
direct effect 373, 374
obstruction of the performance of the tasks entrusted 368–371
operation of services of general economic interest, undertakings entrusted with 363–367
purpose 361
revenue producing monopoly, undertakings having character of 362
manifest inability to satisfy demand 350, 351
other Treaty provisions, requirement to apply Article 86 with 322, 323
pricing 354–356
prohibited conduct
Article 82 and 344–349
enact or maintain in force 342
measures 343
purpose of Article 86 316–319
refusal to supply 360
special rights 334, 340, 341
undertakings
activity is economic 330, 331
activity not economic 328, 329
exclusive rights 334, 335–339
generally 325
meaning of undertaking 326, 327
public undertakings 332, 333
special rights 334, 340, 341

Territorial application
application to trade with third countries 39, 40
extra-territorial application 47–51
extra-territorial jurisdiction 41–46
territory of common market 37
treaties with third countries 38

Transport
sectoral application 82

Treaty Establishing a Constitution for Europe
rules of competition 1

Undertakings
abuse of dominant position
Member States 268, 269
one or more 265, 266
public enterprises 267
anti-competitive agreements and practices, prohibition of. *See* anti-

competitive agreements and practices, prohibition of
associations 59
decisions by 105–107
basic test 52
bodies held not to be 54
changes in corporate structure 58
decisions by associations of 105–107
examples 53
functional concept 52
groups 55
individuals 55
meaning 52–59
Member States 61–69
person 52
private 53
public 53, 60, 333, 334
relative concept 57
situated outside Community 56
State aid
activity is economic 330, 331
activity not economic 328, 329
exclusive rights 334, 335–339
generally 325
meaning of undertaking 326, 327
public undertakings 332, 333
special rights 334, 340, 341

Utilities
sectoral application 88